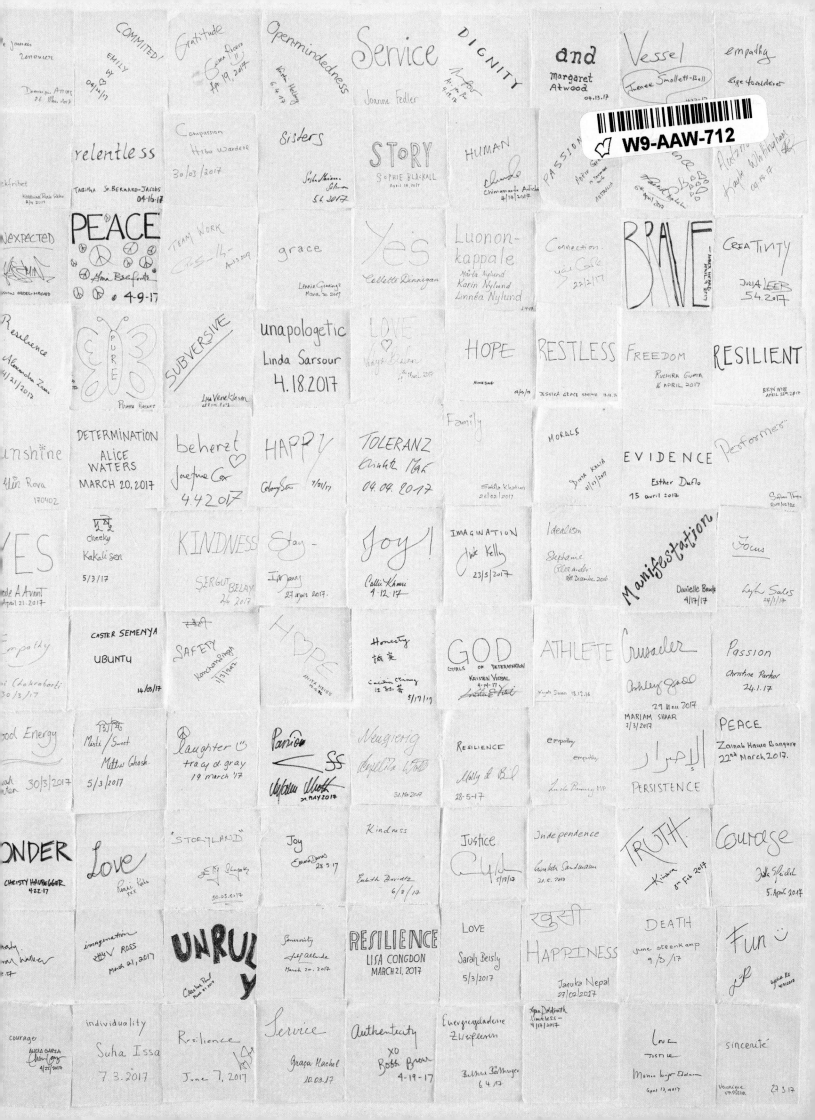

200
WOMEN

TO LILLY ~
I HAVE NO DOUBT YOU WILL
HELP TO CHANGE THE WORLD.
HAPPY 21ST BIRTHDAY!

Sharon Gelman
SEPT 2018

Created by
Geoff Blackwell & Ruth Hobday

Photographs by
Kieran E. Scott

———

US editor: Sharon Gelman

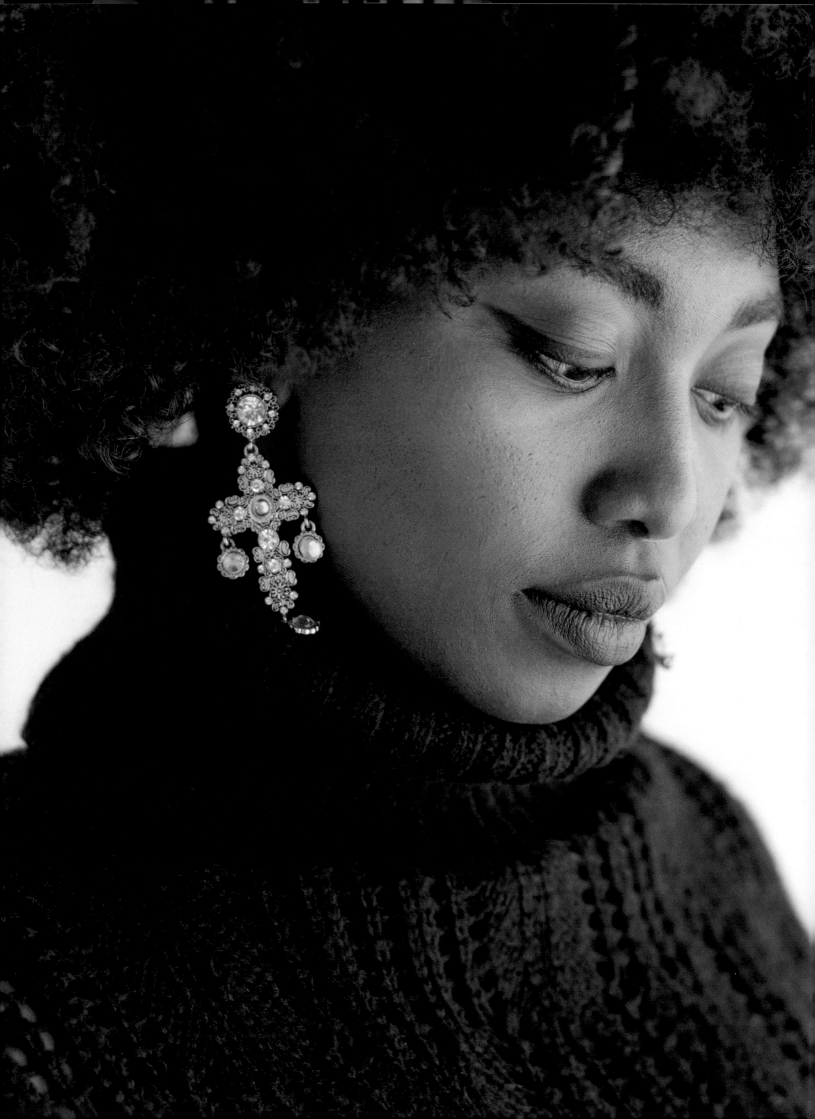

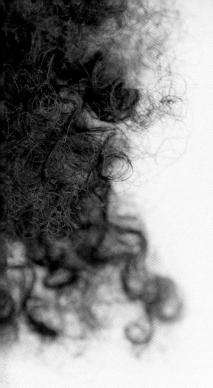

200
WOMEN

who will change the way
you see the world

CHRONICLE BOOKS
SAN FRANCISCO

in association with

Blackwell&Ruth.

'What separates an ordinary
woman from an extraordinary one?
The belief that she is ordinary.'

— Jody Williams, Nobel Laureate

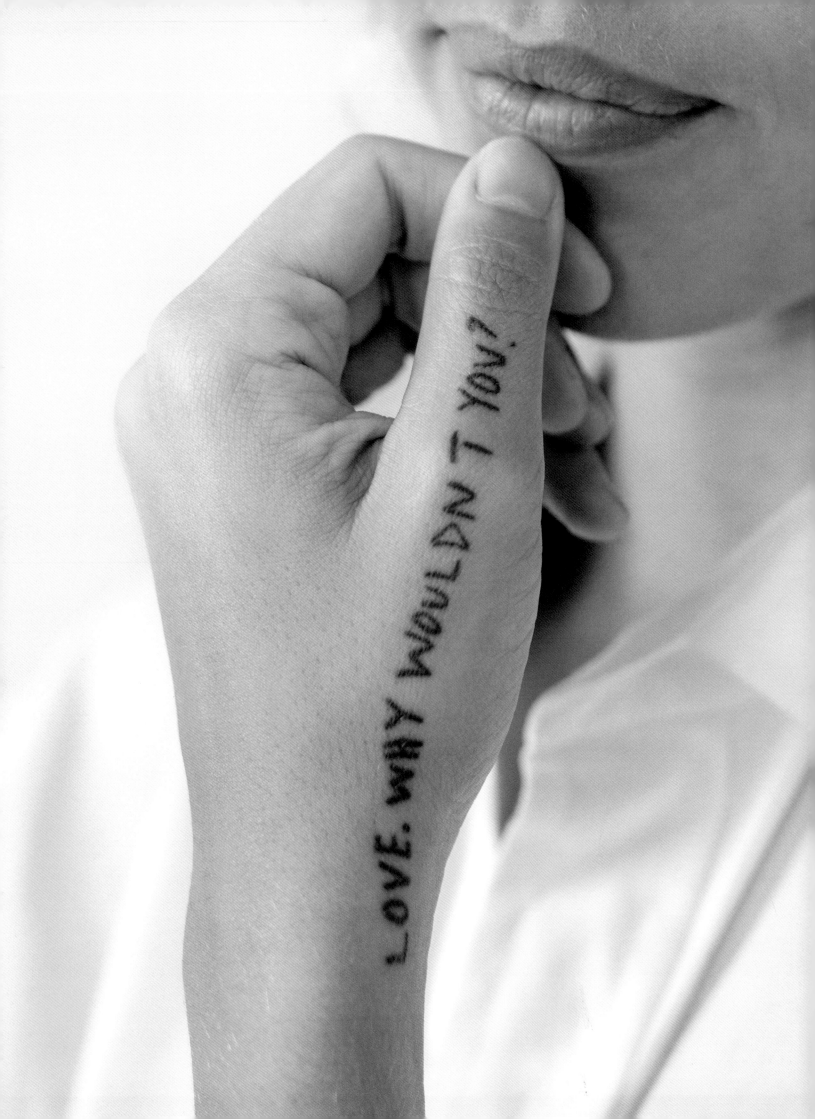

Contents

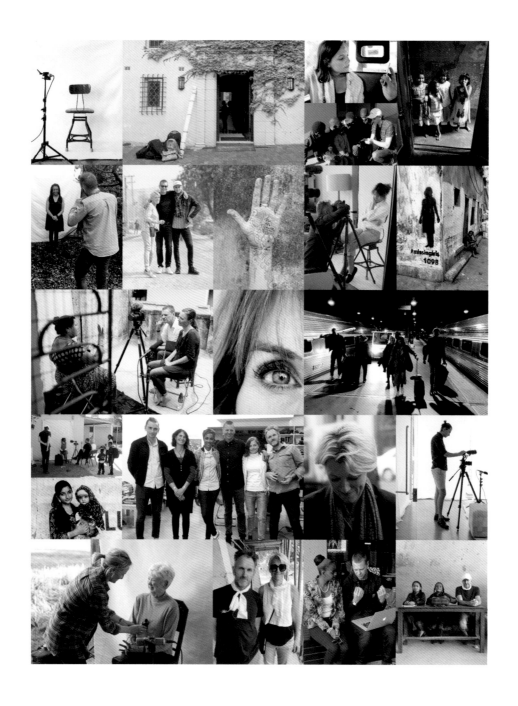

Gloria Steinem once said, 'You can't empower women without listening to their stories.' We agree.

This book was inspired by that belief and our subsequent idea to persuade two hundred women in different parts of the world – whether they be rich or poor, black or white, educated or uneducated, famous or unknown – to sit or stand in front of a plain sheet of fabric and to be photographed and filmed while answering five fundamental questions.

Our goal was not to make a book about just successful and powerful women; those stories are important, but we wanted diversity, and above all, authenticity. Two hundred 'real women,' with 'real stories.'

We sought to cut away distractions and the visual context of each woman's life and to simply focus on her humanity as we asked:

What really matters to you?
What brings you happiness?
What do you regard as the lowest depth of misery?
What would you change if you could?
Which single word do you most identify with?

We travelled as a small tight group. At every stop, we would set up our humble sheet of fabric in the quietest and lightest space we could find, from a dusty rooftop above the streets of Kolkata to a snow-covered art gallery in northern Sweden, to a Palestinian refugee camp in Beirut, to a hotel suite we could barely afford in New York, to a township in Cape Town where we were surrounded by beautiful kids who thought a Polaroid picture was a magic trick, to the earthquake-damaged hills of Nepal, to the leafy suburban streets of Sydney and to many other places.

With our backdrop in place, and a call for 'Quiet on the set,' one of us would begin asking each interviewee about her life and when they were ready, we would quietly ask our five questions, and we would listen.

The list of interviewees was a mix of well-known women and others we learned about as we researched and travelled. Many were introduced to us by generous friends, friends of friends, colleagues and kindred spirits in various corners of the globe. Among them artists, activists, entrepreneurs and even an astronaut, alongside business leaders, a goat herder, a nurse, and a brave Nepalese woman who has spent most of her life living on the streets of Kathmandu selling cigarettes – one at a time – to support her family.

Their responses simultaneously educated, humbled and inspired us. Some came from a place of deep sorrow, but over and over we encountered uplifting examples of kindness, selflessness, strength, wisdom, inspiration and the most compelling of all, truth. Writ large was the value, beauty and privilege of being able to just listen to these women, to truly see their humanity, and to recognise our own in doing so.

In the poorest places, we came face to face with the cruel and very real correlation between poverty and inequality. In those places we shed tears as we listened to the stories of girls trapped into the sex trade, married off to strangers at the age of ten or eleven, denied education and basic freedom, and subjected to all sorts of misery at the hands of men and a patriarchal culture that sadly is still very much in business.

Wherever we encountered these stories of 'us and them' there was almost always pain and division. But we also witnessed that when people truly see each other's humanity, beautiful things become possible.

Ultimately the lesson of creating this book has been that there are no ordinary women, and there is no 'us and them.' There's just us.

People like us.

_ Geoff Blackwell and Ruth Hobday

There is no 'us and them.' There's just us. People like us.

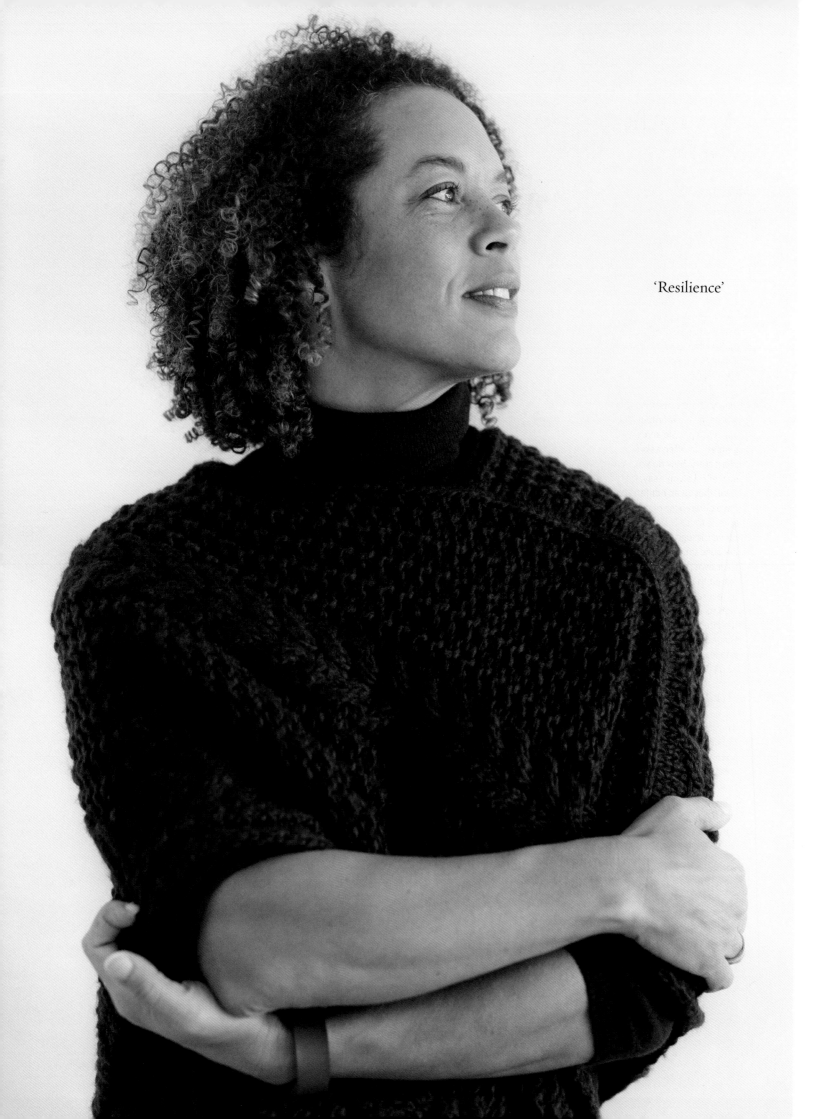

'Resilience'

Aminatta Forna

Aminatta Forna OBE was born in Glasgow, Scotland, and raised in the UK and Sierra Leone. She is the award-winning author of three novels, *The Hired Man*, *The Memory of Love* and *Ancestor Stones*, and the memoir *The Devil That Danced on the Water*. Forna is a Fellow of the Royal Society of Literature and has acted as a judge for numerous literary awards, including the Man Booker International Prize. In 2002, Forna established the Rogbonko Project, which works to improve education, sanitation and maternal health in Sierra Leone. She was made OBE in the Queen's New Year's Honours 2017.

Q. What really matters to you?

I've devoted my life to trying to help people move towards the understanding that we are more alike than unalike. I find it baffling that people cannot see this; I find it sad that we concentrate far too often on differences and not on similarities.

One of the discussions that is engaging writers at the moment is whether we can write people across race or across gender. I'm often asked, 'You write male characters: how do you understand men so well?' I always say, 'Because I don't think they're any different.' I do think they have differences of experience, though. One of these is that men are much freer to move through the world than women are, because they don't have to think about their own personal safety to the constant extent that women do – they don't have to fear rape so much and are not seen as victims in the way that women are. But despite these differences of experience that can lead to differences in behaviour and ways of thinking, fundamentally, I don't think men and women are different. And I feel exactly the same about people of different races and cultures.

There are reasons why patterns form. I'm often asked another question, and it always irks me. It starts like this, 'Coming from two such different cultures – Scotland and Sierra Leone . . .' I will often say to the interviewer, 'Have you ever been to Sierra Leone?' They'll say, 'No.' So I say, 'How do you know they're so different?' The two countries are actually strikingly similar. Let's take my grandfathers in my Scottish and my Sierra Leonean families: they were both not happy with my parents' marriage; both are tall, thin, very athletic men; one is a Scottish Presbyterian and the other one is a Muslim, but both are very religious; both are highly patriarchal; and both had a tendency to indulge me as a child. These two men, from different places in the world, were – to me – almost exactly the same. If you can see that, then you can see that people are the same;

but the presumption of difference that arises simply because we are talking about different colours and different continents, is where we start to go wrong.

We are all connected. I've always wanted to tell stories, because stories are how we come to understand the world. What fascinates me about stories – what drives me to write – is looking at the interconnectedness of things. That's why I moved from non-fiction to fiction: because you can construct worlds in which connections can be demonstrated. They say that non-fiction reveals the lies, but only a metaphor can tell the truth. In *The Handmaid's Tale*, which came out in the mid-eighties, Margaret Atwood pinpoints exactly how rights can be rolled back; she describes how an American elite manages to regain power by vilifying Muslims. And look at where we are now. A writer as great as Margaret Atwood can join the dots and create understanding. That's what writers do.

Q. What brings you happiness?

I have the good fortune to have happiness as a resting position; I'm generally happy unless something I see makes me angry. It's a good way to be. What makes me *happier* is food!

Q. What do you regard as the lowest depth of misery?

I think to be without hope must be the depth of misery. I am fortunate enough that I have never actually experienced the depth of misery, so I can't imagine what that is like. What I would say is this: the thing that makes me saddest and angriest is human cruelty, the capacity of one human being to be cruel to another. I do believe that human beings are innately capable of cruelty. I believe we belong to the animal world, and I don't believe that there's anything that elevates us beyond that – apart from the fact that we *are* more sophisticated. We are more intelligent, and, therefore, we have the capacity to organise ourselves into societies that do not rely on alpha-dom, muscularity,

bullying, the scale of numbers and mob rule. We can organise ourselves in ways that mean one human being doesn't have to force another to submit to them. That is possible. So the refusal to strive for it is what makes me most frustrated and angry.

Q. What would you change if you could?

Actually, it isn't up to me to change anything – because I really, genuinely believe that change begins within. What I try to do is get people to see the world in a different way: to reverse the gaze, to see how they look to somebody else, to look towards something that hasn't been seen before. The only thing that needs to change in the world is a quite tiny shift of perspective. It comes back to the idea that you only have to see that people are more like you than unalike. That's really the only thing that has to change.

I do believe that sometimes people can be wilfully blind. So you have to engage with them to the point where you can pull off their blinkers and actually encourage them to see what is there. Although there's been a rise in monoculturalism, humans are not naturally monocultural. In fact, it takes a lot of work to blinker differences. It requires a Slobodan Milošević or an Islamic State kind of mentality to say, 'Cultures are distinct and people are different from each other.' And what is behind this? Just follow the money: it's a cover story in order to acquire power and wealth.

Q. Which single word do you most identify with?

Resilience. It is the courage to endure. We have this saying in Sierra Leone – typically delivered quite dryly – that goes like this: somebody will say, 'Aw di bodi?' meaning, 'How are you?' In response, people will sometimes say, 'Ah fol don an git ap.' It means, 'I fall down and I get up again.' The fact that this response is almost always delivered with a smile – in a place like Sierra Leone, one of the poorest countries in the world – means something to me. That's what I call resilience.

Amber
Heard

Amber Heard was born in Austin in Texas, USA. As an actor, she is known for roles in *The Danish Girl, Pineapple Express, Zombieland, North Country* and *All the Boys Love Mandy Lane*. Heard is an activist and vocal advocate for women's and LGBTQI rights, and has worked to raise awareness of domestic and sexual violence. She is a supporter of the American Civil Liberties Union, The Art of Elysium, Amnesty International and Children's Hospital Los Angeles.

Q. What really matters to you?

That's changed a lot over the years; for a long time, it was about protection and survival. It was about finding and defining myself, and then defending whatever that was at the time, no matter what the cost. As I have grown older, though, I have found that it is less about what I am now, but rather, it is about what I will leave behind. No one lives forever, and last I checked you can't bring anything with you when you go, so, what matters to me most is the impact I make during my short time here. I have never been content to be a mere passenger in life, so I want to make sure I'm driving somewhere good.

Q. What brings you happiness?

My relationship with – and understanding of – happiness is ever-evolving. I used to think happiness was something I had to fight for at all times – now, more and more, I see what a fleeting, ephemeral thing it is. Happiness is and should always be a goal, but it should never be the *end* goal. Instead, the focus and fight should be on and for the things happiness is built upon.

We human beings instinctively do anything to avoid pain and will chase pleasure whenever possible. I used to chase happiness, too; and, when I caught it, I clung to it and was desperate not to let it go. But, holding on to anything makes you unable to grow; growth is about grasping, at times clawing, your way to the better. No one ever got anywhere standing still, so, to me, being static is the ultimate feeling of sadness.

As I get older, I have come to respect the pain and hardships I've endured, just as much as I now respect the joy and happiness that is the reward of having survived these. When I look back on the worst, most difficult periods of my life, I realise that they were some of the most definitive in making me who I am today – someone who is content to never be content.

These days, I find happiness in standing up for what I believe in – in standing up for truth, justice and others, and fighting to make this world slightly better than it was when I arrived.

Q. What do you regard as the lowest depth of misery?

I can say that – having narrowly survived what I can only hope and imagine are the very depths of my own personal capacity to feel pain – there is some intrinsic worth to the experience; not to the pain itself, but to the surviving of it. You can never win a battle if you've never picked up a sword or been cut by one. And the truth is, if you have never experienced pain, loss, failure or destruction, you can never know what it is to survive, succeed, live and thrive. And you most certainly won't be able to help someone else who is in the throes of that kind of experience themselves.

There is a line, though, at which pain concedes its value. And while that line may fall in a different place for everyone, it is there. I want to join those who use their voices and experiences to help others find and walk that line. Unfortunately, we fail those who find themselves alone on the front lines of their own personal battles, by blindly accepting the value of pain and suffering, for pain and suffering's sake. We all know someone who has been irreparably damaged by the unforgiving fate of persistent pain; the thing that spared me this fate wasn't chance, wealth, a weapon or some tangible advantage, rather, it was the grace, kindness and wisdom of others who had survived and learned from pain themselves. I survived because of the people who supported me in those times when I felt the most vulnerable, scared and alone, on the frontline of my own personal war.

I am grateful that I have come to see the worth in suffering – and surviving – if only to tell others that, although I don't believe suffering 'happens for a reason,' there is always something to take away from suffering – and to tell them the best parts of me were not only formed, but also solidified by, surviving agony, not in avoiding it.

Q. What would you change if you could?

I have always been particularly allergic to injustice, but to suggest that everything could be fair feels ridiculous. Nonetheless, being a conscious human being who is aware of a mere fraction of the injustices in this world, I must say that I would do away with all the injustices that are engulfing us.

Q. Which single word do you most identify with?

Bravery. Let me put it this way: if I were a mother and could pick one quality for my child to have, I would choose that she be brave. There are many qualities I would hope she would possess, but I find that many – like goodness, intelligence or beauty – are subjective or transient. I would hope for bravery most of all, because it's not enough to just be smart, beautiful or 'good.' So many things are subjective in the world; for instance, as children, we learn the difference between 'right' and 'wrong' but, as we get older, the context changes. In our ever-changing, nuanced, complicated young lives, 'good' and 'bad' become less clear, less black-and-white. Yes, we all aspire to 'do the right thing,' but now that I'm older, I find the choice is not always so clear. And many of us resign ourselves to settling on what is easiest or most popular – this makes doing what's right unclear, at best, and lonely and terrifying, at worst. No one really tells you that what's so difficult about doing the right thing isn't the actual doing of it, but rather, the doing of it alone. It takes great bravery, not simply benevolence, to do what's right and I don't think the concept of bravery is tied enough to the concept of morality. All of this to say, I choose the word bravery because it incorporates not only doing what you believe is right, but also having the fortitude and endurance to be able to do so when others can't, or won't.

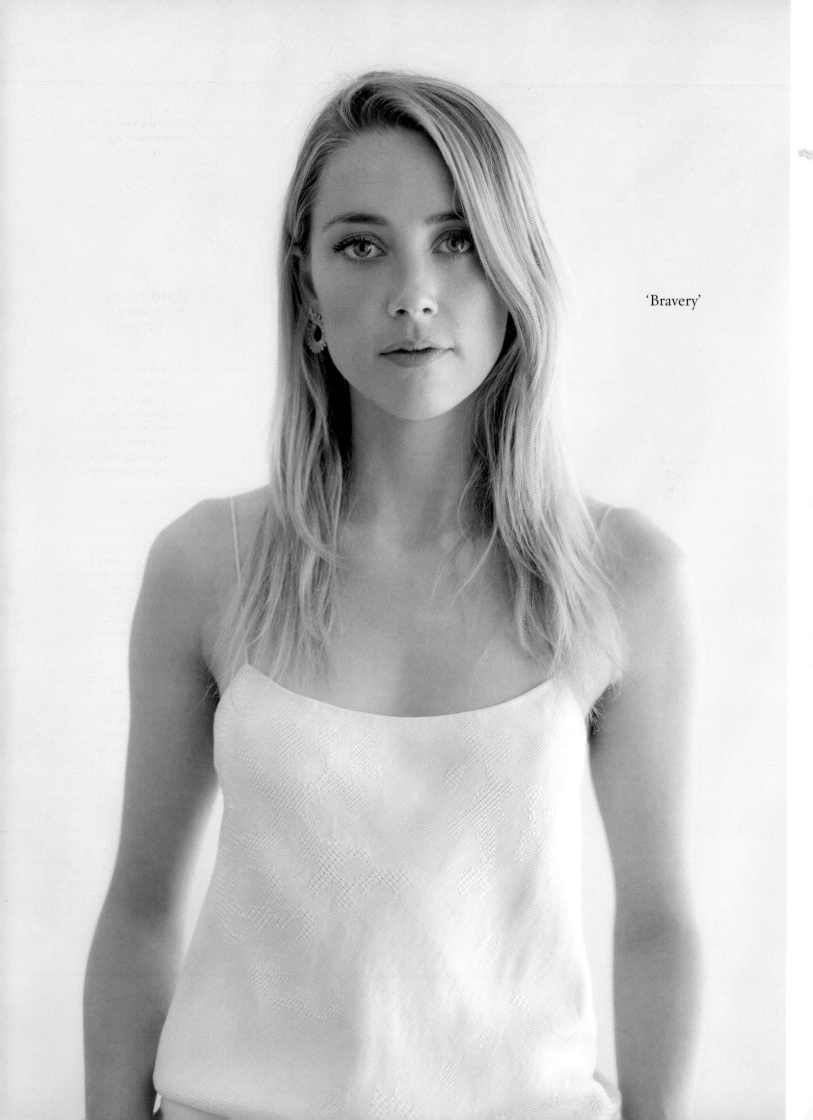

'Bravery'

Isabel Allende

―――――

'People have this idea that we come to the world to acquire things – love, fame, goods, whatever. In fact, we come to this world to lose everything.'

―――――

Isabel Allende was born in Lima, Peru. She is the author of twenty-three books in her native Spanish, which have been translated into thirty-five languages. Her award-winning works include *The House of the Spirits*, *City of the Beasts* and the international bestseller, *Paula*. Allende has received numerous awards, including the 2010 Chilean National Prize for Literature and the 2014 United States' Presidential Medal of Freedom. In 1996 – in memory of her daughter, Paula – Allende established the Isabel Allende Foundation to support initiatives aimed at preserving the rights of women and children.

Q. What really matters to you?
It's people – women especially. I have been a feminist – a feminine feminist – all my life, and my main mission has been to care for women; I have a foundation that works for the empowerment of women and girls.

Justice matters to me.

And stories – I love to listen to people's stories.

Q. What brings you happiness?
Love, romance, passion, sex, family, dogs, friends – all that brings me happiness.

Q. What do you regard as the lowest depth of misery?
On a universal level – speaking outwardly – I would say that there are many depths of misery, but the worst is probably slavery. When you are a victim of absolute power and are living in constant fear, that is the worst.

On a personal level, I would say that the lowest depth of misery is when something happens to your child and you have absolutely no power to control it. It is when your child is behind a door and you don't know what someone is doing to her – when you have no say, when you can't be there and when you can't even touch her.

My daughter, Paula, had a rare genetic condition called porphyria, which my son and my grandchildren also have. It is manageable and should not be lethal at all. Paula took very good care of herself but, when she was newly married and living in Madrid, she had a porphyria crisis. She went to the hospital, and they f**ked up the whole thing: they gave her the wrong drugs so she fell into a coma, then they didn't monitor the coma, then they tried to hide their negligence. For five months, I lived in the corridors of the hospital waiting for them to bring my daughter back to me, and everybody kept promising that she would open her eyes and recover.

She suffered severe brain damage. By the time they admitted this and gave me back my daughter, I decided to bring her back to the United States. She was married, but her husband was a young man who couldn't take care of her. I told him that, in her condition, she was like a newborn baby. I said, 'Give her back to me.' He did – that's something that I will always be grateful for. I was able to bring her back to California on a commercial flight – today that would be impossible, but this was before 9/11. I sectioned off a part of the plane, and we flew with a nurse and all the necessary equipment. But how do you come into a country with a person who can't apply for a visa? We came to Washington, DC, where Senator Ted Kennedy sent two people from his staff to wait for me at the airport – I don't know how, but they got us in. When we got to California, we went directly to the hospital.

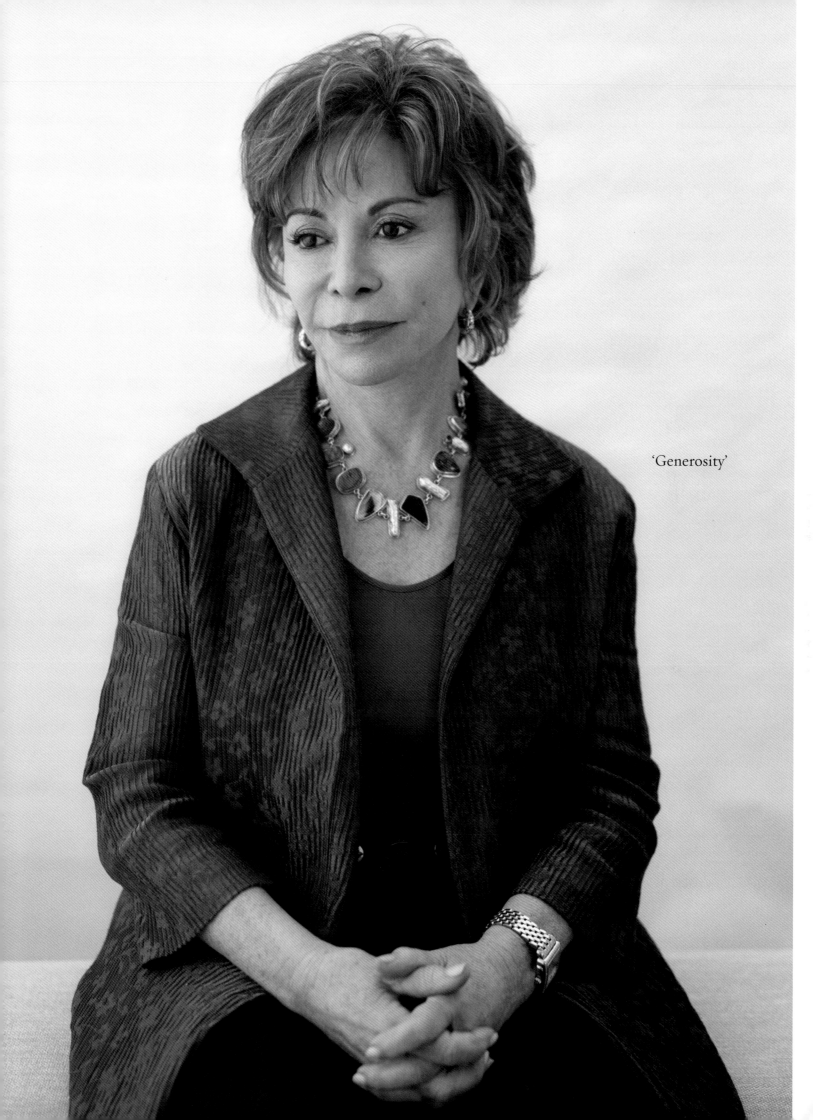

'Generosity'

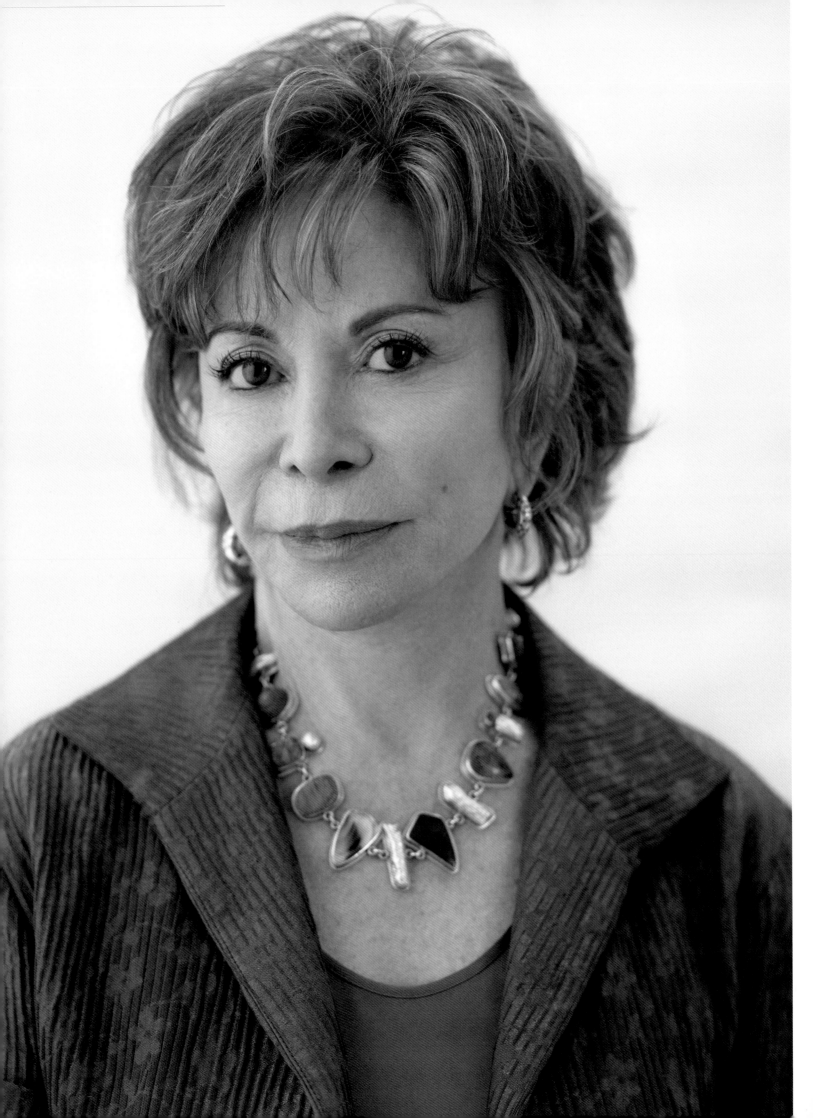

Isabel Allende

'Love, romance, passion, sex, family, dogs, friends – all that brings me happiness.'

After a month, it was absolutely certain that Paula wasn't going to react to anything. She was in a vegetative state, so I brought her home and decided that I would take care of her – because that's what mothers do. I created a little hospital in the house, and I trained myself – we had her there until she died.

That experience, culminating in Paula's death, changed me completely. It happened when I turned fifty, which is the end of youth. Menopause followed, so it hit me at a moment when I was ready to change, to finally mature. Up to that point, I had been an internal adolescent. It made me throw everything that was not essential in my life overboard. I let go of everything. With Paula, for example, I let go of her voice, of her charm, of her humour. I cut her hair short, then, eventually, I let go of her body and her spirit, then everything was gone. I learned the lesson that I am not in control. People have this idea that we come to the world to acquire things – love, fame, goods, whatever. In fact, we come to this world to lose everything. When we go, we have nothing and we can take nothing with us.

Paula gave me many gifts: the gift of generosity, the gift of patience and the gift of letting go – of acceptance. Because there are things you can't change: I couldn't change the military coup in Chile or the terror brought about by Pinochet; I can't change Trump; I can't change the fate of my grandchildren; I can't change Paula's death; I can't even change my dog!

Now, no matter what happens, it is nothing by comparison to the experience of Paula's death. I loved my husband intensely, for many, many years, but two years ago we separated. When people wanted to commiserate, I thought, 'This is not even 10 per cent of what I went through with Paula.' Nothing could be so brutal, to me, at least. It gave me freedom, in a way. It gave me strength and an incredible resilience I never had before. Prior to that, many things could have wiped me out.

Q. What would you change if you could?
I would change the patriarchy – end it! All my life, I have worked towards a more egalitarian world, one in which both men and women are managing our global society – a place in which feminine values are as important as masculine values.

Q. Which single word do you most identify with?
Generosity. Years ago, my therapist said that I had very low self-esteem. He told me to go to ten people and ask them to write five things about me – whatever they wanted. It was a very difficult thing to request from people; it seemed like an exercise in vanity and narcissism, but I did it. Everybody mentioned generosity as my first trait, so maybe there is something true in that.

The mantra of my foundation is, 'What is the most generous thing to do?' This is because of my daughter. She was a very special person and a psychologist. Whenever I was going through something trying, she would ask me what the most generous action I could take was. She used to say, 'You only have what you give.'

Susan Carland

Susan Carland was born in Melbourne, Australia. A writer, sociologist and academic, Carland completed her PhD in the School of Political and Social Inquiry at Monash University in Melbourne in 2015. Her research and teaching focus on gender, sociology, terrorism and Islam.

'The word I choose is hope – hope is a boat that we can get into when everything is difficult.'

Q. What really matters to you?

What matters to me most – what drives me the most – is service. But I don't believe service has to be grand; service is not only relevant on the scale of opening an orphanage, but includes those tiny acts of everyday service, whether they be to your own children or to your neighbour. Because the ultimately happy and content life is actually the life that you give away.

There's a great quote attributed to Muhammad Ali that goes something like, 'Service to others is the rent you pay for your room here on earth.' That really makes sense to me and is something that I've tried to live within myself, though I fail regularly. I'm always telling my children to look for opportunities to help, even if it's just when they see an older person struggling with a trolley in the supermarket. Because, in the end, a life of service is the only life that makes sense.

Raising my children with strong beliefs and values matters to me. I want them to be happy with who they are, but to never develop a sense of spiritual arrogance; I want them to see the core dignity in every human being and to respect that. It's not about us and them – Muslim and non-Muslim – because we are all people and can only function as a society if we respect one another. I believe that every person is potentially good, so engaging with people with that in mind allows for respect; without respect, there's an assumption of superiority – there is no dignity in an interaction like that. It's about giving people the benefit of the doubt, even when they probably don't deserve it. It's about dealing with people with compassion, even when we don't want to. The challenge is to ask yourself what you can do to try and create the society that you want to be a part of and that you want to see flourish. We must deal with each other with compassion if we are going to counteract what is happening in the world.

I am Muslim. I had a very good experience in the Baptist church growing up, but, when I was seventeen I started to wonder why I believed what I did; I didn't know whether it was the truth, so I started looking into other religions. There was a lot of noise surrounding Islam – the typical things Westerners and non-Muslims say about it being sexist, outdated and barbaric – but I realised that Islam was in fact the antithesis of what was being presented to me. And what was at the heart of it made a lot of sense. In fact, it felt like a continuation of what I was raised to believe.

After 9/11, I definitely started to feel the burden of the international representation of Islam. I remember people saying, 'It'll have to get better soon,' but the negative representation hasn't gone away. If anything, it's escalating. But, even when I engage with people who are incredibly rude, I try to remember to give them the benefit of the doubt. I know how often I feel I've been wrong or changed my mind, so I have the awareness that other people, too, can change their minds.

Q. What brings you happiness?

It's when I feel most useful. We live in a society in which there is so much noise and so much pressure for self-promotion and narcissism: 'Pay attention to me! This is my CV!' But I find contentment in the quiet life of service, in any capacity.

Q. What do you regard as the lowest depth of misery?

True misery is when people have no hope, when they are in a situation they feel they cannot change. But, people can endure anything if they feel there is hope; even in situations of horrific injustice, inequality and fear, if they have hope, they will get through it. And if they don't have hope, then it's our responsibility to bring them hope.

Q. What would you change if you could?

I would change inequality. If you look at every injustice, pain or hurt, it comes from a place of inequality, of people crushing other people on a big level or small – in fact, I would struggle to find any problem in the world that didn't have inequality at its heart. If we could get rid of that, things would be so different.

Q. Which single word do you most identify with?

Hope. Although, if someone were to describe me, they would probably say 'trying' – the sense of never achieving and always failing, but of keeping going. But, the word I choose is hope – hope is a boat that we can get into when everything is difficult.

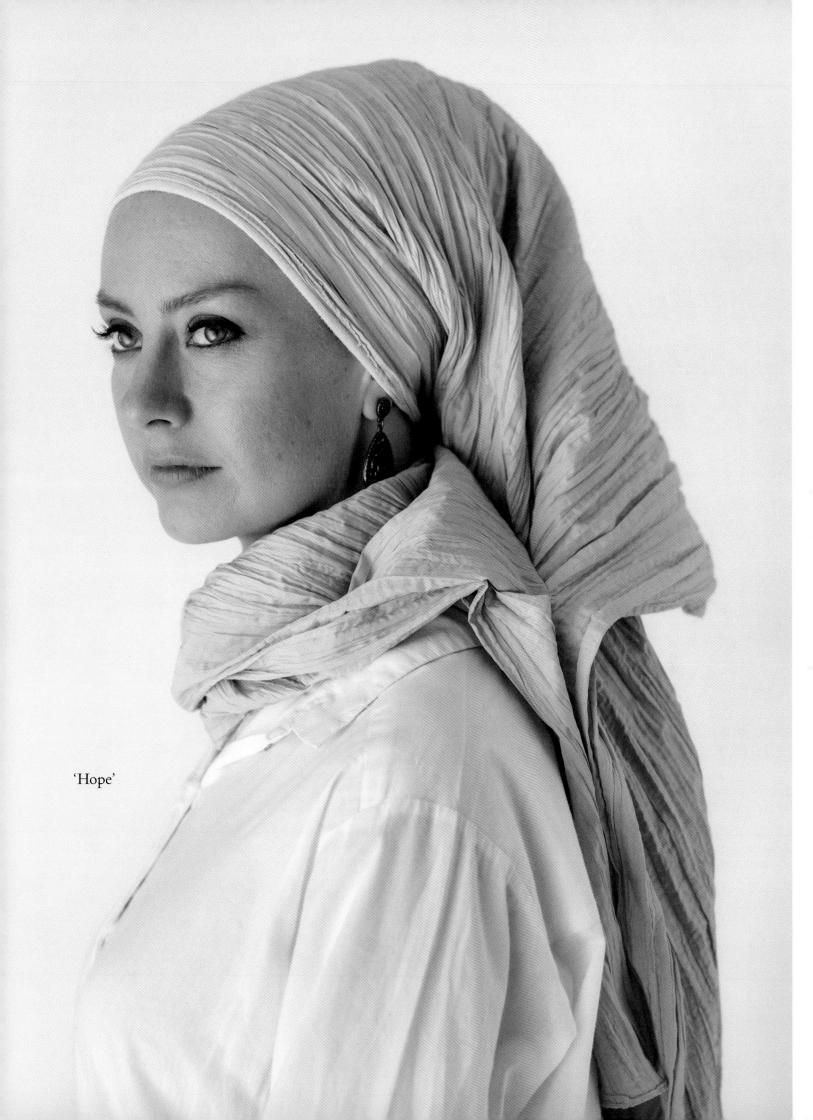

'Hope'

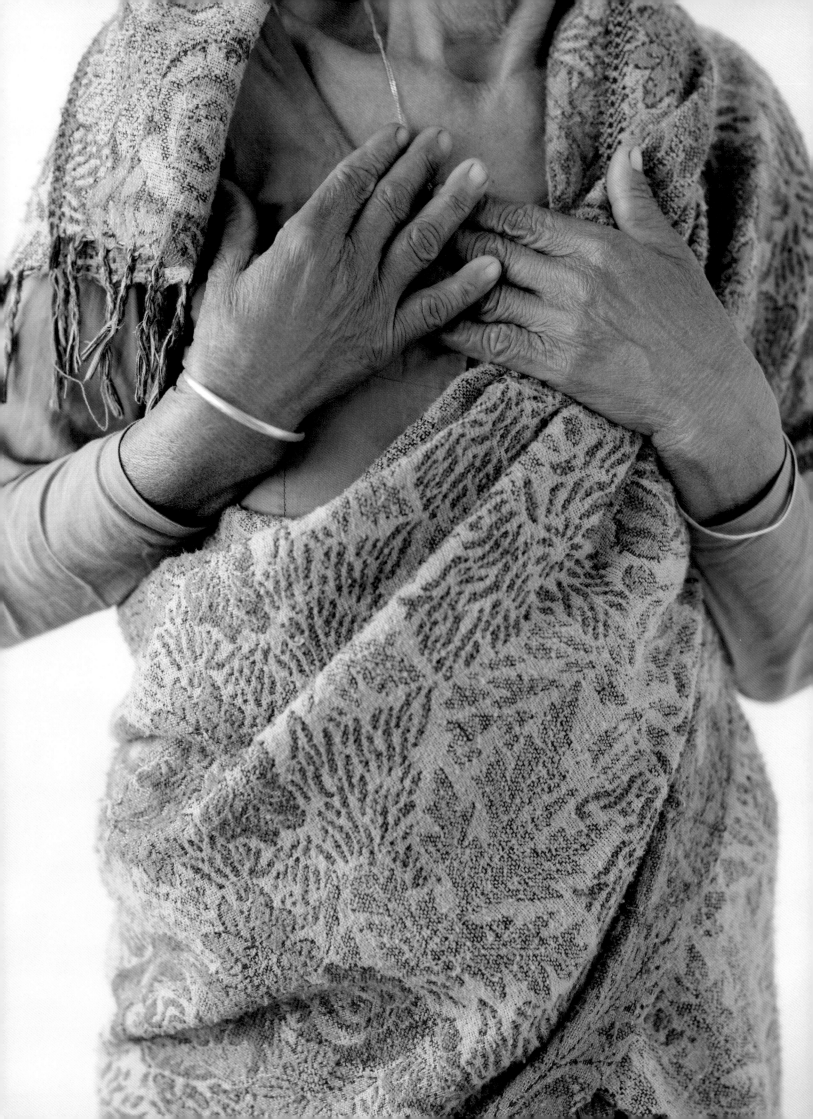

'When I was a child, there were no schools – I have never studied and I don't know how to write; if I have to sign something, I do it with my thumb.'

– Januka Nepal

'Sukha'

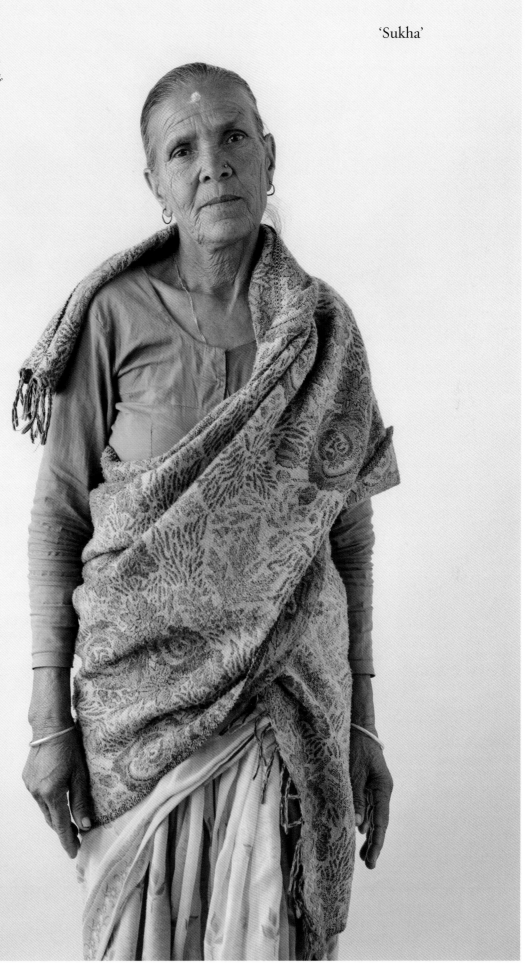

Interview page 366

Inna Modja

———

'Love is vital and loving yourself is more vital still. It's important to be full of yourself sometimes – there's nothing wrong with that!'

———

Inna Modja was born in Bamako, Mali. A musician, singer, songwriter and visual artist, Modja has released three albums: *Everyday Is a New World*, *Love Revolution* and *Motel Bamako*. A vocal women's rights activist and a survivor of female genital mutilation, Modja works to denounce and de-legalise the practice.

Q. What really matters to you?

My life has never been perfect and it never will be, but I've decided that I deserve to be happy. I've realised that happiness is a day-to-day choice – no life is going to be perfect, so it's up to the individual to decide how they are going to react to a situation.

I'm the sixth of seven kids. When I was four, my family was living in Ghana, and my younger brother and I went to Mali with our mother for our holidays. When my mother was out one day, my grandmother's sister took me to a place where I was subjected to female genital mutilation. This happened without the knowledge of either of my parents; they are both vehemently against this practice. Looking back on this, as an adult, this is certainly something that forged my personality. I was always a feminist and had been raised a feminist by both my parents, but this instilled in me a desire to stand up for other women and to help them where I can. This desire is a part of my life and is a part of my art, and it made me into an activist. I consider myself very lucky to have had parents who always told my siblings and me that we were good enough – that we were worthwhile and could be whoever we wanted to be if we just put the work in. Having principles like that to guide you as a child is fundamental and is what formed the foundation of feminism for me.

Being an activist is about putting myself in the middle of what's going on in the field; it's about sharing my own story and bringing awareness to the issues I feel are important to deal with. I want to help by *doing*. My journey started in a place of pain, but it has become so important to transform that pain and let this event become something that can have positive effects through the sharing of it.

It baffles me that people continue to resist gender equality – with racial inequality, everyone can see the issues and seem far more willing to pursue change in this regard. I don't get it. To me, feminism is not about gender. It's about wanting equal rights for both women and men in the world, and equal opportunities for all. The world needs both women and men – feminism is not just women, for women, by women. Women are part of a greater societal context, so, if we want to improve our society, we need everyone working together for basic, equal rights.

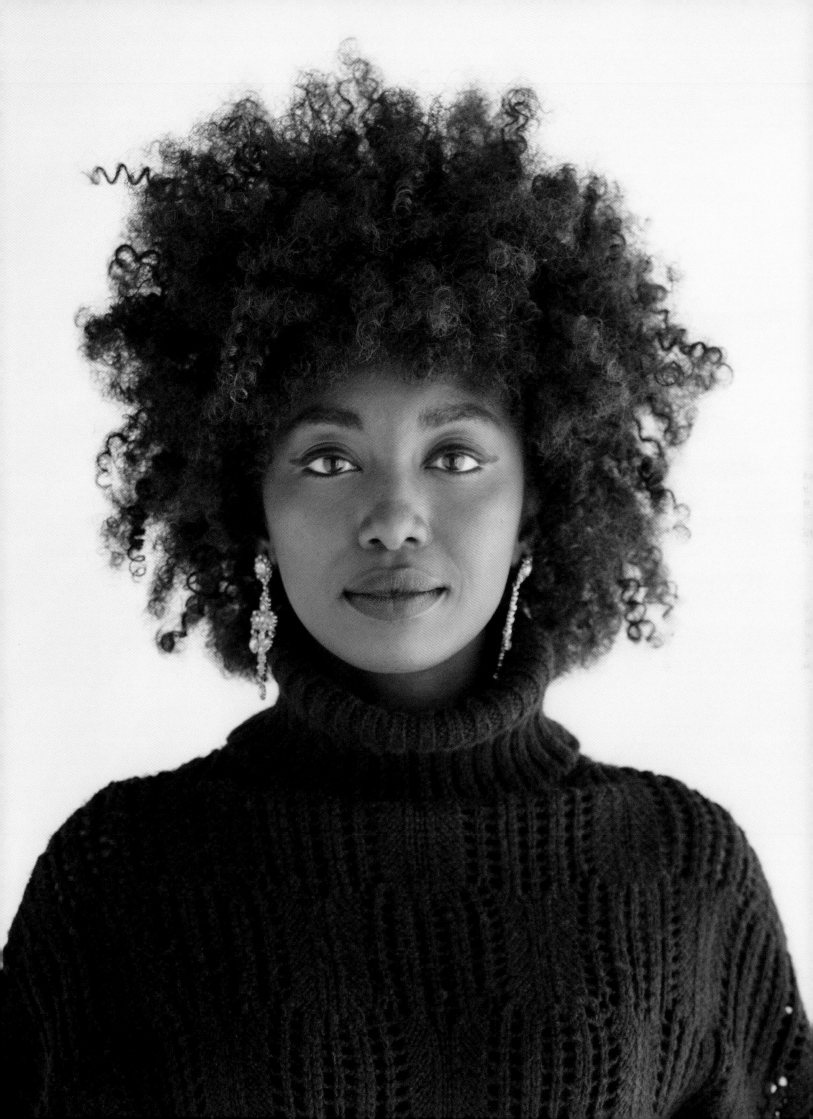

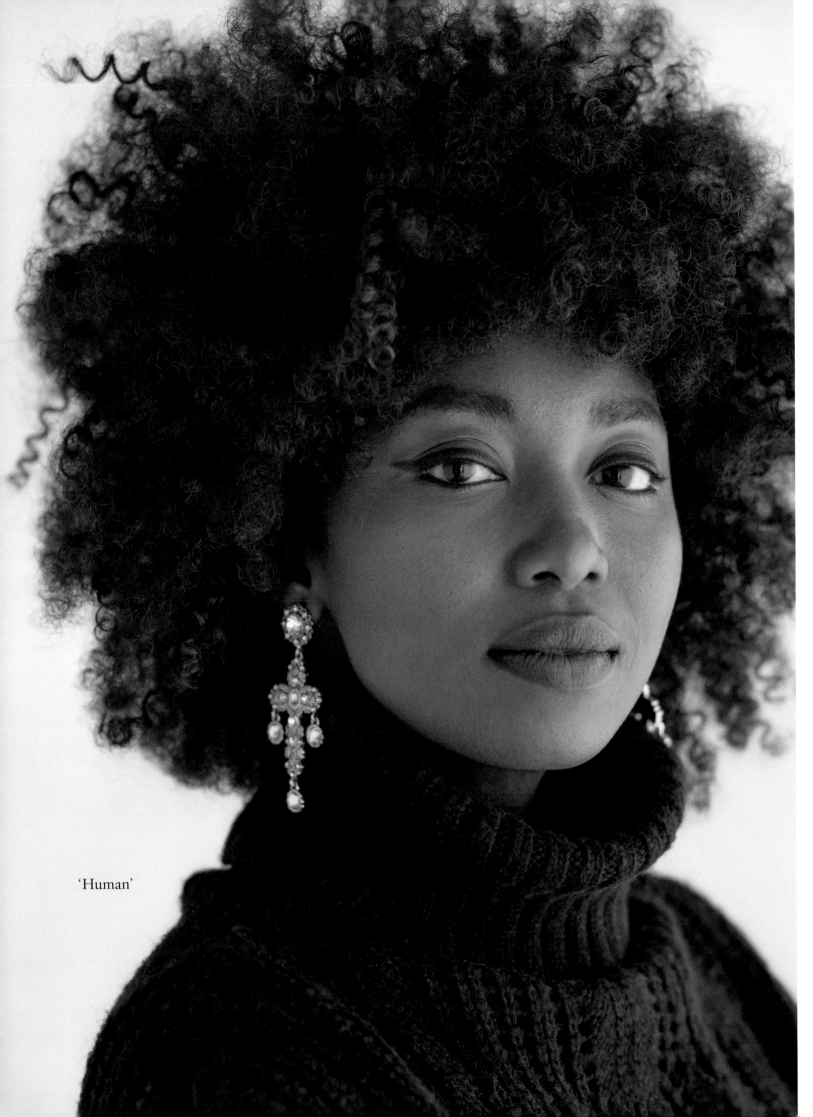

'Human'

Inna Modja

———

'When my mother was out one day, my grandmother's sister took me to a place where I was subjected to female genital mutilation. This happened without the knowledge of either of my parents; they are both vehemently against this practice.'

———

Q. What brings you happiness?
I know that I cannot be completely happy if there is someone in need of my help; if I know that I can do something to change somebody's life, but am not doing it, I can't have peace. As an artist, I believe that the gifts I have, I have for a reason. People can choose to use their gifts in different ways; I choose to focus my energies on things that matter, things that will bring about some good – however small. That decision leads me to happiness.

And happiness is different things. It's a choice I make every day, asking myself, 'What is going to make me happy today?' It could be a nice lunch with my family, spending time with my husband, being with my friends or taking time to be by myself. So, great happiness is about being aware of my feelings and deciding that each day will be a good day, regardless of the baggage that goes with it.

Q. What do you regard as the lowest depth of misery?
There are many depths of misery, but I would have to say loneliness and inequality.

In Mali, where I grew up, you look around you and see inequality everywhere. You see people in very difficult situations – this includes members of my own family – and what breaks my heart is that the capacity exists to address this current imbalance. Society *can* change the lives of people who have nothing, but we *choose* not to. It bothers me that, for whatever reason, nothing will be done for the sake of humanitarian reasons alone. I'm not anti-capitalism, but economic factors are more important than human factors. I see this everywhere. I'm not saying we need to overhaul society, but people need to be doing a lot more than is being done currently.

Some people need only open their tap to have access to clean water, but others walk six kilometres or more every day for clean water. It's usually women and children who do this, so that's less time in women's days to work and less time in children's days to educate themselves. I get so sad when I think of children being denied an education because of something like this. We all

know that education is the key – countries will not rise and become independent if their future leaders are fetching and carrying water instead of being able to turn on a tap and return to their books. Our future is already in jeopardy, without the next generation failing to be educated.

Q. What would you change if you could?
I would change the perceptions most people have of themselves and make these more positive. I want to tell people, 'Just see yourself as you are and love yourself.' Love is vital and loving yourself is more vital still. It's important to be full of yourself sometimes – there's nothing wrong with that! Obviously, it's never good to be arrogant, but it is good to embrace who you are, accept who you are and love who you are. Because you will be able to have more love for others if you have love for yourself.

Q. Which single word do you most identify with?
Human. Whatever qualities I have and whatever flows I go through, I am just human.

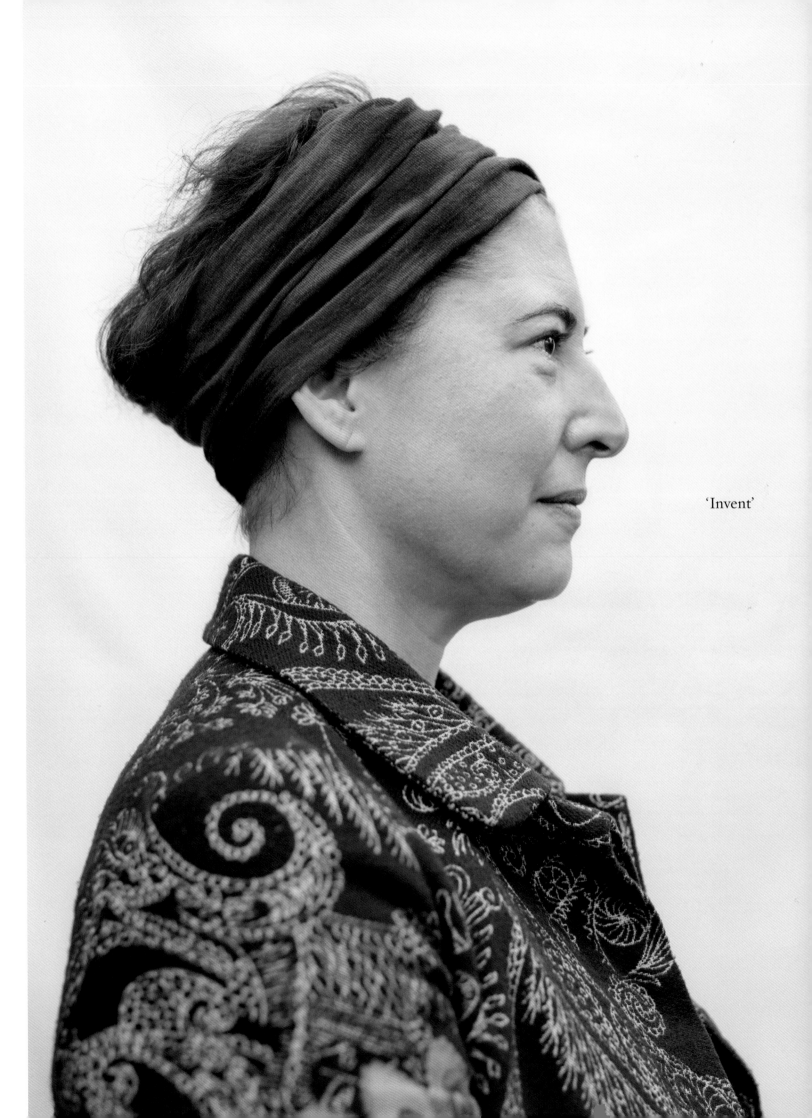

'Invent'

Safia
Shah

———

Safia Shah was born in London, England, and is the daughter of Sufi philosopher Idries Shah. She has worked with Afghan refugees on the Pakistan–Afghan border, has owned a traditional British food store and is the author of numerous books and short stories. In 1990, *Afghan Caravan* – a miscellany collected by Shah's father and edited by her – was selected as the *Daily Telegraph* Book of the Year.

'Being positive and generous matters to me. I don't think there's any place in life for negativity.'

———

Q. What really matters to you?
There's a lot that matters to me, but if I had to sum it up I'd say that making a difference matters to me, even in the tiniest way. Getting involved matters to me. When I was growing up, people would ask me what it was like being the daughter of Idries Shah, but I don't have anyone for comparison. He was simply my father. He taught us to always scrutinise a situation. We learned that you don't have to jump in immediately, but should always be willing to become involved. That was a very useful lesson for us.

Working with Afghan refugee women really, really changed the way I thought. My sister was a journalist, and I joined her on the Pakistan–Afghan border in the mid-eighties. I was nineteen when I met these women who had lost everything. A lot of them were educated, middle-class women who had been walking around Kabul completely at ease, then were suddenly catapulted into refugee camps: millions and millions and millions of people all living together. What really struck me was that, rather than retreating, they came to people like me and to aid networks to start working out how they were going to rebuild, what they were going to do, how they would get involved and how they would get some sort of power back – they hadn't lost their voices. It was an absolutely amazing experience, even though I probably got more out of it than

the women did. I don't know if it changed who I was as a person, but it was one of those experiences that changed my life in terms of how I see the world around me.

I have a great deal of energy when it comes to doing new things, so having new experiences with people I love matters to me, as does being adaptable. As a young child I was always surrounded by the strange, interesting, creative people who came to our crazy house in Kent; so embracing diversity is certainly part of who I am. But I don't actually think our important, new experiences have to be the most dangerous, the most glamorous or the most eccentric things. Although I come from quite an eccentric, risk-embracing family, I don't necessarily think that's always what you have to be doing.

Being positive and generous matters to me. I don't think there's any place in life for negativity. I've never seen it do any good whatsoever. It's one of the most limiting emotions one can have, and I've seen it ruin perfectly good people.

Q. What brings you happiness?
Communication and what it makes us capable of – seeing people communicating, innovating and inventing – brings me a great deal of happiness. I'm talking about this at a human level; reaching out to somebody who feels completely powerless to change their immediate

situation has enormous power. And our abstract thoughts and creativity, our gift of communication, our opposable thumbs and our innovation don't negate the bleakness of the refugee or conflict situations, but I do feel they mean that anything is possible.

Q. What do you regard as the lowest depth of misery?
People who are powerless. People who are bullied. People who feel that they can't do anything to protect the people they love. Those are the things that get me every time.

Q. What would you change if you could?
It's very hard to know what one could do to absolutely change the world. You can ask for world peace and you can ask for an end to world famine and poverty, but it won't last. Education is the only thing that actually works – the sharing of thought. And education doesn't have to be in the form of a textbook – it can be communication, talking or sharing.

Q. Which single word do you most identify with?
I think our ability to adapt is what makes us powerful, but 'adapt' as a word feels a bit passive to me. At the core of our adaptability is our ability to invent, so 'invent' is my word. We need to be inventive in everything we do, whether it's in telling a story or bringing something new into the world.

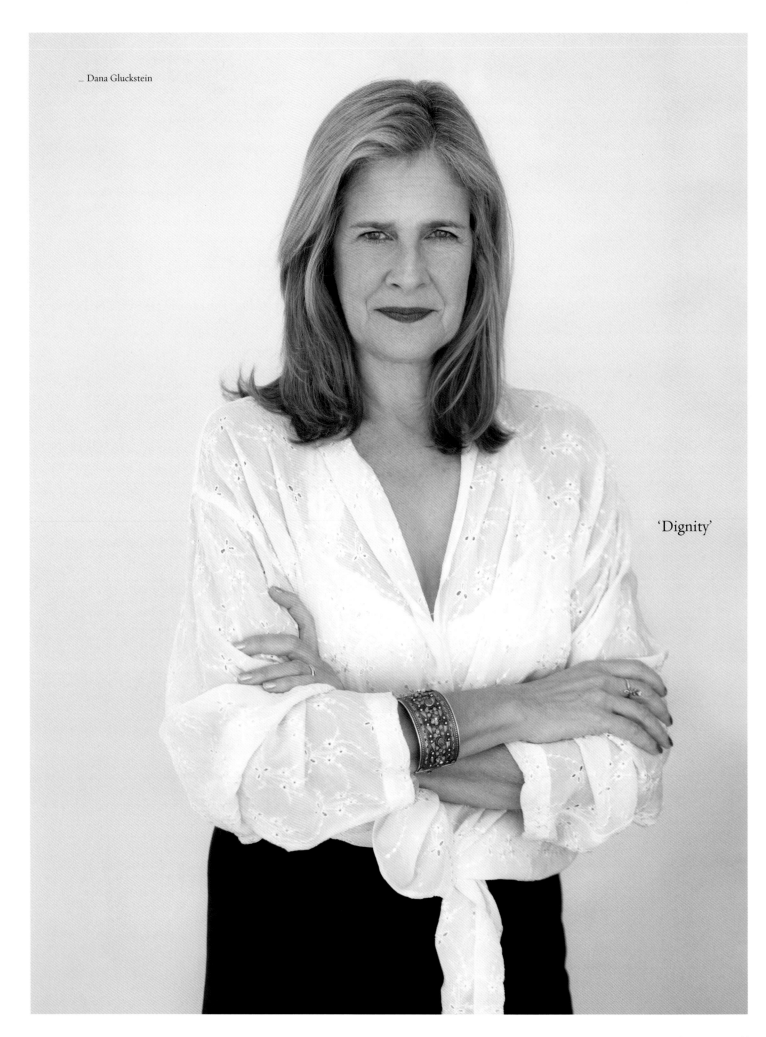

_ Dana Gluckstein

'Dignity'

Interview page 366

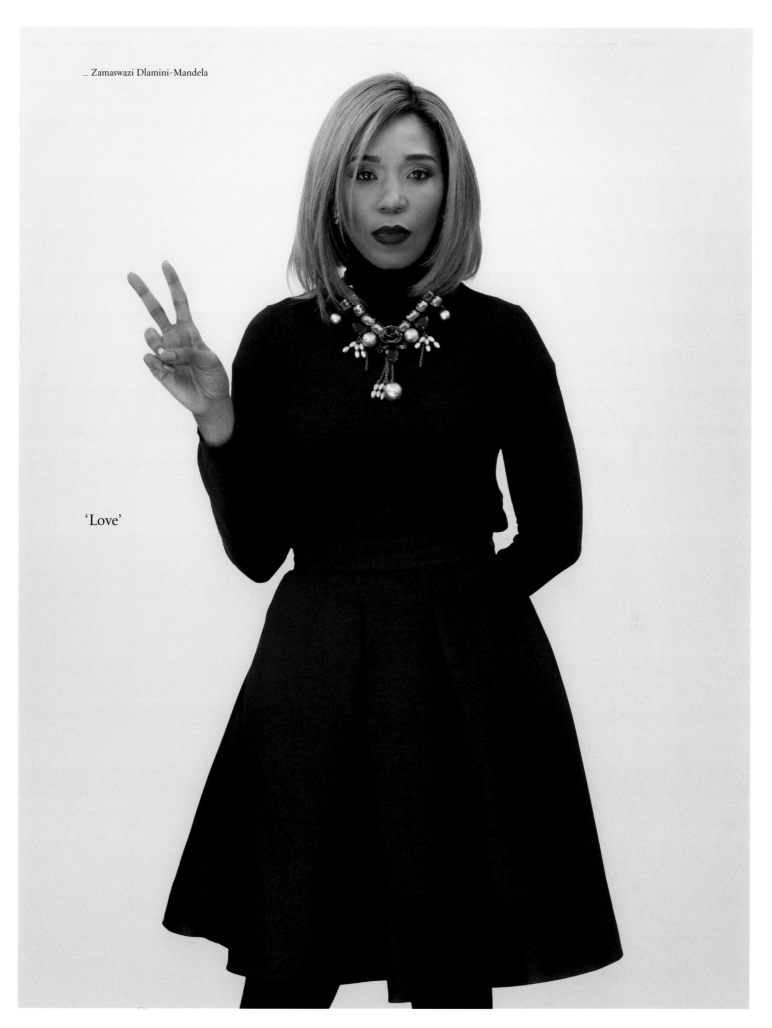

_ Zamaswazi Dlamini-Mandela

'Love'

Interview page 366

Damaris Coulter

Damaris Coulter was born in Kaitaia, New Zealand. Coulter and her sister, Renee, opened their restaurant Coco's Cantina on Auckland's Karangahape Road in 2009. Every Friday, Coco's Cantina offers a meal to the New Zealand Prostitutes' Collective, and outside restaurant hours the space is made available for use by local non-profit organisations.

Q. What really matters to you?

My family is the obvious thing that matters to me. My sister, Renee, and I were brought up in our aunty and uncle's restaurant – while others were playing with Barbie dolls, we were writing orders on docket books. We've never had a huge amount of money but we've never been without the basics: love, food, shelter, kindness, support and community. Rather than being focussed on money or pretence, our family was more focussed on asking, 'Are you being a good friend and sibling? Are you kind? Are you generous?' That's the kind of space and the kind of ethos my sister and I promote in our restaurant. My sister and I are quite different; my family says that I was born a bit spikey. I found alcohol and drugs quite early on, because I had this dis-ease with the world – creatives and people with lots of ideas can be quite chaotic, so drink and drugs really sedated all of that chaos. I stopped drinking when I was twenty, but I didn't clean up my act because I wanted a better life. What kept me sober was hearing people's voices saying, 'Oh, she'll never sort herself out!' So I did it out of spite! When I was clean it felt like all of my senses came back, but I had to relearn how to live. I had to relearn how to be a good friend and sibling. And I couldn't have done it without my phenomenal family.

But what matters to me goes beyond my family. The world matters to me – treating people with kindness and fairness, and being an example of practising good in the world. I found my purpose on this planet when I stopped drinking: it sounds cheesy, but it's doing my very best to fight the inequalities in the world through my actions in my daily life.

We can fall into our daily routines and forget the effect that our niceties can have on others. I put signs up in the bathrooms in my restaurant to remind people about treating others kindly; in the boys' toilets I've got a sign that says, 'If you're not nice to the waiter, then you're probably not a very nice person.' It's not to shame people, it's to gently – or not gently! – remind them.

We offer a hot meal to the Prostitutes' Collective on Friday afternoons. I don't know what it's like to be a sex worker. And I have no judgement about what it's like – that's a choice and sometimes not a choice. But one thing that I can do in my restaurant is offer a meal as camaraderie, to say, 'I'm your neighbour.' My sister and I often say that Coco's is not a restaurant, that it's more like the Bat Cave. The business out in front is Bruce Wayne, and what we do for our community behind the scenes – at night-time in the Bat Cave – is the real deal. My purpose on the planet is to equalise the inequalities in the world through my restaurant.

There always needs to be those people who are disrupting current models — people forget how important that is. And it's not always easy; it can be very uncomfortable confronting someone who's being rude to a homeless person. And some people probably think, 'Oh, it's those busybody Coco's Cantina girls!' But standing up to injustice just feels natural to Renee and me.

Q. What brings you happiness?

I don't know if I find happiness. I still have a constant dis-ease with the world, but now I'm comfortable with it – it keeps me going. Pure happiness is when I don't have to work, when I'm on holiday, when I can have a reprieve from my head and from

work, and from life. I like doing things for other people – because it makes me feel happy that I may have helped someone.

And I quite like a massage!

Q. What do you regard as the lowest depth of misery?

I think about death a lot – that makes me feel a bit miserable. Donald Trump makes me feel miserable. The state of the environment makes me feel miserable. And inequality. When I see people treating others badly, it makes me feel miserable; sex trafficking makes me feel miserable – teenage girls are being kidnapped and shipped in containers, so that men can use them for sex. It makes me sick. We could have such an amazing world, society and environment – humanity could be so loving – and yet we choose suffering, suffocation, exploitation and greed. It's bizarre. It makes me miserable that more people aren't awake, connected and engaged – but I feel like it's changing.

Q. What would you change if you could?

I would make people think. I would change the world's perspective so that it is more accepting of my own perspective. In *The Hitchhiker's Guide to the Galaxy,* there's a perspective gun that, when fired, conveys one's perspective. To me, that is beautiful. People would be more understanding and tolerant if they could see the world through the eyes of the other. People need to be gentler with each other and recognise each other's humanity.

Q. Which single word do you most identify with?

I believe in service: to offer yourself inconvenience in order to give someone else convenience. I believe that's a Buddhist philosophy, making your life harder in order to make someone else's easier.

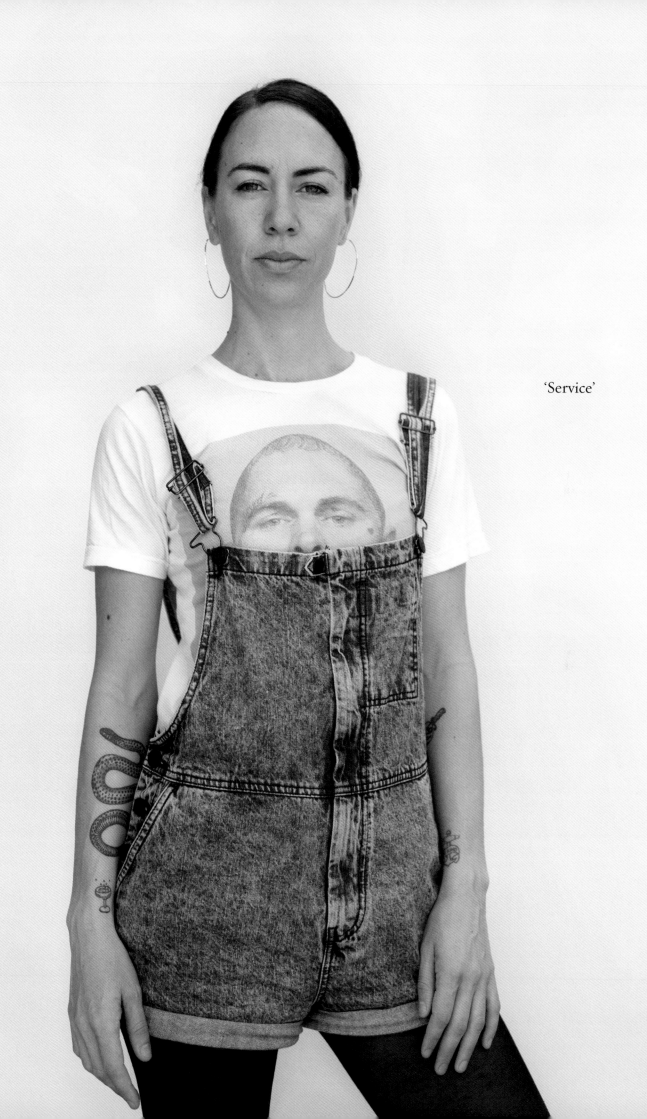

'Service'

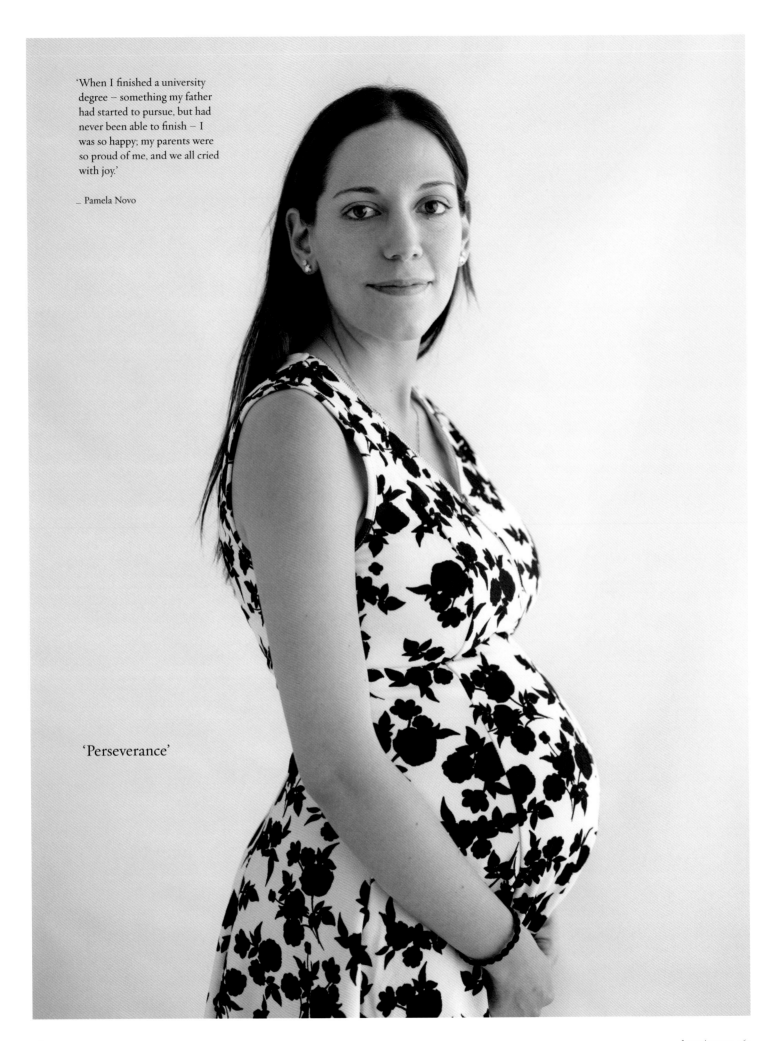

'When I finished a university degree – something my father had started to pursue, but had never been able to finish – I was so happy; my parents were so proud of me, and we all cried with joy.'

_ Pamela Novo

'Perseverance'

Interview page 367

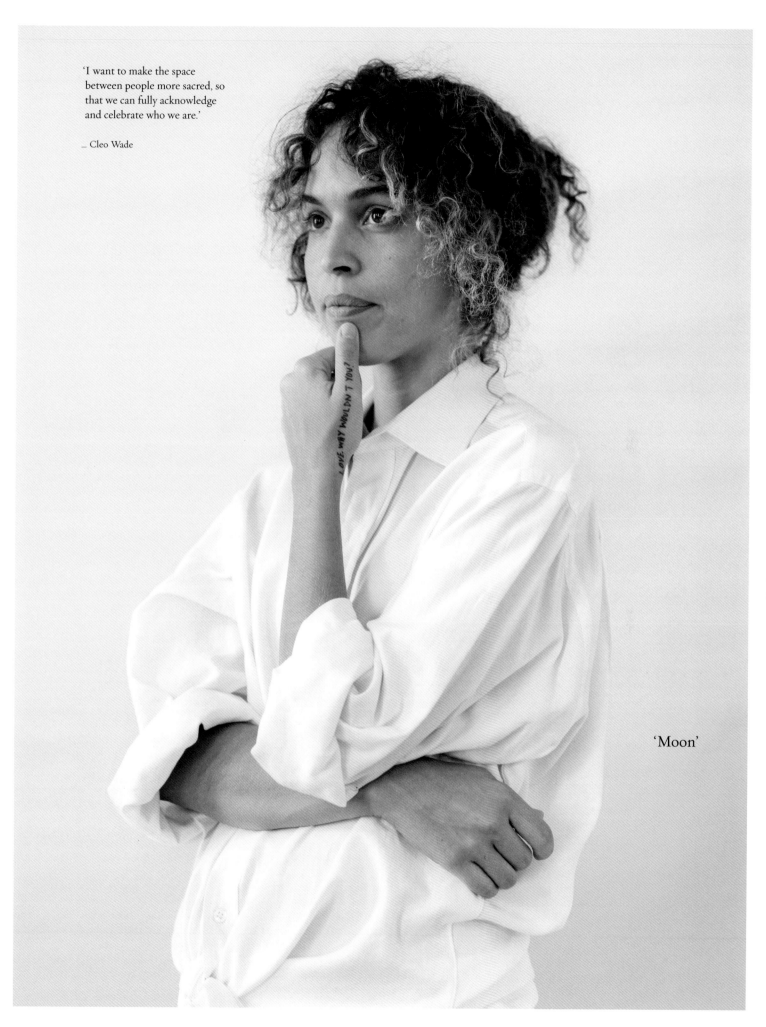

'I want to make the space
between people more sacred, so
that we can fully acknowledge
and celebrate who we are.'

— Cleo Wade

'Moon'

Interview page 367

Ronni Kahn

Ronni Kahn was born in Johannesburg, South Africa. She emigrated to Israel in 1970 and then to Australia in 1988. In 1994, she founded event-planning business Ronni Kahn Event Designs. In 2004, Kahn founded the food-rescue charity OzHarvest and was instrumental in changing legislation that had prevented potential food donors from donating their excess food. In 2010, Kahn was named Australia's Local Hero at the Australian of the Year Awards, and in 2012, she was awarded the Tribute Award for Innovation, Entrepreneurial Skill and Contribution to the Community at the Veuve Clicquot Business Woman Awards.

Q. What really matters to you?

Family, friends and people. It's really all we've got.

Growing up, I realised how important having access to financial stability is. My mother drilled into me that money is crucial for survival because, when I was six, my dad had an almost-fatal accident. He was in hospital for two years, so my mother – who had been a non-working mother – now had to provide for my father and for three children. She scrimped and saved her whole life so that she'd have money to live on in retirement – and she died unexpectedly shortly after her retirement. There was a great lesson in that; it taught me that money is just a means that's useful for living, but that it isn't something to live for.

I was born in South Africa, during the apartheid era. Growing up, my parents taught me that all people are equal and, although they didn't fight the system themselves, they embedded in us that it was wrong. It was an exploitative society and the poverty wasn't something you could avoid – it was right in front of your eyes. One of the tenets of the Jewish religion that I was brought up with is that it is incumbent on each and every Jew to live, 'tikkun olam,' which means, 'repair the world.' It is a duty. The history of the Jewish peoples instils in you the conviction that people must be treated fairly, something that remains very important for me.

When I left South Africa I went to live in Israel; it was an extraordinary experience. For ten years, I lived on a kibbutz, which is a socialist society – a commune – in which everybody works according to their ability and receives according to their need. You can't get much more equal than that.

I then came to Australia and, over the years, grew my event-management and production business. But, thirteen years

ago, I realised that earning a good living was not enough – it just didn't feel like I was doing what I had been put on this earth to do, I wanted to know what more there was to life. That began a journey of discovering what my purpose could be.

In event management, one of the best ways a client can show generosity, abundance and success as a host is by providing wonderful food. What this meant – at the end of an event – is that there was always masses of food left over that goes to waste. When I could, I would take some of the surplus food to one of the agencies I knew, and it certainly made me feel good. So, when I got to thinking about what I could do to bring me joy, purpose and meaning, all this surplus food and the people in need of it came to mind.

It was a visit to Soweto – a township outside Johannesburg – that galvanised me into action to start OzHarvest. On a visit there with my activist friend, Selma Browde, she told me about how she'd helped to bring electricity to the area. It was my light-bulb moment; I wanted to know what it felt like to make that kind of an impact.

Australia is a first-world country, but there is huge need in that more than 10 per cent of the population do not have food security. OzHarvest rescues good food and delivers it to hungry people, and works to educate vulnerable people, consumers and the public in order to minimise food waste. What drives me – and what has driven the culture of OzHarvest – is the notion that every single person deserves the right to food and shelter. They deserve the same as those of us who, by sheer luck, have all they require to live a full and sustainable life. It's not about judgement, rather, it's about ensuring that everyone has the experience of feeling special. Because every single one of us deserves love, health and dignity – that's what really matters to me.

One of the most poignant and meaningful things for me at this point is that Selma's son, Alan, is in the throes of starting a South African version of OzHarvest. I've always had a modicum of guilt for having left South Africa, so it's precious to be able to give back in some way to the country that gave me my core education.

Q. What brings you happiness?

I find happiness in seeing the smiles of the people who work for me – people who've found purpose and meaning through their work for my organisation. I didn't ever intend to be an inspiration to anybody, but it turns out that people find something about what I've done meaningful. And that's priceless.

Q. What do you regard as the lowest depth of misery?

What makes me miserable is inequality, the fact that some people have so much and some people have so little. Personally, though, there's very little that makes me miserable; I have no right to be miserable, because I have everything that I need. But when I think of what causes me sadness, it is ill health and lack of personal fulfilment.

Q. What would you change if you could?

I would love to be able to upskill people who have not had opportunity. I would love to share knowledge and wealth – not just the financial wealth, but the wealth of joy, love and friendship – with those who don't have it.

I am totally aware that, in what I have achieved, I'm standing on the shoulders of all those extraordinary women who fought for my right to live a full human experience. So I will stand up and fight in turn where I can. When I think of my purpose, my fight is for disadvantaged children who are going hungry, and therefore cannot fulfil their potential.

Q. Which single word do you most identify with?

I have so much love to give and I just want to receive it – so it has to be 'love.'

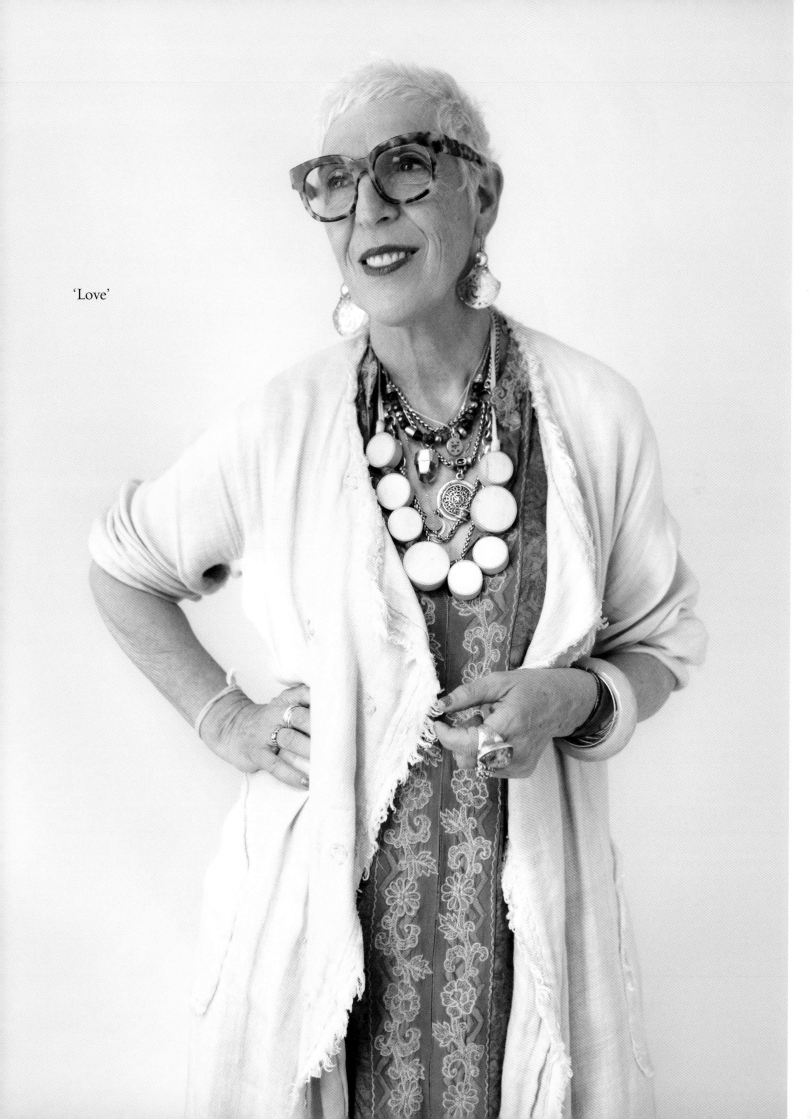

'Love'

Nomvula
Sikhakhane

———

'After my mother found out about all the horrible things that my stepdad was doing – and she had the proof – she still decided to go with the guy. It broke me for a long time.'

Nomvula Sikhakhane was born in Katlehong, South Africa. From the age of six, Sikhakhane was abused by her stepfather. Later, while living with her grandmother, Sikhakhane met Sahm Venter (p. 44) and Claude Colart, who became her unofficial guardians. A graduate of the HTA School of Culinary Art, Sikhakhane now works as a chef.

Q. What really matters to you?
I believe people deserve to be loved.

And I feel that mothers should always put their daughters first – they are the most precious things in life. Mothers should take care of their daughters and look after them. If a daughter says something is wrong, then something is wrong – a mother should believe her.

After my mother found out about all the horrible things that my stepdad was doing – and she had the proof – she still decided to go with the guy. It broke me for a long time. I used to be very bitter, angry and grumpy. I was angry at the world and always used to question, 'Why does life have to be this way?'

But as I grew older and went on to high school I told myself: 'I'm not going to let what happened to me make me a victim. I'm going to be strong and overcome it.' But it wasn't easy. I was angry and when people spoke about my stepdad's abuse I'd break down and cry. Eventually I said, 'I have to be strong and I have to keep going – I'm not going to be a victim of what happened to me. I'd rather have a bright future and be something big.' Even though what happened is not something that I can erase, I can change the way it makes me feel and be a happy person. Because there's nothing that beats happiness. There's no point in staying mad and questioning something you cannot change. But you can turn the negative into a positive. And, so far, I think I've done that; I've accepted what I can't change

and made something positive out of it. I've learned to be a happy person and to let go.

Even though I was still a bit angry when I went to live with my grandmother, as life went on I realised that there was a lot that I should be grateful for. I realised that what was happening was probably a blessing, that I should accept that blessing and embrace it. There are great things in my life: not everyone gets a chance like I did. Not everyone has people like Sahm and Claude who are willing to take them on, do things for them and put them through school. Most of the time, if someone does something like that, they want something in return. But Sahm and Claude don't.

Q. What brings you happiness?
The happiest time of my life was when my granny told Sahm what was going on – she worked with my grandmother. Sahm started buying me things, which is how she came into my life. I'd never actually received so many nice things or had someone doing nice things for me. Sahm taught me how to read and so much else. It was just so overwhelming, but in a nice way. To me, Sahm and Claude are a mother and a father.

Today, my happiest moments are when I walk into a kitchen and start work. My granny used to cook where she worked and, when I didn't go to school because of my stepfather's trial, I'd go to work with her and watch her cook; her being busy – moving around the kitchen – touched me, and I told myself, 'This is what I want to do when I'm done with school.'

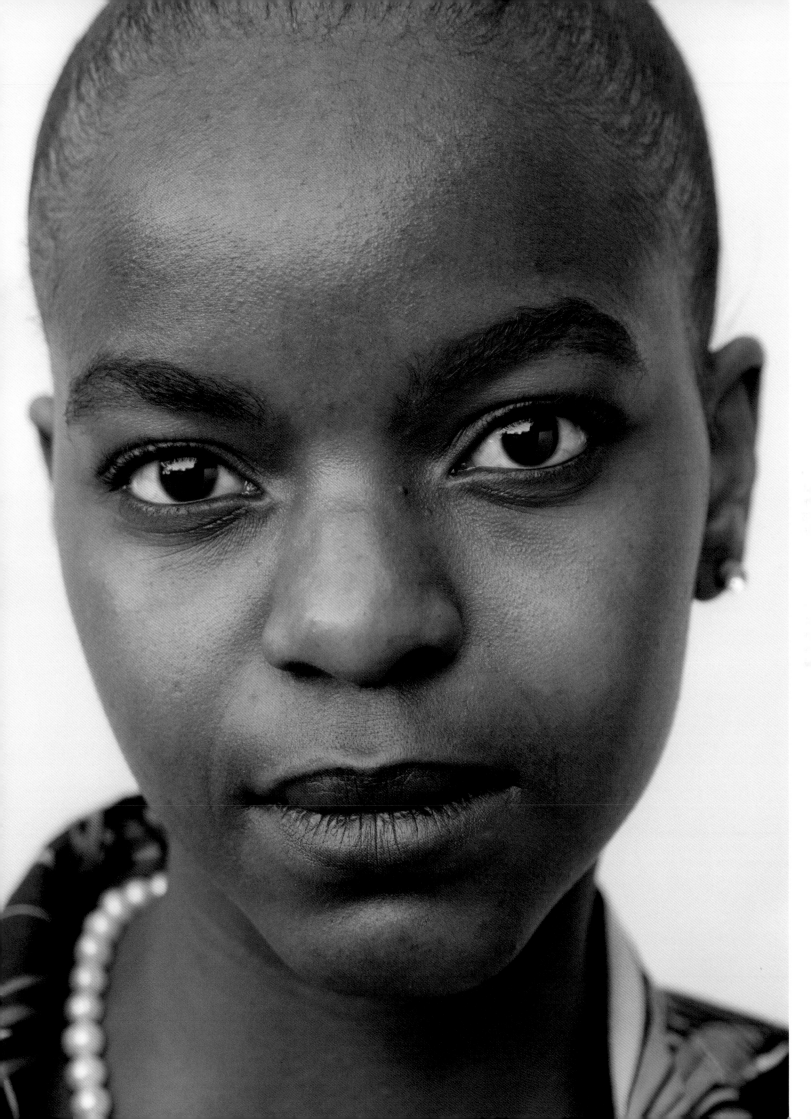

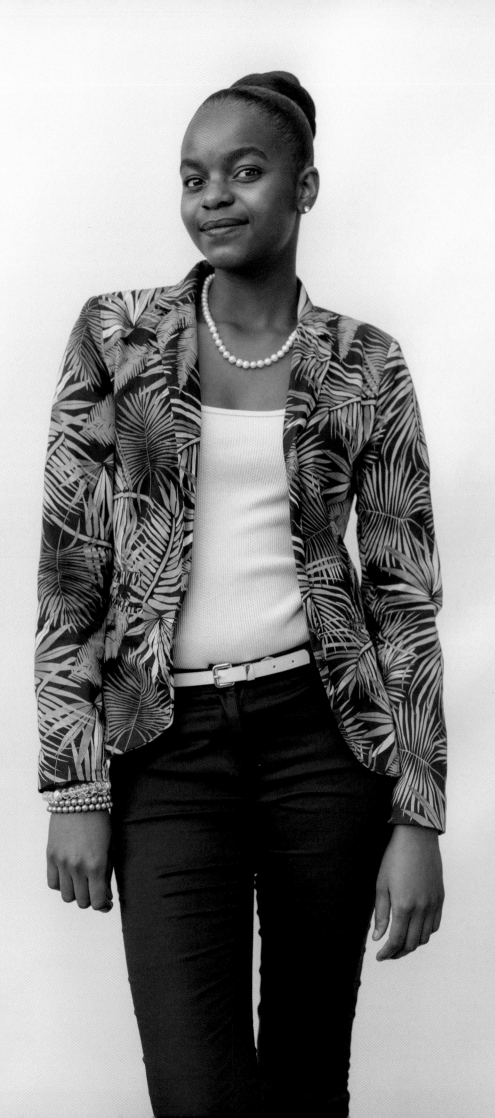

'Love'

Nomvula Sikhakhane

'Eventually I said, "I have to be strong and I have to keep going – I'm not going to be a victim of what happened to me."'

Then, when I was in Grade 7, my aunt and I were walking around Randburg – we were on the way to apply for college for my cousin – and saw HTA, the school where I later studied culinary arts. I told my aunt, 'This is the school I want to go to. When I'm done with everything, this is where I want to be.'

At first, when people asked me what I wanted to do, I had doubts. But, eventually, I realised that if you're going to do something that doesn't make you happy, then there's no point in doing it. I felt that being a chef would make me happy, so, when people asked me what I was going to do, I started answering, 'I want to be a chef. Because cooking makes me happy.'

When I'm in the kitchen I feel happy. And when you serve someone food and you see them smiling, it says something to your heart. You see that you're bringing change to someone's life because they're smiling and they're happy about a meal.

Q. What do you regard as the lowest depth of misery?
It makes me sad that, after everything that happened to me, my mother still got the man that hurt me out of jail. That still breaks my heart, to the point that I feel I should never forgive her for it. I'm her daughter, at the end of the day, and most mothers would do anything in order for their daughters to not have to go through something like that. But it's like my mother didn't care.

Besides that, however, there's nothing I feel that I should complain about; I have a complete life and I have everything I need – life is beautiful.

Q. What would you change if you could?
I would change situations in which children go to bed hungry. I believe that no child should go to bed with a hungry stomach.

Q. Which single word do you most identify with?
Love. I picked love because of Sahm. She has given me so much love – something that my mother failed to do. Sahm showed me that you don't have to be a mother to someone to give them love. Skin doesn't mean anything – it's what's in the heart that really matters. At one point I was angry that I didn't get love from my mother, but when Sahm came into my life she filled that void. I decided that my mother could go on with her life and I would go on with mine: because I have someone who's playing that role. And I have Claude playing the role of a father, and the love of my grandmother as well – I think love goes a long way.

Sahm Venter

Sahm Venter was born in Johannesburg, South Africa. As a journalist for more than twenty years, her career focussed on covering the anti-apartheid struggle and South Africa's transition to democracy. Venter works as the senior researcher at the Nelson Mandela Foundation, and she was a member of the editorial team for Nelson Mandela's bestselling *Conversations With Myself*. She co-edited *491 Days: Prisoner Number 1323/69* by Winnie Madikizela-Mandela, and co-authored *Conversations With a Gentle Soul* with the late Ahmed Kathrada. Venter and her partner, Claude Colart, are unofficial guardians of Nomvula Sikhakhane (p. 40).

Q. What really matters to you?

What matters to me is integrity and sincerity.

And I love communication and telling stories; I became a journalist because I wanted to communicate what was happening under apartheid. The highlight of my entire career – the pinnacle – was Nelson Mandela's release. I was lucky enough to be outside the prison on that day. We waited and waited – it was a very, very hot day – then all of a sudden we saw this grey hair, with a halo behind it, and this fist in the air. It was him! I just stood there. I couldn't believe that he was finally out. Everything I had witnessed – about people being killed and the horrible violence – all seemed far away.

All these years later, it's really important that we stay true, as a country and as a world, to the values that we held high at our best moments: democracy, freedom, integrity, humanity, sincerity. These values are all underpinned by humanity. You cannot have a system like apartheid if you have humanity, because apartheid was the absence of humanity, in its crudest form. And human beings kept that system alive – it wasn't a machine, it was people. We have to always be very true to our values and hold on to the good people in the world. We have to nurture them. And we must make sure that we don't ever let that spirit die. Too many people forget about those things and get too caught up in materialism in their own lives. They forget too quickly. We have to remember where we come from, and we have to judge where we are now in that context – because we can so easily slip back into the worst moments of our lives if we're not vigilant.

This needs to happen throughout the world – South Africa's not the only country in the world that's ever had bad things happen. Most countries have something terrible in their past or are still experiencing something terrible. We're all in it together as a human species. We don't live in isolation, especially not today with all the globalisation; if we had had social media in the past, I don't know that apartheid would have lasted as long as it did.

Q. What brings you happiness?

I love hearing good news, whether it be about someone I know or someone I don't know. I like to hear about people's good news – that things have come together in their lives or in their careers. It can be little or it can be big, but I am so happy when I hear that people are succeeding in what they are trying to do.

For example, I know a family whose mother died. The small children were left behind and their aunt took them in. But she could not get them registered because the mother hadn't registered their births – and if you aren't registered, you can't get access to anything. Quite a lot of effort was put in and – after they had been pushed from pillar to post – all of a sudden they met the right person who sat down with the aunty and said, 'What surname would you like them to have?' It all came together and now they exist – they can function in the world. That's pure happiness.

And I was very happy when Nomvula got accepted into chef's school; I think we both cried.

Q. What do you regard as the lowest depth of misery?

Cruelty. It's extremely difficult to be aware of any type of cruelty, whether it be against women, children, men, animals – any type of life. Cruelty is unspeakable; it should not be tolerated. I can't even hear about it. In fact, I cannot even listen to news programmes on radio and television about some cruelty that's happened. I cannot hear it; I have to turn it off or turn it down. When we're talking about cruelty, we can talk about abuse – physical abuse, emotional abuse – which happens all the time in the world and in this country particularly. It drives me crazy.

Q. What would you change if you could?

I would let everybody have equal quality education. Everybody. As a right. Everybody needs to be paid properly for their work; nothing should say that if you're pulling a big pile of recycling around you shouldn't get enough money to live in a house with electricity, water and food. Everybody should have free and easy access to good-quality social services. And there should be no national borders, so people could move around the world wherever they want and just settle down, raise their families and be happy.

We're not there yet with gender equality, either: not just in South Africa, but in the world. Women are still second-class citizens, and I don't really see all that much change, here or anywhere else. Some countries can be held up as beacons because they've got really special laws and have been at it longer than we have, but South Africa is a deeply sexist society. The slogan always used to be 'Fighting for a non-racial democratic South Africa,' then some people added 'a non-sexist South Africa.' Ours is a very patriarchal society. I'm talking about in every sphere of life, including corporates. I recently had conversations with women who believed that it was okay for some big corporates in this country to tell women how to dress. I was completely shocked. I thought, 'Try and make me wear heels, and I *will* go to the Constitutional Court.' Because it's insane.

Q. Which single word do you most identify with?

Gratitude. I am very grateful for my life: my family, my friends, my car, my job, my house, my roof, my hot water, my electricity. And for the fact that I am able to help people from time to time.

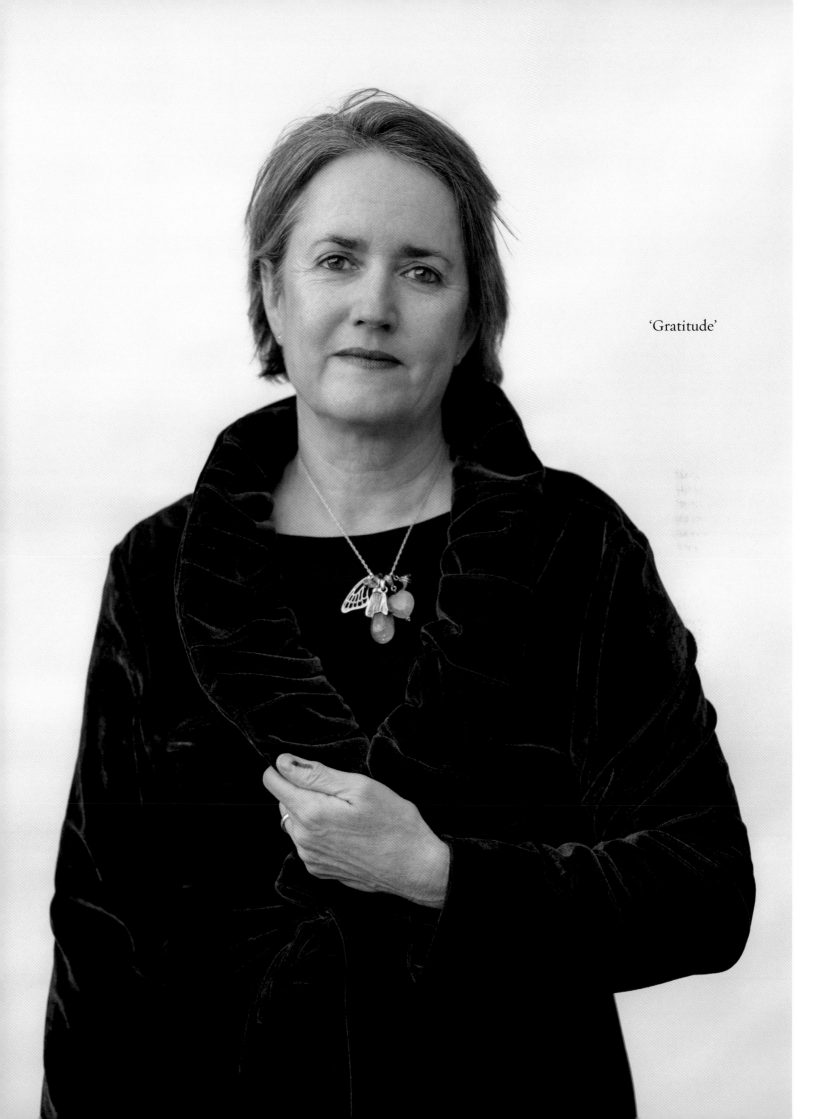

'Gratitude'

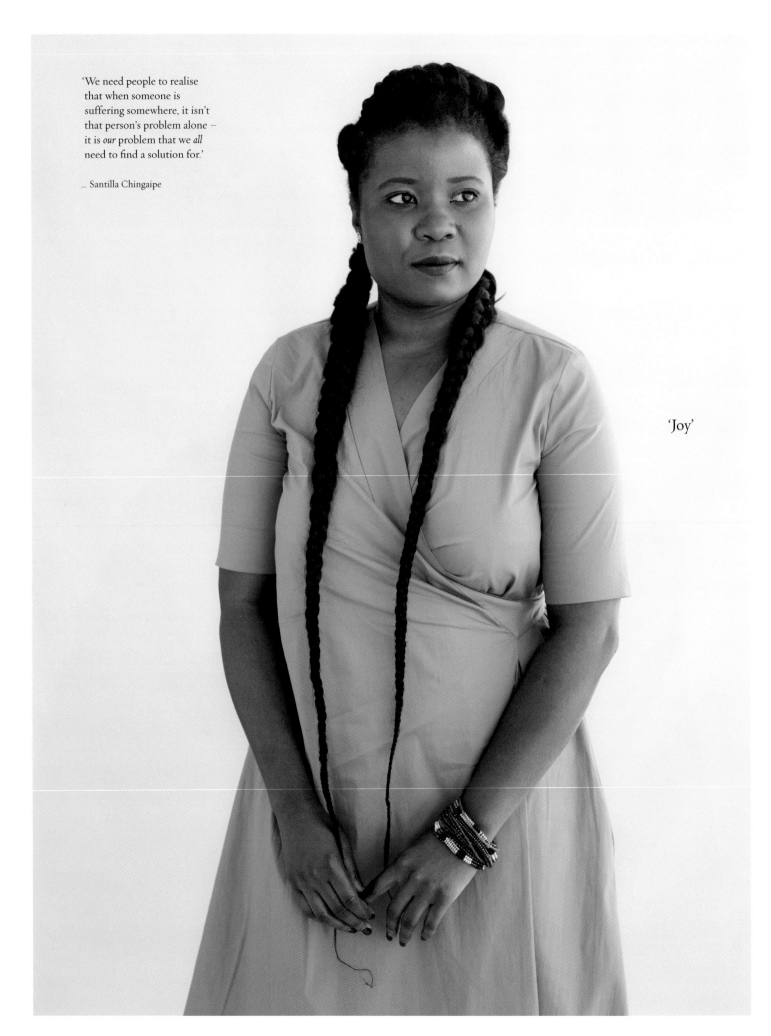

'We need people to realise
that when someone is
suffering somewhere, it isn't
that person's problem alone –
it is *our* problem that we *all*
need to find a solution for.'

_ Santilla Chingaipe

'Joy'

Interview page 367

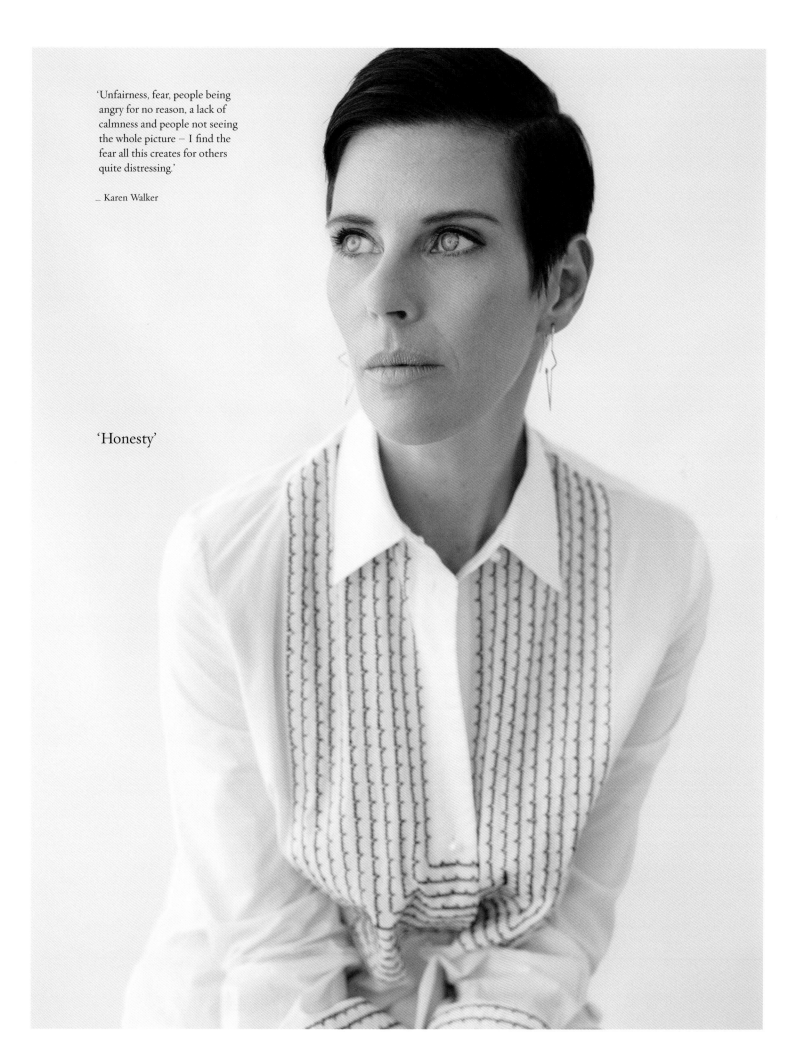

'Unfairness, fear, people being angry for no reason, a lack of calmness and people not seeing the whole picture – I find the fear all this creates for others quite distressing.'

_ Karen Walker

'Honesty'

Zoleka Mandela

Zoleka Mandela was born in Soweto, South Africa. She is the founder of the Zoleka Mandela Foundation and of the Zenani Mandela Campaign for road-safety awareness. Mandela is also an ambassador for the global SaveKidsLives road-safety organisation, and the author of the autobiographical *When Hope Whispers*. She is the granddaughter of Nelson Mandela and Nomzamo Nobandla Winnie Madikizela-Mandela.

'One of the most difficult things that I've come to accept is how I failed my daughter as her mother.'

Q. What really matters to you?
What I try and do every day is see how I can use my life to better the lives of others. It's never too late for anyone to rewrite their life's story, and that's what I've done. I want to remind people that you can always pick yourself up, no matter what you're going through in life – having abused drugs and alcohol for over seventeen years, I celebrated my sixth year of sobriety in 2016. So people can always decide to start making better choices.

I started the Zoleka Mandela Foundation in 2013, and it's really just an extension of myself; I call it my other baby. It was an opportunity for me to give back to my community. The pillars of my foundation are representative of the things that I've gone through in my life: we look at breast cancer awareness, because I am myself a breast cancer survivor; having lost a child in a road accident, we also focus on issues of road-safety awareness; and being a recovering addict, we speak to youth about issues like the dangers of drugs.

I always say, 'As much as we're different people, all our struggles are the same.' Some are shocked at my struggles because of the family I come from. But I think it's important that people know that it doesn't matter who you are in life or where you are in terms of your status – we all have real-life issues and things that we're struggling with. It's great if people are able to relate to my story and journey, and see that you can turn things around. It's just a matter of making the right choices for yourself – but *you* have to change in order for things to change.

Q. What brings you happiness?
My four children. I say that because I think for the very first time in my life, if ever I felt like I had some kind of purpose, it was when I gave birth to my first child. Every single child of mine that has come into my life has really shifted things in me and made my life even more meaningful.

Q. What do you regard as the lowest depth of misery?
One of the most difficult things that I've come to accept is how I failed my daughter as her mother. I lost my daughter Zenani in a drunk-driving accident in 2010, and, unfortunately, at the time I was still quite heavily into addiction. I wasn't with her when she died – when she needed me. I had been so dependent on drugs and alcohol for so long in my life that it was difficult for me to be the mother that she deserved, or for that matter, the mother any of my children deserved. Now, I just try and live my life knowing that I'm staying clean every day and ensuring that I do things that would make Zenani proud of me.

Q. What would you change if you could?
I would change the number of children that die on our roads. It's a shocking number – we're losing 500 children a day everywhere around the world. It's so unfair, because we all know the answers as to how to ensure their safety, and our children, who aren't able to protect themselves, must be able to get the protection they deserve. This has a lot to do with how I lost my daughter; I feel like she needed me there in order to protect her, and so this is my way of celebrating her memory – with the road-safety campaign work that I'm doing both nationally and internationally.

Q. Which single word do you most identify with?
The word would be 'hope.' The title of my autobiography is *When Hope Whispers*. Simply put, I know that there is hope in my life and there's still hope in the lives of others.

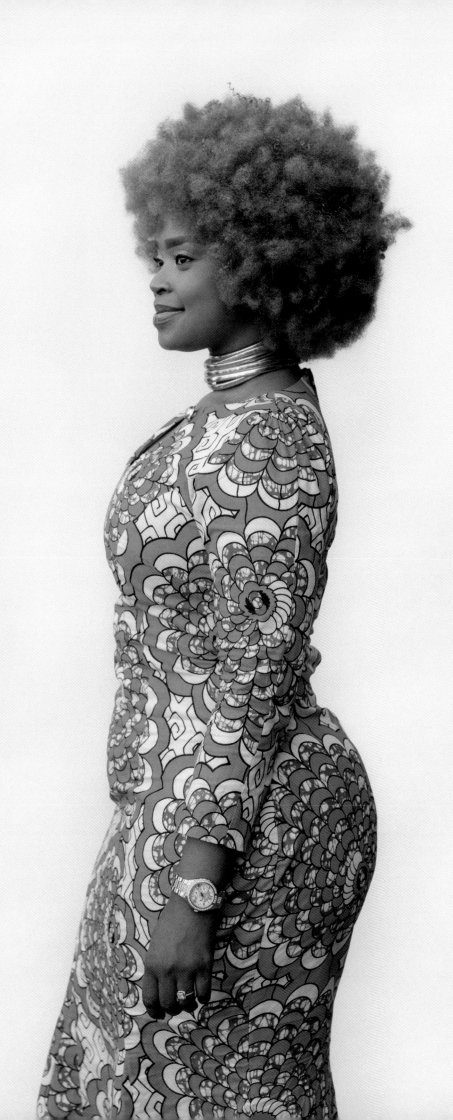

'Hope'

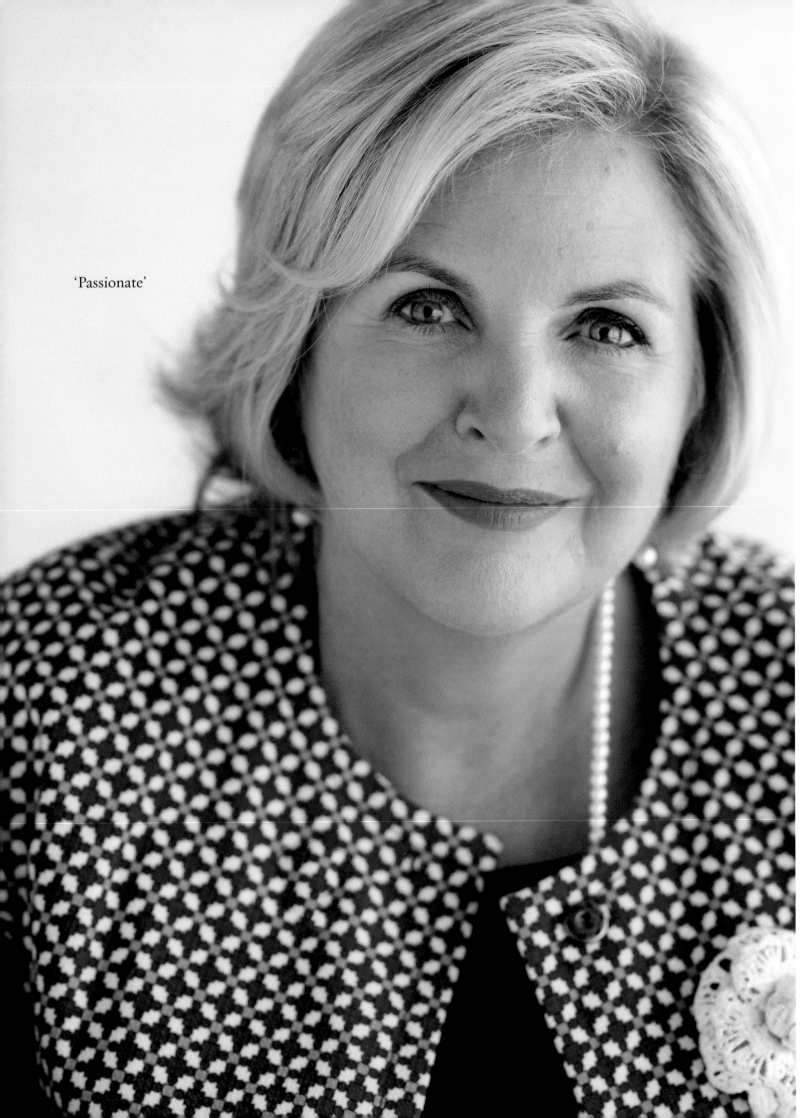

'Passionate'

Christine Parker

Christine Parker was born in Auckland, New Zealand. Trained as an accountant, she holds postgraduate qualifications in human resources management, leadership and quality management. In 2011, Parker became Group Executive, Human Resources, Corporate Affairs and Sustainability at Westpac Group. She is a governor of the St. George Foundation, a not-for-profit organisation that helps disadvantaged children, and is a director of Women's Community Shelters, which works to establish new short-term emergency accommodation facilities for homeless women and children in New South Wales, Australia.

Q. What really matters to you?

It's incredibly important to me that my family and friends are healthy, well and successful in their lives.

Trying to get the right work/life balance also matters to me. Achieving this is different for every individual, but I've become much better at it over time. I've developed an understanding of what balance means for me and of how I can do the things I want to do with my friends and family, and, ultimately, find time for me as an individual as well.

Effecting positive change is something I'm very passionate about. Sometimes you can look at all the things that are going wrong in the world, or in your community, and say, 'Oh, the issues are so big, I can't do a thing.' But I reject that. I think every one of us can make a difference, whether that's in how we help an individual or in how we utilise our influence. My brother had serious mental-health issues from a very young age, which tragically led to his death in his forties. It was just my mother and I who looked after him, and it's given me a deep, deep insight into what it is to suffer with mental-health issues, and the impact and suffering on individuals and families. The exposure I've had to the mental-health care system highlighted to me some of the extreme prejudices held by society, so I'm passionate about helping people who are going through experiences like my brother did, and about ensuring they are supported and given the same choices as everyone else.

Early on in my career, I had a dreadful experience working for someone who was a bully, a racist and sexist. This experience was very formative for me. It taught me that any organisation I work for simply has to be values-driven, and it has to refuse to tolerate individuals and behaviours like that. It showed me that there's a lot of responsibility in being a leader; you have to be courageous enough to call out individuals and behaviours that threaten the values, diversity and inclusion of an organisation.

Organisations are by their nature incredibly diverse, whether in diversity of gender, sexual orientation, disability, ethnicity or of religious beliefs. All this enriches the workplace, but organisations aren't always as inclusive as they should be or need to be. At Westpac, we have over forty thousand people who work for us across Australia, New Zealand, the Pacific Islands, the United Kingdom, Asia and the United States. We have a long, proud history around sustainability, community involvement, inclusion and diversity. When I arrived at the bank in 2007, 33 per cent of the leaders were women, but there were just as many capable, talented and highly educated women as there were men. Now we are on track towards achieving a goal of 50 per cent women in leadership in the top four thousand roles; the process has been exciting and fulfilling.

It's important to me that I'm working in organisations where I can make a difference and am creating meaning and purpose for the people who work with me. For me, it is incredibly invigorating ensuring that our people can, and do, really make a difference in the lives of our customers and their communities. And it matters that I take responsibility for inclusiveness in my workplace and use whatever influence I have to enable people to bring their absolute, whole self to work and be the very best they can be.

Q. What brings you happiness?

My family being happy and well. I love the work that I do, coupled with my involvement in community organisations; I give a lot of my time to helping to support the vulnerable and the disadvantaged, but I get a lot back from it. My previous CEO, Gail Kelly (p. 158) has a saying, 'do what you love, love what you do.' I think this encapsulates life beautifully.

Q. What do you regard as the lowest depth of misery?

At a personal level, misery is the loss of a loved one or having a loved one be either mentally or physically unwell.

Beyond that, what brings me misery is the domestic-violence pandemic against women and children – I see it firsthand through my involvement with Women's Community Shelters and find it incredibly distressing, particularly because it leads, in many instances, to homelessness and the development of mental-health issues that can be inter-generational. Governments, communities and individuals around the world need to be doing so, so much more around this issue; there needs to be more funding, more education and more people stepping up. And the silence has to stop. This is not just a women's issue.

Around the world, I see that divisiveness based on gender or sexual orientation has permeated all facets of society. It's really sad that we are still having conversations about inclusiveness. New South Wales announced its second female state premier recently – an incredibly capable individual – and I found it fascinating that she was asked questions about why she was single and childless, and about whether this would have any impact on her work. In this day and age, I found that incredibly disappointing. But I take heart in the great progress we've made over the years and in the groundswell of individuals and communities that really want to make a difference, and that want to celebrate what's right as opposed to what's wrong.

Q. What would you change if you could?

The important principles to start with are fairness, equity and inclusion – no matter who you are, where you come from, what colour your skin is, who you choose to love or what gender you are – being able to celebrate and debate difference, then still come together as a whole.

Q. Which single word do you most identify with?

Passionate.

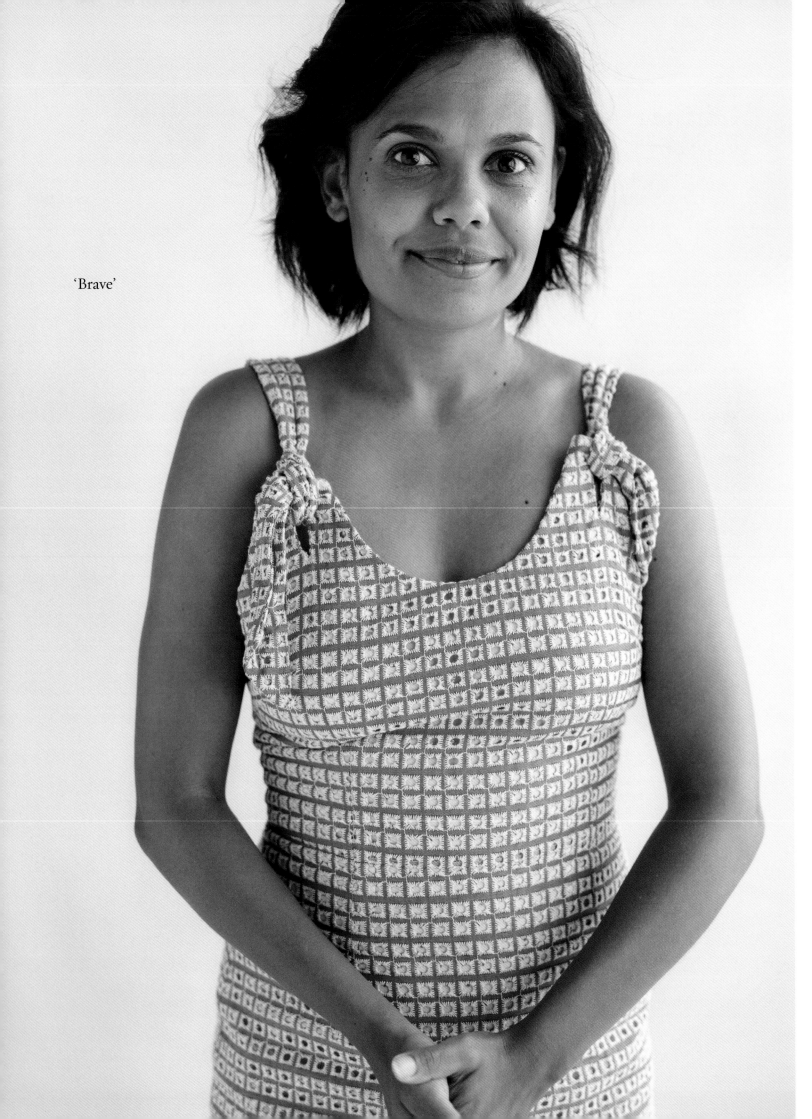

'Brave'

Miranda Tapsell

___

Miranda Tapsell was born in Darwin, Australia. She is a First Nations woman of the Larrakia tribe. Tapsell is best known for her role in *The Sapphires* – the story of four Indigenous Australian women who travelled to Vietnam in the sixties to perform for United States troops – and her role in the drama series *Love Child*, which deals with the subject of historical forced adoptions of Indigenous Australian children. In 2015 Tapsell won a Logie award for her performance in *Love Child*, and, in her acceptance speech, called for more people of colour to appear on television.

Q. What really matters to you?

What matters to me is that art teaches empathy. When people see the way others live their lives, their perceptions change. I love being an artist because I saw what *The Sapphires* did to a non-Indigenous audience: it appealed to people across the board – grandmothers, mothers, daughters – who were able to relate, not just to the era, but also to the timelessness of the story. Young girls loved the film because, like them, the characters were young women trying to achieve their dreams and find their way in a very uncertain world.

Art might not save lives – it might not cure cancer – but it is powerful. It allows people to walk in the shoes of those who are marginalised and disenfranchised. Non-Indigenous people have come up to me and taken my hand, saying, 'Thank you so much for *The Sapphires* – you have no idea what that story meant to me.' This helped me really understand the power stories have to put people into someone else's shoes and allow them to understand what it means to live that person's life. This made a big impact on me, because I have to talk about race a lot.

My mum raised me to be very, very proud of my heritage. I choose to identify as being Aboriginal and am asked about this quite a lot. I'll gladly tell people that I'm Aboriginal, but this seems to be quite divisive. I'm not sure what makes some people think that my pride in my heritage equals a hatred for non-Indigenous people. I don't hate non-Indigenous people, I'm just aware of a system that supports non-Indigenous people and that fails to support the more vulnerable, which includes Indigenous People.

I love storytelling because it gives the most vulnerable a voice. The media doesn't tend to shine much light on Indigenous issues from an Indigenous perspective: if it does, this is very rare. While there's been a lot of conversation in Australia on the topic of Indigenous Peoples, I still feel as though I'm expected to choose a side. Yes, there has been a lot of progress – I didn't grow up having to fight the battles my nan and my mum did, in terms of getting the vote and becoming citizens – but I don't feel as though I should have to choose.

I was a child when John Howard was prime minister of Australia; he was in power from 1996 to 2007, and was quite conservative. The implication I got from his politics was that he didn't believe that the Australian government owed an official apology to the Stolen Generation. From 1869 to 1980, Aboriginal children were forcibly removed from their mothers. He questioned the legitimacy of these claims and refused to acknowledge the damage that had been done to Aboriginal families over decades. While I'd never been taken from my mum, if I had lived in the sixties – born to my Larrakian mother and my non-Indigenous father – that would have been my fate. So, to me, hearing our own prime minister ask why an apology was important was like hearing him ask, 'Why do you even need to exist? Why are you here? Why are you making us feel uncomfortable?'

For most of my life, I have had to justify why I choose to call myself Aboriginal. The title, and all the issues surrounding Aboriginal people, seems to make people uncomfortable. Becoming an artist made me realise that, when people see me in a different light, they can actually like me! People who aren't Caucasian have had to survive by fitting into an existing structure – they're only given the chance to assimilate. No one should have to live that way. Australia needs to encourage integration, because everyone should be able to define themselves the way they choose, without judgement. To be shamed for not blending in is something I just can't agree with.

Q. What brings you happiness?

Being around my friends and family brings me happiness, because I'm one of those people who can't hold things in and they help me overcome hardship.

Being able to use the platform I have makes me happy. I am a very privileged woman, and I've been given an opportunity to use the media in whichever way I can to shed light on the issues that Indigenous People, and other marginalised groups, face.

Q. What do you regard as the lowest depth of misery?

I have to admit that I found 2016 really hard and I think a lot of people found it hard as well; a tribalism was starting to form among many people who identify themselves as white, and I was starting to see more and more people who look like me being shut out. It frustrates me that we now live in a time in which people are more concerned with words than with their effect. When someone like me points out racism – that someone has felt hurt, degraded – people would rather analyse language and sentence structure to determine whether there has in fact been an incidence of racism. I'm sorry, but that's a waste of my time and it's what brings me misery.

Q. What would you change if you could?

I wish I could change the way people thought, the way they see the environment and the way they treat it, and I wish I could change the way people choose to continue to disenfranchise Aboriginal people. But the thing that gets me up out of bed every day is thinking, 'No, I will continue to be strong and continue to say the things I believe in the media.' That's what gives me hope.

Q. Which single word do you most identify with?

My word is 'brave.' Bob Marley said, 'You never know how strong you are until being strong is the only choice you have.' That resonates with me, because sometimes when I know that something needs to be done I just take action, then look back and go, 'Oh, I didn't realise how brave I was.' To me, those actions are what bravery is.

Sara Khan

Sara Khan was born in Bradford, England. She holds a master's degree in understanding and securing human rights from the University of London's School of Advanced Study. In 2008, she co-founded Inspire, a counter-extremism and women's-rights organisation. Khan is one of the United Kingdom's leading female Muslim voices on countering Islamist extremism and promoting human rights. She is also the author of the book *The Battle for British Islam: Reclaiming Muslim Identity from Extremism*. Khan's work has earned her numerous accolades, including a position among 2015's top-ten influencers on BBC Radio 4's *Woman's Hour* Power List.

Q. What really matters to you?

Ever since I was a child, I have witnessed the normalisation of gender discrimination among Muslim communities. Gender inequality exists in all communities, but it was clear to me that many Muslim women experienced additional barriers, which included negative patriarchal religious interpretations of Islam that encouraged discriminatory attitudes and practices towards women. The contemporary rise of religious fundamentalism has perpetuated this problem; as we have seen so often, the rights of women are the first to go whenever extremists hold power. I believe in an egalitarian interpretation of Islam that embraces gender equality. This progressive movement within Islam faces an uphill struggle; supporting Muslim women activists who face an intense backlash for speaking out is vital.

My father is a firm believer in girls' education. He arrived in the United Kingdom from Pakistan in 1963, and it mattered to him that his daughters were independent and able to earn their own money. He told his children that, no matter what anyone said, there was nothing we could not become. So, although I experienced racial abuse and bullying at school, I refused to be defined by it. In fact, it made me even more defiant about who and what I am. At the same time, though, I saw many teenage Muslim girls of my age being forced into marriage, denied further education and being expected to live a life of servitude.

As a teenager, I was also disturbed by the number of young Muslims who advocated Islamist extreme views; and today, even more so than twenty years ago, I am astounded by the rate at which young people are becoming radicalised. But, I am still more astounded by the way society reacts to this issue. Examining the rise of Islamist extremism makes many people uncomfortable. Some on the political left, for example, fear that talking about Islamist extreme ideology will feed anti-Muslim prejudice. I disagree. Countering radicalisation is one of the key challenges of our time, especially as we are seeing children as young as ten fall victim to extremist world views. Our failure to address and resolve this issue is only exploited by the populist far right, in its promotion of an 'us versus them' narrative that sees Muslims as the enemy. Islamist extremists also, of course, promote an 'us versus them' world view. The middle ground that advocates for shared values and a common humanity is increasingly under threat, so we need to defend that middle ground – that is what I seek to do with the work I do.

One of the reasons I co-founded Inspire was my increasing frustration with Muslim organisations who did not want to provide solutions to these complex issues. I grew tired of hearing male Muslim community leaders repeatedly state that before we address gender equality, we must tackle Islamophobia. This was a red herring to me, as I believe that you *can* tackle both at the same time, through the prism of human rights.

I set up Inspire to directly engage with Muslim women, in the belief that, if there was going to be change in our society, it would come from women; whether in addressing gender equality or being on the frontline of countering extremism, women have an important role to play. In 2014, we launched an anti-Daesh (Islamic State) campaign called Making a Stand. Hundreds of women in nine cities across the United Kingdom participated. Many women stated the same point: they could no longer wait for men to lead in this area. We spoke to the women about how essential their role is in disseminating counter-narratives to extremist ideology; how women can not only safeguard their children, but act as a bulwark to extremism by standing up to extremist preachers operating in our society. We cannot pretend extremists do not exist, because they do, and the harm they are causing to our society is significant. Inspire has also trained five thousand teachers in how to recognise the early signs of radicalisation and the importance of teaching critical thinking. We work to influence policy and deliver campaigns, as well as engage with the media. Central to Inspire's work is the promotion of human rights, because we believe human rights, by default, undermine extremism.

Fighting these battles, on these fronts, means you constantly receive a barrage of abuse from religious fundamentalists, including death threats to yourself and your children. Propaganda sites spread fake news and smears about you repeatedly in an attempt to discredit you and your work. I sometimes wonder if, had I lived in a different era, I would have been labelled a witch and burnt at the stake! The abuse is a form of intimidation, directed towards silencing our voices and ensuring that the status quo – gender discrimination and extremism – remain. But I do see change; it comes when women are prepared to shatter boundaries and to make sure that their voices continue to be heard.

My biggest frustration is how some people react to people like me: a human-rights-advocating Muslim. Instead of supporting us, they condemn us or, worse still, align themselves with Islamists and call us 'Islamophobes' because we speak out against Islamist extremism. Solidarity has never been more important to those of us who are prepared to put ourselves on the frontline in the hope of promoting an inclusive society. Getting people to recognise our common humanity and fighting for our shared values, regardless of our differences, matters to me.

Q. What brings you happiness?
Seeing children happy, secure and loved.

Q. What do you regard as the lowest depth of misery?
When people reach a level of despair from which they feel there is no way out, that there is no solution to their situation and that they are alone. This is the lowest depth of misery, and it takes many forms. And, although there is always a way out, it is hard to perceive this when you are engulfed by despair.

Q. What would you change if you could?
I would like to see a more gender-balanced world with more women in power. If we had more women at the leadership table, we would have a more inclusive approach to international development, and to eradicating poverty and resolving conflicts.

Q. Which single word do you most identify with?
Humanity.

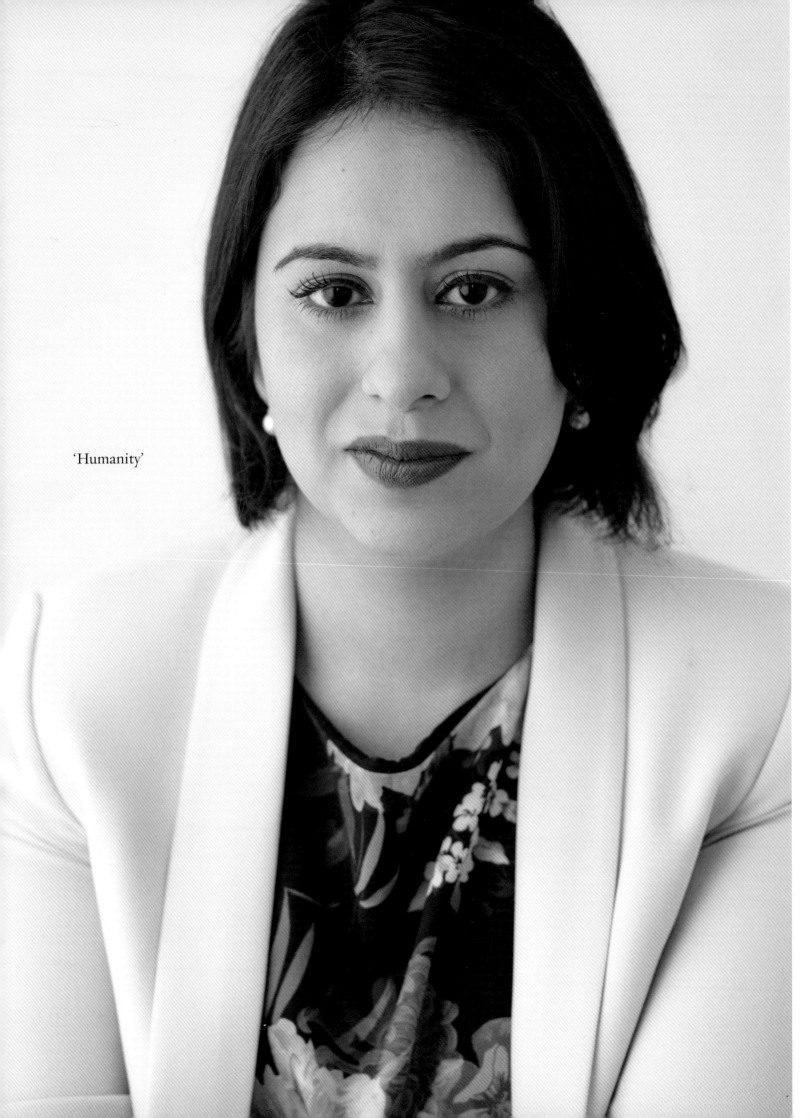

'Humanity'

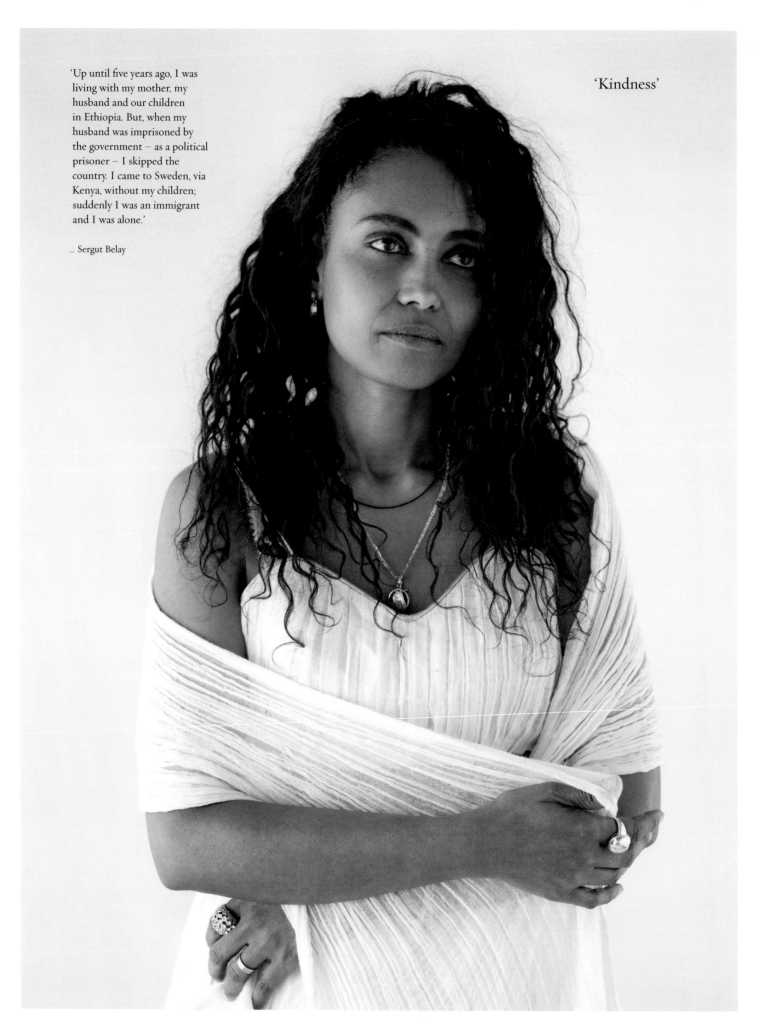

'Up until five years ago, I was living with my mother, my husband and our children in Ethiopia. But, when my husband was imprisoned by the government – as a political prisoner – I skipped the country. I came to Sweden, via Kenya, without my children; suddenly I was an immigrant and I was alone.'

_ Sergut Belay

'Kindness'

Interview page 368

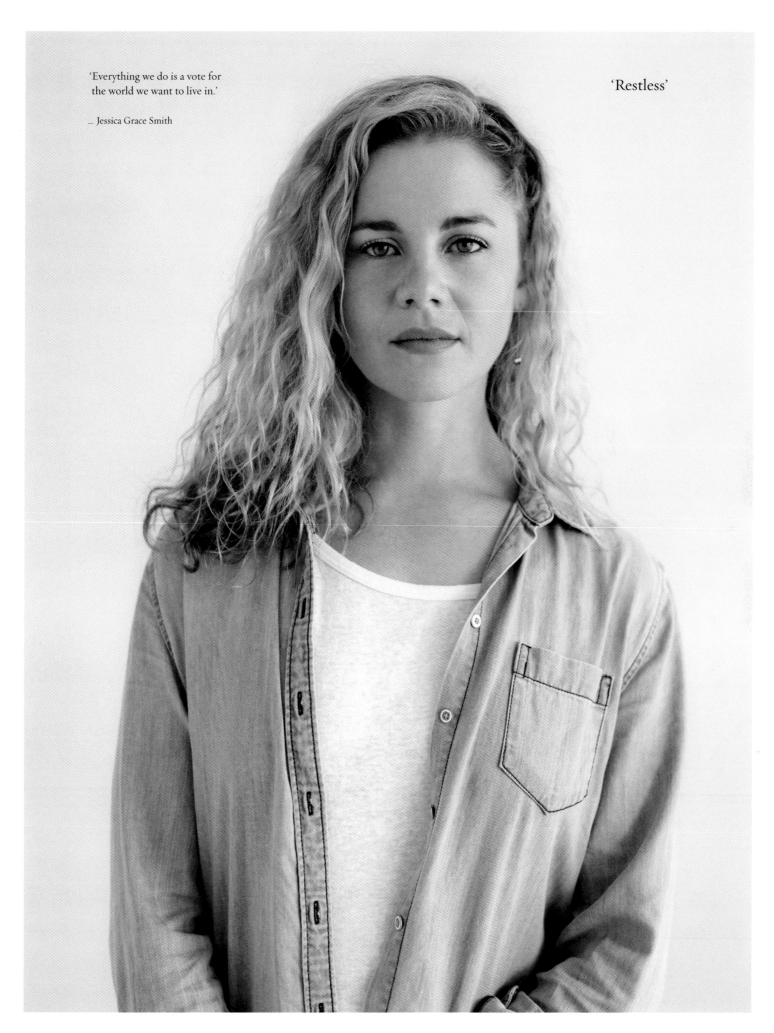

'Everything we do is a vote for
the world we want to live in.'

_ Jessica Grace Smith

'Restless'

Interview page 368

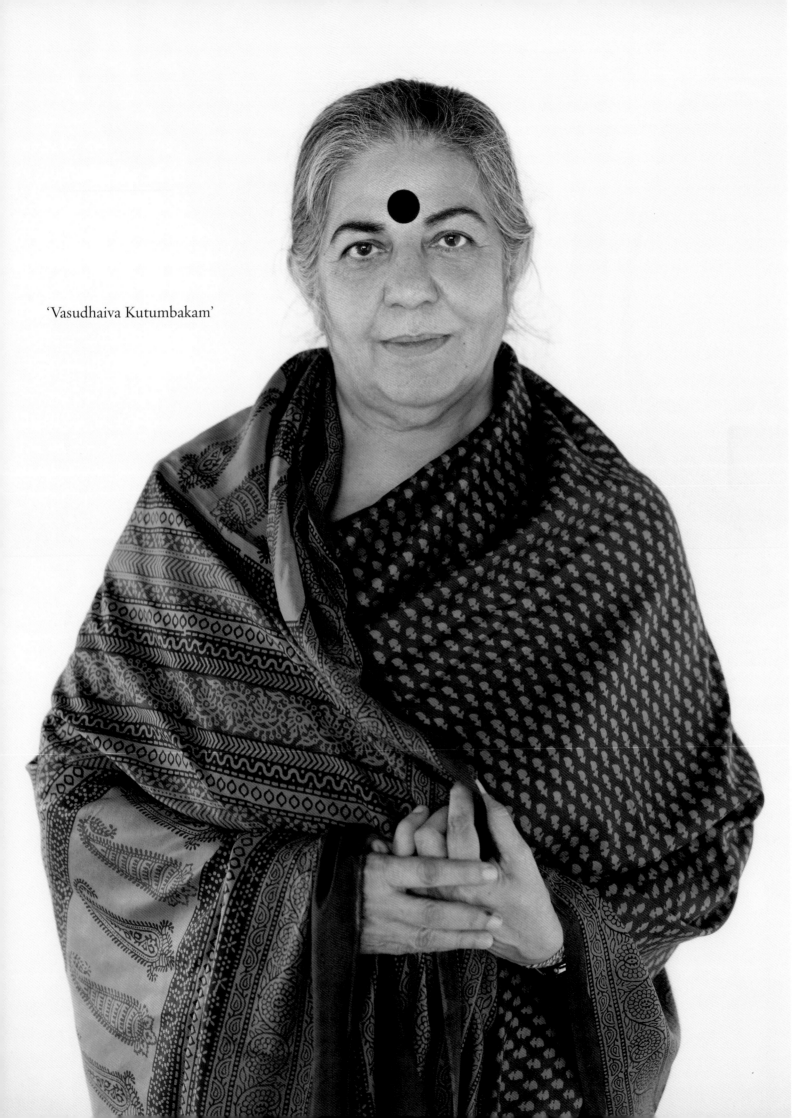

'Vasudhaiva Kutumbakam'

Vandana Shiva

Vandana Shiva was born in Dehradun, India. She trained as a physicist at the University of the Punjab and completed her PhD at the University of Western Ontario in Canada. Shiva is a co-founder of the Women's Environment and Development Organisation – a global women's advocacy organisation that promotes human rights, gender equality and the environment – and the founder of Navdanya, a movement that works to protect the diversity and integrity of living resources in India; she is a board member of the International Forum on Globalisation. Shiva's published works include *Biopiracy*, *Stolen Harvest*, *Water Wars* and *The Violence of the Green Revolution*.

Q. What really matters to you?

It matters to me to cultivate more generosity and compassion in our times, to have deeper resilience to the highly irresponsible and brutal changes we are going to be living through, and to constantly find the strength to be able to respond in ways that empower everyone around me.

I am a child of these Himalayan mountains and of this valley in which I was born – I have returned here to dedicate my life to the protection of the earth and to the rights of people to live at peace with the earth. I trained in physics long ago, but it is really my work in service of the earth that has shaped my life for the last five decades.

As a young girl, I lived in the forests of these mountains. My father was a forest conservator and my mother – who had been a very high education officer in what became Pakistan – come back as a refugee and chose to be a farmer. My reading in the early stages was all based on what I found in the little forest-rest-house libraries. I was particularly inspired by a book about Einstein's writings I must have read when I was five or six – I wanted to be that kind of scientist.

Alas, there was no science teaching in the convent schools I later went to, yet I followed that dream. My parents were very nurturing and encouraging, and allowed us to be what we wanted to be. I wanted to be a physicist, but no girl was studying physics in those days; I wanted to go off to Canada, but nobody was sending their daughters off to do a PhD by themselves in the seventies. Nonetheless, my parents allowed me to do what I wanted to do, with a deep trust that I was making my own choices. So, I did a master's in particle physics and a PhD in non-locality and non-separability in quantum theory – my mind was always tending this way, because I was always dissatisfied with a mechanistic world view.

Q. What brings you happiness?

Following my conscience.

If there was any choice I made every day of my early life, it was to avoid public roles. When I was made head girl of my school, I told Mother Superior, 'I will do this work as long as I can hide. I'll do everything you need a head girl to do, but I will not run assembly, I will not give speeches and I will be invisible in the role. But anything else you want me to do, I'll do.'

It's interesting that here I now am, totally against the intentions of my childhood; I am a public figure, giving talks and writing books, all only because, at every point, I respond to my conscience. So, if my conscience tells me to speak on behalf of a person who is being kept in slavery to build a dam, I will speak; I will find my voice. Because none of this is about me.

Q. What do you regard as the lowest depth of misery?

It hurts me to see a forest dying and to feel violence against nature – I became an activist when I saw a stream in which I had swum as a child dry up. And it hurts me to see a person wasted; it hurts to see the violation of people and the prevention of their full evolution. All around me, I see a desertification in the hearts of people, in their souls and their hopes. And I see the desertification of the planet at large, in a deep ecological sense – the planet is losing its capacity to support life. This outrages me, so I channel that rage into finding creative alternatives. In this, quantum theory is always alive in me; the seed has a potential, the diversity has potential, the land has potential and all this gives me joy; full evolutionary potential expressed in people gives me joy.

Q. What would you change if you could?

First, I would get rid of this cooked-up construction of people who destroy the world whilst hiding behind a corporate form. A corporation is a total construct –

the East India Company was something written on paper for three hundred merchant adventurers – and yet, a big part of the problem today is that absolute power is in the hands of a few people through the corporate form. Corporations should dissolve, and people should take responsibility for their business, rather than externalising liability via a limited-liability corporation.

Secondly, I would do what I'm doing anyway: work to protect the commons that are vital to humans living ecologically on this planet. Because I believe everything related to life is a commons – not just for humans, but for all of life. These commons – plants, biodiversity, seeds, rivers, land, atmosphere – cannot be privatised. Privatisation means making profits out of depriving others and destroying the commons, because you don't have to pay the consequences. But, if I have to manage my river as a commons, I'll make sure it's not polluted. And, if I have to save my seeds and pay the consequences if those seeds are not fertile next year, I'll make sure they're fertile.

Thirdly, I would introduce deep ecological, food-literacy and gardening education into every school, so every child knows what the earth is about, what the soil is about and that they have in their hands and in their minds the capacity to work with the soil to provide amazing food.

Q. Which single word do you most identify with?

I've chosen a phrase, *Vasudhaiva Kutumbakam*, which is the Sanskrit for 'earth family.' Vasudhaiva is one of the one thousand names for the earth; in India, everything – the sun, the divine goddess – has one thousand names.

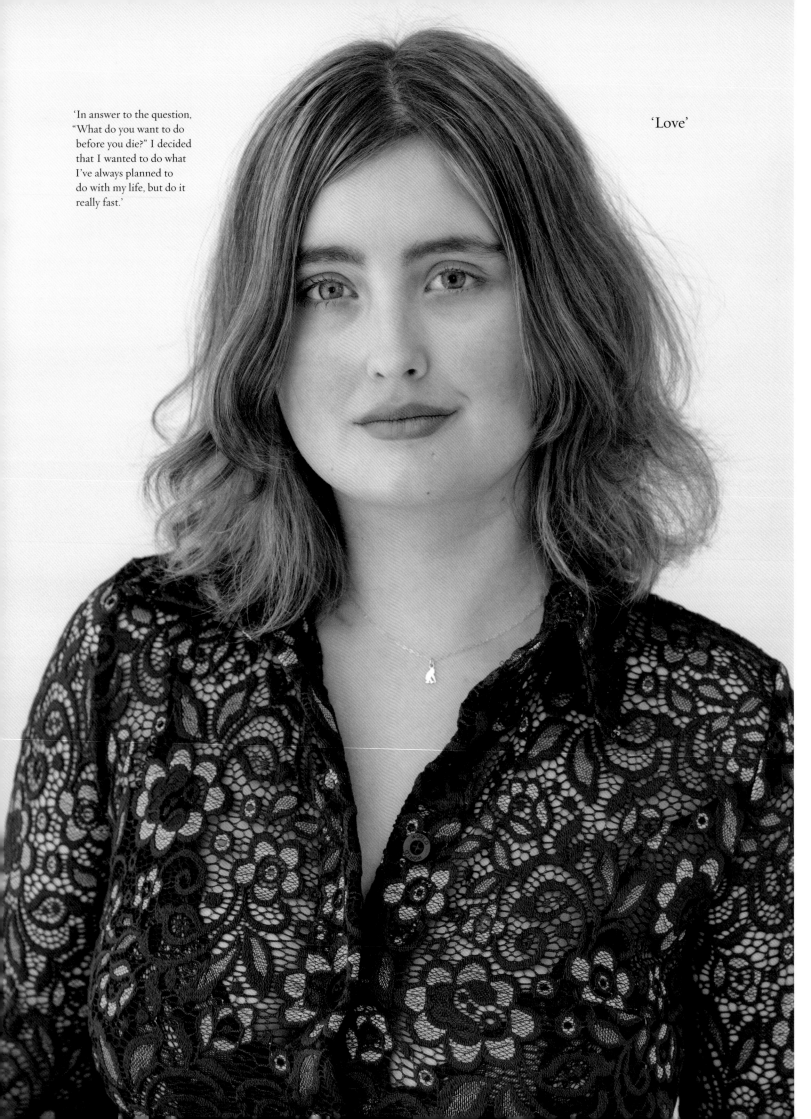

'In answer to the question,
"What do you want to do
before you die?" I decided
that I wanted to do what
I've always planned to
do with my life, but do it
really fast.'

'Love'

Eva McGauley

Eva McGauley was born in Wellington, New Zealand. Raised in a strongly feminist environment, McGauley became a member of the Wellington Rape Crisis centre at the age of thirteen. In 2015, at age fifteen, she was diagnosed with nasopharyngeal carcinoma, which was subsequently confirmed to be terminal, and has undergone several treatments of chemotherapy and radiation. McGauley is dedicated to supporting young victims of sexual violence, having several friends who are survivors of sexual assault. She is also an intern for New Zealand's Green Party.

Q. What really matters to you?

My family. I know that everyone really values their family, but I would not be the person I am today without them. I was brought up a feminist by my mum and my grandmother, so I've always had this inherent sense of equality and a desire to fight for it. I have a very politically divided family, but that's made for a lot of good conversations. My family are my support system. They keep me together, and I, them – which is why what's happening to me is so scary.

When I was fifteen I was diagnosed with nasopharyngeal carcinoma, which is a rare kind of cancer that affects one in 7 million people. I'd initially been misdiagnosed with glandular fever by my paediatrician, but when we finally found out that I had cancer I spent five months in hospital undergoing a course of really intense chemotherapy and radiation. The chemo kills every fast-reproducing cell, so the treatment affected my hair, my stomach lining and my mouth; I couldn't eat or drink because of the radiation. After the course of chemotherapy and radiation, I was told I was in remission, but three weeks later the doctors said they'd got it wrong and that I was terminal.

People think that you're going to break down when you're told something like that, then instantly have an answer when they ask you what you want to do as a result of the news. But I still don't know – it still hasn't sunk in. I don't think it's really going to until it really *has* to. I didn't let out any emotion for a few days – my mum may have, but not around me. It was tough because we were both just trying to look after each other and protect each other. Then we all suddenly started realising that my family is just going to have to cope without me in their lives. All of the people I rely on – and who rely on me – just took a big, deep breath in, then held it as we

realised the impact this is going to have. I'm still not sure when to let that breath out.

In answer to the question, 'What do you want to do before you die?' I decided that I wanted to do what I've always planned to do with my life, but do it really fast. So, what matters to me are women's rights and combating sexual violence, because I want to give more in life than I've taken.

Growing up, I was always aware that different genders were treated differently. And I've always wanted to help people. When I was thirteen, my friends and I tottered into a feminist-club meeting at school, and came out feeling so amazing and empowered – we realised that we wanted more of it.

Before I became sick, I got involved with Wellington Rape Crisis, an organisation that provides support for survivors of rape and their families. That experience showed me that I wanted to work in the sexual-violence sector, with an emphasis on prevention rather than support – I think I'm more of a politician than a counsellor. I developed a business plan for an online-messaging service that would allow survivors to message trained professionals, around the clock, who can link them up with support services in their area. I had the opportunity to speak with Jan Logie – a New Zealand member of parliament for the Green Party – about my idea, and she offered me an internship with the Green Party.

I've carried out and read a lot of research on international messaging platforms like the one I am proposing, which have proved incredibly successful, so I really think New Zealand needs one. Here, one in five women will experience a serious sexual assault in her lifetime, one in three girls will be abused before they turn sixteen and one in seven boys will be sexually abused by adulthood. This is a huge problem. Jan helped me get

my business plan out there, and an agency called Help Auckland responded; they are New Zealand's biggest provider for sexual abuse survivors. We developed a fundraising page with the aim of raising NZ$50,000; after getting the message out, we reached our goal in under five months.

Q. What brings you happiness?

I really love soap operas; they are my guilty pleasure.

I very much admire Helen Kelly – the New Zealand union leader – who passed away in 2016. She was an amazing woman. The people she helped all talk about how she became like a member of their families. I'd like to emulate her and give my time, affection and love to those who need it. Because, when helping someone really pays off, that's the biggest reward.

Q. What do you regard as the lowest depth of misery?

That's tricky, because there's so much misery in the world. I'm very close to my mum, and I've always really wanted children, which I won't have, so the thing that I find hardest is seeing scenes of mothers and children being ripped away from each other in Syria. The idea of losing a child is scary – which is why what I'm going through is so hard – but, at the same time, I know that I don't have it as bad as what you see happening in Syria.

Q. What would you change if you could?

There are so many things, but can I just say world peace? That fixes them all: poverty, anger, hate.

Q. Which single word do you most identify with?

Love. For me, love is a very, very deep, meaningful and sacred thing. I make sure I say, 'I love you,' to the people I love all the time. I call my grandma, my godfather and my aunt every day before I go to bed to tell them I love them. Love is the thing that keeps me ticking.

'I'm always asking whether I'm doing enough to fulfil my potential. My mother worked as a kitchen hand and put all her money into extracurricular activities for my brother and me. She wanted us to have as many experiences as possible.'

_ Marita Cheng

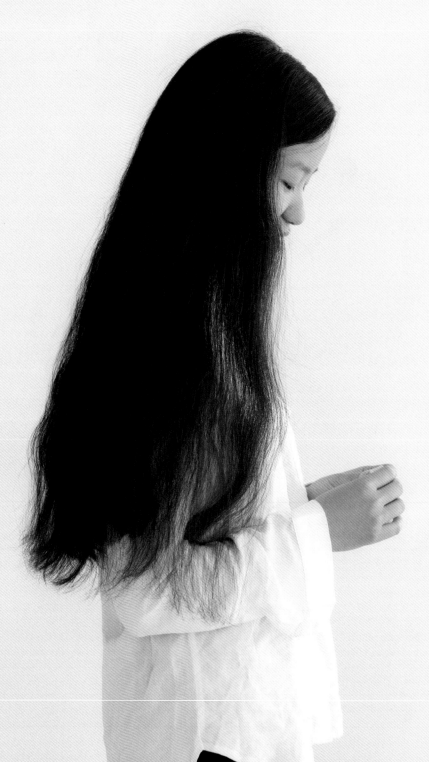

'Hope'

'I'm always asking whether I'm doing enough to fulfil my potential. My mother worked as a kitchen hand and put all her money into extracurricular activities for my brother and me. She wanted us to have as many experiences as possible.'

Interview page 369

'My adoptive parents helped set up Lifeline in Australia, so as a child I was often in the back of a car when they drove to a domestic-violence dispute. I watched my parents walk out of houses with women and children under their arms. I learned about the power of the informal system, when the community wraps itself around someone.'

_ Jan Owen

'Generosity'

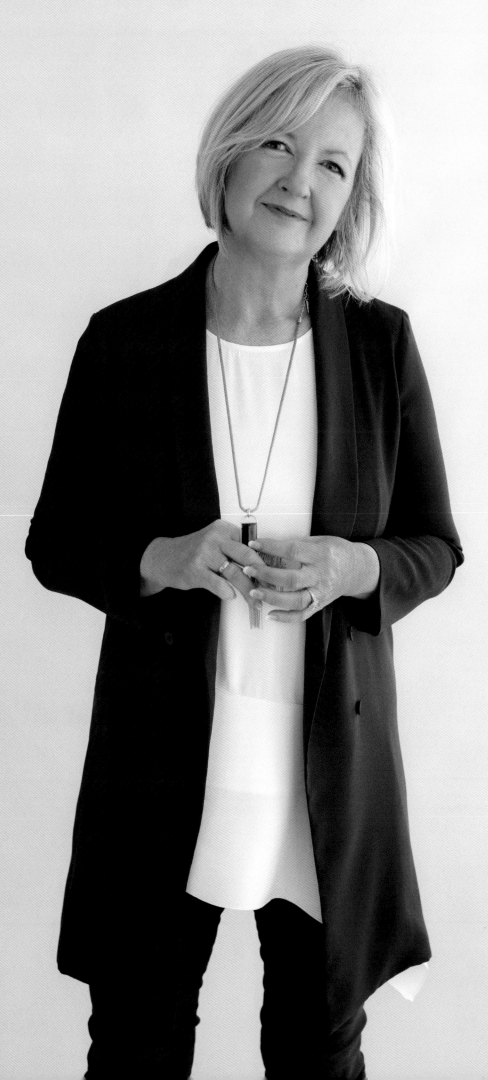

Interview page 369

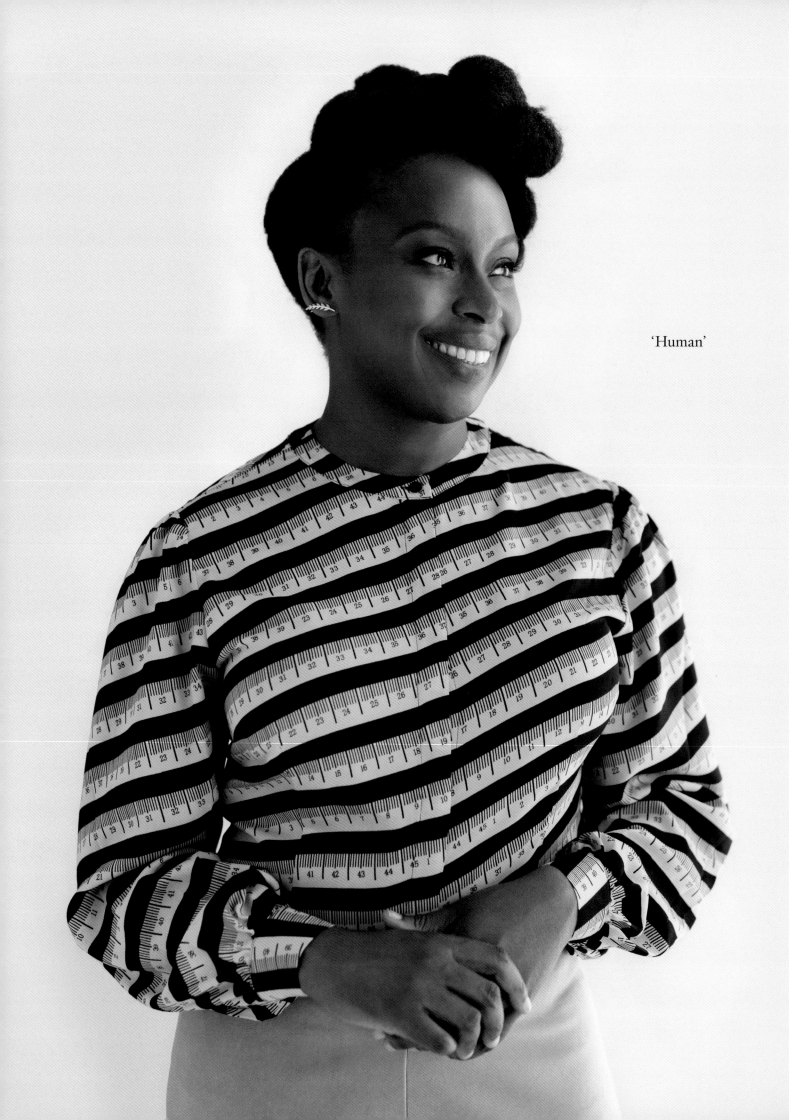

'Human'

Chimamanda Ngozi Adichie

Chimamanda Ngozi Adichie was born in Enugu, Nigeria. A graduate of Eastern Connecticut State University, Johns Hopkins University and Yale University in the United States, Adichie is an award-winning writer whose work has been translated into thirty languages. Her novels include *Purple Hibiscus*, which won the 2004 Hurston/Wright Legacy Award and the 2005 Commonwealth Writers' Prize; *Half of a Yellow Sun*, which won the 2007 Orange Broadband Prize for Fiction; and *Americanah*, which was among *The New York Times* ten best books of 2013. Adichie was awarded a MacArthur Foundation fellowship in 2008.

Q. What really matters to you?
A friend of mine once told me that everything I care about, I care about passionately; I don't think it was necessarily a compliment!

At the risk of sounding like a beauty-pageant contestant, I care about justice. I believe that my purpose is to be a storyteller and, because of this, I believe that I feel things in a very particular way – certainly far more intensely than other members of my family. When I see that which is unjust, my reaction is strong, and what I feel inspires what I write.

I grew up in the shadow of the Biafran War. I didn't experience it, but my parents did; both my grandfathers died in the war. Despite no one wanting to talk about it, the war was very present, and I was the child who asked endless questions – every family has that one child. I wanted to understand the story of who we were and how we came to be in that situation of conflict.

I'm often asked whether anything specific occurred in my past to make me into this fierce feminist, but there was nothing seminal; I just see myself as having been a child who always wanted to understand. As a storyteller and a person who creates, I have always felt slightly removed from my world; I have always felt that I am watching everything and am never entirely present. That has given me the ability to notice; very early on in my life I noticed that the world is very unfair to girls and women. I wanted to understand the justification, but I've never found one. I suppose that, in wanting to understand why certain things were a certain way, I wanted things that were bad to be better – that's still something I want. As a little girl, I always questioned being told, 'Oh, our culture forbids that.' I saw the unfairness even in small things; I was told that I couldn't go to the local

masquerades at night, because only boys could do that. That's when I realised how important it was to be an individual, because allowing people to be individuals and judging people as individuals is a way to combat gender expectations.

I left home when I was nineteen to go to college in the United States, which was a decision that changed the trajectory of my life. My parents are relatively progressive people, and I had been protected from a lot, so it was at university that I did my growing up: the culture I grew up in was outward looking and cosmopolitan, but also very traditionally Igbo.

It's very difficult to talk about one oppressive institution without talking about the others. I often like to joke that I don't choose the days on which I am black, the days on which I am a woman and the days on which I'm both. I experience being black and being a woman, and being a black woman, every single day.

Class is something that has become prominent in my life, because, unlike these other two categories to which I belong, it's a category in which I actually experience privilege – and it's made me understand how complicated privilege is. There is a certain level of access I have that I haven't really earned, but which I benefit from rather happily. This makes my determination that we get rid of unearned privilege even stronger. Here in America, for example, it is impossible to talk about race without talking about class, because there is a very strong sense that race is class. And I can't talk about gender without referencing race and class, because the gender pay gap is also an issue of class.

My writing matters to me. It's hard for me to talk about who inspires me or

who influences me because, on the one hand, the writer in me is reluctant to know the answer – I want my influences to be unconscious, otherwise I may feel like I am copying someone. On the other hand, though, I just don't have an answer – everything I've read up to this point must have influenced me: the history of the Catholic church, the rule of the Nazis, Enid Blyton . . .

Q. What brings you happiness?
My family and my friends – the people I love. For me, family is broadly defined; it's not just the people with whom I share blood, it's the people with whom I share love. Following them, it's my work. I love that I can write and, when my writing is going well, it is a source of happiness. When it's not going well, that's often a trigger for depression – but that's what my family is for.

Q. What do you regard as the lowest depth of misery?
As opposed to experiencing an absence of love, I would say that it's being separated *from* love and being separated from loved ones. It is when you are trapped in a situation that you cannot change and you're cut off from your people – that's the lowest.

Q. What would you change if you could?
I can't pick just one thing; I would eliminate all forms of gender, racial and religious injustice. The issues are their own, independent issues, but they cannot be analysed in isolation from one another. It's very complex and is always a work in progress for me – the issues are connected and they are not, but, however strong their connection to one another is, they've got to go!

Q. Which single word do you most identify with?
Human.

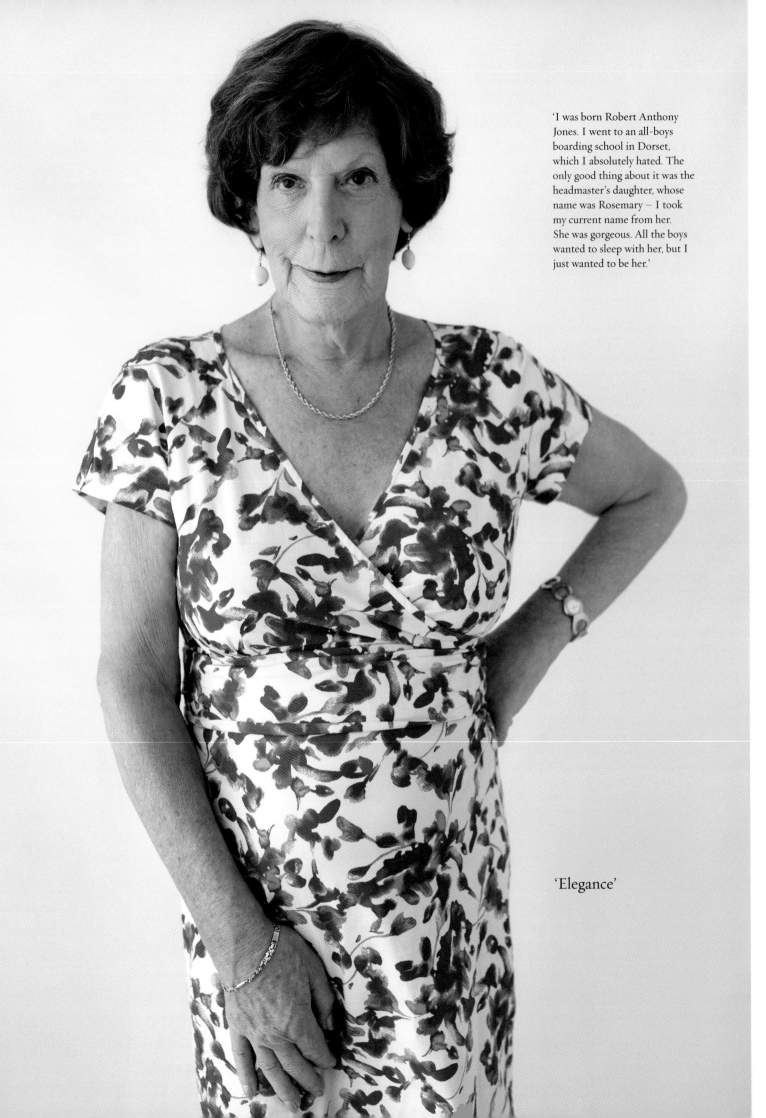

'I was born Robert Anthony Jones. I went to an all-boys boarding school in Dorset, which I absolutely hated. The only good thing about it was the headmaster's daughter, whose name was Rosemary – I took my current name from her. She was gorgeous. All the boys wanted to sleep with her, but I just wanted to be her.'

'Elegance'

Rosemary Jones

———

Rosemary Jones was born in Worcester, England. She earned a bachelor of medicine from the University of Bristol, going on to specialise in gynaecology. Jones has worked in South Africa, Zimbabwe, England and Australia, and specialises in endometriosis, hormone-replacement therapy, laparoscopy, menopause, pelvic pain and testosterone. She is a co-founder of the Beaumont Trust, an organisation established in the United Kingdom that provides information and support relevant to gender dysphoria and transgender-related matters. Jones now operates a private menopause clinic in Adelaide, Australia, and is a member of Doctors for Voluntary Euthanasia Choice.

Q. What really matters to you?

I am riveted by the danger of people like Donald Trump: I am terrified of him and what he means for the world; I am also terrified that other leaders seem to want to follow his style of government; and I am terrified for the world. Everything is going to hell in a handbasket, and I can't imagine how this has happened – how everything has gone so terribly wrong. Have we learned nothing? We're staring down civil wars and, potentially, another world war, and it's just ghastly. I'm consumed by international politics at the moment; 2 per cent of Americans own 40 per cent of the country. It's disgraceful and it doesn't make sense. And that disparity between the very rich and the very poor isn't symptomatic of America alone; I think that when people discover the lie, all hell will break loose.

In terms of what matters to me personally, I'm a great believer that, if you keep your own backyard clean, good things will happen. There's no need to go cleaning anyone else's backyard, because that's their responsibility, so keeping yours clean is the best you can do. And truth is very important to me; I lied about who I really was for the first forty or fifty years of my life, and I'm done with that.

I was born Robert Anthony Jones. I went to an all-boys boarding school in Dorset, which I absolutely hated. The only good thing about it was the headmaster's daughter, whose name was Rosemary – I took my current name from her. She was gorgeous. All the boys wanted to sleep with her, but I just wanted to be her.

Growing up, I didn't feel I was a man on the inside, so, in 1962, I went to see the professor of psychiatry in Charing Cross. He said, 'Don't worry about a thing like that, my boy. You will get married and have children, and all will come right.' Such was the level of understanding of gender disorder then: nobody knew a thing about it. And there was absolutely nothing to read on the topic.

I did marry. I joined the Crown Agents and was posted to Uganda with my pregnant wife. That's when I told her about my disorder. It's one of the things I regret most, because it was a shitty thing to do, frankly. She had no close friends she could talk to about it, so was dealing with the problem on her own. I'm not an unkind person, so I regret behaving in an unkind way. We stayed together for our children, and I worked in South Africa and Zimbabwe before finally coming to Australia.

Over the years, concealing my gender became harder and harder; I can't express the extent to which this thing runs riot through your life. I couldn't think about anything other than the fact that I wasn't a man. But, when I think of this period of my life, there are many things I am grateful for. If I had transitioned at twenty-two, I wouldn't have achieved a medical degree, I wouldn't have been accepted for specialist training and I wouldn't have my children. I would have lost out on all of that.

I've always been extraordinarily curious about women. Feeling as I did, I always wanted to know everything about them: What makes women tick? Who are we? Who are they? Who am I? Am I one of them, or am I some other kind of deviant?

I decided to embrace Rosemary when I came to Australia. One of my patients once told me that I was engaging with her like a woman – she said I had the mind of a woman, but the body of a man. And I thought, 'My god, she's got it!' What really triggered everything, though, was my brother's death. He had leukaemia and, when he died, I thought about his children, his house and his business – he was fulfilled and I wasn't, and I realised it was time to go for broke. When I started telling my patients about the decision I'd taken to transition, many said they'd sussed me out long ago; I had to tell each one of my two thousand, five hundred patients – I lost twenty-two, of whom six came back.

When I had fully transitioned, I felt like a pig in muck; it was like walking on the clouds. I was liberated. I didn't have to be on guard, worrying about whether anyone would notice anything. Being able to express the truth – to express myself the way I wanted to express myself – felt gorgeous.

My work is important to me. I've done some good work throughout my career, independently of what I have grappled with in my personal life. It matters to me that I feel I've been very courageous and haven't backed away from things: I'm proud of doing the first laparoscopic hysterectomy in South Australia; I'm proud of my research on testosterone's potential to reduce the incidence of breast cancer; and I'm proud that, of my 364 transsexual patients, I have only had three suicides – which is an extremely low incidence.

Q. What brings you happiness?

I'm seventy-eight, so my ambitions in life are fairly small; give me a glass of wine and a good book, and that's all I need.

Q. What do you regard as the lowest depth of misery?

Grinding poverty. When you have no family or no home, and barely enough money to buy food, and are holding a baby in your arms, the baby itself is, of course, a source of joy, but I'm talking about the implications of having a child and not being able to give them anything. Poverty is something many transsexuals experience, too. Many of them have awful difficulty just in keeping their heads above water. They have trouble finding employment and in finding accommodation – basically. Finding somewhere to live is a very basic human requirement and if we don't organise this for people who can't afford it, there is something wrong with our society. And for transsexuals, on top of that they *still* need to find money for everything that needs to be done to transition, with no help at all from the government.

Q. What would you change if you could?

I would rip the wealth out of the hands of some of these gluttonous people. I would do the Robin Hood thing and redistribute it – when I read about people with triple-pooled mansions, I feel disgusted.

Q. Which single word do you most identify with?

Elegance. It's the antithesis of rudeness.

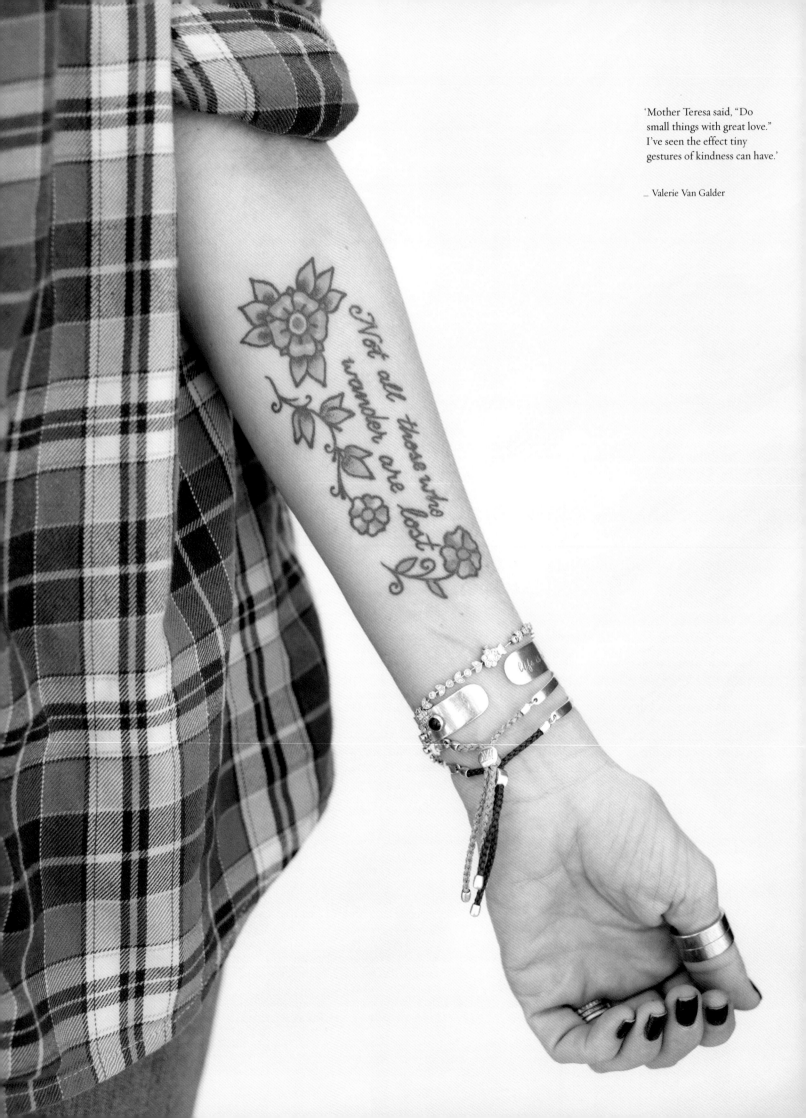

'Mother Teresa said, "Do small things with great love." I've seen the effect tiny gestures of kindness can have.'

_ Valerie Van Galder

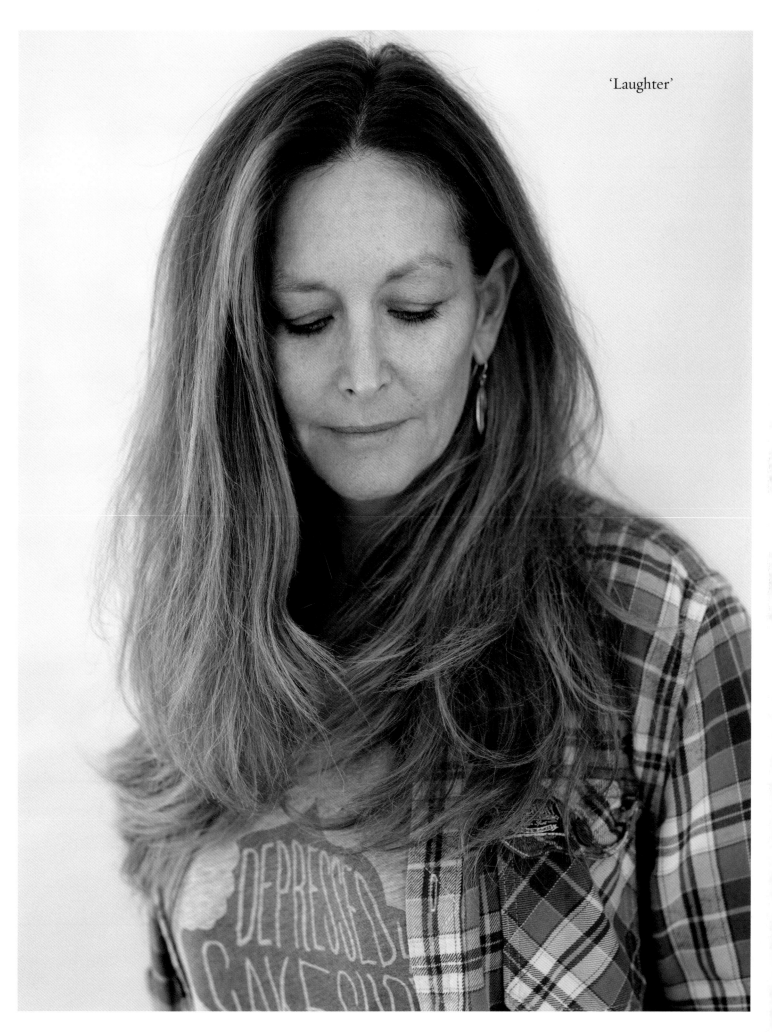

'Laughter'

Interview page 369

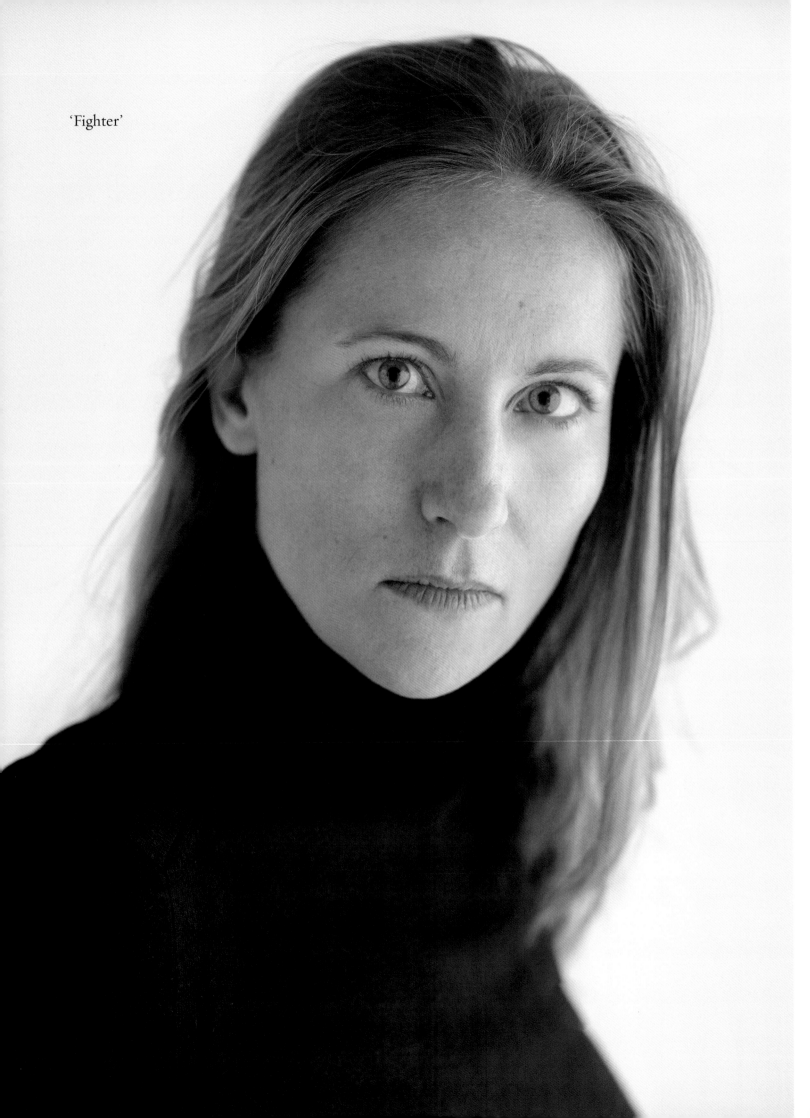

'Fighter'

Véronique de Viguerie

Véronique de Viguerie was born in Toulouse, France. She holds a master's degree in law and studied photojournalism. In 2004, she travelled to Afghanistan, where she worked for three years before continuing her photojournalism work internationally. De Viguerie's work has been featured in publications worldwide, including in *The New York Times*, *Paris Match*, *Der Spiegel* and *The Guardian*, and has been recognised with numerous awards, including the 2006 Canon Female Photojournalist Award. De Viguerie is the co-author of three books, including *Carnets de Reportage du XXIe siècle* and *Profession: Reporter*, both with Manon Quérouil.

Q. What really matters to you?

Truth. Misunderstanding, racism and xenophobia are created by ignorance, so ensuring people are informed of what's happening in the world is essential.

When I was younger, I wanted to be a soldier – I wanted to fight injustice on the ground. But, I don't really like being told what to do, so I decided to become a photojournalist and reporter instead. While I was still studying photography, my teacher told me to speak to a photojournalist about what the profession was like, so I could get some tips on how to start my career; the photojournalist told me photojournalism was dead and that I should take cooking lessons instead. After three days of agonising, I decided that I was going to prove him wrong; no one was going to take my future away from me. That's something that has driven me ever since, and it's why I won't take no for an answer. In fact, nobody should; if you have the will, there is no reason why you can't succeed. This is something that gives me hope. All around the world, I see people refusing to accept injustice and continuing the fight for what's right. A lot of women who live in places where they're expected to remain silent raise their voices, even when they know they will face death because of it. Ordinary people become extraordinary, because they refuse to do what they are 'supposed' to and are determined to decide for themselves and for their own.

It's important to me to go to the places people aren't willing to visit – or aren't able to visit – and illuminate the world about how people there are living. After I finished my studies in England, I went to Afghanistan for a three-month assignment and ended up staying for three years. For the last ten years, I have worked with a journalist named Manon Quérouil. She and I travel the world and compile what I hope are comprehensive reports of what's happening in the world. We focus mainly on the issues faced by women and children – this truth is so important.

Q. What brings you happiness?

Strangely, it's going into conflict areas. It's always extreme and in extreme situations you confront really bad people who are doing terrible things, but, at the same time, wonderful things happen in times of conflict. For instance, I love seeing people performing acts of extraordinary kindness for others. I was in Afghanistan and met an extraordinary woman who had built schools for girls with her own money. She travelled to meet with mothers and convince them that it was essential for their daughters to be educated. She was fighting for what she believed in, in the face of opposition of a kind we can't even imagine in France. I also met a girl who had been sent home from school because her burka was too short. She couldn't afford to buy another, so she found a piece of fabric, sewed it onto her burka to make it a few inches longer and was then allowed back into the school. That example may seem very simple, but women like her are amazing. I'm so heartened by the courage I see, both in conflict areas, and in places of prosperity and peace; it takes tremendous courage to forget about self and fight for others. We need more people like that.

And there is happiness in simple things like waking up in the morning and feeling my two children's warm bodies in the bed beside. This fills me with joy. I used to hate mornings, but, when my children jump around on my bed, my day is made.

Q. What do you regard as the lowest depth of misery?

The opposite of truth, which is ignorance and everything that goes with it. I hate it when people make no effort to understand others, simply because it's easier to disregard the burdens of misery other people carry with them. I want awareness, because the current state of wilful ignorance can't go on; we can't ignore the fact that there are wars raging on not so far away, or that there are places on this earth where women are killed by their families because men have decided that the women have done something to call *their* collective honour into question. We cannot ignore these tragedies any longer; we cannot pretend that there is any reason other than privilege that has dictated our individual peace. We need to acknowledge the truth that those of us living in peace – living with freedom – do so only because of chance.

Q. What would you change if you could?

The thing I would change would affect only half of humanity; it would be great if men could fall pregnant.

In some places, when a woman doesn't live up to expected perfection, she dies. But, if men could get pregnant, this would remove the burden so many women bear of having to be perfect. Here, I'm thinking specifically of honour killings, where it's considered that, because a woman is giving birth to the next generation of her family, she is carrying its honour. So, when she displays imperfection, this is considered dishonourable and she is killed. If men could fall pregnant, they would never subject one another to the same standard.

Even in the First World, it would make a great difference if men could get pregnant. Women would be able to carry on with their lives, uninterrupted, just as new fathers do. If women didn't need to take maternity leave to recover, they would have equal worth in the workplace.

I know all this is impossible, but I can dream!

Q. Which single word do you most identify with?

Fighter.

Linda Sarsour

———

Linda Sarsour, born in Brooklyn in New York, USA, is an award-winning racial justice and civil rights activist, and mother of three. Sarsour, a member of Justice League NYC, co-chaired the 2015 March2Justice, a four hundred-kilometre march from New York City to Washington, DC, advocating for legislative reform to end racial profiling and demilitarise police. Sarsour is a former executive director of the Arab American Association of New York and a co-founder of Muslims for Ferguson and of MPOWER Change, the first Muslim online organising platform. She co-chaired the historic 2017 Women's March on Washington and its ongoing calls to action.

Q. What really matters to you?

For me, it's very simple; I have three children and I want to live in a country that respects them in all their complexities: what they choose to do for a living, what religion they follow and what their ethnicity is. I want to live in a country that respects whomever they choose to be.

I always felt like I lived a pretty good life: I'm a Palestinian American, born to Palestinian-immigrant parents; I grew up in a lower-middle-class environment; and I went to public school. But my activism was born out of the ashes of 9/11. Seeing members of my community targeted by all levels of law enforcement in the immediate aftermath of the horrific attacks at the World Trade Center radicalised me. With my own eyes, I saw men being picked up in public, raids in my community and mothers crying at the mosque saying that they didn't know where their husbands were. I was shell-shocked that this could happen in my country, particularly knowing that a lot of the Muslims and Arabs in my community had come to the United States fleeing precisely that type of persecution and this type of police state. And I was furious. I immediately started translating for families, to connect them with legal services and help them find their loved ones. My networking and relationship building at that time was my introduction to civil rights activism. I started out by wanting to protect my own community, and then I ventured out and found that there were other communities who were also oppressed. So, more recently, I've been doing a lot of work around black civil liberties and issues pertaining to undocumented people. And, the more work I do, the more strongly I feel that there is a connection between all of our communities, that we're all being oppressed by the same state.

Racism, sexism and prejudice aren't concepts ingrained only in the minds of people, they are ingrained in America's history: we live in a country that was founded on the massacring of Indigenous People; Americans enslaved Africans here; and women were only given the right to vote within the last century. So, in order not to perpetuate racism, sexism and prejudice – in order for young people to broaden their horizons – we need to actively engage with our history and come to terms with it. We cannot teach the young blind patriotism for a country that makes mistakes; kids wave the flag and chant 'God Bless America,' but they don't understand that the flag has blood on it.

People will often say that slavery has nothing to do with them, when in fact, the existence of slavery in our history directly correlates to how we treat people of colour. And when people discuss setting up internment camps for Muslims, I wonder whether they've come to terms with the Japanese internment camps America was responsible for, because, to understand that a Muslim internment camp is a horrible thing, you need to understand the horror of previous instances of such treatment.

I was very proud to be a part of organising the 2017 Women's March. A day or two after the 2016 United States elections, I saw a Facebook post that talked about women's rights as human rights and that made reference to many different communities. However, it did not talk about how the issue of women's rights affected the Muslim community, so I decided to comment that I thought it was a great effort and that I hoped they would include Muslim communities. The next thing I knew I was a national co-chair of the Women's March on Washington. So, I caution people against suggesting that the march was exclusive in some way; I felt gratified to be a Muslim woman in a hijab joining women from other contexts in organising something greater than any one of us – something that a lot of people had doubts about. Although there are women in leadership roles, I've wondered whether people really believe in the true leadership of women. We are often in the back, so this was the moment to say, 'No. Women *are* leaders. Women are capable of anything.' We planned a march for two hundred thousand people in Washington, DC, and about half a million people came.

The sisterhood – the love, the compassion and the unity – was overwhelming. And it is just the beginning, a catalyst for protest and dissent under an administration like this.

I live in a country in which a lot of the people I love – people who came here to experience safety, security, respect, dignity and freedom – are not experiencing these things. But, I am hoping to help my country truly be the greatest nation on earth, a place where you *can* be exactly who you are.

Q. What brings you happiness?

A lot of things make me happy. As much as people think I'm some angry outraged activist – which I am – I am also very content with my children and with my family. I'm content being around people who share my values and principles. And I love New York City – I live and breathe it. It brings me joy to be in New York City and in my community out in Brooklyn. So, for me, happiness is very simple: it's beautiful people who care, and loving the things I love.

Q. What do you regard as the lowest depth of misery?

It's this dark place in which people are not able to see themselves in others: it's engaging in air strikes, it's the occupation of Palestine, it's massacres of Syrians at the hands of the Assad regime, it's the murders of unarmed people of colour at the hands of law enforcement in the United States and it's shackled pregnant women in prison. We don't treat others the way we want to be treated – somehow that's been lost across the world.

Q. What would you change if you could?

Freedom and liberation are very important, so addressing this would be my first act of change. I would love to be part of a just solution and see a free Palestine that respects the dignities of all people living there. I would end mass incarceration in the United States. We have a large prison population who are away from their families, and a lot of these people are non-violent offenders.

Q. Which single word do you most identify with?

Unapologetic.

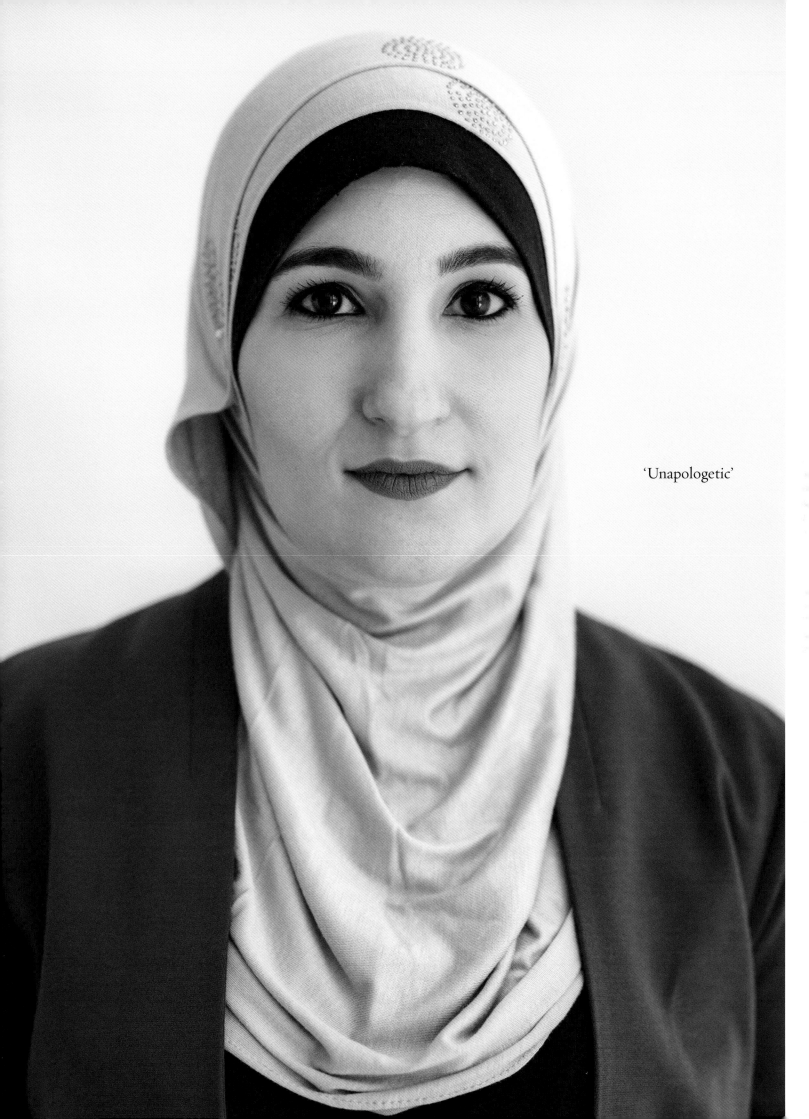

'Unapologetic'

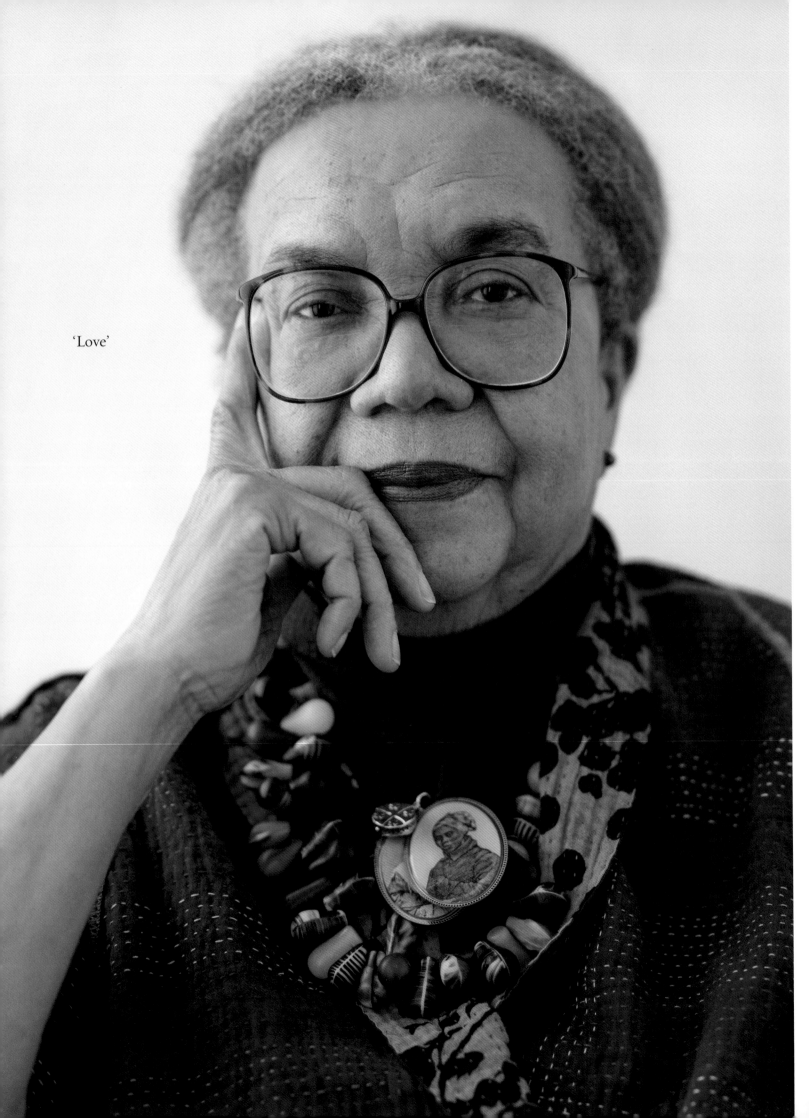

'Love'

Marian Wright Edelman

Marian Wright Edelman was born in Bennettsville in South Carolina, USA. A graduate of Spelman College and Yale Law School, she was the first African American woman to be admitted to the Mississippi Bar. In 1968, she became counsel for the Poor People's Campaign, initiated by Martin Luther King Jr. In 1973, she founded the Children's Defense Fund, a not-for-profit child advocacy organisation of which she remains president. Edelman's work has been widely recognised; among many awards, she is a recipient of the Albert Schweitzer Prize for Humanitarianism, a MacArthur Foundation fellowship and the Presidential Medal of Freedom.

Q. What really matters to you?

I have always felt like I'm the luckiest person in the world to have been born at the intersection of great people in my own family, my community and my church – my dad was a Baptist minister, and my mother was the church organist and organiser – when history was really moving in new directions. I always had extraordinary role models, and people often asked why I do what I do. I said, 'It never occurred to me not to do what I do, I do exactly what my parents did, I do exactly what my community co-parents did, which is to serve and try to make the world better than you found it and making sure that you fight injustice.'

My daddy used to say, 'God runs a full employment economy, just follow the need, and you will never lack for something useful to do.' We were people of faith, and he made it very clear that we were put on this earth to leave it better and make sure we served people in need. When I think about the Children's Defense Fund, it was a natural progression from the civil rights movement and my Mississippi experience of the sixties. But every issue that we focus on really stems from my childhood experiences. There was a child who lived three houses down from our church and who died of tetanus when nobody knew about tetanus shots. I also remember a highway accident; we all ran out and saw it involved a migrant family that was black and a white truck driver. The ambulance came and saw that the white truck driver was not injured. The black folk – the migrant workers – were lying there on the highway, but the ambulance drove off. I never forgot that. I cannot stand seeing ugliness or injustice of that kind.

I think that the Children's Defense Fund's work investing in children is going to be the determinant of whether this nation goes to hell or remains a world leader. Our major national economic and military security problems come from our failure to invest in an educated populace. How can it be that – as our demographics show – the majority of our children are going to be non-white in a few years, and yet over 80 per cent of black children cannot read a computer at grade-school level? This is not counting those who have dropped out of school or have been put into the prison pipeline. We are going to miss the boat to the future if we keep destroying the seed corn of our youth and failing to educate the non-white children, who are going to be the majority of our children. We have this cradle-to-prison pipeline, and we're spending three times more per prisoner than per public school pupil. That is really dumb. I get up every morning because there is a sense of urgency. The future of the country, and also our own futures, depend on what we do with children. We can't save ourselves if we can't save our children.

Q. What brings you happiness?

My children, my grandchildren, children and music.

Q. What do you regard as the lowest depth of misery?

It is unthinkable that children are dying from famine. It is unthinkable that the gun violence rate in this country for children of all ages is seventeen times worse than for their peers in the other high-income countries combined. In a nation that is so rich and has so much, the idea that children in this country are going hungry, are not being educated and don't have housing is just so outrageous. How is it that we cannot create a level playing field for every child? Every child is sacred. God did not make two classes of children.

It's an obscenity that in the United States of America – the second largest economy in the world after China – we are letting our children be the poorest age group, and the younger they are, the poorer they are. That is just intolerable. So many are faced with suffering and misery, while so few have so much. If you have got $5 billion, why do you need another billion? Why do you need more if you have got three houses, and what kind of government or Congress or political leaders continue to take money out of children's mouths? They take money that is needed for food, health care, housing, education, safe child care and early development, in order to do what? To give more tax breaks to people who are millionaires and billionaires, and add another $54 billion to the military budget? I mean, what in the world is the matter with us?

Q. What would you change if you could?

I would lift every child out of poverty. What is it in our character that would let millions and millions and millions of children live in poverty and have hopeless lives, go off to prison and be gunned down by guns we won't control? There is something wrong with this picture, and I just hope that the boil will burst in this administration and that enough of us will begin to see clearly who we are, and that we've got to be one world or no world. That we have an obligation to pass on a better future than we currently have to our children.

I hope women will find their voice and just say, 'Sorry, we have had enough,' and vote these men out of power and try to build a country that is fit for our children and grandchildren. That is the job before us, and if we can empower our daughters and our granddaughters and our sons to do and carry on the work, then we will get there. We can't go on this way as a country, and as a world.

Q. Which single word do you most identify with?

Love.

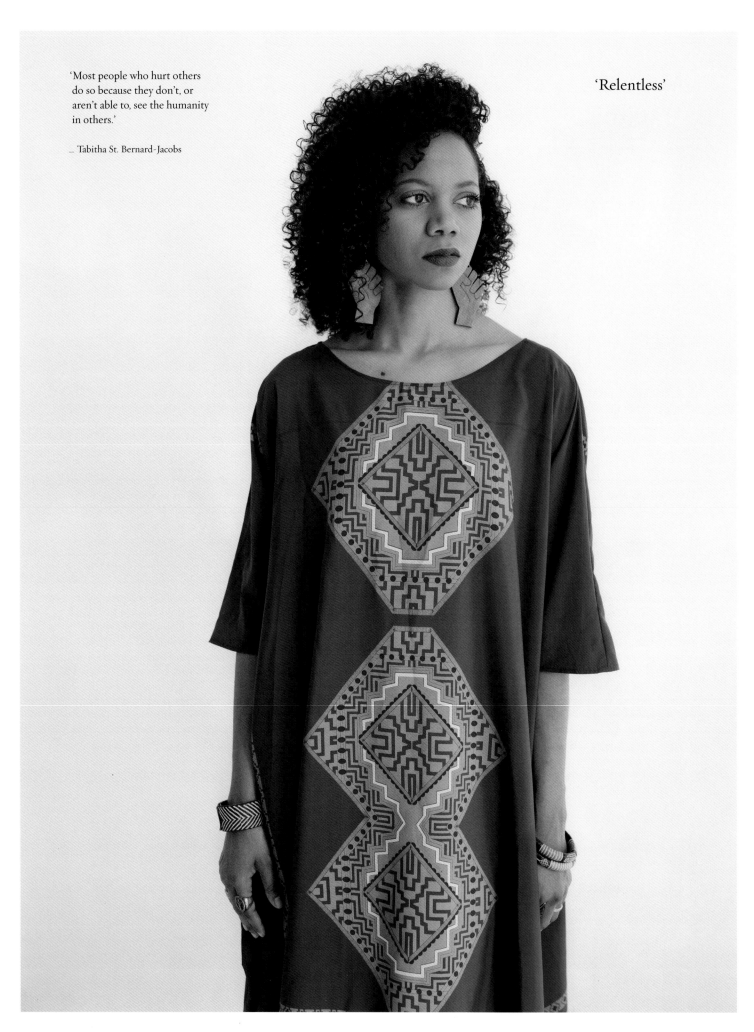

'Most people who hurt others
do so because they don't, or
aren't able to, see the humanity
in others.'

_ Tabitha St. Bernard-Jacobs

'Relentless'

Interview page 370

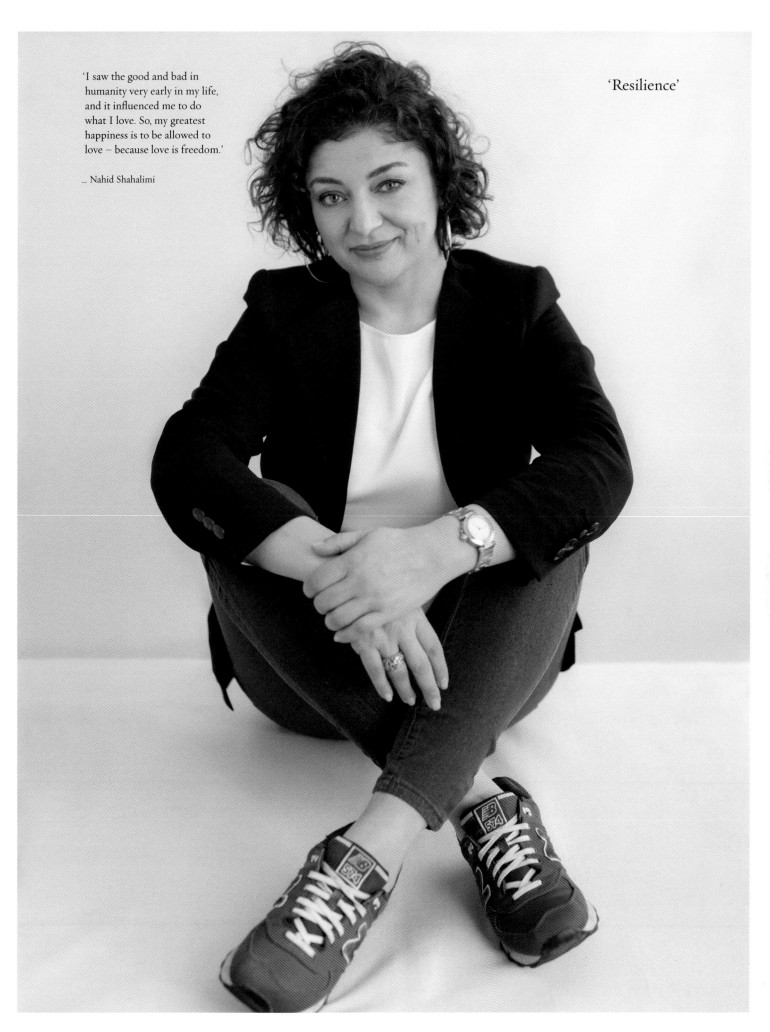

'I saw the good and bad in
humanity very early in my life,
and it influenced me to do
what I love. So, my greatest
happiness is to be allowed to
love – because love is freedom.'

_ Nahid Shahalimi

'Resilience'

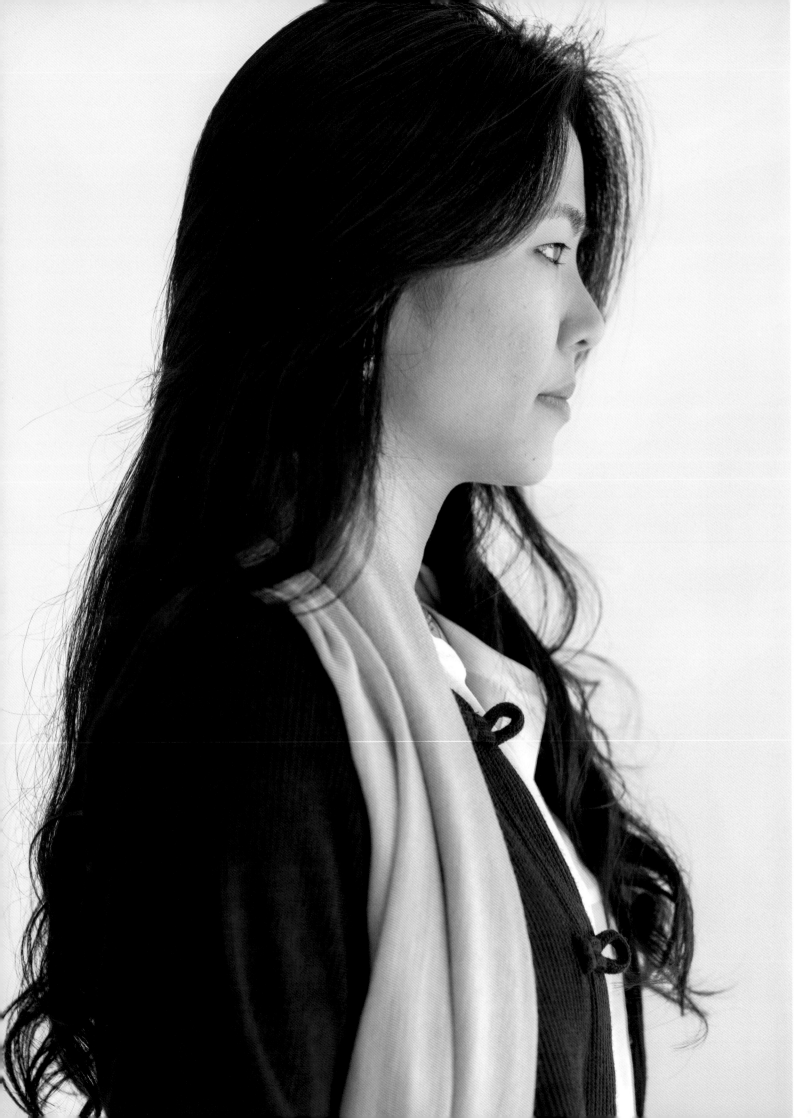

Nicole Tung

Nicole Tung was born and raised in Hong Kong. She graduated with a double major in journalism and history from New York University in 2009, and has since worked as a photojournalist. Tung freelances for international clients that include *The New York Times, The Wall Street Journal* and *TIME* magazine, and her work has received numerous awards. Since 2011, Tung has been reporting on the civil war in Syria, where her friend and colleague James Foley was killed in 2014.

Q. What really matters to you?

More than anything else, it's the people I love. But it's also the people I have yet to meet, who share the goal of human decency with me; there's something about sitting down at a dinner table with people you've only just met – who invite you into their homes to share their food – and finding a connection with them.

In my work, what matters is truth. I always knew I wanted a job that allowed me to travel. While I was at university, I went on a spring break trip to Bosnia. I'd been reading a lot about the conflicts in the Balkans, and I met a woman who had been widowed by the Srebrenica massacre in 1995. These experiences compelled me to pursue journalism; I'd always been interested in history, so journalism felt like a way to write history's first draft.

I started out doing mostly metropolitan news coverage in New York, but, when the Tunisian revolution started – off the back of the Arab Spring – I had to see what was going on. In 2011, I made it to Tahrir Square in Egypt; it was exhilarating and I felt very privileged. I went on to cover Libya when Gaddafi was overthrown; it was outside a courthouse in Benghazi, with thousands of people chanting in unison about having achieved freedom from Gaddafi's regime, that my work as an international reporter solidified. I went on to cover the Syrian Civil War, which is what I've been doing for the past several years.

It matters that people connect with my photos and that the stories I tell are accurate; I want to be able to explain complex issues through my images. But, the more I see of conflict, the less I understand it. War is a place for extremes – it's about how people lose humanity, and also how they gain it. I have witnessed some horrific things, but also the most heroic acts performed in the most terrible of situations. I've seen people risking their lives to save others with no regard for themselves. War and conflict are as old as humanity, they're almost inherent to being alive. But, although conflict needs to exist to create change or move something forward, I'm not interested in the people in power who start conflicts. Rather, I try to focus on people who are the most vulnerable, who deserve to be heard and who are often sidelined by those in charge.

There are two sides to being a conflict journalist. One is very selfish: it has to do with the exhilaration – the rush, the adrenalin – of being on the ground, where the action is happening. You feel so alive and so present, with every emotion heightened. This is dangerously addictive, so you have to constantly be aware of what you're getting involved in and of how deep you want to go. The other side is noble: ultimately, you're there for the vulnerable – for their stories. It's such a privilege when people give you access to their lives – you have a responsibility to bring their stories to whomever is willing to listen. You hope that some sort of change will follow, that, by showing the human side of conflict, you encourage people in positions of power to use their influence positively.

We go into this profession knowing the risks – we're under no illusions – but our responsibility to tell the truth is more important than the danger. Today, those who are neutral in situations of conflict – the journalists – are being murdered for wanting to tell the truth. We have become targets. But you know what? That makes me even more driven, because, otherwise, we will all be silenced. As human stories go unheard, the world will continue in ignorance of the suffering on the ground – and that is something to fight against.

In a way, this work is a mission in defiance of those who want to silence journalists. When James Foley was killed and the footage of his execution was shown in the news, so many people questioned what he'd been doing in Syria; having to defend his decision was so infuriating. You don't get to ask that question about my friend, who risked his life to bring you a story he cared about – of people he felt needed to have their voices heard.

Q. What brings you happiness?

I find happiness in nature, in being able to step away from everything that's going on in the world – and in my head – and feel peace.

A few weeks ago, I was standing outside an internally displaced people's camp in Iraq; it was full of people fleeing Mosul. I heard this woman cry out and saw that she was embracing a little ten-year-old boy. It was her son – she hadn't seen him for two years because she'd been outside Mosul when Islamic State took over and she couldn't get back home. The woman was in a state of the most extreme joy; they were both crying and the boy seemed so in awe of being able to see his mother again. It's moments like this that you really live for.

Q. What do you regard as the lowest depth of misery?

I'm not a parent, so I can only imagine what the pain must be like, but one of the most difficult things to witness is parents losing their children. So, too, it is very difficult to see children – especially young children – losing their parents and not comprehending what has happened.

I often ask myself why a certain thing is happening, but I never have an answer. It is very easy to become disillusioned and frustrated with humanity because of all the suffering we create for each other. I don't think there *is* an answer, though; we just have to be strong and continue working to tell the world about what's happening.

Q. What would you change if you could?

There just needs to be more equality. So much subjugation is carried out by men that I wish more women were in power. Would there be war if women were in power? Maybe, but I would hope not. There is something nurturing about women that I've seen all across the world. Women tend to be more practical and have a different approach to problem solving, so I certainly think the world would be more peaceful. In any event, we need to create some kind of counterbalance to the testosterone.

Q. Which single word do you most identify with?

Hope. I hope for tolerance and for respect.

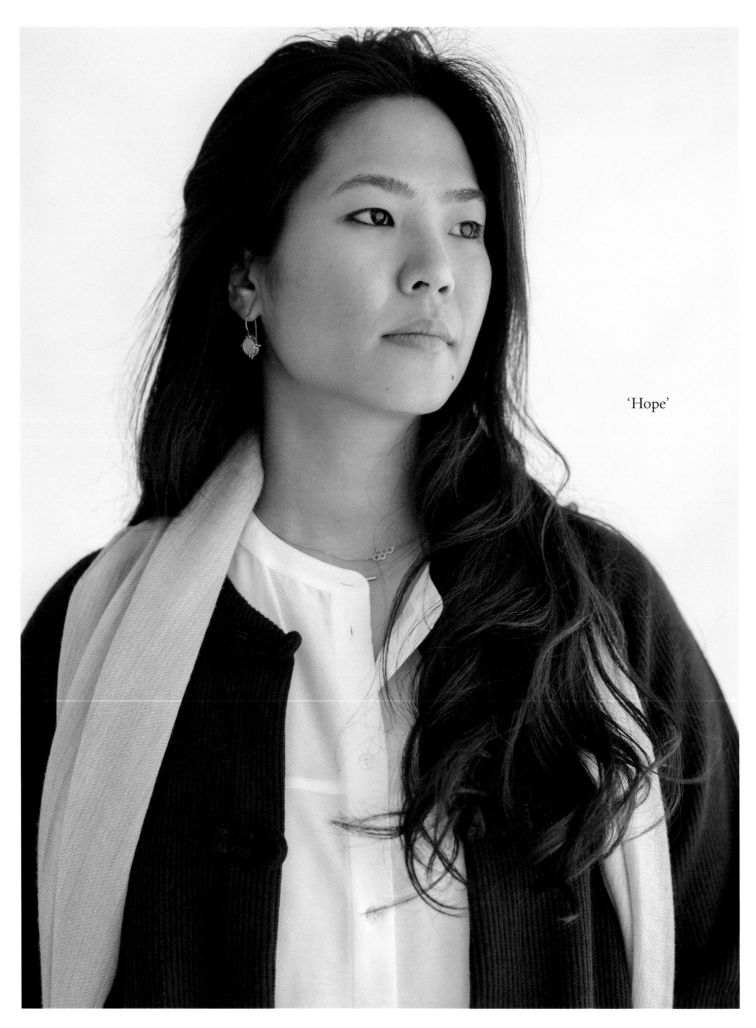

'Hope'

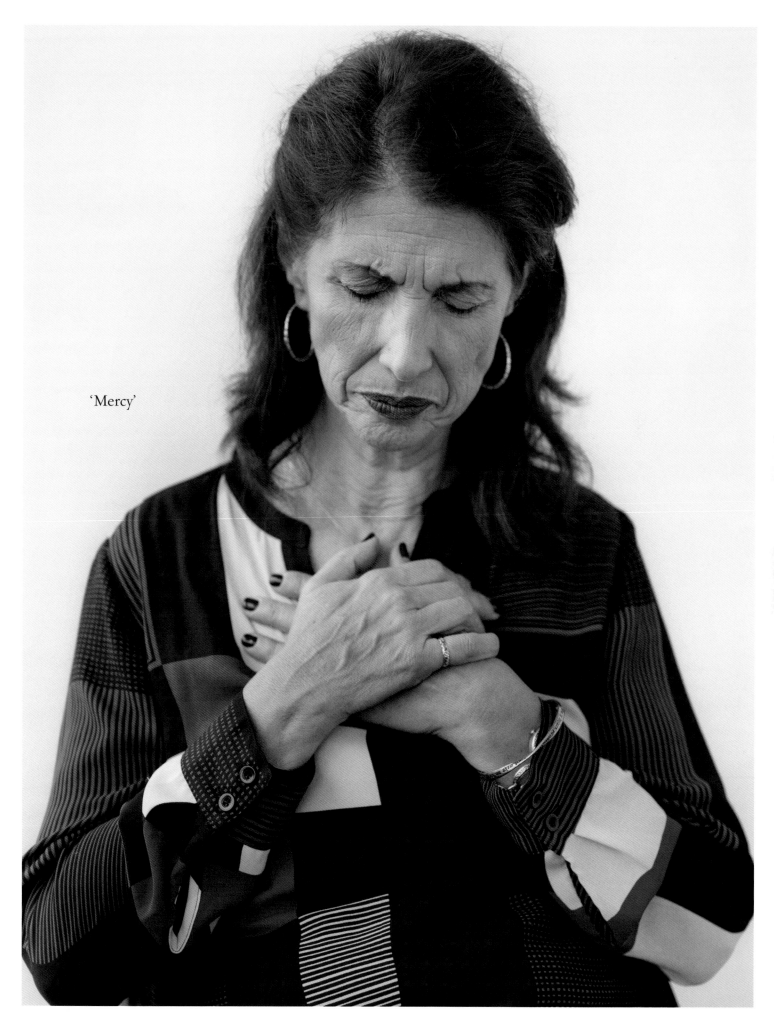

'Mercy'

Diane Wright Foley

Diane Wright Foley was born in Keene in New Hampshire, USA. A former community health nurse and nurse practitioner, Wright Foley now runs the James W. Foley Legacy Foundation, an organisation she co-founded in 2014 following the kidnapping, torture and murder of her eldest son James (Jim) by Islamic State. She is committed to American hostage return and safety for freelance conflict journalists, and to unifying such global efforts.

'I feel our world desperately needs to know the truth; it needs to hear the voices of those who otherwise would not be heard.'

Q. What really matters to you?

There's so much that matters. It matters to me that, for whatever moments or days I have left on earth, I can do God's will, truly. The largest piece of my strength has been my faith in a very loving and merciful God – I know that God was very much with my son, Jim, to the end of his days.

It matters that I can follow the message of love and mercy, and that I can make a difference for the likes of American hostages and independent journalists who are trying to give a voice to people who have none. That's become very important to me – to make a difference for those who need help.

Jim was a remarkable young man. Throughout his life he really cared about the underdog. He was always interested in people who were different from him or who were from a different culture. He did a master's in journalism, then became a conflict journalist. He was very taken up by the hope in the Arab Spring; he'd been in Libya shortly before he went to Syria, so he had an understanding of what it meant for people to seek freedom. Within a month of Jim's execution, I felt compelled to start the James W. Foley Foundation; it just felt like he had so much work left unfinished. The foundation serves to advocate for hostages – particularly Americans who go into conflict zones – because at the time of Jim's death we didn't receive much support here in the United States. Few protect freelance conflict journalists. They are out there on their own.

The work that I'm doing with the foundation is incredibly important to me because I feel our world desperately needs to know the truth; it needs to hear the voices of those who otherwise would not be heard. How else can we become a better society? Jim had a deep understanding of this; he realised how vital the voice of the people is to our democracy and to any goodness in the world. And goodness matters, because I think one of the most frightening things is the opposite – the feeling of hatred and division. That's so destructive to our society, and the world.

As Jim was a unifier, we have supported the international Alliance for a Culture of Safety – ACOS – which is a historic collaboration between media, NGOs and freelancers. We are trying to foster a network that brings together the resources of the many wonderful journalist-oriented NGOs in the world – the Committee to Protect Journalists, Reporters Without Borders – and media companies, whereby they are able to focus on protecting freelancers in conflict zones. There are a lot of good people in the world, so it's just a question of bringing them together to pursue the good cause. We're very hopeful.

Q. What brings you happiness?

Happiness is everywhere. I'm very blessed. I'm blessed with a wonderful husband and four beautiful children. Our grandchildren are the biggest gift, particularly our youngest; he's one-and-a-half years old and is named after Jim – he's the most beautiful child. I have a beautiful mum, too, and I love nature. I've been blessed – there's a lot of suffering in the world and I've just tasted a bit of what many people go through in a much worse way.

Q. What do you regard as the lowest depth of misery?

The hatred. It's the hatred that would treat someone like our son so horribly for all those years, torturing then killing him in such a brutal way. That kind of hatred is hard for me to understand and is so frightening to me – it's just the lowest place a human can be. As people, we have the power for good or for bad; we have the power to be merciful and loving, or to really destroy one another.

Q. What would you change if you could?

The only way we can change is just one person at a time – each of us trying to do the next right thing, trying to be forgiving and merciful to people who may have offended us or really hurt us deeply. We're all just people and we all make mistakes.

I also think it's important that people who are trying to do good in the world come together and stand together. I wish there could be more collaboration. Jim was held with eighteen Western hostages; all of those people came from countries allied with the United States, yet those countries didn't work together to get this group of nineteen hostages out. Each country did its own thing. That is sad because, if we'd come together, we would have had some idea of what we were facing and what true tragedy was ongoing in Syria. And we could have been a lot stronger. I believe in convening people to discuss issues and I deeply believe in a loving God – that is essential for me to continue.

Q. Which single word do you most identify with?

Mercy.

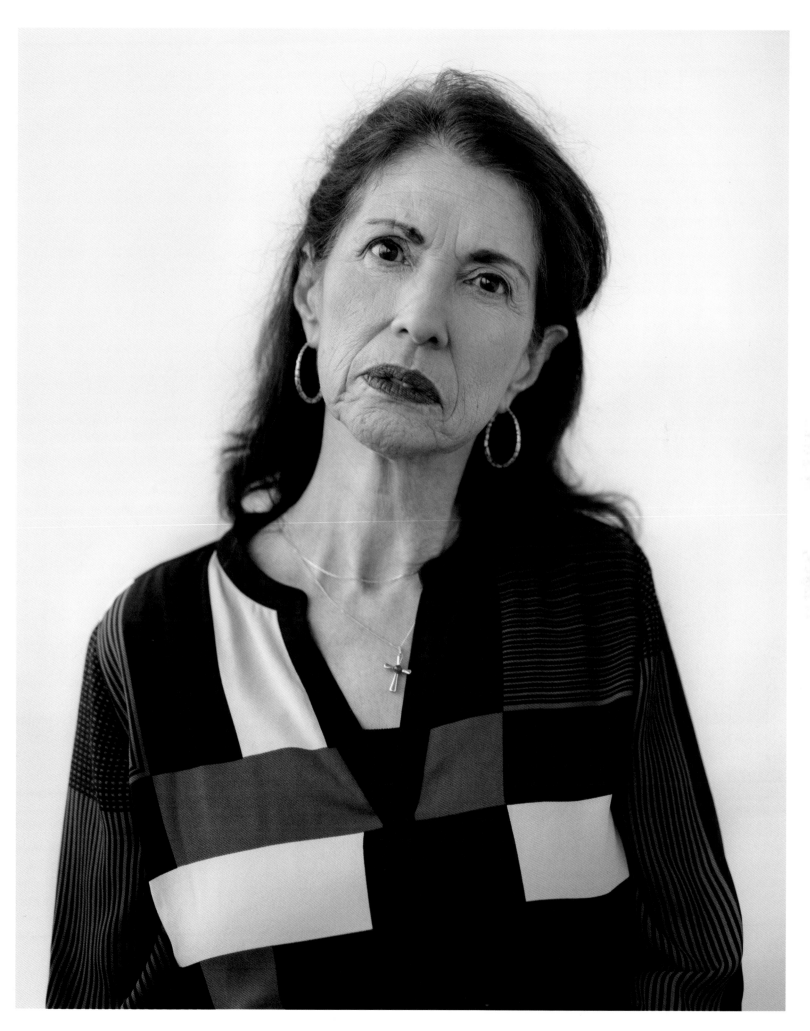

Collette Dinnigan

Collette Dinnigan was born in Mandini, South Africa. She studied fashion and textiles in New Zealand before moving to Australia, where she established her eponymous fashion label in 1990. In 1995, Dinnigan became the first Australian-based designer to be invited by the Chambre Syndicale du Prêt-à-Porter des Couturiers et des Créateurs de Mode to show a ready-to-wear collection in Paris. Her many honours include *Collette Dinnigan: Unlaced*, a retrospective of twenty-five years of her work at the Museum of Applied Arts & Sciences in Sydney, which opened in 2015 for eighteen months. Dinnigan is now focussed on interior design projects and collaborations.

'It's very important to me that the companies I work with are ethically sound and strong.'

Q. What really matters to you?
I've been very lucky to have lived a very interesting, nomadic life – I had it in my blood.

I was born in South Africa, but we left when I was about seven years old. My mother was a very creative, artistic person; she and my father were very anti-apartheid, and they most definitely didn't want to bring up their children in that environment. There had been a lot of altercations with the law, so my father built a yacht in the middle of the bush and took it by truck to Durban. We sailed out from there on Boxing Day 1973. I remember a lot of people on the jetty saying goodbye to us, seeing my mother's sister in tears and dad saying, 'Great sailing weather!' We set sail in forty-foot waves, it was almost cyclonic, but we felt comfortable knowing that dad said it was good sailing weather – we trusted him. I don't think we saw land for six weeks; we had no radio communication, so my father navigated by sextant and compass.

Our first port of call was Albany, Australia. After sailing through South Australia, then Eden in New South Wales, we ended up in New Zealand. I moved back to Australia after graduation and started my own fashion business. I ended up in Paris and was accepted into the Chambre Syndicale. I was in the fashion business for thirty years, living in Australia, but constantly travelling to and from Europe.

But my family is a priority, so a couple of years ago I decided to change the infrastructure and direction of the business. I stopped doing shows, closed my retail stores, and now I just design.

This was all very much because I had a ten-year-old daughter and a newborn son. I felt so blessed to have my son, Hunter, at the age of forty-eight, and I knew I had to give my children my best shot. Parenting, for me, is not about other people bringing up my children to have *their* values, it's about my children having *my* values.

Everything is so fast in the world today; with so much technology and so many methods of communication, it matters that people still take the time to think and to be kind. The world is lacking kindness and empathy, which are very key values we need to remind people of. Because, at the end of the day, a thank-you note can mean a lot more than a cheque.

It's very important to me that the companies I work with are ethically sound and strong, that they're conscious of the environment, and that they empower women by giving them work that's sustainable and not harmful. I find it incredibly frustrating to see a lot of high-street retailers selling T-shirts at two dollars each, because, when you do the maths and work backwards – after you deduct the cost of fabric, the cost of shipping, the cost of retail space and staff – you realise how little, if anything, the person in Bangladesh who made that shirt was ultimately paid. Why not pay double and empower a woman somewhere else so that she's able to feed her family?

I endeavour to work with manufacturers who have maximum working weeks and minimum wages, who have nurseries for women with children and who have medical insurance – that their employees are working in safe buildings and have their fundamental rights respected. As more and more designers realise the importance of ethical factories, more and more unethical factories, wholesalers and manufacturers will be put out of business. And consumers need to support those businesses that are being run ethically. Yes, we may pay a little bit more for the product, but that's how we take away poverty from third-world countries.

Q. What brings you happiness?
My happiness is nothing grand. It's about living on the land and living a simple life; it's the simple pleasures of being with family and friends. I like having more time to appreciate the good little things in life, so I want my life to slow down a bit, but not to the point where I'm watching things go by; fortunately, I'm still offered work and I have creative license when I do things.

Q. What do you regard as the lowest depth of misery?
Loneliness. The lowest depth is those who feel they have nothing to live for: who feel as though there's no one there for them, feel that no one hears their cries for help and feel there is no hope.

Q. What would you change if you could?
I believe it's very difficult to make a difference in politics, so, if I could change anything in the world, it would be making sure that everyone has access to clean water and a basic supply of food and shelter.

Q. Which single word do you most identify with?
Yes. Most of my life, I've had dreams and have followed them, so 'yes' means, 'Let's try!' – even if you fail, you will have learned something. Whereas, if you say 'no,' it's an iron doorstop – it's not progress.

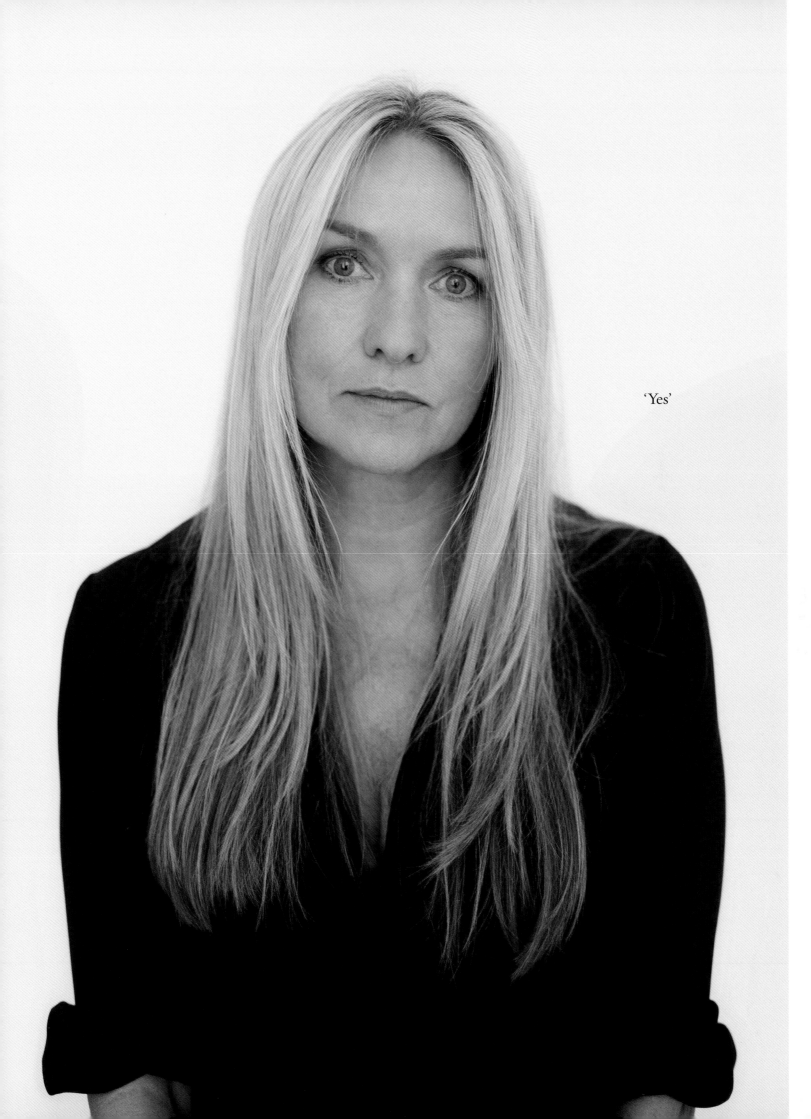

'Yes'

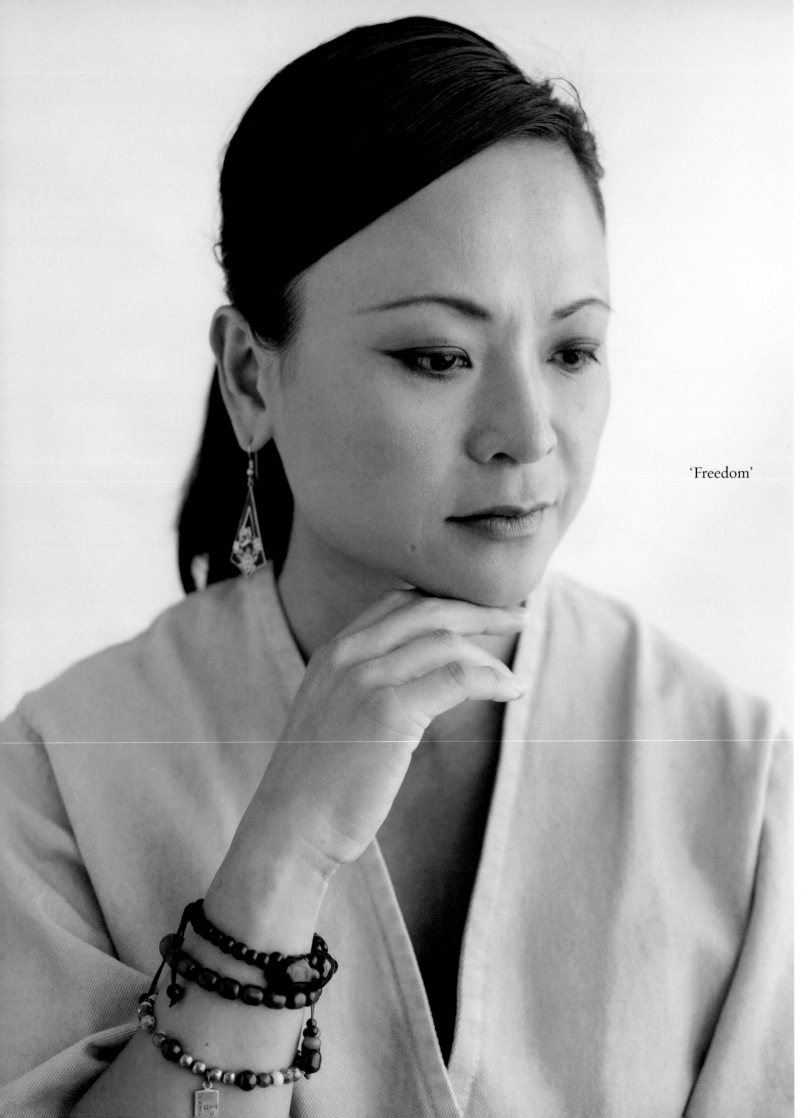

'Freedom'

Pauline
Nguyen

Pauline Nguyen was born in Saigon, Vietnam, and moved to Australia in 1978. Nguyen is a co-owner and co-founder of the acclaimed Red Lantern restaurant in Sydney. An author, spiritual entrepreneur and speaker, Nguyen's writing has appeared in Robert Drewe's *The Best Australian Essays 2010*, and her memoir *Secrets of the Red Lantern* saw her recognised as newcomer writer of the year at the 2008 Australian Book Industry Awards.

Q. What really matters to you?

I find being in a state of joy – just *being* – so beautiful; and I feel so privileged. So, what matters right now is that we all decide to find the joy, the forgiveness, the peacefulness and the beauty in whatever we are faced with – in all things. When we make that decision, even more joy, forgiveness, peace and beauty will come our way.

That's not to say that we should close our eyes and ears, or ignore the relative logic of life. But, what's important is how we translate and interpret what happens. Because we all have a choice. One of the most important things for me as a mother, coach and mentor is helping people find the tools to transform old beliefs and make the decision to be their true selves, to develop the tools and gifts to take off all their layers and masks. What matters is how I show up in the face of my children, my husband and the people I love. What matters to me is to be able to assist them to find freedom in this world. True freedom.

Growing up, I witnessed all the anger, fear and trauma in my father; all the emotional toxicity that built up in him over the years. He was like a faulty pressure cooker about to explode. At the fall of Saigon, my parents had no choice but to escape Vietnam – the only way they could do that was to build a boat and smuggle the family out to sea. We spent nine days on the ocean and ended up in Thailand, where we spent a very difficult year in a refugee camp. My younger brother, Luke, was born there. In 1978, Australia finally accepted us.

But in Australia, the environment I grew up in was very violent – mentally, physically, emotionally, spiritually – and it wasn't until I started examining my past that I realised my father had suffered terribly from post-traumatic stress disorder. He had come out of war, to a new country, with nothing: no house, no job, no money. He didn't know the laws or the language. I guess my father had nowhere to dump his anger, so he started to dump it on his wife and, later on, on his children. But my true self is conscious enough to make the decision that the cycle ends with me, and so the anger and trauma does not get passed on to my children.

There are lessons from my parent's lives that are positive, though. Everything they went through in coming to Australia reflects the values and the truth of my life now: courage, resilience and grit. They had such courage – the courage to take action. They had resilience – the ability to fall and get back up again. And they had grit – the stamina and determination to achieve their goal. My father did the best he could with the tools that he had at the time. He lives a very different life now, and we are friends, although it does require a lot of work on my part. Just as my father had a choice, so do I have a choice. We all choose.

Today, I work to assist people to choose the story that gives them the most peace and to choose the thoughts that bring them the most joy, so they suffer less. That's my mission. The answer is so simple. It's about choice and it's about being true. Because our truth is not in being burdened by anger, fear and trauma.

Q. What brings you happiness?

My life; I'm in awe of my life. It's all beautiful: the privileges, the opportunities, my children, my husband, my businesses. We must all stop and look at how much we've accomplished – how far we've come – and be grateful.

Q. What do you regard as the lowest depth of misery?

I've had some low moments in my life. But, from where I sit right now – looking back –

I can't say that any of my experiences were the lowest depths of misery. I can't even use those words, because those experiences are no longer real to me.

Pain is inevitable, but suffering is a choice and not having the freedom to let go is miserable. I see so many people who have been unable to choose the story that gives them peace, so they take a painful event, put more lenses and more filters on it, until it becomes misery and they suffer needlessly. This absence of consciousness causes people to suffer needlessly, because of the stories they've created and the layers of meaning they've piled onto those stories. All this becomes a rock they are chained to.

Q. What would you change if you could?

Perspectives. I love changing perspectives. Not everybody is ready, which I respect. But I believe I was put on earth to influence people, to give them the opportunity to choose ways of seeing the world that lessen their suffering; to offer them another perspective that gives them the courage to challenge existing paradigms and design a life on their own terms, regardless of what they've been through.

What are beliefs? Beliefs are habits, habits that were downloaded onto us by our parents, our society and our culture. Some of us go through life defending these habits – sometimes to the death – habits that are not even ours. So I want people to be able to say, 'Wait a minute. This is not working for me.' We all have to come to terms with the cost of holding on. Because there's a huge cost of walking this earth defending beliefs that aren't even ours and being someone that we're not.

Q. Which single word do you most identify with?

My word is 'freedom.' Freedom above all else.

Jurnee Smollett-Bell

Jurnee Smollett-Bell was born in New York City, USA. A working actor since childhood, she has received critical acclaim for her performances in *Eve's Bayou*, *The Great Debaters*, *Friday Night Lights* and *Underground*, among other roles. Her awards include a Critics' Choice Movie Award for Best Young Performer, and three National Association for the Advancement of Colored People Image Awards. Smollett-Bell is a committed activist working for racial justice and children's rights and to stop HIV/AIDS. She is on the board of directors of Children's Defense Fund and was a long-term board member of Artists for a New South Africa.

Q. What really matters to you?
Making those I love laugh. And sitting around a dinner table with my family, eating a meal, with Stevie Wonder playing in the background.

Growing up, we were not rich – actually, we were poor. I'm one of six kids, and financial instability was part of my life. So, I don't value things other people sometimes value. I don't care about cars and big houses, because that is not what I had growing up. I learned to value other things: family, laughter, big dinners around the table, debating one another and the entertainment you create yourself. Mom always wanted us to perform for her, so for Mother's Day or for her birthday, she would say, 'Just do a concert for me!' That self-sufficiency is a huge part of my life.

I work in film and television, and it annoys me how we women of colour are represented. As an artist, it matters to me to be used to tell our truth, our stories. I feel like the world has a warped sense of who we are, and a lot of that is perpetuated by the media. We are more than just set dressing and we are more than sexual objects, but for far too long, television and film have perpetuated negative images of who we are as women, and as women of colour. It matters to me to change those images.

My parents met in Oakland, California. My mom decided to leave her hometown of New Orleans and go to the Bay Area because she wanted to join the civil rights movement, and Oakland was a hub for that. My mother is black and my father was Jewish, and both were members of the Communist Party back then, and met working in the movement. Growing up, their story informed my own identity. Hearing stories of what it was like to be on the ground trying to effect change, hearing names like Angela Davis – this is part of the fabric of who I am as a person. When the Los Angeles riots broke out – I think I was five or six at the time – my mom had us on the street corner holding up signs about Rodney King. My parents' activism is in my DNA. Even though I am an artist, I feel like my activism is directly connected to everything I do: the roles I choose, the ways I live my life, my efforts to help better our world.

When I was twelve, I became involved in Artists for a New South Africa (ANSA), a not-for-profit organisation which was founded, led and supported by people I looked up to creatively; artists like Alfre Woodard, Samuel and LaTanya Richardson Jackson, Blair Underwood, Jackson Browne, CCH Pounder-Koné, Sidney Poitier, Danny Glover, Carlos Santana, Deborah Santana and many more. The artists and the activists who ran ANSA, as well as the remarkable African political heroes who guided the organisation, became an essential part of my village. They helped raise me to be someone who not only wanted to make a positive difference, but who was empowered to do so. They showed me how to use my talents and resources as an artist to advocate for better government policies, to raise money for effective social justice programs and to help educate others about our collective rights and responsibilities. They listened to my ideas and wanted my input as a young woman of colour – and they invited me to be a member of the board. With their support, I went into schools to talk with young people about HIV/AIDS prevention and I raised money to help HIV/AIDS orphans. I recorded public service announcements urging people to vote and informing them of their rights. Together, we lobbied elected officials in the US and South Africa and helped to change unjust laws.

In 2006, some ANSA members were planning to go to South Africa to visit the programmes and activists we were supporting and funding. I wanted to go, but there was no way I could afford it. They called me and said, 'We put together the money to bring you with us; we just couldn't leave you behind.' On my twentieth birthday, I found myself on a plane to Africa – my first trip out of the US – surrounded by members of my ANSA family.

That trip changed my life. I met with many of my heroes – Nelson Mandela, Desmond Tutu, Ahmed Kathrada, Albie Sachs, Zackie Achmat – who all embodied what it means to fight for justice and freedom with love and mercy in your heart. I met many new heroes: women and children living in townships and rural villages in difficult, impoverished conditions, who still managed to get up each morning and work hard to make their communities and families stronger. They taught me about resilience and determination, the indomitable power of the human spirit.

Q. What brings you happiness?
My idea of happiness is ever evolving; it's not about the destination, it's about the journey. The morning times with my baby and my husband bring me more happiness than I have ever experienced before. When my son lies in bed with us, looks to both of us, laughs and grabs for us, and smiles up at us with his toothless smile, I am overcome with joy. Beyond that, I am blessed to have so many people in my life who love me just for who I am – I really am lucky in that way.

Q. What do you regard as the lowest depth of misery?
Violation of bodies. I just cannot fathom how anyone could violate a child; this hits me harder than ever now that I am a mom. Children are so helpless, and it infuriates me how children all over the world are neglected, violated and failed, when they need to be protected by us. The fact that children born in a certain ZIP code are not going to have access to the same quality education or clean water as a child born in a different ZIP code is unbelievable. It's a vital part of my life's mission to work to try to protect these children, to ensure they have access to physical, mental and spiritual protection.

Q. What would you change if you could?
I would make sure that children have a safe start, a healthy start, a fair start, an equal start, and that they are never violated. I think so many issues are caused by people being violated in their childhood. It doesn't have to be this way.

Q. Which single word do you most identify with?
Vessel. I gravitate towards the idea of surrendering – to God, and to love – and being used as a vessel for that grace to, hopefully, affect the world in a positive way.

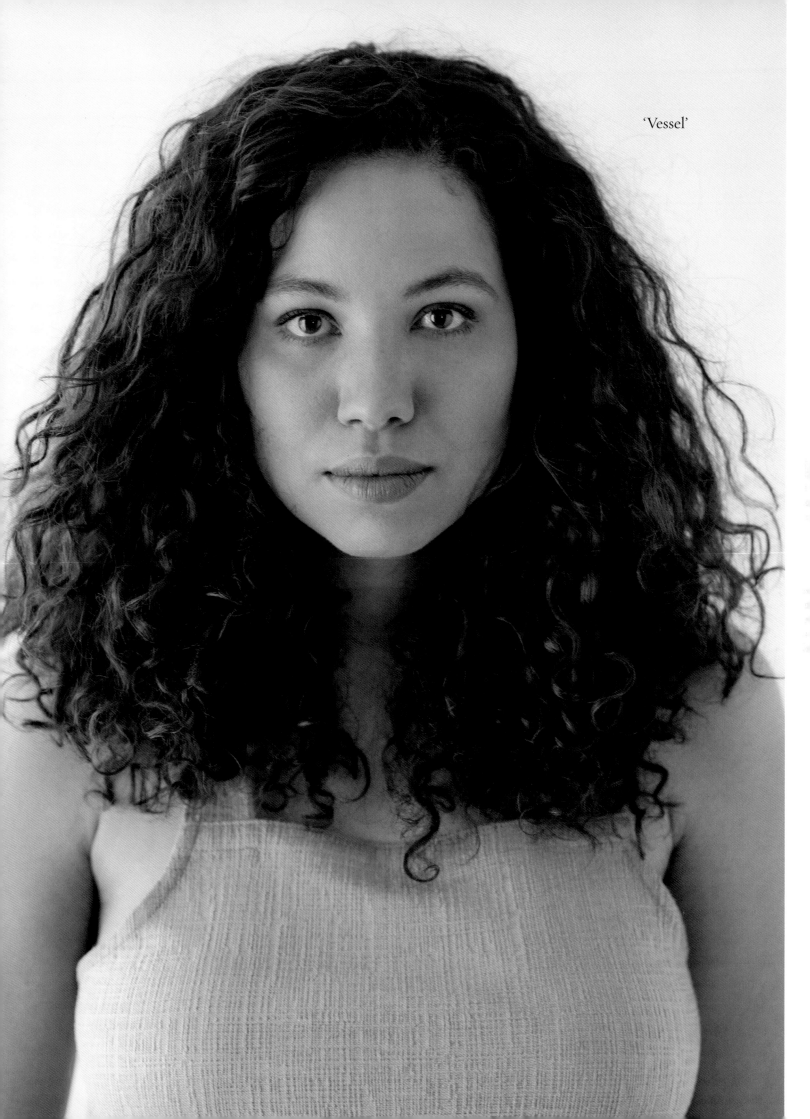

'Vessel'

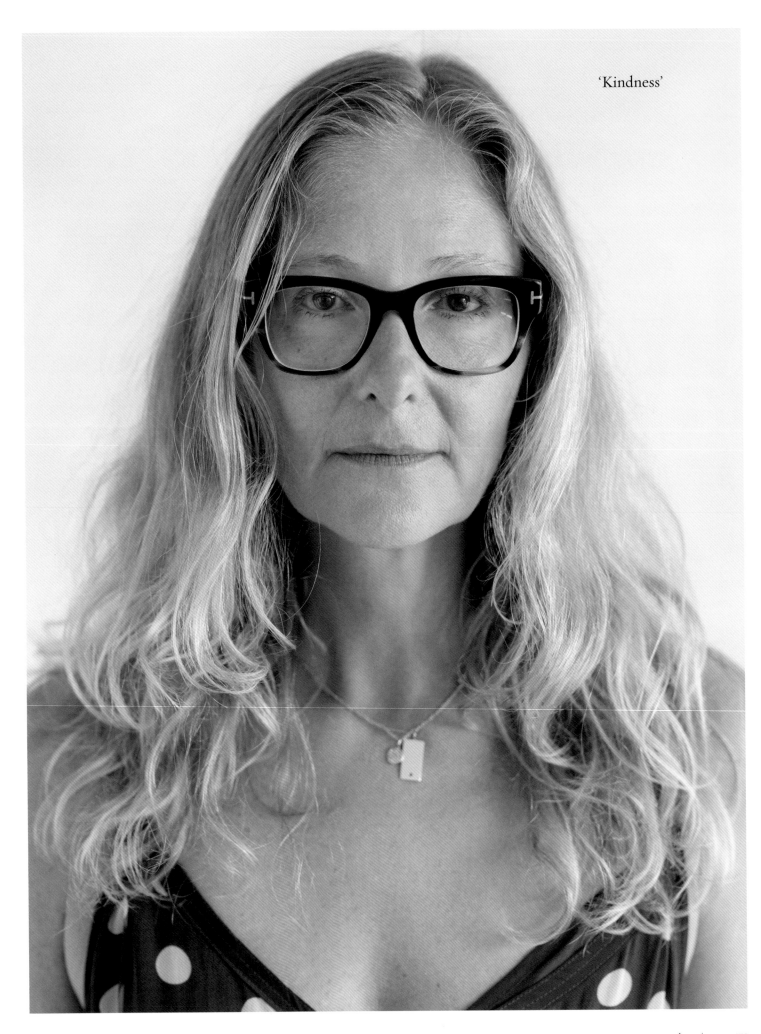

'Kindness'

Interview page 370

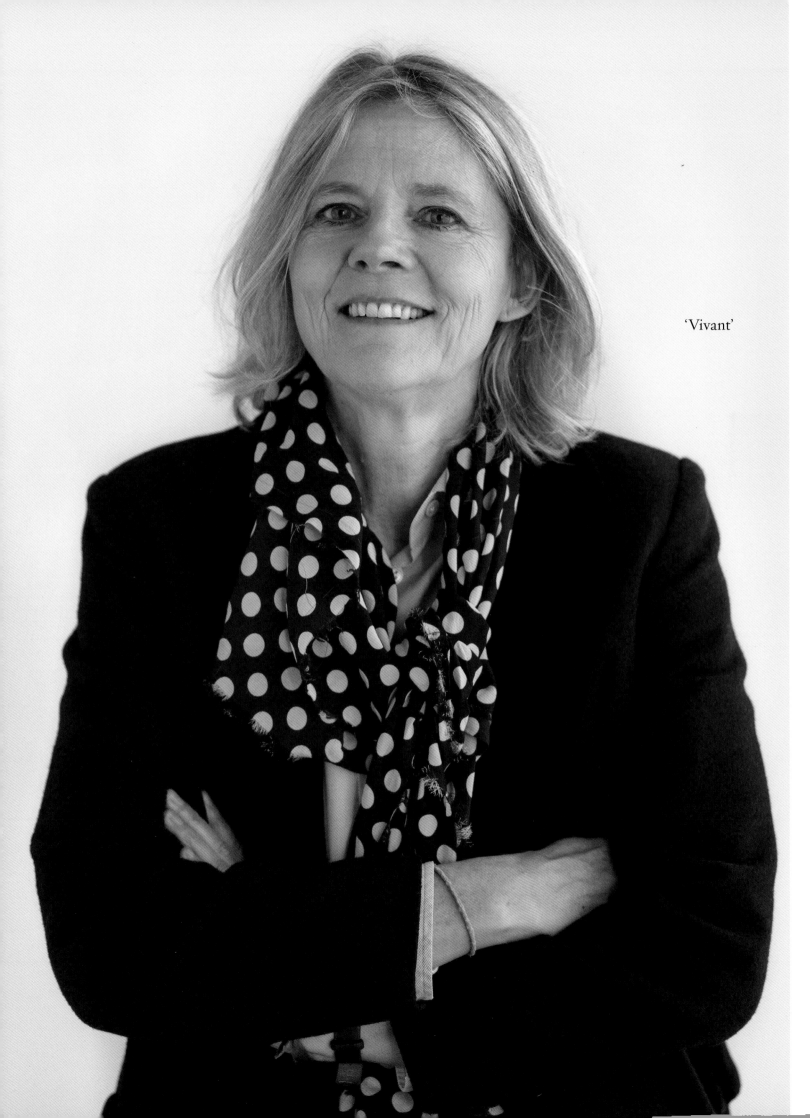

'Vivant'

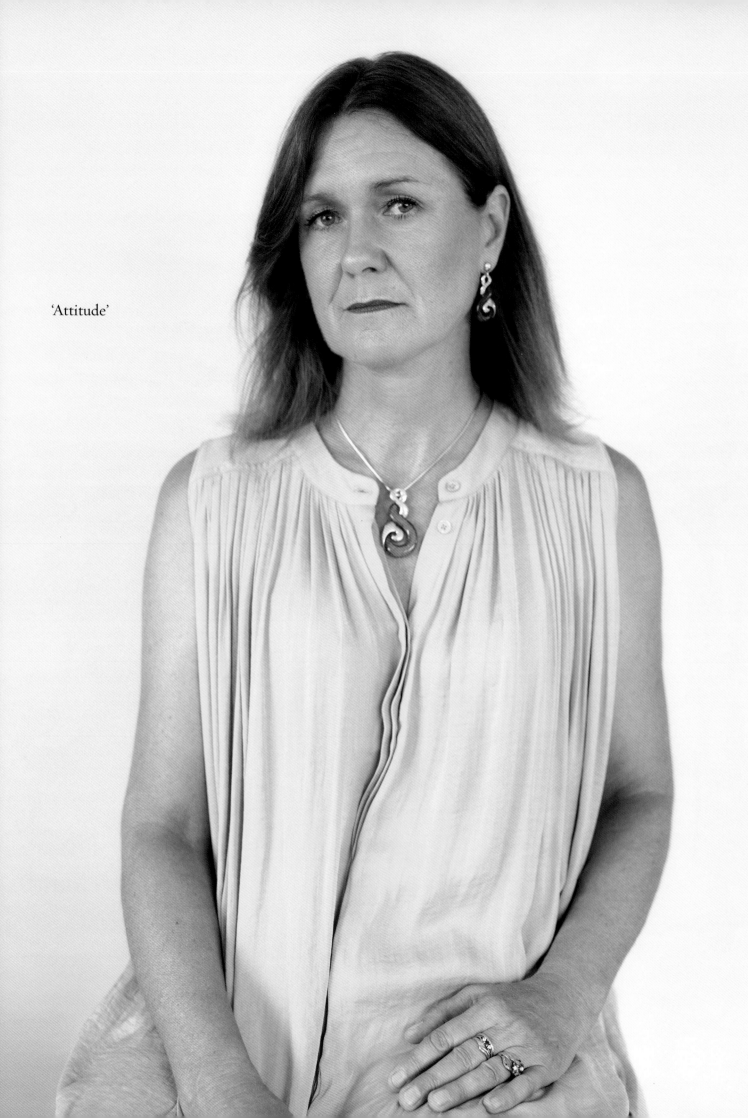

'Attitude'

Louise Nicholas

Louise Nicholas ONZM was born in Rotorua, New Zealand. A survivor of childhood and adult sexual violence, Nicholas is a campaigner and advocate for victims of sexual violence, liaising with survivors and their families, with communities and with police. Nicholas is the co-author of *Louise Nicholas: My Story*, which she wrote with investigative journalist Phil Kitchin. In 2007, Nicholas was recognised as the *New Zealand Herald's* New Zealander of the Year, and, in 2015, she was made an Officer of the Order of New Zealand for services to the prevention of sexual violence.

Q. What really matters to you?

I advocate on behalf of survivors of sexual violence and their families, because what happened to me cannot be allowed to happen to anybody else.

I am a survivor of child and adult rape, perpetrated against me by members of the New Zealand police force from the age of thirteen through to nineteen. For many years, I stayed silent; I covered up what had happened because I blamed myself and carried a lot of shame.

The policeman who hurt me from the age of thirteen was a family friend and had a high standing in our community. I was absolutely petrified that people would find out, because I thought my family would hate me for it. I tried to take my own life – this wasn't about finding an easy way out, it was about protecting my family from the shame of what was happening to me. But I did find the strength to lay a complaint. My family and I never had the criminal-justice system explained to us, though, and not understanding what's happening with those processes can really tip a child survivor over the edge.

I've been through the process of the criminal-justice system seven times in my life; each outcome, bar one, was that the men who hurt me – and so many other victims as well – were acquitted. That experience defined me. My anger grew in the face of this level of abuse; my contribution towards ending this kind of violence is to get out there and be the voice for those who stay silent.

Now I work alongside the New Zealand police. I help train them, and I support them in their work with survivors, particularly through the criminal-justice system. That process is brutal, so I support survivors through the process. I try to empower them to find courage and strength – these qualities are in all of us, and we can find

them if we're given an opportunity to do so. Sitting in the witness box is not like retelling a story – rather, you actually relive what happened; a lot of survivors describe this as an out-of-body experience, because, in order to not be hurt again, you need to be outside of yourself.

In New Zealand, one in three women will be sexually abused before the age of sixteen; many of these women will never disclose their experiences. And, for those who do, it may be decades before they disclose what has happened to them. I try so hard to encourage and empower them. It's not about having to go through a process – it's not about having to go to the police or court – it's about empowering these women to be who they want to be. And it's about the fact that their voices are important – no more silent survivors. Silence is a killer, on so many levels: the suicide rate of survivors is too high, and, when you sit with prisoners – peel back their levels of anger – often the root cause is that they, too, were subjected to sexual violence.

The most important thing is that children need to be encouraged to speak, especially within families; we need to ensure that they have a safe person to go to if anything bad happens. A lot of my survivors – especially the young girls – quite often say, 'I don't want him to go to jail; I just want him to stop hurting me.' That's all they want. So, it's about helping them navigate their pathway to healing and showing society that victim blaming is unacceptable. People don't necessarily speak out straight away and society needs to not judge them for that; society just needs to be willing to listen.

Q. What brings you happiness?

My family; my children and my two little granddaughters.

The biggest joy I get is seeing a survivor come to the end of her journey. Having

seen her at her darkest, having walked alongside her through whatever she's going through, it really is like how human beings slowly stood up to walk in the evolution of man! That's what I see in the survivors I work with – that moment when they hold their heads up high and are so darn proud of achieving something they never thought possible. And that thing is: 'I talked.' It's like going from the dark into the light, knowing that you have done all you can do for yourself. Once you walk into that light, all the evil, putrid, horrible stuff sitting in your soul is gone. That's something a person can only do for themselves; and that light is the beginning of a new life.

Q. What do you regard as the lowest depth of misery?

It's when you are continuously banging your head against brick walls: the government's brick wall, and society's brick wall in the form of all this victim blaming, in the form of this rape culture we've got and the attitudes that come with it. Every day you're fighting to change attitudes, those rape myths like 'She shouldn't have been drunk' or 'She shouldn't have been wearing that.' In actual fact, it's as simple as understanding that men just shouldn't rape. It's that simple. Just don't rape. Don't hurt our girls.

Q. What would you change if you could?

I would have everybody personalise the experience of sexual abuse, because, when people understand the effect it has on a family and the potential effect it could have on them, that's when you start seeing change. We just need our men to understand that all you have to do is ask and listen – all you have to do is be respectful of us as women. We need to teach our young men that they don't need to hurt people.

Q. Which single word do you most identify with?

Attitude. If you change attitudes, you've got a pretty cool world to live in.

'Three of my four grandparents
perished in the Holocaust and
I remember "Never Again"
being a very strong message
in the Australian Jewish
community of the seventies and
eighties. But, at the same time,
I was seeing Cambodia falling
apart on the news. Being a
precocious child, I asked, 'Isn't
it kind of happening again?
It's close to us and we're not
doing anything about it!' It
really struck me and I grew up
wanting to do something that
mattered.'

_ Eva Orner

'Humanity'

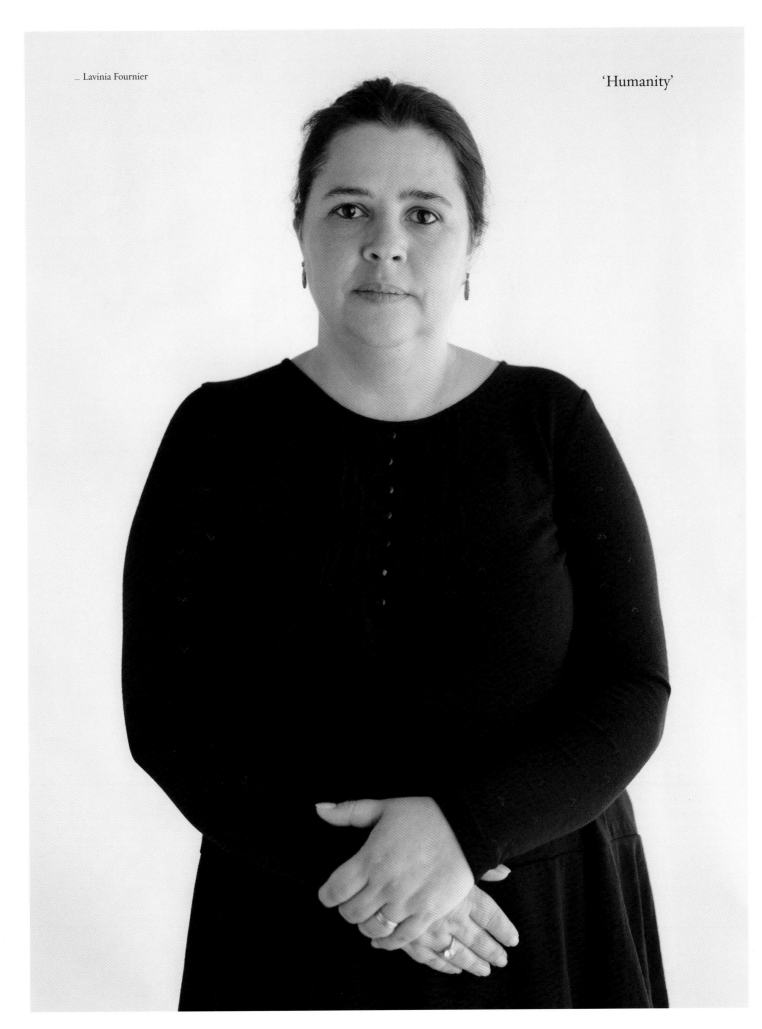

Interview page 371

Florence Aubenas

Florence Aubenas was born in Brussels, Belgium. She graduated as a journalist from the Centre de Formation des Journalistes in Paris in 1984, before embarking on a reporting career with *Libération*, *Le Nouvel Observateur* – today *L'Obs* – and *Le Monde*. In 2005, while working in Baghdad, Iraq, Aubenas was abducted; she was released five months later. In 2010, her book, *Le Quai de Ouistreham* – which chronicled her experiences working undercover as a cleaner on ferries operating out of Ouistreham port, near Caen, France – won her the Jean Amila-Meckert prize and the Joseph Kessel Prize.

Q. What really matters to you?

I'd say curiosity is what motivates me. And, although the press is not enough in itself, it *is* necessary; because, without the press, things tend to stagnate. So, what really motivates me is the combination of these two things: the curiosity to go see what is happening on a human scale, and then the belief and hope that my testimony will, to some extent, contribute to changing things.

About fifteen years ago, in 2005, I experienced a life-changing event: I was taken hostage in Iraq. I'm a journalist and going to war zones is part of my job, so I am aware of the occupational hazards. I am aware that anything can happen; you may be wounded, you may be kidnapped or you may even die. But, still, when you set off for such places, you do think that these things only happen to other people. It *did* happen to me, though; I was kidnapped, held captive, then freed after six months. People often ask me if I feel like I've changed, but I don't. I have the same friends, the same work and the same apartment, and my life is much the same as it was before. However, it's my image that has changed. When people see me now, most of them think, 'That's right. She was a hostage.' This profoundly alters their perception of me.

I still work abroad, in conflict zones, but I also do a lot of work in France. After a while, witnessing *only* extraordinary situations can be a problem, because you are dealing with war and are no longer dealing with people. As journalists, we must keep in mind that, if we are only faced with such extreme situations, we risk losing sight of what really matters. Regardless of the situation – an election, a financial crisis, a conflict or an earthquake – it is the ordinary people who are confronted by these extraordinary situations that matter to me.

In 2009, after a major financial crisis had struck the planet, I decided to approach reporting it by putting myself in the shoes of a woman my own age who has never worked before and who suddenly finds herself in need of a job; it was about experiencing the global economic crisis from the perspective of an ordinary woman. So, for a year, I worked as a cleaning lady in a small French town called Caen. All too often, we hear about world events from the viewpoint of the privileged: the kings and queens, and the industry leaders. But what ordinary people think is equally important; the history of society and of the world we live in is written by us all.

Q. What brings you happiness?

I wish I knew. I would sincerely like to have a particular place or circumstance of which I could say, 'Here, for sure, I'm going to find happiness.' The nature of happiness for me, though, is that these moments happen when I least expect them. We often think, 'This time, everything is in alignment and it's going to be unforgettable,' but we are disappointed. So, what makes me happy is stumbling on the right moments by chance, in the most unexpected and unlikely places. When I was working as a cleaning lady, my lot was thrown in with a group of women who are still doing this work today. Being a cleaning lady is difficult; it is tiring, humiliating, even degrading. Yet, it was while doing our work that I was happiest about the things we shared. Not happy about the work conditions, of course, but about the moments of actual sharing between us. When you work as a special correspondent, you are seen in a flattering light, but for these women it's the exact opposite. You clean toilets on a ferry boat and are on the bottom rung of the social ladder. Nonetheless, these women and I shared moments of happiness equal to those in my own profession.

Q. What do you regard as the lowest depth of misery?

I find it most difficult when I feel like a voice crying in the wilderness. For instance, we see headlines with dire warnings about all of today's environmental issues all the time. However, we can write all the articles we want, shout ourselves hoarse asking what kind of world we are going to leave for future generations, receive all the front-page coverage we want, but the articles won't be read and the message won't be heard. Yes, we know that sooner or later people will realise what's going on and be forced to take action. But, until this happens, there is almost no point and this makes me despair. Why are we unable to see the truth and know what should be done about it? It makes me terribly sad that I still haven't found the answer to these questions.

Q. What would you change if you could?

I believe that we journalists are very lucky, because the press can, in fact, change the world. We have the privilege of knocking on doors and asking all kinds of questions – this doesn't necessarily mean we have the answers, rather, it just means we have a tendency to want to go find out exactly what is going on. Journalists in France were shaped by a major historic precedent in the person of Émile Zola, who took a stand in a very important matter: the Dreyfus Affair. A man had been charged with betraying France and this become one of the first major anti-Semitism cases in France. Émile Zola wrote a celebrated open letter – *J'accuse…!* – in which he accused all of the French authorities with collaborating in the affair. It was a fundamental act that had immense repercussions; I believe that all French journalists are aware, somewhere in the back of their minds, that the press can change the world.

Q. Which single word do you most identify with?

Vivant – alive! Today, just being alive is an act of resistance.

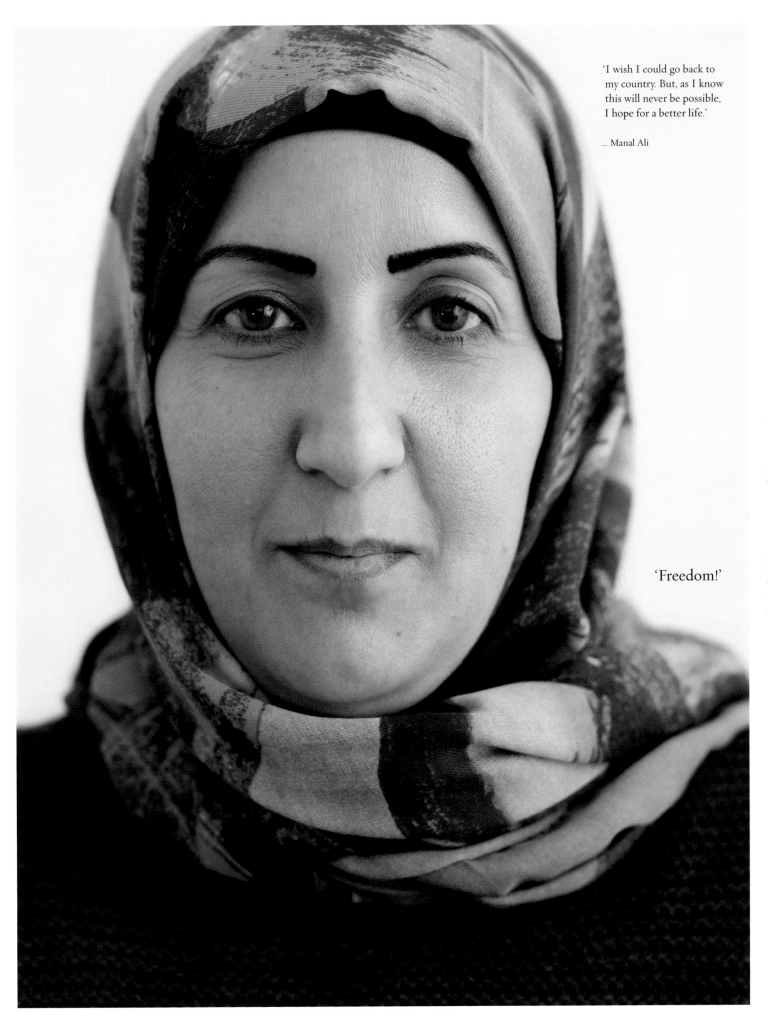

'I wish I could go back to
my country. But, as I know
this will never be possible,
I hope for a better life.'

_ Manal Ali

'Freedom!'

Gabourey Sidibe

Gabourey Sidibe was born in Brooklyn in New York City, USA. She studied psychology before being cast in the titular role in the 2009 film *Precious*. Her debut performance earned critical acclaim, winning her an Independent Spirit Award for Best Female Lead and a National Association for the Advancement of Colored People Image Award for Outstanding Actress in a Motion Picture. For this role, she was also nominated for Academy, British Film and Television and Golden Globe Awards. Sidibe has since appeared in roles on film and television, including *American Horror Story*, *Empire* and *The Big C*. Her memoir *This is Just My Face: Try Not to Stare* was released in 2017.

Q. What really matters to you?

When I think of the things that have shaped me, the first would be my parent's marriage. My mother is American and my father was Senegalese; they got married so that my father could get a green card. They eventually fell for each other – or settled for each other – and had children. But I don't think I got to see a real, loving relationship as a child, so I don't know what that looks like from the inside.

Being in school was also very formative. I went to a school in the Lower East Side of New York City, where most of my classmates were Puerto Rican or Dominican; about 4 per cent of us were black. Being one of the 4 per cent – who also happens to be round, who also happens to be dark – had a real effect on me; sometimes for the better, sometimes for the worse.

What shaped me more than anything, though, was becoming an actress. I had thought I would grow up to be a therapist and had started studying psychology. I loved discovering the inner workings of the human psyche, and I wanted to be a part of exploring that. My whole life I'd watched my mom, who is a singer, pursue her art, and I thought it was too hard for me to do. But I was completely wrong; my first-ever audition was for a film that was called *Push* at the time, but which most people know as *Precious*. I auditioned on the Monday, was hired on the Wednesday, and a year and a half later I was the eighth black woman in history to be nominated for an Oscar for Best Actress. Having all that happen to me at twenty-five years of age shaped and rocked me; it's completely different to what I thought I'd be doing and I'm still very surprised every day. But I hope having studied psychology helps my acting because, even when you're an actor, the purpose of playing a role is to get behind a character – to get behind the thinking of a person and make it real. And that's what psychology is, to me.

Today, my happiness and my comfort – being able to love myself and see that I am deserving of love – really matter to me. I think that's an issue a lot of women battle with, and I think women of colour battle it a little more. Because there is this school of thought that, as a black woman, you're supposed to be strong, a survivor, superhuman – that you have to put everyone ahead of yourself and that there's no room for selfishness.

I like the thought of the strength of a black woman, but I also want to be able to think of myself. I know that sounds really selfish but, without kids or a husband, it's something I can afford to be at this stage of my life; I can be 100 per cent selfish and worry about my own happiness, my own sanity, my own emotions and my own comfort. Prioritising myself – at least not prioritising others above myself – is really something I want my life to be about.

Q. What brings you happiness?

I find happiness in odd sorts of things; I love seeing a hummingbird or a butterfly, doing my own nails, reading a good book or discovering a good show. Those things bring me joy. And I definitely don't think happiness is something that will come to me, rather, it's of my own making. I can't hitch my expectations for joy to someone else. Happiness won't come from relationships outside of myself – if it did, my happiness would end when relationships did.

Q. What do you regard as the lowest depth of misery?

I always say that there are billions of people on the planet, so there are billions of ways to be a person. By that logic, though, there are a billion ways to suffer. I've known my own personal suffering, but I know it doesn't compare to the suffering of people living in third-world countries or fleeing their countries to escape persecution.

From my own small, privileged point of view, however, I'd have to say that the worst kind of suffering is when you're struggling alone and all you can see, feel and understand is darkness – it's when there is no light, everything is harsh and all you want is a way out, but you can't find it. It's when a person is imprisoned by their own brain, by their emotions. I say that's the worst, because that's the suffering I understand; sometimes it can feel like that kind of suffering isn't real compared to what others are going through, but it is.

Q. What would you change if you could?

I would change the stigma attached to reaching out for psychological help. Having some time to talk to a therapist – someone who doesn't know you personally and isn't really involved in your life – can be so liberating, because they don't have a stake in you. Just being able to talk to someone with whom you don't have to worry about monopolising the conversation is key.

I think this has the potential to benefit the entire world, because, once we all reach a level of emotional intelligence, we will be forced to acknowledge each other's humanity; it would force us to be kinder and it would force us to explore the greatness that can come from within. Developing one's emotional intelligence and working on one's self is working towards good energy – and that's contagious. If we were all allowed to be sensitive, we would make a better world; if we were allowed to have emotions, to talk about them and fix them when need be – which is the most important part – then this world would be a safer place.

There are a billion ways to make this world better, but I would say that sound, global mental health is a good start.

Q. Which single word do you most identify with?

Happy. The word sometimes sounds foreign to me, because I don't say it enough.

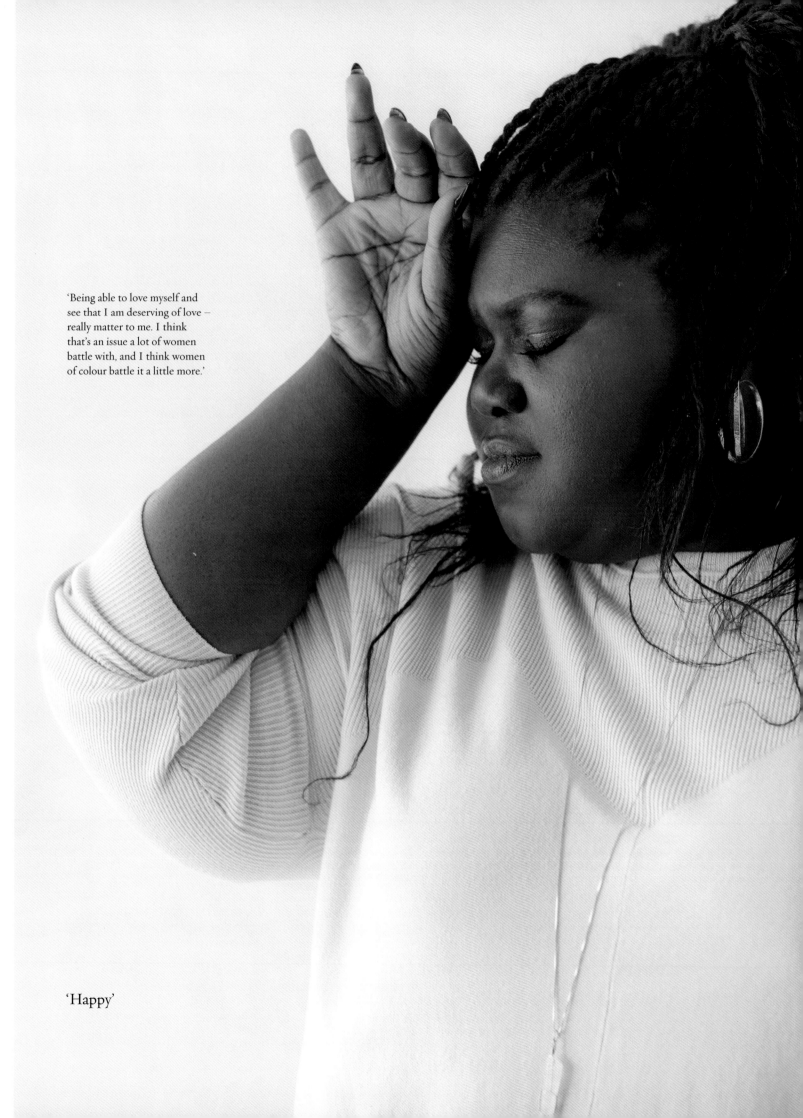

'Being able to love myself and
see that I am deserving of love –
really matter to me. I think
that's an issue a lot of women
battle with, and I think women
of colour battle it a little more.'

'Happy'

Linda Jean Burney

Linda Jean Burney was born in Leeton, Australia, which is part of the Wiradjuri nation. She worked as a teacher before becoming involved in the development and implementation of Aboriginal Education Policy, and in reconciliation. She headed the New South Wales Aboriginal Education Consultative Group and the state's Department of Aboriginal Affairs before becoming the first Aboriginal person to serve in the New South Wales Legislative Assembly in 2003. In 2016, Burney became the first Aboriginal woman to serve in the House of Representatives in the Australian Parliament.

Q. What really matters to you?

On a personal level, it's my two children and it's my friends. Whilst there have been some tough times in my life – and I mean some really tough times – I've been so lucky to have always had an extraordinary circle of friends. They are mostly women and have been my friends twenty, thirty or forty years. They have held me up when I couldn't stand up by myself.

What matters to me is that we in Australia, as a nation, grasp the art of truth telling. Until we do that, we'll never come to terms with the past and how great we can be as a nation. And we'll never walk together. We've made enormous strides in that area, but there is still so much to do. What drives me, many other Aboriginal people and our fellow travellers – because there are many non-Aboriginal people who are part of our journey – is the sense of injustice around the shocking history of colonisation and the treatment of our people.

It's a myth that there were never any wars in Australia, that no blood was shed and that settlement and democratisation were peaceful. It's ridiculous. Wiradjuri was the first Aboriginal inland nation to see the brunt of British occupation and colonisation, because, when the white man came, he saw amazing grazing country. In 1823, martial law was declared by Governor Brisbane and, within four months, one thousand Wiradjuri were murdered. We were the first nation to see the use of poison flour and poisoned water holes.

The Australian government practised social engineering with the express purpose of 'breeding out the black.' Over two or three generations, the government had an assimilation policy of forced removal of children from their families because of their Aboriginality; children were put into church homes or state institutional care.

I was born ten years before the 1967 referendum that declared that Aboriginal people could be counted in the Australian census for the first time. So I was born a non-person; for ten years of my life – like all Aboriginal people back then – I was a non-citizen. It's remarkable that, at the time of my birth, the government knew how many sheep there were in the country, but not how many first peoples.

I grew up not really feeling like I was a complete person – the first time I knew I was Wiradjuri was when I met my father, at twenty-eight years of age. That day was remarkable because I was eight months pregnant with my first child, and I gave birth to my son Binni within twenty-four hours of meeting my dad. I'm sure the emotional side of the meeting is what brought him into the world early.

Whilst I had grown up on Wiradjuri land, I was raised by my non-Aboriginal great-aunt and great-uncle, so I didn't know my father's kinship structure. I had ten brothers and sisters I didn't know existed. Such was the power of racism and exclusion in those days that we grew up forty minutes apart and never knew about one another. But although I grew up in a non-Aboriginal situation, I knew I was different; I wasn't blonde and blue eyed like my cousins. I didn't know whether it was more scandalous that I was born out of wedlock or that I was born Aboriginal. At age twelve, I remember making the conscious decision to embrace my identity and walk that path.

That notion of truth – the incredible sense of honesty and truthfulness – is a theme that I have taken with me into every aspect of my life and into my work, in particular over the last decade in the reconciliation movement. Truth telling is present in the work I've done in education and in the work I'm doing towards recognising first peoples in the Australian Constitution.

It's an indisputable fact that Aboriginal people – on every social indicator – are on the bottom rung, be it education, health, the shocking rates of incarceration for young people and adults, domestic violence, murder, hospitalisation or substance abuse; whichever of these you choose, you'll find in it the story of colonisation. This story exists everywhere. In a first-world nation like Australia, it is not right. So what matters to me is that an Aboriginal child is born at a healthy birth weight. What matters to me is that that child is happy and healthy and safe. What matters to me is that that child learns to read and has the choices and chances in life that every other Australian child has.

Q. What brings you happiness?

I am so driven to make other people happy. I want to make people feel joy, and I want to make people feel loved – but maybe I haven't spent enough time thinking about those things for myself. When do I feel happy? I feel happy at about five thirty every morning, when I'm doing a little bit of meditation to get my day straightened out. I feel happy when I'm gardening. I feel happy when I'm walking the dogs that I don't own but that seem to be at my house more often than not, and that I love very much. I feel happy bringing joy to others.

Q. What do you regard as the lowest depth of misery?

My husband died twelve years ago and I've never really recovered, so, for me, deep misery is losing someone that you think you can't breathe without. Deep misery is seeing people that you love so ill that you know they're not going to make it. I've sat and held three people's hands as the machines were turned off. I know those twenty minutes, from the turning off of life support to that last shuddering breath.

Deep misery is also what's on the seven o'clock news every night. You look at man's inhumanity to man and wonder how we can still be doing these things to each other. We'll hear about 'the war to end all wars,' about stolen generations, and people say these things will never happen again. But then, within a few years, it's happening again.

Q. What would you change if you could?

It's poverty, no question.

Q. Which single word do you most identify with?

Empathy.

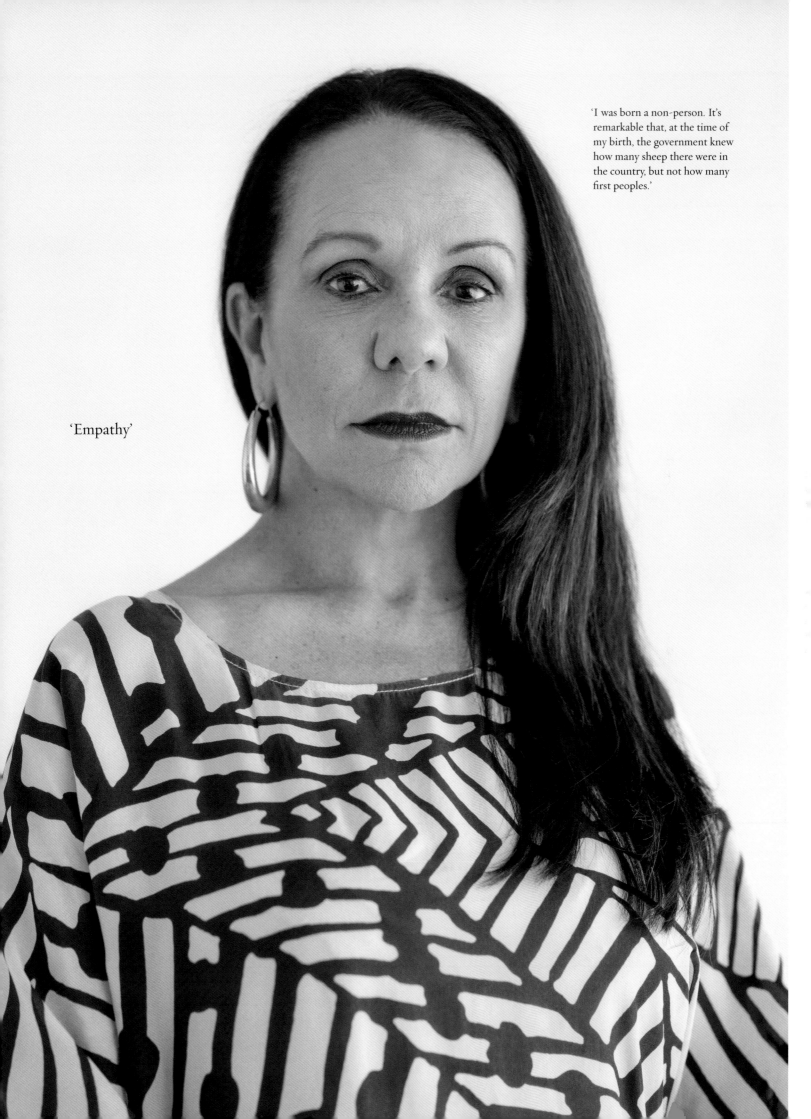

'Empathy'

'I was born a non-person. It's remarkable that, at the time of my birth, the government knew how many sheep there were in the country, but not how many first peoples.'

Nadya Tolokonnikova*

Nadya Tolokonnikova was born in Norilsk in Siberia, Russia. She studied philosophy at Lomonosov Moscow State University. She is an artist, political activist and founding member of punk-rock art collective Pussy Riot. In 2012, following an anti-Putin performance in Moscow's Cathedral of Christ the Saviour, Tolokonnikova was sentenced to two years in prison for hooliganism; she was released in 2013. Tolokonnikova is a member of prisoners' rights group Zona Prava and is a founder of the independent news service MediaZona. In 2014, she received the Hannah Arendt Prize for Political Thought.

'Observing misery hasn't ever helped anyone. What helps is action – moving forward – and breaking through your own fears.'

Q. What really matters to you?
Dignity. Self-respect. Honesty. Justice. Solidarity. Communal spaces. People's movements. Love. Keeping my childish naivety. And art: my dad was an amazing artist, and I myself spent two years in prison as the result of a peaceful art protest.

Although I am a founder of Pussy Riot, it does not make Pussy Riot belong to me, nor does it make me an official representative of Pussy Riot. Because, Pussy Riot doesn't have anything to do with officials, rather, it is a tool for organisation and empowerment. It's simple and fun, and it's what democracy looks like, because anybody can put on a bright mask and express their ideas wherever they like – in parliament, on the streets or at a subway station – this could be a photo of anyone.

Russian culture has a lot of prejudices against women. For example, men don't shake hands with women when they meet them and a woman is supposed to be beautiful only in a mainstream way – at thirty years old she thinks she's become old. In Russia, domestic violence is a big issue and our government has made it even worse – it has legalised domestic violence.

Q. What brings you happiness?
Being helpful and meaningful to others, sharing the beauty I see in the world and staying sensitive to the tiniest details of life.

Q. What do you regard as the lowest depth of misery?
Observing misery hasn't ever helped anyone. What helps is action – moving forward – and breaking through your own fears.

Q. What would you change if you could?
I would increase the level of patience and mutual respect; I would encourage people to be more understanding.

Q. Which single word do you most identify with?
Siberia. I grew up in Siberia; the climate is so severe that I couldn't walk anywhere and had to stay inside reading all the time. So, Siberians are tough and dedicated. And they haven't yet forgotten what integrity is.

* Pussy Riot represents all women; the photograph may, or may not, be Nadya Tolokonnikova.

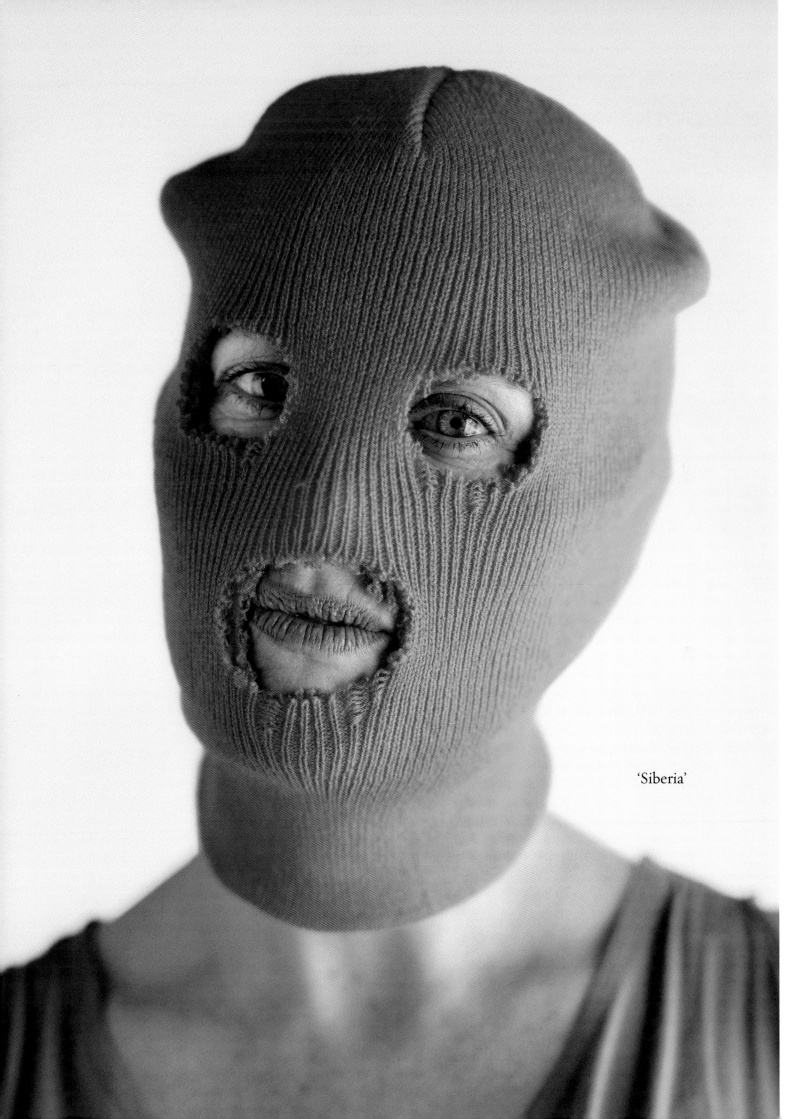

'Siberia'

Alexandra Paul

Alexandra Paul was born in New York City, USA. She began her acting career at age eighteen and became internationally recognised for her role as Stephanie Holden in the television series *Baywatch*. Paul has become a dedicated environmental and animal rights activist, and advocates on the issue of overpopulation. She has been arrested for civil disobedience several times, including while advocating on behalf of nuclear disarmament and protesting the 2003 Iraq War. She is the twin sister of Caroline Paul (p. 217).

Q. What really matters to you?

My identity: I'm an actress, an athlete and an activist – these represent my job, my health and my soul.

When I was twelve, I read this quote: 'When in doubt, do the kindest thing.' It's my guiding principle – you can't really go wrong with it. So, when I wasn't getting a lot of work in my forties and I had to decide what to do with myself, it had to be something to do with alleviating suffering for animals and for people. I don't know if my wanting to help others is selfless, because it gives me meaning and purpose. A lot of people give love and support to their children; I don't have children, so I try to put that kind of energy into my activism.

I've concentrated on animal rights, working to release animals from factory farms and to stop testing on animals. I work with an organisation that negotiates with laboratories to release dogs that are being experimented on. As a vegan, it matters to me that animals have full rights. This means that no one is eating them, wearing them, experimenting on them or caging them. Animals suffer too and should be able to be free.

I also have a career as a health coach now. Helping people to get healthy and fit, and to feel good about themselves, matters to me.

Q. What brings you happiness?

I'm in love with my husband. We've been together for twenty-one years, and he's amazing – he's just so wonderful and supportive of me.

I also find happiness in my activism. I volunteer with an organisation called Food Not Bombs – we cook vegan meals and serve them to the homeless. There are fifteen of us who cook for about a hundred people. Most of us aren't cooks, but we manage to put together an amazing meal. We engage with the people we serve; these are people with passions and dreams. The social aspect of being together with all these people makes me happy.

Q. What do you regard as the lowest depth of misery?

The lowest depth of misery is being imprisoned – whether you're an animal or a human, whether it's an actual cage or not being free to love who you want. In the world today 25 billion animals are confined and exploited, and 45 million people are enslaved – that, to me, is hell.

Q. What would you change if you could?

Here in America a lot of women take it for granted that we have gender equality – we don't. The word 'feminist' is a dirty word, and it shouldn't be. Women's pay is seventy cents on the dollar here compared to men, and on top of that we do most of the work around the house, while raising kids.

I remember screen testing for a female lead role in a television series in which the male lead had already been cast. They were also looking for the second male lead. I found out from a friend who had seen the budget that the female lead was to be paid less than the second male lead – and none of the guys who were up for that second lead had the credits that I had. None of them. But it had already been decided that they were more valuable than I was. And that sort of behaviour is not changing.

So often, I notice women apologising for the smallest things. Just coming towards you along the street they'll say, 'I'm sorry,' and step aside. Men never do that. Women are apologising just for taking up space, and I don't know if that's changing fast enough. I don't think women are enabled to make demands the way men are; men are raised differently. Young boys aren't discouraged as much as young girls, and so girls are raised with an inherent lack of self-efficacy – they are taught to question themselves and are not encouraged to go out and be messy and loud.

In my high school years, my voice was tiny. When I started acting, sound people would always say, 'Speak up, Alexandra, speak up!' But I didn't know how to – it didn't feel authentic to speak up and to speak in my power. A lot of girls go through that. Girls in America are taught that we should be nice and shouldn't be loud. Of course that affects us as we get older. Maybe we perpetuate things like pay disparity because we don't demand the way men do – but to demand *anything* is very hard for a woman.

So this is what I would change if I could. Perhaps it starts with empowering girls and women through education. Every woman should have access to education as long as she wants it. In tandem with that is educating boys and men on the value of women.

Something I care deeply about is human overpopulation – it is one of the most important issues facing our planet. Getting the population down to 2 billion through humane means is essential, and it's an effort which is interconnected with so many other issues. Suddenly, solutions to crises like economic disparity and climate change become visible. And I think the number one way to stabilise the global population is to empower women. If women were wholly empowered, we would choose to have smaller families – because it's normally women who end up raising children. In societies where men have so much power over women, there tend to be larger families because it's a sign of machismo to have more children and they are not a burden for men.

Q. Which single word do you most identify with?

Compassion. I like that it has the word 'passion' in it. To me, it means kindness in action.

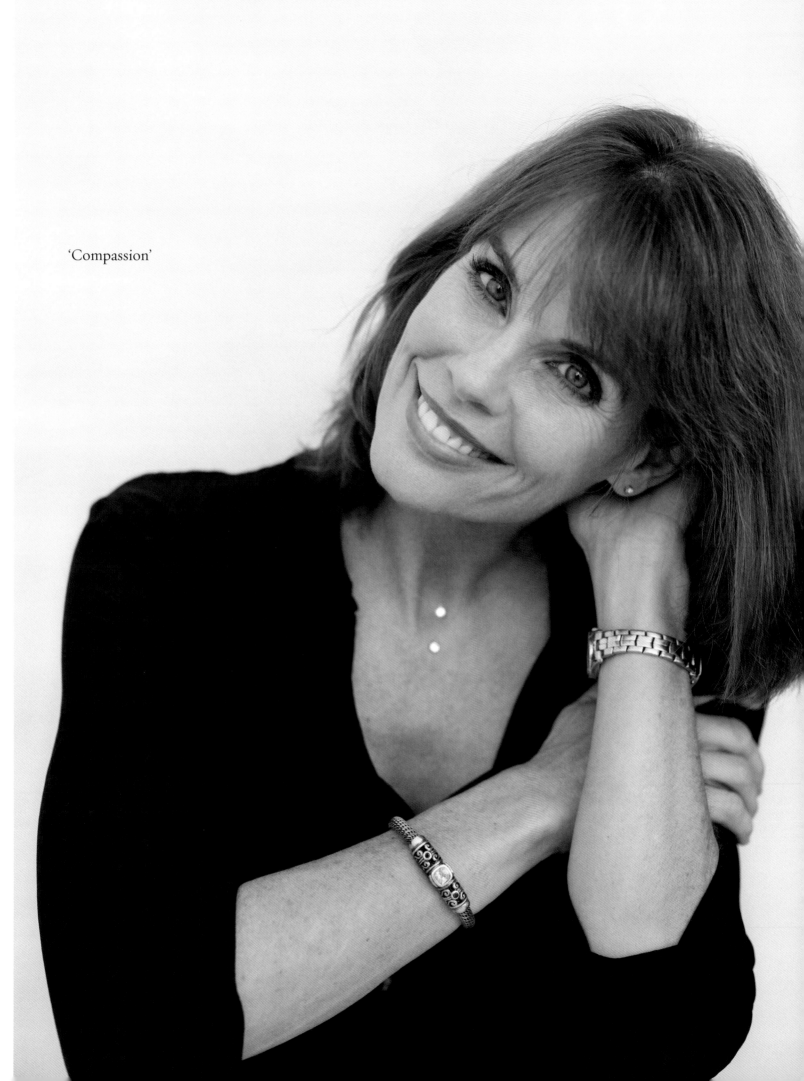

'Compassion'

Christine Nixon

Christine Nixon was born in Sydney, Australia. She holds a bachelor of arts degree in philosophy and politics from Macquarie University and a master's in public administration from Harvard University. Nixon joined the New South Wales Police at age nineteen and became president of the women's branch of the Police Association of New South Wales at twenty-one. In 1994, Nixon became the New South Wales Police's director of human resources. From 2001 to 2009, she was chief police commissioner of the Victoria Police. Nixon has been awarded the Australian Police Medal, National Medal, Centenary Medal and New South Wales Police Medal.

Q. What really matters to you?
Today, I judicially use my time, influence and capacity around things that matter. So, what matters to me now is to encourage women to recognise their talents; I have developed a course with which to teach women what I have learned.

In my time with the police, I had a lot of ups and downs. But when I first joined policing, there were about 0.5 per cent women. As my time progressed – first in the New South Wales Police and then in the Victoria Police – the gender-split in sworn officers was probably about 14 per cent women and the rest blokes. By the time I'd finished, women numbered about 29 per cent of sworn officers.

Since the seventies, I've watched the impact women have had in policing – even just in the way women handle simple incidents. When I first worked in operational policing in Sydney – I was one of the first women to do this – it was in a really difficult part of the city. People said, 'You'll be assaulted and you'll never be able to look after yourselves.' But none of that happened, because the way good police officers – and particularly women officers – handle difficult situations is not by using their brawn, but by using their brains and negotiation skills.

When I became police commissioner, it came as a bit of a shock to the Victoria police. People said, 'Are you going to feminise the police?' I said, 'Yeah, I hope so! I'm a woman, and I'm not about to change; it's who I am. I have lots of roles in my life, and I will go about being a police commissioner on the basis that I am a woman.' I was accused of having created this very conciliatory, community-focussed organisation that was welcoming of gay and lesbian people, Aboriginal people, women and older people. I said, 'Great! If that's what you accuse me of, then I'm really happy!'

More and more, in my work, I came to understand how we were treating disadvantaged people in the community.

One particular time, we had to pick up a fourteen-year-old girl who'd run away. Some of the people I worked with said, 'She's just a rotten kid who has run away from home.' But, I remember sitting down with this girl, saying, 'Tell me why you ran away.' She said, 'Why would I bother?' I said, 'Because I'm interested and I want to help.' She said, 'Mum died. I live with my stepfather. He's sexually assaulted me for years.' Nobody wanted to listen to kids like her in those days – I did and we got her out of there. That experience was part of me coming to understand how we were treating people. All of a sudden – then more and more – I started to see what the police could do better to help. Then gradually, I got more power, and more capacity to work with governments on changing legislation or to be part of a team focussing on those people who are disadvantaged.

Back in the seventies, we had many grand ambitions about where we'd be with women's rights by now in Australia; and people will tell you we've come a long way with women's rights, but we still have a long way to go. An aspect of this that is important to me relates to leadership models. Women have had to be incredibly creative to get things done; we've had to work together, and we've had to work with communities. I think I'm a fairly reasonable example of someone whose leadership style hasn't been the heroic one of 'Just follow me, blokes, and I'll tell you where to go!' That's not women. The leadership model that women have had to rely on involves bringing people together and going, 'That's a really important place we want to get to over there. But you'll have to contribute to helping us get there and you're going to have to do the work to help us achieve it.' Nobody writes that model of leadership up, though. All the books are written by blokes and they are about a heroic kind of leadership. Born to rule! How dare anybody suggest that some are born to be leader? What, then, happens to the rest of us who weren't? That way of thinking is an elite thing and is a mistake. So, I'm in the process of writing a book

with Professor Amanda Sinclair about women's leadership.

Q. What brings you happiness?
I get joy from watching things get done, from watching people achieve things. I live in a lovely part of the world and I appreciate what's around me. We often forget to be grateful for what we have, for living in one of the best countries in the world here in Australia. Yes, it's got its flaws and its problems, but it's got clean water, it's relatively safe and it's got enough food and water. I've been to other places where that's not the case, so I'm happy with that.

Q. What do you regard as the lowest depth of misery?
I try not to despair at what I see in the world. I'm pragmatic enough to look out and go, 'We just have to keep working on these things; we have to keep finding different ways to try to improve things for people.' I've been quite successful in what I've done, so I keep thinking, 'Just take another step.' I often try to push other people to take another step, too. Yes, it may mean you're going to be out there in the light, but you can make a difference when you get there.

Q. What would you change if you could?
The way we treat each other. It would make such a difference if people treated other people decently and fairly. Achieving fairness and equity requires system reform – it's not so much the people who need to reform. One of the things I wouldn't do is want to change women and minority groups. Rather, those who have access to power should be the ones to change and recognise that we would just be so much better off as a society – as communities, families and individuals – if we had better fairness and decency, and were not treating people harmfully. We've got to be ambitious. On occasions it's not appropriate to say that you're an ambitious woman, but I am ambitious – not for me, but for what could be done.

Q. Which single word do you most identify with?
Power. I think I've got power and I can use it.

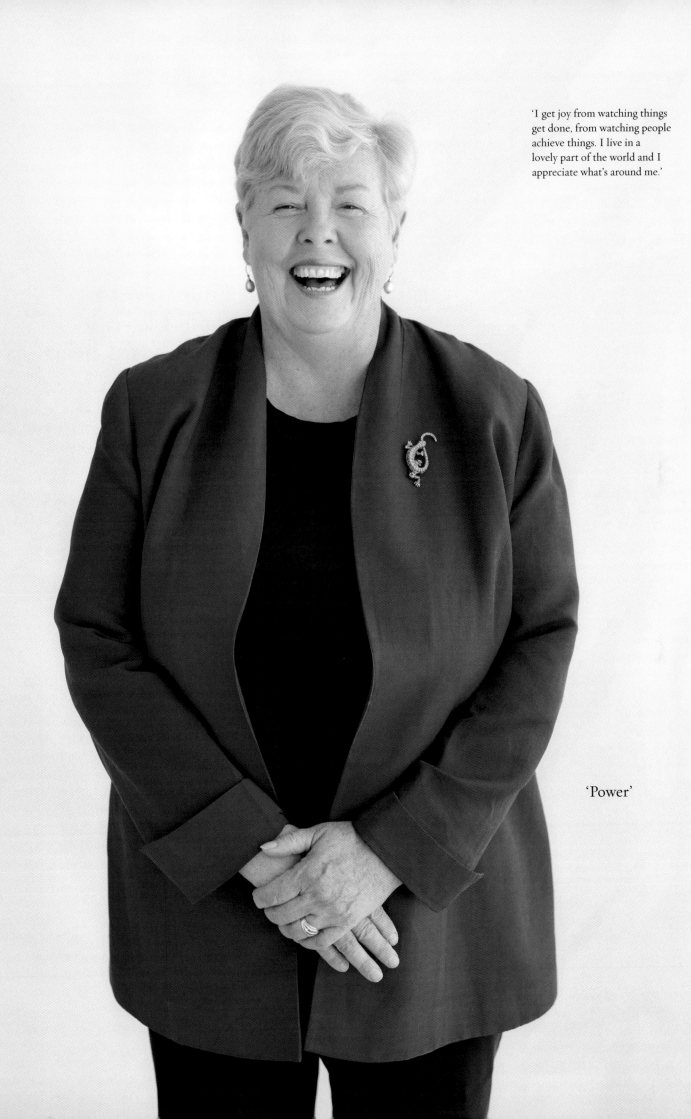

'I get joy from watching things get done, from watching people achieve things. I live in a lovely part of the world and I appreciate what's around me.'

'Power'

Yene Assegid

———

'It matters to me that I'm real with myself and with the people I love; it gives me the courage to follow my heart.'

———

Yene Assegid was born in Addis Ababa, Ethiopia. At age nine, at the beginning of the Ethiopian Civil War, she and her family emigrated to Belgium. Assegid later studied in the United States, gaining a PhD in transformative leadership from the California Institute of Integral Studies. She now works for The Shola Company, providing coaching and training in leadership development, team building and personal development.

Q. What really matters to you?

The biggest lesson that I've learned – and it's a hard lesson – is having the courage to be authentic: to be yourself. Everybody has a gift, so whatever it is, just be it and own it. Society doesn't foster this attitude, though. Instead, it tells us to be apologetic for our authenticity if we don't align with this or that expectation. But I say, 'No. You are beautiful the way you are. You matter just the way you are.'

My family moved to Belgium in the mid-seventies, when the revolution in Ethiopia was starting up. It was hard, because no one explained to a nine-year-old why we were being transplanted. Of course, I knew something was happening when I noticed more and more people wearing black back home; this was because people were being executed and assassinated, and people were disappearing. Before we left, we sold everything. A week before our flight I was asked to open the front door of our home and, when I did, all I saw was the muzzle of an automatic rifle – but it didn't compute; soldiers were coming to our house, searching for weapons or for anything that would associate us with the previous regime. When we left, it was less of a goodbye and more of a funeral, because it was goodbye forever. I went from being a child to a small adult over the course of one flight. We landed in Amsterdam en route to Brussels, and all I remember is that the scent of the air was different. When we got to Brussels, there was no sun, no garden, and no community. There were eight of us: my mum, dad,

uncle and the five children. My parents had less than $10,000 and no jobs. Everything that we were, was gone. Everybody who knew who we were, and who we could be, was gone. What happens when you take away someone's identity? You're no longer anybody. You're an immigrant – a number. When you go to government offices, you go to the counter where the 'other' goes. You stop walking around flamboyantly, and you make your life as discreet as possible. I wasn't conscious of this at the time, but, intuitively, I decided that I had to create something for myself – and it's a lifelong effort to transform this situation into something positive.

What matters to me now – in my work as a trainer and coach – is to look at how I can support people in opening up their gifts. Not many people outside Africa think much of Africa, and I often wonder when Africans will be able to travel for work or education or pleasure. When will we be able to travel because we choose to and not because we feel like we must leave the continent in order to survive? When will we be able to live with the kind of facility and dignity that so many others in the world have? Young Africans must ask themselves: what can they, as the next generation, do to make sure that our grandchildren have those things? How are their lives going to matter? What will they *do*? What will they leave behind? The answers, I believe, are in opening their gifts in service to others. Young Africans must embrace who they are and then be the best versions of themselves.

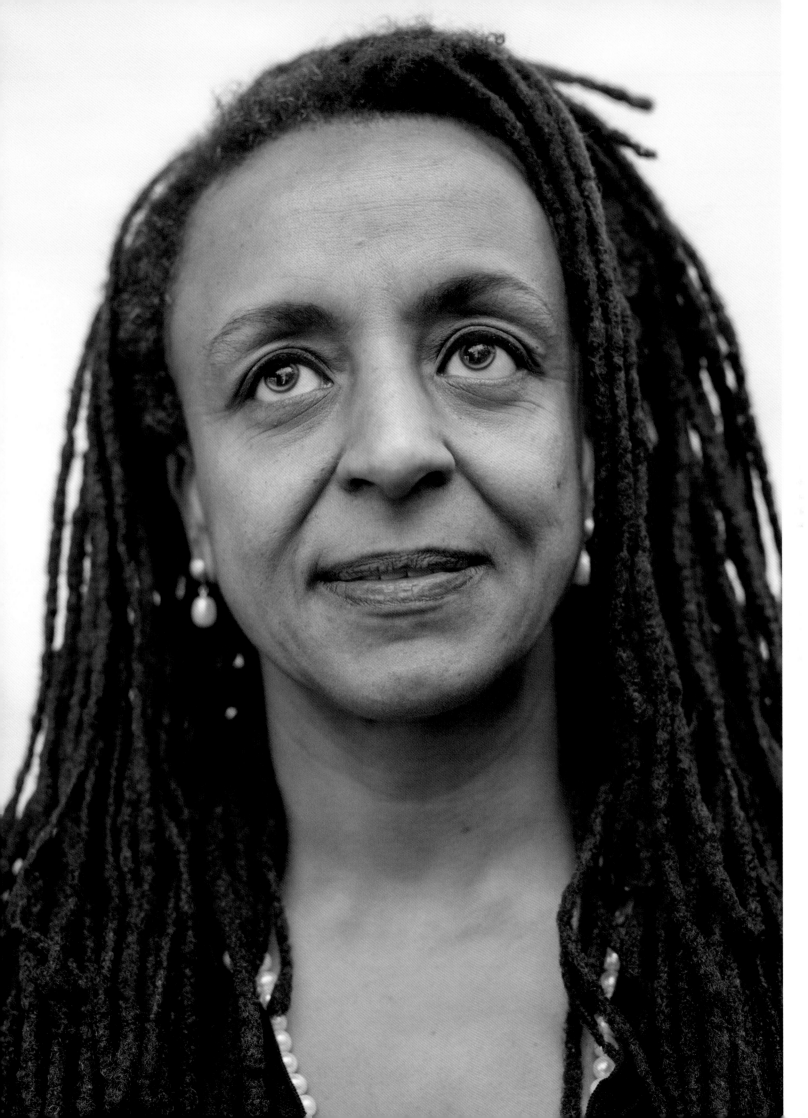

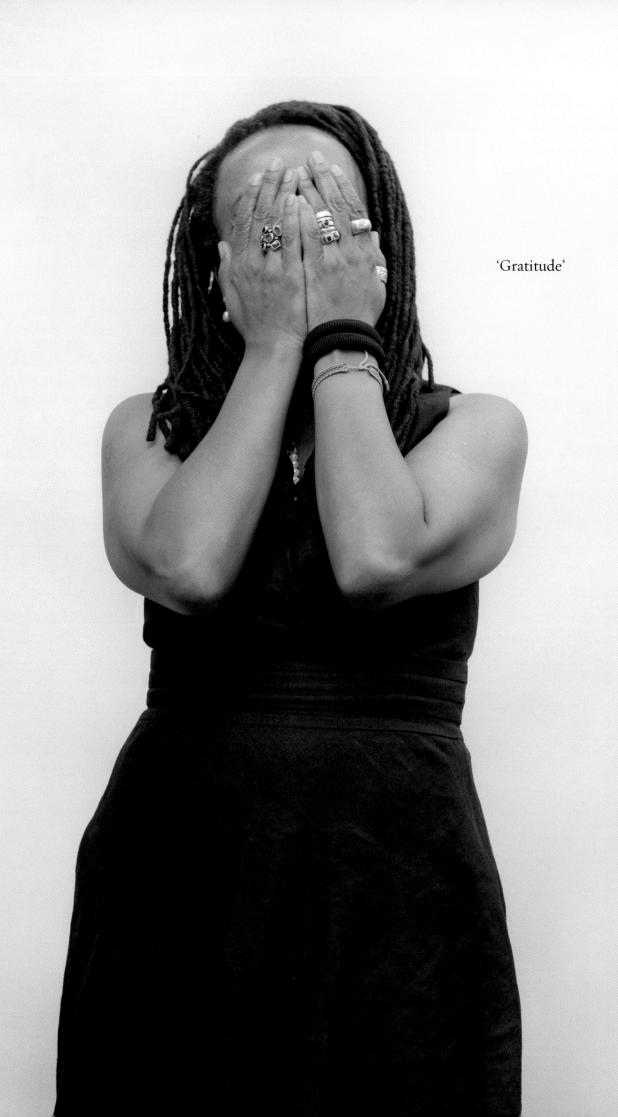

'Gratitude'

Yene Assegid

———

I still feel like an outsider, but a professional outsider. Being an outsider is actually a gift; you belong everywhere because you don't belong to anywhere and you're not in any box. Somehow you become more human because you know how it feels to not be from 'here.' You become more humble, but bold at the same time. You become kinder and also less tolerant of prejudice. It makes something very special in you. So, it matters to me that I'm real with myself and with the people I love; it gives me the courage to follow my heart.

Q. What brings you happiness?
I am happy to wake up in the morning – just happy to be around. And I'm grateful for the friends and family that I have.

I pray. For me, God is not necessarily a religious God, but rather a spiritual being of the greatest possible universal expression of love. Sometimes I pray and I say, 'Please don't send me any more challenges right now. I need a summer break!' In hindsight, though, I am grateful for the challenges that I have, because it's through challenges that we grow into our humanness.

Q. What do you regard as the lowest depth of misery?
What brings me misery is when we, as humans, step lower in our thinking. Misery is when we are made less than who we are: for example, when we expect less of ourselves or when we expect less from another person. Or when we label. It's important to me that we are able to look at others as an expression of the universe – or of God – and to not be reductive of another's identity. If we can look at everyone through a lens of knowing that they are an expression of the greatest spirit, then we'll know that we are not more than them and that they are no more than us.

Q. What would you change if you could?
I would bring about awareness. I wish people would act in the consciousness that the creator – the divine, God or whatever it is that you believe in – is right there with them, always. Would people say what they say if they knew God was listening? Would they do some of the things they do if they knew that God, this being of love, or of positivity, was watching? I think they wouldn't. And what that is, really, is just awareness of God and of God's presence within each of us; awareness would help us to be kinder, to be more tolerant, to be more understanding and to be more forgiving of ourselves and others.

Q. Which single word do you most identify with?
Gratitude. I am grateful for everything I have, especially in the knowledge that there is always a chance that things could become worse. Sometimes we can also have gratitude for what we don't have; maybe, in not having it, we are being spared from some other trouble.

'Somehow you become more human because you know how it feels to not be from 'here.' You become more humble, but bold at the same time. You become kinder and also less tolerant of prejudice. It makes something very special in you.'

———

'Some of my happiest moments have been a result of difficult moments, of realising that the magnitude of joy can, and does, far outweigh the painful things in my life.'

_ Molly Biehl

Interview page 371

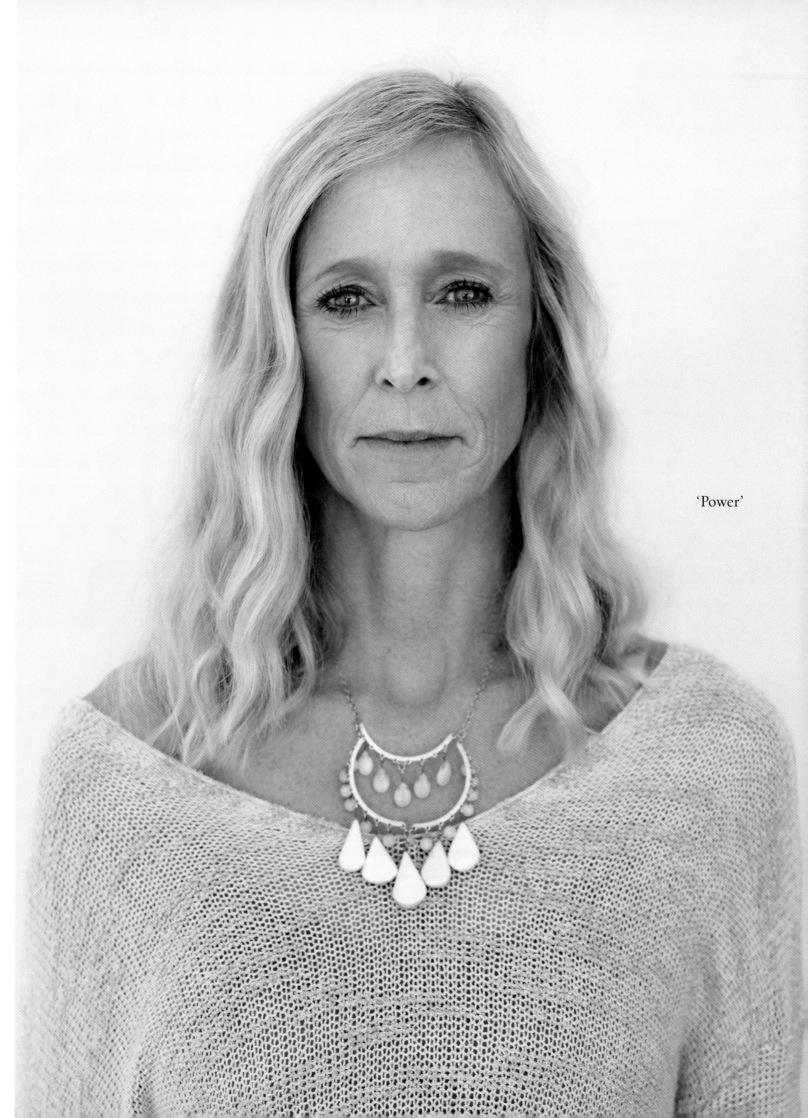

'Power'

Sabila Khatun

Sabila Khatun was born in Sundarpur, Nepal. In 1993, she and her husband, together with four children, moved to Kathmandu to find work. Unable to find employment and unsupported by her alcoholic husband, Khatun and her children were forced to beg for money and sleep on the streets. A mother of eight, Khatun has gone on to become a tradesperson; with this income and the financial support of foreigners, she has been able to provide an education for six of her children.

Q. What really matters to you?
Family. I gave up everything to raise my children, so the thing that matters to me most is that they are able to live better lives than they lived when they were young. But also, it matters that they do not forget their poor mother. Because I don't want to be alone.

Over many centuries in Nepali culture, the concept of love for one's family has grown into a firm duty; in return for being raised well, children take care of their parents and grandparents. I have committed my whole life to my children's futures – one of the things that kept me going through the lowest points of my existence was the belief that, when my children were grown and successful, they would not only acknowledge everything I have done for them, but would *want* to support me and *want* to spend time with me. But, although my whole life has been concentrated on my children, now that they are grown, they have forgotten me.

I have always strived to give of my love to my children, so that they would never feel unloved like I did. I myself never experienced love from my parents; my mother died when I was twelve days old and after my father remarried, he sent me to be raised by his sister.

Just as I never had support from my family, I never got support from my children's father. He is a bad man and I am now separated from him. We had seven children together, yet he never helped me with parenting them; he never earned money for the family, and spent everything we had on alcohol and cigarettes.

In our village, it was not possible for me to work to support my children, but somebody I knew told me there were many opportunities for the poor in Kathmandu and that there were lots of foreigners willing to help people like me. When I arrived in Kathmandu, it was an incredibly difficult time. I didn't speak Nepali or English – only Hindi – so I begged for money in the streets. My husband did nothing to help; my children and I slept on the street for seven years, and any money we made my husband took for himself and drank away.

I remember a foreigner once saying to me, 'Sabila, you cannot be begging with your children – they need to go to school to make their lives better.' But that just was not possible. Every time I tried to speak with my husband about this, he would become violent with me and with the children.

Eventually, someone told me that selling something – even for a little bit of money – is better than begging. So, I started selling small passport bags to tourists, then I went on to sell cigarettes. I became a regular fixture on Durbar Marg – my street; tourists came to know me and my cart, and would ask about my story.

One day, Werner – a German man who I had known for some time – asked me about a scar on my hand. When I explained that it had been my husband's doing, Werner told me that I should go to the police. In Nepal, though, the man is a very important figure in the family and in society, so I explained that this would not be good for my family. Werner told me that I couldn't keep feeding this man who did not contribute positively to my life or to the lives of our children. He has become like my godfather and for the past fifteen years has been sending me money to help send my children to school.

And Werner's not the only one – I've developed a new family for myself and, strangely, it's made up entirely of foreigners! With their help, I've been able to send six of my children to school, which would not have been possible otherwise. And with the money from my sales, I have been able to buy new clothes for the children. Nonetheless, although people send me money, it's always dependent on what they *can* give. So, when their business is not doing well, they can't afford to support me.

Life has been incredibly hard, and, even when I was finally ready and able to leave my husband, there was still sadness to come. He transferred the house that was paid for with money I earned into his name and left me with nothing – literally.

I feel very fearful for my future, even though, in Nepal, if you have many sons, you are considered rich – this is because, when the son marries, his wife is expected to move to his family's home and help keep the house. But, when my oldest son married, he went to live with his wife's family instead, and now this example has been set for his younger brother. All my daughters who have gotten married have also left, so now I only have four children with me, and am very conscious that tomorrow I may wake up and have no one. This is a terrifying thought, because I don't own a house and I don't have money for a caregiver – I'm getting old, and the very last thing I would want is to be infirm, alone and living on the streets once more. Because if that happens, my life will be finished.

Q. What brings you happiness?
It is when my children are doing well, when they are succeeding and when their wishes are fulfilled. It is when I am *with* my children. My life has had immense sorrows, but I have worked hard to raise my children, educate them and feed them, so to see them living better lives is my greatest happiness.

Q. What do you regard as the lowest depth of misery?
I don't know – I'm a sad person, and sadness sees only sadness.

Being with a man who abuses you is devastating. When I see fathers, mothers and children all together, I feel sad, because I didn't have that life and I couldn't give that life to my children.

When I see youngsters caring for their parents, I feel sad, because I fear that I won't have that kind of treatment. I used to say that, even though I didn't have money, I had wealth – my wealth was my children. I used to think that my children would support me when they were grown and that as a result my sorrows would run away. But this is not happening and it hurts me. I fear what my life will be like when I am an old woman with no one supporting me.

Q. What would you change if you could?
I wish I had savings – if I did, I would build a house and live in it with my children.

Q. Which single word do you most identify with?
Family.

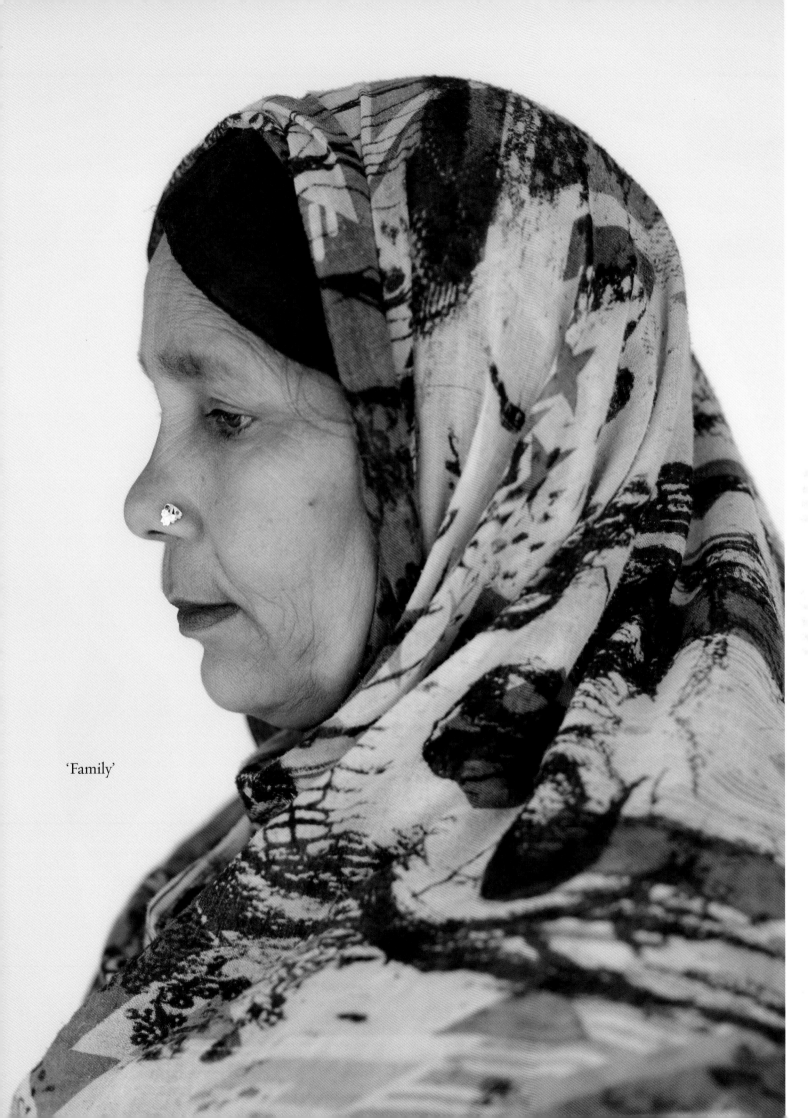

'Family'

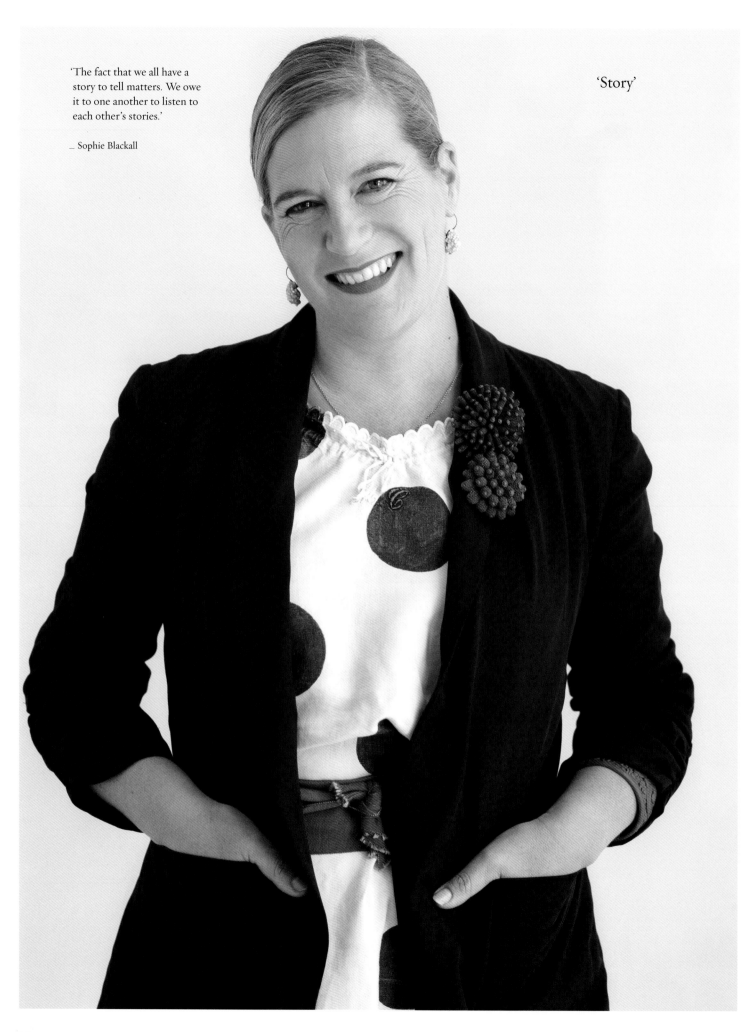

'The fact that we all have a story to tell matters. We owe it to one another to listen to each other's stories.'

_ Sophie Blackall

'Story'

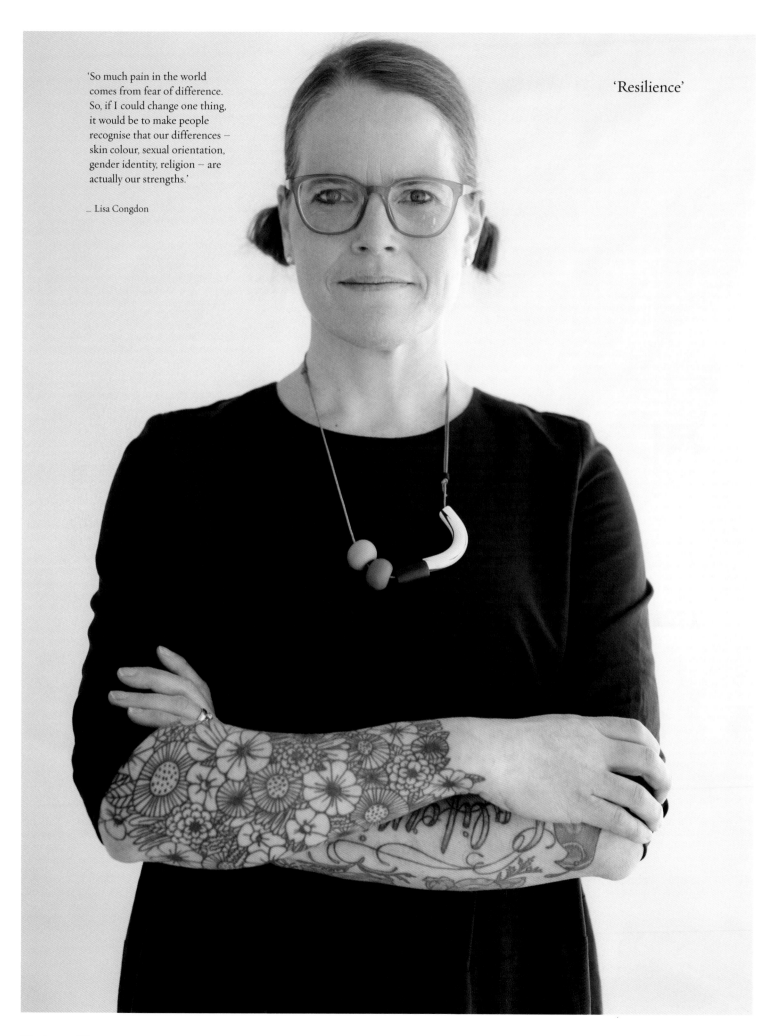

'So much pain in the world comes from fear of difference. So, if I could change one thing, it would be to make people recognise that our differences – skin colour, sexual orientation, gender identity, religion – are actually our strengths.'

_ Lisa Congdon

'Resilience'

Interview page 372

Yassmin Abdel-Magied

Yassmin Abdel-Magied was born in Khartoum, Sudan, and moved to Australia just before her second birthday. She holds a bachelor of mechanical engineering from the University of Queensland. An author, mechanical engineer, activist and television presenter, Abdel-Magied sits on the boards of ChildFund Australia, the Australian government's Council for Australian–Arab Relations and the domestic-violence-prevention organisation Our Watch. In 2015, she was recognised as Queensland's Young Australian of the Year.

Q. What really matters to you?

That's a good question, because I'm in a transitional stage of my life; I've spent the past four years working as an engineer on offshore oil and gas rigs, and I've just exited Youth Without Borders, which I was with for the last nine years. So, I'm trying to figure out what the next thing is. The big picture – what I care about and what brings everything together – is equality and access to opportunity, as well as using my skills to level the playing field. My parents brought me up with the idea that I should constantly be in service; having moved to Australia, we were always aware that we should make the most of the opportunities we had and that we must give back. So, with Youth Without Borders, our initial mission was to empower young people to work together for the implementation of positive change in their communities; it was all about collaboration and that is still important to me.

As a child, there were very few people I could look up to who looked like me. What could I aspire to when I never saw someone like me on the television, was rarely ever able to read a book by someone like me or even by someone whose life vaguely resembled my own?

My parents left Sudan for Australia in 1992, at a time when there was a lot of change and no one knew where the country was headed. When I was ten – in 2001 – I decided to wear the hijab. It wasn't a spur-of-the moment decision. Rather, I had decided that it was time – I was a grown woman. I was the first Muslim girl to wear a headscarf at my school, and from then on my existence was politicised. I had never needed to justify my 'Australian-ness' at my Muslim primary school, but, once I reached a Christian high school, there were questions: 'Who are you? Why do you look like this? Why do you dress like this?' I had to justify everything about myself, but I didn't initially realise that that wasn't what everybody else had to do. Others had the luxury of just *being*. So, not only was I going through all the dramas of being a teenager – of figuring myself out – but I also meant something to the people around me, who wanted to know why I was making

my decisions. And the decisions couldn't be about me – what *I* decided to believe or wear – no, they had to be good enough to be justifiable to others. What's more, every young Muslim person growing up in the West had a pre- and a post-9/11 life – that was a truly formative experience.

At the moment, my focus is on women of colour; I've just started a new company – Mumtaza – which is an organisation dedicated to normalising the representation of women of colour in positions of power and influence. Because, the reality is that we are forgotten. We are so often talked about, but not talked with or to. With Mumtaza, the idea is to not only showcase what amazing women of colour there are around the world and across industries, but also to build capacity – to build a squad and find other amazing women of colour. You can't be what you can't see, so what matters to me is empowering young people to become these women and also giving platforms to those women who are already there.

Q. What brings you happiness?

It comes in the small moments; it's laughing so hard it hurts and beautiful afternoons spent with people I care about.

Sometimes I wonder if 'happiness' is a Western concept, and I wonder how it should apply to me. Being Muslim means submitting myself to the will of God; yes, I could choose to pursue my happiness, but it's not really that useful if it doesn't have meaning. And meaning feels more important to me than 'pure' happiness – it comes from working towards making a difference, which pleases God.

I wonder if we sometimes conflate happiness with hedonism. Is doing something that makes you happy in a single moment – for the pure pleasure of it – actual happiness, or is it filling a hole that we don't even realise we have? That's where faith, spirituality and religion play the biggest role in my life. I've found that many Australians don't really like religion as an institution, so I keep my faith close to my chest, but, if I think about what drives me – what motivates me – it's the things that give me meaning. I would much rather do something that's difficult

but meaningful, than something that's easy and going to make me happy, but in reality is a bit like candy floss.

Q. What do you regard as the lowest depth of misery?

It's unacceptable when people's lives and dignities are treated like they are worth nothing – when people see others as less. It hurts my soul when I see grave injustices like those that are happening in Syria go unpunished; injustices like the fact that those responsible for the global financial crisis will never go to jail and are continuing to make money while millions of people are out of work and some even killed themselves because they could see no future. Or stories about people in positions of power abusing their positions of power in ways that are deeply unethical.

These are things that make me so glad that I believe in an afterlife, because there is no way on this earth that such people can be punished enough for the pain and damage they have caused. But, I remind myself that forgiveness is the most powerful thing – I do truly believe that. I think we can never really move forward as a society or as people if we don't learn to forgive, because choosing to forgive is taking the power back.

Q. What would you change if you could?

I wish that I could get people to feel empathy at scale. Part of the reason so many injustices go on for so long is that people just don't care. There are so many stories about New York City that people can even name some of the city's streets, but we don't have that level of understanding of the stories of people living in Syria, Lebanon or Sudan. We don't know those worlds or the people in them. But, if we did know those stories – if they were familiar to us – we would be able to feel empathy. And, I think the way we get there is through storytelling. I've recently started to believe in the power of popular culture, because I see the potential storytelling has to change hearts and minds. As people develop non-threatening relationships with characters, something unfamiliar can become normal – that's a gateway.

Q. Which single word do you most identify with?

Unexpected.

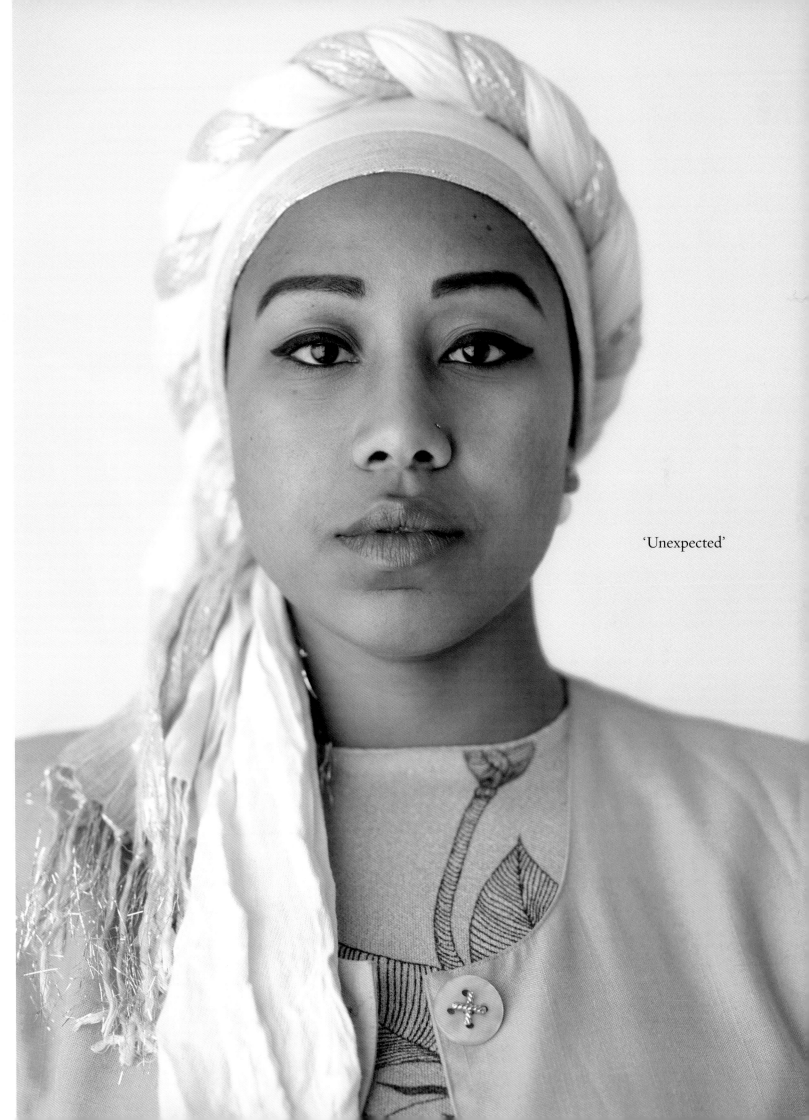

'Unexpected'

'Integrity'

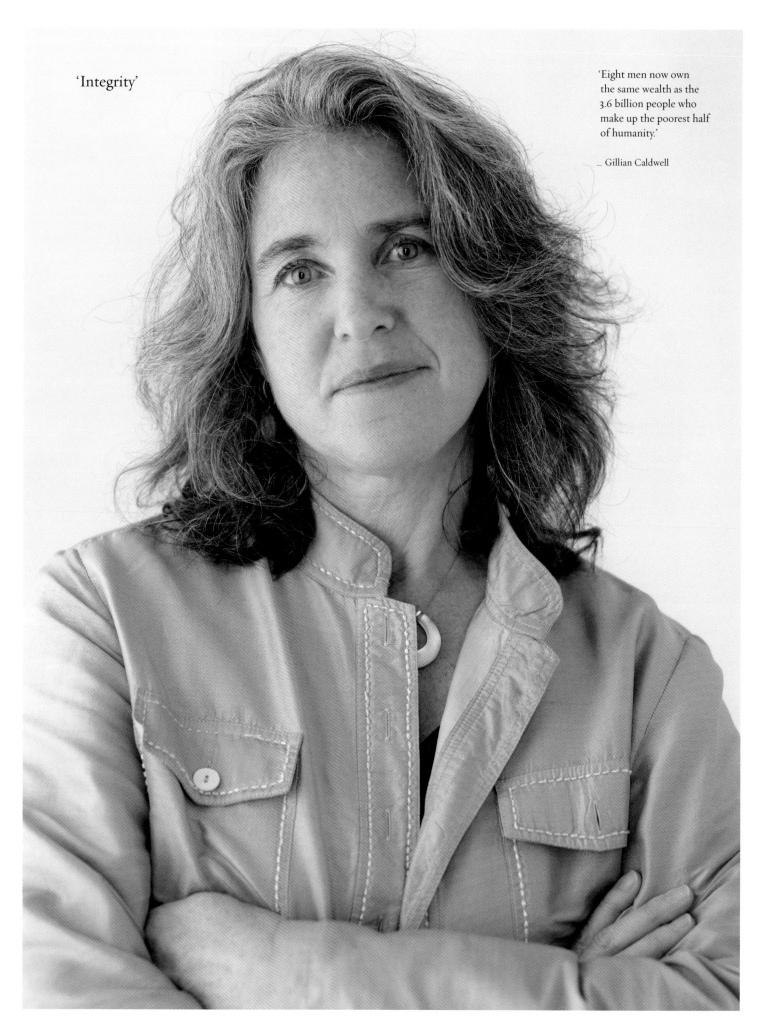

'Eight men now own the same wealth as the 3.6 billion people who make up the poorest half of humanity.'

_ Gillian Caldwell

Interview page 372

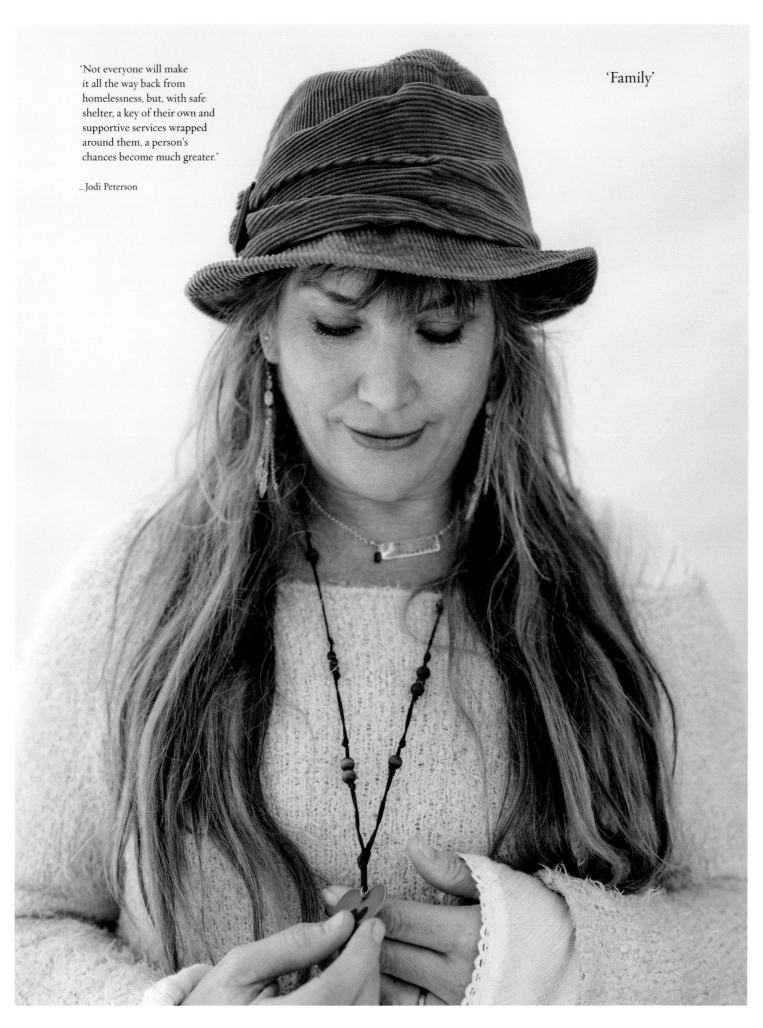

'Not everyone will make
it all the way back from
homelessness, but, with safe
shelter, a key of their own and
supportive services wrapped
around them, a person's
chances become much greater.'

_Jodi Peterson

'Family'

Interview page 373

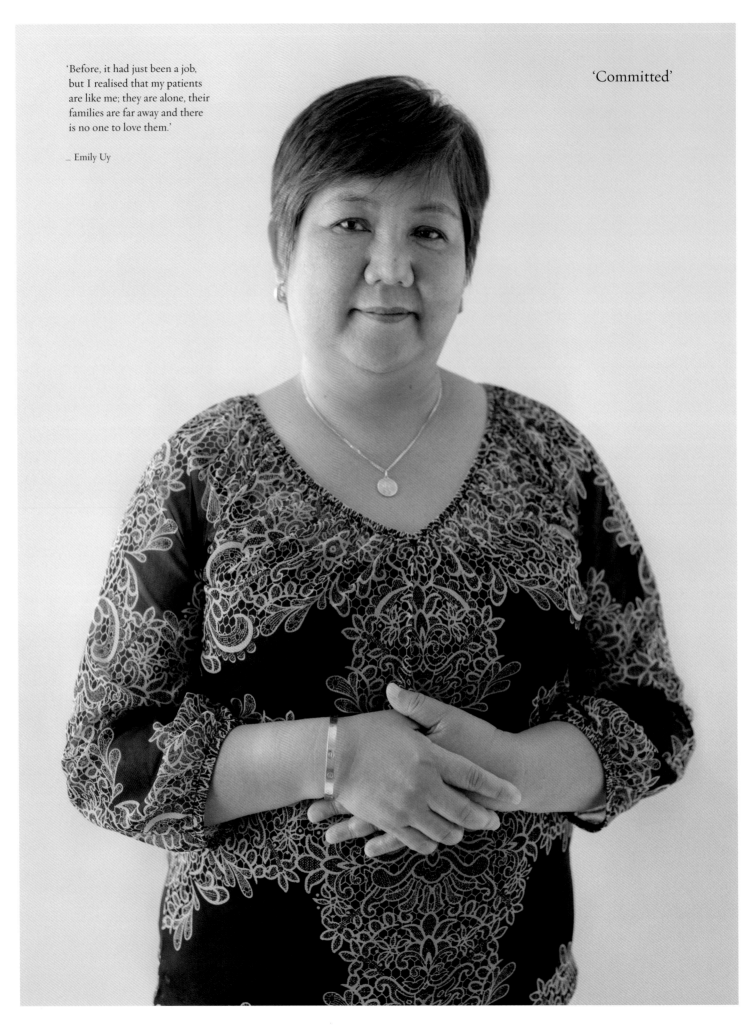

'Before, it had just been a job, but I realised that my patients are like me; they are alone, their families are far away and there is no one to love them.'

_ Emily Uy

'Committed'

Interview page 373

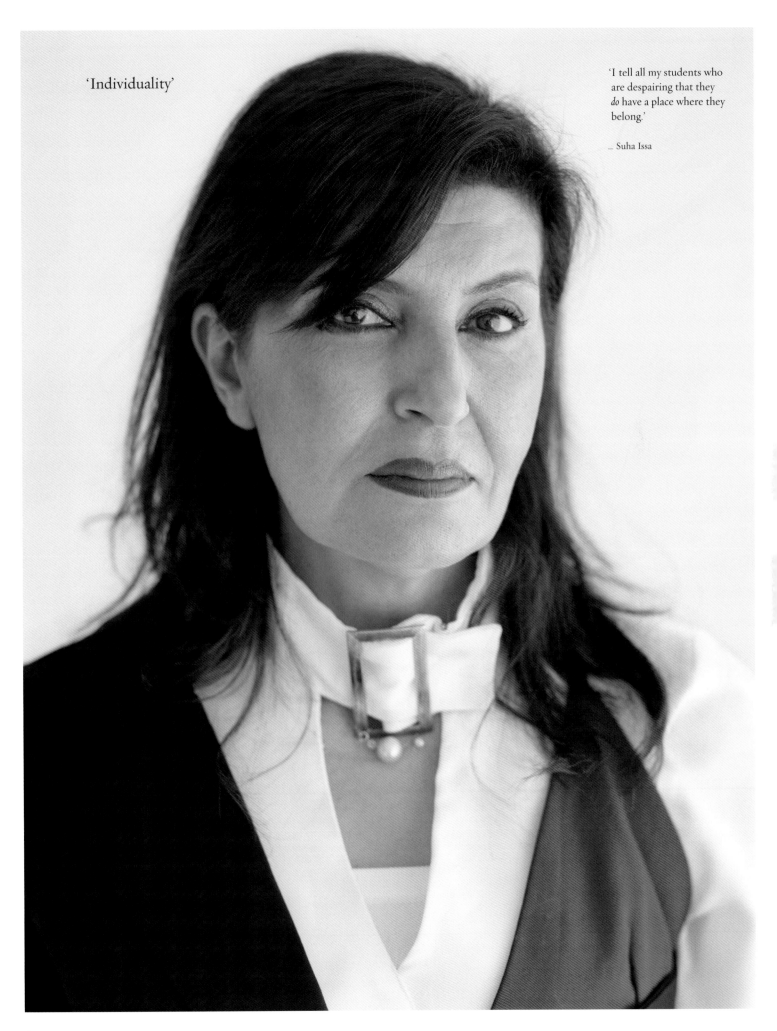

'Individuality'

'I tell all my students who are despairing that they *do* have a place where they belong.'

_ Suha Issa

'Life is not about amassing
things; it's about learning
through experiences and being
in charge of your own destiny.'

_ Fátima Carvalho

'Connection'

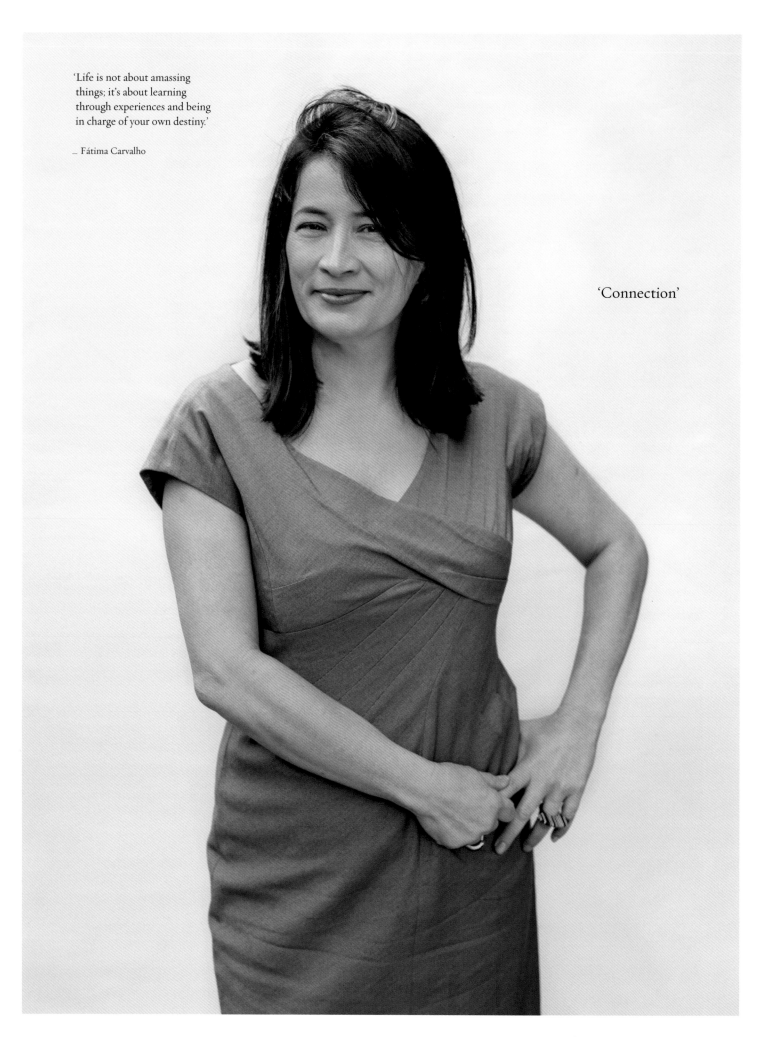

Interview page 374

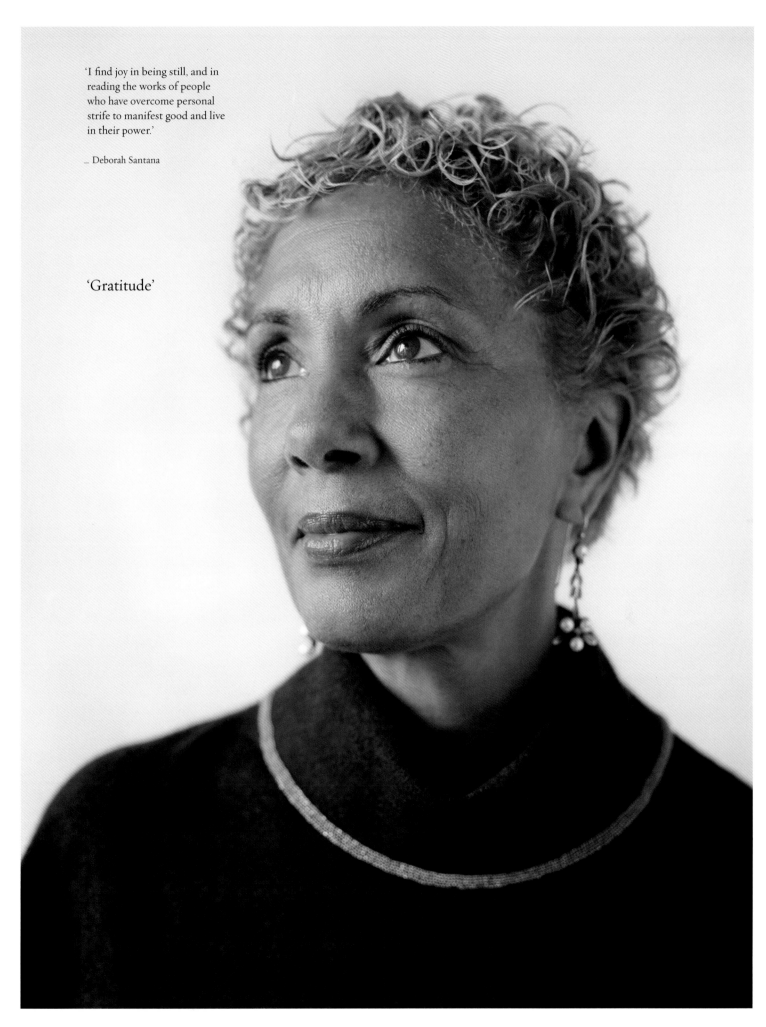

'I find joy in being still, and in reading the works of people who have overcome personal strife to manifest good and live in their power.'

_ Deborah Santana

'Gratitude'

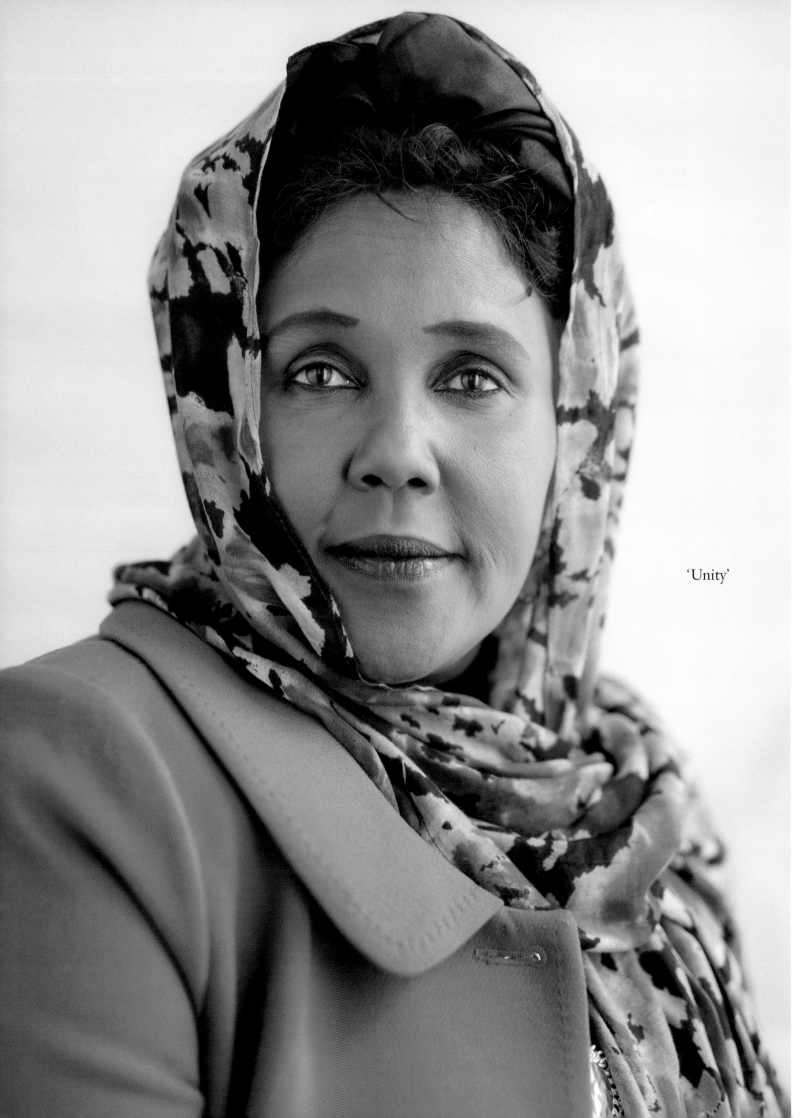

'Unity'

Hodan Isse

Hodan Isse was born in Hargeisa, Somalia. She holds a PhD in economics from George Mason University in Virginia and two master's degrees – in economics and international development – from Ohio University. She is a clinical assistant professor emeritus at the University at Buffalo School of Management. Isse is a co-founder and board member of the United States–based Somali Mental Health Foundation, a member of the board of directors for the Central Bank of Somalia and a founder of H.E.A.L., a not-for-profit based in Buffalo, New York, that helps refugees settle into their new lives. She is the first lady of the Puntland State of Somalia.

Q. What really matters to you?

Justice – more than anything; I think that justice will go a long way towards solving the problems we are faced with. And, when I look at the root causes of most of what vexes the world, I find that these are a lack of inclusion and a lack of justice.

Justice includes within its definition service delivery, freedom of speech and the voices of each individual. A woman in a rural area who is poor, malnourished and sick has no voice in this world, when in fact her voice should be the loudest of all. Instead, she is almost like an untouchable. Justice also includes a fair distribution of resources – at present, global resources are mismanaged in that they are exploited for the benefit of the few. I'm very grateful for what God has given me, but I'm always reminding myself of the fact that he's given me too much; I think more people should be doing this.

I came to America before the Somali Civil War, so I had the opportunity to pursue my education. I was always very focussed on pursuing learning as far as was possible – I knew that if I wanted to change the world and simultaneously better myself, I had to be educated. I knew that education would be the licence whereby I would empower myself and others.

I knew that Somalia had many problems I could assist with, and this knowledge is what motivated me to keep going with my studies. We had a lack of government, a crisis of poverty, a lot of the youth were unemployed, and women – even though they were the primary breadwinners – were subjected to all kinds of violence and injustice. Back when I was growing up in Somalia, we were living under a dictatorship, but what that government did have, over successive regimes, was a clear policy of gender inclusiveness; I sat side by side with boys and felt no need to compete with them. When I went back to Somalia more recently, however, I saw that this was no longer the case. Women are condemned to the corner of every room. And this has nothing to do with Islam, as many people assume. Rather, it is entirely to do with culture.

Something that helps me in my activism is asking the question, 'Is this religion or is this culture?' If it's culture, I don't care about it, because culture is something created by people and informed by numerous inherited values, many of which no longer have a place in the context of recognised human rights. An example of this would be female genital mutilation (FGM), which I am a survivor of myself. This is not religion. The culture of female circumcision is so pervasive that I bought my own razors. Many girls look forward to being cut, because doing so avoids a lot of social stigma; if you are not circumcised, you will be insulted and people will call you dirty. However, the consequences of female genital mutilation on a woman's life are almost inconceivable. For starters, after the collapse of Somalia's government in 1991, medical care was provided by non-governmental organisations that – because of safety and security concerns – were restricted to operating in certain areas. So, a lot of women who did not live in close proximity to health services died as a result of FGM-related complications and diseases. What's more, when FGM survivors give birth, they have to deal with fistulas; when the baby is delivered, the woman is completely torn. So, if she doesn't have access to medical care, she is condemned. And, even if she survives, she may be incontinent for life. When a woman is incontinent, she is not welcomed anywhere and stays home, so FGM has the potential to completely and entirely strip a woman of her dignity.

FGM must be stopped and awareness of the need for modernisation must be raised. The rigidity of our culture in this regard is not acceptable. Women are the backbone of Somali society; we need to be developing our understanding of their importance and capabilities. But, instead, decisions are made about women at a table from which they are missing. I have done work with the United Nations to repair women, and it is an incredibly fulfilling process. At the end of it, you see these women come alive. They feel human again; they can go to the shops, visit their friends and collect their children from school.

There are many injustices in this world, and what matters to me is combating each of them. As long as we are alive, we have to be positive. We *cannot* rest as long as a mother is out there choosing which one of her children will not get food, choosing which of them will die so that the others may live. Justice only for some is simply unacceptable.

Q. What brings you happiness?

Seeing people helping each other and sharing with each other.

Q. What do you regard as the lowest depth of misery?

I'm an economist, so I understand that we must apply a cost-benefit analysis to everything. But even on this basis, I am resolved that poverty should not exist. We cannot say that it costs too much to eradicate, because, actually, it is costing humanity too much to continue as we are.

Q. What would you change if you could?

I would make the world a more just place. I am placing much emphasis on the idea of justice, but I truly believe that *in*justice is at the root of so many of our problems: political, social and economic.

It feels like so many of our leaders – past and present – lacked and lack even the most basic understanding of the impact of their words and the cost to the poorest. Iran, Syria and Libya used to be a part of the world; now their people are refugees. They have lost so much – not due to famine or any other natural disaster, but as a result of problems that are entirely man-made. I am not pointing fingers at any one person, because these decisions are always made by groups whose members are ever-changing. We need a commitment to institutions based on the coming together of people to work in furtherance of the group. My motto is, 'Justice can be enough for us.' But we must safeguard it.

Q. Which single word do you most identify with?

Unity.

Alice
Waters

Alice Waters was born in New Jersey, USA. In 1971, she opened her restaurant Chez Panisse, in Berkeley, California. Waters has written fifteen books, including *The New York Times* bestsellers *The Art of Simple Food* and *The Art of Simple Food II*, and the memoir, *Coming to My Senses*. In 1995, she founded the Edible Schoolyard Project, which is dedicated to building a national edible-education curriculum. Waters' work has been widely recognised, earning her seven James Beard Awards, a National Humanities Medal in the United States, in 2014, and induction into the French Legion of Honour, in 2010.

Q. What really matters to you?

My immediate answer to that is the obvious things: my family and friends, and cooking. And it's cooking *for* my family and friends, with all of us gathered around the table.

Beyond that, what matters is that we preserve and take care of the land that sustains us. Humanity needs to remember that we are a part of nature.

I grew up in a lower-middle-class family, so we never went out to dinner. My mother – who wasn't a particularly good cook! – used the produce from the 'victory garden' we had out back; it had been planted to provide fruit and vegetables during the war. My entire childhood was spent out in nature. My three sisters and I were always climbing trees, running around, sledding in the snow, walking in the rain – you name it! That made a very big impression on me, and I'm still passionate about being outside and in nature.

When I was nineteen, I went to France, then on to Turkey and Greece – my travels engaged me with food I had never seen or tasted. France had a very slow food culture at that time; you'd go to the market twice a day, and children would come home for lunch – I fell in love with that way of life. The first cookbook I owned was written by Elizabeth David, who had also been very changed by a trip to France many years before. She was probably the biggest cooking influence in my life.

I went to school at Berkeley, in California, then went on to study the Montessori method of teaching in London, yet teaching wasn't for me – I just didn't have the patience, but there was a lot about the Montessori method that made a lot of sense to me. It's very much about opening up your senses: tasting, smelling, seeing, listening, touching. In our world today, we're so closed off to these things because we're not asked to work with our hands – it's seen as too much of an effort! Even cooking has been closed down by the fast-food culture we live in, yet cooking is a key way of opening up your senses. So, in my opinion, Montessori fits in perfectly with edible education.

I started the Edible Schoolyard Project because I want to foster a new kind of relationship with food. I want children to be edibly educated, to know about nourishment and sustainability, and to be able to put these skills into practice in their own lives. I believe that is an incredibly empowering experience. And I believe we're winning them over! We're not telling them what to do, we're just creating something irresistible.

We have a demonstration site and learning lab at Martin Luther King Jr. Middle School in Berkeley – for twenty-one years we've been developing a model for edible education with the school administrators. We work with sixth, seventh and eighth graders – about a thousand students a year – and it's been amazing watching them learn, and watching their brothers and sisters coming through after them. I believe I can say that we have made a big impression. For the past five years, we've been reaching out internationally to find similar projects that have a garden or a kitchen or a school-lunch programme that supports organic farming. We have five thousand five hundred partners on our website right now, and those are only the organisations who have added their names to our community – so I know this is happening everywhere. And connecting with community is fundamental to a holistic approach to existing on this planet.

All this matters, and is incredibly fulfilling.

Q. What brings you happiness?

Cooking for people and creating spaces for connection – food is such a great context for meeting new people, so connecting people over a meal makes me happy.

Connecting people committed to slow food makes me happy, too. I am the vice president of Carlo Petrini's slow food movement, an alternative to fast food that promotes regional, sustainable, seasonable cuisine. I have the opportunity to meet people from the 156 countries that are members of Slow Food International – it's like being in the underground and passing on secret messages: 'Do you know this person in Vermont?' 'Have you heard what they're doing in South Africa?' 'Have you met so-and-so from Iceland?' Being a part of that 'counterculture' makes me so very happy.

Q. What do you regard as the lowest depth of misery?

It's being really disconnected from nature and from real food. Both of those are a hunger as real as the hunger for food. It's shocking that we don't know how to – indeed, can't – feed ourselves; it makes me want to cry.

Q. What would you change if you could?

First and foremost, I would change public education, because with young children I think you have a great opportunity and a real possibility of fostering a healthy approach to food. We want children to begin life with a set of values that are essentially human values: taking care of the land, taking care of each other and nourishing themselves – this influences the way they will be for the rest of their lives.

For me, education needs to be hands-on, where you're learning by doing. Whether it's a math class or it's an art class, every class should give children the possibility of using their hands, of being out in nature and developing models in the real world, rather than being a sterilised, isolated place like in a university.

Q. Which single word do you most identify with?

Determined: I am driven!

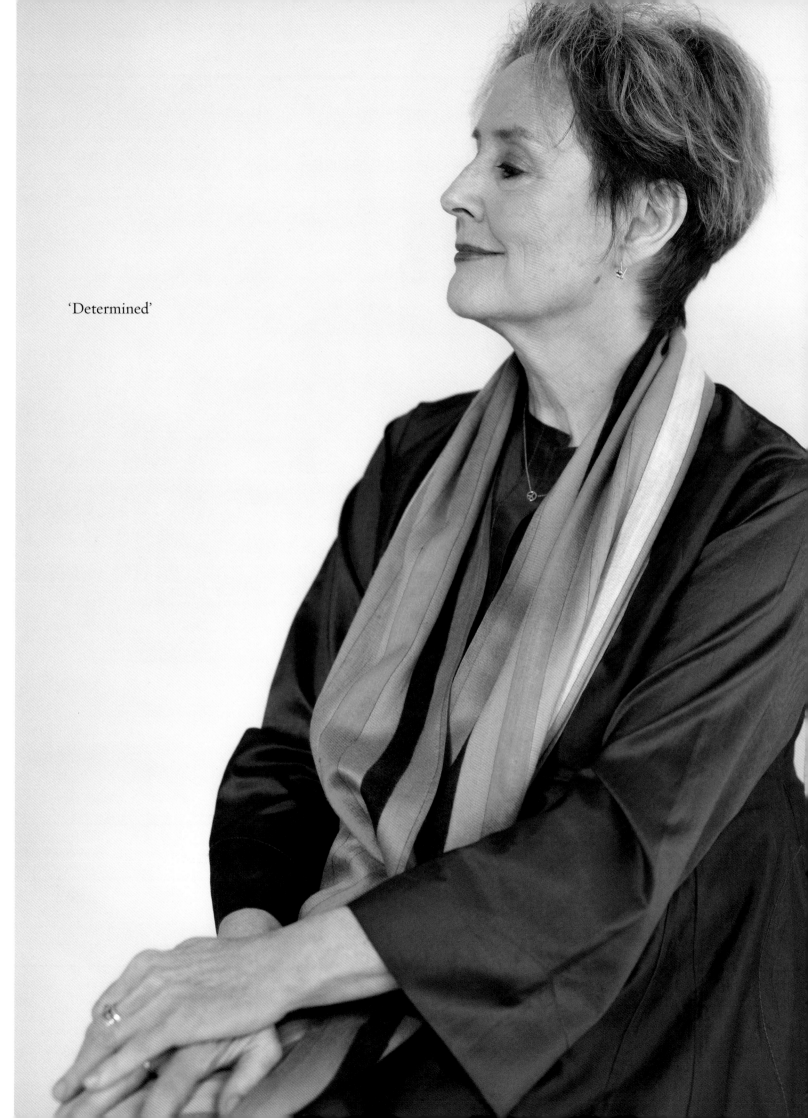

'Determined'

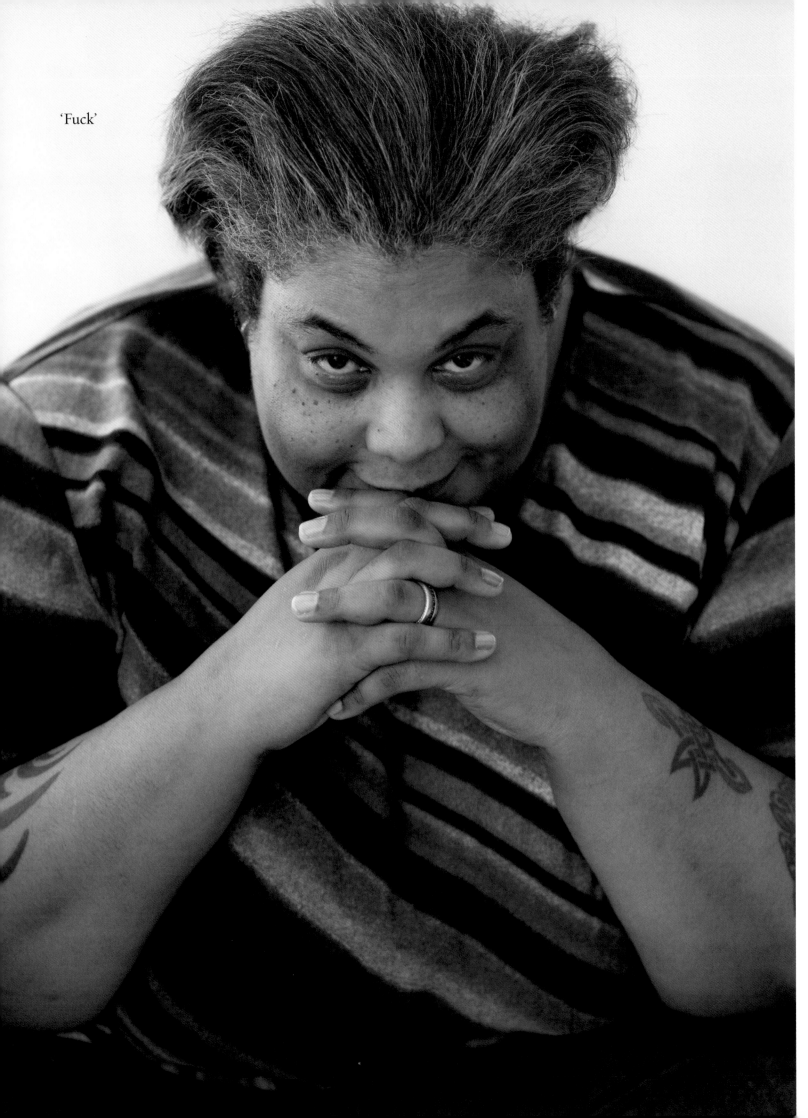

'Fuck'

Roxane Gay

Roxane Gay was born in Omaha in Nebraska, USA. She is the author of several acclaimed books, including *The New York Times* bestselling *Bad Feminist*, a collection of essays exploring issues related to modern feminist identity and her experiences as a first-generation American born to Haitian parents. An associate professor at Purdue University, Gay is a contributing opinion writer for *The New York Times*, and, in 2006, co-founded *PANK Magazine*, a literary magazine fostering access to emerging and innovative poetry and prose.

Q. What really matters to you?
Loving what I do and being proud of the work I put out into the world.

A lot of who I am is a product of how I was raised. I'm a first-generation American, born to Haitian parents – that context absolutely informed and shaped who I am. My parents would always talk about how we were free – about how our ancestors were free – and I think that went a long way towards giving my brothers and I confidence to do what we're doing today.

I have had the writer's bug since I was four. My fascination with writing is just something that's always been a part of my personality – part of who I am. My love of stories is just *there*. I love observing people and forming those observations into something more.

I definitely see a very important role for myself as a black, female author, which is not a perspective we often see in popular culture – even in fiction. I have a platform that, historically, not a lot of people like me have had. It's an exciting time right now – both as a reader and as a writer – because there is an increasing plethora of new African American voices and of voices within the African diaspora. Yes, the numbers are still small, but suddenly I feel like there are more than three authors I can talk about; now, I can quote writers from Algeria and from the Dominican Republic. There's a long way to go, but it's been a spectacular elevation.

I always took myself seriously as a writer, even when no one else would, even when I had no idea how I was going to finance my life with writing. But, I never intended to contribute to the feminist discourse in the way I have – that was never part of my agenda, I just liked to write. I am a feminist, though, and I have been since before I knew what feminism was – I just had a very clear sense of right and wrong. What happened with *Bad Feminist* was so unexpected; the book wasn't conceived as a collection, rather, I wrote those essays individually. When they were consolidated, I was going to call the work *What We Hunger For*, but my publisher thought that was too many words! It's incredibly gratifying to see that so many women are gravitating towards my thinking about feminism, to this idea that it's important to recognise that we can't be perfect feminists and that that's okay.

Other than my work, what matters to me is being a good person to the people in my personal life. At the end of the day, my friends are the people who have always been there for me – so, honouring those relationships is incredibly important. These are the people who have loved me through my best and worst, and I would choose those relationships over just about anything.

Q. What brings you happiness?
I don't know; I'm still looking for it. Writing makes me happy and reading makes me happy. Being with my best friend – that feeling of being with the right person, at the right time, in the right place – makes me happy.

And privilege. Being able to do whatever it is I feel I need to do with my free time; having free time to relax makes me happy, and I'm very conscious that that's an immense privilege.

Q. What do you regard as the lowest depth of misery?
I think inequality is still the biggest problem – and the biggest sadness – in this world. We live in a world of plenty, yet there are billions of people who are suffering and who are going without. You don't have to look far; inequality and suffering are everywhere, and it feels like there's no solution. People seem very unwilling to confront and address inequality, and that's distressing, because I can't see an end in sight.

Growing up in the United States, then going to Haiti for the summer, I learned the difference between relative and absolute poverty. No matter how much money you have in Haiti, the poverty is so intimate – right there, everywhere you go. It's unavoidable. In many ways, that's a good thing, because then you can't willingly avoid it – you *have* to reckon with it. I have never forgotten the first time I went to Haiti, seeing homeless people clambering over our car for a dollar and knowing we could only hand out so many dollars. You really have to confront your privilege when you go to Haiti to hang out on the beach at Club Med – this had a profound influence on me.

I don't believe in utopia – I'm a realist – so I know inequality will always exist, but the current scale is breathtaking. And it's so avoidable! Yet the people with the power to effect the kind of change we need are unwilling. It's frustrating and it's a disgrace that we have people in this world – particularly in the United States – who go hungry and without health care! How is that possible? These are basic human rights.

Q. What would you change if you could?
Absolutely no doubt in my mind on this answer: a year of male silence. No speaking from men for a year: 'Shush! No more talking. It's okay; just look pretty.' That would be so good. I think it would be wonderful to just let women run things for a year; I don't know if we would do any better, but let's try it! We've tried everything else and, at the very least, it would go a long way. It would be so grand!

Q. Which single word do you most identify with?
Fuck. It can be used in so many ways. I'm sure there are fancier options, but that's not me. I love it because I identify with it on so many levels. And I love how it starts out soft and ends hard.

Bec Ordish

Bec Ordish was born in Sydney, Australia. She graduated from Bond University with an honours degree in law, then specialised in intellectual property law. Ordish is a founder of the Mitrataa Foundation, a not-for-profit organisation dedicated to inspiring Nepali people to empower themselves through education, skills, training, networks and self-belief. Ordish has lived and worked in Nepal since 2011, and has two adopted daughters, Nimu and Saraswoti.

Q. What really matters to you?

Throughout my life, I have been incredibly lucky to have had amazing mentors who have believed in me, educated me, cared for me and encouraged me. This is a great gift without which I wouldn't be who I am. I passionately believe in paying forward the lessons I have been taught and in being a mentor to others – someone they can rely on when they need to. It's all about creating networks – we call them daisy chains – whereby people can pay forward their gifts to others. That's a big part of my philosophy and it's what really matters to me.

I studied education and taught for a couple of years. I then went on to study law, which my dad – a country solicitor – said was not a good idea. But I loved it! I went on to work at an international firm and decided I was going to go into intellectual property law. Before I started, though, I wanted to travel overseas and work as volunteer. Most of the programmes were for a minimum of eighteen months, but Nepal had one that was just six months long, so that's where I ended up. Seventeen years later, I'm working and living in Nepal – it never would have occurred to me back then that this is what I'd be doing.

When I first came to Nepal, I lived at a hostel and worked with three schools. Every morning, a woman used to come to one of the schools asking for work. I told her I wasn't in charge and couldn't offer her any work, but day after day she kept coming back. Eventually I asked her why she kept coming when she knew I couldn't help her, and she said, 'I just want my son to go to school.' So, I decided to put her son through school.

I told the school I'd cover his fees. Back in those days, it cost about three hundred Australian dollars per year; that covered books, uniforms, school and exam fees – everything. And this is effectively for private schooling – in English. Government schools are taught in Nepali, but the final school exams are mostly in English, so there is only a 48 per cent pass rate in government schools. Because of this, it's every parent's dream to send their child to an English school.

What I was doing became known in the area, so I had more people approaching me. My friends and family back home learned about what I was doing and starting helping out. I had so many amazing kids that I ended up asking for a discount! I remember feeling so proud of that first woman's son – his name was Sonu, and I was more excited than he was! I still get that feeling every time we help a child set their future free – it's the most incredible feeling. These parents all share a dream of giving their children a decent education, so their dreams are coming true, too.

Mitrataa grew organically after I started taking children on. Mothers came to me saying that they couldn't assist their children with their homework because of their own illiteracy, so I started doing some training with the mothers as well. We have put about fifteen hundred kids through school since we started in 2000 and we're currently supporting about two hundred children. We are mainly supporting girls, but we've inherited some brothers along the way; it's important for the kids to have balance. This journey called life isn't only about girls and women – we have to take the boys and the men along the way with us; we want to create role models and positive influencers of them. The boys in our group are fantastic – all our kids are!

I maintain that believing in yourself is the secret ingredient. Once you stop doing that, you lose hope. Part of my job is to make sure that they all believe in themselves, because, if all the individuals do this, there's got to come a tipping point at which Nepal will start believing in itself. The resilience of people here is incredible; especially after the earthquake, you see it in how people get up and get on with living.

Q. What brings you happiness?

Simple things, like hugs. I tell Nimu and Saraswoti – my daughters – that a mother–daughter hug can fix pretty much anything. It's like saying, 'I'm here – we can do this.'

I love my job. When we help people find their wings, can watch them soar and achieve, that's the absolute best. It could be something as little as passing a test or performing well in an area in which they previously lacked courage. Or it could be something big, like finding a job. All of these things send my heart racing. Sapana Thapa (pp. 357, 390) was one of our students, and now she is a leader in her own right – I'm so incredibly proud of her. She's been through so much, but she's incredibly stubborn; she just kept moving and believing in herself. What she has achieved justifies why I'm here.

Q. What do you regard as the lowest depth of misery?

We live in a time when the world is very commercial, a lot of people are exploiting other people's poverty, unhappiness and desperation. We're all humans, so we should all have compassion, but we seem to have lost it. Society seems to look at everything in relation to money and people look at things only in relation to themselves: 'What's in it for me?'

People being exploited at their lowest points – that's the absolute depth of misery. After the earthquakes in Nepal, people were going around offering money in return for other people's kidneys; people were desperate and didn't receive much money, but there are entire villages with those surgical scars. I just cannot understand how a human being could do that to another human being.

Then there's human trafficking: we had people coming in, offering to rebuild houses. In return, the people they built houses for were told to say that they had sent their daughter, wife or sister to India to work and that she was sending lots of money back. People did this and so others would also want to send their daughters to India – and all of these women ended up in the sex trade. Families who had already lost people in the quake, then lost even more. It's disgusting.

Q. What would you change if you could?

The education system; it's broken.

Q. Which single word do you most identify with?

Gratitude. If we focus on the things that we have instead of things we don't have, we cannot feel any negative emotions.

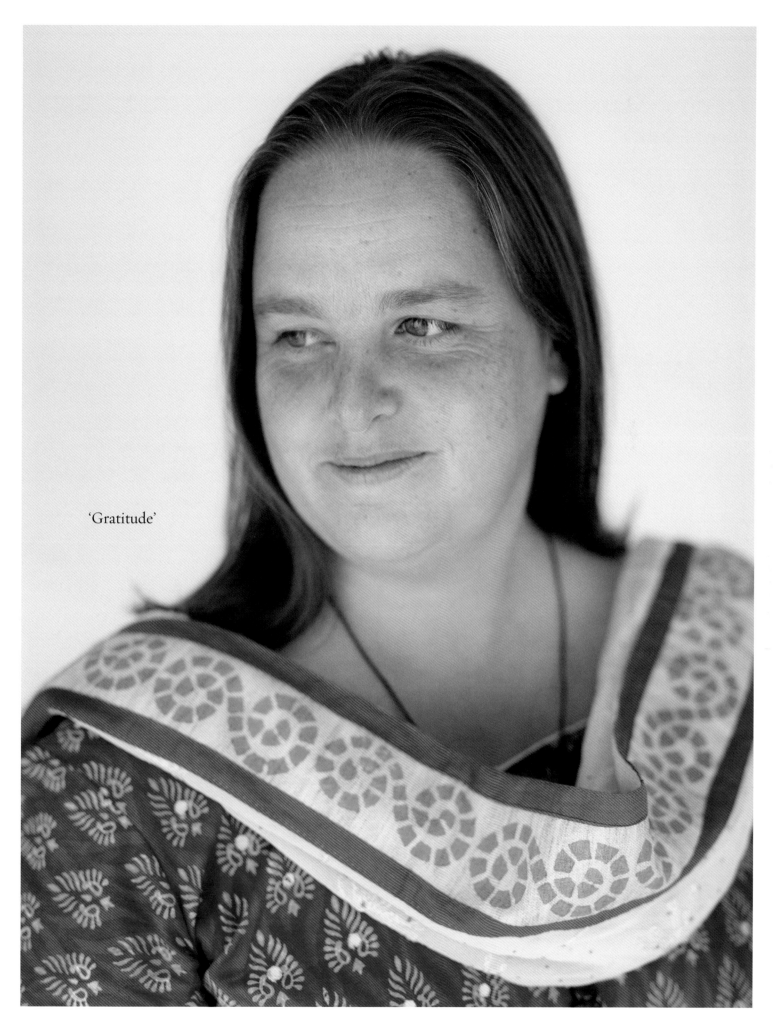

'Gratitude'

Meryl
Marshall-Daniels
_____

Meryl Marshall-Daniels was born in Los Angeles in California, USA. She has worked as a criminal trial lawyer and an entertainment lawyer, was vice president of compliance and practices for NBC television network, was an independent television producer and has also served as the chairperson and chief executive officer of the Academy of Television Arts & Sciences. Now a facilitator, mediator and executive coach, Marshall-Daniels specialises in leadership, organisational development and conflict.

Q. What really matters to you?
I have a deep drive for peace, for a place of quiet within myself.

My career has been all over the place, but, at the core of it, I would describe my role as that of peacemaker. The night Martin Luther King, Jr. died, I was taking a class called 'What it's like to be black in America.' I remember a member of the black student union saying, 'We know what we have to do in *our* community, the rest of you figure out what *you* have to do.' At the time I didn't know how profoundly that would influence me, but, as result of that experience, I eventually became a facilitator. Having worked in law, in television and with non-profits, I've always been at the heart of conflicts, so in my early fifties I trained as a mediator and my work now is really about attaining that inner peace by overcoming conflict.

People think of conflict as this crisis moment, but, in truth, conflict starts long before that – the crisis is merely the eruption. I would therefore say that we cannot avoid conflict, because in most cases it already exists. At its core are our internal issues. We live in an extraordinary time, a very treacherous time; the 2016 election in America brought out the worst in people, and it has posed some essential questions. The levels of misogyny and racism that have been uncovered, which exist in such a pervasive fashion, are now out there for everybody to know about. Those emotions are running free. In a way, it's a gift for those who wanted to believe that these issues no longer existed; we've been disabused of that dangerous assumption. The sacrifice of civility and the unwillingness, or inability, to have dialogue around difference has really intensified. This is really frightening, because it means that we're on a precipice. And if we're not careful, we could destroy ourselves in the process.

People in America have always assumed that democracy is so incredibly resilient. People believe that the will, the heart and the passion of the American population is extraordinary; even though we have this incredible belief in individualism – which has been a deep value – we also have the Horatio Alger myth that anybody can make it. But a lot of those dreams and a lot of those precepts are being undermined. Our economic system of capitalism and our concept of democracy have become confused. They're not one and the same. And unless and until we do some hard work towards understanding how they intersect, or don't – understanding how they support each other, or don't – we are going to live on this precipice. There are a lot of people who are no longer optimistic and who no longer have hope; the biggest danger to humanity is to feel hopeless and helpless.

It's so important, in conflict, to understand what you care about deeply and what is being affected. Conflict often presents itself in a way that is not representative of what the issues are, so the real challenge of conflict resolution is to be able to understand what is driving us. Once this is revealed, the potential for resolution is great. But without that honesty, without that ability to really uncover the interests you are trying to pursue or protect, resolution is not possible. So, acknowledging and expressing your deeply held feelings is crucial – because acknowledgment and expression, by their very nature, change conflict. Once you understand what you're trying to protect or pursue, the relief that clarity brings gives you a vocabulary, or choice, that was totally invisible to you when you were acting unconsciously – out of instinct – and behaving out of fear of this unknown element. That is how we obtain peace among ourselves and also within ourselves.

That quiet, peaceful place matters to me, even on a smaller scale. I've always been an extrovert, so, because I was so engaged with the outside world, without realising it I failed to attend to aspects of myself. I've discovered that it's important to cultivate the very diverse aspects of myself. I've learned that in the darkness – in the pain – is where my passion also lives, so avoiding those dark feelings is actually hazardous to my growth, to my development and my joy; I've come to understand that passion in life requires engagement with all aspects of who I am.

Q. What brings you happiness?
In the outward world, I find happiness in the potential for change, for growth and development. I came into this world as a lawyer – I was raised by a lawyer – so I knew about battle. But what has emerged in the world during my lifetime is this understanding about how reconciliation can be such a powerful tool, and that we have a deep yearning for connection and relationships. If we can find a way to be human – to share our humanity – the opportunities to create magnificence exist every day.

Q. What do you regard as the lowest depth of misery?
Being helpless in the face of suffering. I feel overwhelmed by the agony and the suffering of others. I can't live in that space, so I have to turn to optimism – and yet, I have discovered over and over in my life that sometimes helplessness just needs to be shared. It needs to be witnessed, but it can't always be fixed. That's been a brutal realisation – that my optimism is sometimes not helpful. Increasing my capacity to witness and encourage the voices of pain has been a deep learning in my life. But one has to hope that through expression there can be transformation.

Q. What would you change if you could?
The ability to listen: I would make it safe for people to listen to themselves and to others.

Q. Which single word do you most identify with?
Heart.

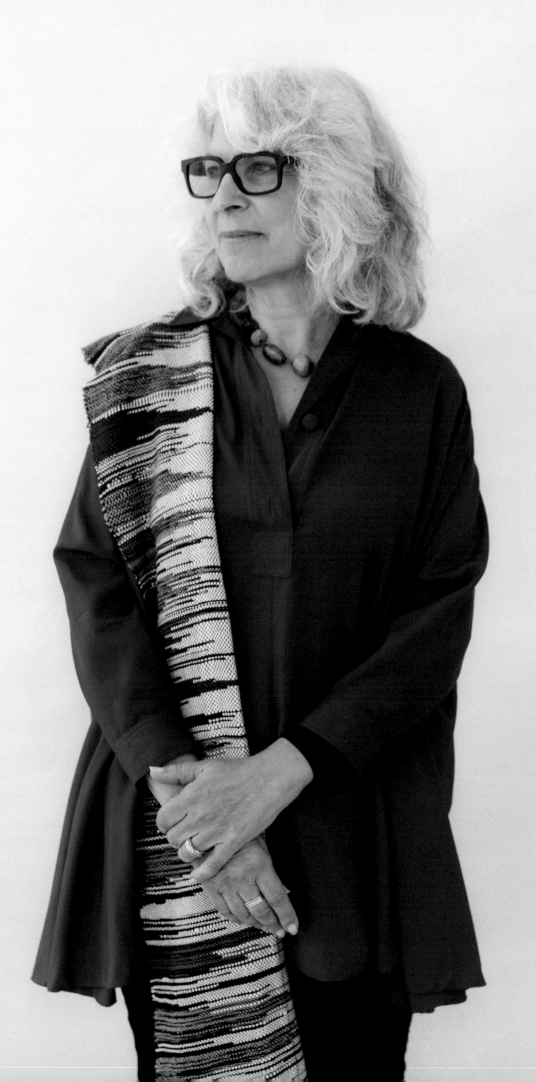

'There are a lot of people who
are no longer optimistic and
who no longer have hope; the
biggest danger to humanity is
to feel hopeless and helpless.'

'Heart'

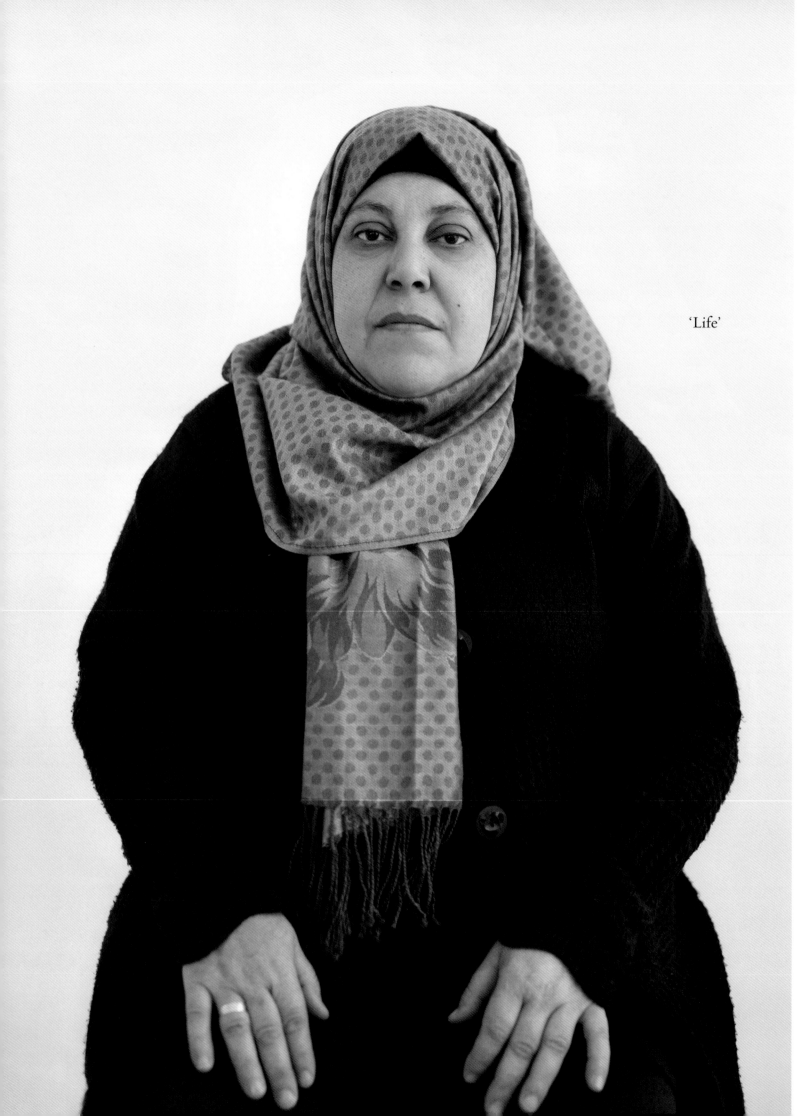

'Life'

'Life. In spite of all the hardship I have known in life, life is beautiful.'

_ Ghada Masrieyeh

Interview page 374

Gillian Anderson

Gillian Anderson OBE was born in Chicago in Illinois, USA. She is a critically acclaimed film, television and theatre actress, activist and writer. She is an active supporter of numerous non-profit organisations focussed on global social issues, as well as animal and human rights.

Q. What really matters to you?

I'm learning that my state of mind needs to matter to me the most. As I have grown older – as I have experienced hormonal changes and lost the certainty of the faculty of my mind – I have come to realise how vital this is to anything else I put my attention to. I have spent a lot of my life putting things before my state of mind, whether it be my career, my family or my work. I find it really, really hard to not put other things first. But what I've started to learn is that I am useless to my children if my mental state is fragmented and not grounded. Part of putting my state of mind first is about meditation and yogic practice. It's about remembering the important things in life every morning and connecting to gratitude. As a woman soon to be in her fifties, if I don't do this the stress level has a hugely negative impact on everything else that is important to me.

Despite growing up in white, middle-class America and white middle-class England, there have been various times in my life when I have felt depths of despair, hopelessness, anxiety, fear and panic, and have felt entirely alone. The contrast of this experience, in the enormous luxury of the life that I have been born into compared to so much of the world – I say luxury even though oftentimes my parents were wanting for money – has made me want to be of service, in any way, shape or form.

I feel the intensity of the responsibility of privilege. The greatest gift is the empathy for other human beings that is born out of whatever adversity one experiences in life. People are so brave – there is so much courage and perseverance. Yet, if it's hard to find courage and perseverance even in my privileged life, then where on earth does it come from in those *without*?

I have an empathy for outsiders. When I was growing up in London, England, I was an outsider; even though I spoke with a British accent, my parents were considered Yanks. Yet, when at age eleven I moved from 1970s London to the small Republican town of Grand Rapids, Michigan, I was also an outsider; on the one hand, America represented sunshine and hamburgers, happiness and wealth and extended family, but on the other, Grand Rapids was a small town – I had a funny accent and on a deep level I never really felt like I belonged there. I didn't feel like I fitted in at all. So, I moved from being separate in one country to being separate in another country.

These versions of rejection were part of my fight against the world. The rebelliousness in my teens was me kicking against a feeling of not belonging, even though, ultimately, part of me didn't want to belong. I've always been a fighter. I think my stance is naturally a warrior stance. But the softer side of me – or the side of me that is interested in human connection, human kindness, acceptance, equality and justice – comes from knowing the other side.

One of the things that I've been concentrating on recently is having the courage to tell the truth. There's something inherently liberating about that. It's about being true to oneself. We are reaching a time when it's becoming more and more important – especially for women – to create definite intolerances towards that which is not our truth. And this can spread; it is contagious. I hope that there can be a global movement of unearthing one's truth, one that enables real change to happen, in both small and big communities around the world. Truth can be a terrifying thing, but the more courageous individuals are, the more that courage spreads – it amasses. And the ripple effect is potentially what will save us.

Q. What brings you happiness?

The greatest sense of joy and happiness that I have experienced is the result of mindfulness and meditation; I am able to open my gaze onto the world – see the sunset and the trees – and come from a place of compassion and kindness. And my children are what I love the most and what bring me the most happiness. But I have come to know that, even if they are in joy, if I have not connected to joy myself, it is very hard for me to recognise and honour it in them.

There is also joy in human connection. The minute I come out of myself and place myself on an equal footing with another human being – no matter what the circumstance – in that minute, in that meeting of humanity, there is no more separation. It is unity. The thought of that unity being able to exist in the world – that there are organisations, communities or individuals whose goal is to build a foundation for it – gives me a sense of hope, and a greater sense of joy and possibility.

Q. What do you regard as the lowest depth of misery?

Hopelessness. When I think of the word 'hopelessness' I think of the lowest, basest level of despair. It is enhanced by a sense of aloneness in the world or a sense that there is no way out, that there is nothing left, that there is no hand to reach for, no connection, no faith. This can be felt by somebody sitting in a penthouse in Manhattan or it can be felt in a refugee camp in Syria. A state of hopelessness is potentially the worst state to be in; it is something that can be universally connected to. And what solves it is connection – it's another human being reaching out and saying, 'I understand. I get you, and you are of value.'

Q. What would you change if you could?

I would make kindness a part of every human interaction.

Q. Which single word do you most identify with?

Sorry. This is because I have a need to say sorry to myself – and to forgive myself; I have a need to say sorry to people in my life with whom I have not connected or whom I have caused harm. And I have a desire for the action of 'sorry' to be spoken in the world.

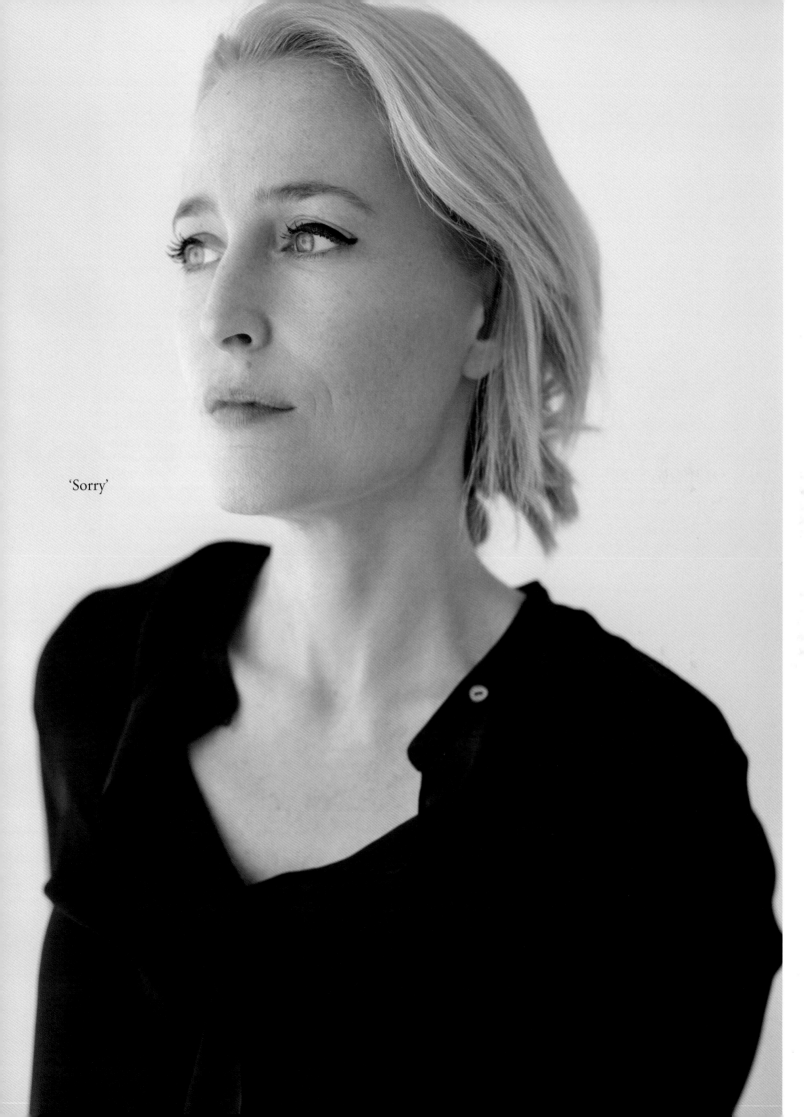

'Sorry'

Ai-jen Poo

Ai-jen Poo was born in Pittsburgh in Pennsylvania, USA. She has worked as a labour organiser for twenty years, transforming the landscape of working conditions and labour standards for domestic or private-household workers. Poo is executive director of the National Domestic Workers Alliance (NDWA) and a co-director of Caring Across Generations. In 2012, she was listed as one of *TIME*'s 100 most influential people and, in 2014, she was awarded a MacArthur Foundation fellowship. Her first book, *The Age of Dignity: Preparing for the Elder Boom in a Changing America*, was published in 2015.

Q. What really matters to you?

Dignity: as the writer Atul Gawande says, 'You may not control life's circumstances, but getting to be the author of your life means getting to control what you do with them.'

So, it matters that my grandmother, who is ninety-two and who cared for me from when I was six months old, should be able to live well and with dignity, on her terms. Workers like Mrs. Lee, who is my grandmother's homecare worker, are critical; Mrs. Lee allows her to live in her own apartment and get the support she needs to go to church, to the doctor and to play mah-jongg with her friends. Mrs. Lee is a huge piece of the puzzle that allows for that dignity. And Mrs. Lee should also have dignity at work: the ability to take pride in what she does, to know that her work is valued and respected, and that she will be compensated so that she can care for her own family. If we really enhanced dignity – this notion of what it means for everyone to live with dignity and work with dignity – we'd be in a good place.

If you think about what domestic workers do, this work is probably some of the most important work in our economy. Domestic workers go to work in our homes every day and take care of the most important aspects of our lives: our kids, our aging loved ones and our homes themselves.

I grew up watching my mother and my grandmother do that work inside our own home in addition to working outside the home – taking care of everyone and everything all the time. I always thought all of that work was really undervalued. What's more, if you look around in the immigrant community, there are very few work options for women. A lot of immigrants have risked their lives – left behind professions, families, traditions and cultures to give their children more

opportunity in the United States – so the stakes are incredibly high for them and they've invested quite a bit in being here. Most immigrant women end up in one form of low-wage service work or another, but, despite how important this is to so many families, it is some of the most undervalued work in our economy. So, it's really important – not only for the workers themselves, but also for all of the families who count on them – to really uplift the value and the dignity of this work, and make it more sustainable for everyone.

Women – particularly immigrant women – are caught in the crosshairs of a lot of the attacks of the Trump administration. Many people don't realise that three-quarters of all undocumented immigrants in this country are women and children, and that most of these women are working in the domestic work setting. Some of the recent data shows that domestic work is the profession with the highest concentration of undocumented immigrants of any workforce. There are a high number of vulnerable women; they are isolated, because this work has been undervalued for so long and because immigrant women are on the frontlines of many of the enforcement efforts – the raids, the deportations, the targeting – of this administration.

Q. What brings you happiness?

All the things that we have been able to achieve and receive recognition for as a movement have been achieved through the power, courage and hard work of thousands of women: domestic workers, nannies, housecleaners and caregivers who sacrificed a day's pay to travel to state capitals to lobby and share their stories, to march with millions of other women, to negotiate, take risks and assert their dignity. It makes me happiest to see these women – who are sent messages from every direction that they are not

fully workers, not fully human or not fully citizens – stand up in their power and assert the value of their work, and the dignity with which they do it.

Q. What do you regard as the lowest depth of misery?

There's a very powerful narrative that is dividing the United States in really toxic ways – it is the thing we have to transform. It has to do with notions of 'us versus them' and with a scarcity mentality. I fundamentally disagree with the notion that, somehow, there is not enough beauty, resources, joy and connection in the world for all of us; it is a notion that is turning us against each other. This kind of division is creating a toxicity that is incredibly destructive. It is really terrifying to watch it rise in new ways. I know people say it's always been there, but it seems like we're adding to it. Yes, the kerosene was on the ground, but it wasn't necessarily on fire – and now we're lighting matches.

Q. What would you change if you could?

I would probably make care an organising principle in our economy. I would try to reorganise our economy so that care in all of its forms – care for neighbours, care for family, care for children, care for elders, care for friends, care for co-workers – is a fundamental principle in every arena of civic and economic life. I would want us to have all the support we need, so that the caregiving relationships in our lives would be upheld as some of the most important and valuable. People who provide care would feel recognised and valued, and be able to support their families. We would utilise care as a way of reinventing our relationships and our structures of value – it would change everything.

Q. Which single word do you most identify with?

Dignity. My grandmother, who is my heroine, embodies dignity, so, in some ways, it is my north star.

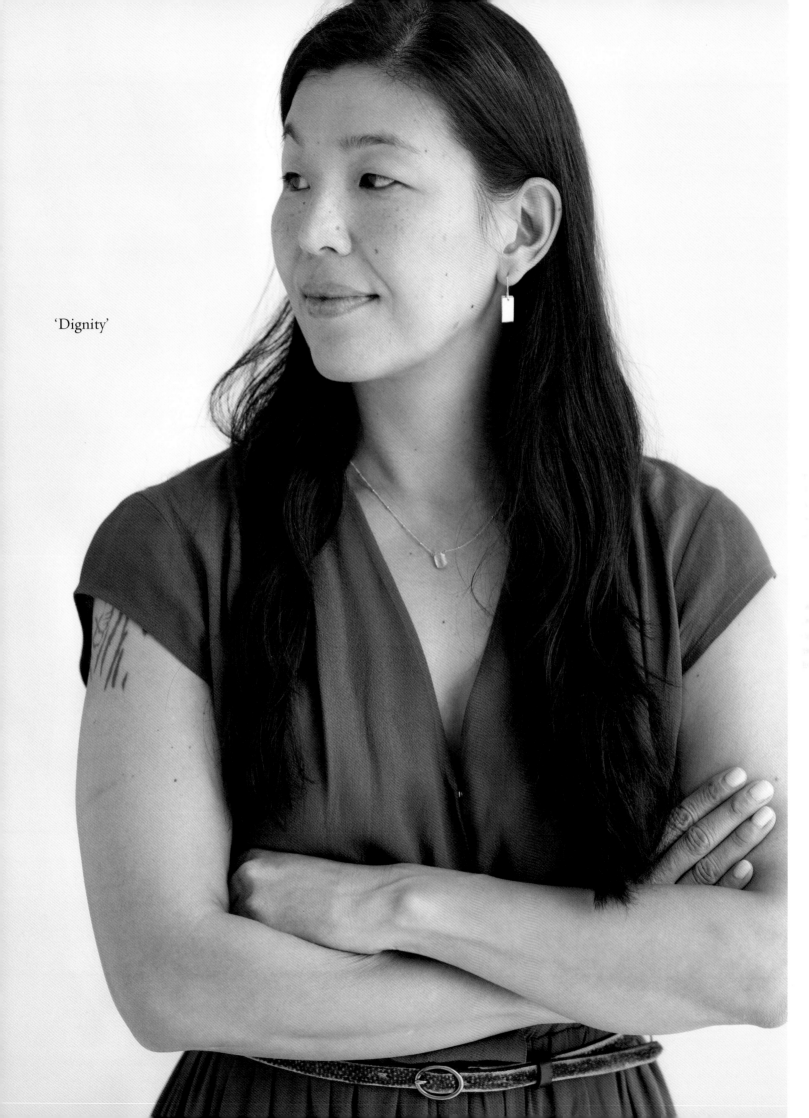

'Dignity'

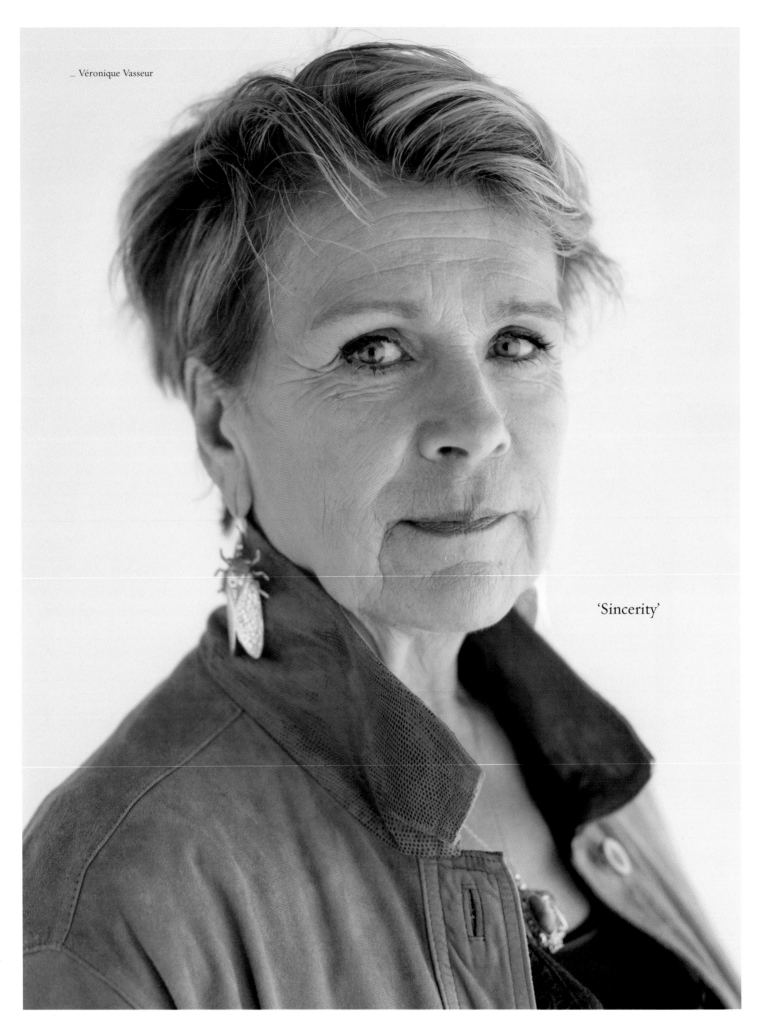

_ Véronique Vasseur

'Sincerity'

Interview page 375

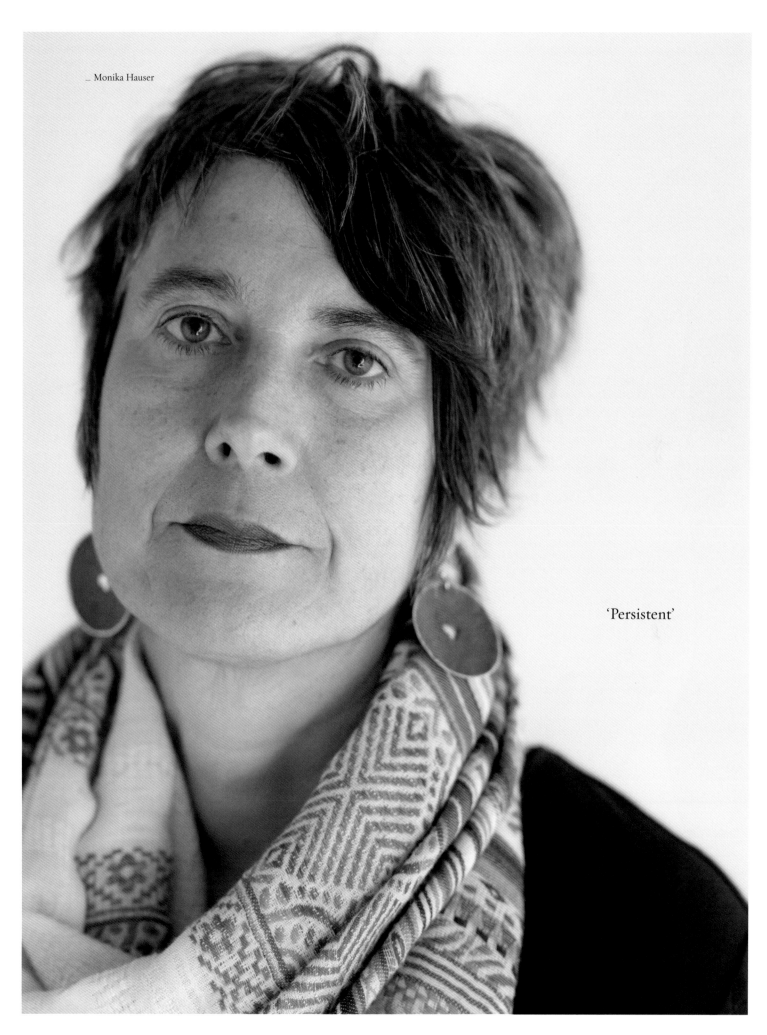

_ Monika Hauser

'Persistent'

Interview page 375

Sarah Beisly

Sarah Beisly was born in Auckland, New Zealand. She holds a business degree from Massey University. In 2002, Beisly visited Kolkata, India, where she discovered and was inspired by Freeset, a pioneering business that provides alternative employment for women trapped in the sex trade. After spending a year in Bangladesh learning Bangla – one of the most spoken languages in Kolkata – in 2011 Beisly and her husband, Paul, moved to Kolkata. Together, they established The Loyal Workshop, an ethical leather-goods workshop that offers employment to women seeking to free themselves from sex work.

Q. What really matters to you?
People, and my relationships with them, matter to me. It's important that each of my family members feel valued: my kids, my husband and our family back in New Zealand. What matters is learning what it means to love my family, to stand with them in their suffering and to celebrate with them in their joys.

My family extends to the family that my husband and I are building with our business, The Loyal Workshop – we don't want to operate it like a standard business, rather, we operate like a family.

One of the things that radically altered the way I make decisions was meeting Jesus. Getting to know his priorities by reading the Bible shifted my priorities. Jesus was concerned for the marginalised; over and over again, we see him give his time to a woman he values who has been pushed to the edge of society. When society is telling her she is nothing, he acknowledges her dignity and tells her that her life has value; I realised that, if I claimed to follow Jesus' teachings, then concern for the marginalised needed to be important to me as well.

I studied business, but I was never interested in making money for myself; I was always examining how business can be used to empower the marginalised or to provide opportunities for the poor. In 2002, when I finished my degree, I visited Kolkata with a bunch of mates, and we met up with mutual friends who were providing alternative employment to women trapped in the sex trade. Something in me came alive – I believed in what they were doing, because it was why I had studied business in the first place.

The slavery that continues to exist in today's world is a human-rights atrocity. There are currently so many women trapped in the sex trade, and the vast majority of these women have not chosen this profession – they are tricked, they are stolen. The stories of how women end up in the red-light district are common enough: girls grow up in a poor household,

with a lack of education and opportunities; traffickers – whom the girls often know – go around the villages and offer work in the city; and, when the girls get to the city, they are sold to a brothel and locked up in a disgusting room the size of a single bed. They are repeatedly raped, forced to see customer after customer after customer. They're told that, having started this line of work, they are bad women – that no one else will take them now and that that is their lot. Slowly, they start to believe this. The psychological abuse is so intense that it gets to a point where the doors are unlocked and the girls won't leave, because they are trapped in their minds. There is a daily rent for their room, so they need to see enough customers to meet that amount; for anything they need above that, they need to see more customers. The women's bodies are commoditised for men's enjoyment, but, as they age, they are discarded. Society has rejected these women because they're deemed worthless, and then the red-light district rejects them too. As they get older they struggle to afford the room and struggle even more to earn money for food. It gets to the point where they can't sustain their life anymore; many end up becoming madams because there is nothing else for them.

When I saw all this going on in Bowbazar, I couldn't believe it was happening in my lifetime – I knew I would never be able to justify doing nothing about it to my grandchildren. In 2014, we set up The Loyal Workshop, which is perched on the edge of the red-light district and offers employment to women who have been trapped in the sex trade. Most of these women are in their mid-thirties – they have reached that point where life is no longer sustainable. When we started, we just did brothel visitations to build up a rapport and trust with the women; we wanted to show ourselves to be friends who wouldn't betray them. Building this trust takes time. We speak a lot about what it would look like for them to fight for their freedom. We let them know that, when they're ready to leave, we're here to offer them work in a for-profit business in which the products speak for themselves and aren't contextualised by the stories

of our artisans – there is a lot of pride and dignity in that.

So, it's important to me that I spend my days on this earth wisely; I don't want to squander the freedom that I've received, and I want to use it to help more women find their freedom.

Q. What brings you happiness?
One thing that brings me joy is watching my children laughing and giggling together, when they are being totally silly, ridiculous, childish, innocent and playful.

Another thing that brings me a lot of joy is seeing the transformation in the lives of the women who work for us. When I first meet them, they are trapped in hellish situations, but I have the privilege of witnessing them move from that point to becoming a part of a family in which they belong and are accepted for who they are, and for who they can become; their posture changes, they start to stand upright, they look us in the eye, they start to crack jokes – they start to believe. We have a mantra here at the workshop, 'Your life has a lot of value; my life has a lot of value.' You can see them start to believe that it's true. What greater joy is there than witnessing this transformation take place in front of our eyes?

Q. What do you regard as the lowest depth of misery?
I have not seen a lower form of misery than a girl being sold into the sex trade and forced – against her will – to work as a sex worker for years and years. Can there be anything worse than to be repeatedly abused on a daily basis and to really believe what society is telling you – that your life has no value?

Q. What would you change if you could?
If people treated every single person with the dignity and respect that they deserved – regardless of the colour of their skin, their gender, their caste, their background or their sexual orientation – this world would be a much better place.

Q. Which single word do you most identify with?
Love.

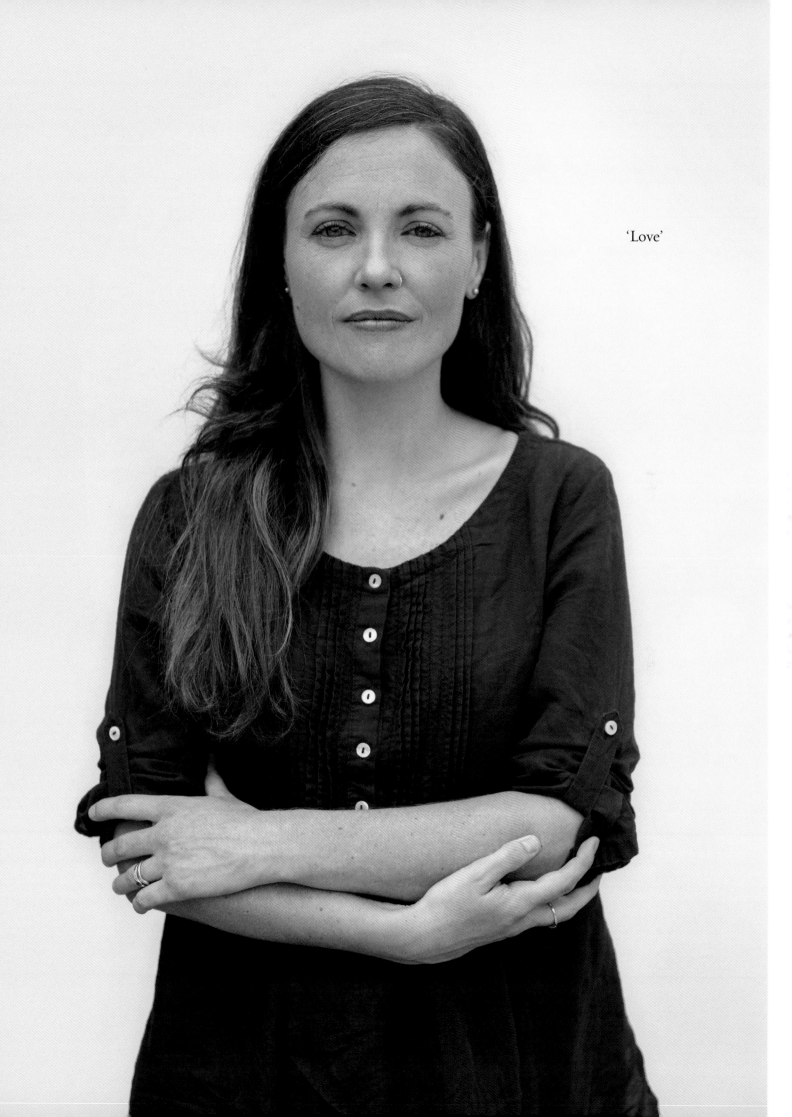

'Love'

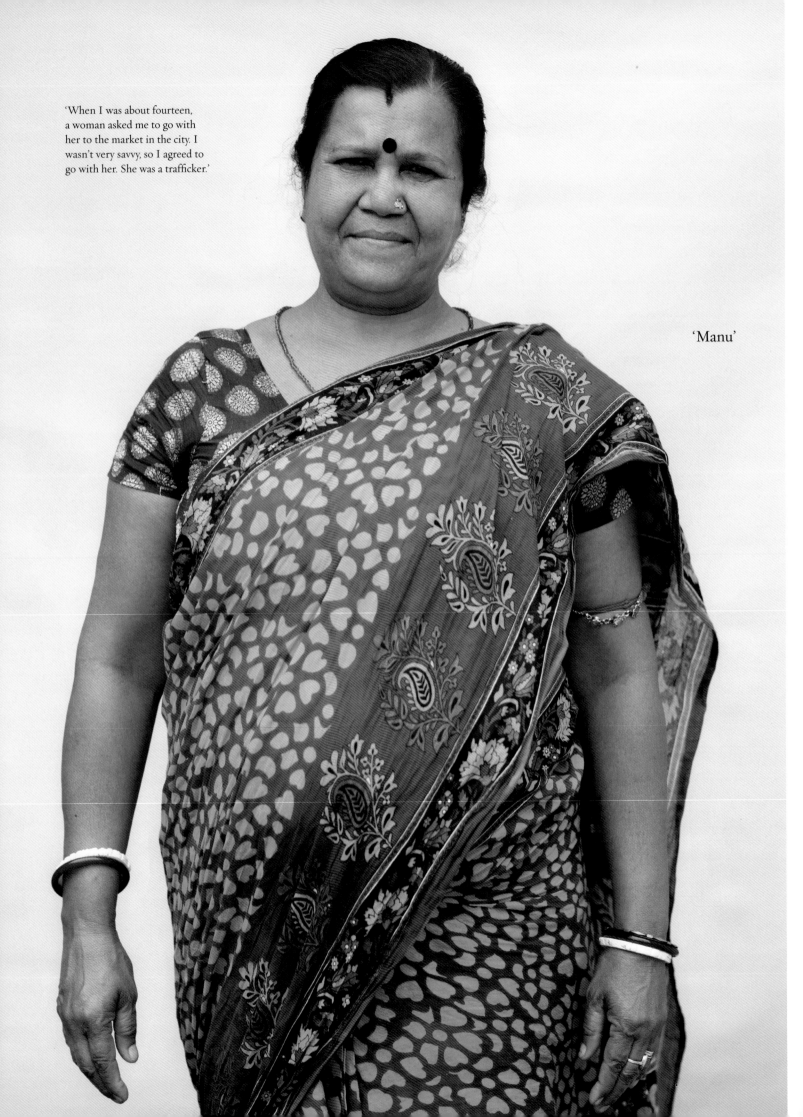

'When I was about fourteen, a woman asked me to go with her to the market in the city. I wasn't very savvy, so I agreed to go with her. She was a trafficker.'

'Manu'

Balika Das

Balika Das was born in Gomai in West Bengal, India. Her family arranged her marriage when she was eleven years old, and three years later a trafficker sold her to a brothel in Kolkata's red-light district, where she worked for twenty-three years. In 2014, she began working as an artisan at The Loyal Workshop. Das now lives in the suburb of Khidirpur, in Kolkata.

Q. What really matters to you?

Having the freedom to choose what my life will be like.

My childhood was not a happy one. My mother and father worked very hard to earn enough money to buy us clothes to wear and food to eat; it wasn't much money, and our family suffered a lot. When I was eleven or twelve, my parents and my older sister decided that I should marry. In India, many families struggle to provide enough food for their children, so one of the ways to address this is to marry off their daughters. When a woman marries, she moves into the home of her in-laws; she is expected to keep the home, which is hard work, but I don't have a problem with it because in return she becomes a daughter of that family and is their responsibility.

I was married to a man from my village and didn't have any problems with the arrangement. When I was about fourteen, however, a woman asked me to go with her to the market in the city. I wasn't very savvy, so I agreed to go with her. She was a trafficker. She tricked me and sold me to a brothel in the red-light district for a lot of money. Life became unbearable. I was locked in a room and was beaten severely if I refused to see customers. My husband did come looking for me, but they refused to release me to him. My entire life became about survival. One of the things that kept me going was the thought of my parents. I kept wondering how they were doing and whether they had enough to eat. They lived in a state of suffering and poverty, their house made of mud, and their survival became the cause of my survival.

I was trapped in that place for six years. They didn't give any of the women enough food to eat and, combined with the beatings, this made all of us very weak. We were completely under their control. I wasn't allowed to see anyone I knew, and I had to get permission to leave the brothel. For six years, I lived every day the same way: no breaks, no joy – just suffering. There was a man who I came to know, whom I then fell in love with. One night he snuck in and broke the lock on my door. I was able to leave and go back to my parent's home. I spent a month with them – I was so, so happy.

But in India things are hard. I needed to earn money, but once a woman has been inducted into the trade she has very few options in terms of work that is available to her once she leaves. I had to go back to the red-light district. This time I entered into a situation whereby I was not fully owned. I was able to keep half of the money I earned and was able to send it to my parents. Knowing that they had food to eat was enough of a reason for me to live. In the red-light district we talk about 'the line': all women stand in a line, in the filthy alleyways outside the brothel, waiting to be selected by a customer. In total, I spent twenty-three years on the line.

By the time I met Sarah Beisly (p. 144), I was not in a good way. I was still in the red-light district, but I was no longer earning enough money to survive. All of my clothes were torn, I didn't have any money for food and I didn't have enough to pay the brothel owner for my room. Sarah offered me this opportunity to work at The Loyal Workshop, and it completely changed my life: I don't go hungry anymore, I'm able to pay rent for my home, and I can give money to my son if he needs it. Compared to what my life has been, I don't have any problems. Being able to earn money has given me the power to make choices as well. I have been able to take back the power that had been stripped from me and choose to make my life better. I used to be powerless, and now I'm free; one day I hope to build my own home, where I can live in peace. I have options now, and I receive respect. That matters to me.

Q. What brings you happiness?

Financial freedom – being able to earn money utilising my skills, and being able to pay all of my bills and run my household well makes me happy. My greatest joy is having a job that I am proud of and earning wages for the products I make. The place where I work is a place of joy, it has a big heart and all of us are one family.

Q. What do you regard as the lowest depth of misery?

The suffering I've experienced was when I was working in the sex trade; working in a brothel room is the lowest form of suffering. The lowest points were when horrible men would come to my room – drunk or under the influence of some drug – and do awful things to me, abuse my body. You can survive going without food, but to survive the brutalisation of your body every day is very, very difficult. Not every woman survives.

Q. What would you change if you could?

I am liberated from the trade, so I want all women trapped in the brothels – wherever they are – to be liberated as well. I have had a lot of good happen to me, and I want my experience to be the norm. I used to be afraid of people, but now I'm afraid of no one. All women should have the opportunity to do fine work, to live with dignity and respect, and be able to realise their own value.

Q. Which single word do you most identify with?

Manu. It's the name of my son. In Indian culture, the husband is the most important thing, but I don't have a husband, so it is my son who is my greatest treasure.

'I want policy changes to require that all women are respected and that men are punished appropriately if they commit crimes against women.'

_ Mithu Ghosh

Interview page 375

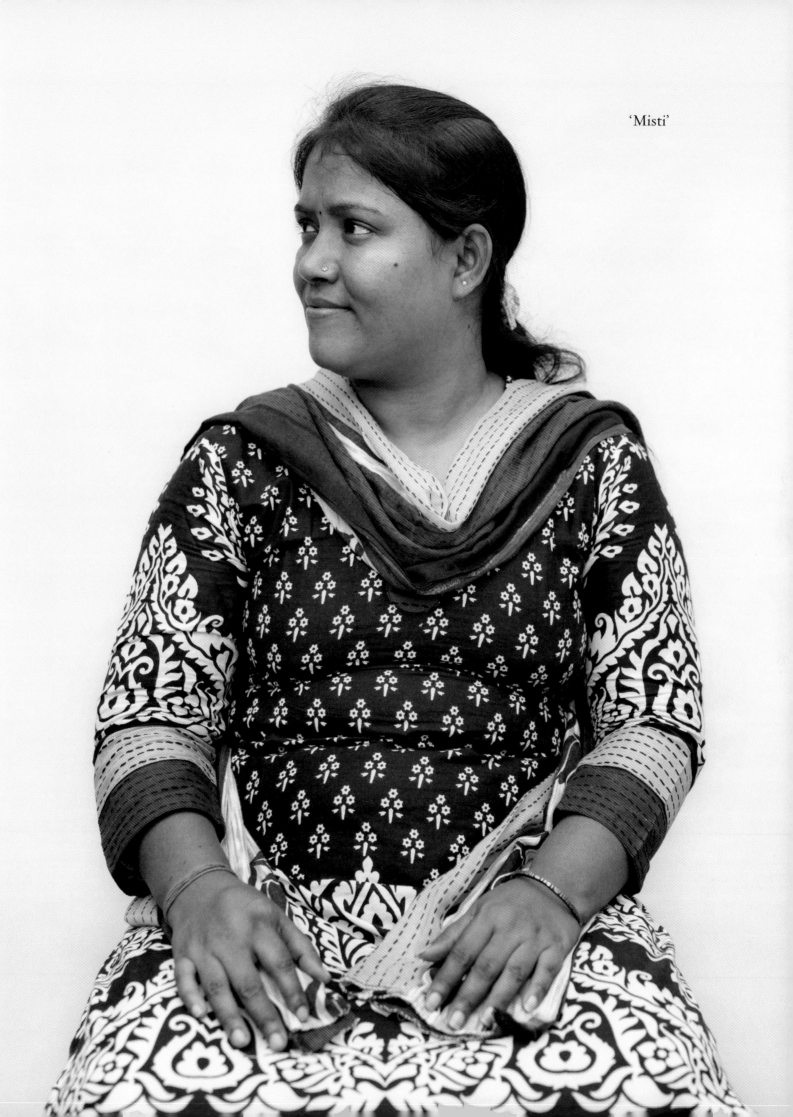

'Misti'

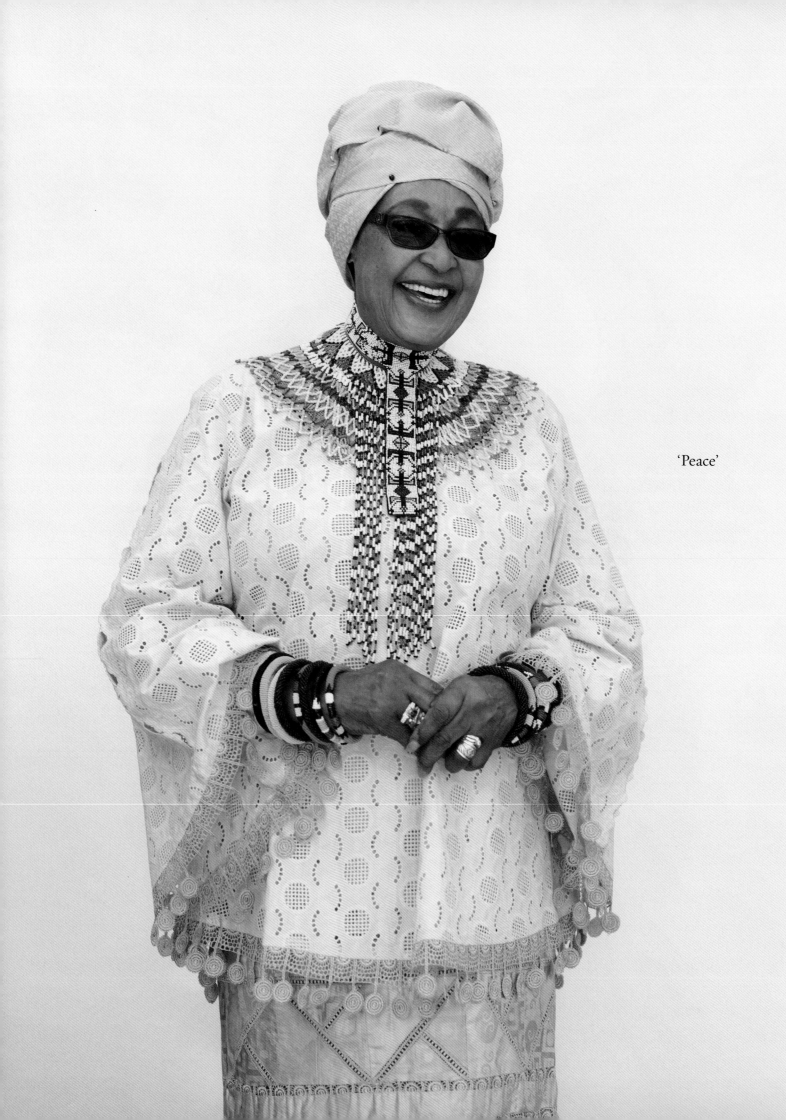

'Peace'

Winnie Madikizela-Mandela

─────

'It is a serious problem that women must prove that they are equal. How odd is that? Men would not be in this world without women.'

─────

Nomzamo Nobandla Winnie Madikizela-Mandela was born in the former Transkei, South Africa. Because of her anti-apartheid activism, she was regularly detained by the South African government. She endured house arrest, torture and imprisonment in solitary confinement, and was banished to the town of Brandfort in 1977. Madikizela-Mandela was married to Nelson Mandela for thirty-eight years, twenty-seven of which he was imprisoned. In 1985, she won the Robert F. Kennedy Human Rights Award for her role in South Africa's liberation struggle. Madikizela-Mandela is a member of the South African Parliament and a member of the African National Congress' national executive committee.

Q. What really matters to you?
So many things matter so much to me, in my strange type of life, that I wonder how to actually answer that question. All my life, I've been a politician, made so by the circumstances of my country. I never planned to be a politician, but the policies of South Africa's previous government and its brutality compelled almost each and every black person to become one – every black home was really a political institution. I got caught up in the quagmire, and I then became one of the freedom fighters on the front line of the struggle for our people.

The African National Congress is my family. I have known nothing other than the African National Congress, for whom I am a member of Parliament. If I woke up tomorrow and I was no longer a member of the African National Congress – although I was originally a social worker – I don't know what I would be; it never even occurred to me that I would be anything else other than a fighter for the liberation of my people and my country.

Q. What brings you happiness?
I have the greatest wealth; I may not have dollars, but my grandchildren and my great-grandchildren are the best thing God has ever given me – I live for them today. And at the very mature age of eighty, they are a complete joy. I don't know how I would get along each day without them, because they bring me so much happiness. They've compensated for all the years of struggle and they've healed a lot of my wounds. Because of them, I have learned to forgive the painful past and remember that we all belong to the family of humankind. Otherwise, I would have been so scarred; I don't think I would be alive if I didn't have this wealth of my grandchildren and great-grandchildren. And I'm hoping to become a great-great-grandmother very soon!

Q. What do you regard as the lowest depth of misery?
The patriarchy of society; in South Africa, women are not only culturally oppressed, but are oppressed by their past. During the apartheid era, women were of the lowest rung in society. And they were the least educated. The traditional belief was that you only educate a boy, because a girl is going to get married and take her brains away from the family – we have the extraordinary situation of the *lobola* bride-price custom, whereby families exchange wealth in the form of cattle. In apartheid South Africa, there was no point in educating women; the laws of the country at the time made it impossible for women to be women – we were regarded as children and, literally, nobodies at all. As women, we were regarded as cannon fodder, because our husbands, brothers and uncles perished in the apartheid prisons. South Africa was a police state – like Nazi Germany.

I remember an extraordinarily painful part of my life, when I was banished. I was living with my youngest daughter, Zindzi, in Johannesburg, though she was at boarding school in Swaziland. The apartheid government made it their business to arrest me whenever my children returned

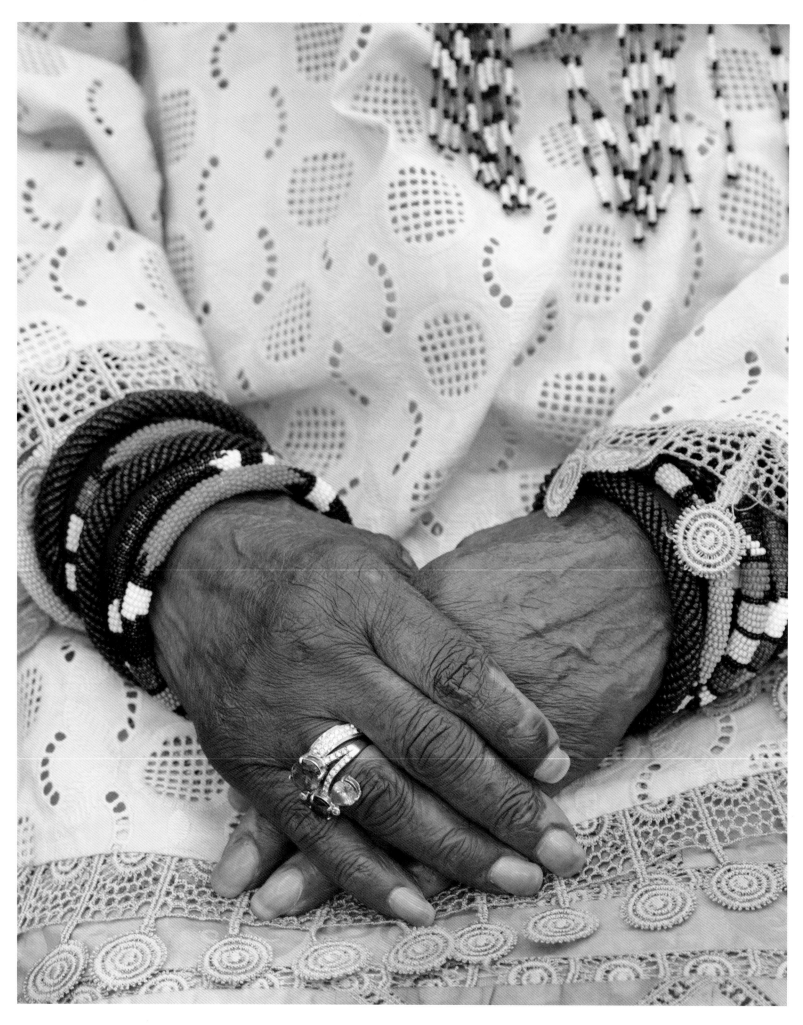

Winnie Madikizela-Mandela

'I have the greatest wealth; I may not have dollars, but my grandchildren and my great-grandchildren are the best thing God has ever given me — I live for them today.'

---

from school – this particular time when Zindzi came back, I was removed from Johannesburg and banished to this remote little village of Brandfort. The laws at the time were that if you were banished or banned by the apartheid regime, you were not to communicate with more than one person at a given time. The interpretation by the police of the law of the time was that, given that I was banished, my Zindzi could not have visitors, who would have been little children; she was barely 12 years old. I had to make an application to the regime to allow Zindzi to have children to come and play with her in the premises to which I was banished. To my horror, I was told by my lawyers that I couldn't make that application because by law a mother had no such rights – I was not her guardian. Only her father was her guardian and he was in prison on Robben Island at the time. The lawyers had to fly to Cape Town and apply for a visit to see

Zindzi's father on Robben Island simply so he could sign documents to allow me to apply for Zindzi to have other children enter the premises to play with her. Those were the laws of the country at the time.

It's still a struggle to uplift the lives of women. As a result, our generation and the generation that followed us are still not as educated as our men; we're still fighting for total equality.

Q. What would you change if you could?
I would like a global situation in which women were equal to men, in all aspects. A situation in which it isn't strange that in an old democracy like America, someone like Hillary Clinton would want to be president. The fact that she is a woman is somehow remarkable, even in the twenty-first century – she has to prove to certain people that she, as a woman, can do the job, and this is the case globally. I think that patriarchy really is an international cancer.

Even the African National Congress only began to accept women in 1943. It is still very difficult for South Africa. We're battling, right now, to understand the concept of power, and that it does not reside with men only. Were we to put up a woman candidate for the presidency when the current term expires, it would be a fierce battle, as there are still quarters within male circles that believe that a woman cannot lead a country.

It is a serious problem that women must prove that they are equal. How odd is that? Men would not be in this world without women. We are their biological passage. They cannot avoid being mothered by us, and we are very proud of the fact that we are that biological passage for humankind.

Q. Which single word do you most identify with?
Peace.

Georgie
Smith

Georgie Smith was born in Perth, Australia. A filmmaker, chef and designer, Smith is the founder of A Sense of Home, a not-for-profit organisation based in Los Angeles that is dedicated to creating homes for young people who are exiting the foster-care system. In 2016, Smith was named a Top 10 CNN Hero for her work with A Sense of Home and, in 2017, was nominated for a Women's Choice Awards Shero Award.

Q. What really matters to you?

What matters to me is that everyone has an opportunity to become the best version of themselves - everyone.

Q. What brings you happiness?

I love being in raw nature; it's where I feel we are meant to be. Being in nature makes the most sense to me - being able to learn from its exquisite balance and abundant inspiration, and to revel in its immense beauty. I love seeing nature flourish.

And I love seeing human beings flourishing. What I have noticed is that, in order to flourish, an individual needs to matter in this world. I am happiest when I see people feeling that they matter, when their spirits are lifted, and the entire mood of the environment becomes lighter and more at peace. For me, the 'community' equivalent of an ecosystem in harmony is when everyone matters; those in need are connected with those who have the means to volunteer their time - hence, these volunteers' time on this planet matters - and with businesses that share their resources. Together, these three subsets of the community create a sustainable solution that lifts up the disenfranchised, and they create a healthier, more thriving community.

A total stranger's cry for help made me discover that a feeling of home is as vital as - if not more vital than - our need for love. A young man who had aged out of the foster-care system asked me for help with his first-ever permanent living space. In responding to his request and in turning his barren, doleful space into a functioning home, it occurred to me that he had never felt at home - anywhere - in his entire life, and that that very fundamental feeling I knew so well - the feeling that had anchored and guided me - was something he was bereft of. This caused him to feel adrift in the world; without a sense of home, we do not have a sense of belonging in the world; without it, we do not have a foundation from which we can build a future that reflects our hopes and dreams. Our basic, primal need for shelter, married with human connection, gives us the feeling of home - or, what our not-for-profit calls, 'a sense of home.' My random act of kindness in helping that young man has evolved into a not-for-profit called A Sense of Home; we create homes for youth without family - for kids aging out of foster care. We do this with volunteers from the community and a staff of former foster youth, because, as much as this is about creating a home, it's also about creating community. What I love most about A Sense of Home is that it exists because, every day, the best of humanity shows up. How many other ways can we find to inspire the best of humanity to reveal itself, in every moment of every day?

I would say that I draw happiness from working shoulder to shoulder with people who are working towards solutions, with people who have a vision for a better world or just a better community. Working to benefit others makes me feel connected to others of like mind. And, connecting with human beings makes me very happy.

Q. What do you regard as the lowest depth of misery?
To be oppressed. Oppression is many different things, but to not be able to realise one's gifts and talents - to not have a voice - is the lowest depth of misery.

Q. What would you change if you could?
The need for home is something that binds us all. Connecting our innate desire for home with our desire to matter is why A Sense of Home is successful. I would like to see this approach spread across the world; I would like to see other paradigms created that focus on our innate desire to make the world a better place and on what unites us - as opposed to what divides us. I would like to see businesses, schools and community organisations think about how they can lure people out of their bubbles, get them to link arms with strangers, and work on meaningful and sustainable projects. I'd like them to think about how we, together, can bridge the divide and build healthier communities while, in the process, becoming more empathetic and educated on the plight of others around us. The desire to do this exists. We simply need to be more focussed on igniting our desire to better humankind and the health of the planet, rather than on our desire to make a buck off of it.

Our community is our responsibility. If our community is to be a success, we must aid its progress. Therefore, we cannot turn our backs on those who are not thriving; if we lift them up, we lift up their entire community. The same applies, too, to the environment; we shall not flourish as long as it not flourishing. So, let's shift the thinking around what is community and the individual's role in community. For too long, we have been taught to look at what we can gain from situations, rather than what we can bring to situations. The consciousness is there, now let's act - with love!

Q. Which single word do you most identify with?
Gratitude. I myself feel gratitude, and I like it when I'm in the company of others who feel gratitude.

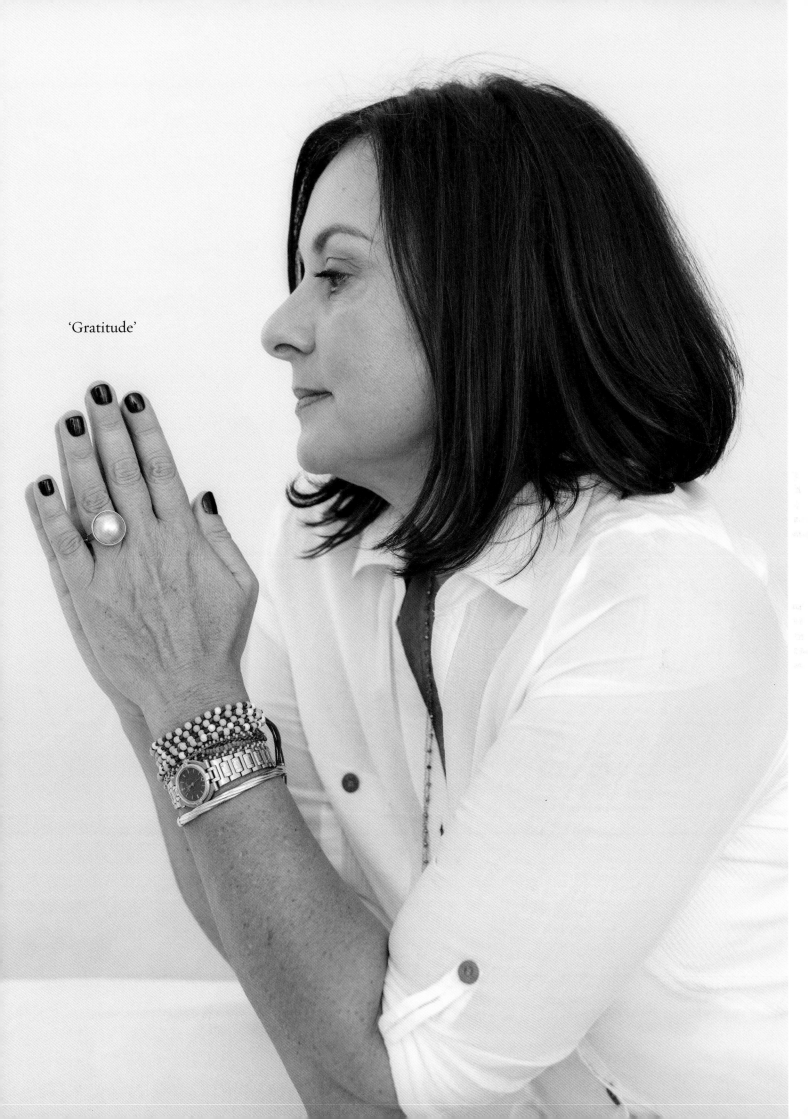

'Gratitude'

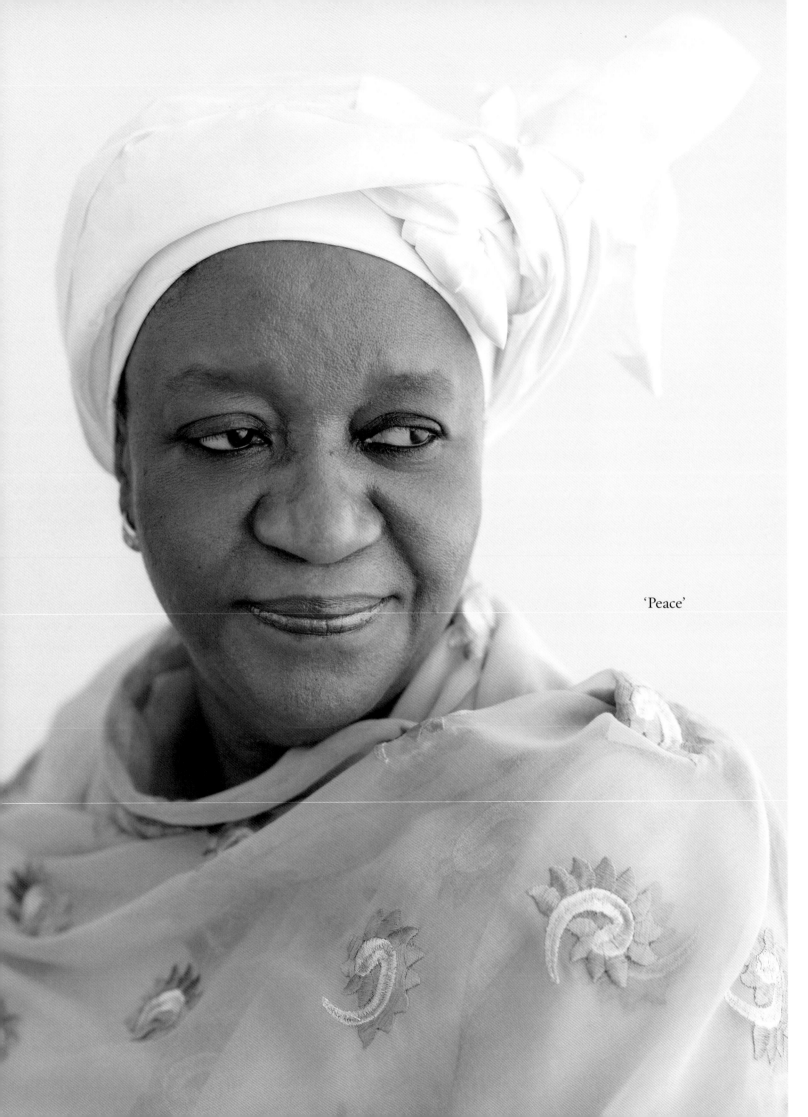

'Peace'

Zainab Hawa Bangura

Zainab Hawa Bangura was born in Yonibana, Sierra Leone. She holds a bachelor's degree from Fourah Bay College in Freetown, Sierra Leone, and advanced diplomas in insurance management from the University of London and Nottingham University. She was Sierra Leone's minister of foreign affairs and international cooperation between 2007 and 2010, and minister of health and sanitation between 2010 and 2012. She was the United Nations special representative of the secretary-general on sexual violence in conflict from 2012 to 2017. Bangura has received numerous awards for her social activism, including the Reagan-Fascell Democracy Fellowship and the National Endowment for Democracy's Democracy Award.

Q. What really matters to you?

Social activism is what defines me as a person. And the future – in relation to this, education is the golden key we must pass on.

I grew up in abject poverty, as my mother's only child. All my father wanted was a son, but my mother was not able to have any more children. When I was twelve, my father walked out of our lives because my mother refused to allow him to marry me off. She was an incredible feminist. She told me that, if I just took the time to understand how much work I would need to put in, there were no limits to what I could achieve. She used to say, 'When you fall, never fall on your face; fall on your back, so that you can see the sky and know that you still have a long way to go.'

After my father left, my mother couldn't afford anything, so we moved back to our village. She instilled in me this idea that I had to be educated, because that was the only way to get out of the poverty we were in. Most of the men in my mother's family had been given the opportunity to go to school, but she hadn't, so she knew what a disadvantage this was. In my final year of high school, I had to rely on a friend to pass down her old uniforms to me; another friend gave me a pair of shoes. And I would have dropped out of high school in my final year had my principal not supported me; I was a senior prefect, and she thought I was the most brilliant student, so she made a special request to the government for me to remain – she told them she couldn't afford to lose me. Then, I was able to attend university because I received a government scholarship. My mother gave everything for me to better myself – then she died.

The traditional and cultural restrictions I experienced at the time of my mother's death changed my life. I was told I couldn't make the decision to bury her because I was a woman; I was told that I would have to find my father, bring him back to the village and await his permission. By that time, I already had a son, my own job as an insurance executive and my own car, yet I wasn't able to bury my mother. Here, I had to submit myself to the leadership of this man who left us years ago to marry another who would have his son. I had no option but to marry my partner to empower him to bury her. The blatancy of this gender inequality changed me – I knew I had to become a voice for women's rights.

At the time, Sierra Leone had a military government. I couldn't fight for women's rights under that regime, so, first, I had to fight for democracy. We rallied and I led women from the markets and villages into the streets – women like my mother. We demanded that the military leave the seat of government and return to their barracks. Once we were successful, I rose to become minister of foreign affairs. When I take stock of that time in my life, I know I learned two very important lessons. The first was an understanding of the transformative power of education; I came from a village where women weren't allowed to own land, where aunts and grandmothers were distributed as items of a man's property when he died. Yet, in a single generation, education had lifted me up beyond my mother's wildest dreams. The second lesson was that your gender and your place of birth do not determine your future. So now I make sure that every girl in my extended family goes to school and, when I look at them, I know that here we have doctors and engineers. But I know that if someone doesn't fight for them, their potential will never be known.

My mother made me believe that I could move my life forward, and now the course of our family's history is changed; it all started with a woman who had to beg for a room to stay in with her daughter, yet, today, her grandson is a lawyer who is married to an engineer. If I hadn't had that experience of exclusion when my mother died, I might today be a retired managing director of an insurance company. So, when I think about what matters to me, it is the future – and social activism is my vehicle. I'm working for the future of my children and of the children of Sierra Leone. I want it to be a future full of possibility. We must look ahead and keep moving, refusing to be imprisoned by the past.

Q. What brings you happiness?

Progress and change. Whenever I see a woman who is struggling, I ask myself what I can do to assist her to move forward and better herself. It has been very fulfilling to watch a group of women I worked with in Sierra Leone, who have suffered appalling sexual abuse during the war, take back control of their lives – to watch them transform and rise above their suffering by helping one another.

Q. What do you regard as the lowest depth of misery?

The grand prison of poverty, and the powerlessness and hopelessness it brings a person; at times, they can believe they are not a human being. I understand the humiliation, lack of self-dignity and self-respect a person feels, and, when I see such poverty, it pains me. Because I know how my mother felt when she didn't have enough money to feed me. Wherever I go, I see poverty as having a woman's face, while power still has the face of a man.

Q. What would you change if you could?

Injustice – and the resultant lack of opportunity – because this is what creates poverty.

Q. Which single word do you most identify with?

Peace. We have too many wars raging in this world; when I look at the famine that's happening in South Sudan, I see that this is a man-made crisis. How does a country that is so fertile have rampant famine? It is caused by an absence of peace.

Gail Kelly

Gail Kelly was born in Pretoria, South Africa. She began her banking career in South Africa in 1980, before moving to Australia in 1997. In 2002, Kelly became the first female chief executive officer (CEO) of a top-fifteen ASX-listed company – St. George Bank. In 2007, Kelly was appointed CEO of Westpac Group. Since retiring from Westpac in 2015, Kelly has been engaged in a variety of roles, including with CARE Australia, an international organisation that works to combat global poverty, with a particular focus on the empowerment of women and girls.

Q. What really matters to you?

Making a difference has always been the factor that's driven me. I was never focussed on becoming a CEO – it wasn't in my long-term plan – but, throughout my career I've sought to try, in whatever role I've occupied, to make a difference and help others. There's nothing that gives me more joy and satisfaction than being able to assist others in achieving their goals, and seeing them flourish and grow. In the Westpac context, we built this very concept into our vision to be one of the world's great companies, helping our customers, communities and people to prosper and grow. In a nutshell, this translates into helping our customers to achieve their financial goals and life dreams, our people to grow and find fulfilment in their careers, and our communities to be strong and resilient.

In 2010, we set out to achieve a goal of women occupying 40 per cent of leadership roles by 2014. At the time, we were at about 30 per cent, and it struck me that it just wasn't good enough – our progress was plateauing at that level. I knew from my own experience that, if you can build a culture in which everyone feels valued and respected, and if you build strong momentum, you develop a pipeline of growth that makes you stronger and richer as an organisation. The interesting thing is that we never had to articulate the business case for 40 per cent representation of women. People understood. They knew why it mattered to have strong young women coming through the system and standing alongside equally qualified men. So, in 2012, with the momentum of the organisation behind us, we absolutely smashed the target.

At a lunch not long after that, I was asked, 'Well, what's next?' The immediate answer was: 'Why stop at 40 per cent? We want to achieve 50 per cent, because that's the right balance overall.' Right there, I called out 2017 as the target date, Westpac's bicentennial year. It's a very important landmark, and a proud moment for us. We're deeply proud of our history of diversity and once again, the organisation has stepped up to deliver.

Q. What brings you happiness?

My family; they're my first and most important priority.

I married my husband, Allan, when I was twenty-one, and we've been together for over forty years. Our relationship has been the bedrock of my life; Allan has supported me throughout my career, and together we have built a strong and happy family.

I'm immensely proud of each one of our children – our beautiful, happy, centred, kind, thoughtful children – Sharon, Sean, Mark and Annie. I'm proud of the human beings that they are. They're very different individuals, but have strong bonds between them and give me enormous joy.

Beyond my family, my biggest happiness is being able to help others. It is such a joy when you see young people grow in confidence and achieve their potential, when they step up and deliver. Now that I've retired from my executive career, I'm doing lots of teaching, sharing, advising and supporting. Fundamentally, I'm trying to share some of the lessons I've learned along the way to hopefully help others live happier, more fulfilled lives, to be stronger and better leaders of others. That gives me immense joy.

Q. What do you regard as the lowest depth of misery?

In a personal sense, the very lowest depth of misery that I could contemplate is hurting someone or causing suffering to someone who is in my care. I haven't been in that position, fortunately, but I know that that would just be the most painful, lowest depth of misery for me.

On a broader level, cruelty of man toward man gives me a lot of pain. There's so much evidence of people who willingly, knowingly, deliberately inflict suffering and pain on others. Think of Aleppo, and the wrenching dislocation and suffering for men, women and children caught up in this brutal, bitter conflict. Think of the impact of terrorism on the lives of innocent victims and their families. Think, too, of the profound impact of domestic violence and sexual abuse of women and children all around the world. Hate and intolerance in all its forms create deep pools of pain for me.

Q. What would you change if you could?

Education for girls – indeed, equality for girls – is a huge area requiring change. As we know, there are many, many countries around the world – and particularly in developing nations – in which girls have serious challenges with regard to equality, and don't have the educational access and support that they need. But we shouldn't overlook the developed parts of the world, in which girls also have many challenges; in some respects, these may be subtler, but girls in the developed world equally don't have access, opportunity and equality in the same way their brothers may have.

The reason I'd want to focus on this particular area for change is that girls' education has a multiplier effect. The rate of teenage pregnancies is likely to fall, communities will be safer and stronger as empowered women deploy their skills in economic endeavour and future generations of children will be better supported.

I have seen this personally in the work that I do as CARE Australia's ambassador for women's empowerment. I have visited parts of the world where CARE does its wonderful work – Malawi, Cambodia, Vanuatu – and I've seen the programmes focussed on women's empowerment, on equipping girls with confidence and new skill sets. I have seen first-hand how women focus on the long-term, in terms of giving back to their communities. After a cyclone in Vanuatu, one of the male leaders said that the women had been outstanding, because they thought about the needs of the whole community. Women bring inclusiveness and a long-term perspective. Quality education for our girls will bring hope to the world.

Q. Which single word do you most identify with?

I think the single word for me would be 'optimism.' If you have that, you build hope and resilience, which are what the world needs these days.

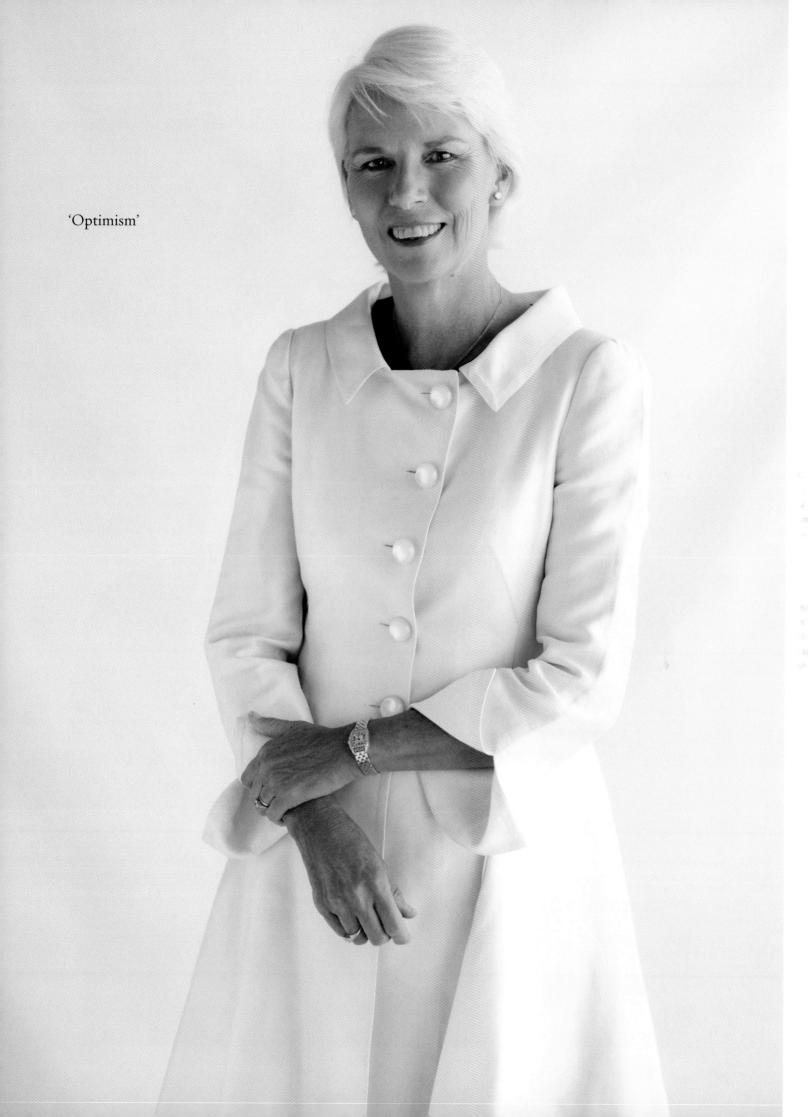

'Optimism'

_ Josefine Cox

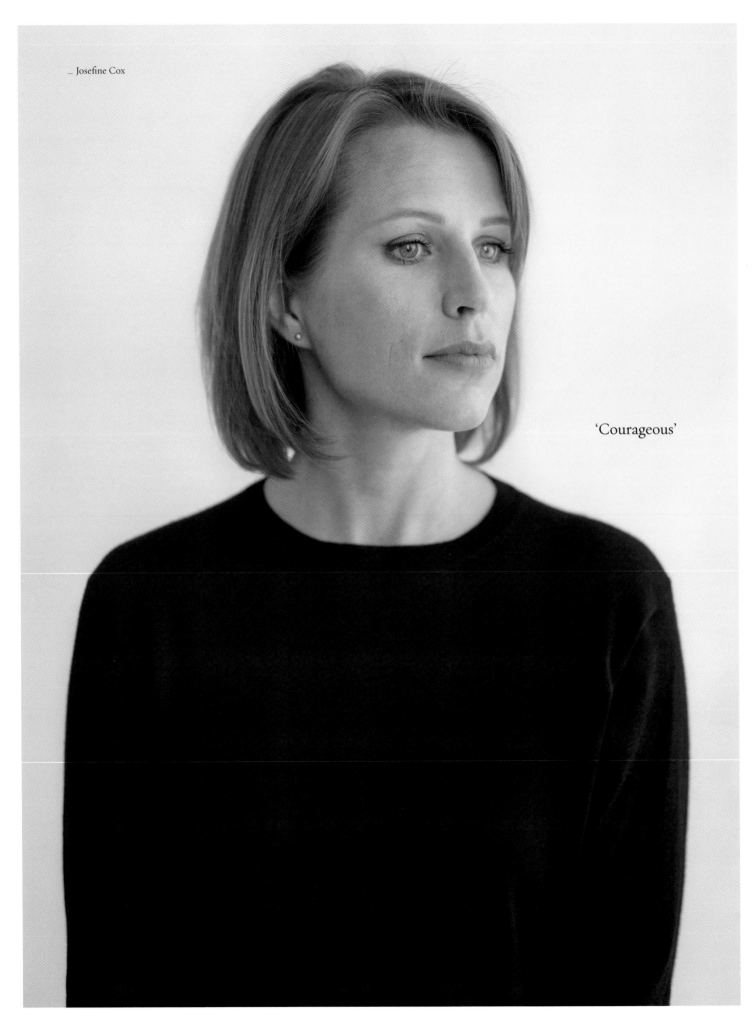

'Courageous'

Interview page 376

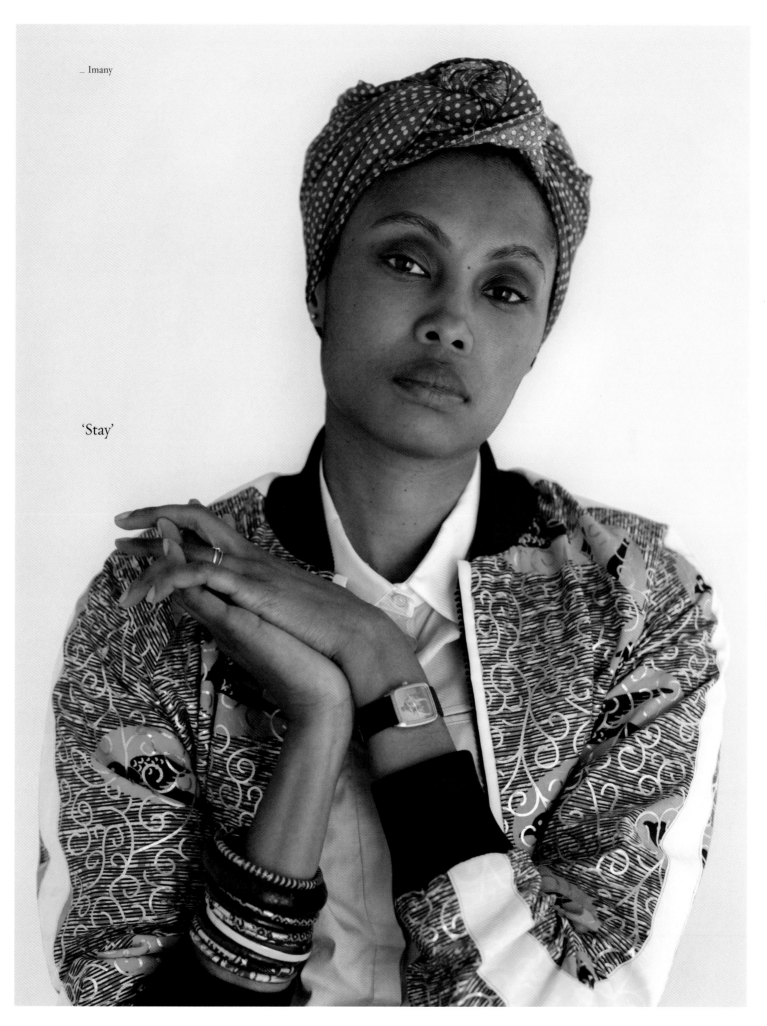

_ Imany

'Stay'

Interview page 376

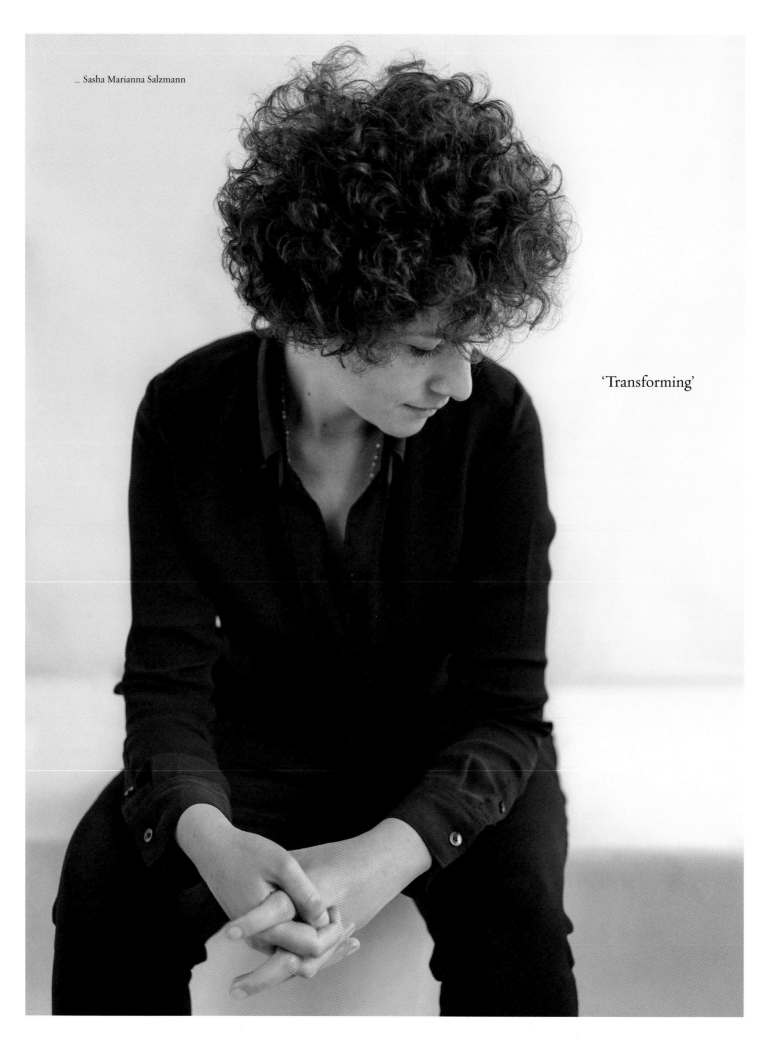

_ Sasha Marianna Salzmann

'Transforming'

Interview page 376

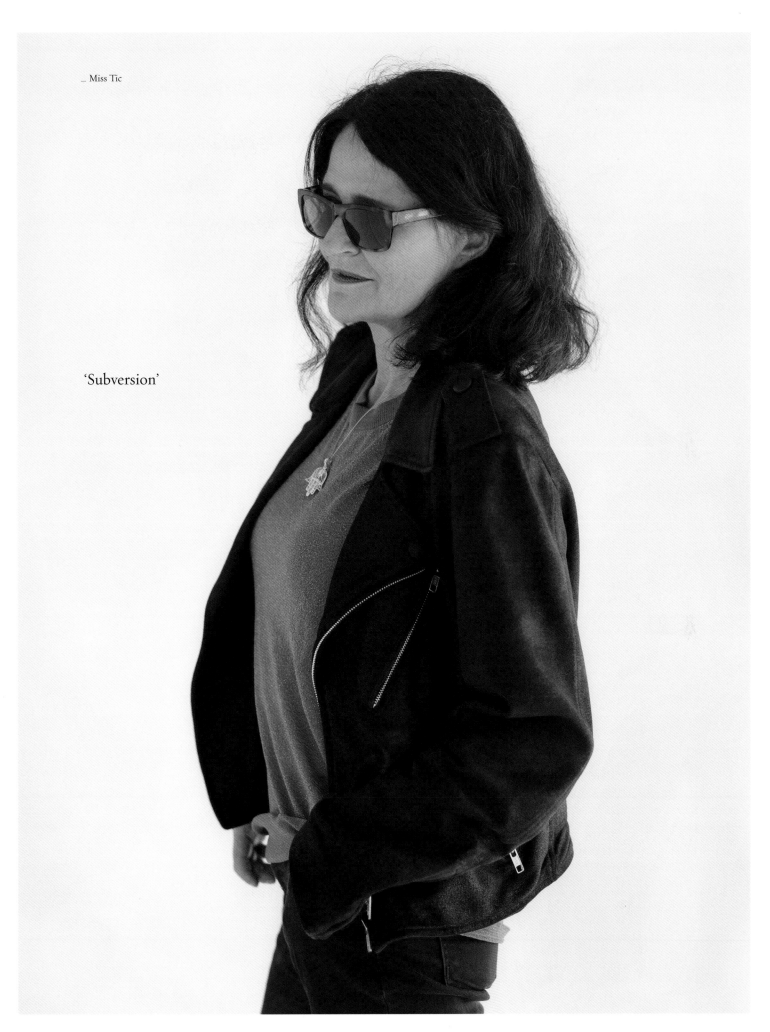

'Subversion'

Laura Dawn

Laura Dawn was born in Pleasantville in Iowa, USA. She is a political activist, writer and filmmaker. From 2003 to 2012, she was the creative and cultural director for MoveOn.org, a public-policy advocacy group and political action committee. In 2012, she co-founded Art Not War, a cultural strategy group specialising in campaigns for social justice and progressive issues.

Q. What really matters to you?

The most important thing to me right now is the world that I'm going to leave for my daughter, Mona. When she was born, everything shifted. Now I see everything through the lens of making sure that she has a good life. There's a deep delight for me that I'm able to give her some of the things I wasn't given, in the form of support from an early age. But, I'm also aware that she is walking into a world that is deeply troubled. Before my daughter was born, I described myself as a radical feminist, but I don't think I truly was one until she was born.

The way that women and girls are devalued worldwide has become the most pressing issue to me. I think finding ways to reinvent culture and to address systemic sexism – which is really the white patriarchy that's been in control for most of history – is vital to our survival as a species. If we don't have more feminine principles and leadership, and more values of communication, cooperation, collaboration and consensus building, we won't be able to address very dire and direct threats like climate change.

I did a study, called *Men*, that I'm hoping to make into a film. It's about testosterone and how it acts in homogenised groups of male leadership. It's about looking at what happens when you just have men at the fore of the political, financial, religious and cultural systems of the world. Historically, these systems were – and, let's be honest, still are – run by men: mostly white men. The continuation of this could be the end of us, because it's one of the reasons we've had such intractability around climate change. In a closed system of male-dominated leadership, men's testosterone and cortisol levels rise, which produces a really negative cascade of effects. It produces an acute focus on short-term threats and a very long-lens focus on long-term threats: so terrorism feels very, very immediate, but climate change – which is much more likely to be the bigger catastrophe – is put off. Men also fire dopamine and serotonin when they engage in conflict, so in these situations they exhibit much more risk-taking behaviour.

Women have a somewhat different leadership style, so, when you inject a tipping point of 30 per cent women into a ruling system of men, the entire group changes biochemically – communication, collaboration and consensus-building become more possible.

My big theory is that, if more women were involved in the leadership of the world, in every country, we might see less war and more action on some of the direst threats. There are studies that bear this theory out; the countries that have the most progressive policies towards women generally have more women in office and in business. These countries also have the highest gross domestic products, they have the highest happiness indices and they have the lowest incidences of war. The countries that have the most repressive policies towards women are in endless cycles of war and tend to be doing very, very poorly.

The backbone of feminism is that people should be treated equally; what I call radical feminism is an awareness that feminism is connected to racism, xenophobia and class – it's all connected. And men can participate in radical feminism. They need to be our allies. I'd say a good place for men to start is by looking at how they speak about women when they are not around. The 2016 United States election has shown us that misogyny is still very much alive and that there's still massive resistance to equality. The author Rebecca Traister makes the point that the entire American economy was built not only on slave labour – which is something we're all aware of – but also on the free labour of women. We have an entire economy that, for many, many decades, was propelled by men at work.

This entire system doesn't work without someone at home taking care of the family, doing unpaid labour. A lot of the work that has historically fallen to women – the care of a household, the care of children, the care of the elderly – is unpaid labour. And this won't do anymore. It's time to look at more aggressive ways of addressing the power imbalance.

Q. What brings you happiness?

Spending time with my family makes me the happiest: just me, my husband, Daron, and Mona making up songs, giggling, taking a walk or doing something fun. Showing Mona the world is so much fun.

I have a little mantra; I believe that every act of creation is an act of love. So whenever I see someone participating for the forces of love, I get very moved by it. Sometimes, reading the news feels like an onslaught of negativity, but the truth is that the human race gets a little less violent every year. We get a little better all the time. And the arc of the moral universe is long, but it bends towards justice. It makes me so happy when I see someone choosing creativity – choosing love – and trying to spread that in the greater service of everyone.

Q. What do you regard as the lowest depth of misery?

To me, there's one deepest misery – it's violence. Yes, we all have to die, and at some point we all realise this. In my case, although I knew about death, I don't think I actually realised that it would happen to me until I was around ten – I remember being overwhelmed with the pain and fear of that realisation. So, seeing as we all live with this existential knowledge of our own demise our whole lives, why would we choose to murder each other?

There's a kind of violence, too, in not sharing the bounty of this world. We live in a world where the resources are vast – there's plenty to go around for everyone. No one needs to go hungry; there's not a shortage of food, there's a shortage of the will to get food to people who need it. This is part of why I did the *Men* study: trying to get to the root causes of violence and trying to figure out how human beings could evolve into a less violent species.

Q. What would you change if you could?

I would put more women in charge. I'm not naïve enough to think that this would fix everything, but I think it's worth trying – because it's worth noting that at no point in history have we tried it.

Q. Which single word do you most identify with?

Love.

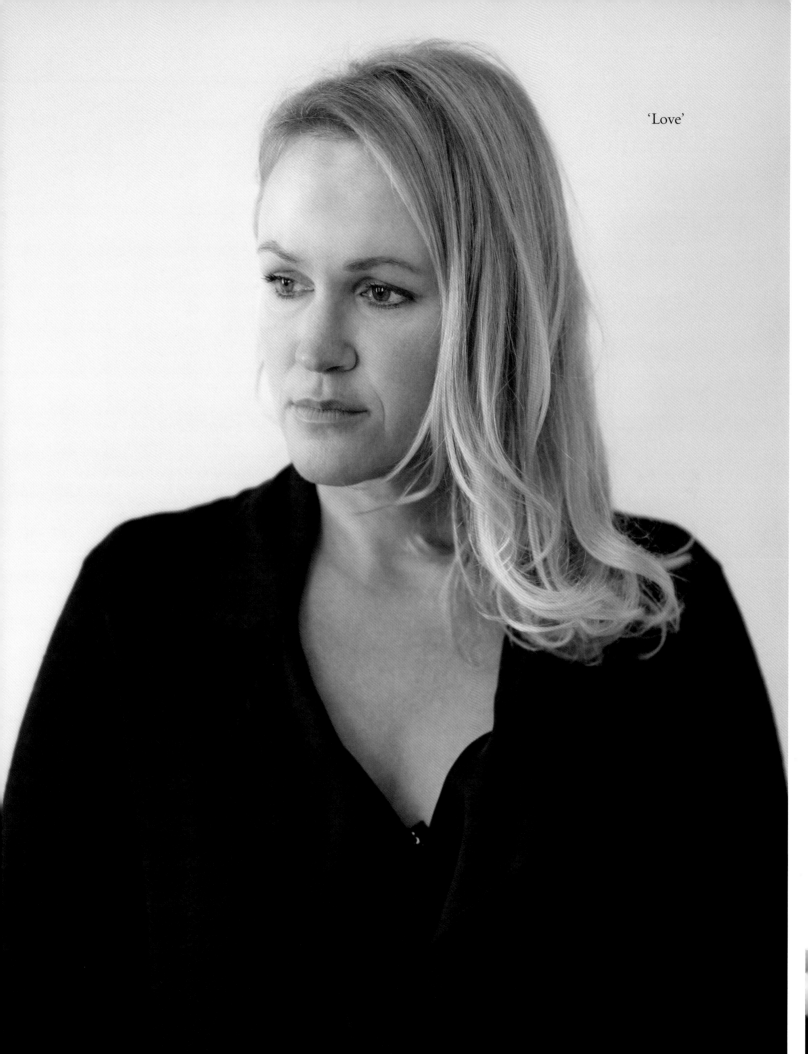

'Love'

Ellen
Bryant Voigt

Ellen Bryant Voigt was born in Chatham in Virginia, USA, and lives in Vermont. A teacher and writer, Voigt is the author of eight collections of poetry, including *Messenger: New and Selected Poems, 1976–2006*, which was a finalist for the 2008 Pulitzer Prize, and two collections of essays on the craft of poetry. In 2015, she was awarded a MacArthur Foundation fellowship.

'Even when cruelty is not physically violent, and whether or not it is inadvertent, it always has an indelible, irreversible cost.'

Q. What really matters to you?

'A more just, verdant and peaceful world,' to borrow the MacArthur Foundation mission statement. But I admit I despair of ever seeing it. The current political climate in the United States is absolutely appalling. Even the level of discourse is appalling. And the risks are huge, rolling back hard-won progress for the rights of women, of minorities, the steps made to protect the environment – I am ashamed of my country and concerned about the future. The recent ignorance and prejudice feel especially discouraging to me, because as one ages, the limitations of stamina and energy restrict one's belief in being able to make a difference. And idealism denied expression in action reliably produces bitterness and cynicism, which exert their own costs to the soul.

However, remarkably, one thing that is actually very encouraging is that the arts have never been more important, nor more vibrant, than they are right now. In our electronic, digital age – even with some alarming side-effects in the Twitter/tweeting world that need to be addressed, and this will take time – there is so much more access, more voices being raised, more ways for those voices to be heard. There are of course the usual pronouncements about the death of literature and even literacy itself, but these are contradicted by my own experience and observations. People are hungry for poetry: the 'news that stays news.' You can see it in the number of public readings in small local libraries, in the number of online journals, in the number of poetry collections being published right now – more than ever before, and publishers wouldn't publish them if they couldn't sell them. This may sound too conveniently Orwellian, but it does seem to me literature will remain vital because it is the last dependable source of language committed to telling the truth.

Q. What brings you happiness?

Work – focussed work. Poetry, like all the arts, requires a lot of it. To try to write a poem, then try to write a good poem, and then try to write a better poem than you have ever written: these are challenges that help you escape and enlarge the limited self. It's slow and it's arduous, and one continually fails, but for me it's exhilarating. In the middle of that process, you're in the company of John Keats – down at his feet, to be sure, but in his company. That's what you're working toward, the point at which the language on the page is leading you, speaking to you. You've realised all of your existing 'opinions' are shallow and clichéd, and suddenly you're taken past them; the language on the page, the music of it, the images and the sentences and the residue of all the poems you've ever read, have led to discovery and opened you to the contradictory, endlessly glorious world. What could be more exciting than that?

But superlatives can be tyrannical. Music also makes me happy, especially the pure mathematics of it. My children have been and continue to be reliable sources of happiness, as have my grandchildren, a long marriage, and the company of many, many wonderful friends. And teaching – it's very fulfilling, which is another name for happiness, yes? And living in Vermont, which is beautiful and humane. And my standing-seam roof! It gives me great happiness to hear the snow slide off.

Q. What do you regard as the lowest depth of misery?

I don't actually believe comparisons can be made in regard to suffering, whether it presents as abject poverty or acute physical pain, overwhelming grief or other forms. But since you ask me to articulate the absolute nadir, I'll say the absence of hope, when there seems no spark of possibility, however sputtering, that the present misery will ever change. The triumph of the human spirit over suffering, which a rational person knows will never end, derives from a perhaps irrational hope for the future, if not for the future of the particular one suffering then for that of others who follow, be it one's children or comrades or country or – if you'll forgive the large abstraction – humanity.

Q. What would you change if you could?

I have a very long list but would start by eliminating all acts of cruelty. Even when cruelty is not physically violent, and whether or not it is inadvertent, it always has an indelible, irreversible cost. Most often, it's triggered by ignorance, which is what racism and sexism are. Sometimes it can be directed at oneself, not solely at others, and this is most often triggered by shame, itself a consequence of earlier cruelty. Whatever the causes, all of us working hard on that would allow many other things to change.

Q. Which single word do you most identify with?

Stubborn – I think I am.

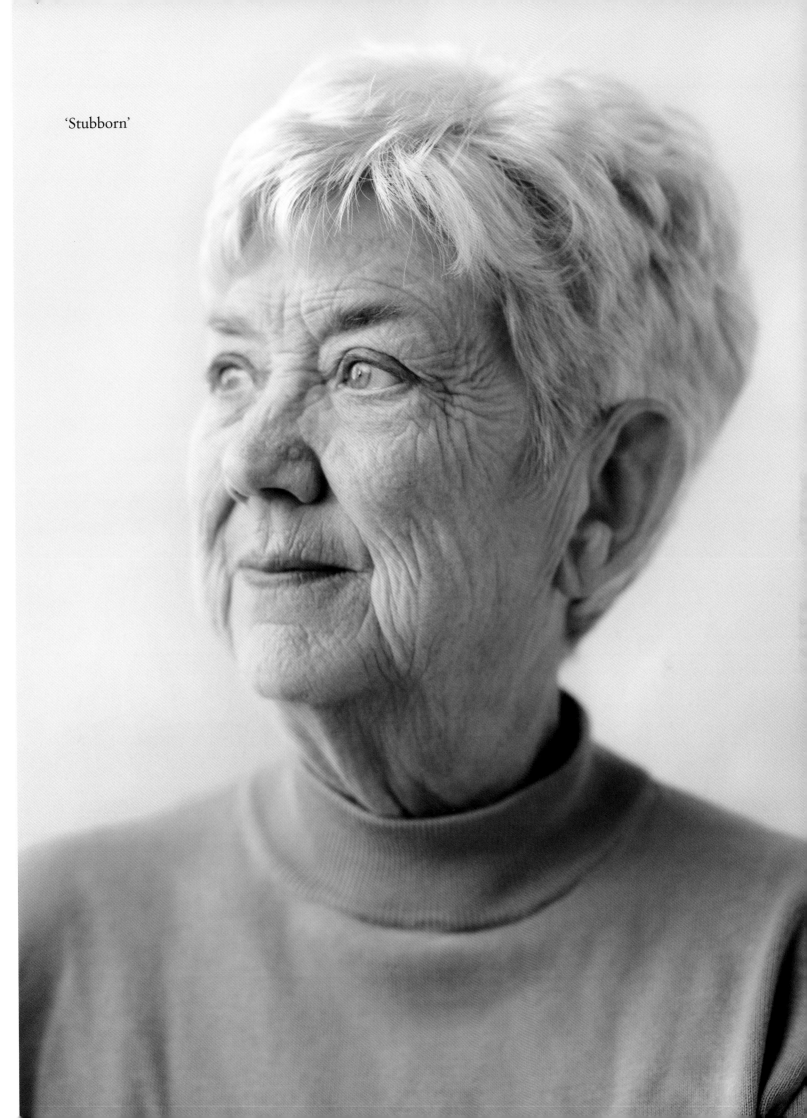

'Stubborn'

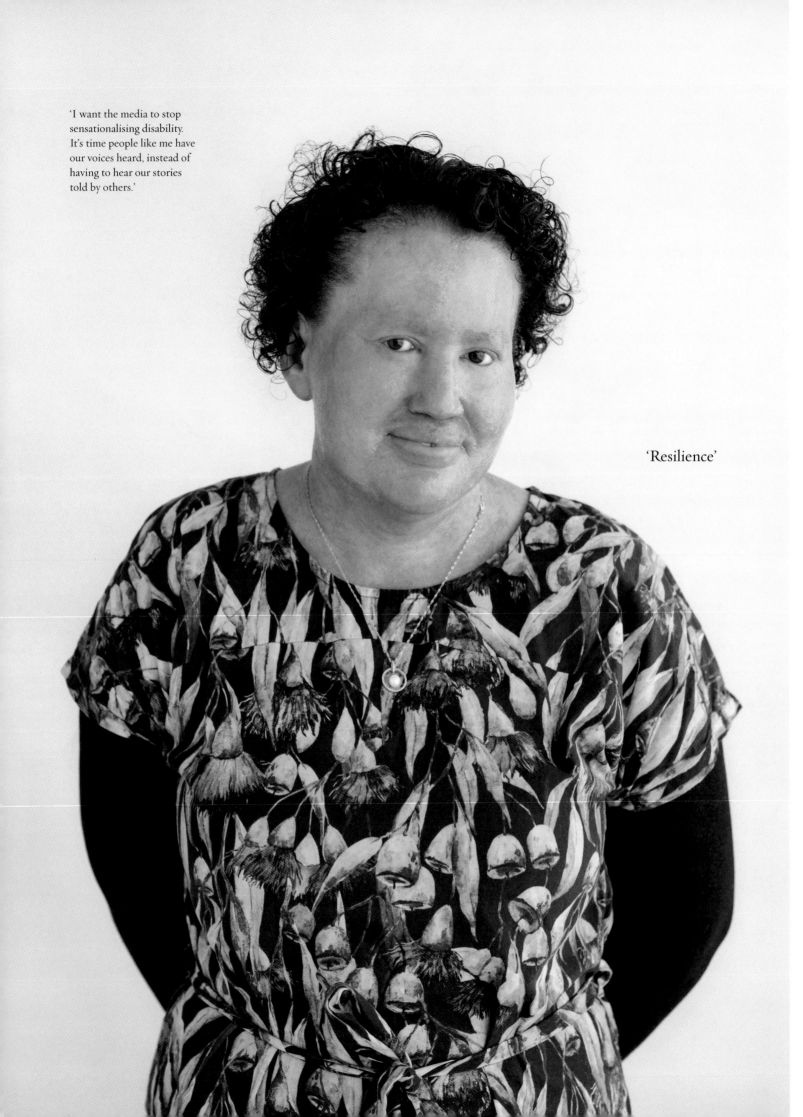

'I want the media to stop sensationalising disability. It's time people like me have our voices heard, instead of having to hear our stories told by others.'

'Resilience'

Carly
Findlay

Carly Findlay was born in a small town in rural Victoria, Australia. Born with ichthyosis, a rare genetic skin disorder, she advocates for a more inclusive attitude towards media portrayals of people who are disabled and who are living with facial differences. She holds a masters of communication from Melbourne's RMIT University and a bachelor of e-commerce from La Trobe University, also in Melbourne. A blogger, writer, public speaker and appearance activist, Findlay was named one of Australia's most influential women in the 2014 *Australian Financial Review* Westpac 100 Women of Influence Awards.

Q. What really matters to you?

For the last ten years, I've wanted to change the way people with disabilities and facial differences are portrayed in the media, so taking part in this project is really good because it exposes people to a kind of face they may not otherwise see. I was born with a very severe skin condition called ichthyosis that has been really challenging medically and socially. When my skin becomes infected, I'm hospitalised; it becomes very difficult to move, and they treat me by wrapping me up in bandages like a mummy. To be honest, though, it's the social challenges that are the hardest to bear: stares, comments, low expectations and ableism.

My parents couldn't get married in apartheid South Africa – my mother is mixed-race and my father is white – so they moved to Australia thirty-six years ago. I was born in Australia and raised in a very small farming town, where my mother and I were the only people who didn't look like everybody else. My primary school made no allowances for my condition – I'd have to sit watching sports even though it's dangerous for me to be exposed to the elements. I think that if, at the time, I'd identified with having a disability, then I wouldn't have had to just accommodate what the school could offer.

My mum said high school would be easier, but it wasn't at all. Kids can be pretty awful. I felt, because I didn't have many friends, that I wasn't a good friend; it took me a very long time to learn how to be a friend. My escape was in spending a lot of time writing and reading, when I was in the hospital or at home sick. But the best thing I did was work at Kmart for four years. My parents were really worried about putting me in the customers' sight, because of how they might treat me, but it was fantastic; I made so many friends and was treated professionally compared to how I was treated at school. I got to deal with customers who asked about my skin in a very professional way, which really set me up for life. I learned to just give them really polite, succinct answers, but be assertive at the same time. If someone was harassing me, I had an agreement

with the manager that I could say, 'I don't want to serve you,' and pass the person on. That experience was really empowering – I wish I'd started working earlier, in fact, because I think it would have given me a lot of confidence.

Through my writing and speaking I've taken my story out into the world. My appearance was something I'd always wanted to change when I was younger, but then – I'm not sure how – I came to accept that this is how it is; I'm quite happy with how I look.

I want the media to stop sensationalising disability. It's time people like me have our voices heard, instead of having to hear our stories told by others. So, I've used my story to help influence the media and the media representation of people who look different and who have disabilities. It's important that brands like Target and Kmart in Australia have been including people with disabilities in their catalogues. It's fantastic. We've got more diversity of race and culture on mainstream television now, which is great, but there's not so much diversity around disability. Seeing people with disabilities in mainstream media really matters – it shows that we're valued, and it shows that we're seen.

So, that's what matters to me, but also, being happy matters. I'm married now, which is really lovely – I never thought that would happen when I was at primary school.

Q. What brings you happiness?

My husband makes me happy. He's quite nice! While I'm lucky to have found love, though, getting married is not the most successful thing I've done. It's very important to have my own independence and my own success. Self-love is also really important – accepting yourself is very important in finding happiness.

Q. What do you regard as the lowest depth of misery?

Discrimination and ableism – they're so tiring.

And sometimes I get really upset about the level of pain I'm in. I project a pretty stoic or resilient image online, even though sometimes it's very hard and painful.

Looking outward, it's the constant lack of representation of people with disabilities anywhere that really annoys and frustrates me. For instance, at the moment – as women's marches are being planned around the world in response to Donald Trump's election – so many people with disabilities are talking about how they're not being included. Sometimes we're just an afterthought. But a lot of women are now coming to me asking, 'How can we include you better?' And I say, 'The march is four days away and you're asking now? You should have included people from the outset.'

It's also very hard when friends are being particularly discriminatory, ableist or just nasty around disability. Because they're a friend, when you call them on it they don't necessarily take you as seriously as if you'd written an article about it. I do sometimes feel a responsibility to educate, but it can be at the cost of relationships. So, losing friends because of standing up for what's important is quite hard. There are a lot of times when people have used the 'r' word, and, when I've told them that wasn't on, they've said something like, 'It doesn't matter, I work with special needs children.' I mean, please! That's no excuse.

Q. What would you change if you could?

I would create access to reliable, affordable health care for everybody. With the election of Donald Trump, people that I'm friends with in America – particularly those who have disabilities – are really scared about what might happen under the Health Care Act.

I would also hold companies accountable for the content posted on their online forums. I've had my picture misused online and the comments people make are just so cruel. If I wasn't so strong and didn't have a really strong support network, I might take that kind of bullying to heart. People kill themselves because of what they read in the comments sections. Online forum administrators have a much greater responsibility than just to put up cat memes.

Q. Which single word do you most identify with?

Resilience. You've just got to keep bouncing back and get on with it.

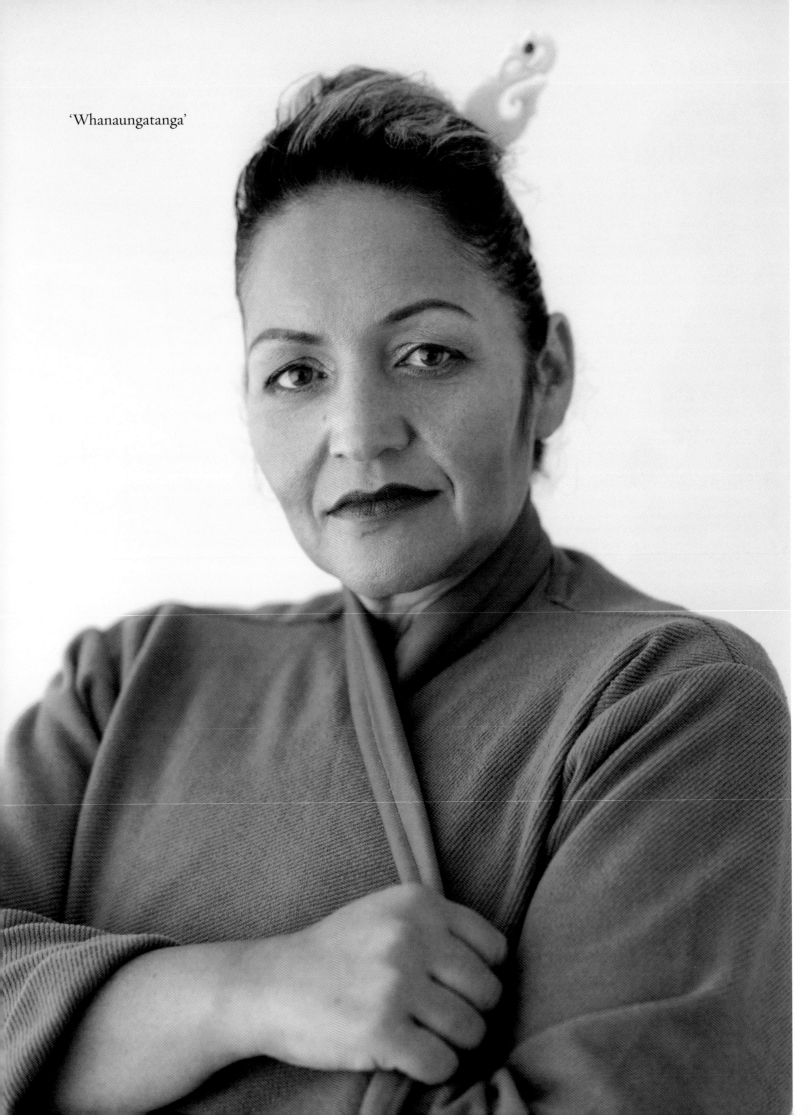

'Whanaungatanga'

Marama
Fox

Marama Fox was born in Hamilton, New Zealand. She has taught at Māori-language immersion schools aimed at fostering an understanding of Māori language, culture and wisdom, and in public secondary schools. Fox was an advisor to the Ministry of Education before being elected to the New Zealand Parliament in 2014; she is a representative and co-leader of the Māori Party.

Q. What really matters to you?

Our Māori children – I went into politics to help our nation remember how to love our children.

It is time to correct the disparity that exists between Māori and Pākehā – between indigenous New Zealanders and those descended from European settlers. People have to listen to the realities of what it means to be Māori, so that we can develop and implement better policies that help our children realise their aspirations. I want our children to know how great they are – to stand up and embrace the greatness of their ancestors and their achievements. So, I am paving the way for my children's generation to take back their narrative.

For a long time, I myself held negative perceptions of my people and thought I had a great Western education; I learned about Elizabeth I and about the wonderful settlers who colonised New Zealand. I had intended to go to university, but I had a baby instead. It was when I took my son to *kōhanga reo* that I was exposed to a Māori world view. Kōhanga reo is a Māori language nest – a pre-school – hosted by our elders in an effort to revive our language. They invite mothers to bring their children along to be spoken to in *te reo* Māori and to be schooled in the knowledge of our people. It felt like someone had taken off the top of my head with a can opener and had started pouring in all this knowledge. Oh, my gosh, my brain!

I couldn't believe that I hadn't been raised with this knowledge. I had grown up feeling that I should be content with the disparity between my people and Pākehā. But, learning of my mother's *whakapapa*, or genealogy, I realised I was born of greatness. My people had navigated their way to Aotearoa – New Zealand – across the oceans by reading the stars, while Europeans still believed the world was flat. The more I learned, the more I started to question: How did Māori go from being the epitome of health to having a life expectancy ten years lower than that of Pākehā? And why didn't we own our land anymore?

In 1840, we signed the Treaty of Waitangi. Māori people were assured of certain rights over their land and agreed to live in unity with the colonisers, but we have suffered because, for 177 years, the New Zealand government has ignored us. There have been laws that said our children could only be taught labouring, cooking, cleaning and nursemaiding – this was all we were deemed competent to do.

There have been laws preventing our children from speaking their own language in schools because, when faced with the decision of whether to exterminate us or to 'civilise' us, it was decided that we were to be civilised – and this would need to be done through a language more conducive to human thought. Excuse me? Our language is not good enough for academic rigour, and yet, we traversed the oceans and forged an existence here before anyone else!

I joined the Māori Party to be a voice for our people. There's an old First Nations saying, 'Left wing, right wing – same bird.' These days, I say, 'Red undies, blue undies – same skid marks.' We Māori are still bearing the skid marks of colonisation and of the resultant cultural genocide. They stripped away our faith in ourselves – our hope – by telling us our language was not good enough and that we were not good enough to benefit from Western knowledge. I don't think people understand what that kind of systemic abuse does to a people: to be told generation after generation that we're not good enough.

And what does it do to the other side who are told they deserve their place in the world while everyone else has to fight for theirs – that they are superior and are entitled to their privilege. I'm new to this struggle, but we have never stopped fighting: I follow phenomenal women like Whina Cooper, Eva Rickard, Donna Huata, Tariana Turia.

My goal is equitable outcomes, which is more important than equal opportunity. The statistics that exist in relation to sexual abuse, child abuse, domestic violence and suicide rates are unacceptable. When a nine-year-old chooses to take their own life instead of living their reality, that is wrong.

Children who go through the system – and 63 per cent of these kids are Māori – are immediately at the bottom of every disparaging statistic in this country; they are more likely to be incarcerated, more likely to be abused, more likely to leave school without an education and more likely to die earlier. And the present-day incarceration of our people is another stolen generation. It is unacceptable. The system is wrong, and yet it is deemed a 'Māori problem' – but it is not. Our whole nation is responsible for our children. We have to change the way we do things.

Q. What brings you happiness?

I find my happiness in mayhem. My nine children have all just moved home with my husband and me; four of my sons are married, so their wives have joined them. There are six *mokopuna* – grandchildren – the youngest is a newborn. It is mayhem, and it is the most perfect bliss I've ever experienced. My peace and my happiness are right there, sitting in the middle of that – the kids running around, clambering all over me; everybody cooking, debating, arguing, playing, laughing and singing.

Q. What do you regard as the lowest depth of misery?

I live in a society in which we have some of the highest suicide statistics in the world, especially for Māori. Our young people can't see hope in their futures and so choose to take their own lives – that is the pit of misery. How can it be that these people aren't empowered to reach out for help, to deal with their emotions, to find resilience and hope?

Q. What would you change if you could?

I want our people to reconnect with our *tūrangawaewae* – the place where we have the right to stand. We have to build a society that values this again, that pulls people together to assist one another in fulfilling their dreams and shows them a brightness of hope for our future.

Q. Which single word do you most identify with?

Whanaungatanga. This embodies everything about being a family and our interconnectedness. It is the idea that each of us needs each other and that there is none greater or lesser than another.

Mariam
Shaar

———

Mariam Shaar was born in the Bourj El Barajneh refugee camp, Lebanon, where she now lives, to Palestinian parents. She has been a social worker for almost twenty years, and runs the Bourj El Barajneh Center of the Women's Program Association, an organisation that provides education, vocational-skills training and microloans to women in eight out of the twelve Palestinian refugee camps in Lebanon. In 2013, with seed funding from Alfanar, a venture philanthropy, she founded Soufra, a catering business that employs women from Bourj El Barajneh camp.

'Hope makes me happy – I'm always hoping for a better life.'

———

Q. What really matters to you?

Working is the most important thing in my life. I started out as a kindergarten teacher and then went on to work specifically with women through the Women's Program Association (WPA). Our goal is to develop women's skills and assist them to live independently. We have worked on various initiatives to empower women in our immediate surroundings – the refugee camp – and we intervene to provide support for economic empowerment of women and youth. We now operate in nine refugee camps in Lebanon – it is so gratifying to know that our influence is expanding.

One of our current ventures, Soufra, was born out of a study conducted on the needs of women refugees living in Lebanon. One of the results of the study was that women lacked suitable employment for their circumstances. We had been running cooking-skills lessons at the WPA and saw the potential for these lessons to develop into a business. We found a partner in Alfanar – a venture philanthropy organisation that invests in, and provides coaching and training for, social enterprises in the Arab world. With their support, Soufra became a reality. At the start, it was a small catering business, but it has since grown to the point that we are delivering healthy food to schools outside the camp. We realised that the idea of a food truck was perfect for us;

we created history by becoming the first women-refugee-led organisation to apply for a commercial food-truck license in Lebanon. The idea of women cooking and delivering food outside the camp is a very strange idea in Arab society – especially in Palestinian society – and I was actually quite afraid when we first started. But we were committed to the success of the project, and now we have more than thirty part-time workers. Now, we're not only providing new economic opportunities for the women of Bourj El Barajneh, but the project is also a platform for our workers to share their Palestinian culinary heritage with the world. The process of setting Soufra up has been beyond what we could have conceived when we started out – it involved, among many other things, incorporating a company outside of the camp and getting partners – but here we are!

Q. What brings you happiness?

Hope makes me happy – I'm always hoping for a better life.

I feel happy when I see how we can succeed in our work, and when we launch new projects that interest us and engage the people around us. This fills me with excitement and gives me hope that tomorrow will be better.

Palestinians have many difficulties travelling, so the opportunities to travel and see other countries that I have had

through my work with Alfanar have made me very happy.

Q. What do you regard as the lowest depth of misery?

Being outside your country of origin and being unable to return – that makes me sad, and I believe all Palestinians feel this way. To be classified as a 'refugee' is not something that I am comfortable with – I don't like that word or what it means in practice. But what makes me sadder still is the life that each of us lives in the camps – this is not a humane existence. We live in very bad conditions.

Q. What would you change if you could?

War *must* not be allowed to happen. We have experienced war from within, so we know what people in other countries are experiencing in conflict. I would not let any situation deteriorate to the point where war is the only answer.

If I had the power, I would give every person on earth the opportunity to study.

And I would change the laws to provide for better services that improve the conditions for all Palestinians living in Lebanon.

Q. Which single word do you most identify with?

Persistence. I struggled to choose between 'persistence' and 'hope,' but maybe these are the same thing. In the end, I chose persistence, because that describes my personality.

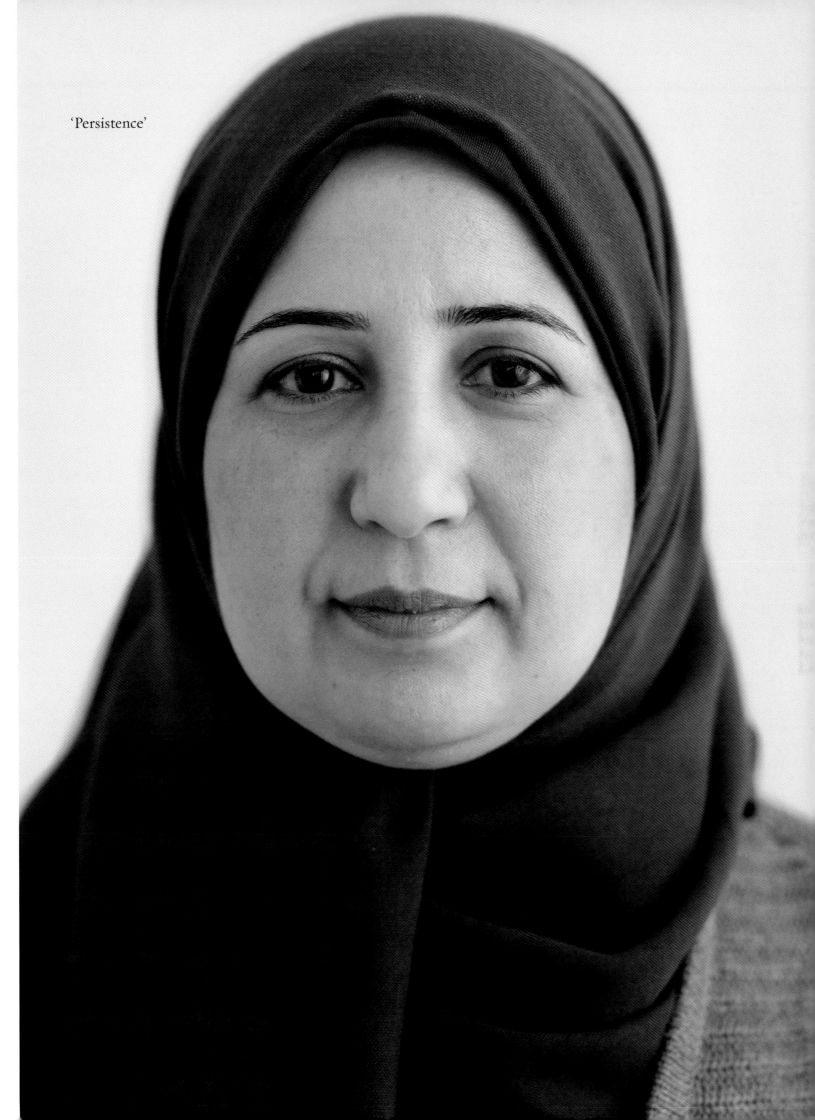

'Persistence'

Alfre
Woodard

———

'I believe in possibility, so I don't despair. Thankfully, I've got a place like storytelling to put my swings between ecstasy and misery.'

———

Alfre Woodard was born in Tulsa in Oklahoma, USA. A multiple-award-winning actor and activist, she is a founder of Artists for a New South Africa, an organisation dedicated to ending apartheid, advancing democracy and equality, and fighting HIV/AIDS. In 2009, Woodard was appointed by Barack Obama to serve on the President's Committee on the Arts and Humanities.

Q. What really matters to you?

The most important thing to me in my life is my children, Mavis and Duncan. My job as a parent has been to love them, feed them and really look at them – even when they were tiny – to see who they are. Because I believe you come here who you're going to be. You don't turn into Picasso at twenty-one; Picasso was probably making those ladies with the eyes on the side of their heads when he was five or six years old; you don't want to be that person going, 'Pablo! You've got to put those eyes on the front – she's not pretty!' Rather, you look to see who a child is and then you watch them unfold; that's the privilege. You help them navigate until they learn the language, the way you do with any friend who doesn't speak the language – when you're translating for somebody, you don't change what they're saying. When I became a parent, I developed a deeper love, a deeper honesty; it was humbling. And it deepened my work as an artist.

The thing that means the most to me is that my son and my daughter have freedom of thought, that they understand their true power is their ability to think their own thoughts. There's nothing greater to give them than the understanding that nobody can contain or control their minds. The great gift that Madiba (Nelson Mandela) gave us is the truth that, no matter what the circumstances, the thing you are absolutely master or mistress of is how you respond to those circumstances. That's what I would like for my children.

And there are also sensibilities that were passed down to me from my parents that matter to me. Both of them were rural people. Everybody was from Texas originally, but my father's family ran for land in the Oklahoma Land Run when Oklahoma became a state in 1889. When my father was growing up, guys would come through their property, hat in hand, but when people called them hobos, his mother would say, 'That's not a hobo. That's somebody's daddy. That's somebody's brother.' Both of my parents talked all the time about how the land is a great equaliser; it doesn't care who you are. You plant, and it's the luck of the draw whether or not your crop comes in well. My father also talked a lot at our table about how, if somebody's crop didn't come in – no matter who it was – it was your responsibility and privilege to make sure that that family ate that year. And not whatever was left over, but the same things that you were eating at your table. Because it could have been you.

Back during segregation, everybody lived together in a vibrant black community: the people of means, the people who did not have means, preachers, strippers, lawyers, doctors, teachers and bus drivers. I remember when I discovered that some kids in my school were hungry and that others didn't have floors in their houses – they had dirt floors and my house was filled with antiques. I remember the first time I sensed some of those kids' shame. It made me uncomfortable, because I felt their shame – in my body, in my heart and

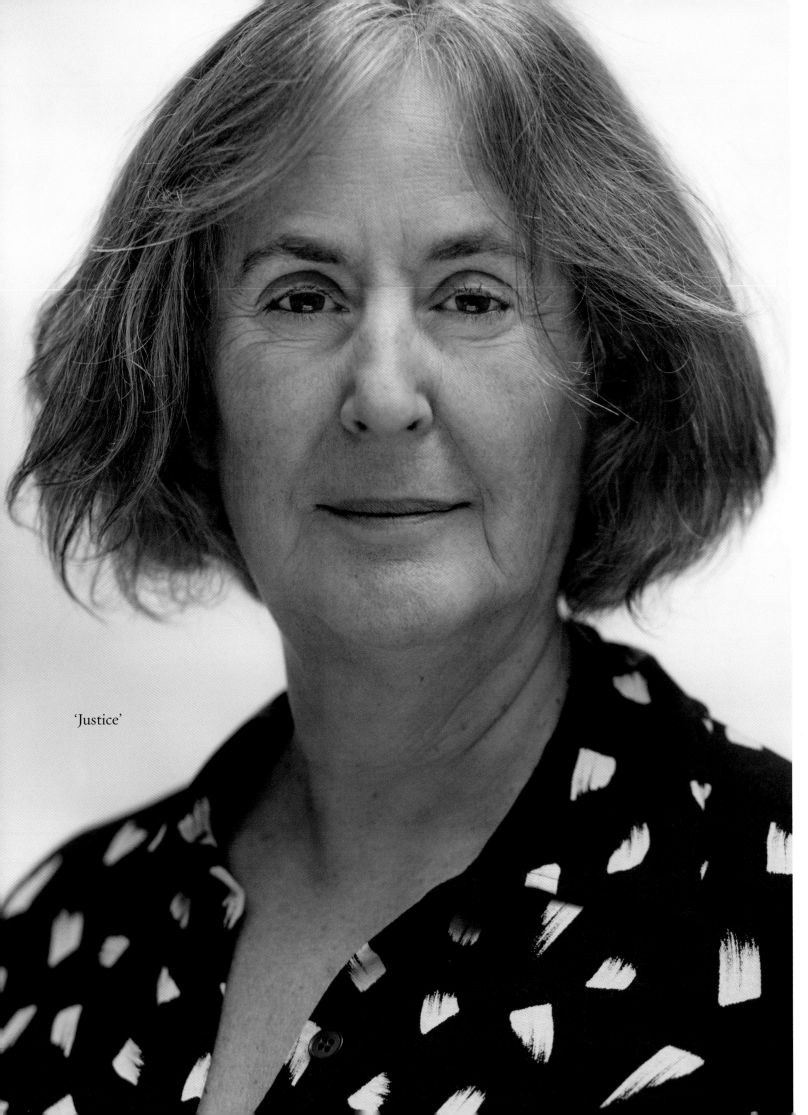

'Justice'

Alfre Woodard

'When I became a parent, I developed a deeper love, a deeper honesty; it was humbling. And it deepened my work as an artist.'

in my mind. I felt that their shame was my shame. It stunned me when I realised that my friends, who I thought were like me, looked down on those other people – I felt embarrassed at the lack of awareness.

My activism started when I was at high school. When the assassinations started – John Kennedy, Medgar Evers, Malcolm X, Martin Luther King, Bobby Kennedy – I felt that if you got killed for it, it must have been really important. Standing with people who would pay with their lives got to be more of a reality I wanted to live in than what kind of car I was driving, what designer clothes I was wearing or anything else that seemed so important to other girls my age. And all the while, at Bishop Kelley catholic school, I was being taught what I perceived as the walk of the radical Jesus; if you believed any of the things that you were reading and hearing about in your spiritual walk, you knew what you had to do. At the same time, Brother Patrick O'Brien, a film buff, would shut down the high school and take the entire school to see a film that he wanted us to see. We saw *Citizen Kane, Sundays and Cybele, An Occurrence at Owl Creek Bridge, The Red Badge of Courage, The Red Balloon, The Loneliness of the Long Distance Runner* – all these films that people would normally see in film school. It was there, sitting in the dark and sucking on Twizzlers, that I realised how powerful film was. Me at fifteen, sitting there weeping about this

French father and his little girl, I thought, 'That's what I want to do. We can change everything if we commandeer the moving image.' So, that's when I decided I wanted to be involved in film – to be an actor.

Q. What brings you happiness?
I am happiest when I am with my children and my husband on holiday: no distractions, just sitting around shooting the breeze. My family is very irreverent and we laugh a lot. Our kids respect us, but they're not afraid of us, so they are good company. We've never said, 'Because I said so!' or, 'I've got the purse strings!' so they're not being anything other than themselves and they're not trying to please us.

I do enjoy being around my comrades – my fellow artists. I feel that we're in the human business; we're recreating a human action. We're bringing people to life and telling the stories of how they intersect. This is my way of paying rent in the world. Since we first stood up on two legs around a fire, there have been those who told the stories and kept the lore, who held up the mirror; it increased the well-being of the tribe. Now, we're recognising that we are a global tribe. I'm making a product, and I want to know where it's landing. I've got to be concerned about that family sitting there in front of the TV. Do they have health care? Is anybody hungry? Will that girl be bullied at school? Will she be touched by the neighbour? I think an artist

has to understand that. We can name it activism, but, to me, we're in the people business – and it's part of a whole.

Q. What do you regard as the lowest depth of misery?
I believe in possibility, so I don't despair. Thankfully, I've got a place like storytelling to put my swings between ecstasy and misery. And I'm a real God person: I'm not talking about an anthropomorphic God with human emotions, but a scientific principle in which all the scientific laws are included. I believe in that ultimate principle – in God – so I can never despair. And I don't despair in terms of the world, because we're in it and everything is always possible.

Q. What would you change if you could?
If I could do anything, I would give everybody the gift of discernment. I recall the story of King Solomon: When God asked him what he wanted, instead of asking for riches or position, he said, 'God, give me a discerning heart, that I can judge your people.' If we all had discernment as naturally as we took breath, then we'd make good decisions – that would solve mostly everything.

Q. Which single word do you most identify with?
Joy. I use it more in my mind than any other word in the day. I feel it, I look for it. Joy is deep, and the lessons are included in it – the understanding and the appreciation.

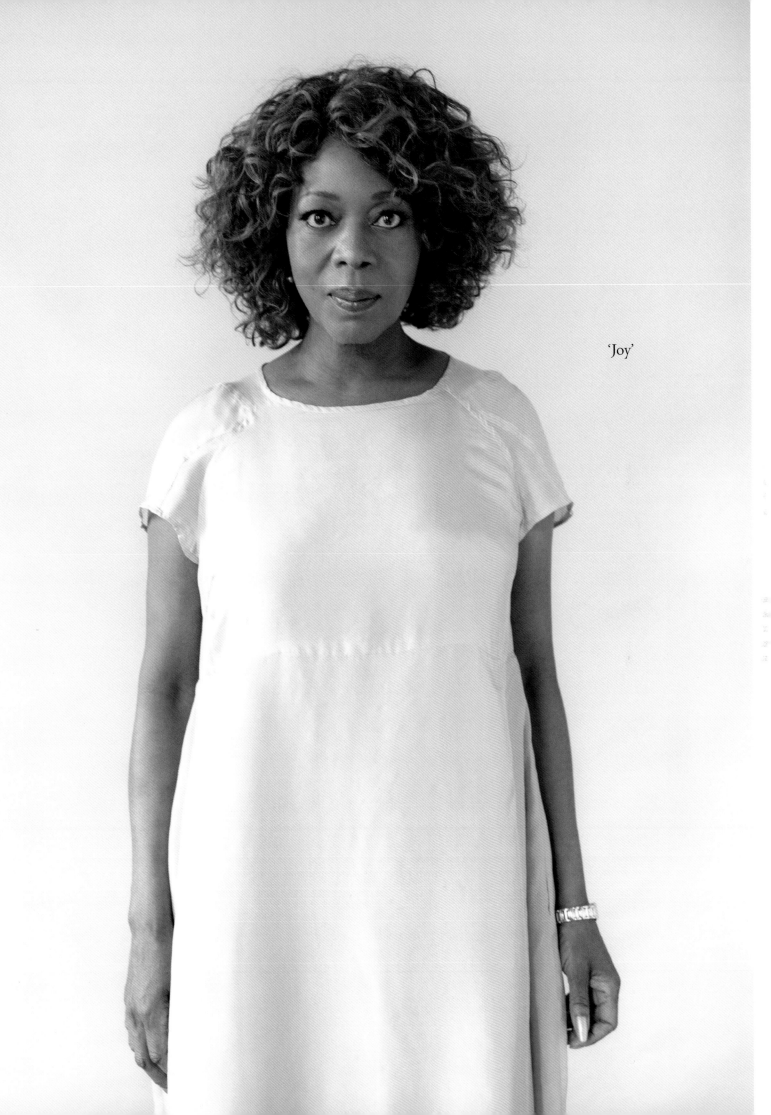

'Joy'

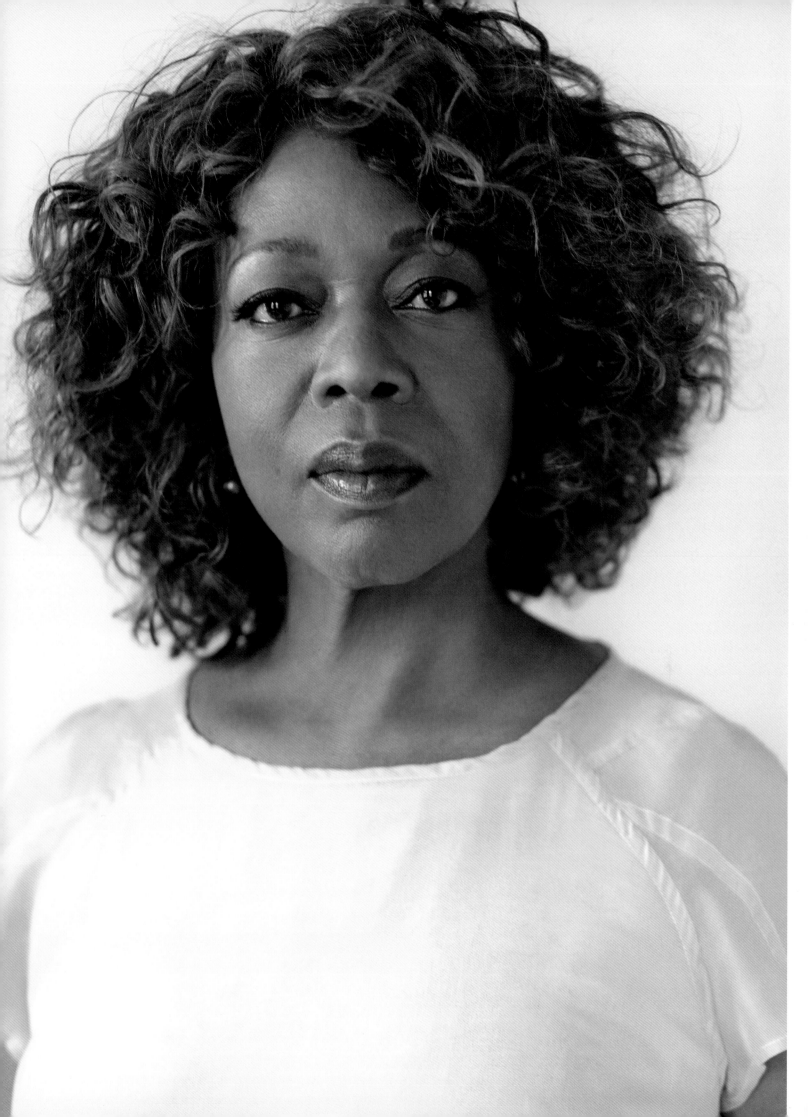

Gillian Slovo

Gillian Slovo was born in Johannesburg, South Africa, and now lives in London. She is a novelist and playwright, and her verbatim plays include the 2017 drama *Another World* – a look at why Western youth would join Islamic State. Her fourteen published books include *Ice Road*, which was shortlisted for the Orange Prize for Fiction; *Red Dust*, which is set around a hearing of South Africa's Truth and Reconciliation Commission and was made into a film starring Hilary Swank and Chiwetel Ejiofor; and her family memoir, *Every Secret Thing,* which tells the story of life with her parents, South African activists Joe Slovo and Ruth First.

'I don't forgive the men who confessed to killing my mother.'

Q. What really matters to you?

My life has, in many ways, been shaped by my childhood. I spent the first twelve years of my life in South Africa. My parents were part of a small band of white South Africans who decided that they couldn't close their eyes to what was happening around them and who joined with other South Africans to fight apartheid. I had the difficulty of growing up in a family in which almost everything my parents did was illegal. I remember there always being a sense of the real danger that my parents could disappear at any time and not return. The other side of that was, of course, the privilege that my parents' circle included the greats of South Africa – Nelson Mandela, Oliver Tambo, Walter Sisulu. They were a generation of political activists who really believed in human beings. They dotted my childhood and some of them later my adulthood; the contacts with people like them are among the most significant events in my life.

What matters to me is both the micro and the macro. The micro is my family and my friends. The macro is wishing for justice and equality for everybody; I live in a world where this is absolutely not the case. I'm not just talking about South Africa – where the differences between rich and poor are so acute that they're in your face all the time – but also of Britain and the rest of the world. What matters to me is something that seems to be unachievable at this moment: that people should have better conditions in their lives, whether it be that they're allowed to live without war or whether it be that they're allowed to live

with food on the table. Gender equality is part of that; where you have gender inequality you will never have peace.

Q. What brings you happiness?

I find happiness in relationships. I find it with my family and with my friends. I sometimes find it in my work, and I find it walking in the landscape.

Q. What do you regard as the lowest depth of misery?

There are so many things to choose from. What's happened with the corruption in the African National Congress (ANC) in South Africa upsets me. It's an organisation that, in a way, is my family – so it's terrible when your family lets you down like that. In fact, they're not the ANC that made the change in 1994, but a distortion of what it once was. They're a pale reflection of the people my parents fought with.

The prevailing state of inequality in South Africa gnaws away at me – it's just so apparent when you go there. This is not what my parents fought for. My father, who was Mandela's first minister of housing, always said during the time of the negotiations, 'If you think that it was difficult for us to bring about this change – to have made a revolution – just wait until you see what's going to happen when we get into government. It's going to be much more difficult.' My parents were always realists, and I think my father has been proved right. I don't know how you approach trying to turn a country like this around, when the education that is given to most people is so unfit for the modern world and where the inequalities are so extreme.

People forget that the Truth and Reconciliation Commission set up after apartheid was a political compromise as much as anything else. I do believe that it was an appropriate compromise in the interests of peace, but forgiveness is not something you can force on individuals. I don't forgive the men who confessed to killing my mother, but, although I would like to see them jailed, I know my mother would not have wanted justice for her to be exchanged for peace in South Africa. Reconciliation is about a whole society, not about us forgiving individual murderers and torturers. I still believe that the miracle of South Africa resides in its people.

The way asylum seekers and refugees are continually being treated in this world we live in, and the horror of what's happening in Syria, also upset me. The world is witnessing the decimation of a people – the use of awful weapons against ordinary people – and nobody stops it.

Q. What would you change if you could?

My answer to that changes every day, but I suppose I would try and change people's feeling that those who are different from them are taking things away from them. I would like people to understand that just because you're not born in the same street, in the same city, and don't have the same colour of skin, does not make you any less human.

Q. Which single word do you most identify with?

Justice. That's how I was brought up and it runs through my life – a need for justice.

Jessica Gallagher

Jessica Gallagher was born in Geelong, Australia. At the age of seventeen, she was diagnosed with cone dystrophy, a rare eye disease, and was classified as legally blind. Gallagher went on to represent Australia as a Paralympic alpine skier, track-and-field athlete, and tandem cyclist. She won alpine-skiing bronze medals at both the 2010 Vancouver and 2014 Sochi Winter Paralympics, and at the 2016 Rio Paralympics became the first Australian to medal at both summer and winter games when she won a track-cycling bronze medal. Gallagher is an osteopath, and global ambassador and board director for Vision 2020 Australia.

Q. What really matters to you?

Being happy and living in the moment; I know that if I'm doing the things that I love, then my life will take care of itself and opportunities will present themselves. And spending as much time as possible with the people that I love matters.

In relation to sport and my career, what matters is surrounding myself with good people who really make it all worthwhile. Standing on top of the podium for Australia is an incredibly special moment, but there's a whole tribe of people who are involved in that process. So, although I participate in individual sports, you get to share it with so many others – it's those relationships with people that really matter the most to me.

Q. What brings you happiness?

When I was younger, I had the ability to experience life with full vision, but, when I was seventeen, I was diagnosed with a rare, degenerative eye disease. That has been one of my biggest challenges. I'm now legally blind, so I find pure happiness in the simple things: in the fact that I haven't completely lost my sight, in the fact that I can have time with my family and friends, that I have a roof over my head and that I have the opportunity to do the things that I love, which are my greatest happiness. I'm very fortunate that, despite the challenges I've faced, I still have the ability to choose the life that I've always dreamed about. Being able to have that perspective is really important, and it means that moments as simple as walking down the street on a nice sunny day to get a coffee with a friend make me really happy, although they are essentially simple.

My brother and I grew up with a single mum, who worked really hard to provide for us. I idolised her; the challenges she went through gave me the skills I have today – especially the resilience, persistence and courage to move forwards. I think the uncertainty of my diagnosis hit my family harder than it did me – they experienced a lot of pain coming to terms with the fact that I had this life-changing condition. We didn't know anybody who had a disability, let alone low vision.

For me, it was a matter of accepting that I couldn't change my situation. Yes, it threw up the uncertain question of what my life would look like, but at the age of seventeen you're trying to figure that out anyway! It was about trying to accept and acknowledge that there were things I was never going to be able to do, and using the strengths and the skills that I did have to create my own path, regardless of the fact that I had low vision. I look at life as a series of moments, and, in any given moment, I get a choice of how I want to perceive a situation. I'm always trying to take away the positives from a situation, but I know that if the outcome is negative I'll be able to learn from it.

On my journey, I've learned that knowledge is power, so I love that I can now give back to young children who are recently diagnosed with, or were born with, low vision or blindness. I'm able to share my experiences and the fact that I have been able to overcome all of the challenges I've faced. I love that I can pass my knowledge on to others – to help them learn – but I find it incredibly humbling when my story helps someone find inspiration. It can be really empowering for people to receive advice from someone in similar circumstances, because it helps them move past the challenges they're facing.

Q. What do you regard as the lowest depth of misery?

It really breaks my heart that so much of our global blindness is preventable and avoidable, but is not avoided because people can't afford to see an optometrist or get a pair of glasses that may only cost ten dollars. That level of inequality, whereby so many people in this world don't have the ability to live the life that they've dreamed about, is misery, and is why I'm so passionate about things like eye health.

Q. What would you change if you could?

I would create equality of opportunity. I would give people the ability to live a good life, be free and safe, have a roof over their heads and afford food – just those simple, basic things that the majority of us take for granted. The helplessness and inability of people to choose the directions of their lives really saddens me.

Q. Which single word do you most identify with?

The one word I would identify with is trust; it's the very essence of my life as a vision-impaired Paralympian. When I'm ski racing, I ski with a guide at over one hundred kilometres an hour. We wear headsets, and I have to trust that he gives me the right communication. It's the same when I'm on a tandem bike: I have to trust that the person steering the bike knows where they're going and what they're doing. If you can truly trust people, then authenticity and honesty come easily – through these, you are able to develop deep relationships with people.

Trust, for me, even lies in approaching a stranger for help in something as simple as walking down a street when you can't read signs or see steps. It takes a lot of courage, because you have to trust a complete stranger. I gain a real sense of optimism every time I ask for help, because I've never had an experience in which my requests for help have been refused. Whenever I'm struggling, there's always someone willing to help. It's a special moment, and suddenly you're bonded with a complete stranger. It may only last a moment, but it gives me such optimism.

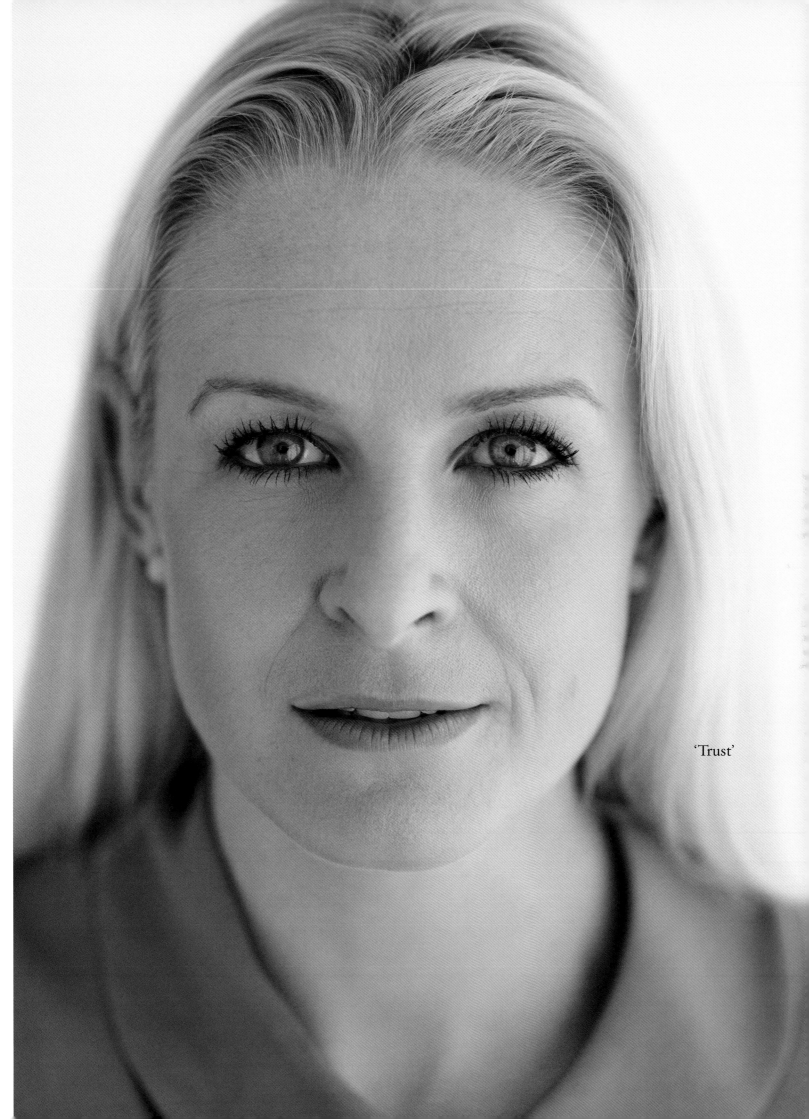

'Trust'

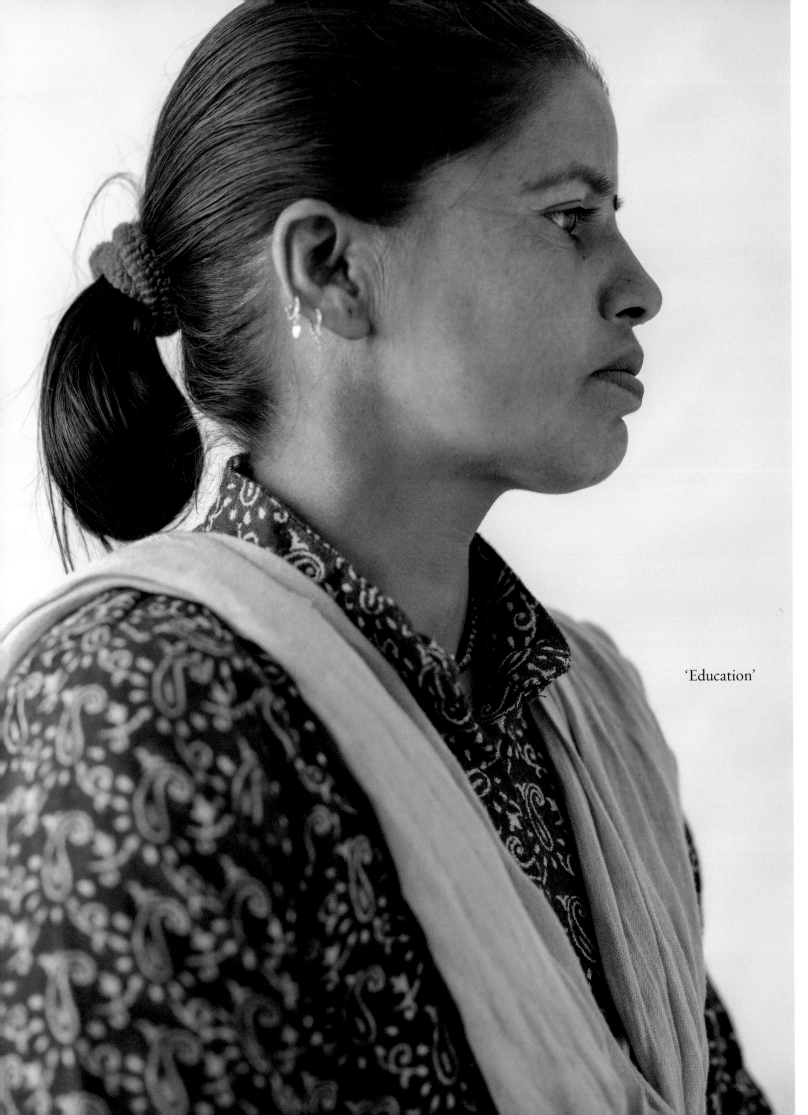

'Education'

Ambika Lamsal

Ambika Lamsal was born in Patlekhet, Nepal, into the Ghimire caste. Upon her marriage, at the age of thirteen, she became a member of the Lamsal caste – taking the last name Lamsal – and moved to Panchkhal, in central Nepal. She was widowed at age seventeen and became the sole caregiver for her two daughters. Since her widowhood – which carries with it strict cultural practices in Nepal – Lamsal has worked as a labourer in order to provide for and educate her daughters.

'I never used to focus on whether my life was happy or sad, I just focussed on survival.'

Q. What really matters to you?

My two daughters are more important to me than anything else; I don't care about my own life or my own future – only about them. I was married at the age of thirteen and had two children by the time I was seventeen. One month after my second daughter was born – when my eldest was two – my husband died. I'm told my mother died when I was five, although I know nothing about her, and my father died the year I married. So, I was left to raise my children alone. After my husband died, his family did not look after us – they did not want to support a young girl with two children.

I never used to focus on whether my life was happy or sad, I just focussed on survival. And I did not imagine I would come this far raising my girls. I am the only one who earns money for us to survive. I only have a small piece of land; I farm it myself, but it is not enough to feed my family, so my only option was to become a labourer, working in other people's fields. It is hard work and my health is bad, so I'm not able to do heavy lifting. But, I have been able to keep the household going. Our house is not luxurious and is in a bad condition. We have a tin roof that is not fixed down, and every time it rains my eldest cries because she fears the wind will blow the roof away.

In Nepal, the man is a very important figure in the family. I was always worried that, with my husband gone, my daughters would not be able to study and would not have enough food, and that people would judge them. I didn't want anyone pitying them, and I used to worry so much. Now, they are both receiving an education; my eldest studies at the Bhakunde government school and my youngest was chosen to attend a private school, where she has been doing very well. My eldest's studies have sometimes suffered because she has been ill and had a few operations, and because, when I fall sick, the burden of running the household falls on her shoulders. Because I am the only earner, I worry about what will happen to my daughters if something bad happens to me. I know they won't be able to focus on their studies – especially my eldest, who will be in charge. Overall, though, I feel my children's futures will go well because of their education. I was never educated, but now there is hope for them and my worries are less great.

Q. What brings you happiness?

My greatest happiness is the same as what matters to me – my happiness is my daughters. I know that their studies are the most important thing – that these will allow them to develop themselves – so I am happy when I know they have enough time to study, and when they have the textbooks and exercise books they need. When I see them working hard, when they score good marks and have everything they need – and when I am able to earn money and buy food for my family – I feel happy.

Q. What do you regard as the lowest depth of misery?

There is one incident that took place in my life which was the unhappiest of all – it was when I lost my life partner. I will never forget him, but this incident came and went – in life, happiness and sadness come and go. Although there are many other things in my life that make me sad, overall, I have been able to be independent and that makes me feel happy.

Q. What would you change if you could?

Everyone faces challenges, and, if you can push through the sadness, you will achieve satisfaction. So, I would not take away challenges.

Do we need more property? No. Why would we need more? Yes, people *want* more and more, but tomorrow they will be gone and everything they have will be left behind.

People just need enough to survive, so I would want to make sure that everyone has enough to eat and that everyone has a home where they can live safely and happily – that's the change I would love to see.

Q. Which single word do you most identify with?

Education, of course: it is the most important word there is. If I had had the opportunity to study, I would not need anyone's help; I might have become a teacher or gone to work in a government post. That is the kind of future I want for my daughters, one in which they can earn good money and be completely self-dependent.

Karen Mattison

Karen Mattison MBE was born in Liverpool, England. She began her career in the public and charity sectors, but realised after having children that career progression in part-time roles was significantly limited. In response to this, she first co-founded Women Like Us, to support women with children to find quality part-time and flexible work. She then co-founded Timewise, which is dedicated to unlocking the flexible jobs market in the United Kingdom. Mattison was made a Member of the Order of the British Empire in 2010.

Q. What really matters to you?

Now that I'm about to hit fifty, what matters is my family, my community, my friendships and my work. The thing that drives me is social justice and fairness; it drives my work and it defines me as a parent in terms of what I want to pass on to my kids.

Q. What brings you happiness?

The thing that I love doing, and in the end have made a career out of, is connecting people. I think it's an incredible thing to do. When you put two people together – whether it's someone who needs a great dentist or somebody looking for a job – that's where real magic happens.

Q. What do you regard as the lowest depth of misery?

For me, it's when people lose hope of the possibility of change. On an individual level, that's why people become depressed: they don't believe that anything they can do can influence the course of their lives. Misery is when you don't believe you have the power to change the things that are wrong in your life.

Q. What would you change if you could?

The single thing I would change would be how we think about work; I would give everybody the flexibility that they needed in their lives without losing their value in the workplace. On one level, it's just a job. But it's also one's economic empowerment, one's ability to be free. For a woman in this world, economic independence is vital. The workplace has been designed for men and based on a world that doesn't really exist anymore – a world in which the wife stays home to raise the kids and the husband is free to commit himself to work. So when I first returned to work from maternity leave, the only other mother in the organisation advised me not to talk about my children, to just say they were fine and not elaborate when people asked, because otherwise I'd just be thought of as 'the mum.'

I was very fortunate in that I didn't experience gender discrimination growing up. My mother worked and I grew up expecting to be able to do what she told me was possible, which was to have a family and be able to progress my career – but it didn't really work out like that. When I had my first two children, I effectively hit a brick wall; I was working part-time in a senior job and, when I wanted to move up the career ladder, I was told that it wouldn't be possible. I was told that I couldn't have it all and that I should be grateful for the role I had; if I couldn't accept that, then I should stop working for a few years and return to the working world when I was ready to be serious.

My first response was to internalise this, which is what I think most women do. I thought, 'Okay, right. So I don't fit into this world of work anymore; the problem is me and I'll need to think about what I can do differently.' But as I became more politicised about this issue, I realised that there are hundreds of thousands of women at all levels of the job market who are skilled, experienced and who have ambition, but who are given this impossible choice between their career progression and their families; most of them then leave the job market altogether. Not only are we women staring at a glass ceiling, but there's the sticky floor of a lack of flexibility in our careers as we progress – together, it's the ceiling *and* the floor that are keeping women down.

My former colleague, Emma Stewart, had the same experience I did, so together we launched two businesses to fix the problem in the market. First was Women Like Us, a social business focussed on helping women with children, who had either stopped working or were trapped in low-paid part-time work. Women Like Us was established to offer support, coaching and advice, and a route to better-paid part-time work. We also focussed on confidence, because – particularly when you've left the job market – you experience a huge drop in self-belief. It takes a lot to return to work and feel as though you belong there, and that you deserve it;

I don't think you can overstate how important confidence is, so – to avoid them leaving altogether – women need to be supported in finding flexible work.

Secondly, in 2012, we launched Timewise to fix the wider market problem, which is that, despite the fact that over half the population in the United Kingdom wants to work flexibly or part time, the job market is completely blocked for them – only a tiny number of skilled jobs that are advertised have flexible working options. We run a job-site with eighty thousand candidates on it, offer support to businesses and campaign for a better flexible jobs market.

Whatever a person's reasons for seeking flexibility, there's a stigmatisation – and, for men, a feminisation – towards part-time work. But I believe that if we shared work better, then we'd have more people working less. There are many people making this work; in the United Kingdom there are almost eight hundred thousand people working in high-tax-bracket, part-time jobs. However, when I was looking for these kinds of role models, I couldn't find them; these people stay under the radar to avoid stigma. But I believe in the power of storytelling and in my opinion these are the kinds of people who can help formulate a vision for what a different kind of workplace would look like.

That's the utopia – a significant step towards equality. It would be absolutely transformative if we could change the way we design jobs to allow people the space to nurture their children or older relatives, or to find fulfilment in other aspects of their lives in order to keep healthy mentally and physically. And I think it's possible, if employers can focus on output and how best to facilitate it, rather than on how many hours their employees are at their desks.

Q. Which single word do you most identify with?

Possibility.

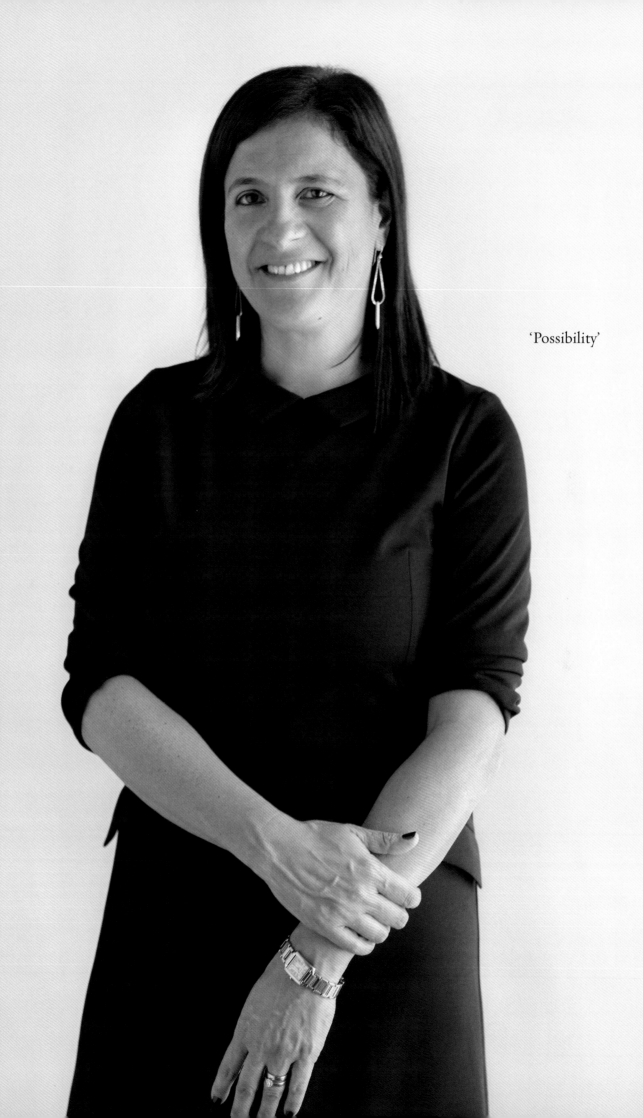

'Possibility'

Maggie
Beer

Maggie Beer AM was born in Sydney, Australia. In 1979, Beer and her husband, Colin, established the highly acclaimed The Pheasant Farm restaurant in the Barossa Valley, which operated until 1993. Beer is the award-winning author of nine cookbooks and, in 2014, established the Maggie Beer Foundation to improve the quality of food for those in aged care. In 2012, Beer was made a Member of the Order of Australia for service to the tourism and hospitality industries as a cook, restaurateur and author, and to the promotion of Australian produce and cuisine.

Q. What really matters to you?

What matters to me is emotional connection: to my family, to my community, to my country and to the people who work with me. And the sense of belonging I've been given, by the Barossa Valley, by Colin and by my family. The other things that matter to me are being surrounded by positive people, being challenged mentally and physically, living in a beautiful environment, music in my life, the joy of friends and the table.

Food is the centre of my plate; music, community and environment all gather around that. My food is beautiful and simple, but everything about it is important, from the way it's farmed to its stage of ripeness to how much you do with it. Food and bringing people together around the table were very much a part of my early life. My great influences were family and food; even in the depths of having no money we always ate well. My father was passionate about produce; he was the one who had all the food ideas – for instance, he was way ahead of his time in terms of things like aging beef. But my mum did all the work – everything we made, we made from scratch. She taught me how to choose a ripe pumpkin and how to choose the freshest fish. We ate oysters from the rocks and fish we caught ourselves.

In some bizarre way, my very difficult upbringing has helped me enormously in life – it gave me great grit. When I was fourteen my parents lost everything and I left school to support the family. My elder brother left school at the same time and our paltry wages – my wage was five pounds a week, his was seven pounds –

kept the family going and a very beloved aunt rented a house for us. It taught me at an early age that you can do anything. I didn't think about our circumstances a lot – I just *did*.

The way I've felt about leaving school so early has changed over the years. I was offered scholarships to stay at school and, at the time, I certainly felt that I'd missed out on the chance of a better education. But today I can recall, without rancour, my father's comment to the school: 'But she's only a woman – she'll just be a secretary and get married.' This was totally at odds with someone who did believe in me, but his opinion was of the times – that's why I can think of it now without any rancour at all. Yet, for a long time – particularly after my children were born – I felt I had missed out. But now – many years after the fact, at the age of seventy-two – I can say that I realise it did me a great favour. I would have gone in a totally different direction if I had stayed on at school and gone to university. My life would have been so different, but I can't imagine anything in life giving me more pleasure than the pleasure I've had in the field I happened upon by chance.

Q. What brings you happiness?

Happiness is love, music, food and making a difference.

Creating the kind of pleasure that people get from eating my food is a great joy. I love to cook and I love to share; there is a warmth and generosity of the table that forms such an amazing part of your life if you love food. I love having people around me who want to be there, too – people who are really interested in food, life and what we can do to make it better.

Q. What do you regard as the lowest depth of misery?

If you're lonely in your heart, that is the worst that can happen. People who have so little and have no one are what makes me sad – this can happen in many, many ways and is not always about your economic circumstances.

Q. What would you change if you could?

Firstly, the lack of access to beautiful food. By beautiful food, I mean the simplicity of food seasonality. There's an understanding that comes from accessing seasonal food, then knowing how to cook and share it. The filter-through effect of that understanding is so enormous. If you can teach those things at an early age, young people can be empowered by their understanding, even if their parents aren't into food; this is something Stephanie Alexander (pp. 335, 388) does with her Kitchen Garden Foundation. We can fix the world with good food; there's so much to learn from fresh, seasonal food cooked with love.

Something that drives me particularly at the moment, which is the flipside of educating the youth, is the food those in aged care receive. When people are elderly, they no longer even seem to count in so much of our society. Luckily, there are examples of wonderful elderly care, but there are also many, many people who need to be looked after. They should be given the best nutrition, as well as pleasure that gives them a reason for being instead of merely existing. Everyone should have something to look forward to – have involvement and hope – whether they are five or ninety-five.

Q. Which single word do you most identify with?

Excitement.

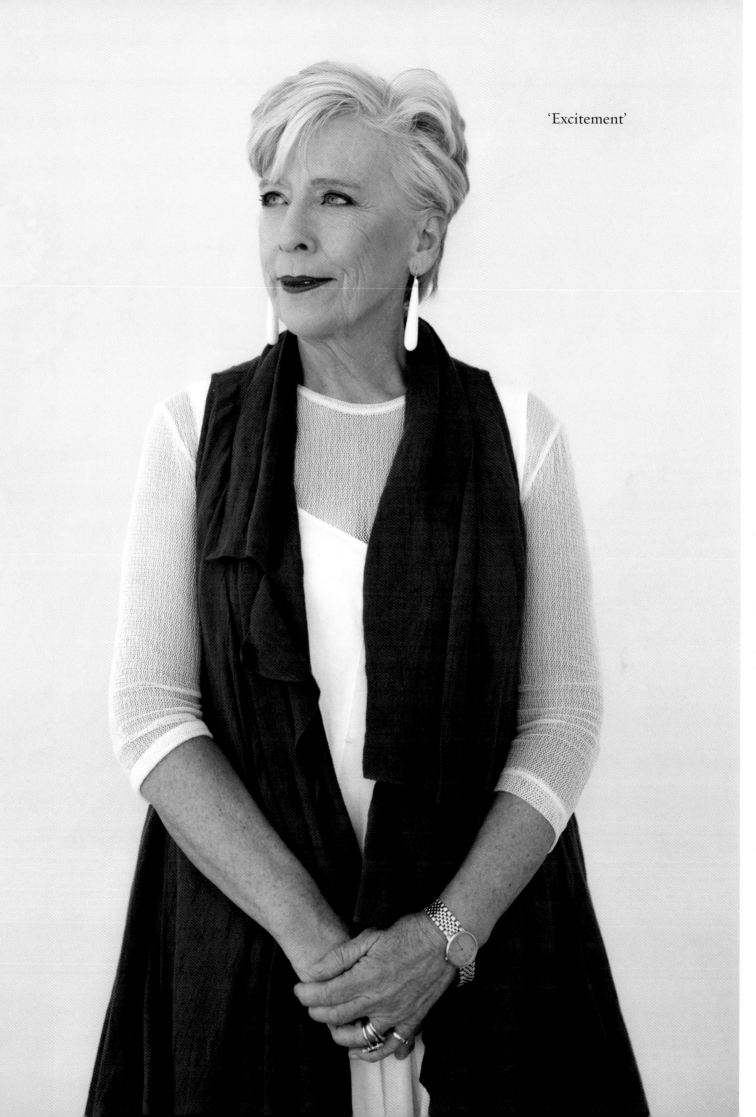

'Excitement'

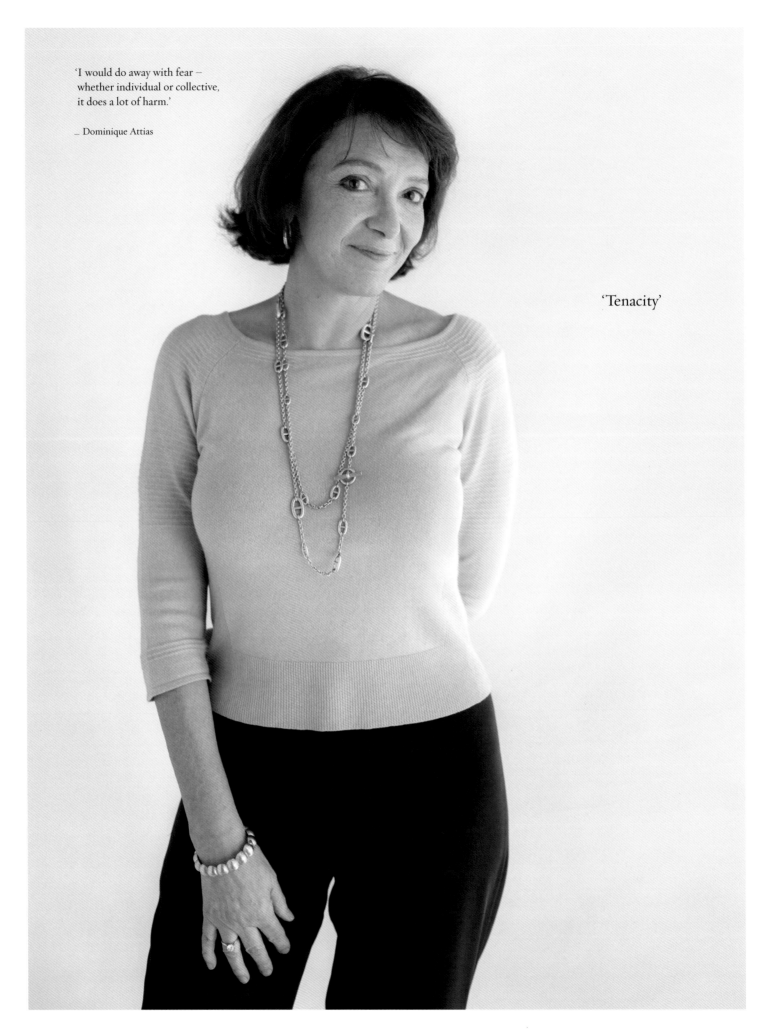

'I would do away with fear –
whether individual or collective,
it does a lot of harm.'

_ Dominique Attias

'Tenacity'

Interview page 377

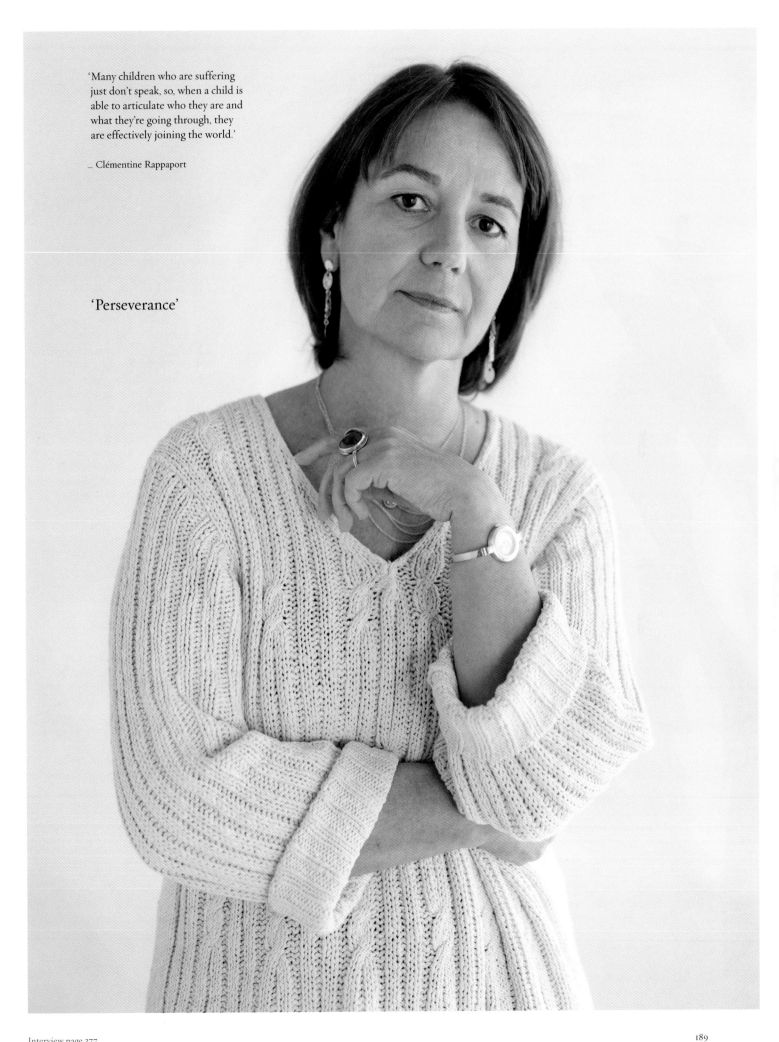

'Many children who are suffering just don't speak, so, when a child is able to articulate who they are and what they're going through, they are effectively joining the world.'

_ Clémentine Rappaport

'Perseverance'

Sophie Mathisen

Sophie Mathisen was born in Hammersmith, England, and moved to Australia in 1990. A master's graduate of the Royal Central School of Speech and Drama in the United Kingdom, Mathisen wrote, directed and performed in the 2016 film *Drama*. Mathisen is on the committee of Women in Film and Television (WIFT), which is committed to improving the position and representation of women in the film and television industries.

Q. What really matters to you?

Speaking up. I feel like I've gone back to being the precocious child I was at twelve years old, because for most of my early twenties I was really scared to speak up. I really thought that, because I was smart, if I played the system I could outsmart, outwit and outplay – be that survivor. But I couldn't.

When I was in high school I became interested in drama – particularly big, meaty female roles – and I was so interested to see that they were all being written by men. I found that really strange, because how is it that a man knows my psyche better than I do? As I went through drama school, my frustration continued building, because I was constantly being directed by men, being told by them how and when I should feel a certain thing.

The Australian Academy of Cinema and Television Arts (AACTA) presents the highest awards Australia can bestow on any film- or television-maker. Out of the twenty-eight films that were preselected for consideration in 2016, just two were directed by women and only three had female protagonists – that represents under 7 per cent of the content. I, along with the Women in Film and Television committee, discovered that a lot of the films that hadn't been preselected were made by women, but, when we asked AACTA for some rationale, they ignored us. We had no idea what to do; we're a tiny organisation with no resources, and they're a federally funded body that has a huge amount of access and star-power behind it.

Megan Riakos – a filmmaker – and I were sitting in my kitchen writing a charter setting out our demands to AACTA, when Megan said to me, 'Oh, God, Soph. It's just such a sausage party!' And I thought, 'Oh yeah, it totally is!' We got a costume designer friend of mine to buy twenty yoga mats and hundreds of yards of brown fabric to turn into sausage suits, and then, together with nineteen other emerging filmmakers, donned the suits and crashed the red carpet at the AACTA awards chanting, 'End the sausage party! End the sausage party!'

The footage of us has been syndicated over seventy-five times internationally. We got millions of dollars worth of coverage, which was fantastic, and we basically forced AACTA to sit down with us, which we're in the process of doing now; we know they've lost significant corporate sponsorship. What we were trying to do is expose the facts that cinema, as an art form, was birthed at a time when women had grossly disparate economic and social privileges to men, and that men continue to dominate the industry. I don't think there are a lot of men conspiring to keep women out, rather, that it's just easier not to address the issue of diversity. But it's for the health of everyone that these awards should be reflective of everyone; because if the awards involve just forty people and Mel Gibson, they don't really make sense.

Now, I'm really interested in calling a spade a spade and talking truth to power. Because, realistically, what we have left is our integrity and our ability to speak on solid ground. It really matters to me to learn more and read more, to analyse things and know that what I'm saying has some contextual and factual basis. I've always had this sense that I want to use film as a tool for social change; the film production company that I run with my sister has a 50 per cent gender quota for staff and it's very feminist in its outlook; we're currently doing a documentary looking at modern sensibilities around women, love, personhood and agency.

Empowering other women to speak matters. If there's any validity in being a highly educated and privileged white woman, it's about listening more and providing platforms for other women to speak. I think it's very, very easy to learn to love being the mouthpiece for an industry, but I'm really trying to counterbalance that with active and deep listening as well.

Q. What brings you happiness?

Dancing. I do a thing every week called No Lights No Lycra, which is about dancing in the dark for an hour. It makes me very, very happy and is a community-based thing.

I love the arts and my interest in them comes from an interest in community. Arts practices really draw people together to create something new and enable us to escape the strictures of a system that sometimes benefits from our isolation.

More broadly, my greatest happiness is the idea that there is still weight, or worth, in collective action. That, to me, is really important. I've existed for a really long time feeling so isolated, and it's such a lovely feeling to feel like there is some re-engagement with people as a group or that the community isn't dead – that we're finding a sense of how to live with one another again and how to share perspectives.

Q. What do you regard as the lowest depth of misery?

Isolation and grief. My middle sister suicided twelve years ago, so that sense of loss is something that's been very formative. There's an ongoing sense for me of contacting that level of misery. As esoteric and hippy as it sounds, it's all about seeing life with some kind of sense of yin and yang. I think it's about understanding that there are moments of intense darkness, but that they are always followed by moments of light. It's really important to always know that there's something at the end of it all – that it's not for nothing.

Q. What would you change if you could?

I guess it would be how people listen to one another, how people debate. It's fine to have contrary opinions, and it's fine to disagree, but I would love to see more empathy for someone else's perspective. I'd really love to hear more people being interested in difference and being less dismissive.

Q. Which single word do you most identify with?

Pugilist.

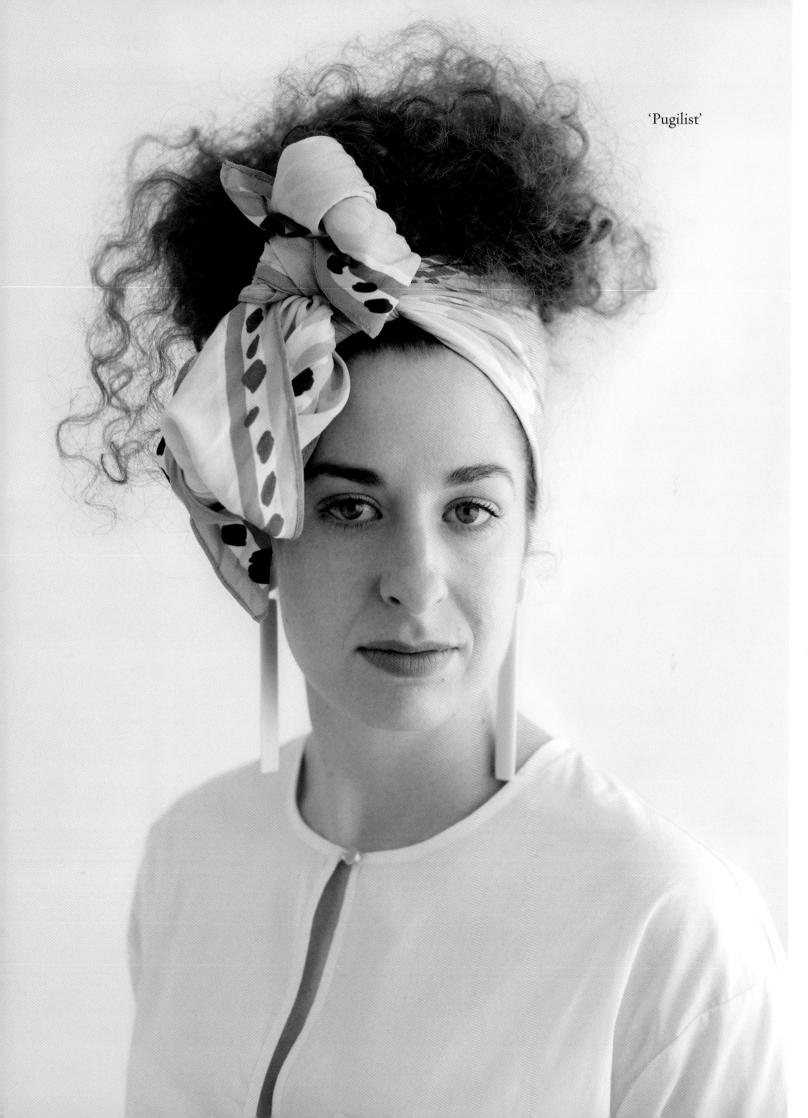

'Pugilist'

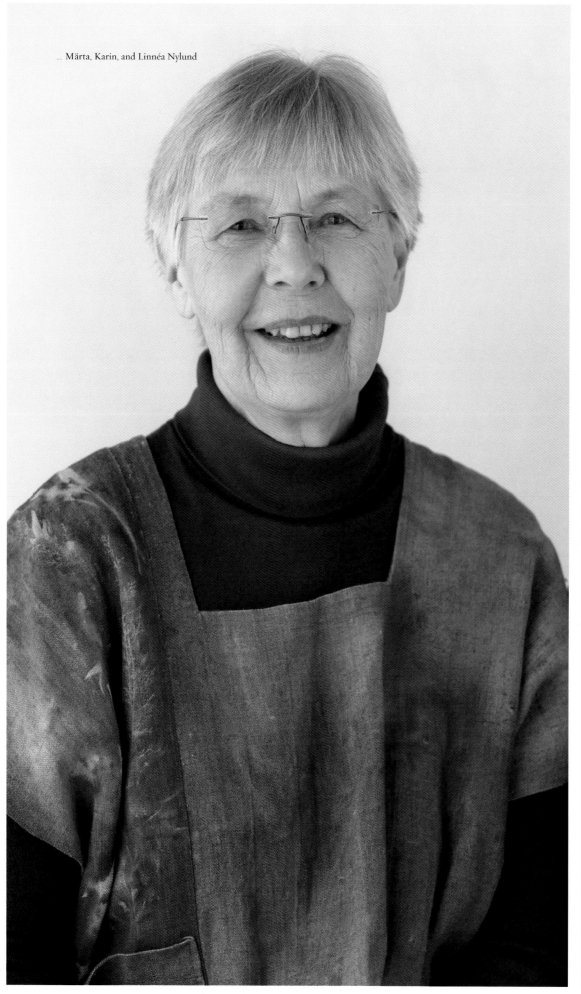

Märta, Karin, and Linnéa Nylund

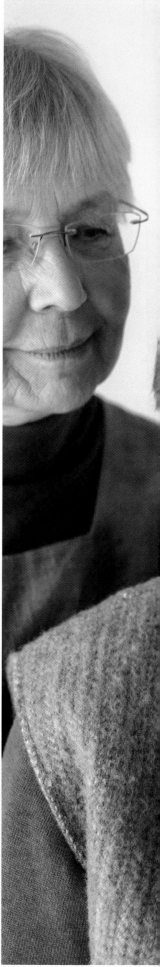

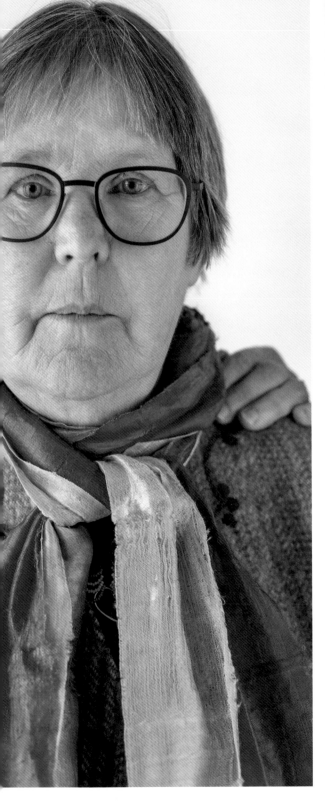

'Luonon-kappale. Everyone is a little piece of nature; if we could acknowledge that, circumstances would improve for everybody, including women and children.'

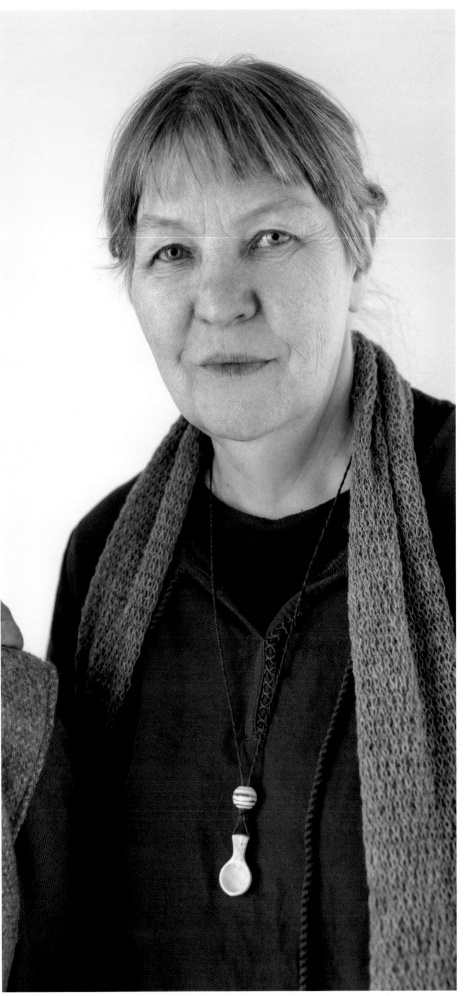

Interview page 378

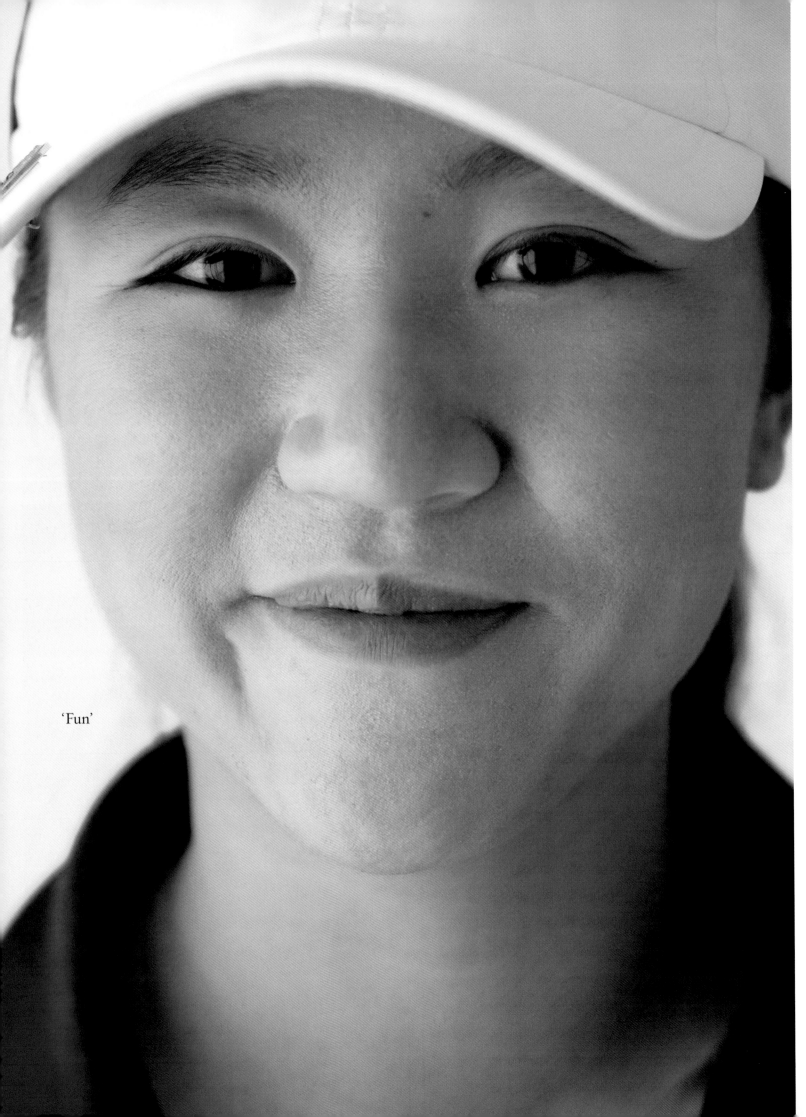

'Fun'

Lydia Ko

Lydia Ko was born in Seoul, South Korea, and grew up in New Zealand. In 2012, at the age of fifteen, she won the Canadian Women's Open title, making her the youngest-ever winner on the Ladies Professional Golf Association (LPGA) tour. In 2015, she became the world's number-one-ranked woman professional golfer, the youngest person ever to do so. Ko has achieved fourteen wins as a professional player on the LPGA tour, an Olympic silver medal at the 2016 Rio Olympic Games, was named the LPGA's 2014 Rookie of the Year and 2015 Player of the Year, and was 2016 Young New Zealander of the Year.

Q. What really matters to you?

It matters that I'm happy with the choices I've made and the life I'm living. No matter what I do – whether it's my sport, my studies or whatever I do once I retire from golf – the bottom line is that I'm content with my choices.

I didn't come from a golfing family, but my mum's sister was a golfaholic. She was a professor, and in her spare time she played. One day I went out with her, and she offered me a go with her club – when I hit the ball without falling over, I think she was very impressed! That's where it started for me. There's just no feeling of joy or success I can compare to that feeling when you hit the ball *just* the way you imagined in your head. Every sport is special in its own way, but, for me, what's special about golf is chasing those good days on the green. And it's those good days that keep bringing you back. Both professional and weekend golfers all have those bad days, when they throw down their clubs and say, 'I'm never coming back – I'm never playing this game again.' But they're back the next weekend, chasing those memorable shots.

Finding the moments of happiness in what I do has been a big lesson, because I sacrificed a lot of things to get to my current level. I remember sitting in class when I was twelve or thirteen, not wanting the day to end because I knew that the afternoon would be spent practising. I loved golf, but I also loved my friends, and I was at the age when you want to be going to sleepovers and watching movies. But, looking back, I can see that it was all worth it; yes, it can be a sacrifice at the time, but you end up getting so much more a few years later. And that's why it matters that I find happiness and enjoyment in each moment. I work very hard, so I need to remind myself why I'm doing what I'm doing and appreciate the benefits of my choices.

My family matters to me. They've been with me every step of the way and are responsible for who I am, both as Lydia the golfer and as Lydia the individual.

When I'm playing golf, it's obviously me actually playing, but at the same time it's all of us playing together. Yes, there have been arguments along the way, but my family has shown me that happiness in what I'm doing is fundamental; no matter what you're doing, you should be doing it because it's going to bring you happiness and because you know you won't have any regrets doing it. I know that's not always possible, but I wish everyone could have the opportunity to pursue those things that bring them happiness – I think a lot of people have regret for the paths not taken.

The greatest thing I can hear from a fan – especially a junior fan – is, 'You're my role model.' I know these kids are going to be the ones on tour soon, so it's pretty special to hear that you're their inspiration or favourite player. It's very cool, and it inspires and motivates me to work harder so that I'm a *good* role model. I push them and they push me – it's a very special combination of inspiration. I hope that when those fans remember me, it won't only be for my skills as a sportsperson, but also for being kind and approachable – because that's what I hope I am.

Q. What brings you happiness?

I've been fortunate enough to have a very strongly connected family, so it makes me happy to see the strength of the bond of love within families. My dad and my sister were present at my first Olympics in Rio, and I needed them there, because I wasn't only representing myself, but New Zealand as well. It felt like a huge responsibility, and my dad and sister walked that path with me. Whenever I'm on tour and I see one sister caddying for another – even though the caddy is a player herself who has sacrificed her career to support her sister – I feel so, so happy. Those gestures of kindness and support between family members show you how strong love is. It's amazing.

Looking at the world, peace makes me happy. I don't see it yet, but I will be happy when I see no borders. I was born in Asia, grew up down under in New Zealand and now I live in the United States. Every culture and country has its special traits, but we're all just people trying to be happy, as best we can. I'll be happy when I see humanity operating as one, with nobody better than anyone else. I see instances of people doing this already; I see people from different places coming together, living in community as though they'd known each other their entire lives – regardless of race or culture – and in spite of the negative narratives defining how we should engage with one another, and these make me feel happy and hopeful.

Q. What do you regard as the lowest depth of misery?

Racism and sexism really disappoint me, because, at the end of the day, we're the same. We might not understand someone else, but, when you peel back the layers of a person, you see that they all have families, they all have parents and they go to work every day. I'm a professional golfer, but I go to work every day the same as anyone else.

The sporting world is notoriously sexist and, historically, golf has been viewed as a men's game. A male golfer's prize money can be as much as four times higher than that of a female winner. I think, 'What? Why? We don't play fewer rounds than the guys, and it's not like we're less talented.' I hope that one day the game will be equal, because there's no reason it shouldn't be. There are so many legends who have walked this path and brilliant female role models currently on tour who have really made the game better, greater and more popular. Equal pay is the right thing to do.

Q. What would you change if you could?

I wish there was a way of pre-empting disasters, of warning people *before* tragedy strikes.

Q. Which single word do you most identify with?

Fun. I hope I'm fun. If something's not fun, is it worth it?

'Kindness'

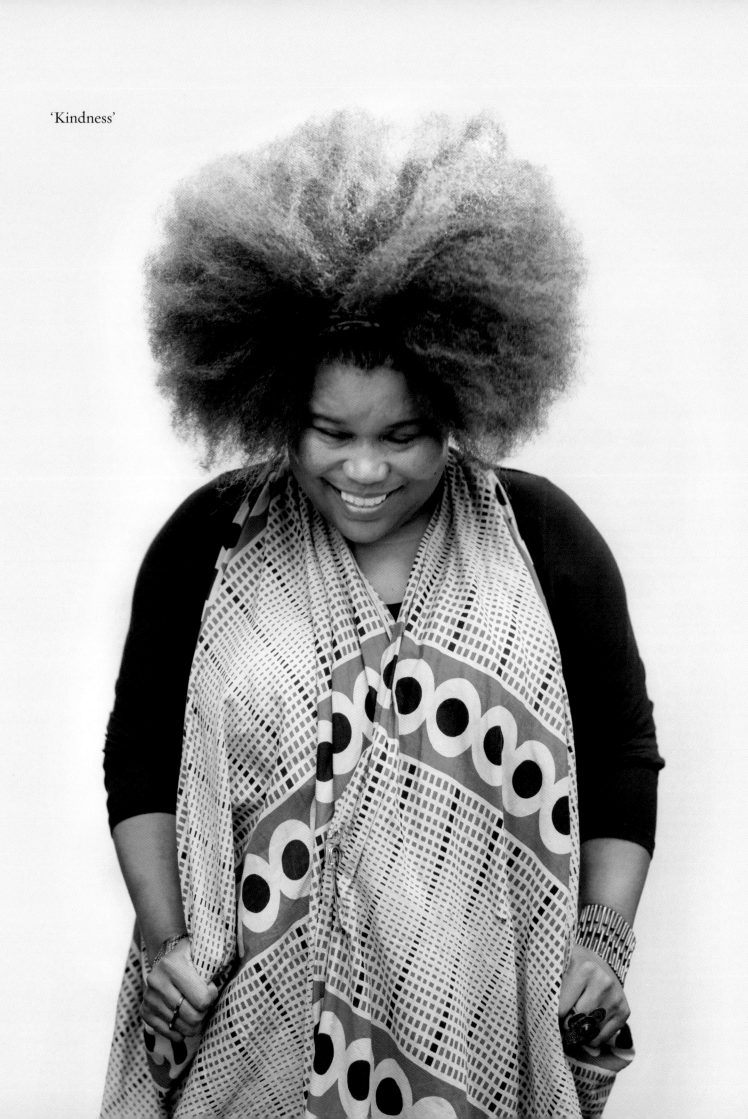

'I would say the place and time when I am most happy is when I'm watching a thunderstorm in the dark, or playing swords with my nieces.'

— Audrey Brown

Interview page 379

Embeth
Davidtz

'Many women struggle with the idea of still being able to own their femininity after going through a baptism of fire like breast cancer.'

Embeth Davidtz was born in Lafayette in Indiana, USA. She obtained a master's degree from Rhodes University in Grahamstown, South Africa. Davidtz has appeared in numerous films, including *Matilda*, *Schindler's List*, *Mansfield Park*, *Bicentennial Man* and *Bridget Jones's Diary*, and in television programmes that include *Californication*, *Mad Men* and *Ray Donovan*. She was diagnosed with stage-three breast cancer in 2013 and underwent chemotherapy, immunological treatment, lymph-node removal surgery and a mastectomy. Davidtz has been in remission since 2013.

Q. What really matters to you?

When I think about what has profoundly influenced my life, the two moments that come to mind are having children and being diagnosed with breast cancer at age forty-seven. There are profound differences between my life before and after motherhood, and my life before and after breast cancer.

Raising kids in this day and age is a truly difficult thing to do. Of course, I want my children to be happy, but that's not always a requirement; rather, it matters that they be on the right path. Trying to find and keep them on that path is really important to me as a parent.

The planet is also very important to me, and it's fundamental that I'm not contributing to ruining it. In everything I do, I'm consumed by the question, 'How do I leave this world a better place?' Answering this is becoming more and more difficult, however, because the world seems to be degenerating, and I do wonder whether I'll have the feeling of the world being in a better place in my lifetime.

It matters to me that I'm talking to women about breast cancer – not only about experiencing it, but also about the results of treatment. Many women struggle with the idea of still being able to own their femininity after going through a baptism of fire like breast cancer; this has been a

very interesting journey for me and not always a comfortable one. When I was first diagnosed, I remember feeling an enormous amount of shame; breast cancer felt like something dirty, and, for a long time, it wasn't something I wanted other people to know about. The first time I had to appear in front of others with really short hair, everyone thought I was trying something edgier. I told them, 'Oh, I just felt like a change.' But, whilst I just wasn't comfortable shouting from the rooftops that I had breast cancer, it also didn't feel like I was being authentic by hiding it.

Then, a job on the television show *Ray Donovan* came along that required nudity in a love scene. My immediate thought was, 'I only have one nipple!' I decided to get a prosthetic one and sent a photograph of my nipple off to have one made. I figured I could put it on and cover the scar with makeup, and everything would look all right. But, as we started to discuss the character more deeply, I began thinking more about my body. I realised that I had a choice: I could hide the map of who I am and nobody would be any the wiser, or, I could reveal this map and be a woman who can still be a lover *and* a compelling character. It felt a bit like taking the lead but, to be honest, it also just felt like the right thing to do. So, we did it; I showed myself as I am, and it blew up. There was a massive outpouring from survivors, families of victims and advocates.

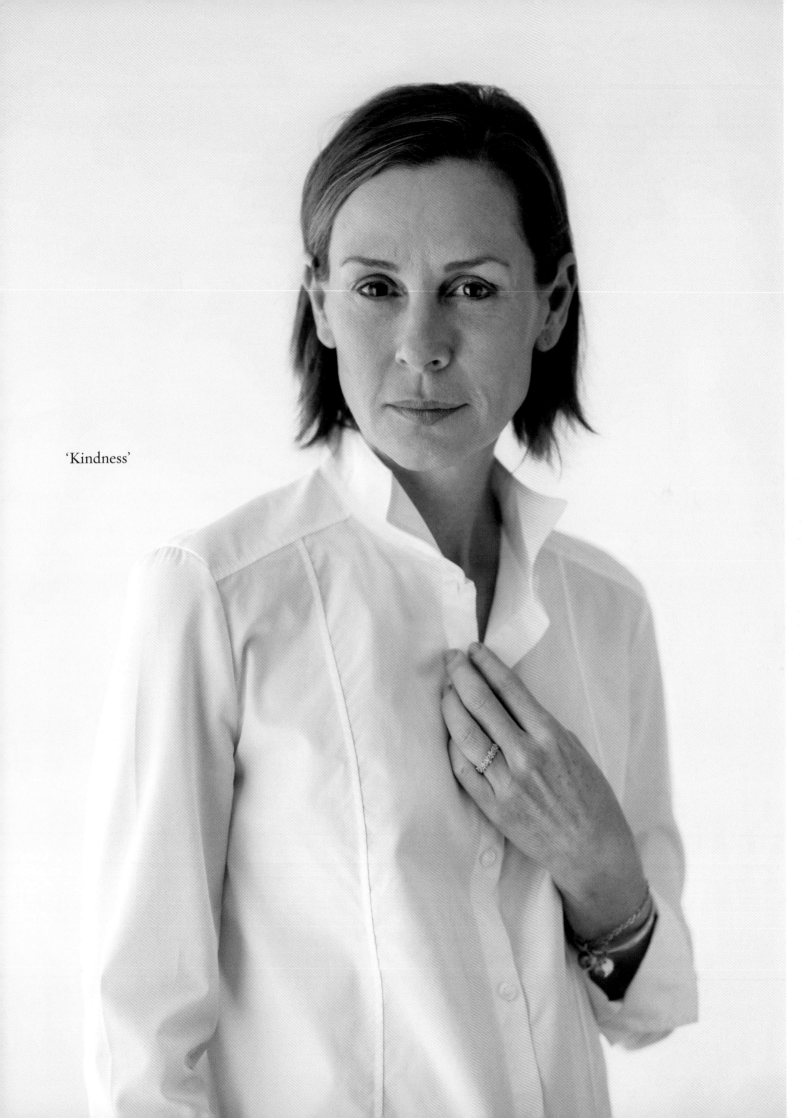

'Kindness'

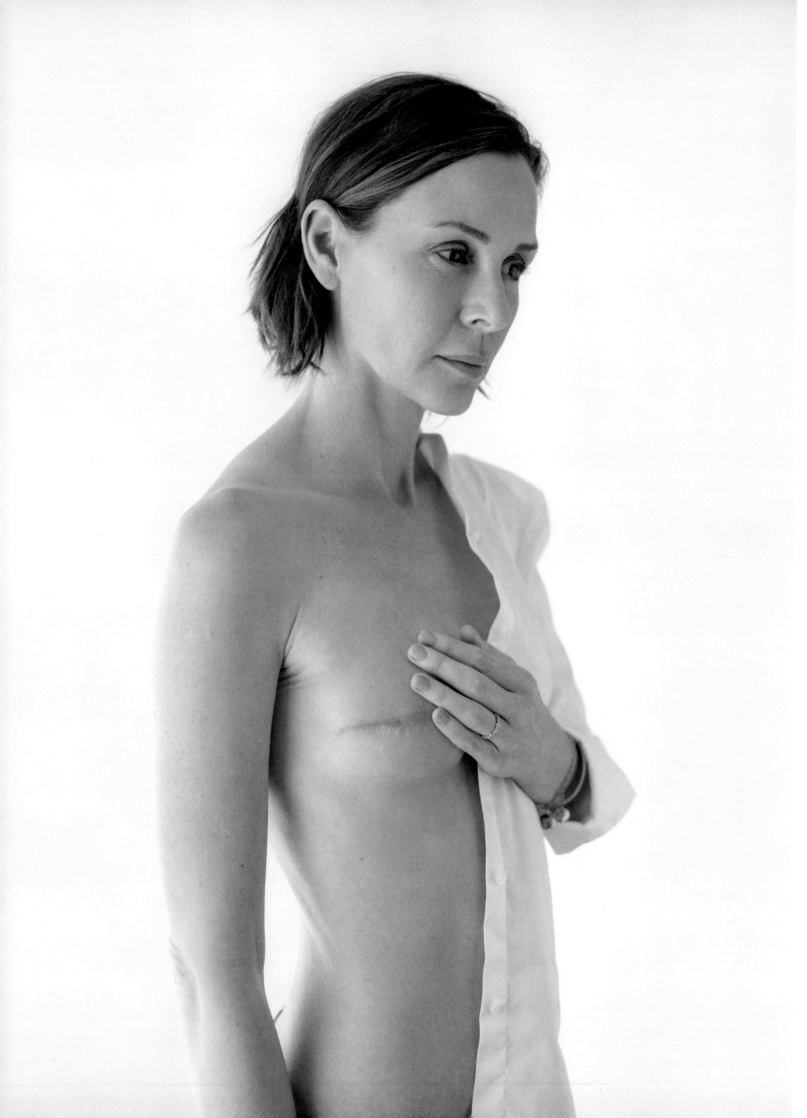

Embeth Davidtz

———

'I had never thought of myself as ugly after breast cancer, which is why it was so important to me to convey a confident, well-put-together woman in a sexual light — to not have her scar dictate that she was less of a woman.'

———

It was overwhelming. I hadn't really *done* anything – I certainly didn't set out to serve the greater community – I just wanted to be honest.

I'm so glad I did it, though, because the experience has given me purpose. So many women have told me that, when they saw the scene, they felt beautiful, unjudged, strong in their sensuality and sexuality, and able to reject the labels associated with their scars. I had never thought of myself as ugly after breast cancer, which is why it was so important to me to convey a confident, well-put-together woman in a sexual light – to not have her scar dictate that she was less of a woman.

I did worry, though, that some of my children's friends might see the show and talk to them about it; they were at the age where you don't really want your parents to stand out in any way. So, I carefully told them what I had done and why. The discussion happened after the show had aired and when people were beginning to respond, so I told them that I really thought what I had done was helping others. I showed them the correspondence I had received, and they saw the value in it. In time, I hope they will feel proud.

Q. What brings you happiness?
My dogs, my cats and my chickens. My children, too, bring me great happiness and I have a really great partner; I got married later in life, and that feels like it was a smart decision for me. I lived in South Africa for many years, so being in Africa makes me happy. I love being in nature: the sound of birds, swimming in the ocean and gardening. It's the small things that bring me the greatest pleasure.

Q. What do you regard as the lowest depth of misery?
My immediate response to that is personal: the lowest depth of misery for me was day three of chemotherapy. But, that's not the lowest depth of misery; there are people who, on day three, have absolutely no hope of recovery. So, the lowest depth of misery may be being told that there is no hope for you – being told that there is, in fact, no room for optimism.

Q. What would you change if you could?
I would end suffering. When I think of children struggling to survive in war-torn countries, or living in circumstances of poverty or abuse, I just want to rush in and protect them; I think of my own children, who are so fortunate, and I want to take everything that the world is throwing at the disenfranchised children and chuck it back!

Q. Which single word do you most identify with?
Kindness. The word encapsulates everything about how I want to live my life. I felt so optimistic about the United States twenty-five years ago, and now I long to feel that way again; I wish that we could get back to human kindness – if we could hold on to kindness, even just for an hour every day, things would be better.

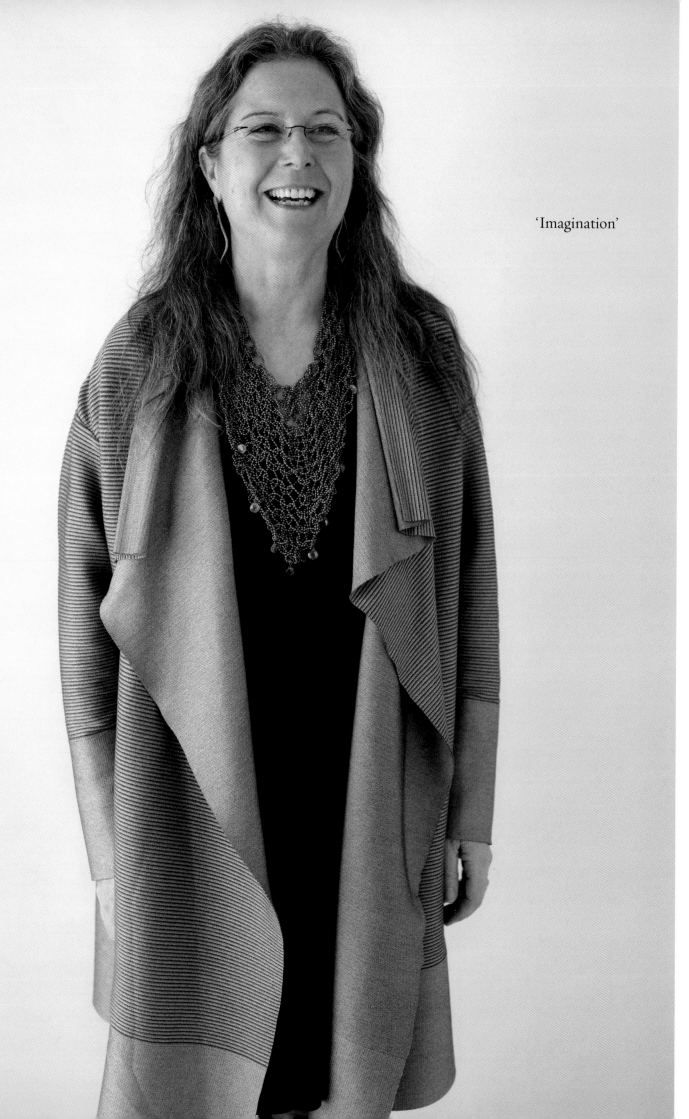

'Imagination'

Ivy Ross

Ivy Ross was born in Yonkers in New York, USA. A graduate of New York's Fashion Institute of Technology and of Harvard Business School, her metalwork features in the permanent collections of twelve international museums, including the Smithsonian American Art Museum. Ross has been a senior executive in creative design and product development with companies such as Swatch, Coach, Calvin Klein and Mattel. She is a vice president, head of design and user experience for hardware products at Google.

Q. What really matters to you?
What really matters to me is living my truth and being exactly who I am on the inside, on the outside. Being genuine is so important to me in terms of living a life that is fully mine; it's about acknowledging my values and refusing to compromise on them. I've had several experiences where, after giving a talk, young women have come up to me saying, 'I want to be like you!' And my response is always, 'No. You want to be like *you*.' That's a lesson – a gift – I feel I can pass on.

People – especially women – should not let anyone tell them how they should live their lives. My father was the designer of the Studebaker Hawk and I always wanted to be like him. But, when I told him I wanted to follow in his footsteps, he said, 'Ivy: marry someone rich, become a schoolteacher and have your summers off.' It crushed me, and although now, I appreciate that he wanted to spare me from the kind of suffering he'd experienced because of his work, it felt like I was being robbed of my dreams. My mother says that's the day I went into competition with my father! I suppose I did, unconsciously. I thought, 'I'll show you I can live my dream.' No one should compromise themselves – their dreams or their truths – for anyone else; I feel I've been fearless in that respect, and my father triggered that in me.

I became a jewellery designer because I knew I had to be creating with my hands. When I was twenty-three, my work got into museums and my ego was satisfied. That was such a gift; some people spend their whole lives pursuing that kind of success, but when I achieved it, the high lasted for about three weeks and then I realised that life is actually about the journey, about the process of creating versus the end result. Life is too short to ignore that.

I stumbled into the corporate world by accident. Eventually, I was running the design and product-development departments for a wide range of companies, including Swatch, Calvin Klein and Mattel. One of the greatest instances of living my truth came when I was at Mattel in charge of designing and developing all of the toys for girls. Two of the typical buzzword phrases that the chief executive officer had put in an annual report were 'innovation' and 'teamwork.' I had studied what I call 'the technologies of the sacred' – sound, light and colour, along with the power of connection and psychology – and I realised that it was time to implement what I *believed* could work in pursuing Mattel's goals of innovation and teamwork.

Team creativity comes from trust and being in resonance with each other, but, when I looked at my team, I realised that they didn't know each other at a deep level to create the trust, nor were they on the same wavelength. I'd been studying sound and vibration for thirty years as a hobby, so I brought in my sound teacher to discuss some options about how to use the power of sound to connect the team into the flow state when we needed to create together. We got twelve volunteers from my team to sound out their voices. We recorded their vocal ranges with the objective of finding a place where all of the twelve voices overlapped. We took that fundamental frequency and embedded it in music – in octaves up and down. When we would brainstorm ideas, I would play the CD in the background. After a short period of time each day, our brains would entrain, spiralling to new places and ideas together. An independent creativity test administered both before and after the team worked in this way, showed that I had increased creativity by 18 per cent. I had taken my beliefs in the power of sound and music, put them into action, and united us. The ideas and products that were generated from this alternative way of working were so successful that I won the chairman's award for sustainability. It was such a validation for embracing fearlessness.

When I think about the benefits of female involvement in the corporate world, I think of this project. Feminism, for me, isn't just a woman's cause; it's about embracing the female principles that exist in everyone. It's about creating the space for others to be who they are and allowing their talents to emerge. It's about collaboration and trust rather than control. It's a generalisation, but I think men are more individualistic and competitive, which is why I'm excited that we are getting more women into technology. Women ask different questions and have different perspectives than men do.

Emotion and intuition have roles to play in decision making, so I think a little bit of EQ to balance IQ is something every business can benefit from. We have incredible minds in Silicon Valley, but what we're lacking is heart; I'm interested in technology that amplifies our humanity, rather than removes us from it.

Q. What brings you happiness?
Being in a state of awe and wonder, which, to me, is when my ego is diminished in the face of something greater than myself: that could be the beauty of a sunset, standing in front of a magnificent piece of art or feeling the love between one another.

Q. What do you regard as the lowest depth of misery?
The destruction of the natural world and the disappearance of entire species. Life is an embodied network. We are a part of a community composed of relationships. There is no separation between humans and nature. By killing nature, we are killing ourselves.

Q. What would you change if you could?
I would love for us to go back to the time before our egos developed – or to before we got things so wrong that we decided to separate ourselves from collaboration with each other and with the world. Today, we live separately from nature and we live separately from one another – that separateness is the cause of so much negativity. One of my favourite books as a kid was *Horton Hears a Who!* by Dr. Seuss. It has hugely influenced my life. There's a fundamental lesson in it, that together we can do anything. In the story, only when all the tiny Whos of Whoville joined together holding hands, making noise could they prove their existence. They would have been destroyed if they had not all cooperated, as they were too tiny to be seen. But together, they made a loud enough noise to be heard – I would love to see each corner of society included in the global discourse and have every aspect of life connected.

Q. Which single word do you most identify with?
Imagination. In the long run, it's imagination that brings us knowledge. Because, if you can imagine it, you can make it happen.

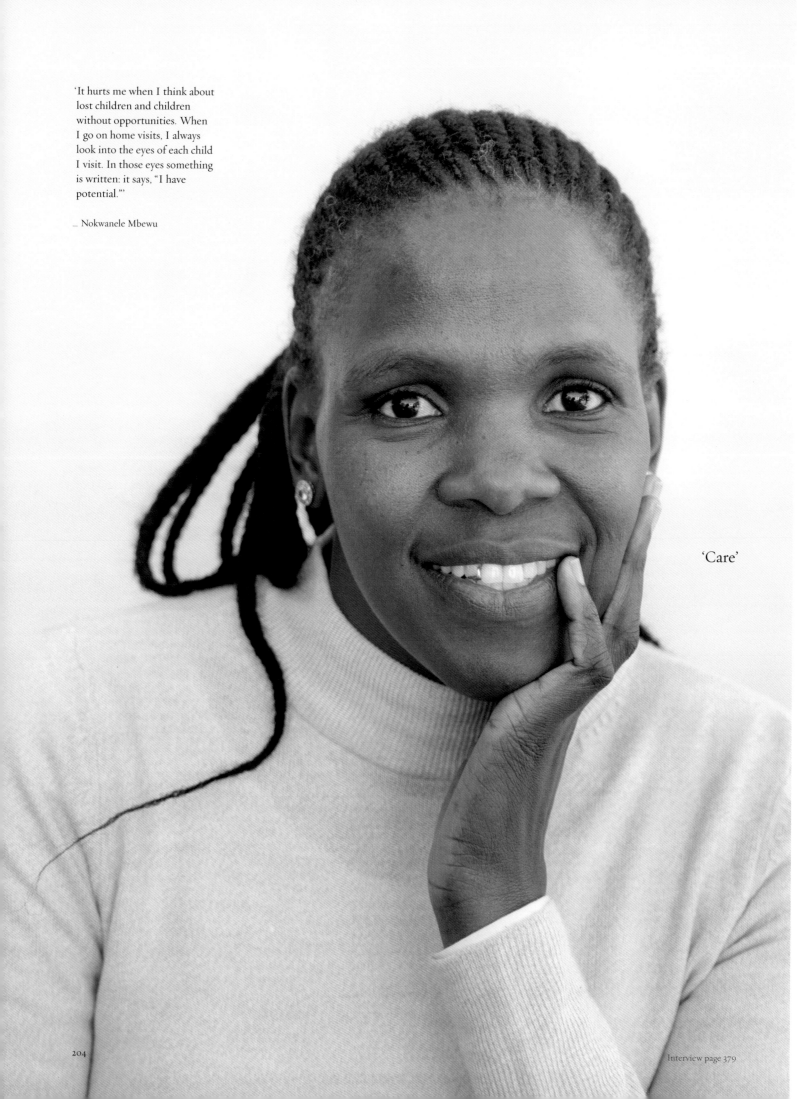

'It hurts me when I think about lost children and children without opportunities. When I go on home visits, I always look into the eyes of each child I visit. In those eyes something is written: it says, "I have potential."'

_ Nokwanele Mbewu

'Care'

Interview page 379

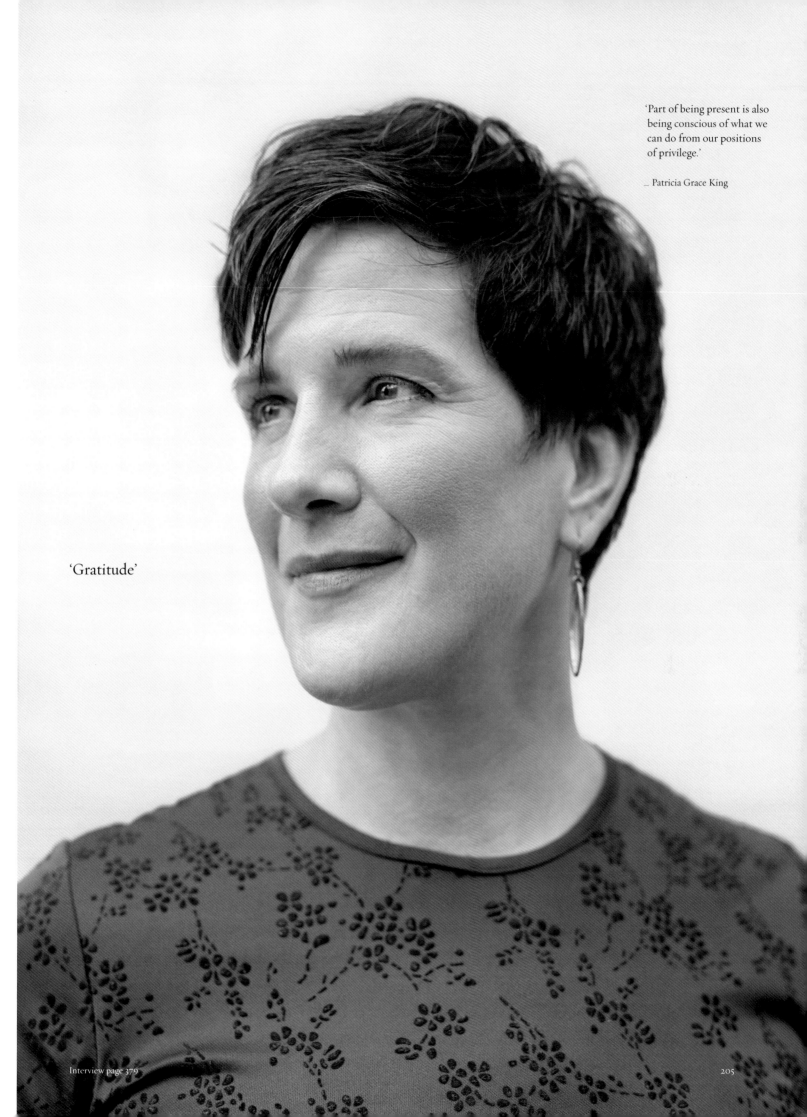

'Part of being present is also
being conscious of what we
can do from our positions
of privilege.'

_ Patricia Grace King

'Gratitude'

Interview page 379

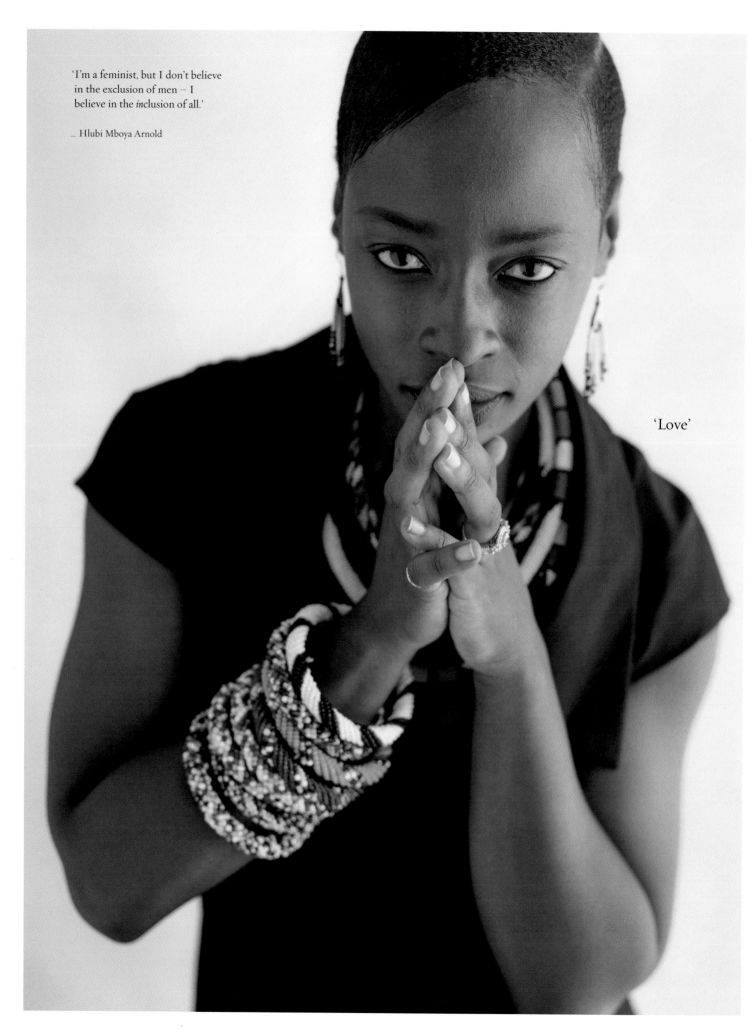

'I'm a feminist, but I don't believe
in the exclusion of men – I
believe in the *in*clusion of all.'

_ Hlubi Mboya Arnold

'Love'

Interview page 380

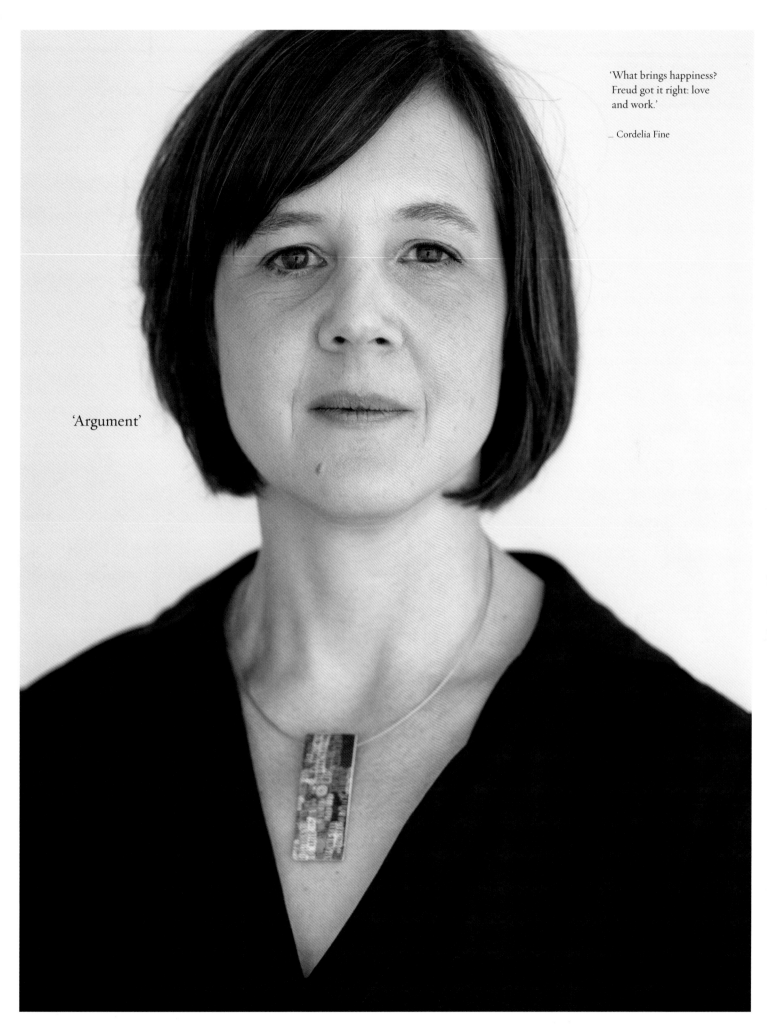

'What brings happiness?
Freud got it right: love
and work.'

_ Cordelia Fine

'Argument'

Interview page 380

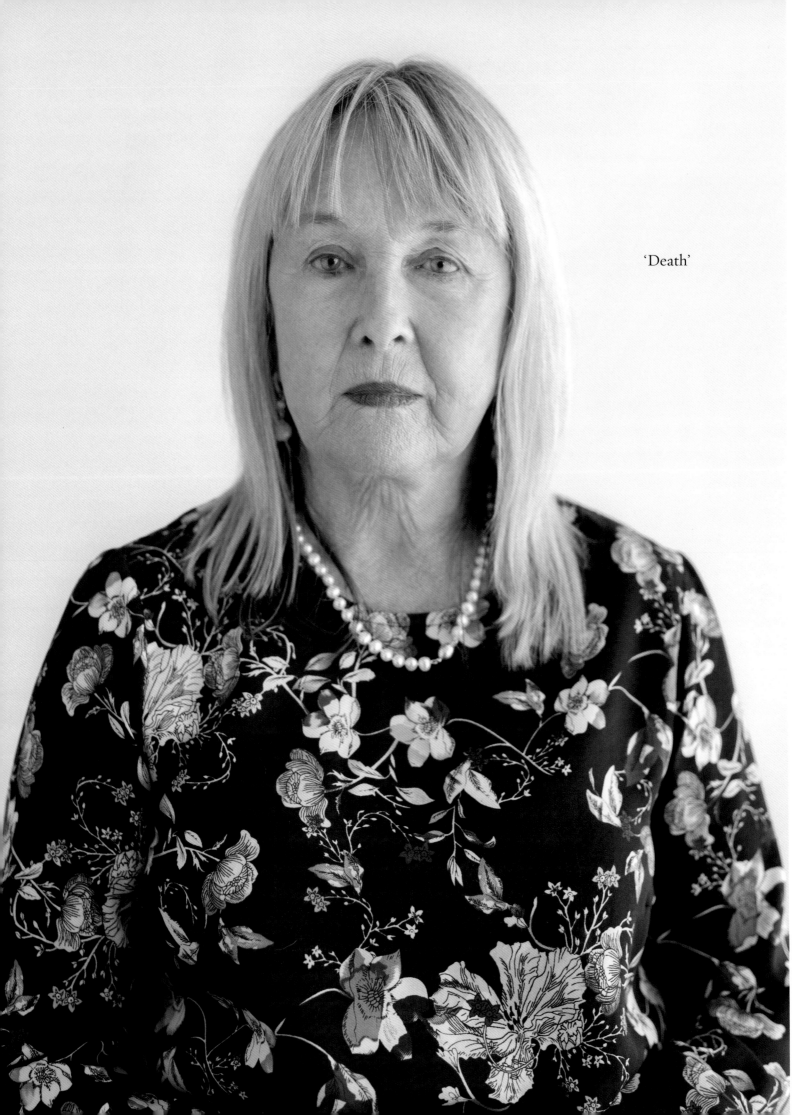

'Death'

June
Steenkamp

June Steenkamp was born in Blackburn, England, and moved to South Africa in 1965. In 2013, Steenkamp's daughter, Reeva Steenkamp, was shot and killed by Paralympian Oscar Pistorius, who had been dating Reeva for several months. Pistorius was later convicted of Reeva's murder. In 2015, Steenkamp established the Reeva Rebecca Steenkamp Foundation to educate and empower women and children against violence and abuse.

Q. What really matters to you?
What matters to me is other women; I want to save women from losing their daughters, and I want to save women from losing their lives.

I moved to South Africa from England with my first husband and our daughter, Simone. The marriage ended in divorce and I was left on my own in a strange country. Learning how to stand on my own two feet was incredibly hard; I had to work three jobs to support Simone, and I grew up a lot over that period. Then I met Barry in 1981, and, ten days later, we were married. We never expected to have children together, but then I became pregnant with Reeva and we were overjoyed.

Reeva was such an exceptional, loving person: she gave so much love to Barry and me, and we gave it back. We adored her. Before she went to university, she broke her back in two places. It was incredibly traumatic for all of us and the doctors weren't sure whether she would walk again. But she did. She went to university wearing a special casing for her back – she looked like she was heading for space – but she never missed a day's lectures, and she finished her law degree with thirteen distinctions. She was clever, beautiful and caring.

When Anene Booysen was gang raped, disembowelled and murdered in 2013 – at just seventeen – Reeva called me and said, 'Mummy, I have to do something about this.' She started her work against the abuse of women and, less than two weeks later, she herself was murdered; the day she died she was supposed to talk to schoolgirls in Johannesburg about violence against women.

Reeva was the most wonderful person in our lives, and suddenly she was gone. It was unbearable. Whatever she was going through in her relationship she hid from me – I believe that's because she didn't want me to worry. Living with the horrendous way she died is difficult. We

had protected her all along, then suddenly this thing happened and there was nothing we could do. Barry and I wake up every night at the time she died, and I think that's because we feel we should have protected her. You believe it one minute, then the next it hasn't happened – it's how you shield yourself but, eventually, you have to accept it.

After it happened, I missed Reeva so much and my grief became destructive, but, during the trial, I went into another space in my head. I felt very vulnerable in that courtroom, but, after everything that had happened, it was crucial that I had my dignity – it was a way of protecting myself. I wanted to be strong, but the things I had to listen to were terrible and it was very hard for me. God gave me the strength to get through it, though, and eventually, I freed myself from the anger and the destruction inside me, and I forgave; you have to forgive – it's what God expects – but that doesn't mean Reeva's murderer mustn't pay for what he did.

Somehow, I came to the realisation that, instead of sitting at home crying and crying, I needed to get myself together and try to help other women affected by violence. That's how the foundation was born; it's named after Reeva, in her memory, to continue her legacy and the work she started. We want to raise awareness of physical abuse towards women, provide resources to victims of abuse and educate women on their self-worth. We are focussed on education; we speak to girls so that they are equipped with the tools they need to develop an intolerance towards men treating them in certain ways. We also want to educate men – while they are still boys – to respect the women in their lives. We want to get ahead of this violence and try to do something to prevent it even occurring. Men must be taught to respect their mothers, their sisters, their girlfriends and their wives. Right now, we are focussing on trying to get attorneys and advocates to volunteer their time to support women who might not have access to legal support. And

every year we nominate a Reeva Girl – a woman who is pursuing a legal degree with an emphasis on family law – and we pay for her studies, to empower her to help victims of physical violence.

The foundation gives me a reason to go on, a reason to live and to move forward; helping other people is what my life is about now – this has helped me a lot. But violence against women is not an easy thing to stop, and it's escalating every day – the examples are endless, and sometimes it feels like there is so little justice for these women. Nonetheless, I hope we can change the world; until I take my last breath, my life is going to be about trying to save other women from losing their daughters; it's going to be about trying to help others so that they don't have to go through what I went through and what Reeva went through.

Q. What brings you happiness?
I find happiness and peace in my work and with my animals. Barry was a racehorse trainer and I've had horses all my life, though I don't ride anymore – I'm seventy now, so if I did, my legs might fall off!

Q. What do you regard as the lowest depth of misery?
The state of the world as it is now – there is so much cruelty, abuse and murder. If we all loved one another and gave love to each other, the world would be a better place, but, right now, it's not happening – I look around and I see tragedy. It's hard and relentless.

Q. What would you change if you could?
I want everybody to give their love to each other, in the same way that they love themselves – we can't go forward without doing that.

Q. Which single word do you most identify with?
Death. I'm trying to help extinguish the death of young women at the hands of their partners. That's why I've chosen that word – because death has made me who I am today.

Kimbra

————

Kimbra was born in Hamilton, New Zealand. Her debut album, *Vows,* was released in 2011, and her second album, *The Golden Echo,* was released in 2014. Kimbra's collaboration with Gotye on 'Somebody That I Used to Know' won record of the year and best pop duo/group performance at the 2012 Grammy Awards. Kimbra has twice travelled to Ethiopia in support of Tirzah International, a global network of grassroots movements that works to combat poverty, exclusion from education, modern-day slavery, HIV/AIDS and violence against women and girls.

Q. What really matters to you?

I started writing little songs when I was eight as a means of asking questions about the world and reaching for answers. It was also a way to articulate what I was feeling. Today, I'm much the same, so what matters to me as a musician is very much tied to what matters to me as a person.

Music is so important to me; it teaches me a lot about myself. But, although that self-reflection and growth is very important, I see music also as a tool to communicate with – and grow in relationship to – others. I've always wanted to find a way to connect with people beneath the surface level; music is a powerful medium for achieving that. It's a form of empathy, because, when you watch another person perform, you can feel what they feel, and vice versa, when others watch you perform, they can feel what you feel. As a writer, when I explore the things that are hard for me to talk about – when I challenge myself, when I'm vulnerable – I feel this gives others permission to do the same for themselves. When people see you letting go and embracing those spaces, they feel they're not alone in doing it themselves.

Music is a search for truth and a means through which to articulate beauty. While sometimes a simple conversation isn't enough to explain what you're feeling, melody's power is that it can say a thousand words. In my work, I'm not only trying to articulate my experiences, but also to dig deeper into an experience in order to try and make it relatable to others. Music is quite mystical – there's no tangible formula you can use to unlock it – and it can lift you into a higher state of consciousness that allows you to step outside your bubble and see the world in a greater context – it can be quite transformative. It can disarm your mind of its constructs.

Q. What brings you happiness?

At its core, every living thing has a space of stillness – I find real happiness in that space, especially because my life is full of noise, talking, singing and creating. So, I find great happiness in silence and amidst nature; sitting in silence – on a mountaintop or in a forest – gives me a sense of being grounded. And that's true joy.

I've also found happiness through my work in Ethiopia with a charity called Tirzah International. Although there is usually a lot of pain attached to such extreme experiences, there's also a great happiness in feeling a sense of oneness with those you meet: it's really important to me that I continue to plant myself in situations where I'm able to recognise that. In Ethiopia, I experienced profound connection and joy with everyone I spoke with, so, when I look at the world at large, I find great happiness in knowing that, despite our different environments and circumstances, the human experience is very much the same. We all come from vastly different contexts, but, at the core, we experience the same things.

Tirzah works with women and children all over the world who are especially marginalised. Many of the Ethiopian women they work with are HIV positive. They are given support in developing their own businesses, which is about empowerment and helping them find independence. There is a lot of inequality in Ethiopia. For example, the women do most of the physical and manual labour. I couldn't believe it was possible, but I saw women walking up a mountain every day with huge logs on their backs. They constantly looked like they were going to fall over their feet as they went, but they kept going to sell the wood at the market. Meanwhile, the men are doing a lot of knitting and sewing. It's quite a cultural shift, but it's not a matriarchal society. It's just become accepted that women

who've fallen to the bottom rung of the ladder will need to turn to physical labour to make money. This is especially the case for women who are sick, whose husbands have left them – they are bringing up their kids on their own and physical labour has become a way of life. The experience of watching these women in Ethiopia has been a double-edged sword for me; I have felt such pain observing them, but their strength empowers me. It helps me to just get on with what I'm going through. Whenever I have to do something hard, I picture those women walking up and down that mountain. Their resilience of spirit is incredible. The resilience of women around the world – and what they will do for their children, to keep their families going – blows my mind.

Q. What do you regard as the lowest depth of misery?

To live your life in fear. In Ethiopia, the women I've spoken with are fearing that their children may not make it. In New York, minorities fear that their rights will be violated because they don't know how things will work out politically. Or, in my case, times of darkness are when I'm not living out of fearlessness and courage, but out of fear. That's when I see the world in black and white – I shut off and disconnect.

Q. What would you change if you could?

Myself. If you go out thinking you can change the whole world, you can quickly become disillusioned, but the only thing I can say I have real power over is myself. So, I need to ask: How can I overcome fear? How can I be a better person, a kinder person or a more loving person? And, as a musician, I feel like I'm making some kind of difference, because music – by communicating hope and love – has the ability to reach all parts of the world.

Q. Which single word do you most identify with?

Truth. You can't speak for anyone else's truth; you can only speak for what is true for you.

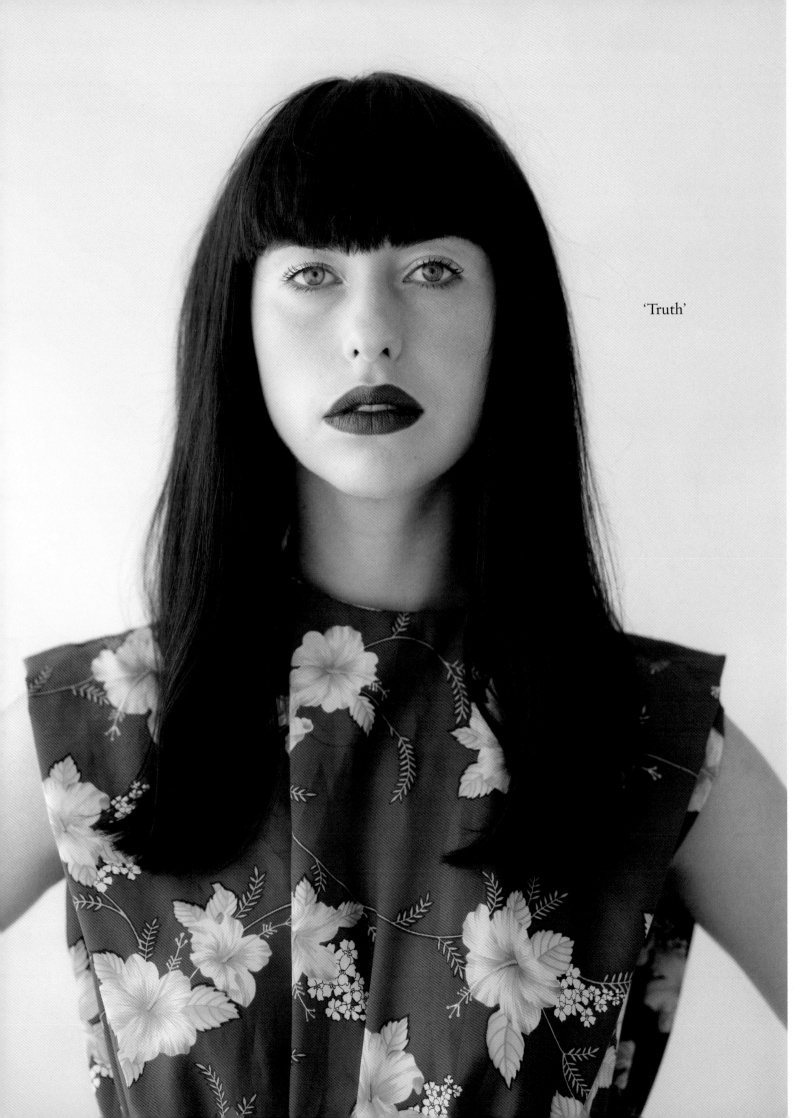

'Truth'

'Honesty'

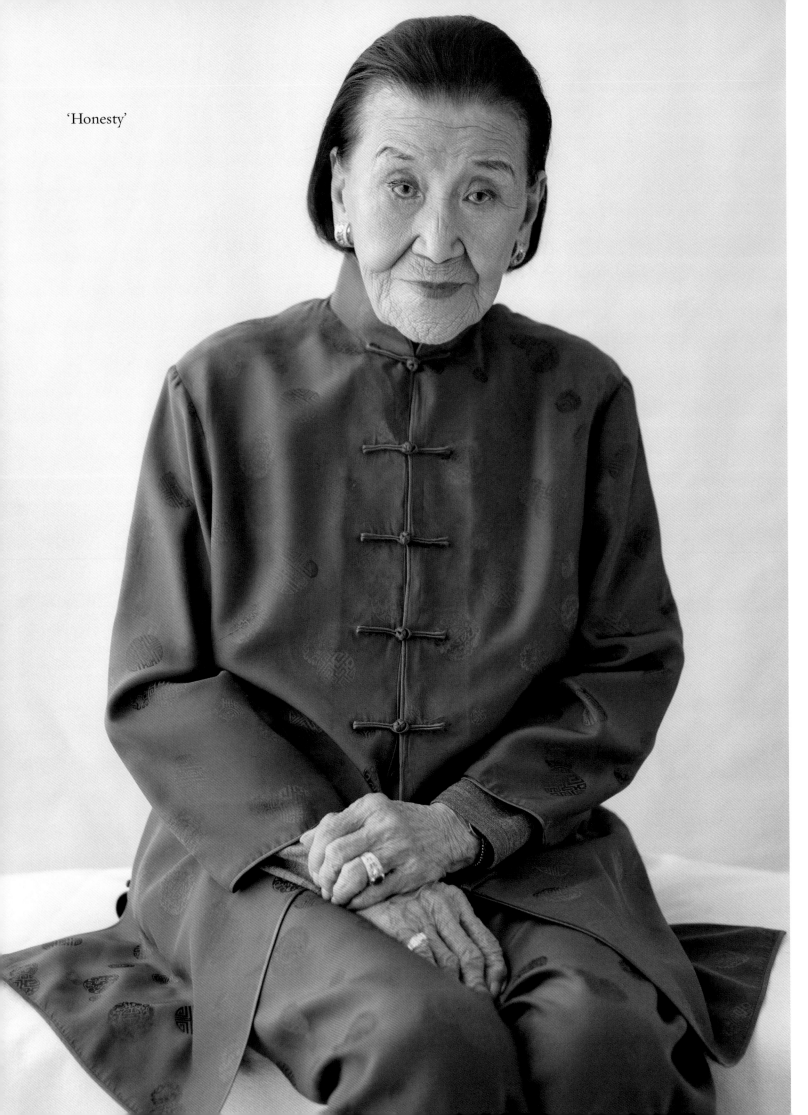

Cecilia Chiang

Cecilia Chiang was born in Wuxi, China. In the 1950s, she travelled to San Francisco, United States, where she opened The Mandarin restaurant; Chiang owned and operated the restaurant for thirty years, retiring in 1991. She was awarded the James Beard Foundation Lifetime Achievement Award in 2013 and was the subject of filmmaker Wayne Wang's 2014 documentary *Soul of a Banquet*. In 2016, she appeared in the mini-series *The Kitchen Wisdom of Cecilia Chiang*.

'You know in yourself whether or not you are being honest.'

Q. What really matters to you?

I am very grateful that I was welcomed and given a chance in the United States. By contrast, I wouldn't have had much opportunity had I remained in China or in Japan; as a woman, even if you had a talent, they didn't give you the chance to develop it.

In my childhood, it was one war after another: first civil wars – warlord fighting warlord – then came the Russians and the Japanese. By the time of the Japanese occupation, in 1937, we walked to escape. It took about six months to go from Beijing to Chongqing on foot – that's a long walk! We had no map – nothing – just walked from village to village dressed like peasants. The Japanese flew very well, and would shoot and kill any people they saw, so, we had to sleep during the day and walk at night – because the Japanese airplanes didn't fly at night. Finally, we got to Chongqing, in Free China. The city was under generalissimo Chiang Kai-shek and the Kuomintang, the Chinese Nationalist Party; they fought the Japanese for eight years and, finally, they won the war. I met my husband and got married in Chongqing. Later, we moved to Shanghai and had our two children there: one son and one daughter. We hoped we could settle down – take a little break and a rest – but then the communists came in and, in 1950, we had to go again, because my husband worked for the Kuomintang government. We decided to move to Tokyo. We tried to take the last plane out of Shanghai, but we were four people, and there were only three tickets left. My daughter was not quite two years old and my son was

just a couple of months old. I told my husband, 'Either we take the daughter or the son; we'll have to leave one behind with my sister.' My husband said, 'Take the daughter,' and so we left Philip, my son, behind. Later, we were reunited with Philip and settled in Japan.

I came to the United States in the 1950s. My sister had married a war journalist who was an American-born Chinese. He died suddenly of cancer, leaving her alone in the United States. She had no friends, didn't speak much English and, in those days, it was very hard to find a job. My husband said, 'I think you really should go to the United States to see how your sister is.' I came to San Francisco and, before I knew it, I was in the restaurant business. I had met a couple of ladies I had known in Tokyo, who said, 'How lucky we are to find you here! We want to open a restaurant and we've seen a location, but we can't speak much English. Can you help us negotiate the lease?' So, I got them the lease. Then, when the landlord asked for a deposit, I wrote a cheque to help them, because they didn't have a bank account and they said they would pay me back.

When I first opened the business, everything was against me. Firstly, I was a woman, when all the restaurants in San Francisco were owned by men. Secondly, I spoke Mandarin, not Cantonese. So, when I went to buy things in Chinatown, they wouldn't give me credit because they said I was a foreigner. They wouldn't even deliver; I had to go and pick things up. And every time I went, I had to pay cash. But the American shop owners were very

nice. They would say, 'We'll give you a little break – three days' credit,' or, 'You can pay us at the end of the month.' But the Chinese? No way!

Q. What brings you happiness?

Basically, I am a very happy person. I have a lot of good friends; they love me and I love them. I keep myself very busy, every day. I love all my plants; I water them and take care of them. I still cook for myself when I'm home alone. As for my health, I am fine for my age. Everybody laughs when I drink, they say, 'Wow, you are still drinking?' and I say, 'Why not?' I am happy.

Q. What do you regard as the lowest depth of misery?

San Francisco has more and more homeless people; these are not old people, some homeless are very young. And some I have read about come from very nice families; they could do so much, but they live on the street – that is really sad.

Q. What would you change if you could?

I would get rid of our president, Donald Trump. The way he acts is terrible, disgraceful. You can't believe what he says and you never know what he is going to do next. Today he says one thing, the next day he says something else. He said he wanted all the factories to use American labour – to use American everything – but then his own daughter manufactures her designer clothes, shoes and bags in China because of the cheap labour over there!

Q. Which single word do you most identify with?

Honesty. You know in yourself whether or not you are being honest; it is something I always taught my children to be.

'Generosity'

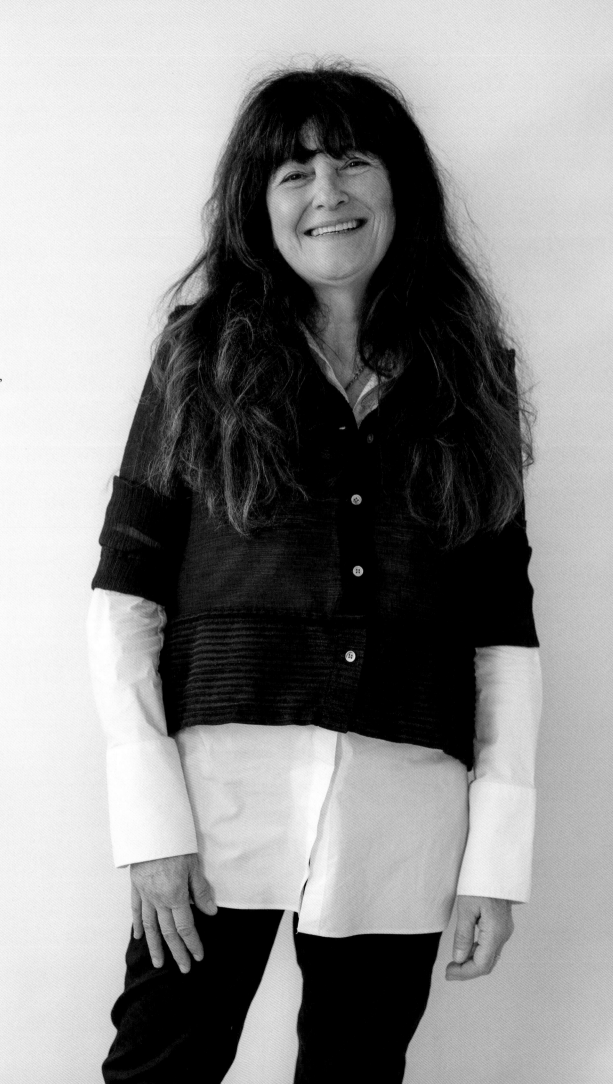

Ruth Reichl

Ruth Reichl was born in New York City, USA. She wrote her first cookbook at the age of twenty-one and later was a restaurant critic for the *New York Times* and *Los Angeles Times*. She was editor in chief of *Gourmet* magazine from 1999 to 2009. A television host and producer, Reichl is also the author of four memoirs: *Tender at the Bone, Comfort Me with Apples: More Adventures at the Table, Garlic and Sapphires* and *For You Mom, Finally.* Reichl has been recognised with six James Beard Awards.

'There must be a hundred times a day that you have a choice of being a bitch or being kind.'

Q. What really matters to you?

Kindness is probably the most important thing in the world; it's something that can inform your life, or not. I've never felt the importance of kindness more than when I became the editor of *Gourmet* magazine; I realised that I could either be one of those hard-driving, difficult, hard-to-please bosses, or I could try to make the lives of the sixty people who were working for me better. Kindness is the thing you want to keep front and centre in your life all the time – there must be a hundred times a day that you have a choice of being a bitch or being kind. For me, it's about making those choices all the time and always erring on the side of being kind. The older I get, the more important I think that is.

Q. What brings you happiness?

The act of making a beautiful meal makes me happy. For me, there is nothing quite as wonderful as thinking, 'Who's going to come to dinner tonight? What can I cook that will give them enormous pleasure?' In today's world, where we're so busy, so rushed, and always feeling pressured and fraught, the one place where we take time to slow down is at the table. I love watching everyone relax and start really paying attention to each other. That's one of the joys of being a cook.

One of the things that shaped my world as a child was my mother's bipolar disorder. There were a lot of ramifications attached to this, but one was that she was taste blind; she couldn't taste when food was bad, so she fed people poison. As a child, I learned very quickly to taste very carefully, and I cooked a lot. But the thing that was so important about my mother being bipolar is that she woke up every morning not knowing who she was, how she was going to feel and what she was going to do. I woke up every morning – and still wake up every morning – grateful that I'm not her and grateful that I'm sane. I learned early on that it is a blessing just to be a sane, ordinary person who can count on herself. That shaped everything else in my life.

The author Ann Patchett was interviewing me about my books and said that in every author's work, no matter what they're writing about, there is a buried message that gets repeated over and over again. That's true. The secret to life runs through all of my books – it's learning to find joy in ordinary things. You can spend your entire life in despair, because there is a lot to be despairing about and there are terrible things happening to people everywhere. But at the same time, it behoves us to learn to take joy in the smell of coffee in the morning and the feel of rain on our faces. There are as many reasons to be happy as there are to be unhappy – you can choose to be either one. So I literally find joy in the sound of water boiling in the kitchen or the colour that emerges when you peel a peach – there's a sunset hiding under there. One of the reasons I love food is that it is such a ready source of joy, if you pay attention. Working for the likes of Condé Nast, you live this very big life; you meet famous people, and have clothes, cars, jewels and money. But none of it matters. You can find as much joy in a piece of bread and butter. To me, that really is the secret to life.

Q. What do you regard as the lowest depth of misery?

Because I'm a food person, it's hunger. Here in America, one in eight children goes to bed hungry every night. It's horrifying, given that we are in the richest country in the world. It really hurts me. There's plenty of food in the world for everyone, and it's all a problem with distribution. I really believe that one of the reasons government exists is to give people the basic necessities in life, and food is certainly the most basic of basic necessities. It really horrifies me that, as we become more scientifically adept, we still can't manage to feed the world – looking at people who go hungry makes me crazy.

Q. What would you change if you could?

Gender inequality is probably the most egregious inequality there is. Who would believe that today we still see women who have no rights at all; who want to learn to drive but are completely subservient to their husbands. Half the world is being robbed of all their potential, and we need to stop that.

I would also stop climate change; the devastation that we've created today was unimaginable thirty years ago. We know climate change is going to make people hungry and it is completely man made. We're probably too late to stop it completely, but if I could, I'd get us, as a world, to all pull together and say, 'We will not put up with this anymore; we really need to make a change here.'

Q. Which single word do you most identify with?

Generosity. It's a really important quality; every time someone tells me I'm generous, I just find myself beaming.

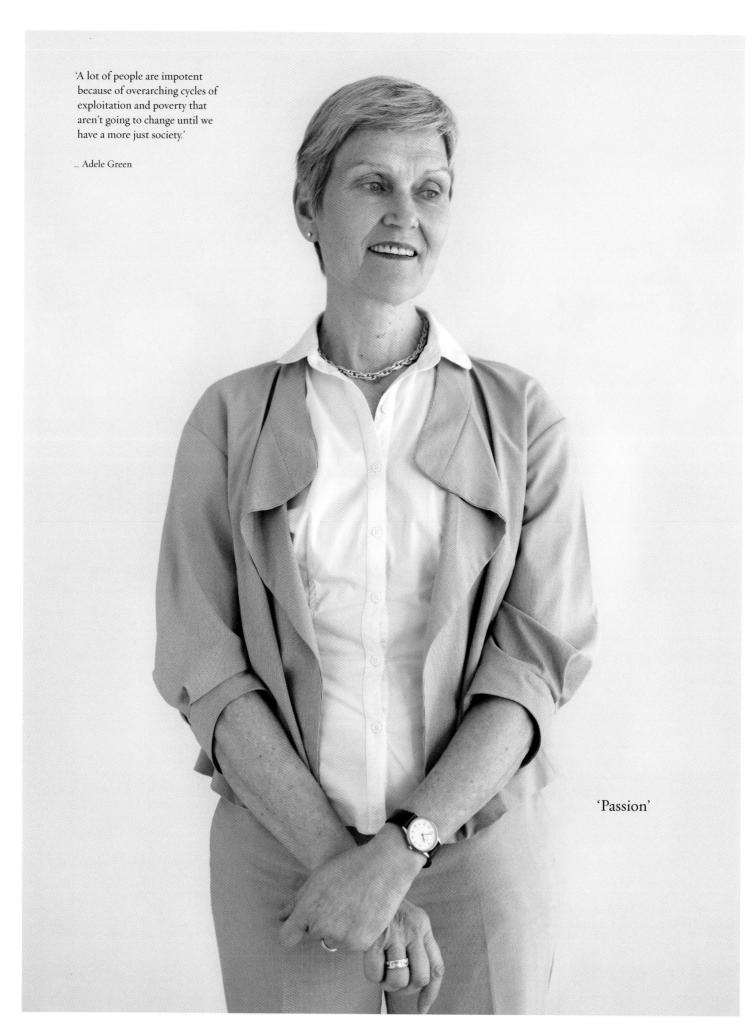

'A lot of people are impotent because of overarching cycles of exploitation and poverty that aren't going to change until we have a more just society.'

_ Adele Green

'Passion'

Interview page 380

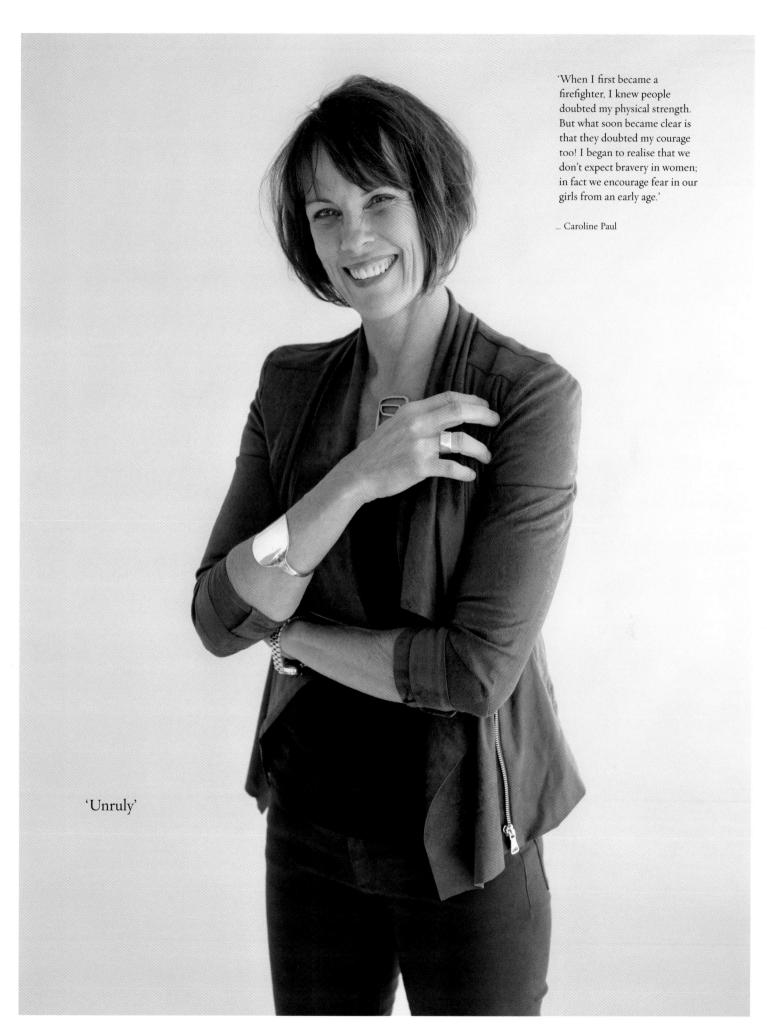

'When I first became a firefighter, I knew people doubted my physical strength. But what soon became clear is that they doubted my courage too! I began to realise that we don't expect bravery in women; in fact we encourage fear in our girls from an early age.'

— Caroline Paul

'Unruly'

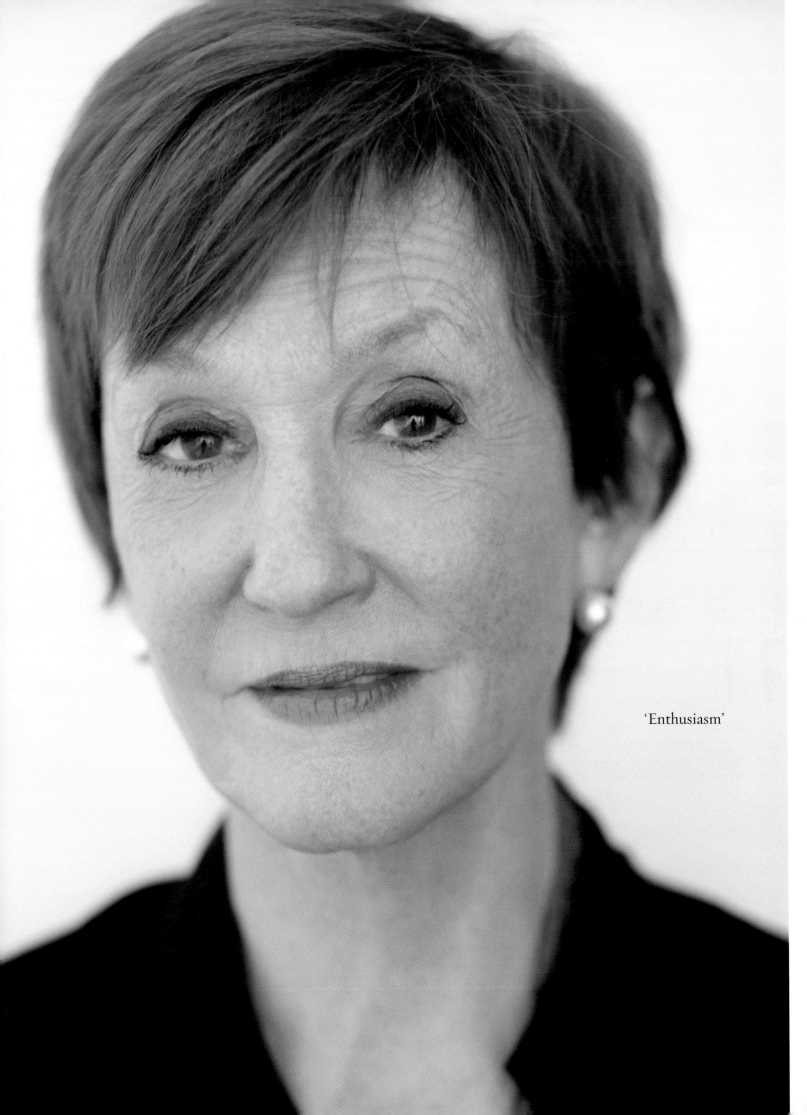

'Enthusiasm'

Kathy Eldon

Kathy Eldon was born in Cedar Rapids in Iowa, USA. In 1993, Eldon's son, Dan – who was a Reuters photographer and war correspondent – was stoned to death in Somalia. Inspired by his memory, in 1997 Eldon and her daughter, Amy Eldon Turteltaub, founded the Creative Visions Foundation, dedicated to inspiring and empowering creative activism. Through Creative Visions, Eldon has incubated more than two hundred and sixty projects and produced award-winning films, including a feature about her son, *The Journey is the Destination*. She is the author of seventeen books.

Q. What really matters to you?
Creative activism. I believe that each of us has a creative spark that can be used not only for ourselves, but also for others. This concept is the basis of a movement that we call 'creative activism,' which simply means using that spark – along with our skills and talents – to create good in the world. With creative activism, we don't have to be apathetic observers anymore; we can roll up our sleeves and do something positive.

Never have I been as passionate about this concept as I am now, because it's clear from what has happened in America over the past year – in 2016 – that if we don't get involved, individuals who may not have the 'greater good' in mind can control the narrative. But if we can come together as a 'global tribe' around important issues in our neighbourhoods, our communities and in our world, we can create positive change for all. We shouldn't wait until we're in really bad shape, facing major disasters, nuclear holocaust or drastic climate change; we should begin immediately to address issues like bullying, divisive talk, hateful rhetoric or stigmatisation of the 'other.' Being able to work together on manageable local causes equips us to address more expansive issues like renewable energy, water conservation or nuclear proliferation. I don't think I'm being idealistic when I say that it's possible to ignite a powerful, peaceful uprising that can unify individuals into a force for good.

I believe that we can create positive change in the world and transform ourselves in the process. The key is learning how to create, collaborate and communicate effectively. We must have the vision to see possibilities, but most great things don't happen without collaboration between individuals, and nothing major is possible without effective communication to a wider audience. That's why Creative Visions focusses on supporting creative artists who use arts and media to tell stories that need to be told about problems that need to be solved. We love individuals who are seeking solutions, and sharing them with a world that's hungry for inspiration and direction.

Q. What brings you happiness?
Happiness for me is about connecting. We are all given gifts in life – I believe mine is the ability to connect with an individual, to see beyond the obvious and tap into what he or she would really like to do and be, but may not feel courageous enough to attempt. I believe in the power of our creative vision and the possibility of transforming that dream into reality. Remarkable things happen when we focus our energy on intention, dream or vision, and transform it into reality.

My son revived a phrase that stays with me: 'The journey is the destination.' I've spent decades not being fully present because I've been so worried about an outcome. Now I believe that we should strive to achieve our vision, but shouldn't forget to enjoy the process.

Q. What do you regard as the lowest depth of misery?
I can't think of anything in my life that has been worse than enduring the loss of my child. But, when I look around me and see people in Aleppo who have lost not only their loved ones, but also their communities – and as a result – their possibilities and their futures, I am heartbroken. I can only begin to imagine what it's like to experience loss on that scale. It's a heavy burden to know that people in the world are going through so much tragedy. That probably makes me as sad as the loss of my child. But then I have to ask, 'What do we do about it?' I can't just sit around feeling sad or even just compassionate – I have to take action. To paraphrase the words of Teddy Roosevelt: we have to do what we can, with what we have, where we are.

Q. What would you change if you could?
I'm lucky, because I'm doing exactly what I believe I should be doing right now: trying to awaken people to their own potential to change the world around them, and then giving them the necessary tools and resources to get started. I want to do all that I can to spread the concept of creative activism around the world, to motivate and then activate people around the issues they believe are important. You don't have to choose a cause that doesn't matter to you – just tackle something right there in your own neighbourhood.

At a time when people are so frightened of the 'other' – whether it's gay people, black people, old people or Muslims – it's time for us to realise either that we are all 'other' or that there is no 'other.' That goes for gender equality as well. We are one, *ubuntu*: 'I am because you are.' We are members of a global tribe. It doesn't matter whether male or female – we are one. But until we figure that one out, we are really screwed.

Q. Which single word do you most identify with?
The word I would choose changes all the time – today's word is 'enthusiasm!' It's the sense of energy that flows through you when you are excited about something. It's contagious – it's like a virus. If we can be enthusiastic about things that are positive and exciting in the world – instead of reacting only to the hard, negative things that are going on right now – I think we can shift the world.

Divya
Kalia

Divya Kalia was born and raised in Delhi, India. She earned her master's degree in economics from the Gokhale Institute of Politics and Economics in Pune. Kalia began her career as an analytics and consulting professional for Genpact, then the Royal Bank of Scotland, before working in consumer-finance strategy for Boston Consulting Group. Kalia is the chief operating officer of Bikxie, an app-based bike-taxi service that she co-founded in Gurgaon in 2015.

Q. What really matters to you?

I want to ensure that women in India benefit from an equitable distribution of jobs and also benefit – in whatever profession they are in – from the same honour and respect men receive in pursuing their professions. And I want to ensure that women are not discriminated against when they come forward to do the kind of work society believes is reserved for men.

India is a very religious country, but, although I am a Hindu, my religious inclinations are not very strong because, early on, I was introduced to a lot of literature by my communist grandfather. When I was seven or eight, my mother had to undergo a very dangerous operation that she was told she might not survive. Watching her going through her illness instilled a fighting spirit in me; I decided that, if she could fight when everything was completely out of her control, then I could do the same in my own life. It made me fiercely independent; I completed a master's degree in economics, then went on to work in the field of analytics.

Being a married Indian woman and trying to also pursue a career means that you have to fight twice as hard; when you're single, you need only look after yourself, but, once you get married, you are expected to take principal responsibility for the care of the entire extended family – that is a cultural value placed upon you. When I married my husband, our families joined, and I was expected to focus on everybody in that bigger family. As a wife, you get up in the morning, clean the house, make the breakfast, prepare and pack lunches, then go out to focus on your work knowing that it is not only *your* livelihood but the family's you are pursuing. And, if someone in the family is not well, you have to take the day off to take them to the doctor. When you are married, travel for work also becomes difficult, because, in India, we are so emotionally connected to our kin that being away from home introduces a disconnect with our family. But, I have been extremely lucky in that my family is very understanding and supportive of me – not everybody is so lucky.

My husband and I were both doing well professionally, but we quit our jobs to pursue our own venture, Bikxie. Delhi has terrible road congestion that can last for hours; we used to spend four to six hours a day travelling but would see bikes zipping past our four wheelers and think, 'That's not fair!' And because there is no organised transport that operates from the Delhi metro stations, people end up spending four times the cost of their train ticket on travelling the last mile from the station to work. I used to tell my husband, 'I wish there was a taxi service on motorbikes!' and he thought this was a great idea. That's when we conceptualised the bike taxi. I told my husband that, as a woman, I might not feel comfortable sitting behind a male driver because I might bump into him if he braked; culturally, that wouldn't be acceptable to me. Our state, Haryana, is also infamous for incidences of molestation in cabs, so, if I wasn't comfortable, how could I expect other women to be?

We decided to employ women pilots for our bikes, to ensure that women commuters feel safe and to create employment for women. We also provide pepper spray to our pilots to ensure that they and our travellers are not subjected to anything untoward. We've now been operating for over a year and, fortunately, we've not faced any issues of that nature. When we started we had ten male and five female pilots, and now, because the response has been so phenomenal, we are catering to three cities.

We have sometimes gone around with our female pilots to get a sense of their day-to-day experiences. One day, a call came in for a female pilot to pick up a young girl and take her for tuition. We went home with the girl and spoke to her mother, who, because it's not safe for a girl to travel alone, used to drive her daughter to the tuition herself. It was utterly heartwarming when she told us how confident Bikxie made her feel about her daughter's safety.

Once Bikxie becomes really successful, it's my dream to start other ventures through which I can ensure that women in India have access to an equitable distribution of jobs and are not discriminated against because of their gender. Watching women come out of their houses and breaking the stereotypes really matters to me – it's so liberating! And they break those stereotypes not because they're encouraged to, but because doing so just makes sense to them.

Q. What brings you happiness?

I absolutely love cooking and experimenting with food!

Q. What do you regard as the lowest depth of misery?

It's something I feel would upset most women: the feeling of helplessness that comes from not getting sufficient education or support, which keeps you dependent. This is why my husband and I feel so proud to have been able to generate employment for both men and women; they feel more financially independent and they have choices. We don't restrain anyone from taking on a job for us part-time, which allows them to study or work in parallel; this means that a lot of our women pilots are studying. This is great, but there are a lot of smart people out there who aren't educated or empowered enough to do what they're meant to – for these people, misery is the helplessness that comes from not receiving the right life orientation at a young age.

Q. What would you change if you could?

I would provide a global, moral- or values-based education system. There is a difference between literacy and education; of course we need to improve literacy globally, but we also need to make sure that people are in the right frame of mind. Violence, racism and gender discrimination won't go away until we have a universal education system that helps children understand, from a tender age, that they need to be accommodating of others.

Q. Which single word do you most identify with?

Morals – without them nothing else matters.

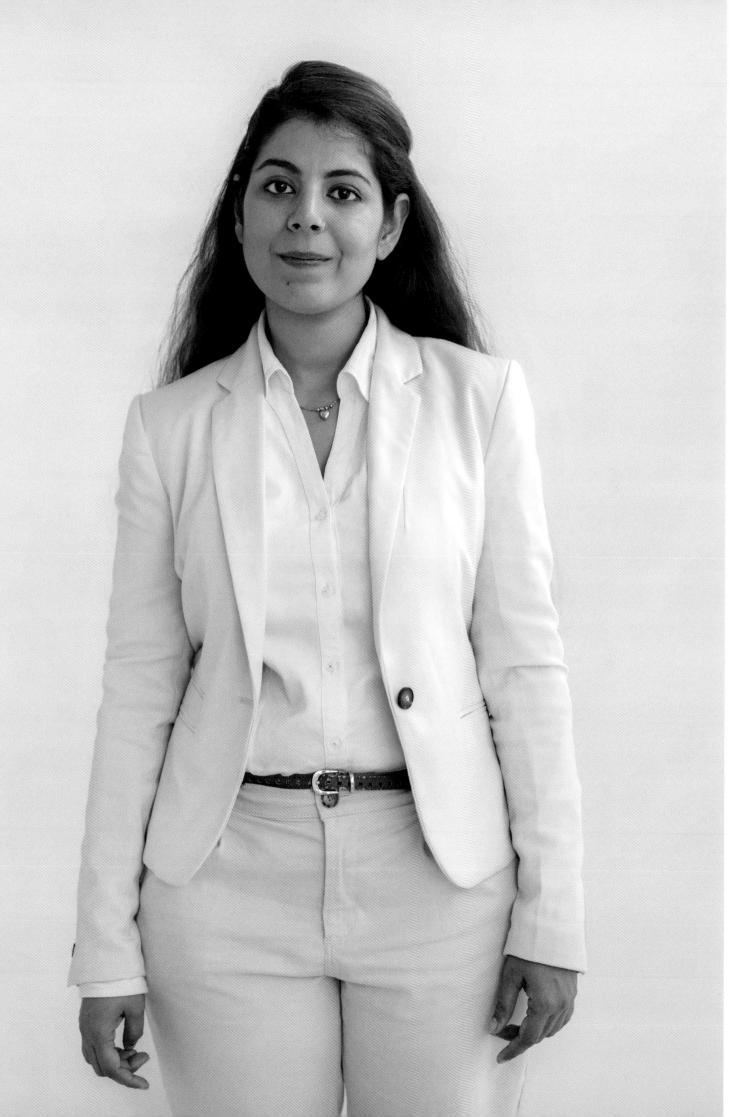

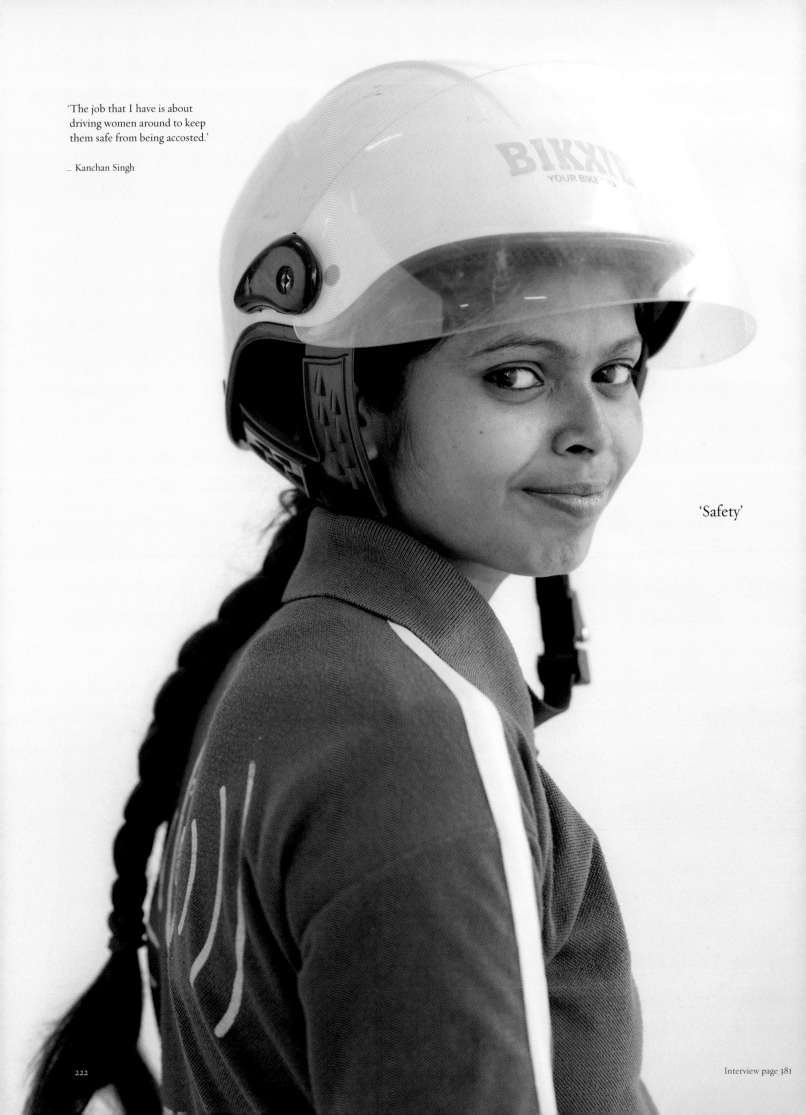

'The job that I have is about driving women around to keep them safe from being accosted.'

_ Kanchan Singh

'Safety'

Interview page 381

'Being a married Indian woman and trying to also pursue a career means that you have to fight twice as hard.'

_ Divya Kalia

'Morals'

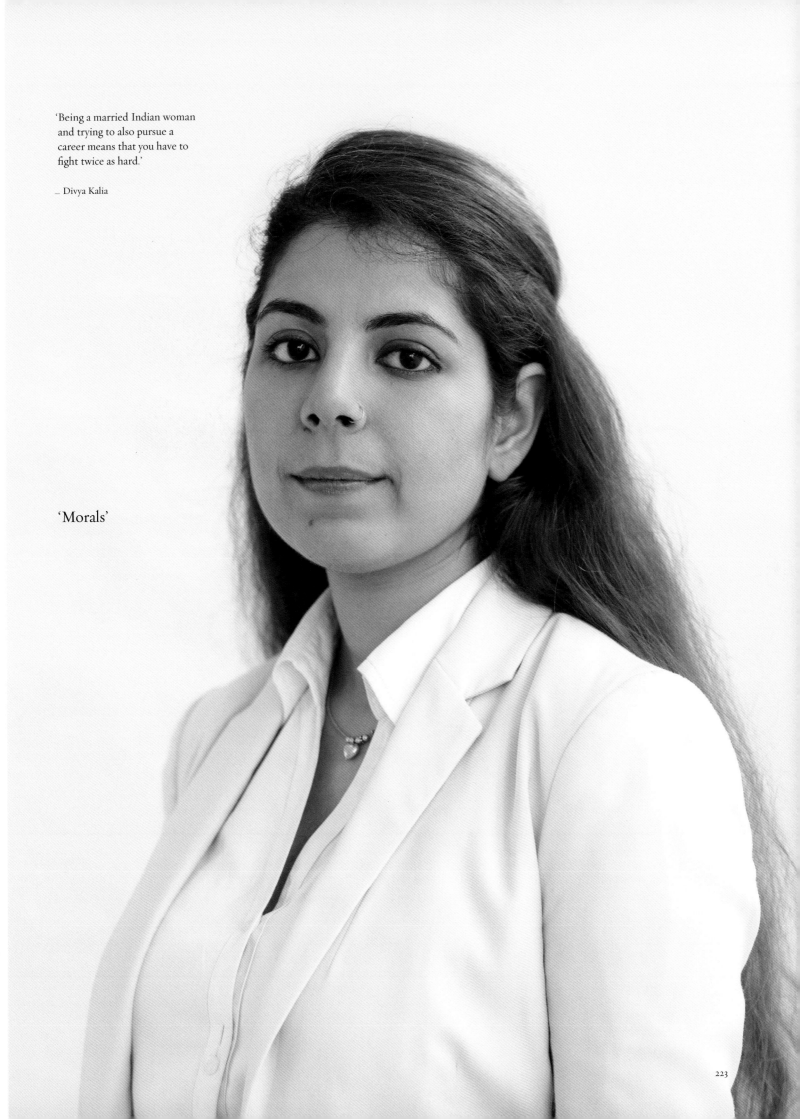

Ruth Bader Ginsburg

Ruth Bader Ginsburg was born in Brooklyn, New York City, USA. She holds a bachelor of laws from Columbia Law School. Ginsburg co-founded the Women's Rights Project of the American Civil Liberties Union (ACLU) in 1971, later serving as the ACLU's general counsel and on its board. She was appointed a judge of the United States Court of Appeals for the District of Columbia Circuit in 1980 and an associate justice of the Supreme Court of the United States in 1993. She was awarded a Thurgood Marshall Award for contributions to gender equality and civil rights in 1999.

Q. What really matters to you?

Two things: my work and my family. But I wouldn't put one before the other.

In terms of my family, the best decision I ever made was my choice of life partner: my late husband, Marty Ginsburg. We met when he was eighteen and I was seventeen, and he was the only young man up to that point who cared that I had a brain. He was my biggest booster, and we had fifty-six wonderful years together.

I also had wonderful in-laws. My mother-in-law's secret to a happy marriage was, 'It helps sometimes to be a little deaf.' I've followed that advice, not only in dealing with my dear spouse, but also with colleagues throughout my career; so, when I hear anything that is unkind or thoughtless, I just tune it out.

I received wonderful advice from my father-in-law, too. My daughter was fourteen months old when I started at Harvard, and I worried about balancing my responsibilities. My father-in-law sat me down and explained that, if I didn't think I could manage my studies, I had the best reason in the world for dropping out. But, he said, if I did want to do it, then I would have to pick myself up, stop feeling sorry for myself and find a way. So, at many turns in my life, I have asked myself, 'Is this something I really want?' And if it is, I find a way to do it.

My success in law school, I attribute largely to my daughter, Jane. My life was balanced, whereas most of my contemporaries were consumed by their studies. Our babysitter worked eight-to-four, which allowed me to attend classes and read law books during the day. At four in the afternoon, I went home; then, it was Jane's time. We went to the park, played silly games and I sang – I wouldn't dare sing to anybody except my children! After Jane went to bed, I was eager to get back to the books. So, each part of my life was a respite from the other.

My own mother, who died when I was seventeen, impressed on me the importance of independence. In those ancient days, most parents of girls wanted them to find Prince Charming and live happily ever after. But my mother wanted me to fend for myself. She thought being a high school history teacher would be a good path for me; she never dreamed of me becoming a lawyer, no less a judge!

It was when this country experienced the Second Red Scare, in my college years, that I became interested in the law and in doing something to keep our country in tune with its most basic values – like the right to think, speak and write as one believes, and not as a 'Big Brother' government thinks.

Then, later, I had the enormous good fortune to be alive, and to be a lawyer, in the early sixties when the women's movement was coming alive in the United States. What we achieved later, in the seventies, would have been impossible at any time earlier, because society wasn't yet ready for that change. By the seventies, however, most people's thinking in terms of what life should be like for women had changed.

I was also the beneficiary of a change brought about by President Jimmy Carter. When he became president in the mid-seventies, he took one look at the federal judiciary and realised that they all looked like him; they were all white men. President Carter realised that the federal bench wasn't representative of all Americans and was determined to appoint members of minority groups to it – back then, women counted as a minority group! He was only in office for four years – so he never had a Supreme Court vacancy to fill – but he literally changed the complexion of the United States judiciary through his appointments; he appointed twenty-five women as trial judges and eleven as Court of Appeal judges – I was one of the lucky eleven.

I have enjoyed everything that I have done in the law, but I think the job I now hold is the very best a law-trained person could have. Our mission is to do what the law requires and what is just, and we have tremendous job security, because the Founding Fathers were wise enough to protect the independence of all federal judges.

Q. What brings you happiness?

I'm satisfied when I feel I've done my job, when I've written an opinion that is as good as I can make it. And my growing family is my happiness; I get endless joy from my children, Jane and James, and from my four grandchildren and two stepgrandchildren.

Q. What would you change in the world if you could?

We have advanced as a society, but there is still a long way to go, so I would have society buy into the notion that daughters are to be cherished as much as sons. I don't want daughters to be held back by artificial barriers, rather, they should be given the opportunity to grow, aspire and achieve according to whatever talents they have. That is my dream for the world; I am convinced that we will all be better off when women and men are truly partners in society at every level.

When I started at Harvard, in 1956, they had only been accepting women for five years and I was one of nine women in a class of five hundred. There were no anti-discrimination laws back then, so they installed women's bathrooms in only one of the two teaching buildings. If you had an exam in the one building and needed to go to the bathroom, you had a problem; but we didn't complain, we just accepted that that was how it was. And there were law firms that wouldn't interview women. They'd say, 'We had a lady-lawyer once and she was dreadful.' Justice Sandra Day O'Connor worked without pay for four months to prove her worth to a county attorney in California. Of course, he found out in short order that she was worth more than all the men put together!

Q. Which single word do you most identify with?

Notorious. A young woman made a Tumblr account out of my dissenting judgement in the *Shelby County* case. She told me I had become The Notorious R.B.G. – totally understandable! The Notorious B.I.G. and I were both born and bred in Brooklyn, New York, so we have *that* in common.

'Notorious'

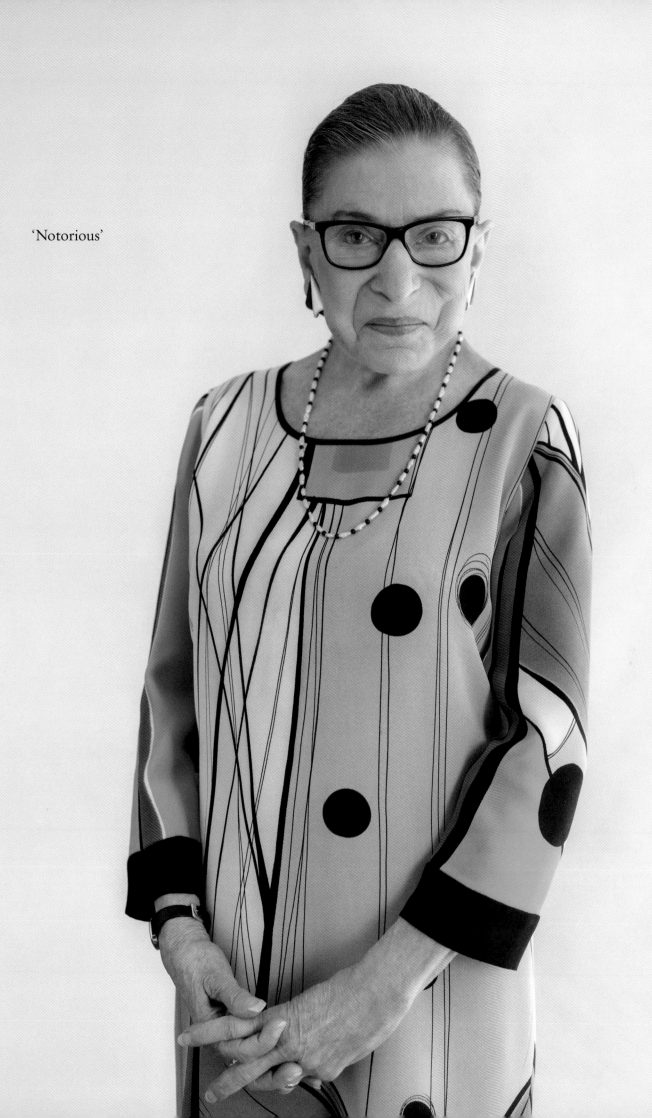

'Sometimes people feel intimidated
in the face of prejudice, thinking,
"What difference am I going to
make?" But we can't think that
way, because we are here to make
a difference; every decision we
make is literally going to change
the world.'

_ Hélène Grimaud

Interview page 381

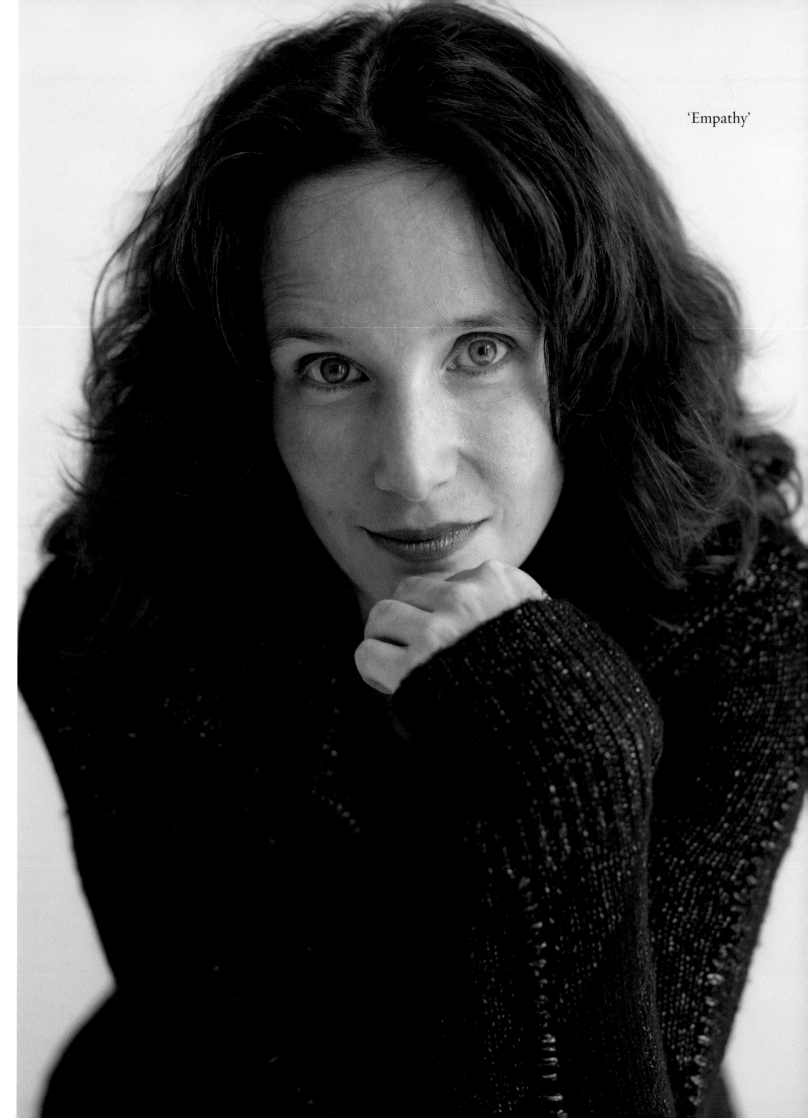

'Empathy'

'Service'

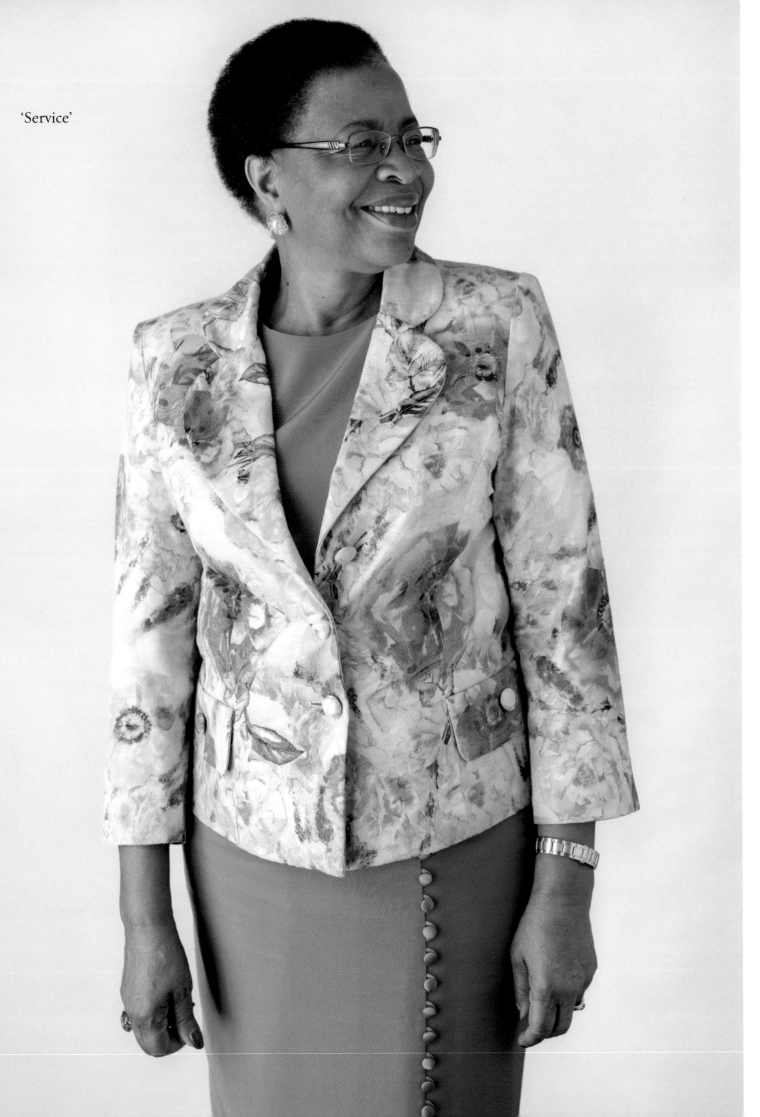

Graça Machel

Graça Machel DBE was born in Gaza, Mozambique. She is an African stateswoman, a former freedom fighter and Mozambique's first minister of education. She is the widow of Mozambican president Samora Machel and of former South African president Nelson Mandela. Among numerous awards, Machel has received the United Nations' Nansen Refugee Award and is an honorary Dame Commander of the Order of the British Empire. She is the founder of the Graça Machel Trust and several other organisations through which she advocates for women's economic empowerment, food security and nutrition, education and good governance.

Q. What really matters to you?

What matters to me is protecting women and children, and allowing them to flourish. But, I never sat down to choose a cause or purpose, rather, I was confronted by situations in which the causes chose me – and I embraced them.

I'm a village girl, who was very fortunate to be born to a loving, caring and protective family. I was nurtured, I was allowed to build my inner strength and I was told to take up my dreams and fly with them, with no limitations. I was the last of six children and my father died seventeen days after I was born. He was at home when he sensed he was going and, because he didn't want my mother to take in the shock alone, he called my eldest sister to join them. He asked my mother and sister to make a pledge to him that none of the children would be allowed to grow up illiterate. So, these two women are the pillars I built my character on.

My mother was left with six children to raise on her own, with very, very limited material resources. People would have called us poor, but we weren't, because we had a very strong sense of dignity in our family and we could live with what we had. This built our characters to be resourceful in any situation. My mother fought to give us the best tool in life: an education. We all managed to go to school, and, although we each have different levels of accomplishment, we all have a profession and are able to make a living.

All my life, I've had opportunities to be of service on different levels in the community – from my church work through to when I joined the liberation struggle that continues to liberate my country, Mozambique. When I was twenty-nine, I was made minister of education. I had to tap in to my inner strength to discover the best ways of providing education to millions of young minds, to enable them to take up their own dreams and fly. In that process, I learned about the very severe injustices that are inflicted on children and women – and that's when those causes chose me.

The foundation that I received growing up allowed me to be free throughout my life; by acknowledging that, I am able to understand how important it is for every single woman in the world to have the freedom to make choices and to do whatever it is that she desires. My mother and my sister certainly informed my deep belief in the ability of women to regenerate, to rediscover inner strength and new energies, even when faced with challenges. In the nineties, I was given the opportunity to lead a study for the United Nations and visited many, many camps for refugees and displaced persons in desperate situations. I was inspired when I sat down and heard women's stories, because I came to understand that they never gave in to despair. I marvelled at how women could hold on to their dreams, and at their determination to build something for themselves and for their families. They could see a future in which all the challenges they were faced with were meaningless. My belief and trust in the capacity of women has come from those face-to-face conversations.

I do feel that things are getting better for women and children, because we have this big push from humankind to acknowledge their rights; we have very well-developed treaties and protocols in place that are aimed at protecting women and children, and millions of people around the world are working towards this end. We shouldn't say that things are getting worse, just because there are challenges. Rather, we should celebrate the numbers of young people who give up the comforts of their places of origin to provide help to those facing challenges in situations of conflict. There are millions of people who are consciously committed to goodness and to the protection of human rights – including the rights of women and children – and that *is* progress.

Still, there are millions of children not in school and millions of women who are illiterate; children and women are dying unnecessarily when the capacity, the knowledge and the tools exist to prevent this. Many of the issues will continue beyond my lifetime, but I strive to go to bed every day knowing I've done my best to make inroads. Yes, there are times when we make remarkable progress and there are other times when we have serious setbacks. You just have to make sure for yourself that you did your best – then you can be at peace.

Q. What brings you happiness?

Looking into the eyes of a happy child – those eyes speak volumes and give me joy. When I can embrace a child who is healthy and happy, and who has the full potential to become whatever they want, that makes me happy.

Q. What do you regard as the lowest depth of misery?

It's when a human being becomes dehumanised to the point of being unable to recognise the humanity of others. Yes, there are people in desperate situations who are capable of anything when they're looking for something to eat. But, if you give them a loaf of bread, you will see their humanity – it has not been killed. There are people living in abundance, however, who have managed to kill their own humanity and who therefore are not able to recognise it in others – they're not able to recognise suffering. That is the absolute lowest depth of misery.

Q. What would you change if you could?

I would love for people's hearts to recognise the spark of life that exists in each one of us and the fact that this is what makes us equal. And to recognise that, because we are equal, no one has the right to humiliate, degrade or kill another. The mind is unlimited in its capacity, so I don't think it is a stretch to imagine this. I want everything that we do to be directed towards valuing, protecting and caring for life. Achieving this is not complicated – we have the means to reach hearts and minds – but the problem is that the means has been appropriated to speak to people's materialism; people have become slaves to money. Instead, our primary concern must become the quality of who we are as human beings. We must bring to light the people who serve, who are defining their lives on the basis of the concept 'I am because you are.'

Q. Which single word do you most identify with?

Service.

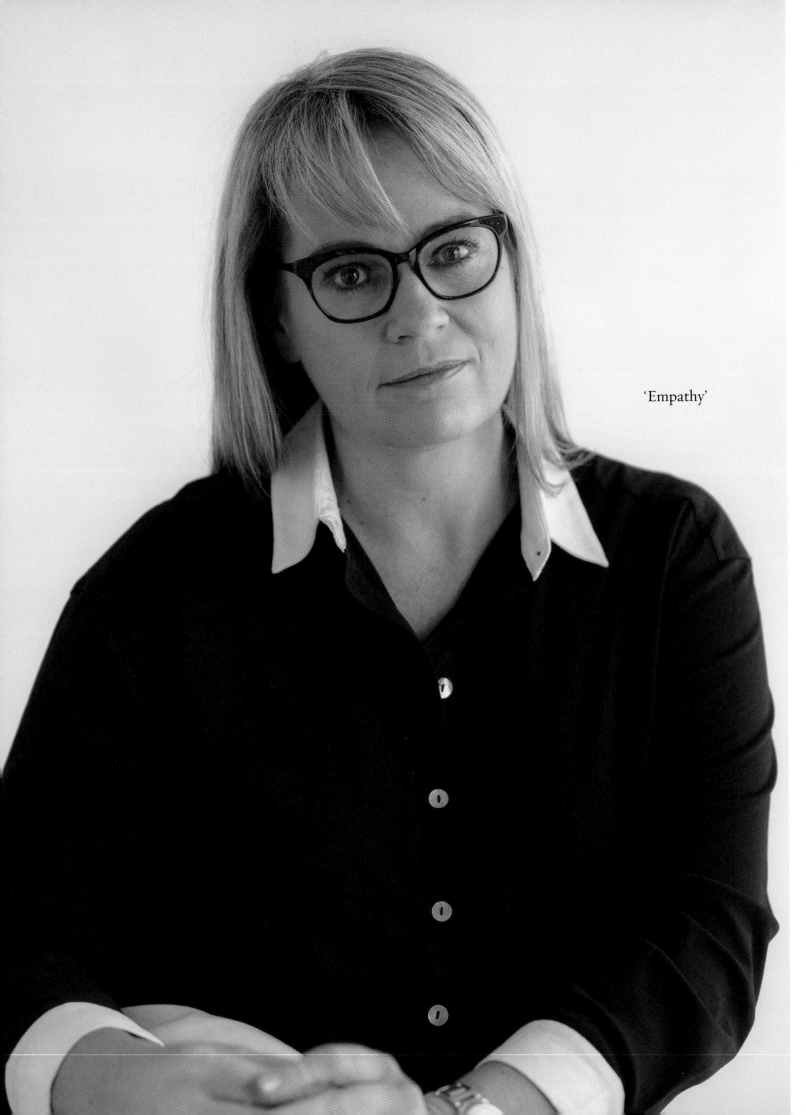

'Empathy'

Zelda la Grange

Zelda la Grange was born in Johannesburg, South Africa. She completed a three-year executive-secretary diploma at the University of Technology, Pretoria, in 1992. In 1994, she became assistant to the private secretary of South Africa's first democratically elected president, Nelson Mandela; in 1997, she herself became one of the president's private secretaries. Following President Mandela's retirement from the presidency in 1999 until his death in 2013, la Grange served him in various capacities, including as executive personal assistant, spokesperson, aide-de-camp and manager of his private office. In 2014, she published her bestselling memoir, *Good Morning, Mr Mandela*.

Q. What really matters to you?

Humanity is all that matters – period. If we can acknowledge and respect each other's humanity, we will be able to see that we have more in common than sets us apart. If we can focus on that, we can achieve anything. Everyone on earth craves respect, and it's by respecting our enemies that we make them our friends. The biggest lesson Nelson Mandela taught me is that it's when we are able to remove ideology from consideration that we can connect with one another.

I was born in apartheid South Africa and grew up in a very conservative Afrikaans community; my immediate environment supported the apartheid system, and my immediate future was dictated by it. My parents and their contemporaries were incredibly religious and close-minded; they weren't exposed to the lives of non-white South Africans outside our community. So, from a very young age, children in our community became racist by default. You didn't question a thing – you bought into the system and you believed the propaganda you were fed. I was taught to believe that, because of my white skin, I was superior to all people of colour, irrespective of their beliefs, status and intellects, or of the similarities between us. It's unbelievable to think of it now, but I felt superior because I was white.

It was only when I was challenged that I came to realise how wrong the system was and how it had poisoned my outlook. When Nelson Mandela – whom we call Madiba – was inaugurated, the Afrikaner community was overwhelmed with fear. For decades, the apartheid government had told us that we needed to protect ourselves from the non-white masses, so we had no idea how the new system would affect us. At that point, I was working in the Department of State Expenditure. We had only just been exposed to non-white government employees, and I still very much believed I was superior to my non-white colleagues. I was living with my parents and wanted to work closer to home, so, a move to the government's Union Buildings was purely logistical; in 1994, I applied for a job in Madiba's office,

never thinking I would meet him. After all, I was a twenty-three-year-old *boeremeisie* – Afrikaans girl – from a racist, conservative background, and I had been against the abolishment of apartheid. Nonetheless, I was offered a job working under Madiba's private secretary – I assumed it would be in an office of two hundred people, but there were only five of us! Two weeks into the job, I nearly bumped into Madiba as he was leaving the office; I found myself face to face with this man my people feared, and I didn't know what to expect of him. I didn't know it then, but that moment was the start of my metamorphosis. Madiba did the complete opposite of what I expected; he extended his hand and began speaking to me in Afrikaans. He asked me about my childhood and my upbringing, and asked what I was doing in his office – luckily, he didn't ask me who I voted for! All the while, he spoke to me in the language of his oppressor, never once letting go of my hand. I expected hostility from him, but all he showed me was love and respect. I was so undeserving of his kindness. It makes me so emotional to think about that moment, because it changed my life.

I realised that everything my people believed was false. I started questioning everything about my life: my upbringing, my religion, my parents and the system that I had bought into. I had to examine the privilege that had isolated and shielded me from the suffering of others. That day, a whole new world I had been completely unaware of was opened up to me. That was Madiba's gift: he could connect with people by stripping away their layers – their religion, their history, their ideology, their baggage – and seeing them purely as a person. And he didn't only free people of colour who had been oppressed for so long – he also freed the oppressors from their ignorance.

So, it's humanity that matters to me. I'm constantly asking myself how I can best extend kindness. On both sides of any divide stand human beings and I truly believe that, through kindness, we can find middle ground. I believe that if we can consider the lived experiences and

suffering of others, we will be able to connect with one another.

Q. What brings you happiness?

My deepest sense of happiness comes from those moments when I have the time and the freedom to think, in my own company. Every now and then, Madiba would say that he missed prison. People would be almost disgusted. They'd say, 'You can't say that; it sounds like you want to go back there.' And he would respond by saying, 'No, no. I miss having time to think.' Our lives have become so crowded with issues and challenges that time spent alone has become a luxury. But we can't address the problems of the world if we take contemplation for granted.

Q. What do you regard as the lowest depth of misery?

Any kind of suffering. Watching a body losing its ability to function is just terrible; when Madiba's life was coming to an end, it was incredibly difficult to watch someone so strong in life degenerate.

It's also miserable to consider that, in today's world of abounding luxury, development and technology, there are people starving in poverty. I find it incredibly painful to contemplate what is happening in South Africa. I've seen first-hand what the sacrifices of fighting a liberation struggle can do to a family. People sacrificed their families and personal lives to free South Africa – many sacrificed their lives – yet twenty-three years later, in 2017, people are still dying of hunger. How is that possible? When I look at the corruption, mismanagement, and unethical and immoral behaviour of the current African National Congress government, I wonder whether all the sacrifices our struggle heroes made were in vain. And I wonder how we rebound from where we are now.

Q. What would you change if you could?

I would start by transforming our education system – it's the only way out of this. And I mean not just by granting access to education, but access to *quality* education.

Q. Which single word do you most identify with?

Empathy.

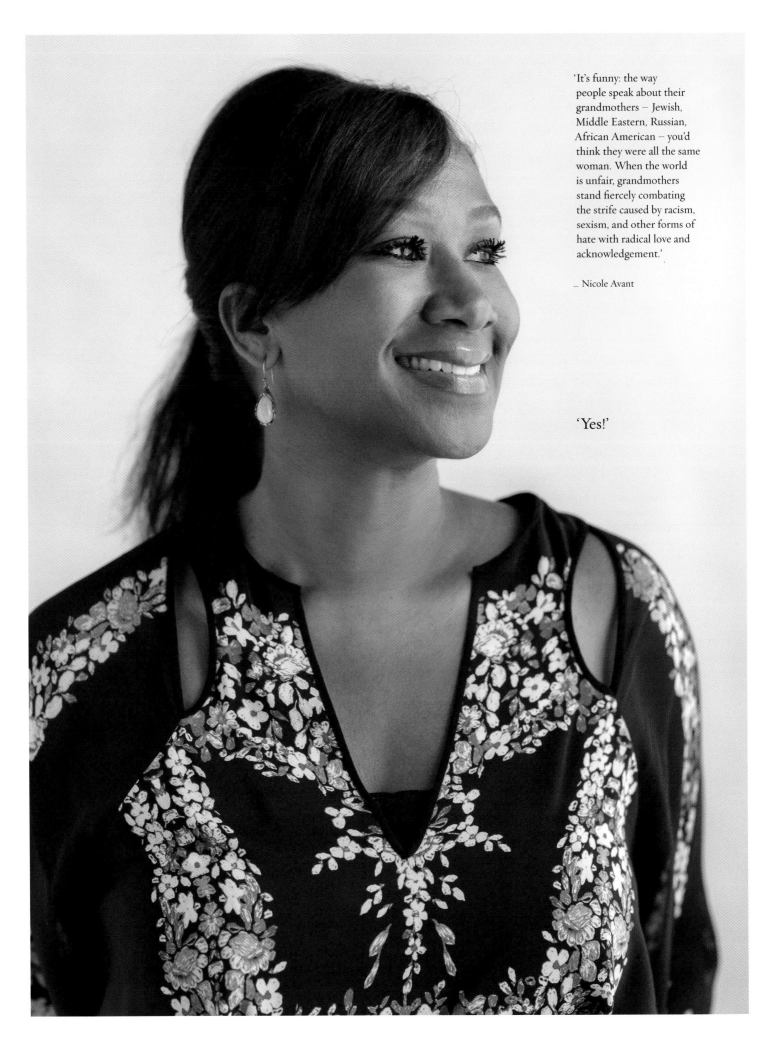

'It's funny: the way
people speak about their
grandmothers – Jewish,
Middle Eastern, Russian,
African American – you'd
think they were all the same
woman. When the world
is unfair, grandmothers
stand fiercely combating
the strife caused by racism,
sexism, and other forms of
hate with radical love and
acknowledgement.'

_ Nicole Avant

'Yes!'

Interview page 382

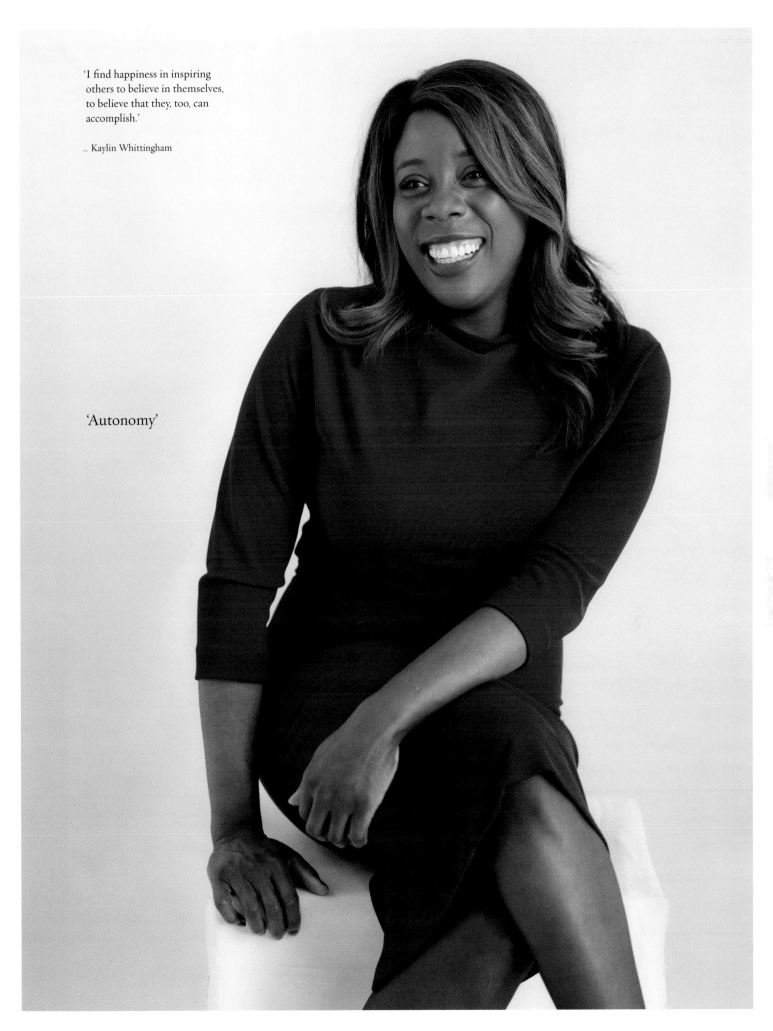

'I find happiness in inspiring others to believe in themselves, to believe that they, too, can accomplish.'

_ Kaylin Whittingham

'Autonomy'

'I find happiness in inspiring others to believe in themselves, to believe that they, too, can accomplish.'

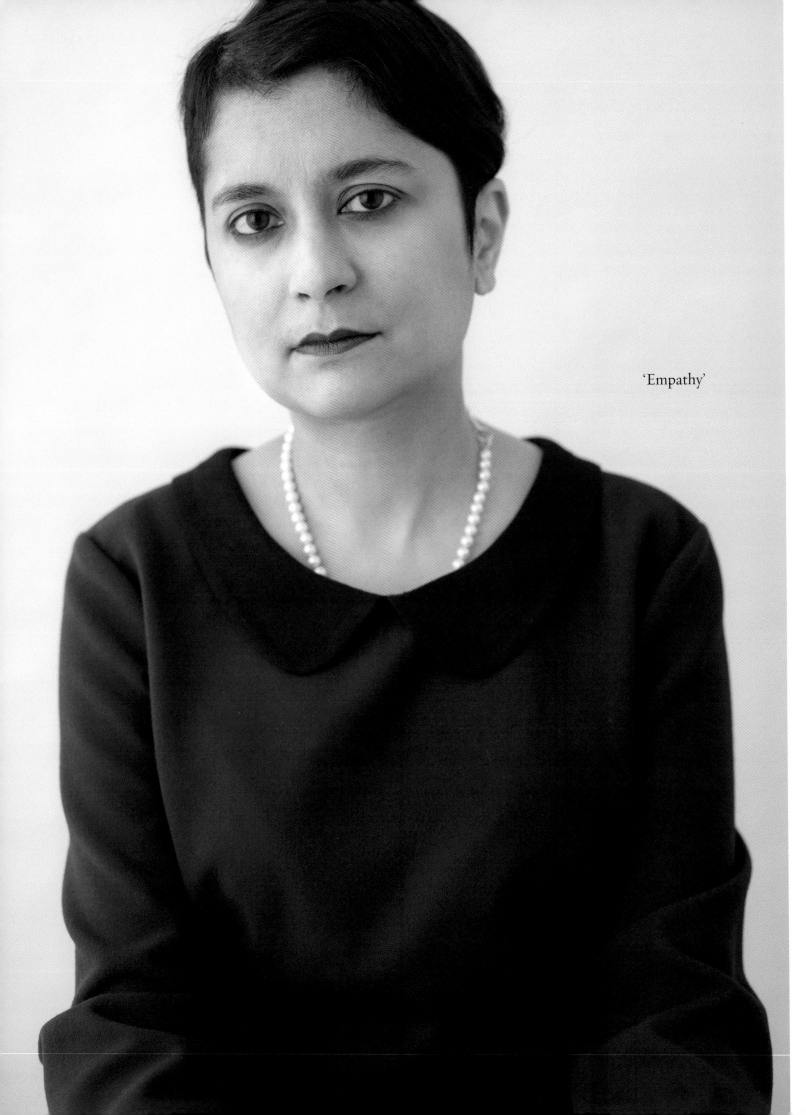

'Empathy'

Shami Chakrabarti

Shami Chakrabarti CBE was born in London, England. She holds a bachelor of laws from the London School of Economics and Political Science, and trained as a barrister before joining the Home Office in 1996. Chakrabarti became in-house counsel for British civil-liberties-advocacy organisation Liberty in 2001 and was its director from 2003 to 2016. In 2007, Chakrabarti was made a Commander of the Order of the British Empire for her services to human rights. In 2016, she was appointed to the House of Lords and became Labour shadow attorney general for England and Wales.

Q. What really matters to you?

Universal values: I believe human rights are conceived of universal values and that's where my beliefs begin and end – the content in between is just the meat for the bones.

People spend a lot of time talking about British values or European values or American values, but I am most interested in universal values. I'm interested in the idea that we are all entitled to be treated with equal dignity and to be regarded with equal worth. We're entitled to this, not because of our passport or because we're a good person, or because we are either male or female, or because we are of a particular race, but because we are human.

Being the daughter of migrants has been a very important part of my journey, because, in many ways, my journey feels like a continuation of my parents' journey. My dad is still around but my mother, sadly, is not; they were both originally from Kolkata, and I believe that being the child of migrants like them makes you inherently internationalist. It gives you a natural interest in human rights, and it makes you curious.

My parents always talked about having come to Britain with great excitement and hope; one of the things Britain symbolised for them was the rule of law. Neither of them were lawyers, but they had a real sense of justice and injustice, because they had both witnessed injustice early in their lives. They instilled in me a sense of equality before the law. When I was twelve or thirteen, the Yorkshire Ripper – a serial rapist and murderer – was being covered in practically every news story. I remember saying to my parents, 'When they catch that animal, they should string him up.' My father responded that I couldn't possibly support the death penalty. To my current shame, I asked him why not: this man had preyed on vulnerable women, and I felt like a vulnerable woman myself. But, my father told me that, no matter how well-imagined or designed, no justice system in the world is perfect. He said that even if one person in a million is wrongly convicted, that's one too many. And he asked me how I would feel if it was me walking up to the scaffold, with no one believing in my innocence, not even my family. That moment was very significant – it was when I first started to understand the complexity of human-rights issues. Because, often, you're dealing with competing rights. I told this story in an interview, and the next time I saw my dad he said, 'You've been talking about me to the press!' Just as I was apologising for not consulting him, he told me his issue wasn't with that, it was with the fact that he couldn't recollect the discussion at all; it made him worry about all the things he must have said to me that may have influenced me. I have a fifteen-year-old son, so now I'm constantly conscious of the power of my influence over him or that of any adult over him. Because those small moments of influence are so important.

Q. What brings you happiness?

The meaning of life – and the way to get the best out of life – is connection with other people. In our personal lives, we use words like love, friendship and family. But more broadly, we can talk about community and solidarity. There are words for this in everybody's language and everybody's cultural context; Christians call it fellowship and Muslims call it peace. There are many words for it, but, in the end, it's that connection with other people that makes this all worthwhile.

Q. What do you regard as the lowest depth of misery?

To feel isolated: to be without empathy and to not experience it in return. I think that would be enormous misery. People do need food, water, health care and shelter, but they also need dignity and, as social creatures, they need the opportunity to connect with others.

Q. What would you change if you could?

I would succeed in persuading more people to have a care for other people's children, in addition to their own. That is the key to the human-rights kingdom, as far as I'm concerned. This notion of my speech being free, but yours being a bit more expensive, is not acceptable. There are some people in my country who are very scathing about the notion of human rights; they'll say it's political correctness gone mad, that it's a cover for all sorts of selfishness or that it's protection for the guilty. But those people still love their own human rights, so I would make them imagine that the person who is bothering them – who has been made wretched, poor or isolated, or who is drowning in the Mediterranean – could just as easily be them or their own child. At the very least I would ignite an empathy, which would be the key to so much in the world.

Q. Which single word do you most identify with?

Empathy. It informs my thinking and my work. We lawyers call it non-discrimination and equal treatment, but, as people, we call it empathy. It applies in many intimate spheres of love and friendship, and it applies in the greater social context as solidarity.

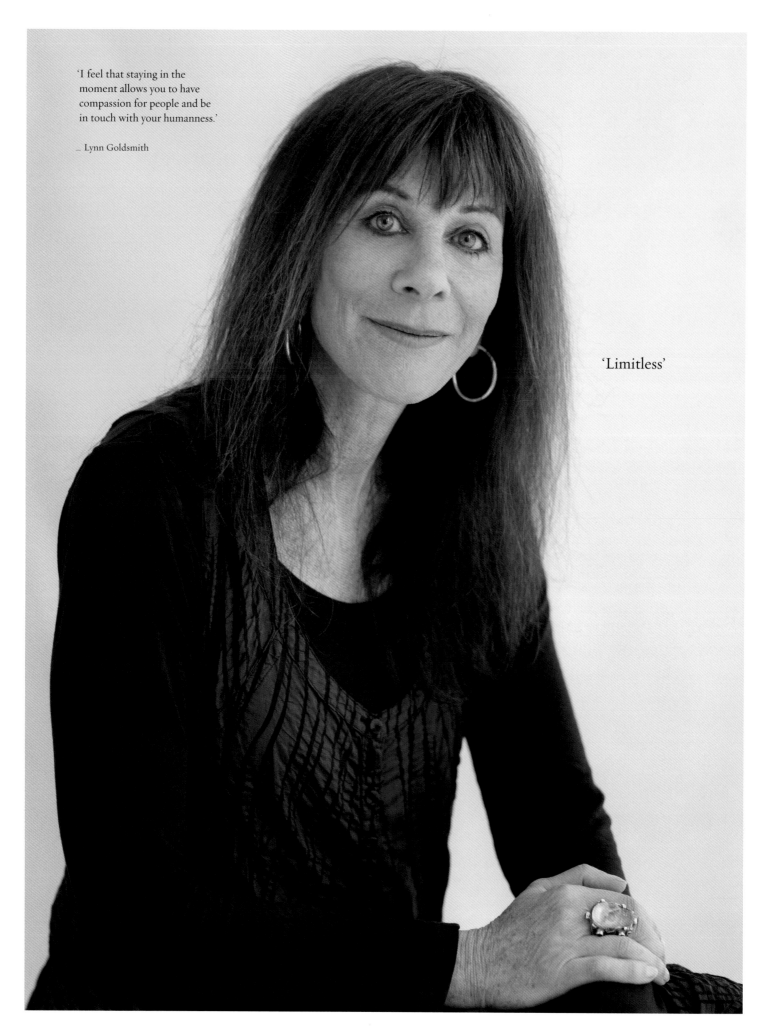

'I feel that staying in the
moment allows you to have
compassion for people and be
in touch with your humanness.'

_ Lynn Goldsmith

'Limitless'

Interview page 382

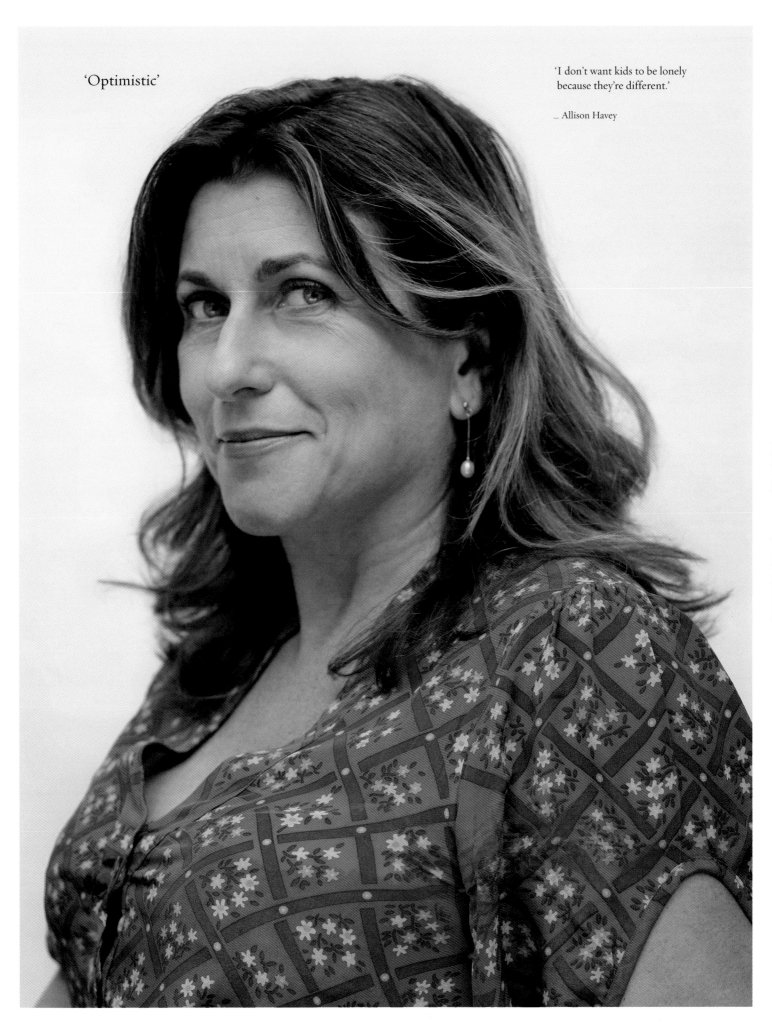

'Optimistic'

'I don't want kids to be lonely
because they're different.'

_ Allison Havey

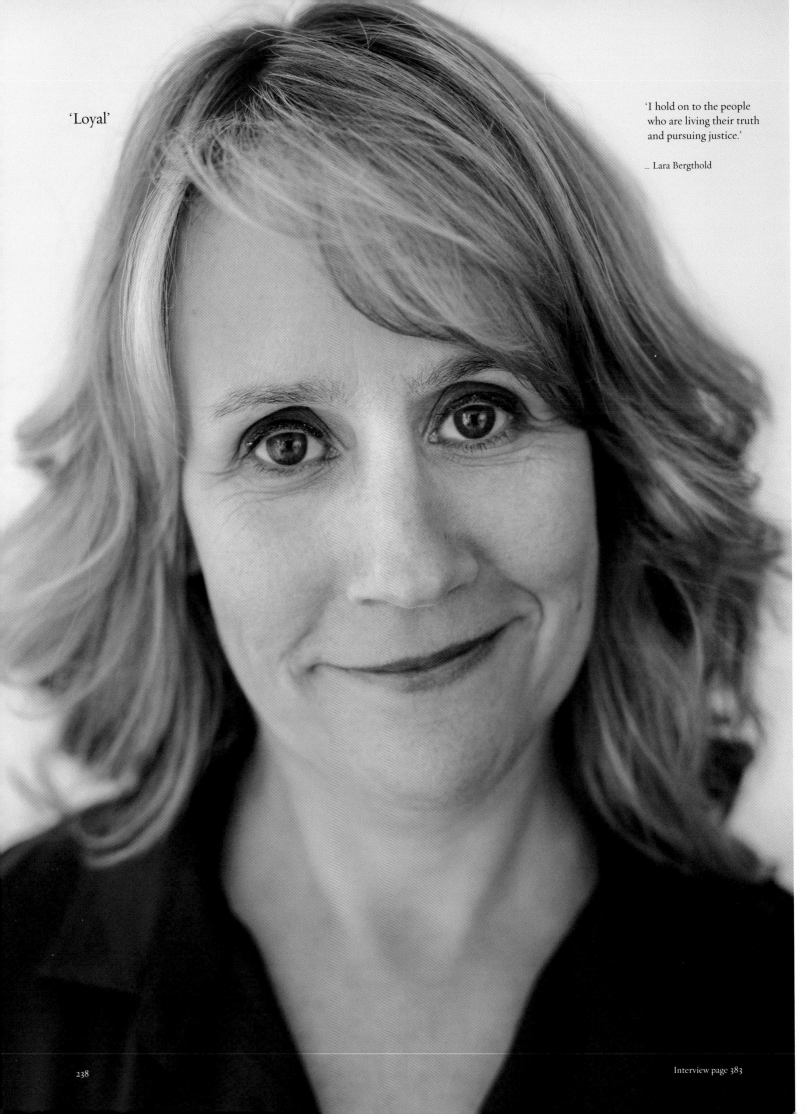

'Loyal'

'I hold on to the people
who are living their truth
and pursuing justice.'

_ Lara Bergthold

Interview page 383

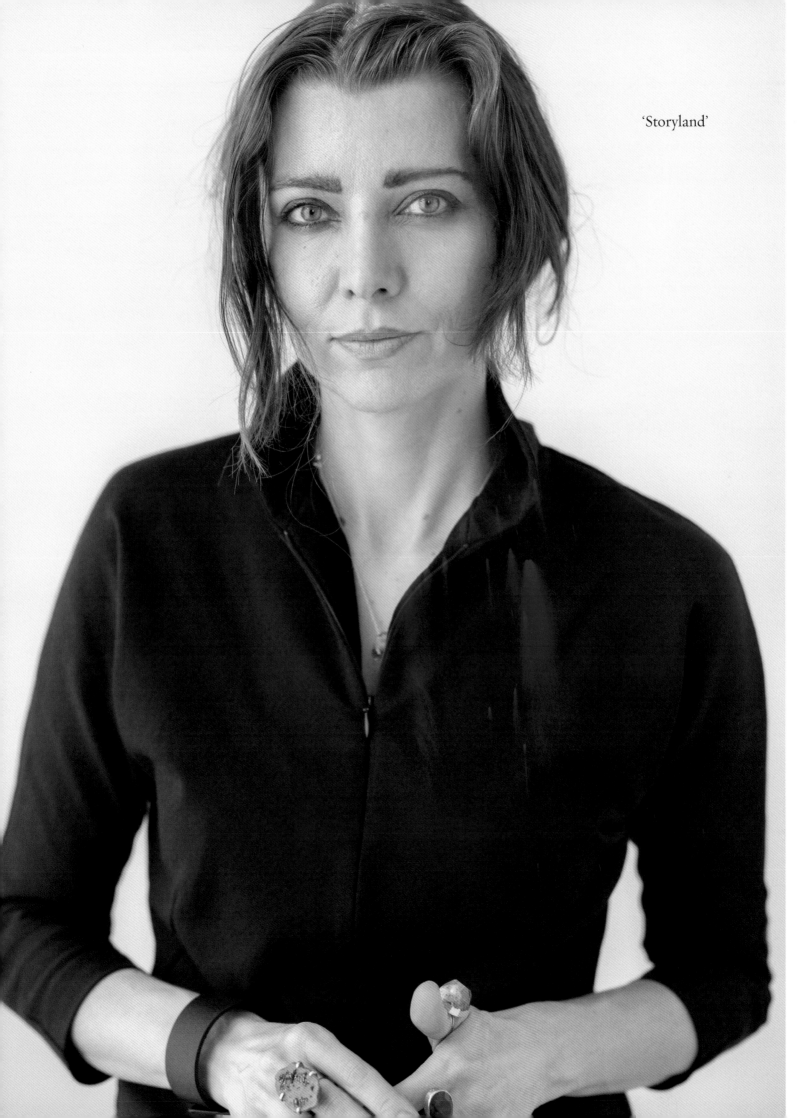

'Storyland'

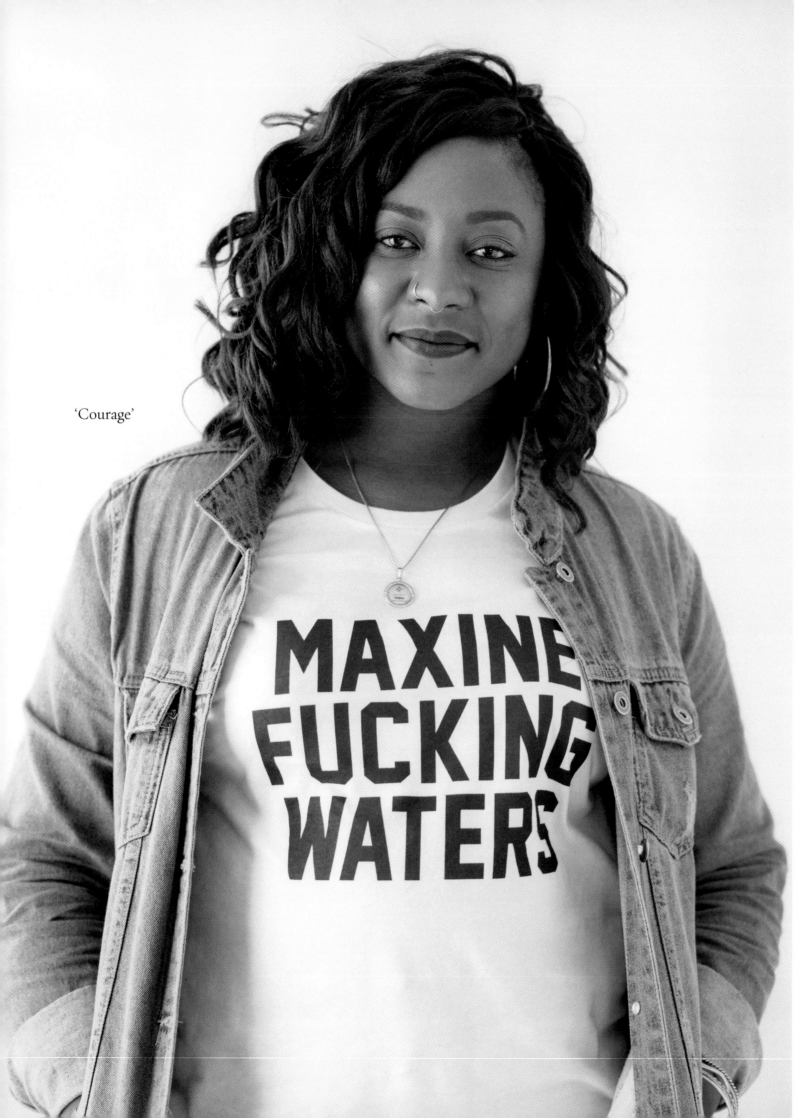

'Courage'

Alicia Garza

Alicia Garza was born in Carmel in California, USA. She is an activist and organiser based in Oakland, California. In 2013, Garza co-founded Black Lives Matter (BLM), an ideological and political organising network campaigning against anti-black racism and violence. In 2016, she and her two BLM co-founders were recognised in *Fortune*'s World's 50 Greatest Leaders. Garza is the director of special projects for the National Domestic Workers Alliance. She is also an editorial writer, whose work has been featured in publications including *The Guardian, The Nation, The Feminist Wire, Rolling Stone* and *Huffington Post*.

Q. What really matters to you?

I want to be able to tell my kids that I fought for them and that I fought for us. In a time when it's easy to be tuned out, it feels really important to me to be somebody who stands up for the ability of my kids – of all kids – to have a future.

The other thing that really motivates me is wanting to make sure we achieve our goals. As I was coming up as an organiser, we were told we were fighting for something we might never see in our lifetime. I'm just not satisfied with that; I think change can happen much faster, but it requires organisation, and an understanding of power and how we can shift it from its current incarnation. We need to transform power, so that we're not fighting the same battles over and over again. This is what I wake up thinking about every single day. And every night when I go to sleep, I'm thinking about how we can get closer to it tomorrow.

Women inspire me to keep going. My foremost influence was my mother; she initially raised me on her own, having never expected to be a parent at twenty-six. She taught me everything I know about what it means to be a strong woman who is in her power. I'm also very much influenced by black women throughout history. I'm inspired by Harriet Tubman, not only for all the work she did to free individual slaves – which, of course, was amazing – but for everything she did to eradicate the institution of slavery, the alliances she built to do so and the heartbreaks she endured in pursuit of her vision. And it's not only women in the United States who inspire me. In Honduras in 2016, Berta Cáceres was murdered while pursuing her vision of ecological justice and a better life for the people in Honduras being preyed upon by corporations and the United States government.

Black Lives Matter has been a big part of my activism. When it came onto the scene, there was a lot of pushback; people responded by saying, '*All* lives matter.' I think the intensity of these reactions against Black Lives Matter is a testament to how effective our systems are in isolating these kinds of issues – they make them seem as though they impact individuals, as opposed to entire communities. The all-lives-matter thing is simultaneously fascinating and infuriating to me, because it's so obvious. Obviously all lives matter; it's like saying the sky is blue or that water is wet. But, when people say, 'Actually, all lives matter,' it feels like a passive-aggressive way of saying, '*White* lives matter.'

People seemed shocked that police brutality was an issue, but I thought, 'Um, where have you been?' The police are supposed to serve all communities, but instead, they aren't accountable to black communities in the same way they are to white communities. The United States is rooted in profound segregation, disenfranchisement and oppression in pursuit of profits. And it feels like the country is being powered by amnesia.

Q. What brings you happiness?

My community – absolutely. This includes both of my families, blood and chosen – because my family is also my friends, the people I've been through things with. These are the people who stand with me, support me and love me. They are the people who feed me, and we just let each other be, because we understand each other.

Q. What do you regard as the lowest depth of misery?

I'd call it capitalism. There is nothing on earth that makes people as miserable, that kills people as avidly and that robs people of their dignity so completely as an economic system that prioritises profits over human needs. Capitalism prioritises profits over people and over the planet we depend on. There are millions and millions of people living on the streets without homes because of capitalism. And there are millions and millions of people suffering from depression and other emotional and mental afflictions because of it – because the things we are taught should drive us and make us happy are unattainable for the majority of people on this planet. Capitalism shapes every understanding you have of who you are and of what your value is. If you have no monetary value – if you can't sell something that you produce in this economy – then you are deemed unusable, unworthy and extraneous. There is no other force in the world that is so powerful and that causes so much misery for so many people.

Q. What would you change if you could?

I would start with all of the people who are suffering right now. I would give whatever is needed to every mama who is living in a car with her kids and is trying to figure out how she's going to make it another day – if not for herself then for the people who depend on her. I would give to all the people who are dying in the deserts right now, trying to cross artificial borders pursuing what they think will be a better life here in the United States – if I had a wand I'd make it so that that journey was easier and that there wasn't punishment on both sides. In fact, I would ensure that no one ever had to leave their homes in pursuit of survival – they would have everything that they needed right there at home.

The other area I would work on is within our own movements. I spend a lot of time thinking about how we could be clear about what we're up against and how we each fight it differently; I think about how we can advance our goals without tearing each other up along the way. So, if I could wave a wand, I would also change some of the suffering of organisers and activists in our movements who are tired and burned out, who feel disposable and don't feel seen.

Q. Which single word do you most identify with?

Courage. It takes real tenacity to be courageous.

Alexandra Zavis

————

Alexandra Zavis was born in Stockholm, Sweden. She spent a decade as a journalist with the Associated Press, reporting from war-torn countries in Africa, Asia and the Middle East, including Liberia, Sierra Leone, the Democratic Republic of Congo, Sudan, Somalia, Afghanistan and Iraq. In 2006, Zavis joined the *Los Angeles Times* as an international-affairs writer and editor. She is a recipient of the American Academy of Diplomacy's Arthur Ross Media Award for distinguished reporting and analysis on foreign affairs and the Society of Professional Journalists' Sigma Delta Chi Award for foreign correspondence.

Q. What really matters to you?
Being able to do my job.

I learned as a teenager what it is like to live without a free press. My father was an American diplomat in South Africa at the height of white-minority rule. We lived in a beautiful, whites-only suburb of the capital, Pretoria. It was the kind of place in which you could live out your life without ever knowing about the poverty and repression in the black townships just a few miles away. State television would give us blow-by-blow coverage of China's crackdown on demonstrators in Tiananmen Square in 1989, but nothing that might be construed as critical of the violence deployed by South Africa against the protests sweeping through its townships at the time.

Schools were segregated in those days, so my parents sent me to a small boarding school in neighbouring Swaziland. That's where I started getting to know kids who had grown up in those townships – I had to go to another country to meet them. Some of these kids had seen friends and family members jailed or killed for opposing the government. What I took away from the experience was how frighteningly easy it is to manipulate and dominate a society if you can divide people and control the information they receive about each other. So much of the real brutality of the system of apartheid came down to the fact that people of different races might cross paths every day without ever really getting to know each other or seeing each other as fellow human beings.

Ultimately, this is why I became a journalist. Because violence, racism and abuse aren't things confined to some far-off place and time. They happen all around us, and I never wanted to hear another person say, 'I didn't know.'

I didn't set out to become a conflict journalist. But, when I began my career in Africa in the 1990s, many countries were in turmoil. Some of these places – Liberia,

Sierra Leone, Sudan, Somalia – had been at war for so long that it could be hard to interest readers, and even our own editors, in the stories. It all seemed too complicated and far away. And yet, the toll on the people who lived in these places was almost unfathomable. In Sierra Leone, rebel fighters would line people up and ask them if they wanted a 'short sleeve' or 'long sleeve.' If they said, 'long sleeve,' the rebels would chop off their hands. If they said, 'short sleeve,' the rebels chopped off their arms.

The challenge in Iraq and Afghanistan was different. With American troops involved, there was no shortage of interest in these conflicts – at least in the beginning. But, the danger of reporting there was much greater. In Iraq, in particular, journalists were literally hunted by insurgents. For the first time in my career, I had to work with bodyguards and use armoured vehicles. When we would go out to do interviews, I would dress in local attire and wear a headscarf, so as not to stand out. If we were spotted in the streets, it could put not only us, but anyone we spoke with, at risk. Finding ways to do our job took more and more creativity, not to mention resources.

I am often asked whether being a female journalist in these places is limiting. I can't speak for others, but my experience has been the opposite. As a woman, I am less likely to be seen as a potential combatant, so it can be easier to talk my way through a checkpoint. In very conservative places, such as Afghanistan, being a woman has given me entrée to a world that is often closed to my male colleagues. I can sit and talk with women who are not permitted to interact with men from outside their families. And yet, being a woman hasn't for the most part been a barrier to meeting with men. As a foreign journalist, I often have access to places to which local women cannot go.

I count myself lucky to have worked for organisations that continue to be willing to do this kind of journalism – that's

not a given these days. Newsrooms are shrinking. Fewer and fewer media outlets have the budgets to send correspondents to far-off war zones, let alone base them there for extended periods of time. I worry that our understanding of the world – and our impact on it – will suffer because of this. Ironically, this is happening at a time when technology allows us to connect across distances in ways that were unimaginable just a decade or two ago. But seeing images from Syria flash across our screens in real time doesn't mean that we have any better understanding of what is driving that terrible conflict or of what the solution might be. The only way to figure that out is to be there.

Q. What brings you happiness?
Seeing kids kick a ball around on a beach during a break in the fighting in Liberia. Or watching a young United States soldier in Iraq shop online for an engagement ring for his girlfriend back home. Because, life goes on, even in the midst of the worst wars.

Q. What do you regard as the lowest depth of misery?
The mother who has to watch her baby waste away from hunger because she herself is too hungry to produce milk. Or the father clawing away at rubble because a bomb has landed on his house and he doesn't know whether his family is alive or dead. Too often, it seems the cost of our wars falls heaviest on those who play no part in them but have the misfortune to live in their midst.

Q. What would you change if you could?
I would settle for a little more empathy, and a little more willingness to question ourselves and to see the world from someone else's perspective.

Q. Which single word do you most identify with?
Resilience. I see it all the time in the people that I write about. That woman with the starving infant will walk for days to find help for her child. And the family with the bombed-out home will bury their dead and rebuild – if given the chance.

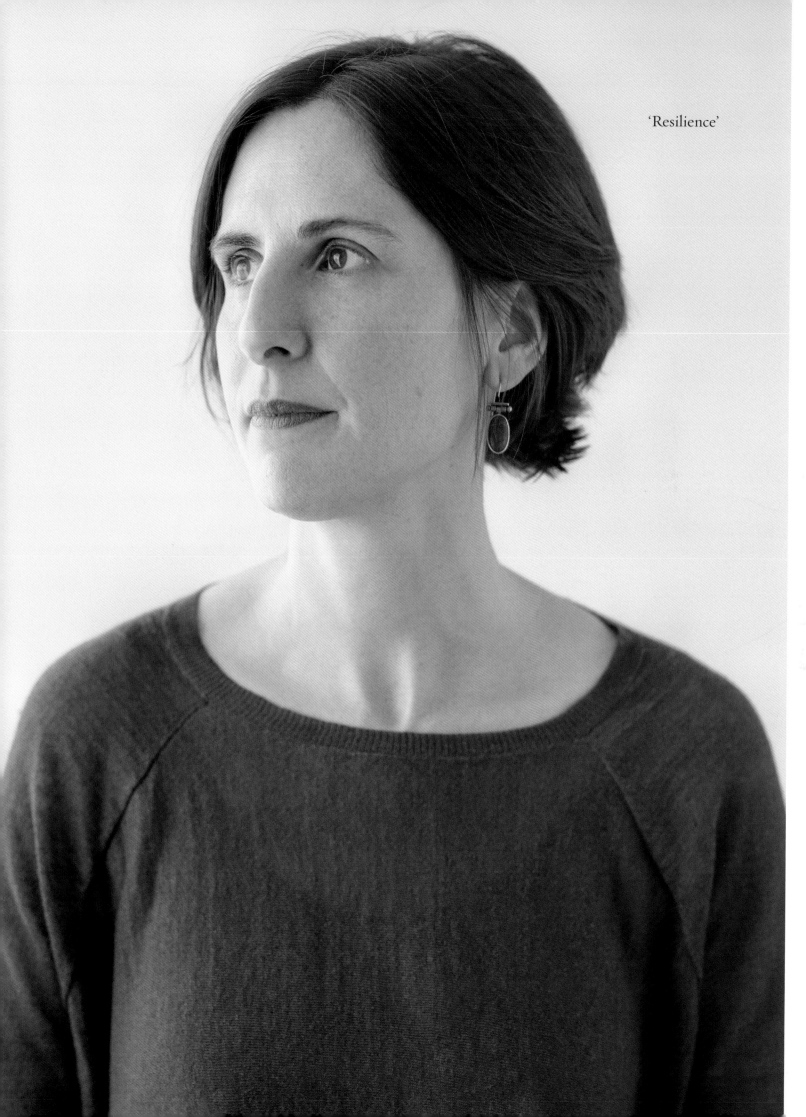

'Resilience'

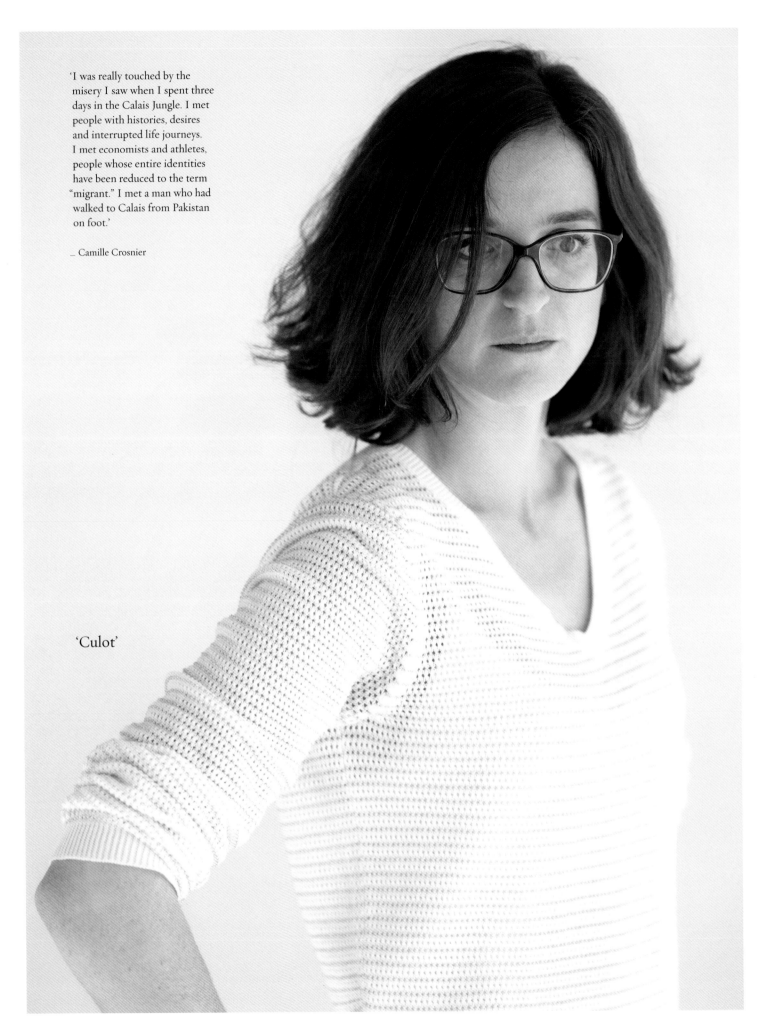

'I was really touched by the misery I saw when I spent three days in the Calais Jungle. I met people with histories, desires and interrupted life journeys. I met economists and athletes, people whose entire identities have been reduced to the term "migrant." I met a man who had walked to Calais from Pakistan on foot.'

_ Camille Crosnier

'Culot'

Interview page 384

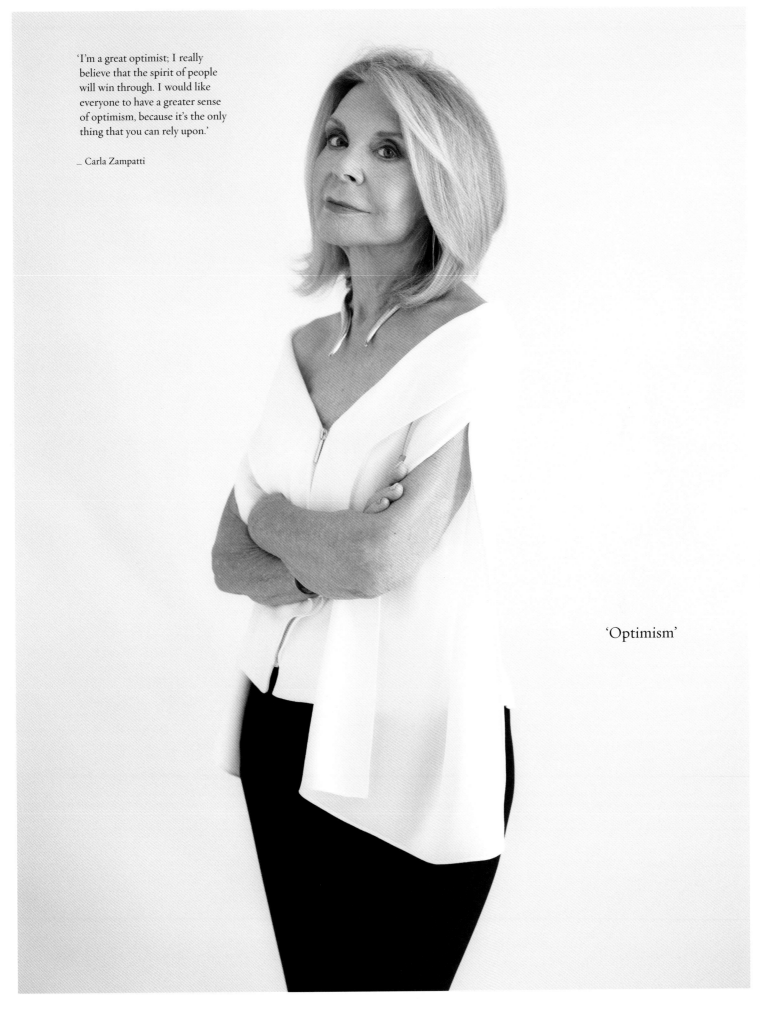

'I'm a great optimist; I really believe that the spirit of people will win through. I would like everyone to have a greater sense of optimism, because it's the only thing that you can rely upon.'

_ Carla Zampatti

'Optimism'

Interview page 385

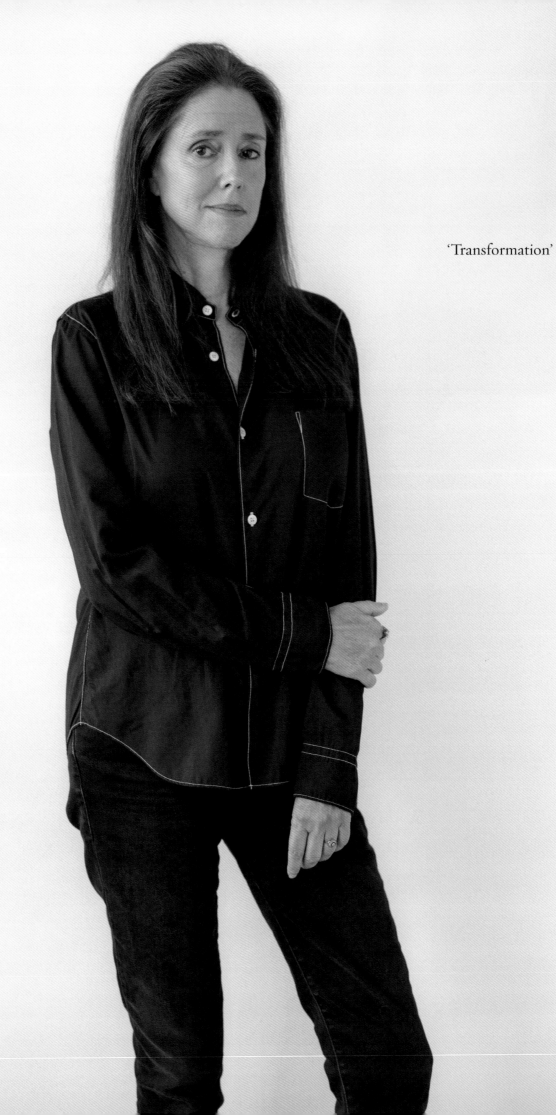

'Transformation'

Julie Taymor

Julie Taymor was born in Boston in Massachusetts, USA. Upon graduation from Oberlin College, she spent four years in Indonesia on a Watson Foundation fellowship and, in 1991, received a MacArthur 'Genius' Fellowship. Her theatre credits include the all-time highest-grossing Broadway musical, *The Lion King*, for which she won two Tony Awards; *Grounded*, starring Anne Hathaway at the Public Theatre; and *M. Butterfly*, with Clive Owen. Her operas include *Oedipus Rex*, with Jessye Norman; and *The Magic Flute* at the Metropolitan Opera. Her films include *Titus*, starring Anthony Hopkins; the Academy Award–winning *Frida*, starring Salma Hayek; *Across the Universe*; *The Tempest*, starring Helen Mirren; and *A Midsummer Night's Dream*.

Q. What really matters to you?
I do feel like I was given a gift to create, so what matters to me is being able to inspire people and move them. This journey began when I was eight or nine: every day after school I did theatre with kids from all over Boston and from various socioeconomic backgrounds. It was the start of understanding what it means to be in another's shoes.

That understanding is why travelling is so important. When you go to another country, you can't fall back on the things you are used to or are comfortable with; it's important to lose your bearings, so that you can start to see what it's like to live in another body, in another context. That's the start of compassion and empathy, because it's very hard to have an enemy when you can empathise with them, when you're able to recognise a common thread.

Later, when I was twenty-one, I remember wondering why the *New York Times* had an 'Arts and Leisure' section. Why were those two things put together? Why is art considered to be an 'extra' in our society? When you think about the potential of art and what it can do for people, it's extraordinary. So if people can be touched, be intellectually and emotionally inspired, then I feel like I've done my job.

Storytelling can be illuminating, dark, transformative or healing. So, as an artist, being able to not just give people a good time, but to affect their lives is very important to me. I feel that this is my responsibility, and I'm lucky that *The Lion King*, a stage musical I created twenty years ago, has given me economic freedom. When you have economic freedom, you have the freedom to choose your work. The projects I choose to do have something to say and, hopefully, can inspire. I believe that's my role as a contemporary shaman – it's as entertainer and healer; it's connecting people and, potentially, effecting a transformation in them. The origin of theatre is shamanistic performance. It was about taking people through misery, death and illness, through a healing process. A shaman would take or enact a spirit journey to confront the causes or issues plaguing the community and would return to address these. Whether or not the shaman's power is 'real' isn't important – if you believe it's real, then it is. The power of the human psyche is huge, as is the negative potential of belief – just look at extremism in any of the religions, from Islamic to Christian fundamentalism. It's horrifying to look at what has been done in the name of religion – from the Crusades to the Ku Klux Klan and Islamic State – it's all about controlling people's beliefs and the power of the imagination.

The Lion King – like all the old Disney stories – works on an archetypal level; it is a prodigal-son story. It doesn't matter who you are or where you're from – if you're part of a family, this is your story. And it binds us together, especially in a world in which people are no longer keeping their prejudices – their fears and hatreds – to themselves; bigotry is allowed to run rampant. Being human is about acknowledging this darkness and figuring out how to manage it, so that we may flourish together.

When we took *The Lion King* around the world and performed it in different languages, we realised that the one thing that doesn't translate is humour. Because, like the use of American inner-city black humour for the hyenas or borscht-belt Jewish humour for the characters of Timon and Pumbaa, a lot of humour is based on our ethnic differences. Hopefully, when we use it for comic purposes in the arts, it is done with affection. We all have prejudice and we're not going to get rid of it, so we have to treat it with care – with love – then confront it and move through it.

Q. What brings you happiness?
My work, and everything that matters to me in it, brings me happiness. As do my other half, my dog, my mother and my friends. And being on the beach; beautiful places in nature bring me tremendous happiness.

I'm happy when I see people accomplish something – seeing them at their best instead of their worst just awes me. The word 'awe' is very important, because awe is hard to find – especially in a world in which technology has become so primary. I know people think technology connects them, but it also brings out the worst in people. Everybody becomes smaller – more downturned – until they live inside themselves and are not outward anymore; I really prefer an open, connected, outwardness in human beings.

Q. What do you regard as the lowest depth of misery?
There is just so much misery, but the worst that can happen to a person is being tortured in the body and being tortured in the mind – especially with no hope. That's why faith is so powerful for people: because they can be suffering, but faith – all of that malarkey about another life – gives them hope.

But that's just the beginning. There's also what everybody feels: the inequalities and the inequities of the world. The inequalities experienced by, and imposed on, women are just astonishingly horrifying, especially given how much knowledge that we have about them.

And the earth being destroyed: I don't know how we'll avoid this. It would take such a massive effort to save this planet, but that doesn't mean we shouldn't keep trying.

Q. What would you change if you could?
That's two questions: 'What would you change that can't be changed?' and 'What would you change that can be changed?' You can't change human nature – you just can't – but in answer to the first question I would change the viciousness, the violence and the things that cause torment and torture to people who don't ask for it.

Q. Which single word do you most identify with?
Transformation: that's what I try to bring about through my work, and that's what I see on the faces of people if I've done my work well.

Ruchira Gupta

___

Ruchira Gupta was born in Kolkata, India. A former journalist, Gupta directed and produced the Emmy Award–winning 1997 documentary *The Selling of Innocents*, which investigated India's sex-trafficking industry. In 2002, Gupta co-founded Apne Aap Women Worldwide, an organisation working to empower girls and women to resist and end sex trafficking. She has received numerous awards for her activism, including being made a Knight of France's National Order of Merit and being awarded the Clinton Global Citizen Award for Commitment to Leadership in Civil Society. She campaigns for a world in which no human being is bought or sold.

What really matters to you?

Dignity and justice. I firmly, firmly want fairness. I understand that inequality exists and that there will always be inequality in some form or another – someone will always be richer, someone will always be whiter – but I still believe we can make this world a fairer and more equitable place.

So, what matters, is my work to end inequality.

About twenty-one years ago, when I was working as a journalist, I was travelling through Nepal and came across numerous villages with very few women between the ages of fifteen and forty-five. I started asking the men I met why this was. Most were sheepish and some were very hostile, but a few told me they were all in Mumbai, which was fourteen hundred kilometres away; I couldn't understand how these women had gotten there from these remote Nepali villages, so I decided to find the answer. It changed my life – I discovered a supply chain stretching to Mumbai's brothels.

The supply chain involved local village procurers, transporters, corrupt border guards and lodge keepers across the border in India. The lodge keepers would lock these girls up for several days, and beat them, starve them and drug them, until their spirits were completely subjugated. The girls would then be sold to pimps in Mumbai, Kolkata, Bihar and Delhi. Prices were negotiated based on beauty; fair skin was premium, being voluptuous was premium, as was being docile and young – the youngest girl I met who had been trafficked was seven. These women were then locked up in rooms with iron bars on the windows and brought out every night to see eight to ten customers. Girls and women were being chewed up and spit out by the system, and, although the prostitution was all in plain sight, the extent of the network was invisible. I had covered war and famine, but nothing like this kind of intimate and deliberate exploitation of one human by another, the violence of a fifty-year-old man on top of a ten-year-old girl. I decided to tell the world about it.

I made a documentary, *The Selling of Innocents*. I interviewed twenty-two women who found the courage to tell their stories. They spoke about how they were pulled out of school or sold by their fathers. They told me about how, when they escaped to a police station, the officers would return them to their pimps and tell them it was too late for them to be redeemed – that they were devalued and should accept their destiny. These women were beaten black and blue, their bodies were developing diseases and they were being forced to have abortions. I felt rage, anger and sadness – and I started to realise that reporting wasn't enough.

The women would later tell me that I saved their lives, but we saved each other's. I was shooting in the brothels without any protection for myself; one day, I was talking to these twenty-two women in a room when the brothel manager appeared at the door with a knife – these places are tiny wooden houses with narrow staircases and twenty rooms to a bathroom, and there's nowhere to run. The manager told me I couldn't be filming. The women surrounded me in a circle in that little space and said he would have to kill them all to get to me. That was the moment I was transformed, because I thought I was saving them, but they saved me.

I went back to the women I had interviewed, and they asked me to start a not-for-profit organisation. I told them I wasn't a lawyer or a doctor or a social worker – I had no idea how to run a not-for-profit – but they told me I could help them because of my English and access to networks. We set up Apne Aap, which means 'self-action' – this is a reference to the individual needing to help themselves, but is also about women coming together to help womankind. Fifteen years in, we're now twenty thousand members strong. We have a voice, we influence policy and we march in a great battalion for women's rights. When the Delhi bus rape happened, we marched to parliament. The women of our organisation have overcome their shame, guilt and fear, and we are now

sharing their stories with politicians – we have convinced them to classify trafficking as a sexual offence.

When we started, those twenty-two women said they had four dreams: schooling for their children, so that they didn't end up in the trade; a room of their own with a door they could lock, so that they and their children would be safe; a job with a steady salary in a clean office; and justice. Today, children are working in jobs that they never would have had access to otherwise and are supporting their mothers. Sadly, the original twenty-two women are no longer with us. They have all died from various things – AIDS-related complications, suicide – but their dreams live on in their children.

What is your greatest happiness?

Friendship: I love sitting with my friends and talking about 'the possible.' I love entering into people's stories and standing up for justice.

What do you regard as the lowest depth of misery?

I've seen so much of it that it's hard to define what that would be. In my film, there was a nine-year-old boy who slept on the floor of his mother's room in the brothel; when she had customers, he would either look for another room to sleep in or would have to sleep on the street outside next to a heap of garbage. And, I've seen women who were raped with foreign objects. I thought violence was the lowest, but then I met a girl sold by her father – the man who should have protected her. So, I'm afraid I don't know what the lowest depth is; I don't know why people want to hate more than they want to love.

What would you change if you could?

I would remove Donald Trump from office like a puff of smoke – poof!

Which single word do you most identify with?

Freedom.

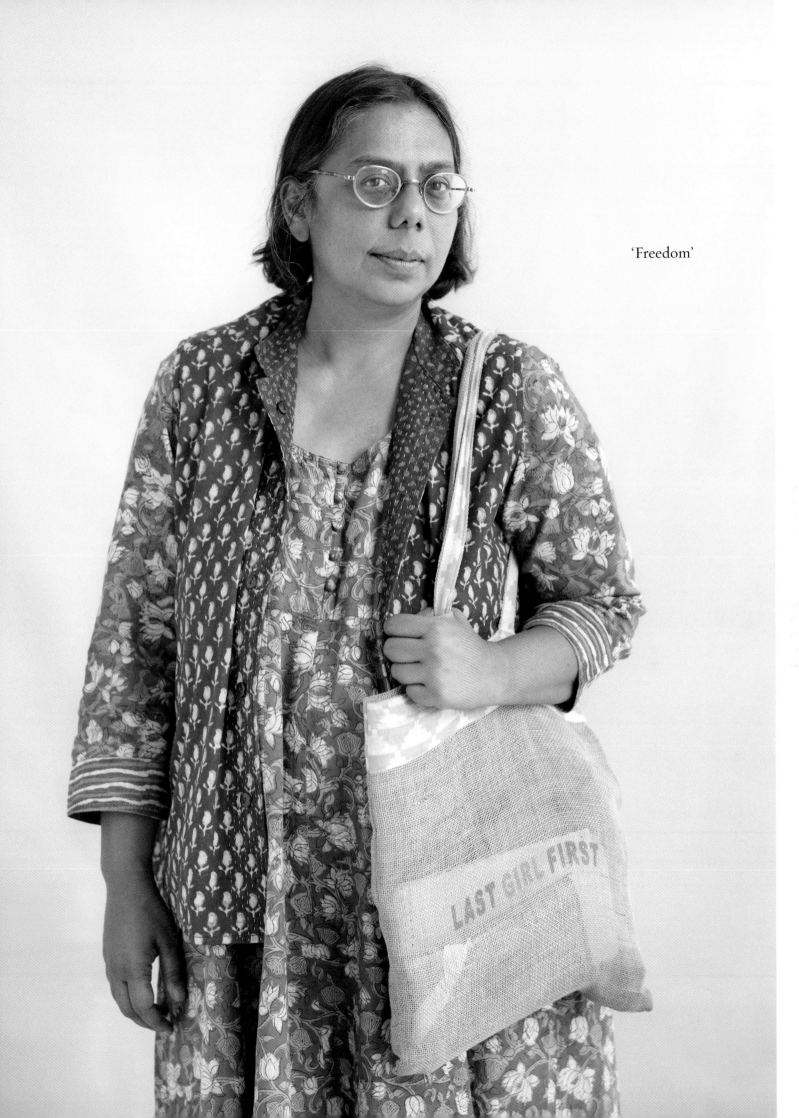

'Freedom'

'I want to see a day when we are
living without cancer. I hope
to close my business in twenty
years because there won't be a
need for me anymore!'

_ Dana Donofree

Interview page 385

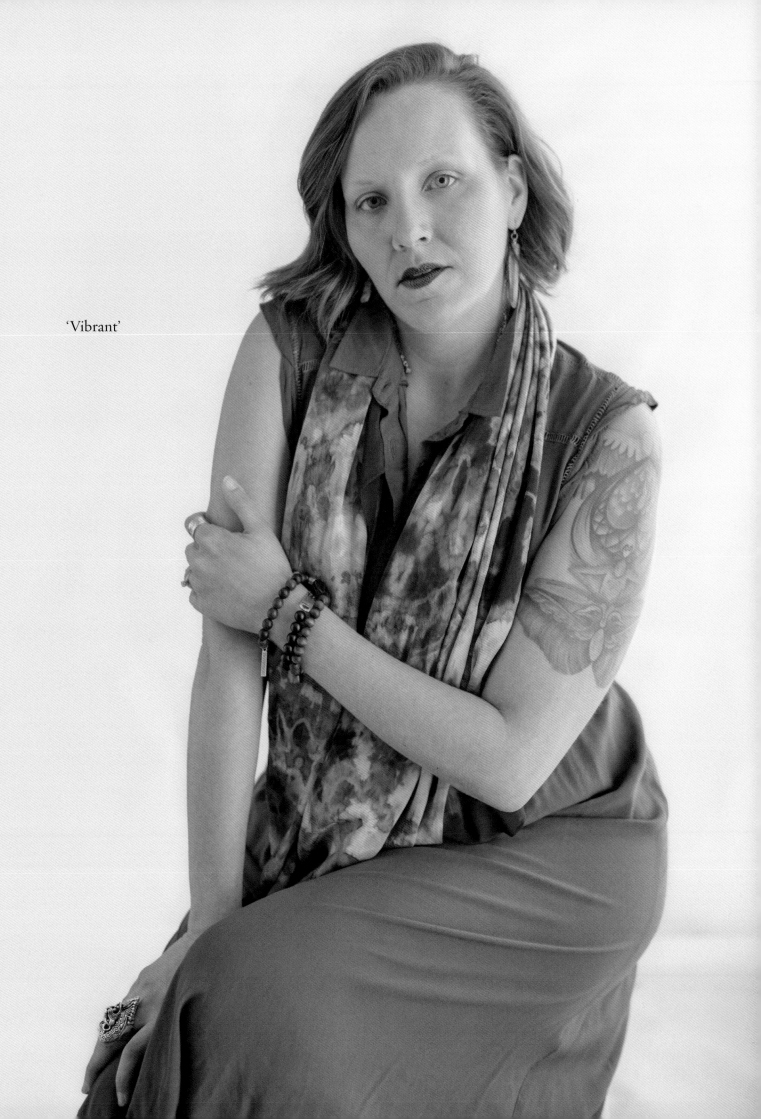

'Vibrant'

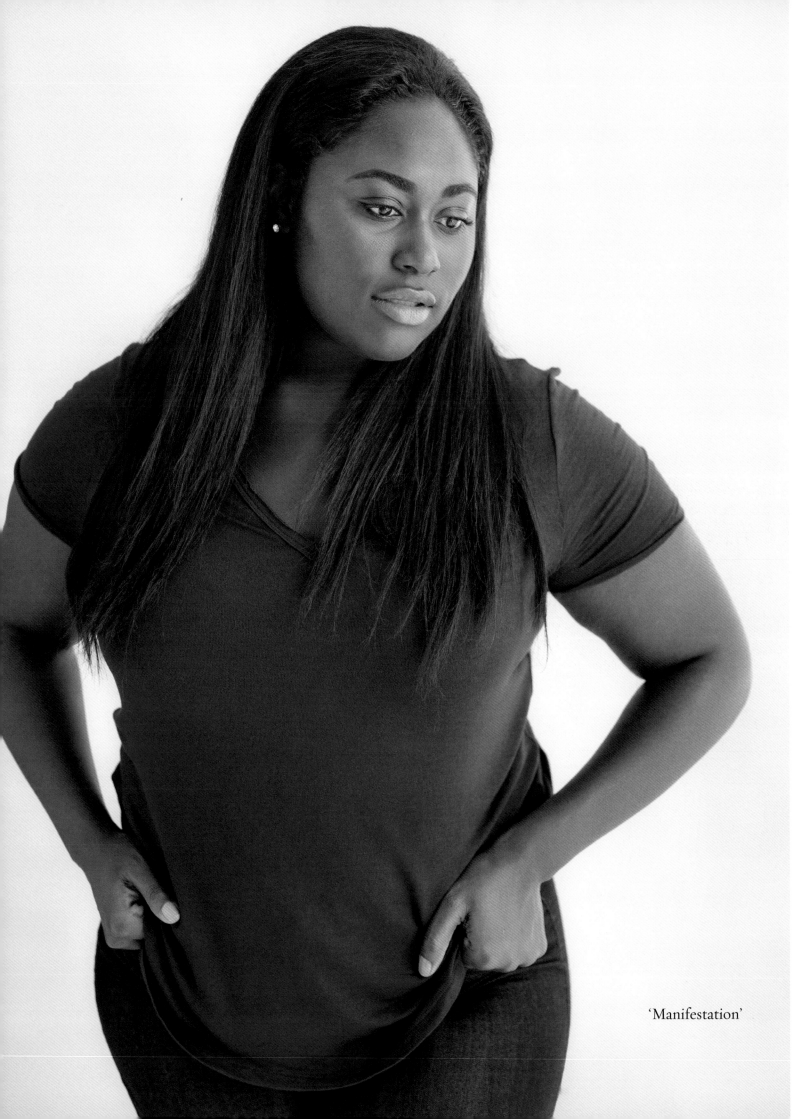

'Manifestation'

Danielle
Brooks

———

Danielle Brooks was born in Augusta in Georgia, USA. She attended the South Carolina Governor's School for the Arts and Humanities, then the Juilliard School in New York. Her work in the Netflix series *Orange Is the New Black* has been recognised with three Screen Actors Guild Awards for Outstanding Performance by an Ensemble in a Comedy Series, and in 2014, Brooks won the Young Hollywood Breakthrough Actress Award. Her performance in *The Color Purple* on Broadway saw her nominated for a 2016 Tony Award for Best Featured Actress in a Musical and earned her a Grammy Award for Best Musical Theater Album.

Q. What really matters to you?

What matters to me most is telling stories that move us forward as a society – telling stories that help people better understand one another.

I was in my first church play when I was six years old, but, when you're that young, you don't understand how you're affecting others. Everyone kept telling my mother that I was good, so from that moment on she found all of these different programmes for me to attend. I was transferred to arts school in middle school, then again in high school; in high school, I discovered my love for theatre, and I came to understand its power to change people's lives – it definitely changed mine.

In my senior year at the South Carolina Governor's School for the Arts and Humanities – I had just been accepted to Juilliard, so the school was always making me perform monologues when donors visited – I performed an August Wilson monologue from *The Piano Lesson* for about twenty women, who all happened to be white. I was terrified. But all these women were able to relate to Berniece's story, the need to convince her brother of the mistake he had made by selling their piano, an heirloom that had so much family history in it. The women all told me how they'd been moved, and that was the moment when I realised the power of art – how transformative it is. Everyone can find a way to relate to it. That's when I decided I would use my gift to help others become more free. In return, it does the same thing for me. This is why I feel so strongly that we have to pour our resources into arts education; it allows people to experience the arts and, through them, to feel seen and heard. Because it's important to give voices to people who feel like they don't have one.

In this world, most of us are operating in our own little circles, but, when I had the chance to tell Berniece's story, I realised the potential for arts to help us relate to each other. There is so much hate and opposition in the world – I'm right, you're wrong – so what we really need is to be able to relate to each other's stories. I feel *Orange Is the New Black* is so powerful because all of the characters are written off as criminals – as the lowest of the low – but you come to understand how each of them landed in prison. You see that most of them were operating out of love: stealing for their children, selling drugs to support their husbands or whatever else it might be. They were trying to do more, be better and to provide. When you take a step back and appreciate that these are people's mothers, sisters, daughters and lovers, you start to break down the judgement about who they are.

I do think that there are micro-aggressions black actors experience – I experienced them myself when I first started on *Orange Is the New Black*. Some people deem my character, Taystee, ghetto or unkempt, because she is incarcerated and says whatever she wants. And they have reflected that on me. I've stepped into interviews where the first questions are, 'Are you trained? Where did they find you?' Yes, I'm trained! I spent four years at a conservatory studying this craft. Yet, I don't necessarily hear those questions when my white contemporaries are being interviewed about their characters. I was at a fancy event recently, and a very distinguished black woman, who is in the business, told me she'd only realised my background after she recognised me in *The Color Purple*. She said, 'I thought they found you on the street or something.' I felt that was disrespectful to me as a human being, because she didn't have the imagination to believe that I could be greater than just the character I was playing.

People can be so close-minded in their beliefs, but I feel acting creates room for people to change – to see things differently as they get to know a character and then the person behind it. My mother is a minister and my father is a deacon, so I grew up in the church, and my family can be very homophobic. But, because they've engaged with the work of my colleagues Laverne Cox and Samira Wiley – and then with the women themselves – they're able to look at life a little differently than they had been taught to. I think that's a beautiful thing. What I've learned from my mother and her journey with faith is that it's okay to leave room for more love.

Q. What brings you happiness?

Doing what I love. When I'm centred and have inner peace, that brings me happiness. There are so many distractions that can throw you off balance, but, when I can take a moment to live outside of my insecurities and be fully in the moment, I find a true appreciation for life, health and the beautiful people around me.

Q. What do you regard as the lowest depth of misery?

Self-hate. I know I have a lot more to learn, but, in the twenty-seven years that I've been on this earth, a core lesson has been being able to identify self-hate. When you don't love yourself enough, or you don't feel like you have a reason to live, that's misery. Not all, but a lot of, self-hate we cause each other. In some way, our self-hate is all connected: whether it's somebody who's been abandoned by their mother or somebody who can't provide for her child. We affect one another; the minute I run into somebody, their energy moves my energy, and vice versa.

So, I think it would help if we all took a second to focus on loving ourselves. If I'm not operating out of a place of love for myself, how am I supposed to spread love? A drug addict who spends time with drug addicts is most likely going to do drugs, whereas, if they're going to AA meetings and hanging around people who are clean, that's probably the direction their life will take. I feel it's the same when it comes to loving one's self: we have to surround ourselves with the same vibrations.

Q. What would you change if you could?

I would change how we view money; greed is a powerful demon and it runs the world. I think the way we view money is ugly.

Q. Which single word do you most identify with?

Manifestation. We have the power to manifest whatever we want, if we believe.

Caster Semenya

Caster Semenya OIB was born in Ga-Masehlong, South Africa. She holds a bachelor's degree in sports science from the University of Pretoria. A professional middle-distance runner, she is an 800-metre-event world champion and a two-time Olympic gold medallist. Through the Caster Semenya Foundation, Semenya trains and assists young athletes, and supports campaigns to distribute menstrual cups to disadvantaged South African girls, supporting them to remain in school during their menstrual cycles. In 2014, Semenya was granted the bronze Order of Ikhamanga by the South African government for her achievements in sports.

'Ubuntu has a lot of meanings, but, for me, it is about acknowledging the basic human dignity of every person.'

Q. What really matters to you?

What matters to me is doing what I can to change the lives of others, especially the lives of people living in rural areas who have very limited access to resources. I set up my foundation because I believe in the potential of sport to develop young kids, to teach them discipline and to produce future leaders. I feel I can contribute to ensuring that kids become better human beings.

I loved sports from a young age; when I was six, I discovered running, and I just never stopped. My role model was the athlete Maria Mutola; she lived with me and inspired me. I decided I was going to be a world champ – that I was going to be better than her – but, as I matured, I realised life isn't about being better than anybody else – it's about being the best *you* can be. The actor Will Smith has said that he might not be the most talented or the smartest or the sexiest, but, when he steps onto the treadmill next to someone, either they are going to get off first or he's going to die running. That motivates me a lot, because, it doesn't matter how good anyone else is; when I step up to perform, I make sure I kill it! I hate training, but you reap what you sow. And, I am motivated by chasing my own improvement – that's the message I want to impart on anyone who looks up to me.

Family is also very important to me. We come from a small, dusty town, and, although we lacked certain things, we had each other. Our family unit was strong, and my parents did a lot to make sure their six kids could have bright futures – I have such an appreciation for their sacrifices. I had

quite a simple childhood, but it was great. I was forever in the bush, looking after my dad's sheep and goats, or playing with my cousins; I would play with the boys – I've always liked a challenge! – and we were very rough with each other.

Growing up, everyone in my family was sporty: my dad was a great soccer player, my mum was into netball and my sisters did athletics. As a child, I was obsessed with soccer. My dad thought I might play for the national team one day and used to buy me soccer boots every three months, but then I chose another path: one day, I decided to sell all my boots to buy spikes instead. I love soccer, but, as with everything you do in life, I look back and see the benefits of the decision I made. I believe that sport has an important role to play in uniting people, and we need more unity in this world. This is why I'm doing what I can to motivate young people, so that they can have better lives and more opportunities.

Q. What brings you happiness?

I got married a few months ago, so that is my happiness; more than anything else, happiness is being with my wife. She supports me in everything I do and is the most precious thing in my life.

I also love running. It's all about finding my rhythm – feeling every single step. Sometimes I'll feel tired, but then I find that fire within me that tells me I can do it. In those moments when I can forget about everything that's going on and the only thing that enters my mind is winning or losing, I love it so much.

Q. What do you regard as the lowest depth of misery?

It's when people lack basic respect for one another. My grandmother taught me that in order to be respected you must show respect for others. I don't care what anyone in the world thinks of me –every person in the world is different, we each have our own missions and visions – but the very least we can do is show respect for others. I respect people and their choices, and I expect the same treatment. I know that what I see is different from what others see, but that's life. How can we live if we don't respect each other?

Q. What would you change if you could?

I don't have the power to change anything, but, if I did, I would change the way people treat one another. I look around and I see so much criticism – people criticising how others look, dictating how others should live – and that's just never going to end well. I would force people to mind their own business, focus on themselves and live their *own* lives to the fullest. People need to understand that they can't go around criticising or undermining or judging others. People just need to live their own lives and respect the right of others to do the same.

Q. Which single word do you most identify with?

Ubuntu. It has a lot of meanings, but, for me, it is about acknowledging the basic human dignity of every person. I am a reflection of those around me – I am defined by them. It is about being respectful of others and being received with respect.

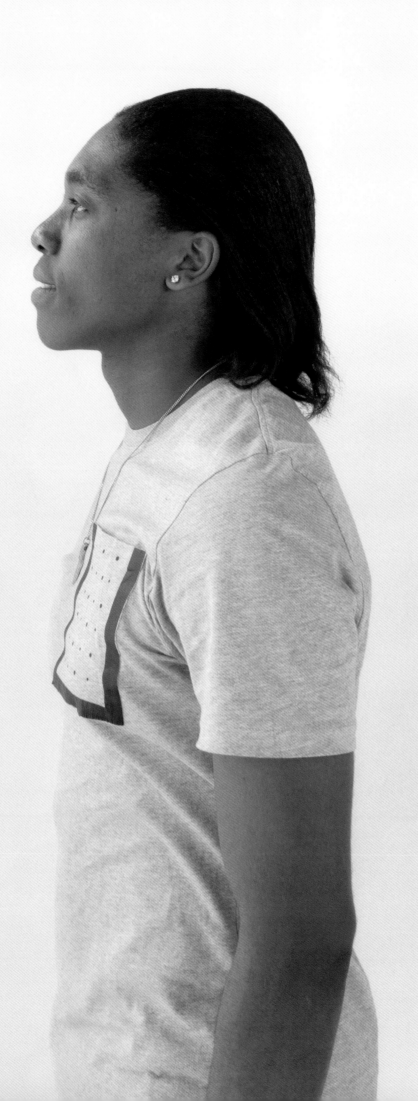

'Ubuntu'

Jody Williams

———

'It makes me angry that those subscribing to the realist school of thought – the Henry Kissingers – think that people who talk about peace are wimps.'

———

Jody Williams was born in Vermont, USA. She was involved in her first protest, against the Vietnam War, in 1970. During the 1980s, she worked against United States military involvement in Central America. Williams was awarded the Nobel Peace Prize in 1997 for her work coordinating the International Campaign to Ban Landmines. She helped found, and is the chair of, the Nobel Women's Initiative, which unites women recipients of the Nobel Peace Prize to support grassroots women's organisations in conflict areas.

Q. What really matters to you?
What matters to me is finding sustainable peace through justice and equality. That means redefining security and distinguishing it from national security, which just provides for the security of the state's structure; it isn't really about taking care of people. We need to ensure that structures of power focus on human security, on making sure that the needs of individuals and communities are met by governments – that's their job!

If everybody had access to basic health care, decent housing and a job worthy of the name – one for which they're paid enough to actually survive – the world would be much less stressed. Power struggles would be shaped very differently. It makes me angry that those subscribing to the realist school of thought – the Henry Kissingers – think that people who talk about peace are wimps who don't understand the realities of power and are tree huggers who wear Birkenstocks. It's not that way at all: I hate Birkenstocks, and I do understand the realities of power! That's why I want to shift the focus away from the power of the state and onto the state providing for the people it is supposed to be providing for. That's what drives me and fills me with righteous indignation.

Personally, what really matters to me is that at the end of each day – even if I have been a bitch or haven't put my best foot forward – I can look in the mirror, straight into my own eyes, and know that I am doing the best I can to make the world a better place for everybody: even

for people I don't like! When you win a Nobel Prize, you don't become Mother Teresa – there are people I can't stand and that's the reality. There are 7 billion people on the planet, but although I may not like everybody, I do want the world to be good – even for those I dislike. If I didn't, then I'd really just be a member of a political party. You have to be driven for the greater good of everyone – I am, so I feel very happy about that.

Q. What brings you happiness?
Being inspired; not by the famous names that I encounter, but primarily by those that are unknown. I chair the Nobel Women's Initiative, which I helped form in 2006; we came together to use the influence and access to resources that we have because of winning the peace prize to support and shine a spotlight on the work of grassroots women's organisations, to enhance what they're trying to do in their countries and bring them into a larger network. Some of the women that I have been privileged to meet through that work, and some who I would call friends, just blow me out of the water. On days when I just want to stay in Vermont and never leave my house again, I think of them.

There is something that has moved me tremendously recently. I joined my sister Nobel Prize winner Rigoberta Menchú for the last week of a trial in Guatemala, after years of avoiding Central America – I'd been avoiding it because, despite eleven years' work, we had been unsuccessful in stopping United States intervention in El Salvador and Nicaragua.

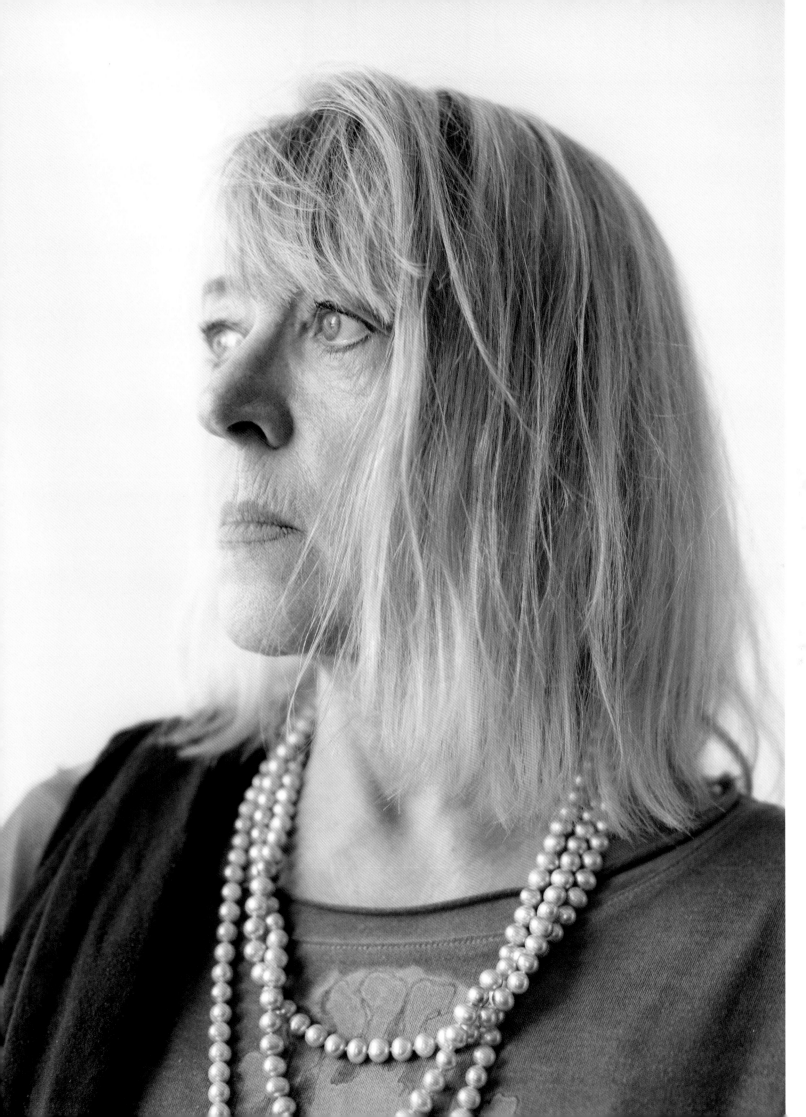

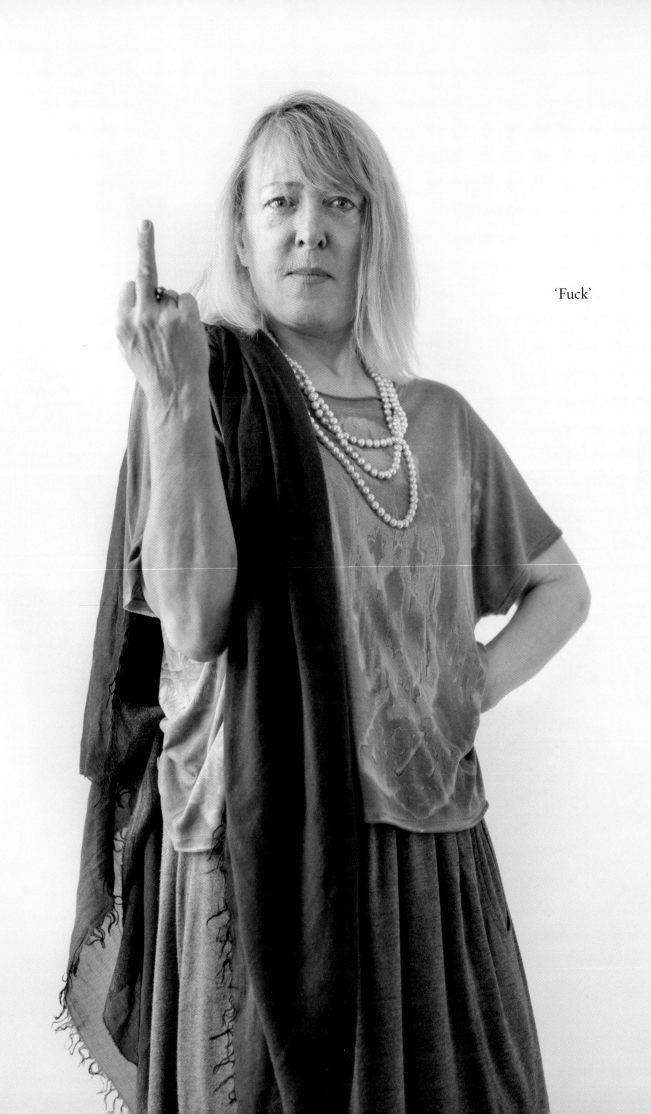

'Fuck'

Jody Williams

'People have become caught up in "self-actualising," but I just think, "Get up off your ass and actualise for people who really need help!"'

In 1982 and 1983, in northeast Guatemala, fifteen Mayan K'iche' women – who couldn't even speak Spanish – were held as domestic and sex slaves in an army garrison that had been built for rest and recuperation leave for soldiers who needed some fun after going out massacring. After the women's ordeal ended, they were vilified as prostitutes and what happened to them wasn't acknowledged. They started talking through their trauma with each other, and over time, with the support of three Guatemalan NGOs, they decided to bring charges against the man who had been the head of the garrison and the man who had been the head of the vigilante paramilitary self-defence group. It took about six years for the case to get to trial.

When we met with the women before the judgement, they could not look us in the face – they barely looked at each other. They had their hands up almost in supplication; it was like looking at ghosts. They said they were doing this because they wanted justice and because they wanted to make sure that it didn't happen to other women and children. I was blown out of the water listening to them. And they freakin' won! They won the case! It was amazing. When I think of inspiration, I think of women like that.

People have become caught up in 'self-actualising,' but I just think, 'Get up off your ass and actualise for people who really need help!' I have my own emotional issues, so I'm not unsympathetic, but

I don't believe that learning how to get in touch with your inner being will make you able to help the world. The obsession with self in this country makes me sick, especially when you compare it to those women in Guatemala, who have absolutely nothing, and yet had the courage to pursue a case that is precedent-setting in the entire world; it's the first time a country has tried sex as a war crime in its national courts. And they won. That makes me happy.

Q. What do you regard as the lowest depth of misery?
People who have no hope. People whose lives have been so crushed that they just move through life and don't live life. The opportunity for a full life has never been given to them, or has been taken away from them – I just can't imagine it.

Q. What would you change if you could?
The big thing would be to make people care about the planet. When I hear an owl in the middle of the night it just makes me so happy – I wish people understood that connection.

Q. Which single word do you most identify with?
Fuck, probably! It's a noun, a verb, an adjective and an adverb – I love it. When I first said it at home – when I went away to college – my parents were horrified, of course. My mother, who's eighty-six, begs me not to use that word in public because – this cracks me up, I just adore her – it tarnishes my Nobel image. But it's who I am.

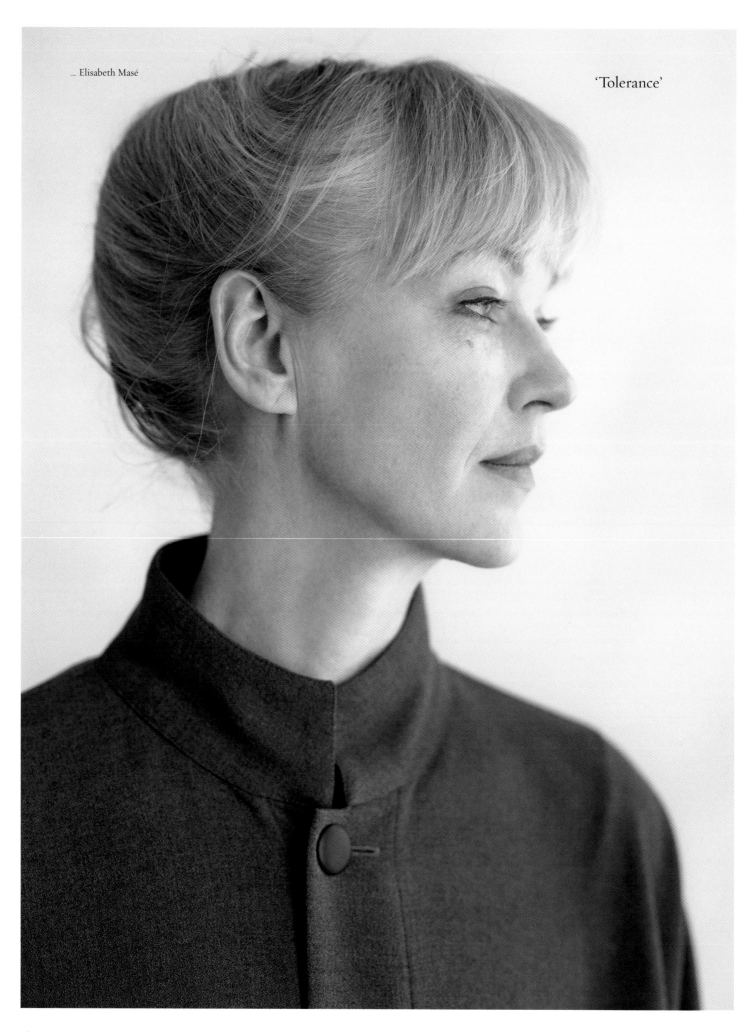

_ Elisabeth Masé

'Tolerance'

Interview page 385

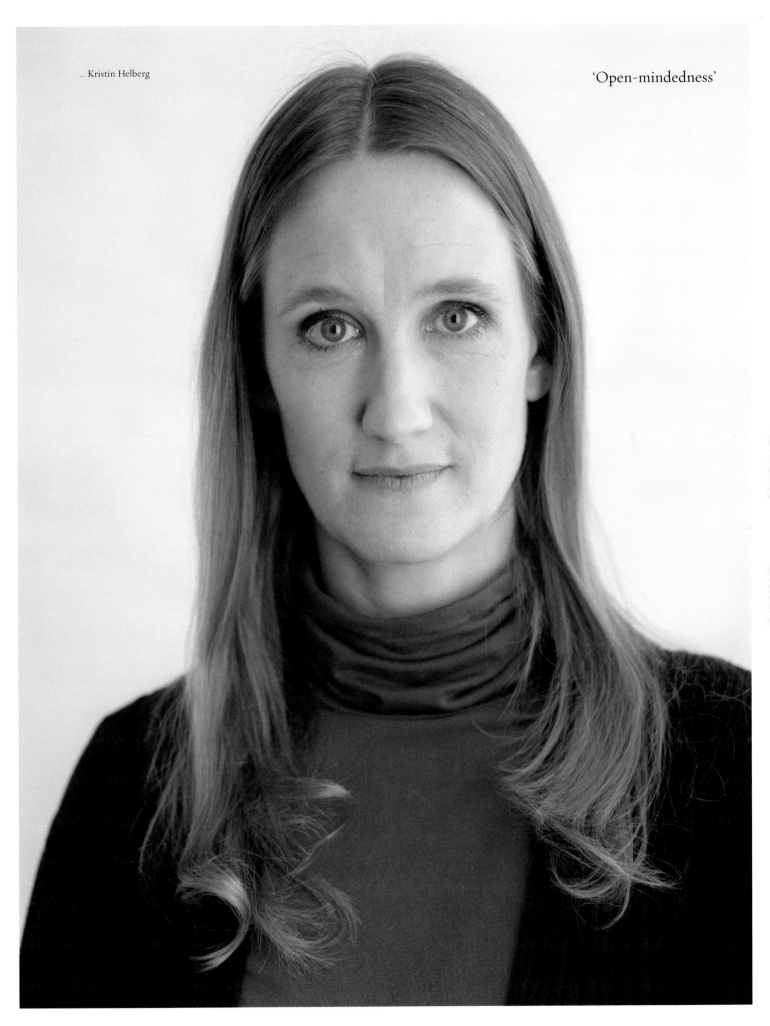

_ Kristin Helberg

'Open-mindedness'

Interview page 386

Margaret Atwood

⸻

'I grew up without electricity or running water, which gives you a whole different mindset.'

⸻

Margaret Atwood CC was born in Ottawa, Canada, and received her undergraduate degree from Victoria College, University of Toronto, and her master's from Radcliffe College. She has authored more than forty books of fiction, poetry and critical essays, including the dystopian novel *The Handmaid's Tale*. Her writing has garnered numerous awards, including the Booker Prize, the Governor General's Award, and the Arthur C. Clarke Award. Atwood has served as president of the Writers' Union of Canada and the International PEN Canadian Centre and is an environmentalist and conservationist. She was granted the Order of Canada in 1973.

Q. What really matters to you?
An impossible question! It's too hard to definitively decide what matters to me – because so much does.

I think that *when* you were born is very important, because it determines what was going on when you were ten, when you were twenty and so on. It defines what is within your living memory and what is – on the other hand – in the land of legend. I believe there is a huge gap between the lived memories of the depression kids, the war kids and then the baby boomers – those are *very* distinct generations. Equally, anybody born in the year 2000 doesn't even remember the Vietnam War – it is a mythical thing to them that was long, long ago and far away – and they can't envisage a world without cellphones. For them, World War II is way back there – it is like people in 1880 thinking back to the Battle of Waterloo.

I'm a war kid. In the fifties, when I was an early teenager – it was an impressionable age – *1984* had just come out. The Cold War, Stalin and Russia were very much on people's minds. If you had a fear in that period, it would have been of being blown up by an atomic bomb, followed closely – in the case of women – by a fear of getting pregnant. Because there was no pill in that age, sexual politics were really quite different then. The fifties was a decade in which the prevailing ideology was to get women back into their homes and tell them that they wouldn't be fulfilled unless they had four kids, an open-plan house and a washer–dryer. Women's jobs were to make life happy for others and get rid of their selves. Luckily – because Canada was a cultural backwater – that message wasn't being pushed in our magazines. My parents were very egalitarian and keen on the outdoor life. I grew up without electricity or running water, which gives you a whole different mindset. I had few material possessions; at first, this was because of the war, and after that, my parents simply weren't interested in such things. Other girls complain about having been put into a frilly dress; I complain about missing out on that. So, I drew dresses! I spent my time drawing, then reading and finally writing.

My writing is important to me. I tried my hand at writing romance stories when I was sixteen, because they paid the most. No-go – that was not going to happen. Then, I thought I'd be a journalist – until my parents invited one to dinner. He said I'd just end up writing the ladies pages and obituaries, which some people say I've done anyway.

I'm very proud of my work. It's unique to see something like *The Handmaid's Tale* take on a new aura of urgency in a time when various state legislatures move towards phasing out not only women's reproductive rights, but their health rights. What is the plan here? All of it is pretty frightening and it doesn't only affect our women – because you can never change the condition of women without offering things for men.

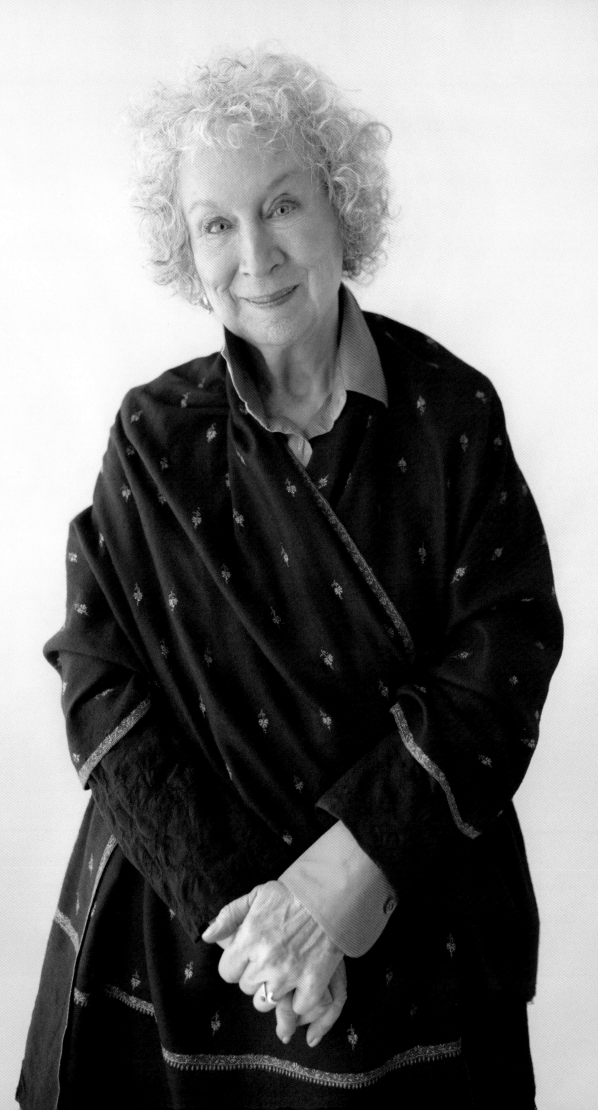

'And'

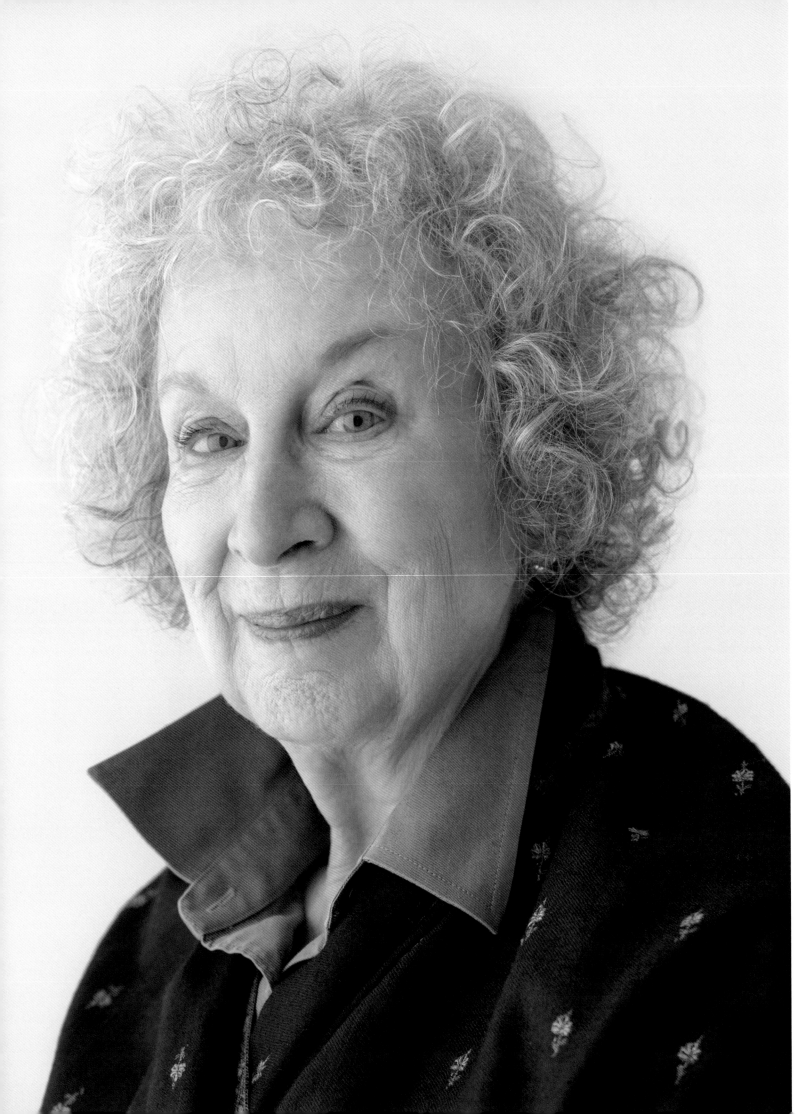

Margaret Atwood

_____

'I am annoyingly chipper, but that doesn't mean there is ground for hope. I think that most people have hope built into them, because a species without hope built into it wouldn't last very long.'

_____

Apart from my writing, I invest myself in conservation issues, freedom of expression and women's rights; since I take the radical view that women are human beings, I consider women's rights to be a subset of human-rights issues.

Q. What brings you happiness?
The pursuit of happiness was always a bit of a red herring, because happiness in itself is not a goal – rather, it is a by-product. So, doing things that you really want to do, being with people who you really want to be with and pursuing goals you find worthwhile will probably bring you happiness along the way.

But, happiness is quite often a matter of inheritance, I'm sorry to say. Some people are more cheerful than others, and some people battle depression all their lives – it's a chemical thing. I'm congenitally rather cheerful, and with all the dire things I write about, you would think I would be very depressed all the time. But that's not the case; dark things don't consume me, and I am generally an annoyingly chirpy person – which can be very irritating to other people when the news is quite gloomy.

Q. What do you regard as the lowest depth of misery?
The lowest depths of misery and suffering are certainly being experienced by people right here and now on this planet. Human beings have been imagining hell for a great many centuries, and they have done a pretty good job of creating it. What we have difficulty with is creating heaven.

Q. What would you change if you could?
The most important thing right now for us as a species is that we must avoid killing the oceans. If we kill the oceans, our oxygen supply will plummet. The blue-green algae and marine algae make approximately 60 per cent of the oxygen that we breathe; were the oceans to die, the oxygen supply would become a lot more skimpy. A great number of people would die, and the rest would become very stupid. Our brains would be functioning at about the level of somebody on the top of Mount Everest. How well are people unable to breathe enough oxygen to function going to get on at that point? Yet, we have advanced technology, so the thought of allowing the oceans to die is terrible.

If I could wave a magic wand, I would let the oceans be de-acidified. And I would let all the plastic be taken out of them. Plastic is a hard issue to get around, especially when you think of how many things in our lives are now dependent on plastic parts, including our phones, our computers, a lot of the parts of our cars and the things in our homes. We really need to find a solution to what happens to those plastics long term.

I am annoyingly chipper, but that doesn't mean there is ground for hope. I think that most people have hope built into them, because a species without hope built into it wouldn't last very long. So, we keep hoping for the next breakthrough, which keeps people working at the next breakthrough – if we didn't hope, we wouldn't do it.

Q. Which single word do you most identify with?
And. It means there is always something more.

Claudie Haigneré

Claudie Haigneré was born in Burgundy, France. A rheumatology and neurosciences graduate and practitioner, Haigneré became an astronaut candidate to the French space agency in 1985. She has had two space missions as a European Space Agency (ESA) astronaut to the Mir space station in 1996, and to the International Space Station in 2001. Haigneré held several French political positions between 2002 and 2005, including minister for research and new technologies, and minister for European affairs. Since 2015, Haigneré has worked with the European Space Agency on its research and development plans for the construction of a village on the moon. Haigneré is a Grand Officer of the French Legion of Honor.

'It takes ninety minutes to travel around the earth when you're in orbit, so I've circled it sixteen times a day, seeing sixteen sunrises and sixteen moonsets.'

Q. What really matters to you?
Having a sense of curiosity matters to me. I have a desire to learn and discover things that are beyond my usual horizon, and to comprehend even a small part of what our limits might be – both as individuals and as a society. In the context of the project to build a village on the moon, I call this desire to think outside the box 'thinking outside the atmosphere!' Naturally, I believe we need to try to provide answers to everyday issues and problems, but everyone also needs to be able to project a little beyond this – to see beyond everyday life, beyond the horizon. So, I try to keep my mind open and hungry at all times, to keep pushing the limits.

One of the most memorable moments of my life occurred in July 1969, when mankind took its first steps on the moon. I was a young girl of twelve, and that night, while witnessing that absolutely extraordinary moment of magic, I told myself that dreams can, in fact, come true. I told myself that even doors which seem out of reach can be opened.This experience no doubt gave me the daring and the strength to push open doors, to take on missions and to keep on exploring – to discover places I have never been before.

Q. What brings you happiness?
Happiness has to be practised every moment of every day. It's something we make – something we build. There is a quote from Alain that puts this nicely: 'You need to want happiness and to create it.'

I've had the good fortune to have experienced happiness from outer space: I've looked through a porthole and discovered the earth. It takes ninety minutes to travel around the earth when you're in orbit, so I've circled it sixteen times a day, seeing sixteen sunrises and sixteen moonsets. I've watched cities light up and the luminous edges of continents at night.

But, I've also experienced the joys of everyday life: a melody, a scent, a beautiful painting, a beautiful place, a gesture, a look. Little things like this fill me with joy and happiness, and I accumulate them.

In medical school, I read a study demonstrating that happiness is contagious. I really believe this is true; if you spread your own joy and happiness, you'll help other people feel better, too.

Q. What do you regard as the lowest depth of misery?
I may be saying this because I'm a doctor, but I think the depth of misery is suffering – in all forms. There is pain in physical suffering and then there is moral and intellectual suffering that we endure when we are alone, when we experience injustice and helplessness. Such suffering, of every kind, causes us to give up. It makes us want to exit this life that is making us suffer, or it makes us feel our suffering is so unfair – such an undeserved punishment – that we are pushed to extremism and violence of the kind we are seeing today.

Q. What would you change if you could?
It is absolutely essential that every child – and every grown-up, too, who was never given the chance – learns how to read and write. Illiteracy is a cause of exclusion, while literacy is a form of freedom. It makes it possible to understand, to express ourselves, to exchange ideas and to not just be passive bystanders. Reading and writing, to me, are paramount to critical thinking; they give us the ability to decide our own fate and to acquire a kind of responsibility.

Q. Which single word do you most identify with?
Curiosity. It's what allowed me to open doors and is what gave me the chance to live these many lives. There is the curiosity of a child who wants to explore: either by reading or by going out into the world to touch, discover and experiment with life. There is the curiosity of a researcher, who desires to understand, the curiosity of an astronaut to explore, and the curiosity of a doctor to unravel medical histories; to me, being a doctor was a little like being a detective. You had to look for clues to make a diagnosis and then – either with what you knew or with knowledge provided by others – find a solution.

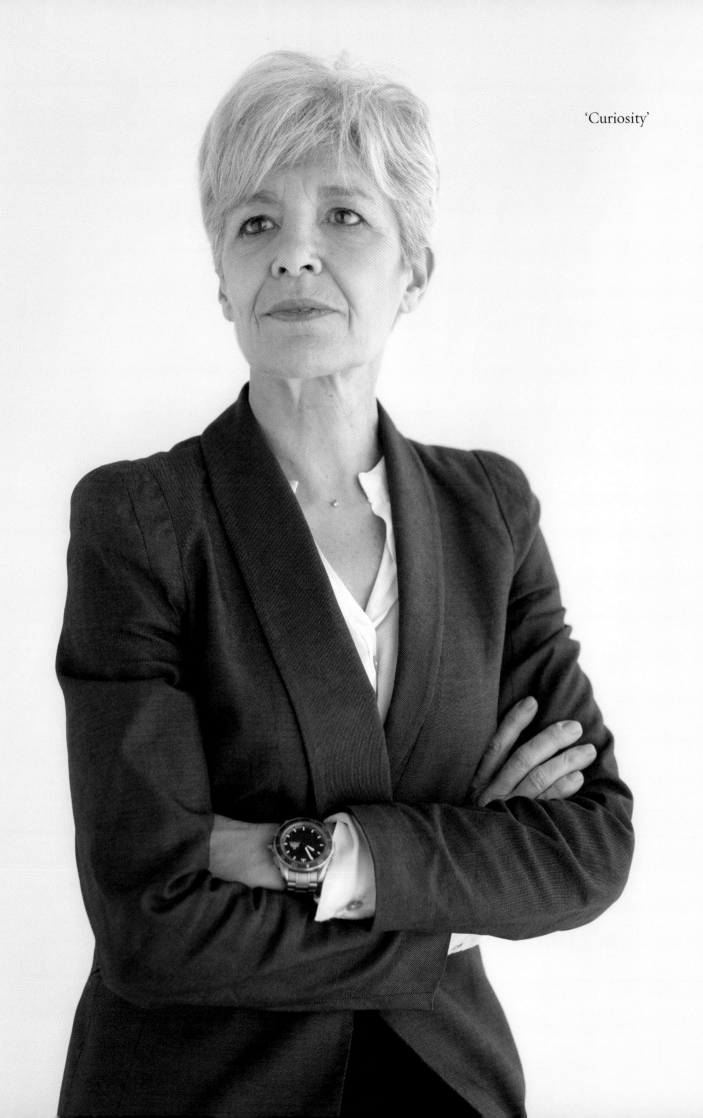

'Curiosity'

Renée Montagne

Renée Montagne was born in Oceanside in California, USA. She is best known as the co-host from 2004 to 2016, of the National Public Radio's flagship news programme, 'Morning Edition.' She graduated from the University of California, Berkeley, with a degree in English, and began her award-winning journalism career at an independent community radio station in San Francisco, KPOO, which dubs itself 'poor people's radio.' Montagne travelled to South Africa in 1990, arriving the day Nelson Mandela was released from prison, and covered the nation's transition to democracy up to President Mandela's inauguration. She has worked extensively in Afghanistan since 9/11.

Q. What really matters to you?

Making a difference – being deeply involved and deeply present in the world – matters enormously.

There are activists who are making an amazing effort on a daily basis – often quite bravely – to make a difference, but what I do, personally, also matters, because an important aspect of change is bearing witness. It's important to go to places where no one else will go, to find the things that people don't know about – because if no one knows about what's happening, they can't be changed.

Q. What brings you happiness?

The small things: dinner with my dearest, conversations with people and reading. I would say that I don't reserve great joy for great events, although there are some exceptions.

For instance, I was there when Nelson Mandela was inaugurated president of South Africa. At one point, unexpectedly, these fighter jets – this symbol of state power – flew over us in formation. Behind them streaked clouds in all the colours of the new flag. We all went silent. People around me started weeping – that's my kind of joy.

The only happier moment I can think of was five or six years ago, when I went to Badakhshan, a remote region of Afghanistan that has one of the worst mother-and-infant mortality rates in the world. We'd gone to cover a midwife programme that had been very successful there. The village we were in had just adopted the programme, whereby the village nominated girls to go away and be educated as midwives, then return to deliver children. Previously, sending a girl away would have embarrassed a family, but, as these girls were nominated by the village, they became its responsibility and so, being part of the programme became an honour. As we were leaving, we were told that one of the expectant mothers we had interviewed had just gone into labour. So, when the birth was over, I went in

with my mic. I made a mess of recording this moment with the mother, because I was so excited and overjoyed to see this baby – so many women in this family had died in childbirth: mothers, sisters and daughters; one aunt had lost eight babies. They all looked down at this baby and the grandmother said, 'This is a golden child.'

But I guess I'm strange, because joy for me is always mingled with sadness, a little strange sense of something emerging out of nothing. That's the moment where everything is pure and beautiful and right.

Being a woman makes me happy, and I never for one second wanted anything else than to be exactly who I am: a woman. I'm very lucky, I suppose. I didn't have many role models growing up, but I had a father who respected me and a mother who was all about taking chances. If every kid in the world – especially every girl in the world – could have that, they could do almost anything!

In my work, there are many ways in which being a woman gives you extra points; it even applies, to some extent, in places where you would think women aren't valued. I've been able to relate to half the population just by being a woman. I get this sense that there's an underground of women surrounding the planet and being able to relate to them can get you just about anywhere. In Afghanistan, I've discovered really strong personalities under the burka: tough, opinionated people, who in many cases are happy and able to live as whole people – I'm not so sure a male reporter would have discovered this.

Q. What do you regard as the lowest depth of misery?

On a personal level, I've experienced one great tragic event in my life that has made me deeply sad; David Gilkey, a photographer whom I worked with regularly and was a dear friend, was killed just recently in Afghanistan. He was covering a war he had covered for fourteen years. I've been lucky that I've

not experienced death personally very much, but what I see is that it's never just about that moment – some people never recover from the loss.

Generally, it seems to me that the real depths of misery people find themselves in – aside from losing loved ones – is losing their connection to their culture. This could speak to so much that's going on today: to having to flee, leave everything behind and rebuild. For some people, it's actually a wonderful opportunity, but for many more it is the end of their life and their being; in Afghanistan there are people who can't go home, or for whom home – even if they can go back to it – will never be the safe place it once was.

Q. What would you change if you could?

I would transform people so that they are able to see the 'other' as something valuable, beautiful and desirable to know. For the most part, at the heart of what's wrong is the fact that people don't see each other. And, as a matter of fact, people have memories that are a little too long. They nurse bad feelings, often against those who are close to them: the Shiites and Sunnis, the Northern Irish and the Irish.

People don't see other people as they see their loved ones, even in something as simple as offering a person a ride. When I was travelling, I would always ask people to hop in the car; I would give people rides to where they had to go, and they would help me find where I had to go. I found that people always – always – looked out for me. I attributed that to being female, which is a really positive aspect of being a woman. People weren't scared of me; they understood that I really meant to help them. I was able to get much of what I covered in my work by just being out in the world as me.

Q. Which single word do you most identify with?

Passionate.

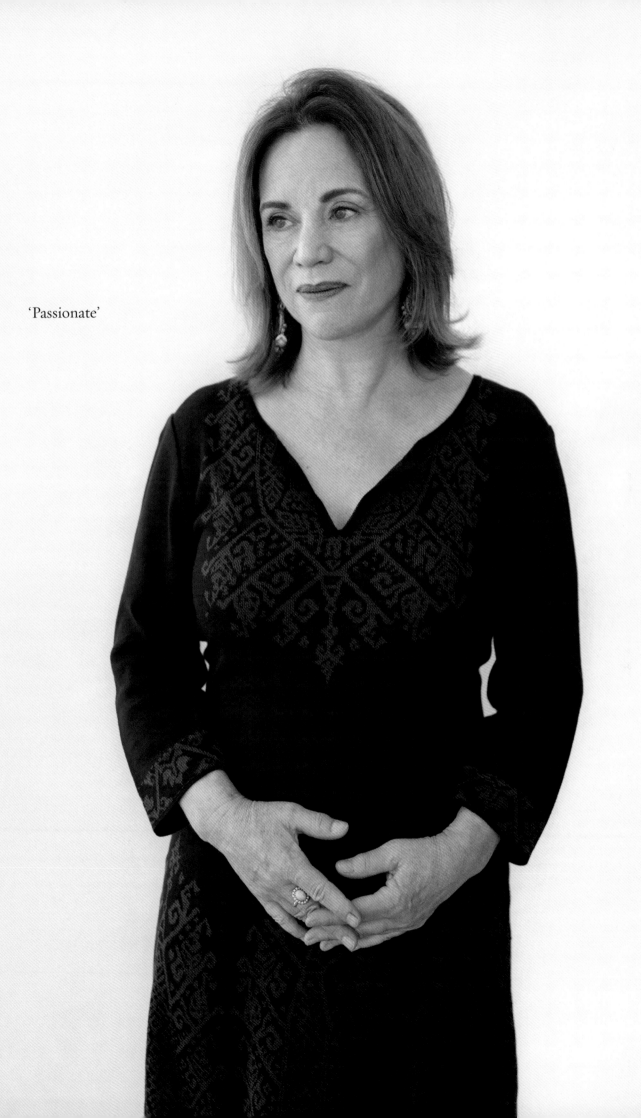

'Passionate'

Bobbi Brown

———

Bobbi Brown was born in Chicago in Illinois, USA. She founded Bobbi Brown Essentials in 1991; the brand was acquired by the Estée Lauder Companies Inc. in 1995. In 2013, Brown launched the Pretty Powerful Campaign for Women & Girls, supporting women's empowerment through training and education. In 2016, Brown stepped down from Bobbi Brown Cosmetics to create a new lifestyle platform that celebrated empowerment and confidence. She recently published her ninth book, *Beauty from the Inside Out*, and was named creative consultant of the American department store Lord & Taylor, where she created JustBOBBI, an in-store and digital lifestyle concept boutique.

Q. What really matters to you?

Everyone wants to be confident, and a woman is confident if she feels comfortable in her own skin. So, first of all, it matters that I am able to teach women how to be their best selves. Empowerment has always been my message, both through my company and in life. This doesn't mean trying to be someone you are not, but it may mean that if you put on a little eyeliner and mascara, or a little blush, you feel good. And if you take care of yourself, you take care of everyone.

I fell in love with makeup when I was a young girl in the Jackie Kennedy era. I fell in love with beauty and makeup watching my mother put hers on – she was so gorgeous.

Nothing that I was either taught or learned growing up in Chicago set me up for what I'm doing, but everything I do brings me back to something or someone in Chicago. We were taught hard work, and we were taught giving back. My entire life, I have been someone who cares about other people – this is not because I was told to do it, it is because I watched my family doing it. Today, I will be sitting in business meetings and will think about my grandfather Poppa Sam, who came from Russia. He was a role model for me in the way he handled his business; he was constantly working, always paying attention to the details and caring about his customers.

My career started after college, where I got a degree in theatrical makeup; I had gone into theatrical makeup because I knew I didn't want to go to beauty school – I wanted a regular college degree. It was an inter-disciplinary major that I had to put together myself, and it is why I am here today – because college was not about the rules, it was about creating your own destiny and being an entrepreneur of your life. When I left college, I did the

most important job that anyone could do: I waited on tables. It taught me a lot – that I could take care of myself and could pay my rent, and what it's like to be in the service industry.

Later, I moved to New York, where I thought I would do some fashion work on the side while I got my movie career going. But I did one movie and hated it; it really wasn't for me. So, I started pounding the pavement and being hired as a freelance makeup artist working in magazines. It was the eighties, and the makeup was artificial everything: pale skin, contouring, overdrawn lips and eyebrows. I either wasn't good at it or didn't like it, so I started to do makeup that just enhanced someone's natural beauty. I think it's because I love the way people look without makeup.

Starting a company as a new mum, not getting enough sleep, was definitely a challenge. I remember talking to editors on the phone – telling them how to stay fresh when leaving the house in the morning – while my son was literally puking on me. But you kept it cool, because back then you didn't talk about having kids. It wasn't cool in the fashion industry to even have a life outside of fashion. I think I probably had a little bit to do with the change of attitude – that you can actually have a life outside of the fashion industry – because that was always really important to me.

When I launched Bobbi Brown Cosmetics, I knew I needed to make foundation that actually matched skin, and not just white skin – everybody's skin! I knew there was a hole out there because, when I was a makeup artist, I could never find colours that worked on people's skins; I always had to go to theatrical makeup stores to buy yellows and blues to fix all the makeup. That's why, over all the years in my company, whenever we would have meetings to decide what to discontinue

based on what sells, I refused to get rid of the darkest foundations even though these were not top sellers.

For me, everything has to make sense. It makes total sense that, when a woman comes to the counter, she needs to get a foundation that matches her skin – it's not that complicated. I figured out early on that blush should be the colour of your cheeks when you pinch them, that the pencil should be the colour of your brows and that the most beautiful lipstick is the colour of a woman's lips. To me this was common sense; it was not brilliance and it wasn't some 'Aha!' moment, it was just what needed to happen.

Q. What brings you happiness?

It's pretty simple: having a happy marriage, having amazing kids, having great friends, being able to be incredibly creative and take a lot of risks, and working with a team of people that have my back. We have a lot of fun and that makes me happy.

Q. What do you regard as the lowest depth of misery?

The hardest thing in life is when people don't have their physical or mental health; if you have your health, there is always hope.

After that, I would say not having an education. If you are educated, in whatever way it is, you have a future. This doesn't mean everyone has to go to college; you could be educated by being an apprentice or by going to trade school. It doesn't matter which form it takes, I just wish that everyone could get an education.

Q. What would you change if you could?

Free health care and free education. Honestly, I couldn't choose between the two.

Q. Which single word do you most identify with?

Authenticity. To me, there is nothing better than when a person is exactly who they are.

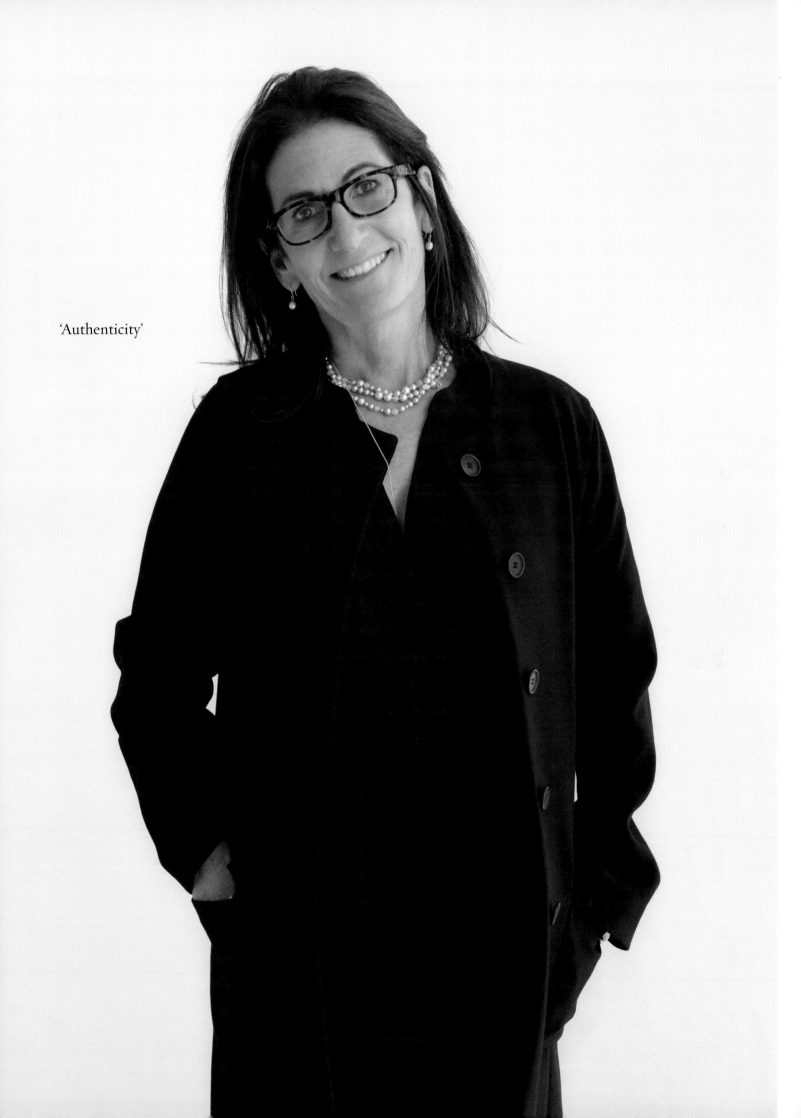

'Authenticity'

'If you're not disrupting the status quo, what are you doing? I don't want to just plod along every day and ride along on the coat-tails of other people.'

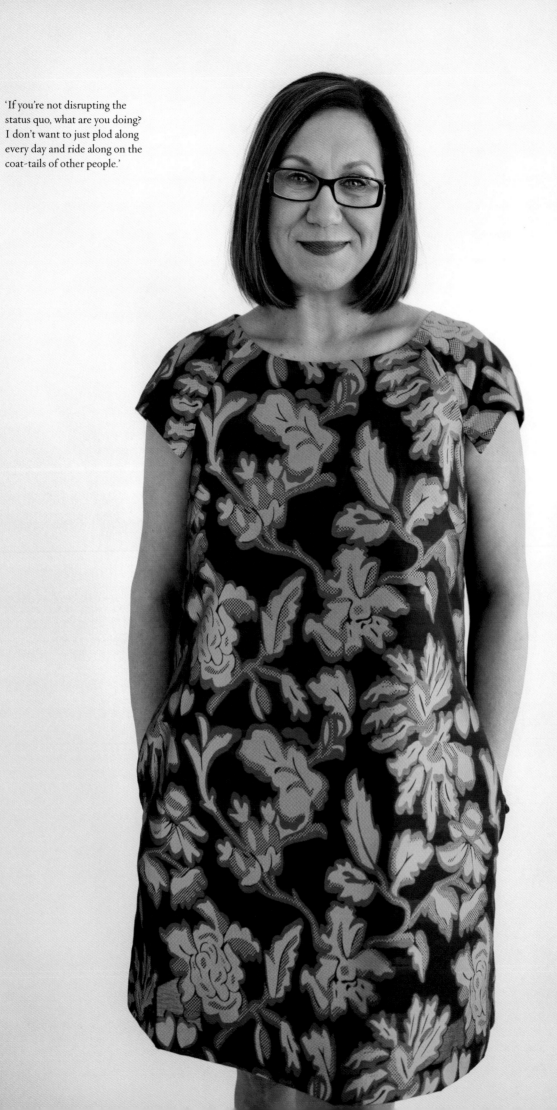

'Hope'

Anita
Heiss

Anita Heiss was born and raised in Sydney, Australia, and is a member of the Wiradjuri Nation of central New South Wales. Heiss' award-winning published works include the novel *Not Meeting Mr Right,* the *Macquarie PEN Anthology of Aboriginal Literature* and the memoir *Am I Black Enough For You?* Heiss has been a communications advisor for the Aboriginal and Torres Strait Islander Arts Board of the Australia Council, and deputy director of Warawara – Department of Indigenous Studies at Macquarie University. She is a lifetime ambassador of the Indigenous Literacy Foundation and manages the Epic Good Foundation.

Q. What really matters to you?

Everything I do in my life, particularly in terms of my writing, is through the lens of an Aboriginal woman. I am a Wiradjuri woman, which means I'm from the Wiradjuri Nation of central New South Wales, one of the largest Aboriginal Nations in Australia. But, I was born and bred on the land of the Gadigal People – Gadigal country is the city of Sydney. As Aboriginal people, we always reflect on the traditional owners of the land in which we find ourselves. So, right now, I'm being interviewed on the land of the Jaggera Peoples in Brisbane.

If we take family aside, because obviously they matter, what really matters to me are my *tiddas*. Tidda is an Aboriginal generic word for sisters that is largely used on the east coast. Tiddas are the friends you choose as your sisters, but you can also call your mum, your blood sister or your aunty your tidda as well – young people today call them BFFs! My tiddas are the people who give me support and don't judge me; they have my back, even if they don't necessarily agree with the position I'm taking; they are the people I can ring at three o'clock in the morning and who will tell it to me straight; they are the women who will march next to me for whatever the cause is, then lie under a palm tree and have a cocktail with me. They are what really matters to me in life – without them, my life would be half of what it is.

Q. What brings you happiness?

I find the greatest happiness and joy in being a creative disruptor. I'm disrupting the literary landscape by for the first time placing Aboriginal women, but also Aboriginal children and men as well, into literary landscapes where we never belonged before: in commercial publishing, in children's literature, in historical fiction. I'm using the themes that are important to me as an Aboriginal woman – social justice, identity and so forth – and putting them in novels that all Australians can read and hopefully reflect upon. My characters – who are just like me, my tiddas, and my family

and friends – have never been in any of the storytelling in Australian literature. They are like the people I walk past in the street in Brisbane's West End, who have never had a voice. I love placing these real, authentic characters in Paris, Manhattan or Hawaii – because we do exist out in the world, and I am happiest when I am taking this reality and weaving it into a creative storyline.

Q. What do you regard as the lowest depth of misery?

On a personal level, seeing anybody I love in pain or suffering makes me most miserable. I started grieving the day my father was diagnosed with the cancer that would eventually take his life a year later. It took me five years, and some professional help, to get back to be the happy Anita that I was prior to my father becoming sick – to realise that I wanted to go back to being the person I was prior to falling into a pit of sadness.

On a global level, seeing what mankind is doing on a daily basis because of land, religion or power – war and death, and the terror in the faces and eyes of young children – is the definition of misery for me. But, we know that humans create this misery, therefore humans can stop it.

Q. What would you change if you could?

If you're not disrupting the status quo, what are you doing? I don't want to just plod along every day and ride along on the coat tails of other people. I want to make change and I know that I can do that through storytelling on a page.

If I could wave my magic wand, I would change the racial hierarchy we see played out every day on the news that tells us the lives of people of colour are less valuable than other lives. I would like to see a world in which any child born anywhere in the world has the right and the opportunities to live a complete and fulfilled life regardless of the colour of their skin or of where they were born.

Growing up, all I ever saw was a brown mother and a white father who loved each

other, so race was not part of my home life. But, when I walked to and from school, I would be called Abo, coon, chocolate drop and cocoa pop – that language was completely normal back then. I would go home and cry to my mum, because I didn't understand why the other children would bully me like this. But how do you explain to a five-year-old what race hate is? So mum said, 'Oh, they're just jealous that you've been kissed by the sun.' And I literally believed that the sun had puckered up and kissed me. I remember my mother going to the school and telling them, 'Anita's come home upset because kids are calling her Abo.' I had to stand in the classroom and point to who said it. Although that must have made me a bit of a telltale, it was then that I decided not to tolerate racial vilification of any kind.

I want to change behaviour. When people read my work, I want them to think about how they view Aboriginal people today, and about how their views and opinions are demonstrated in their actions. And, I do believe that literature can make change, that the way people view issues and social justice can be impacted upon by their reading a novel.

Q. Which single word do you most identify with?

Hope. Because I'm hopeful on every level: I hope I'll meet Mr Right; I hope that one day the racial hierarchy won't exist; I hope that one day teachers won't have to be forced to include Indigenous perspectives in a classroom; I hope that we don't have to keep explaining why it's important to have an Aboriginal acknowledgement of country, that people can understand it's just how it's been done for tens of thousands of years; I hope that in years to come our Indigenous young people aren't leaving school with low literacy levels; I hope that at some point an Australian government actually acknowledges that what's happened in the past is the reason we're stuck where we are today; and I hope Donald Trump doesn't last!

Mpho Tutu van Furth

Mpho Tutu van Furth was born in London, England. She is a preacher, teacher, writer and retreat facilitator, and is an Episcopal priest. Shortly after her marriage to Marceline van Furth in 2016, she handed in her licence to officiate in the South African Anglican church, as it does not permit its priests to marry same-sex partners. Tutu van Furth is canonically resident in the USA. She is the daughter of anti-apartheid activists Archbishop Emeritus Desmond Tutu and Leah Tutu. Tutu van Furth was the founding director of the Desmond and Leah Tutu Legacy Foundation, which is dedicated to supporting projects and initiatives that promote peace and reconciliation for the flourishing of people and the planet.

'What's really important is that all of us – people and planet – ought to be able to flourish.'

Q. What really matters to you?
My children. I've always said that having children really changed – or, perhaps, cemented – my view of the world. I have two girls and after my older daughter, Nyaniso, was born it was almost like I took a look around and thought: 'Well, this isn't good enough for my child!' The reality is that it's not a world that feels good enough for my daughters to live in. And in order to have the kind of world that I want for them, the world has to work for everyone else as well.

What's really important is that all of us – people and planet – ought to be able to flourish. Nobody can flourish in circumstances of abject poverty. Nobody can flourish in circumstances of sickness and want, or in places of war. No one can flourish when they're stigmatised, or when they're set aside. No one can flourish when they are treated as if they don't matter. We need to create a world in which all of us can flourish.

Q. What brings you happiness?
I couldn't choose one thing; I have at least seven! I'd like to say 'joy' instead of 'happiness,' though. My joys are in moments with my children and in the kind of intense engagement I can have with my wife. When I am presiding at the Eucharist, I feel completely in my own body. And I sometimes get lost – absorbed – in drawing or painting. And I love to cook.

Q. What do you regard as the lowest depth of misery?
Recently I was at an orphanage established by a pastor and his wife. He was talking to me about the basic-income grant – the welfare grant that the orphanage's children were supposed to receive – and he said that only four of the thirty-one children at the orphanage are actually receiving it. This is because although the money had been sent by the government, it had been pocketed by someone in the office that was supposed to distribute it.

That kind of casual corruption which has absolutely no regard for the welfare of a person down the line makes me weep. It's such a casual cruelty. I think, 'What was it? Did that sum of money buy you another handbag or another pair of shoes? It's not enough to make the difference between whether or not you have a roof over your head, but it would have been enough to make a difference for the child who was supposed to get it.'

I'm not disheartened because, for me, nothing is impossible. My generation overcame apartheid, so we carry in us the knowledge that we can change the world. The corruption that we confront today doesn't always have to be so – we can change it.

Q. What would you change if you could?
Can we start small and get rid of patriarchy?

I went on a pirate ship with my younger daughter, Onalenna, and the guy wanted to paint a heart on her cheek and give her the pink whistle. She wanted a moustache and a blue whistle. He said, 'Are you sure you're a girl?' I said, 'Yes, she's sure she's a girl; she's just a girl who wants a moustache and a blue whistle!' When she was four years old, she had to write down what she wanted to do when she grows up, and she said she wanted to rule the world. I don't know if we'll ever have a female president in South Africa, but if our girls have an attitude like that, who knows?

As a mother of girl children, I know that if we can fix the world for girl children, we will fix it for all children. Even in South Africa, with its amazingly enlightened constitution and women of courage who have demonstrated their skill, ability, passion, intelligence, fortitude and leadership, there are still women who go home to the most unsafe place on earth. For the large number of women who are still victims of domestic violence, for the number of women and girls who are subjected to rape and sexual abuse, our wonderfully enlightened constitution is really words on a piece of paper – it hasn't yet become the reality of their lives.

Q. Which single word do you most identify with?
I still say 'love.' When in doubt, do the most loving thing.

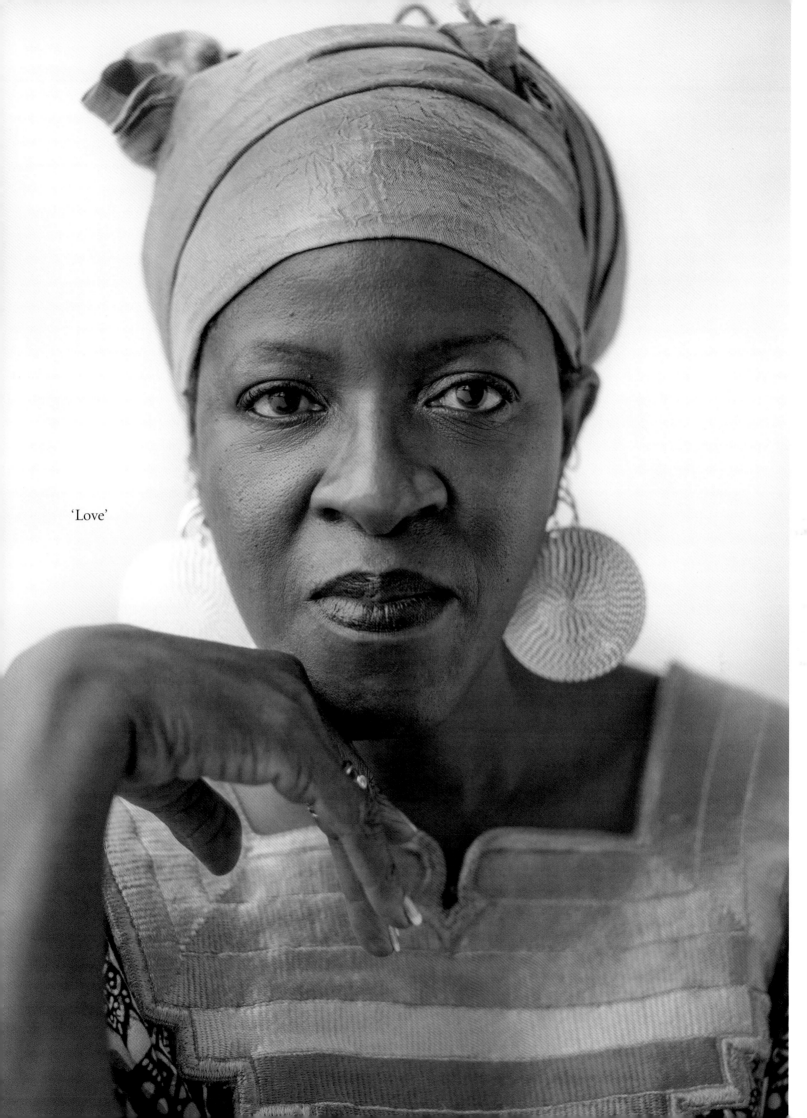

'Love'

'Imagination'

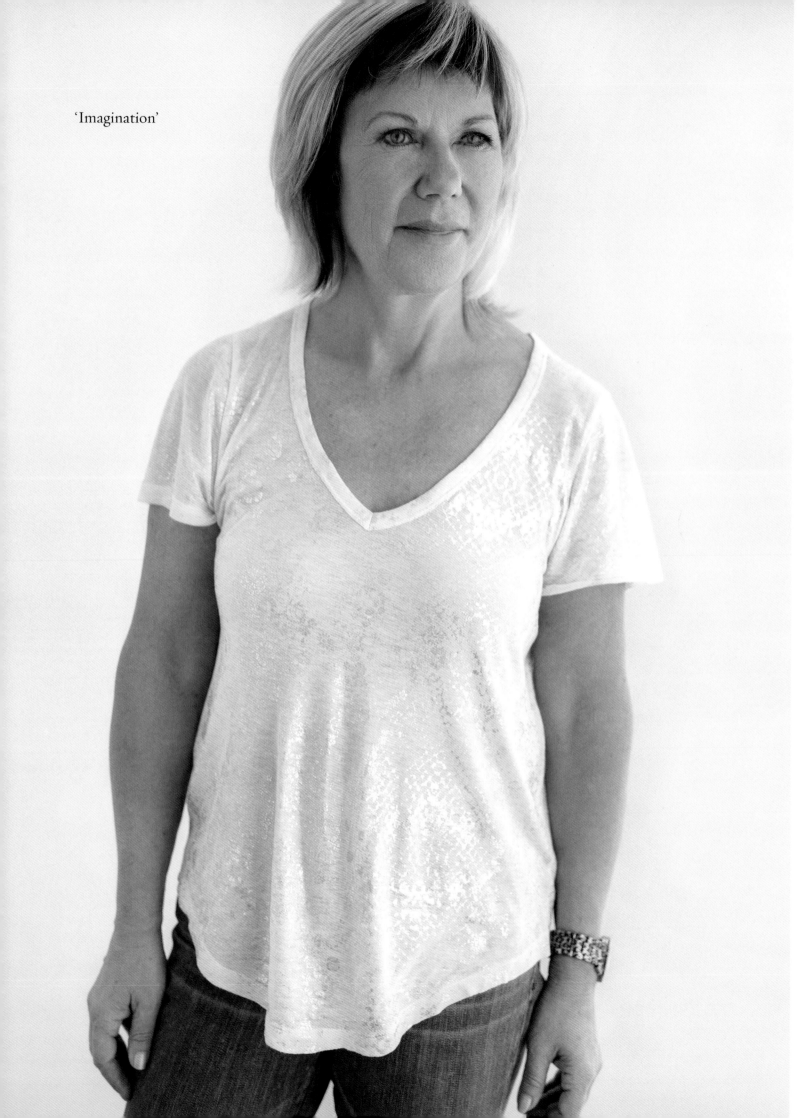

Jude
Kelly

_____

Jude Kelly CBE was born in Liverpool, England. She holds a bachelor of arts in drama and theatre arts from the University of Birmingham, and has directed numerous award-winning theatre and opera productions. In 2006, Kelly became the artistic director of the Southbank Centre, the United Kingdom's largest cultural institution. She is the founder of several arts organisations and events, including WOW – Women of the World Festival, which celebrates women and girls, and promotes gender equality. Kelly was made a Commander of the Order of the British Empire for services to the arts in 2015.

Q. What really matters to you?

Equality. I feel very despairing when I think about human beings wanting to have a higher status than other human beings. That higher status is really about ensuring that one group of people in society are more powerful; it's disturbing and is at the root of why we have so much aggression. The fact that girls and women are systemically unequal is an enormous problem; this also applies to race, caste, disability and sexual preference.

I was born in Liverpool, a northern city in the United Kingdom. My grandmother left school when she was twelve and had fourteen children; my mother left school when she was fifteen and had four daughters. So, I am shaped by the realisation that I am where I am today because people who are dead and long gone got women the vote, got girls education, helped get women birth control and made it possible for me to realise my dreams.

Sometimes, I have had to challenge quite casual, lazily held ideas about what girls and women can and can't do – or should and shouldn't do. I have been prepared to do this because I've been encouraged and supported. This makes me feel that other girls and women need to have an opportunity to realise their dreams, too. I'm not angry or aggressive about the challenges I've had to overcome, though, because I have men in my life that I absolutely love: my son, my partner, my dad. Men are not necessarily individually creating sexism or prejudice; they, too, are the product of a society that determined this inequality thousands of years ago. Men can be part of the solution now, and I encourage them to be.

I believe that the arts are primal; the cave paintings from thirty-five thousand years ago tell us that humans – long before they created anything mechanical or scientific – had to express themselves, somewhere. So, for me, the arts are something that humans need to have and have to do. It upsets me when the arts are quickly appropriated by structures that say, 'This is very special and it is just for us.' Then other people feel excluded from the arts, thinking, 'Well, this is not for me then, is it?' This idea starts at a very early age; in fact, all the signals to do with boundaries and role models, to do with what is a boy and what is a girl, what is appropriate and what is not, start at a very early age. These things are all absolutely critical to a child; if you don't give a child education in the arts early, then they always think the arts are something that other people do, that they themselves may not be deserving of.

Q. What brings you happiness?

It is nice, being happy. I love my family, I love being in love and I love to windsurf – these things bring me great happiness. And, I do actually like my species, so, when I see humans being happy, enjoying themselves and doing good things with each other, that makes me feel happy.

Q. What do you regard as the lowest depth of misery?

I accept the fact that we may never have world peace, that we may always have eruptions of violence and disturbance; I think we are a very turbulent species, that we just have to recognise this and work out how to deal with it. What makes me most unhappy, though, is seeing people deliberately neglected and marginalised by cruelty; by this, I don't mean the flashes of anger that humanity shows, but long-term, systematic cruelty to people. Those on the receiving end of this cruelty never really understand why it is happening to them; they tend to internalise it and think it is their fault. It makes me terribly unhappy to see children cruelly treated – being blamed or excluded for things that will never have been their fault. And I know that they are storing up the problems for when they are an adult; what goes around, comes around, and that is a fearful thing as well.

Q. What would you change if you could?

If I had a magic wand, I would change the very deep-rooted idea that men and women aren't equal. Almost all theologies have this idea that there is a male, divine creature, and that down from him comes creativity that imbues males with a final, separate and more powerful existence. At its most primitive, this idea begins with the question, 'Well, who is physically stronger?' It is the strongest, therefore, who can literally dominate. You can see in the desire humans have to create status how the idea of 'men versus women' came about. It's obviously complex and, when it goes back thousands and thousands of years, it is very hard to deconstruct. So, I would just eradicate the whole thought process and start all over again with the idea that men and women are marvellous and equal. I would love to see what would happen if we could do that, and I am optimistic that we are at least considering this idea of equality.

Q. Which single word do you most identify with?

Imagination. Imagination says, 'I don't know how to do this yet or what it could look or feel like, but I'm going to dream it up and then walk towards it.'

'Focus'

Leigh
Sales

———

Leigh Sales was born in Brisbane, Australia. She holds a master's degree in international relations from Victoria's Deakin University and a bachelor's degree in journalism from the Queensland University of Technology. A journalist and author, Sales is the recipient of two Walkley Awards: for radio current-affairs reporting, in 2005, and for broadcasting and online interviewing, in 2012. Since 2011, Sales has hosted *7.30*, the Australian Broadcasting Corporation's television current-affairs programme. Her book, *Detainee 002*, earned her the 2007 George Munster Award for Independent Journalism, presented by the University of Technology, Sydney.

Q. What really matters to you?

The facts, in both my professional and my personal life. I believe that there is always a truth to things. People have opinions, but, at the heart of matters, there are basic facts. I find it really disturbing when we, as a society, fail to give currency to these. Everything that I do professionally is about trying to get to what the bare facts are – stripped of opinion. Perhaps that's optimistic, but I believe that if you can provide most reasonable-minded people with the facts, then they will be suitably armed to make their own decisions. When I interview people, what I aim to do is ask them those questions that I believe the average member of the audience would like to have answered. I consider it my job to be a representative for the average member of the public – I'm asking questions on their behalf, which is a privilege.

The other thing that's hugely important to me is kindness: both being a kind person and being grateful for the times when other people are kind to me. When I had my second son, things were very touch-and-go – it nearly went badly for us both. It was during that time that I realised kindness is the most important thing, even though you shouldn't need a reminder that kindness is so key! When I was ill and the chips were down, it was the kind people – not the funniest people – who mattered the most. It was the kind people who were the most valuable. I know it sounds a bit earnest, but I do put a lot of effort into trying to be thoughtful and kind, and to thinking about what other people need. That goes for people I don't know very well, too; there's always something you can do for someone to make a little bit of difference to them.

My sons are now two and four. Kindness and thoughtfulness are important in my parenting, as I try to ensure that they become their best selves and turn into people of good character. I believe that, when one is outwardly focussed, acts of equality and empathy are natural – you're focussed on treating others the way you wish to be treated. Raising a couple of people who are like that matters to me; hopefully they'll apply those lessons broadly, throughout their lives.

When I was ill, I also realised how quickly things can change. It's left me with this feeling that I have to be bold and do things when I think of them – that I have to focus on being present in the moment. So, I don't worry about the past and I try not to be too anxious about the future – I try to appreciate the moment, because it can disappear suddenly.

Q. What brings you happiness?

Many people become journalists because they want to change the world; I just liked talking to people and writing stories. For twenty-five years, I've been a daily-news journalist, which means that every single working day I'm absolutely immersed in people's lives. Frequently, because of the nature of news, I see people on the worst day of their lives. This has shown me that ordinary days can change in an instant and – with hindsight – that ordinary days are actually extraordinary. So, though I'm not always successful, I try to find my happiness and joy in appreciating the ordinary days in my life and in the small things I fill them with. I love music, reading and having a nice cup of tea, then being present with whatever I'm doing in the moment. People talk a lot about how self-help books can help you find happiness, but that's nonsense. I don't think you'll find happiness by chasing after it like that, because it's not really some *thing*. It's not a commodity that you can grab, rather you have to find happiness in your everyday circumstances. Some days it might be something awesome – a fantastic meal and a beautiful bottle of wine – that is a source of joy and happiness to me.

Other times, it might be that I have a really interesting conversation with an Uber driver. Regardless, I try to take joy where I can get it, because you never know when it's going to dry up. I've interviewed lots of people over the years who have survived something horrendous and they often say that, at the other end of it, it feels like the everyday is really heightened; they find that the contrast between life and death allows them to find beauty in everyday moments.

Q. What do you regard as the lowest depth of misery?

That's so subjective – and I acknowledge my privilege in saying this – but, for me, it's ill health. I think you haven't got anything if you don't have good health; when good health is taken away from a person, the difference in them is so glaring compared to how they used to be. Suffering from ill health is so draining; the illness is ever-present and stops you from doing the things you want to do – because it's not only painful physically, but also mentally. Illness is absolutely debilitating: mentally, emotionally, on every level.

Q. What would you change if you could?

I'm keen to have religion without the zealotry. I wouldn't get rid of religion itself, because it's a source of comfort to so many people and because religious organisations do some amazing things. But, although I would try to allow people to have religion and be empowered to act on the positives of their religion, I would inhibit them from wanting to kill each other for subscribing to different religions. There's so much suffering, death and pain caused by people not being comfortable allowing others to believe whatever they choose.

Q. Which single word do you most identify with?

Focus: remembering to focus on the things that need to be focussed on and letting go of the rest – focus on truth, kindness and on being a better person.

Eryn Wise

Eryn Wise was born in Albuquerque in New Mexico, USA. She is a Native American woman of the Jicarilla Apache Nation and Laguna Pueblo People. She is an organiser for Honor the Earth, a not-for-profit that works to create awareness and support – both political and financial – for Native environmental issues and sustainable Native communities. In 2016, Wise became a leader and media coordinator for the International Indigenous Youth Council, campaigning against the Dakota Access Pipeline at Standing Rock Indian Reservation.

Q. What really matters to you?

Kids. Too many kids come from abusive spaces, and by this I mean abuse in whatever form: sexual, physical or through neglect. Although I, too, come from an abusive background, I had grandmothers who were my light. They lived across the country, but, whenever I needed them, they were always there. However, a lot of children don't have that person they can call when they are in need. So, they are ill-equipped and are rendered useless by both their parents and by society.

It is a huge disservice to the next generation that there are parents who refuse to talk to their children about issues, yet expect them to have an understanding of those issues and act in accordance with that understanding. It's so much more complicated than millennials not having the correct tools, because the problem is also that the world has been so fundamentally changed by previous generations. I don't want kids to be confronted by all these sociological and environmental disasters, not knowing what's going on around them. I don't want them to be confronted with 'No!' after 'No!' and have no one to hold their hands for as long as they feel they need the support. I work with Indigenous youth, and our suicide rates are three times the national average. Last year I worked with a group of kids from Attawapiskat in Ontario; in the space of a month, 110 children tried to commit suicide – and most of them succeeded.

Growing up, I was that youth. I was the child who tried to check out early because I couldn't comprehend or process the emotions I was feeling. There is a surge of suicide amongst youngsters because they are also going through puberty. I see kids – especially on my reservation – dying all the time because there is no one to intervene and say, 'Hey, I know it doesn't make sense, but let me help you figure it out.' Kids are the best bulls—t detectors, so I like to just hang out with them and trust that they are going to say whatever they think or feel. And I would rather surround myself with honesty than sit at a self-congratulatory table at which people applaud themselves but are blind to future generations.

I got involved with the Dakota Access Pipeline (DAPL) when I was trying to get my brother and sister, who were in college, off the couch – they are my cousins, but, in my culture, your cousins are your brothers and sisters. Their mum had asked me to motivate them to contribute to society, so I sent them an article about the Indigenous youth who ran to Washington, DC, to tell President Obama to block the DAPL. I told them that, if those teenagers were doing something incredible, they should be finding something to do as well. And I told them that our grandmothers didn't raise us to be complacent. Two months passed and I'd totally forgotten about it, when my aunt called me. 'They've started a camp,' she said. They had jumped into their car and driven to North Dakota! I had no idea what they had gotten themselves into, so I borrowed my mom's truck and trailer, and drove from Phoenix to North Dakota to find them. When I arrived, they introduced me to this big group of kids, saying, 'This is our big sister, she'll pay for everything; she'll take care of us!' So many of these kids had never had anybody to hold their hearts or spend time with them in a way that engaged them in something greater than themselves. So, the youth kind of attached themselves to me and started calling me Ina, which means 'mother' in Lakota. A week after I arrived, security guards' dogs attacked protesters. When that happened, I felt such guilt and knew I couldn't leave. The camp started to grow, and we created a safe space. Suddenly, I became a mom, for five and a half months. Things like that *really* matter.

The United States will never acknowledge that a genocide has happened in this country – it is consumed by self-assuredness. But somebody, long ago, decided to survive, so that I could be here to have these kinds of conversations. So, my existence is their resistance. I don't think most Americans will *ever* see me. But I see me, and that's a lot better than my mother's generation. So many Indigenous people are lost to us, because they were told they didn't exist; as a result, they stopped seeing themselves. This is why I look at myself in the mirror every morning and say 'I see you.' And I tell the kids I work with that I see them too. We're going to have to make one hundred thousand times more noise if we are going to be heard, but I'm here to help them scream.

Q. What brings you happiness?

Water.

Mni wiconi: water is life. People think of this as a hashtag rather than as a statement, but, for me, it's the latter, because I grew up with a deep love for the water, its gifts and its terrors. Nothing makes me happier than being able to touch water. I don't want the DAPL touching water, because I don't want to be apologising to the rivers for what's being done to them.

Q. What do you regard as the lowest depth of misery?

When we have lost our humanity: when children die and no one pays attention. The most miserable thing to me is when we look at our biological children and say that they're worth more than any other children.

Misery is also when we dismiss our most sacred gifts; it's when a person expects to have clean water running from their faucet, while, elsewhere, people are dying from thirst. And it's the fact that the Navajo Nation have to have their water shipped to them and that, in Flint, Michigan, turning on the faucet can give a child cancer. Misery is when our children are dying and ecological devastation abounds, and no one is doing anything about it.

Q. What would you change if you could?

I wish that compliments came in the form of glasses, so that the recipient could put them on and see themselves as they're seen by others. I think that would be a way of bringing humanity back to the global population.

Q. Which single word do you most identify with?

Resilient.

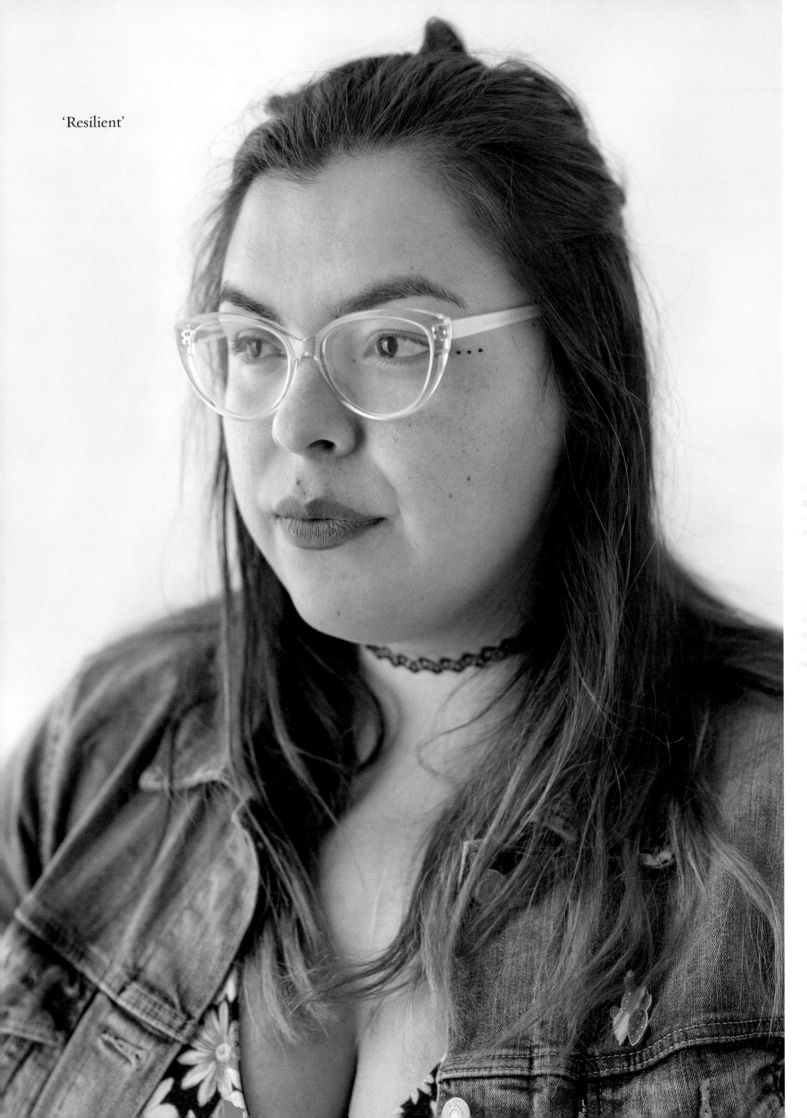

'Resilient'

Geena Rocero

Geena Rocero was born and raised in Manila, in the Philippines. At seventeen, she moved to the United States, where she began a successful modelling career. In 2014, she came out as transgender at the annual TED Conference; her TED Talk has since been viewed over 3 million times on ted.com and has been translated into thirty-two languages. An award-winning producer and television host, Rocero is the founder of Gender Proud, a media production company that tells stories to elevate justice and equality for the transgender community worldwide. Rocero has spoken about trans rights at the White House, the World Economic Forum and the United Nations.

Q. What really matters to you?

Justice: I want everyone to have the same opportunities to pursue their dreams. I was just a young trans girl, growing up on a little island of the Philippines, who had a dream – I imagined something bigger for myself. And here I am: I live in New York City, I offer my voice for my community and I'm meeting world leaders. But, I don't forget where I've come from, and I have such gratitude that my dream has come to pass.

In the Philippines, we have a long-held tradition of throwing a fiesta for the birthday of a particular saint; I was always drawn to the singing and dancing contests, and to the transgender beauty pageants. When I was seven, I remember standing there watching these beautiful trans women, thinking, 'Wow, that's me!' For the first time in my life, I found that I could identify with this particular representation of humanity. I realised that I wasn't alone, and I started dreaming of becoming like these women. It was the first time I felt valid – the first time I felt that all the things that had been going on in my head since I was five could actually be real. It was the moment I realised there was a place in this world for me to inhabit.

When I was fifteen – again, I was at the pageants – the pageant manager approached me and offered to pay for my registration and garments to wear. She told me she would take care of me and that I could be her daughter. It opened up an entirely new world for me. For the next two years of my life I was immersed in this world, travelling around the Philippines with people like me: wonderful, creative, loving people. We found community in each other in a country where – although we were seen – we were not included. And we found empowerment through each other; this was particularly important because, although we were culturally visible, we weren't politically recognised. We weren't recognised as women – on many of my official documents I'm still listed as male.

Fashion was one of my dreams, so I moved to New York City to become a model. It was a completely different experience, because there weren't a lot of trans models – there still aren't. For about a decade, I worked, but hid who I was. Worrying about whether anyone would find out my history gave me great anxiety, because all of the trans women who had come before me lost their careers when they came out. But, I felt like I wasn't fully myself at work or with the people I surrounded myself with. Then, I just decided to share my story and did a TED Talk; I decided it was time to share my pride in my journey as an immigrant, trans woman of colour. It changed my life. People ask me why I did it; I think I felt a sense of purpose that was greater than my fear. And declaring the fullness of my humanity and femininity to the world opened up so many opportunities. The greatest has been being able to listen to people's stories. I'm so aware of my privilege and would never want to speak for anyone, so it matters that I'm engaging with the complexities of people's experiences, so that I can share them with the world. Producing has given me the ability to take ownership of the trans narrative; for the longest time, people have taken away our control of our own narratives by telling our stories through their own lenses. That's changing and will continue to change.

Visibility of the trans community is an important component, but it is only one aspect of realising equality. There is a very complex, empowering relationship between changing policies and changing culture – those two things work hand in hand. You can't change a culture without effecting specific policies that will empower trans people. Equally, you can't talk about changing policy without changing culture. Trans people need to have access to employment and inclusive health care practices – to the things that we need as humans. But, even with the progress that is being made on the issue internationally, we are constantly being pushed back into the closet. Now, more than ever, we need to embolden people by unapologetically living our truth.

I'm aware of how lucky I am to live this life, but I'm also aware that the journey hasn't ended. It keeps going, and it keeps evolving. Justice, for me, is about the freedom to be yourself, the right to self-determination and the ability to express yourself in the world. That should be everyone's lived experience.

Q. What brings you happiness?

Where I was born and raised, creativity was a privilege; we didn't have much money, so creative outlets weren't prioritised. Being able to express myself creatively makes me happy – I value the inner workings of my mind and what it can imagine.

Q. What do you regard as the lowest depth of misery?

Not having the ability to dream. It was being able to dream of a life that was better than the one I was born into that allowed me to be myself. But some people don't have the privilege of dreaming because their thoughts are consumed by survival – and that is the biggest misery. To be able to dream is to be able to envisage how you can change the course of your life.

Q. What would you change if you could?

Bruce Lee once said, 'Be water, my friend.' I want us to embrace this notion of the spiritual essence of fluidity, in order to truly understand that we're all in this together. I grew up in a place in the world where everything was very restrictive; I was surrounded by a rigid, traditional, Catholic environment – the Philippines is the only country in the world in which you can't get divorced. But, when I came to New York, I began to realise that life is made up of so many different components. So, I wish people could adopt as their resting stance a fluid mindset and a fluid attitude when engaging with issues of any kind. Because, how are people going to develop their universal understandings of culture, religion or class if they remain rigid in their beliefs?

Q. Which single word do you most identify with?

Gratitude.

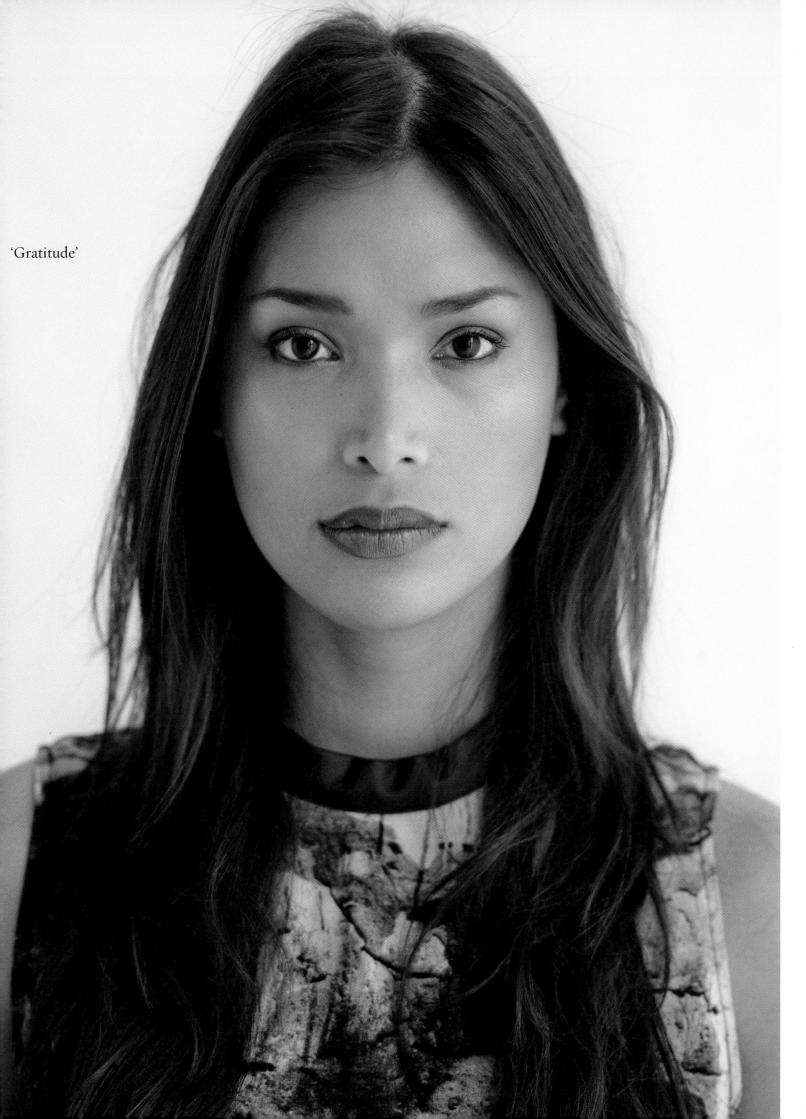

'Gratitude'

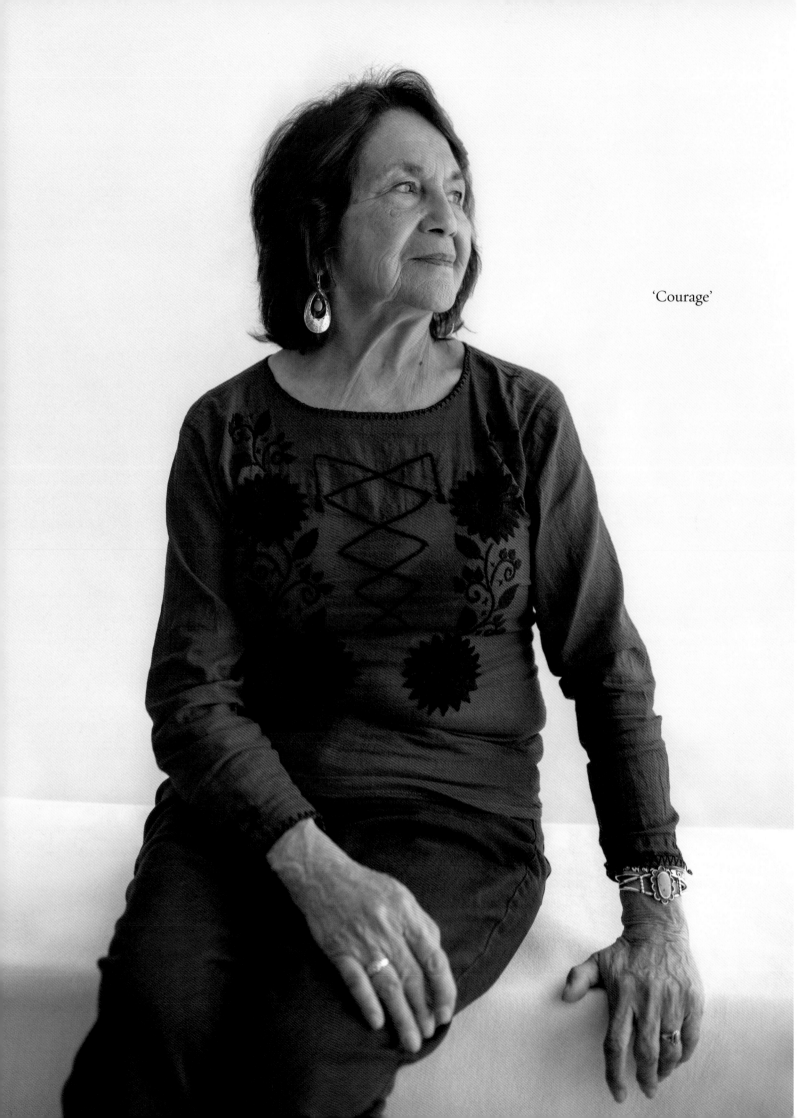

'Courage'

Dolores Huerta

Dolores Huerta was born in Dawson in New Mexico, USA. A teacher, lifelong labour activist, community organiser, and feminist, she co-founded the Stockton, California, chapter of the Community Service Organisation and founded the Agricultural Workers Association. She and César Chávez co-founded and led the National Farm Workers Association, which became United Farm Workers of America. Huerta heads the Dolores Huerta Foundation, developing grassroots community organisers and national leaders. She received the Eleanor Roosevelt Award for Human Rights, the Ellis Island Medal of Honour and was inducted into the National Women's Hall of Fame. She was awarded the Presidential Medal of Freedom.

Q. What really matters to you?
My mother was a feminist and a businesswoman; she was charitable, soft spoken and gentle, and she set the philosophy for all our family. She taught us that you have to help people you see in need, that you have an obligation to help them even if they don't ask for your help. And she said that, if you do help people, you don't expect a reward or compensation for the help you are giving them, because, if you expect someone to give you something back, that takes the grace away from the act.

Q. What brings you happiness?
It brings me happiness to see people taking power, to see them working together and taking collective action, thereby developing leadership. We are seeing the end result of the work we are doing.

Q. What do you regard as the lowest depth of misery?
It makes me sad to see that people do not engage. People have the power, but they choose not to exercise it. I think that, for a lot of people in our society, there's too much leisure and entertainment; many people are so hooked on their cell phones or video games that they aren't coming out into the world and seeing what's really going on around them.

The other thing that makes me sad is seeing so many people who are homeless in our society. It is a disgrace to our government that we have so many empty houses but so many homeless people. It is a disgrace that we in America - one of the richest countries in the world - can't house our people, or give them free medical care and free education like other countries do. It is greedy corporate control of our government that is depriving people of a decent education, of decent health care and decent shelter. It's a sin to have people making multimillion-dollar salaries while other people can't afford to live on what they earn. It's not only wrong, it's almost evil.

There is a terrible ignorance in our society that comes from a lack of education - the kind of ignorance that racism, sexism, homophobia and prejudice against immigrants comes from. Who built this country? First, it was the Native American slaves. It was African slaves who built the White House and the United States Capitol; it was people from Mexico and Asia who built the railroads, tilled the farms and built America's infrastructure. These are the very people who are now looked down on; immigrants and people of colour did all this work, yet racism is systemic and endemic in our society.

Q. What would you change if you could?
Right now, there's a very strong intent to destroy labour unions - and labour unions are workers. Organisation is absolutely important because, when we are not organised, it's very hard to reach people. But when we are organised, we can communicate, we can talk to each other and we can become educated on issues. When we have an organisation, we can all move together and take actions together to make the changes that need to be made. In all my work, over six decades, we have been able to make a lot of positive changes, but, in order to do that, you have to be able to mobilise and put pressure on the politicians. And, you have to make sure you can elect the right people to get the kind of representation you need. But, you can't do all that if you don't have organisation.

Consider the 2016 election - specifically, where the blue states were. What did the blue states on the West Coast - Washington, Oregon, California - and on the East Coast - New York, New Jersey, Vermont, Connecticut - all have in common? They had organised labour! Workers in those states are organised, so they can act together, especially when it comes to the political realm. But in those places where labour unions don't have organisation - the South or the Midwest - too much power has been taken away

from working people, so they can't really organise; they have been hamstrung.

All of this lack of organisation and lack of education results in the kind of president we ended up with in 2016. The only way out is to vote bad politicians out of office. But Republicans are putting in voter-suppression laws. In California, you can register to vote on your cell phone and people are automatically registered when they get their driver's licence. But, in Wyoming, you have to go down to the courthouse - between nine a.m. and five p.m., Monday to Friday - to be able to register to vote. So, they put up all these obstacles, and as a result we have a democracy that is not functional, because people aren't able to participate by casting their vote. They are trying to make voting more and more prohibitive for people, which is how they keep control. I like to quote the words of the Spanish philosopher José Ortega y Gasset, who said that if you don't have an educated citizenry, all you end up with is a government ruled by the greedy and the powerful.

People have the power to make change, but they don't act on that power. We have to instil in them the understanding that we are the majority - we are the ones who pay the taxes, we are the ones who elect people to the legislative and congressional offices. All government staff work for us - we pay *their* salaries with *our* taxes.

Q. Which single word do you most identify with?
Courage. It takes courage to step out of your comfort zone and take on challenges even when you don't know exactly what the outcome will be and when you know that, when you start doing work to change things, you are going to be criticised. You have to have the courage to continue despite those criticisms.

We all have to take responsibility to have a more representative government by voting. If we do not do this, no one will do this for us.

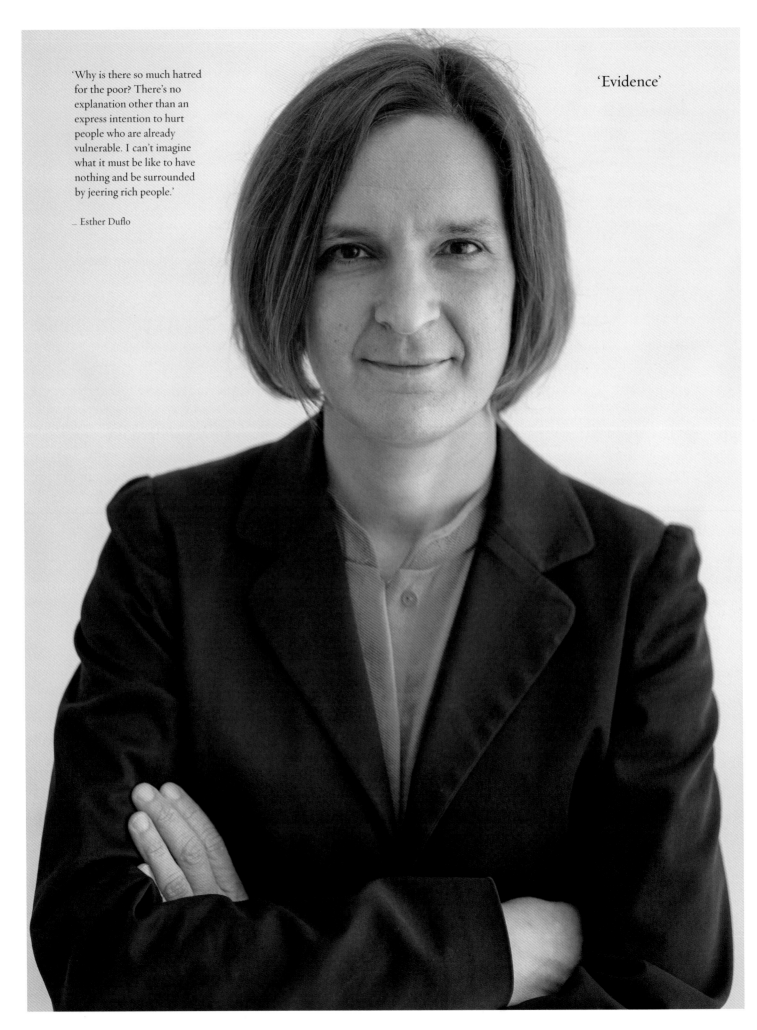

'Why is there so much hatred for the poor? There's no explanation other than an express intention to hurt people who are already vulnerable. I can't imagine what it must be like to have nothing and be surrounded by jeering rich people.'

_ Esther Duflo

'Evidence'

Interview page 386

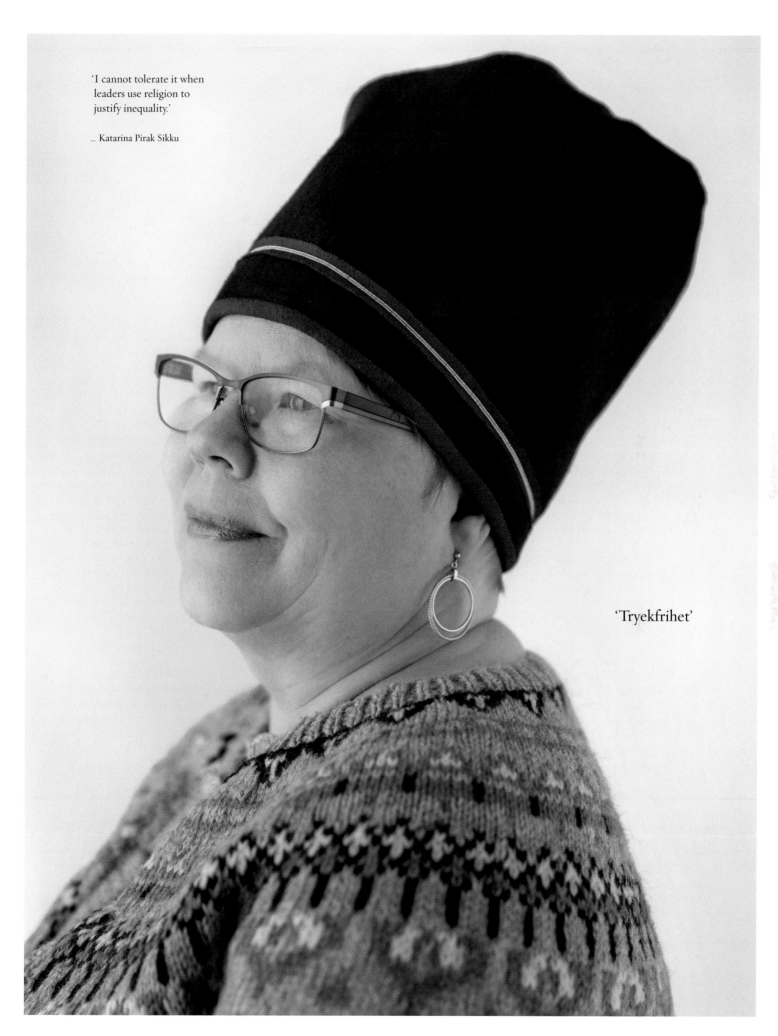

'I cannot tolerate it when
leaders use religion to
justify inequality.'

_ Katarina Pirak Sikku

'Tryekfrihet'

Interview page 386

Sarah
Outen

Sarah Outen MBE was born in Wegberg, Germany. Raised in the United Kingdom, she is a biology graduate of St. Hugh's College, Oxford. In 2009, she became the first woman and the youngest person to row solo across the Indian Ocean. In 2011, she was made a Member of the Order of the British Empire for services to rowing, conservation and charity. In 2015, travelling by rowing boat, bicycle and kayak, Outen completed a four-and-a-half-year, round-the-world-journey. She is a supporter of The Adventure Syndicate, CoppaFeel!, Inspire+, YHA, Youth Adventure Trust and Jubilee Sailing Trust.

Q. What really matters to you?

Putting good energy out into the world is so important, as is doing the best you can for other people and trying to help them be the best they can too. The importance I place on this comes from being really lucky to have grown up with so much support: in a peaceful country, with a brilliant education and a family that loved me – my parents have had a huge impact on my life. But the kind of support I had is not universal, so trying to spread as many opportunities as possible and sharing the good energy is really key.

Seeing my father suffer from chronic disability – he had rheumatoid arthritis from when I was about two years old – then die very suddenly when I was twenty-one, made me very aware, from a really young age, of just how precious, finite and non-universal health is. I grew up seeing inequalities in the way people with disabilities are treated and viewed; I watched my father struggle with this and with not being able to do the things he wanted to do. Seeing this, it was a natural impetus for me to make the most of everything, every day – because every day has the potential to be our last day. I feel very fortunate to be able to say that, if I died today, I would die happy.

It was my father's death that prompted my decision to row solo across the Indian ocean in 2009. I had been thinking about rowing an ocean, but had wanted to do it with other people, because I had no concept of going solo. But dad died quite early on in the planning phases, so, at his funeral, I told everybody I wanted to make the journey solo in his memory, to use it as a way to get through the grief and do something positive for others by raising money for charity.

As a youngster, I had spent hours walking with the dogs by myself, so it is no surprise that solitude comes pretty easily to me. I have learned to embrace it and the peace it can bring – you really get to know yourself in solitude and, when solitude is chosen, it's powerful. I don't think I got lonely on the ocean, but there were times – particularly in the scary moments – when I thought, 'I'd really like it if someone else was here right now, to make my dinner tonight or just give me a hug.'

On the Pacific, I went through three of the most harrowing days of my life: fifteen-metre-high waves, winds faster than you drive down the motorway, capsizing and being thrashed about, and bits breaking off the boat. It was horrible, so I was very relieved and grateful when I was picked up. But there was a sadness, too, in leaving my boat behind, because, when you spend that much time solo, you and your boat are a team; you rely on each other. For me, the boat is a personality, so it felt like I was leaving a teammate behind. It was even worse on the Atlantic; I was picked up before a hurricane and had to watch the guys cut *Happy Socks*, my boat, away. I bawled my eyes out. I had spent more than a year of my life alone with *Happy Socks*, so it really did feel like losing a friend.

Throughout all my journeys, I have had a huge amount of support. In particular, I am infinitely grateful for my parents' support – they taught us to go out and make whatever we want happen, and the sense of freedom they instilled is so important.

Q. What brings you happiness?

A few years ago, I would have said being out in nature, somewhere wild and beautiful; I would still say that now, but I would put friends and family – particularly my partner, Lucy – higher up on the agenda. I have reached the age where it's more about the people around me – about love. There's not much better than that, is there?

Q. What do you regard as the lowest depth of misery?

I have had some really dark moments in which I have slipped into massive depressions; there's been huge anxiety and post-traumatic stress disorder type stuff, and I've been suicidal at times. Being in that dark space, where nothing feels possible and it feels like there's no hope or return, has been my own deepest misery. That, paralleled with the grief of losing my father.

In the context of the world – for humanity – I cannot imagine what it must feel like for people in situations of war to be forced to flee their country, leaving everything behind. Many people say, 'Oh, what you do is really cool.' Yes, I do all these ventures, but I am setting out to sea in properly made, well-equipped boats, with a support team back home; when I think of the current refugee crisis, I just cannot imagine what it must be like for folks fleeing from the Middle East in what are, essentially, rubber tubs.

Q. What would you change if you could?

In one broad sweep, I would ensure equality, right across the board. That entails gender equality, financial security and basic needs being met: enough food, safe water and sanitation for everyone.

Q. Which single word do you most identify with?

Two words: 'good energy.'

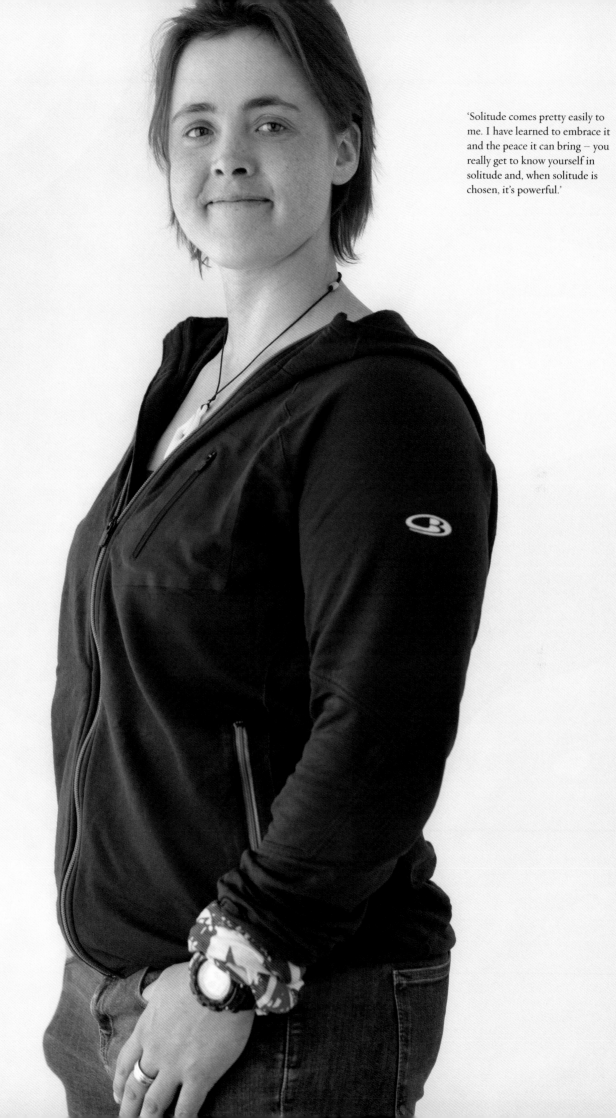

'Energy'

'Solitude comes pretty easily to me. I have learned to embrace it and the peace it can bring – you really get to know yourself in solitude and, when solitude is chosen, it's powerful.'

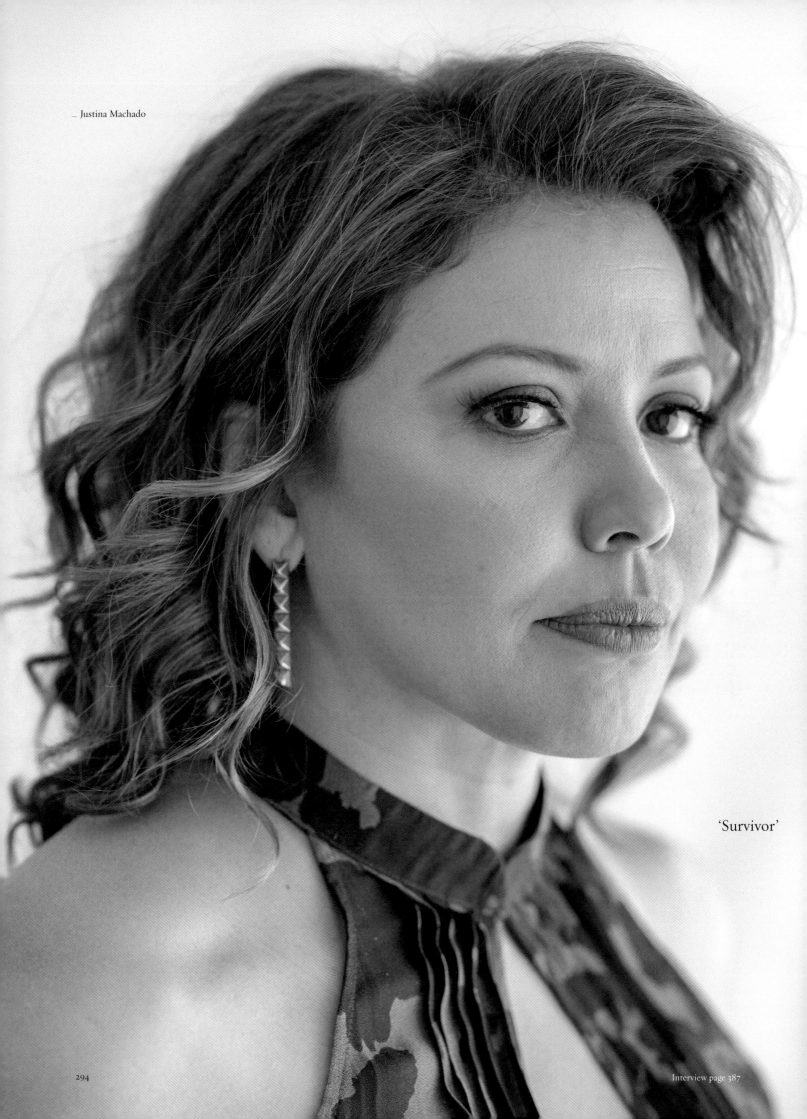

_ Justina Machado

'Survivor'

Interview page 387

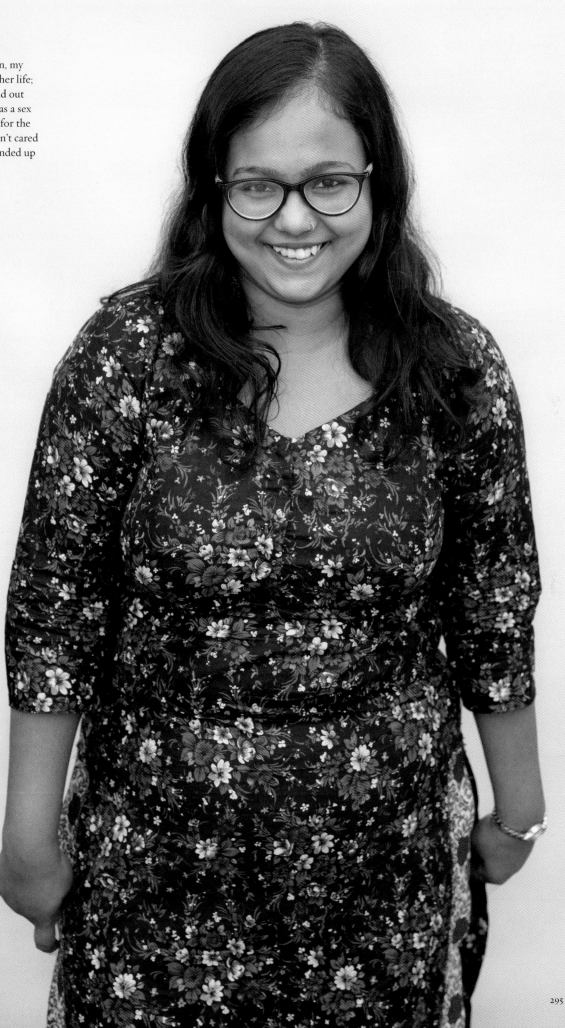

'My sister is the most
important thing in my
life. When I was eleven, my
mother's asthma took her life;
after she died, we found out
she had been working as a sex
worker to earn money for the
family. If my sister hadn't cared
for me, I would have ended up
in the sex trade too.'

_ Kakali Sen

'Dushtu'

Interview page 387

Gina Belafonte

Gina Belafonte was born in New York City, USA. She attended the High School of Performing Arts and is a graduate of State University of New York at Purchase. Belafonte is a civil rights activist, actor, producer and director, who has appeared on stage, film and television. She produced the acclaimed documentary *Sing Your Song* about her father, Harry Belafonte, and is the director of *Lyrics from Lockdown*, a hip-hop musical about racial profiling. She co-organised the 2017 Women's March in Los Angeles and co-directs Sankofa.org, a social justice organisation using culture and entertainment in advancing justice, peace, equity and equality.

Q. What really matters to you?

I'm many things to many people; I'm a mother, a sister, an aunt, a friend and – to myself – a work in progress. My journey is about trying to figure out what kind of impact I can have in this incarnation, both within and without. My parents have been, and continue to be, a huge influence on me, so my life is also about understanding those who came before me, in order to best understand how to create a path forward.

I'm a cryer! Someone once told me that I cry for those who can't. I've been thinking a lot about that; do tears diminish what I want to express or do they enhance it? I don't know the answer to that yet.

But I'm also a laugher. I think that's because, as a child, I took in what was happening around me in our home; the civil rights-movement meeting and strategy sessions were often infused with a genuine sense of levity, and I was drawn to that. It was not until middle school, and I began 'tripping' over my homework, that I was diagnosed with dyslexia. Being dyslexic was a deeply frustrating and humiliating experience, especially when I was called on to read in front of my class. I learned to mask my humiliation with humour, which is how I discovered my quick-wittedness. At the High School of Performing Arts, I gravitated towards comedy. Humour can be a tool for healing as well as for cutting things down to size. It can also be an effective way to confront the injustices of our world.

The heart of what matters to me, though, is fairness, equality, kindness and love. I want to carve a path that ensures those who come after us will be able to find peace and inhabit this earth in love. The world is starting to feel a lot like *Blade Runner*; in the film, it's almost impossible to breathe air, and entire species and groups of people are going extinct – this is a future we cannot allow. We need to prevent war, stop killing children, stop hurting each other and, instead, protect and nuture this planet. The thought of what human beings subject each other to makes me so emotional.

So much of what's going on in the world, and in the United States, makes me deeply, deeply sad. The state of our country is particularly painful, because I witnessed my parents and their friends working so hard to make it a better place. There's something strange about the human condition in that we seem to take a few steps forward, then several steps backward – there's a wretched ebb and flow to it all. But, there's is no alternative, except to continue the work. I love what I do, creating art and supporting culture helps to shine a light on things. Art can open the hearts and minds of people to effect change and shift consciousness. My mentor told me – as his mentor told him – that 'Artists are the gatekeepers of truth; we are civilisation's radical voice and moral compass.'

I was one of the organisers of the Women's March in Los Angeles; all these women from different walks of life came together to say, 'I can do this; I'm going to participate in this; we're going to do this.' They were committed to communicating and getting things done. It was really quite amazing to be a part of that and to continue to build. I believe our ancestors have paved the way for us to create a critical mass of love and that this is still a realistic goal.

The biggest challenge is convincing people that capitalism in its current design does not make for a sustainable existence. Art can guide us to a deeper truth. The way that the few are eating up resources in pursuit of success while diminishing the lives of others is just not sustainable. I am hopeful that people will wake up. People need to reassess what they really need – what's truly worth fighting for – and conceptualise an existence in which they don't need to push others out of the way to get it.

Q. What brings you happiness?

My daughter. Getting enough sleep. Patience. Comedy. Laughter. Suspending my first judgement – when I pause to hold back on my first conclusion, I'm usually much happier with what I express later; I learn more that way.

Q. What do you regard as the lowest depth of misery?

It's those who choose not to be conscious. Ignorance in the face of children suffering brings me to my knees. And, it makes me miserable when people aren't willing to have an open heart to understanding alternative experiences and strategies.

Q. What would you change if you could?

I would go back in time to when we started our human evolution and inhibit our feeling that one thing, or person, needs to be better than another; I would ensure the development of an understanding that there are enough resources for us all. I would make the experience of living equal for all of us: men, women and the differently abled. We would all sit in a space, probably a circle, where we have the opportunity to make a contribution and to communicate, which would give us collective understanding and the ability to identify the best way forward.

In fact, I feel there's a way for us to do all this without travelling backwards in time. If we can find a way to work within the structure that has created the status quo and chip away at it enough, we can achieve a collective understanding. We'll see that an injustice for one is an injustice for all, that when one is suffering we are all suffering, and that until we are all liberated, none of us are. It's really the best thing for us and I think people will come to realise this. The pathological commitment to ego – seeing something and wanting to possess it to the exclusion of others – is so minimal; we need to be thinking far more expansively than that.

Q. Which single word do you most identify with?

Peace.

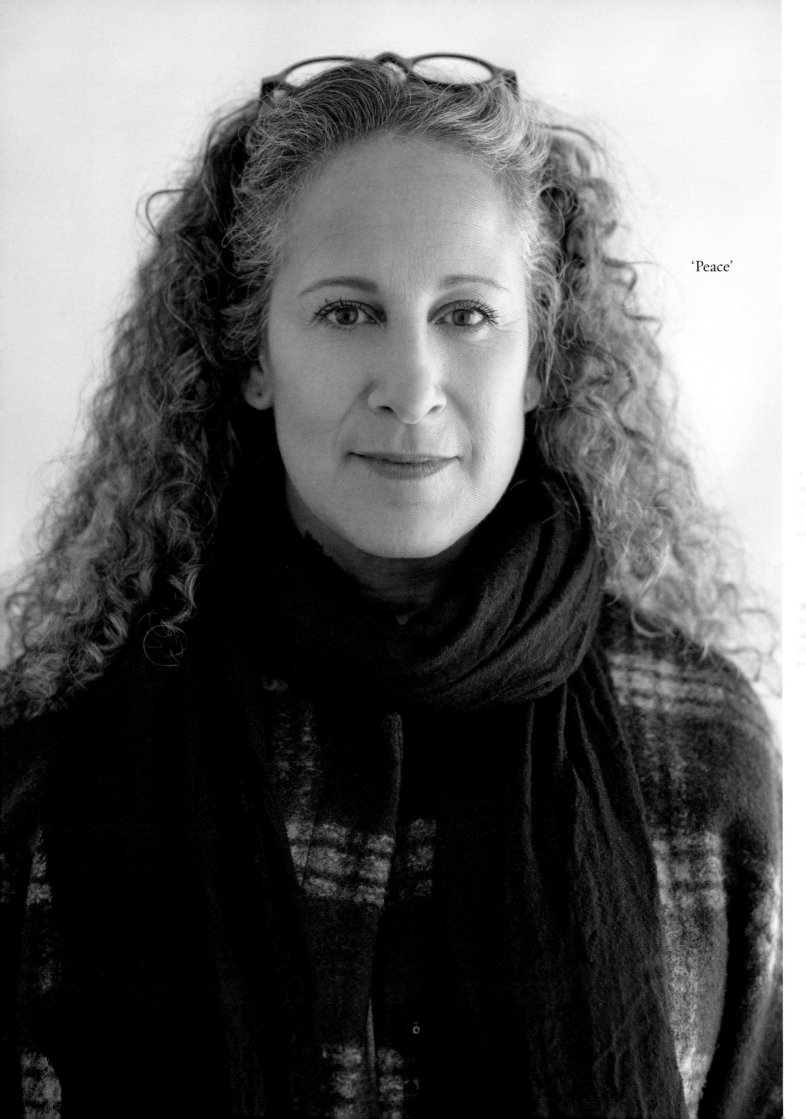

'Peace'

LaTanya Richardson Jackson

LaTanya Richardson Jackson was born in Atlanta in Georgia, USA, and graduated from Spelman College. An actor and philanthropist, she is a Trustee of the American Theatre Wing and Board Council of the Smithsonian's National Museum of African American History and Culture. She supports a number of charitable organisations, including the Children's Defense Fund and the American Civil Liberties Union, and was a long-time board member of Artists for a New South Africa. She met her husband, Samuel L. Jackson, in 1968 on a plane travelling to protest Martin Luther King, Jr.'s assassination. Their daughter, Zoe, is a senior television producer.

Q. What really matters to you?
My family matters to me.

My grandparents – who raised me – are the cornerstones of who I am. My grandmother was a cook and housekeeper, and my grandfather worked at the railroads and at a hardware company. They are who I think about when I go about my day. If what I'm doing is something they would have approved of, then I know I'm okay. They raised me in a very religious household, with a moral centre – I try to stay in that wheelhouse, because I know there is truth to it.

My grandparents and my aunt raised me to be service-oriented. And I've also latched on to something my mentor Marian Wright Edelman – who started the Children's Defense Fund – said: 'Service is the rent we pay for living.'

You want to nourish the things that you care about, and I care about love. It matters to me that we find love in the world – that we don't just say it, but that we use it.

I know that we're responsible for the earth, so I care about that. We have the intelligence to figure it all out if we would just stop denying global warming. I don't know how people can say that it doesn't exist – maybe they're too lazy to figure out that they're going to have to do something about it.

Q. What brings you happiness?
I find joy in God, who is the progenitor and the genesis of everything we are. I find happiness in my connection to a source that is so much bigger than all of us.

Q. What do you regard as the lowest depth of misery?
Ignorance – I deplore it in all of its forms. For me, an ignorant person is a person who just refuses to at least admit that there could be another way. And just plain meanness – we're living without a lot of shame right now, but we need to bring shame back. People should be ashamed of their behaviour, of not trying to figure out how to get through life together. Because, ultimately, it's our responsibility while we're here to live well and our responsibility to make sure that those who are around us are living equally well.

Q. What would you change if you could?
Love. People say 'I love you' all the time, but I would change how we say it. Look at my husband, for example: God knows, he loves me, but at times I think, 'Okay, I'm not looking for the word, I'm looking for the action of that. Let's get really active with love, make it a verb and figure out what we're going to do with love today. And the action doesn't have to be for me, it could be for somebody, or something, else.' Every day we should get up and try to figure out how to love something.

Q. Which single word do you most identify with?
Love. We just opened the Smithsonian's Museum for African American History and Culture in Washington, DC. As we went through the museum's history galleries – from the shackles of slavery, through Jim Crow and the Brotherhood of Sleeping Car Porters – everybody kept saying, 'God, those first galleries are hard.' But I said, 'Oh, no, you can't look at it like that; you've got to look at the love.' We are still here, and it's love that brought us here – without it, we could have just lain down and died. It wasn't fear that kept us going, because you can't create from fear. It had to be the relationships between the people – the love.

'Ignorance – I deplore it in all of its forms. For me, an ignorant person is a person who just refuses to at least admit that there could be another way.'

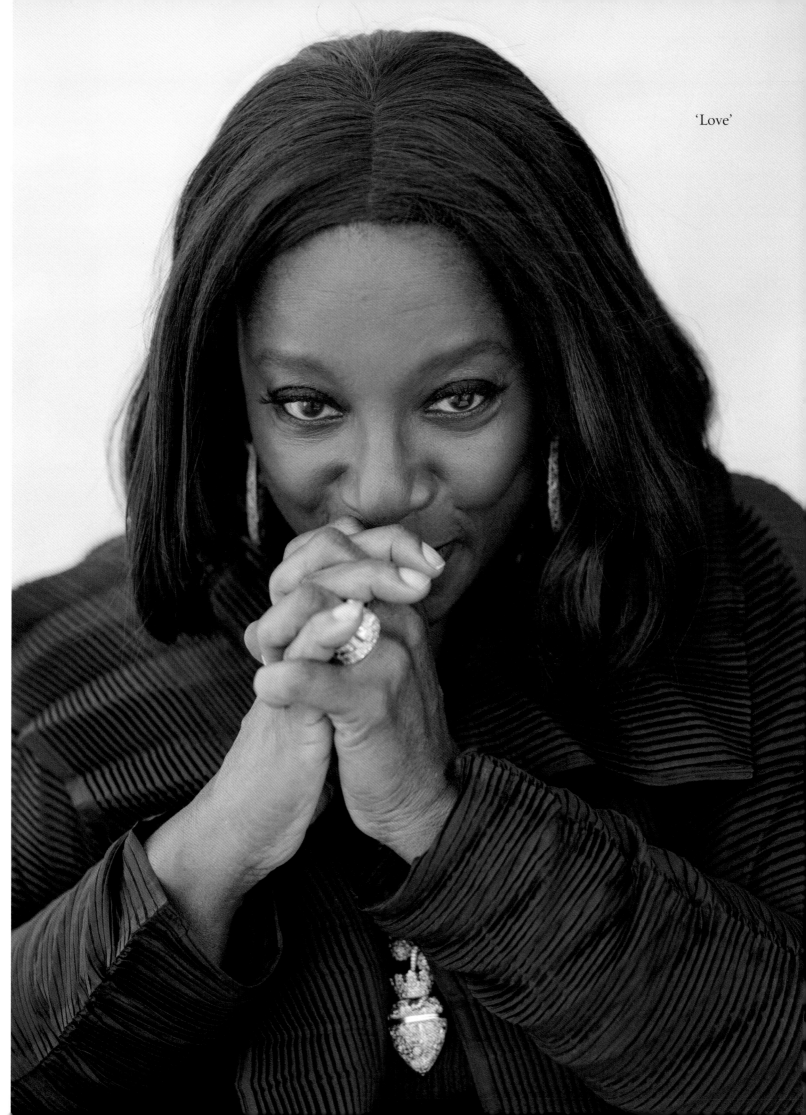

'Love'

'Compassion'

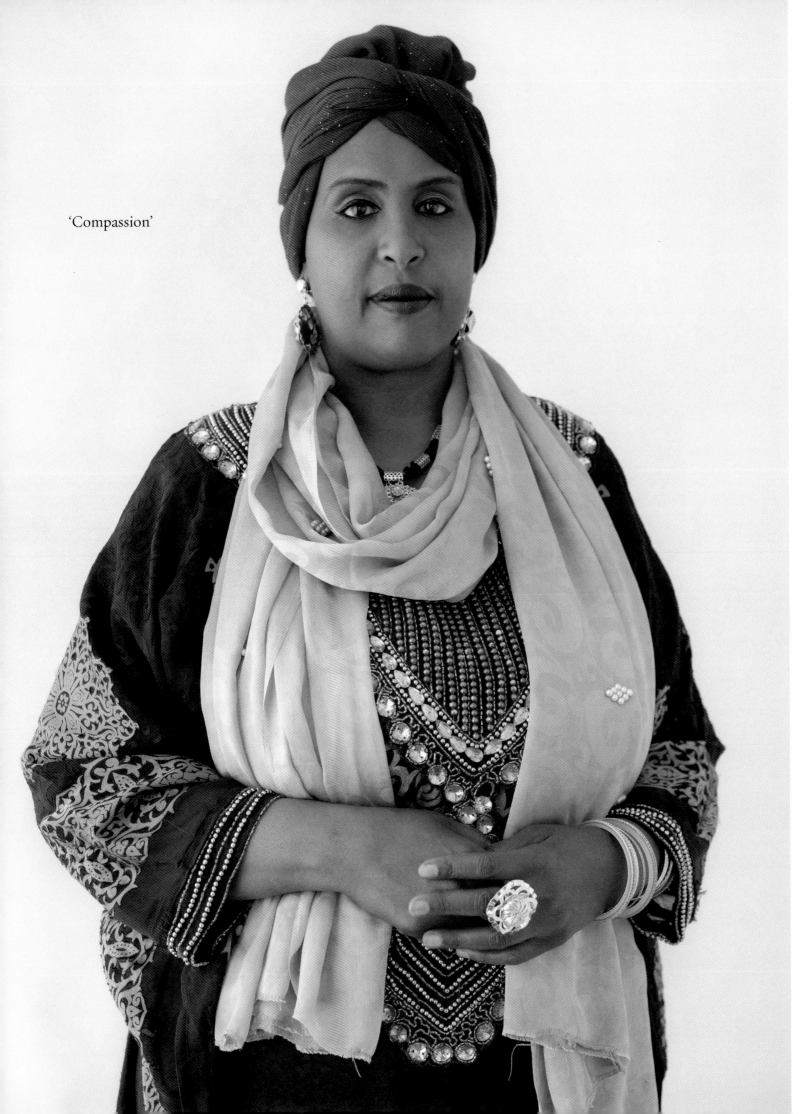

Hibo Wardere

———

Hibo Wardere was born in Somalia. When civil war erupted in Somalia in the late 1980s, she was sent to Kenya, where she stayed illegally before seeking asylum in the United Kingdom when she was eighteen. Wardere is a campaigner against female genital mutilation (FGM), an author and a public speaker. Her 2016 memoir *Cut: One Woman's Fight Against FGM in Britain Today* chronicles her experiences as survivor of type-three FGM. Wardere's testimonials and campaigning work have appeared in publications that include *The Telegraph*, *BBC News Magazine* and *The Guardian*.

Q. What really matters to you?

My family. When I look at my husband and my seven children, I know I am blessed, because many of my colleagues who are also female genital mutilation (FGM) survivors cannot have children. That right has been taken away from them.

I came to the United Kingdom almost thirty years ago as a refugee. Coming here when I was eighteen was a big deal, not only because we were fleeing the Somali Civil War, but because I was gaining freedom from so many things that were going on in my head. I was very emotional walking through Heathrow Airport – I was breaking down with tears of joy because I realised that, for the first time, I would be able to make decisions about my own life.

The moment that changed my life forever occurred when I was six. In West Africa, the process of FGM is extreme in that it entails the complete removal of the genitalia, leaving a tiny hole through which women are expected to menstruate, have sex and birth children. In Somalia, we call it 'the Pharaoh's cut,' because the Egyptian pharaohs introduced it as a form of sexual control: men were subjected to castration and women to FGM. This practice removes the libido and any sexual feelings whatsoever. In Somalia, FGM is carried out to preserve the woman's virginity – and sealing up the woman is the only way to do that. It's a one-hour procedure that has massive repercussions for the rest of a woman's life. Medically, it leads to numerous complications that can persevere for life. And psychologically, it's torture. It's emotionally draining and it's a life sentence; when a survivor is birthing her children, it is very, very bad. In developing countries, the mortality rates for women in childbirth are through the roof – thousands of women die.

I never intended to write about my experiences. Writing about them took about seven months and is the hardest thing I've ever had to do. In my talks, there are details I can choose not to disclose, but in a book, there's nowhere to hide. I was laid bare, which was very emotional. Nevertheless, I'm glad I wrote *Cut* and

that it was well-received; it has been a blessing. The book has become a source of information for professionals, but, for me it's a book about hope. I believe the book shows survivors of FGM – or abuse of any kind – that when you experience the darkest moments of your life, if you permit it, there is always light within the darkness.

When I underwent FGM, I completely shut down. I felt that every adult around me had betrayed me, especially my mother. I had trusted and loved her, but that day, when I was screaming, she didn't help me – she ignored me. After it happened, I felt so isolated that I felt there was no point continuing to exist. I feared that, if I had daughters, I wouldn't be able to protect them. I did blame my mother, but I don't anymore – I can't. It's how she grew up, and it's what she went through; in the community I was raised in, all mothers think it's their motherly duty to cut their girls. It is considered a loving action, rather than child abuse. My mother didn't think there was anything wrong with it, because she was cut, her mother was cut and so was each one of her female ancestors. It was the social norm for the whole community; even if someone didn't want to cut their girl, they would do it, because to not do so would result in social sanctions. FGM has social value, because it means that your daughter has high marriage prospects.

After it happened, I hated men. I thought I had been hurt and undervalued because of them. In my upbringing, I could see that girls were not appreciated to the same degree that boys were; we weren't told we could reach for the world – we were to be beautiful wives and mothers, and nothing else. Men were valued and men were put first – all I saw was men, men, men, and I just hated that. But what happened to me wasn't men's idea: of course I was being cut for men, but I was cut by women – it is the women who are continuing this practice.

Religion is very strong in Somalia, but FGM is a cultural practice; of my generation, 98 per cent of women were cut, most of them in such a way that healing is a continuous process – it never stops and

you die healing. When I ask women to show me in the Koran where it says we need to mutilate girls, they don't have anything to say. Yet, somehow, the cultural belief in FGM has become so much stronger than our religious beliefs.

But I knew I didn't have the right to take away from my children their God-given right to feeling and enjoying their bodies. That's why walking through Heathrow was such an emotional experience; it was the beginning of my life, and I felt I was reborn. I was able to get to a place where everything I'd suffered didn't define me – I define myself.

Q. What brings you happiness?
My family and being alive.

Q. What do you regard as the lowest depth of misery?
Being a refugee in today's world.

Q. What would you change if you could?
I would change how people see others; I want people to have compassion for human suffering and empathy for others.

Q. Which single word do you most identify with?
Compassion. Recently, when I was meeting with communities who had given up FGM, I met a woman who was an ex-cutter; it took me half an hour to compose myself, because all I could see was my own cutter's face on her body. After I had spoken to the group, I saw this ex-cutter coming towards me. I felt I was going to crumble as she hugged me, but, somehow, I felt I had to hug her back. I did. We sat down to talk about her life, and she spoke about being married off to a forty to forty-five-year-old man at age eight, then to a fifty-five-year-old man at age twelve. She became a cutter because her mother was a cutter – it was a generational thing. She told me that, when her own daughter was cut by her mother, she nearly died inside.

I felt compassion for this woman, because her life had been a dreadful one. I asked her how she felt about the girls she had cut, and she told me that all she could do was ask other cutters to stop. I never thought I would have compassion for an ex-cutter, but I do.

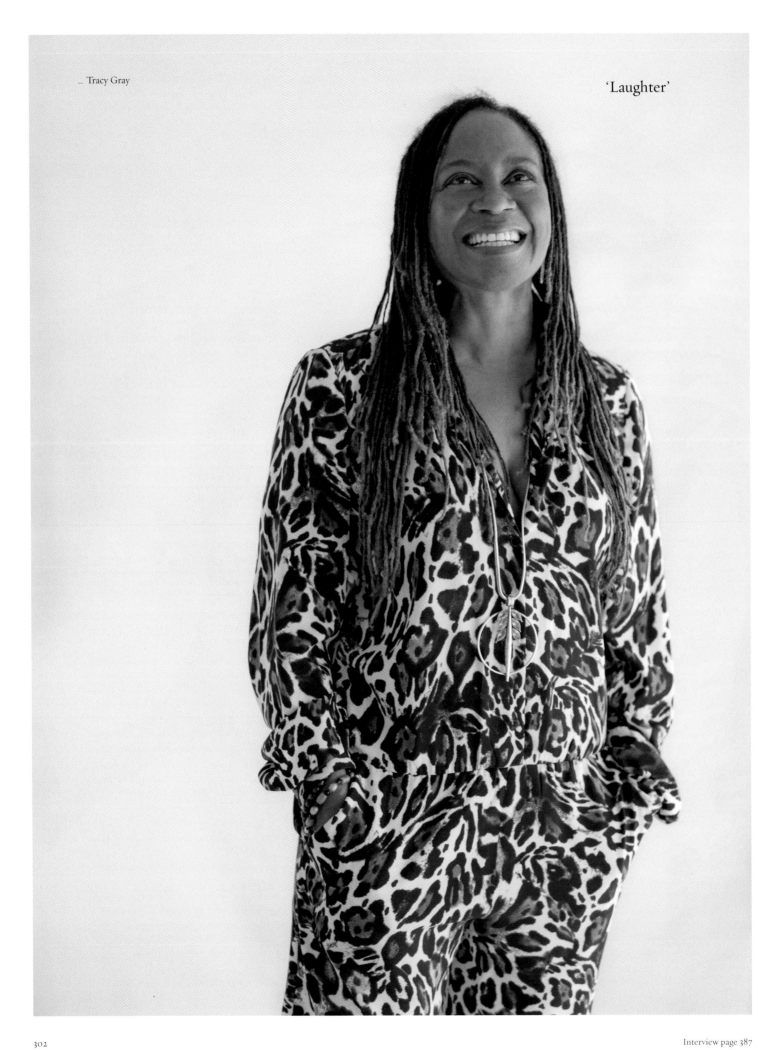

Interview page 387

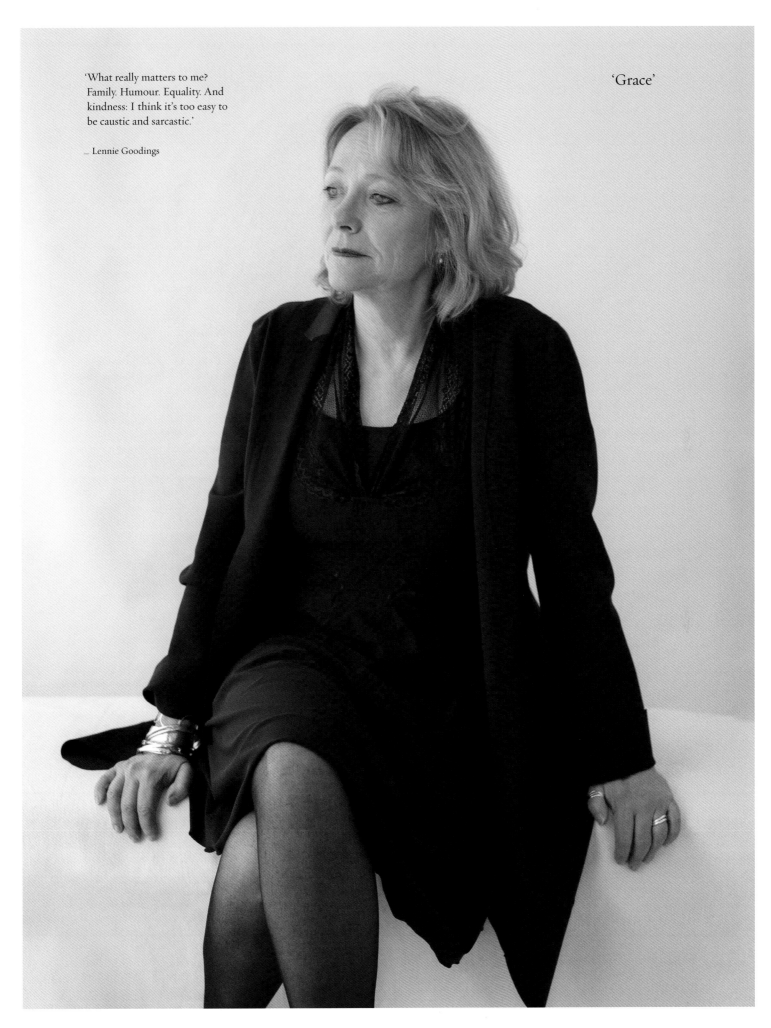

'What really matters to me?
Family. Humour. Equality. And
kindness: I think it's too easy to
be caustic and sarcastic.'

_ Lennie Goodings

'Grace'

Ashley Judd

———

Ashley Judd was born in Sylmar in California, USA. She holds a master's degree in public administration from Harvard University's John F. Kennedy School of Government, where her paper, *Gender: Law and Social Justice*, won the Dean's Scholar Award. She is working towards a PhD at the University of California, Berkeley. A Golden Globe and Emmy Award–nominated actor, Judd is also a feminist social-justice humanitarian. She has served on the boards of the International Center for Research on Women, Population Services International, Apne Aap Worldwide and Demand Abolition, and was appointed a goodwill ambassador for the United Nations Population Fund in 2016.

Q. What really matters to you?

I am a feminist. By that, I mean that I believe in dignity and equality between girls and boys, women and men. I consider the patriarchy to be just as damaging to boys and men as it is to girls and women; it's a false construct for all of us.

When I think about what has formed the person I am today – my capacities and my passions – I think not only about the totality of my lived experiences, such as being a tenth-generation Eastern Kentuckian, but about the totality of the lived experiences of my predecessors. My ten-times great-grandparents Mary and William Brewster were religious refugees living in defiance of two British monarchs; they assisted with organising the voyage of the *Mayflower*, on which they travelled to the United States. Their kind of crusading, and devout, passionate love for – and intimacy with – God is very much a part of who I am today. My mother was pregnant with me at the time of the assassinations of Martin Luther King Jr. and Bobby Kennedy – those events imprinted on her and, therefore, on me. More than anything, though, what has formed the core of both my pain and my resilience – informed my grief and my determination to transcend my outrage so as to make it empowering for both myself and others – is experiencing sexual abuse in early childhood.

That experience of extensive patriarchal wounding shaped my neural anatomy; the very pathways of my brain have been shaped by that trauma and I have spent a good deal of my adult life either unconsciously affected, or bewildered by my inability to let go of the pain, even when I earnestly wanted to. There are more of us who experience sexual abuse than those of us who don't. Sadly, I think that coming to terms with that kind of trauma is dependent on the kinds of help people are able to access. A treatment method may be knowledge- and science-based, but if it's not accessible, it's drivel to the sufferer.

In my particular case, things changed when the pain of staying the same became greater than the pain of being willing to change. I had been using yoga, meditation and prayer as modalities to cope with the sexual abuse, but the power to really confront what happened to me came through my sister as the conduit. She had been seeking help for an eating disorder and, when I showed up to a family week, her treatment team took one look at me and recommended a twelve-step programme. Initially, I thought they were wrong to suggest it, but I was willing to do *anything* to change, and I'm glad I did. These twelve-step programmes are free and are part of a real, grassroots movement. Choosing recovery was terrifying and exhilarating, and was by far the best thing I could have done for myself and for the people I purport to love; because I cannot transmit that which I do not have. Also, through professional help, I've become a general badass. It can be abusive to highlight a problem without also underscoring a solution, so I am very thankful that today, when I talk about being a survivor of adolescent and adult rape, and of all kinds of gender wounding, I do so from a position of empowerment.

I've been profoundly influenced by feminist theologians. When I was an undergrad, I took a seminar on images of women in the Bible; it was incredibly disturbing. The experience shattered my faith and created anarchy in my family. I saw women diminished by the commodification of their sexuality. I had to look hard to find theologians willing to address the ills of the patriarchy in their writings; one such person was Sallie McFague, who wrote that God is he, she, both and neither. That is more like the God of my understanding: a God who doesn't make hard terms for those who seek her. I believe the message that the realm of spirit is broad and inclusive to all who wish to embrace it. I would say that my core identity is in the belief that I am a loved and precious child of a Higher Power; this belief supersedes all others.

I still experience patriarchal aggression – microaggressions, bombastic pride – but what matters to me, now, is applying my life lessons with grace and humour. I've always felt strength in the role of a crusader and that makes me feel very powerful. I've learned the lesson that it's important to connect with and listen to myself, my feelings and the sensations that I experience; only by doing this can I discover what I need. I feel that this is a lesson many boys and men need to learn, because the definitions we have of masculinity, manhood and sexuality are toxic, abusive, constraining and limited – men will come to see this if they try to connect with themselves.

Q. What brings you happiness?

My greatest happiness is seeing girls and women standing up in defiance to systems of patriarchy; it impresses me to see them doing this in ways that must absolutely terrify them. When Julia Gillard was prime minister of Australia, the leader of the opposition said something like, 'Oh, *I* must be a feminist.' In response, Julia Gillard launched into a thirty-minute diatribe – in every sense of that word – in which she outlined each instance of him shaming, diminishing and ridiculing her simply for being female. She spoke from her guts – it was one of those moments when you could see that her head and her heart were connected and wide open. She went through each instance in which he had threatened and insulted her; she eviscerated him, and I loved it!

Q. What do you regard as the lowest depth of misery?

Watching the resistance to progress articulate itself so well; watching those who defend themselves against microaggressions and the patriarchy being bullied for doing so. Still, I believe that no good deed goes unpunished, so I always try to remind myself that I may not be celebrated for the choices I make, even though I feel I'm doing the right thing. And, when I see people doing the right thing and being properly received for it, I am filled with hope.

Q. What would you change if you could?

I would change the prevailing global culture of sexual exploitation and sexual entitlement.

Q. Which single word do you most identify with?

Crusader. The first time I was sexually abused and told some adults what had happened, they told me that I'd misinterpreted what he'd done and that he was a nice man. Boom! A crusader was born.

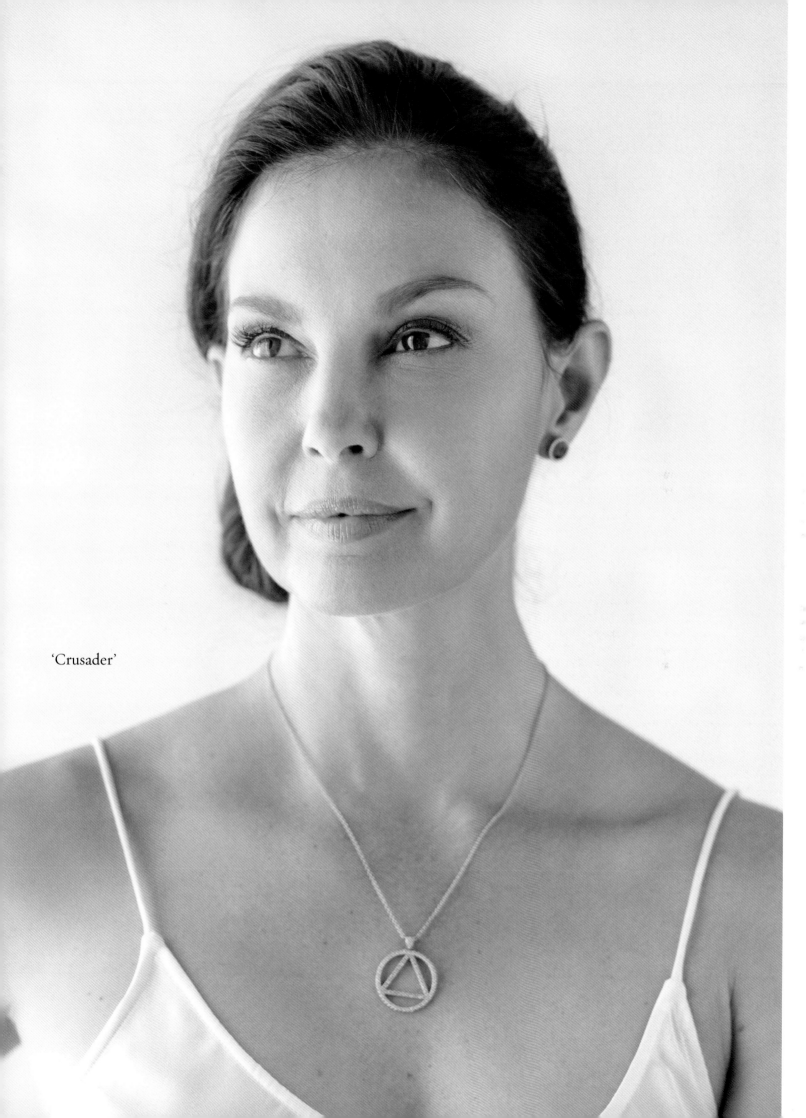

'Crusader'

Joanne Fedler

Joanne Fedler was born in Johannesburg, South Africa. She studied law at the University of the Witwatersrand and at Yale University before returning to South Africa, where she lectured in law and became legal advisor at People Opposing Women Abuse (POWA), a women's rights organisation that provides both frontline and advocacy services. Fedler's debut novel, *The Dreamcloth*, was nominated for South Africa's *Sunday Times* Fiction Prize in 2006, while *Secret Mothers' Business* was on the 2008 *Der Spiegel* bestseller list. Now a full-time author and writing mentor, Fedler works with aspiring female authors to help them find their voices through the power of writing.

Q. What really matters to you?

I grew up with an older sister who is deaf, so I've always understood that some people don't have a voice and that I had to use mine to speak up for others. Life's blessings are not evenly dealt: the quirk of birth is that some of us get things and others don't. I grew up in South Africa, where it was impossible not to appreciate that I had privileges – for no reason I deserved – and that others didn't. This unfairness and injustice corrupts all beauty – how can we enjoy wealth, shelter, education when others around us can't?

I thought the way to use my voice would be to change the laws. So, I studied law, and after I got my master's degree, I went back to South Africa and became the legal advisor to POWA. My experience working one-on-one with abused women profoundly affected and changed me. I began to understand the limits of the law. I became disillusioned about what I could do.

I went into this work as an idealist. But then, one day, I was at a meeting of women's advocacy groups. An old African woman stood up and said, 'Why do you spend all this time talking about how terrible rape is? I was raped, my daughter was raped, my granddaughters have been raped and their children will be raped. There are worse things than being raped. We need medical care, housing and jobs. Those are the things that are important to us.' I'd been working as a women's rights advocate to end violence against women for six years. This matriarch had seen every single generation of her family brutalised, assaulted and violated. And as I listened to her say, 'That's *just how it is*,' I realised I couldn't speak on behalf of anybody, because I didn't know their reality. I had no right to stand before these women and tell them we needed a more effectual system to deal with rapists. At the same time, I couldn't bear that this was what it had come to – acceptance that this is just how it is. That was not a world I wanted any part of.

In that moment, I was humbled and shattered. I lost my will to fight that fight.

Looking back, I can see that anger and bitterness is a necessary stage of human consciousness. When you're becoming politicised, you have to be completely broken down in order to come back with a mature understanding of how to truly build community, how to be an advocate and how to heal.

Anne Herbert said, 'Large change doesn't come from clever, quick fixes from smart, tense people, but from long conversations and silences among people who know different things and need to learn different things.' For me, change is about those conversations, so to exclude people based on identity or privilege is actually to cut off a source of access to a solution.

Since then, I've been on a twenty-five-year journey of spiritual awakening that's taken me into meditation, Buddhism and therapy, and what amazes me is that storytelling is at the core of all healing and survival. When we can own our stories as storytellers rather than victims and make meaning from our experiences, we have a chance to transform. And when we can find our voices and share our stories, we light the way for other people to do the same.

Now, I don't want to fight anymore. I want to hold. I want to hold peoples' stories and allow them to reclaim their power through the narratives of survival, and I want to honour their pain. I now work to help people find that moment of surrender and change through creative expression.

After I left political work, I began to write. I just needed to focus on myself for a while. Now that I've had ten books published, I found that my own achievements make me happy about 40 per cent of the time; when our lives are just about ourselves, we get caught up in ego. Even at the height of my publishing success, I'd find myself anxious, jealous of other authors or feeling slighted by being overlooked for speaking opportunities – ridiculous, I know. Everything changed, though, when I realised that I'm not here for me, but to support other women in finishing and bringing their books into the world. Now,

I mentor and help other women to write their stories. And that makes me happy 100 per cent of the time.

My brand as a writing mentor is WINGS: words inspire, nourish and grow the spirit. What matters to me now is to leave a trail of gifts for others, to share everything I've learned and to make opportunities available to people: to open doors. I aim to lift others up, either through my writing or through doors that I can open for them, or by connecting women, in particular, with who they are in this life and by helping them find value in that. We're surrounded by this culture of narcissism, but I believe in the idea that *I* don't have freedom until *you* have freedom – so I focus my life on others, on 'we' instead of 'me.'

Q. What brings you happiness?

I'm not a happiness chaser; I'm not obsessed with the idea of being 'happy.' I try to live a meaningful life and, when I connect with my own emotions and with others, that feels meaningful. When I'm connected, I feel safe and deeply alive. Maybe that's what people call 'happiness.'

Q. What do you regard as the lowest depth of misery?

My idea of misery is suffering without a spiritual framework. In my darkest moments, I've only been able to pull myself through with a belief in something that is bigger than me. To know that, though I feel alone, I am not alone.

Q. What would you change if you could?

I'd start everything from the beginning again. Our difficulty is that the table has already been set. We're limited by what exists. Given that, I'd revolutionise the way we value things in our world. I'd switch everything we currently chase with kindness, service, generosity and humility. I'd swap consumerism with the stories of the meek, soft-spoken, humble warriors of this world. Less noise, more listening to each other.

Q. Which single word do you most identify with?

Service.

'Service'

'When you're becoming politicised, you have to be completely broken down in order to come back with a mature understanding of how to truly build community, how to be an advocate and how to heal.'

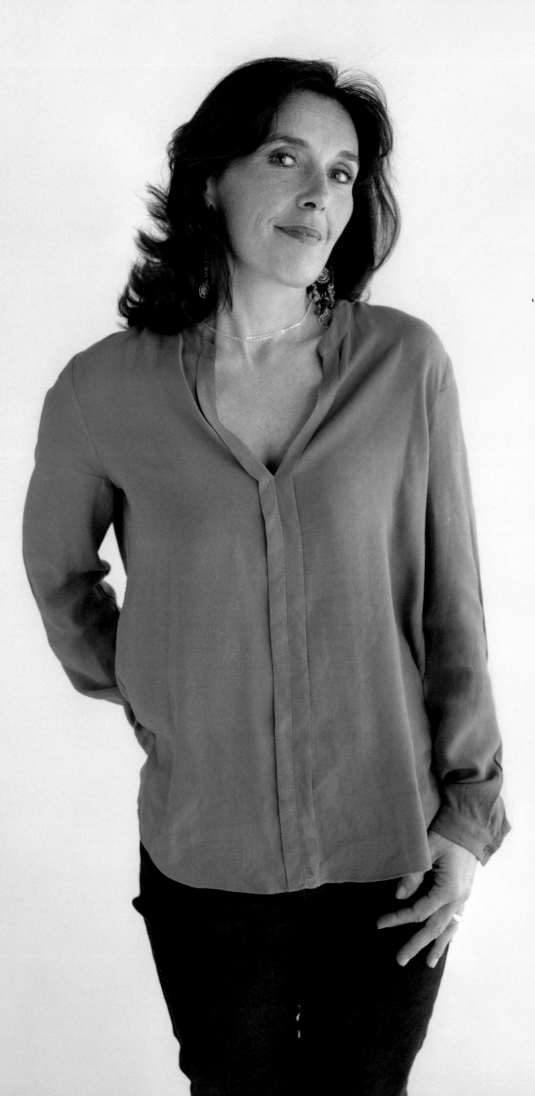

'Commitment'

Laure Hubidos

Laure Hubidos was born in Romans, France. Hubidos worked as a press secretary for the Franche-Comté regional council before founding La Maison de Vie, a home dedicated to those requiring palliative care, in 2011. She is a health consultant and founder of the national association of Maison de Vie.

Q. What really matters to you?

I would define myself as a woman with a strong sense of commitment. This goes way back, to when I lost my mother at age four. This was incredibly difficult, least of all because her death was initially hidden from me. It meant that I had to cope with questions of loneliness and death from a young age; I had to come to terms with solitude and developed what amounted to a philosophy of life: a commitment to always choosing life above everything else. Questions of solitude, weakness and suffering were naturally always on my mind, so, the commitment that defines me today – and that is growing stronger and stronger with age – has always been with me; I have always been committed to being close to people who are the most vulnerable and left out. All people matter to me, but those who matter to me most are the unhappiest and the most fragile.

My innermost motivation is to pay attention to others and to actively take part in the world we live in. I firmly believe that, regardless of who we are – and whether we are prominent or humble – we have the ability to bring change to our world. Even the most insignificant of things can make an impact – simply paying attention to another, for instance. Helping someone to cross the street is itself an act of solidarity; that person will be touched that you took the time to focus on assisting them, and the act may change their entire day. So, we must focus on those small joys we can bring.

I was always satisfied in my work, but something was missing at a deeper level; getting on with things became impossible for me without meaning, inspiration and conviction. Deep down, I had always felt like I had a mission to accomplish, so, in 2001, I decided to go out and take my place in the world. In addition to my job, I became a volunteer in the palliative-care unit of the University Hospital of Besançon. I sensed that I had found my place in becoming a companion to the sick. We live in a world that is obsessed with appearances, material possessions, and the race for money and power; it is considered better to be good-looking, young, rich and healthy than it is to be sick, unhappy, fragile or vulnerable. This outlook is unacceptable to me – I cannot condone it. I have known both physical and emotional pain in my life, so, the people I am looking after at the end of their lives are, in a way, me – in fact, they are each and every one of us. This is why I want to assist people to live the best life they can right up to the end and is where the idea of starting a facility came from; I realised that there was a missing link between hospitalisation and care at home. Sometimes, it's hard for someone to receive proper care at home because their family may be exhausted or they may not have a family. In such instances, a person will have no choice but to return to hospital, a place that is not necessarily adapted to their needs; many don't require intensive medical care, and hospitals are designed to cater for the most urgent and complicated cases. I wanted to found a house where I could offer the services people requiring palliative care would need – and here we are!

Q. What brings you happiness?

Ever since I was a child, I have applied what I call 'the philosophy of small joys.' I would always tell myself, 'Okay, so your life isn't easy – you feel lonely and not at all like other people – but find three small things in your life to be happy about.' These were the simplest of things: if the weather was good, I would soak up the sunshine and let that joy fill my entire day.

My greatest joy is in the deep love I have for life, in all its forms. I am a mother of three wonderful children and they are, of course, an incredible source of joy. But, more generally, my joy is derived from my awareness of the treasure that is life. Nature gives me great joy, and I spend a lot of time appreciating the beauty of a particular landscape or the exceptional, almost magical, quality of a flower. And I love the sea. These things touch the essence of life and are universal.

Q. What do you regard as the lowest depth of misery?

The world we live in. In my view, it is out of touch with – in fact it has forgotten – what really matters. We live in a world that goes too fast; it is very advanced on a technological level, but humanity in general has lost its authenticity, that simple bond that makes us human. We are all in the same boat, in fact, we are its crew. But how is the crew to steer the boat and work well together when we have no bond that binds us? Apart from those who are committed to this cause, most of us are taking an individualistic approach to life: power for ourselves, success for ourselves. All of this is resulting in destruction, abuse and injustice on so many levels.

But I do believe we all have within us the impulse for humanity, fraternity and solidarity. After the attack on the *Charlie Hebdo* office in Paris, I was genuinely surprised by the scale on which people mobilised to reject that kind of violence and barbarity; my dream is that we can build on this momentum.

Q. What would you change if you could?

This may sound silly, but I would increase the momentum of love, generosity, kindness and understanding. We all have something beautiful to contribute, so why don't we come together and share in our humanity?

Q. Which single word do you most identify with?

Commitment. My commitment stems from a deep-seated idealism.

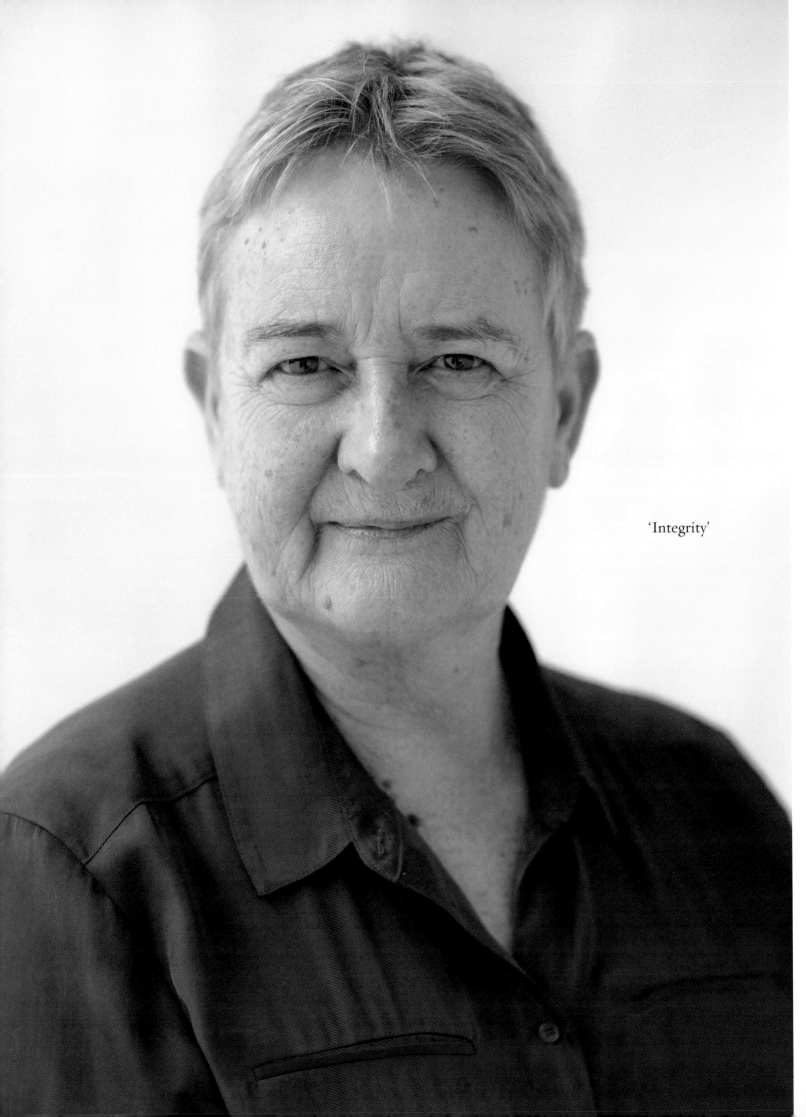

'Integrity'

Marilyn Waring

———

Marilyn Waring CNZM was born in Ngāruawāhia, New Zealand. She holds a doctoral degree in political economy from the University of Waikato, and at age twenty-three she became a member of parliament, serving until 1984. Waring's internationally influential critique of gross domestic product, *If Women Counted: A New Feminist Economics*, appeared in 1988. Since 2006, she has been a professor of public policy at the Institute of Public Policy at AUT University. In 2008, Waring was made a Companion of the New Zealand Order of Merit for her services to women and economics.

Q. What really matters to you?

Doing what I can, where I can, to try to make a difference matters to me. Microcosmically, that means supervising PhDs around human rights and social justice, in particular those of young people from all around the world who want to change the world. That's an enormous privilege and feels doable.

Growing up in Taupiri, a small town in rural New Zealand, informed and affected my life in tremendous ways. I grew up right beside the tangata whenua – the indigenous people of New Zealand – in the Tainui tribal area, so I was always conscious of Māoritanga – Māori culture – and conscious that there was not only one paradigm: one way of thinking and seeing. I was impressed by the value Māori culture places on collectivism, sustainability and taonga – their treasures.

But, although I grew up knowing that in 1893 New Zealand had granted universal suffrage to Māori men and women, and to Pākehā (European-New Zealander) women, and I felt pride in that, I also noticed that there hadn't been a lot of change subsequently. Growing up in the sixties and seventies, I was able to access a whole new wave of highly critical feminist literature that, for a change, was not Western-dominated. This was throwing out major challenges to so many disciplines that were being taught in universities. It was a very exciting time to be alive and to be a feminist; standing for parliament in 1975 was, for me, a feminist activity. The political parties at the time kept saying how they'd love to have more women in parliament, but they never offered any candidates, so a group of us decided to put ourselves forward. We expected to lose, with the intention that this would at least take the political parties' excuse away from them, but the plan backfired for me and I was elected. I served three terms in the New Zealand Parliament.

When I was twenty-seven, the prime minister, Robert Muldoon, placed me in charge of the Public Expenditure Committee. I was able to learn what happens internally and be in a position to explain it externally, which was a privilege not many women had in the seventies. And it's where my learning about economics and gross domestic product (GDP) started. This led me to write a feminist-critical analysis of GDP: of how it affects women, how it affects the environment and how it counts some of the most damaging things in the world as positive for growth.

I've now spent most of my life analysing GDP. It is structured according to a set of international rules and determines what is 'work' – what is productive activity and what isn't – in the construction of GDP. The GDP figure is enormously powerful because it is one of the foundation statistics that is used by governments in all policy and strategic planning, in all resource allocation and in all five- and ten-year projections. The figure is constructed omitting all the service work of the environment, so the environment is only counted when it is mined, forested, exploited, destroyed or deteriorating in some way. And the figure excludes all unpaid work, all voluntary and community work, all parenting and caring work, and a whole range of other activities that are thought of as household-confined – all of which work is overwhelmingly done by women.

One of the really key issues around all of this is that it's very difficult to make good government policy if the activities of the majority of your population aren't part of your scenario. It means that GDP considers investment in – and the use of – armaments as extraordinarily good for growth. And any oil or toxic spills are good for growth because of the potential that lies in clean-up operations. In New Zealand, we've recognised that major earthquakes like those we have had in

Christchurch since 2010 actually sustain the GDP figures for years, because you have to rebuild. So, GDP is altogether a very perverse statistic; it's highly destructive; it's very dangerous; and it's grossly deluded propaganda that values things which destroy lives.

Q. What brings you happiness?

Breaking down barriers brings me joy: watching young people, and especially young women, have access and opportunities. Watching the success of my wonderful scholastic doctoral candidates brings me great happiness. When I attend events, nationally and internationally, and look out into the audiences, I see, not the next generation, but the one after that: they're courageous, they're witty, they're bright and sharp and they have analyses we've never thought of. They're dealing with a very, very different world, and when I look at them I think, 'It's really been worth it.'

Q. What do you regard as the lowest depth of misery?

There are so many catastrophes that I can't pick one.

Q. What would you change if you could?

I would create a world in which no one has fear. Somebody once asked Nina Simone what her definition of freedom was and she said, 'No fear.' This became my vision and is what I work for: no fear of violence, no fear about where you'll sleep tonight, no fear about hunger and impoverishment, no fear that all the crops will fail and that no one will be there.

Q. Which single word do you most identify with?

Integrity. When I left parliament I wondered what I was going to do with myself. I went to see a very highly placed recruitment agent, and he said to me, 'I've gotta be honest with you, Marilyn. With respect to the private sector, you're just too hot to handle.' That was one of the best compliments I ever had. I thought, 'Cool, let's keep it that way.'

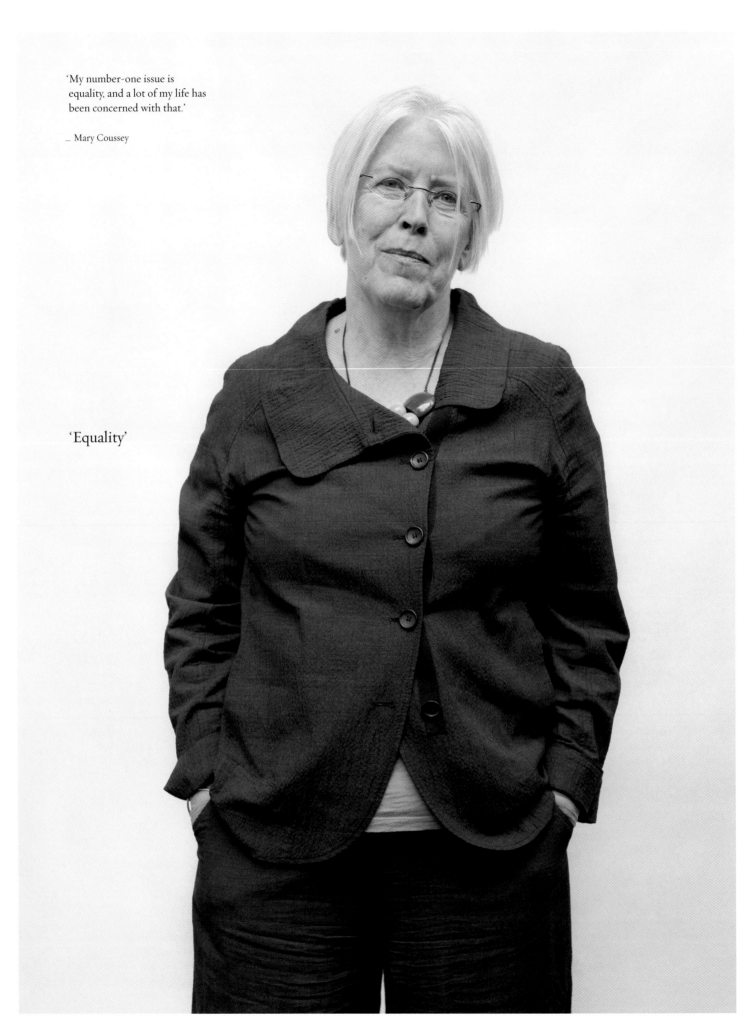

'My number-one issue is
equality, and a lot of my life has
been concerned with that.'

_ Mary Coussey

'Equality'

Interview page 388

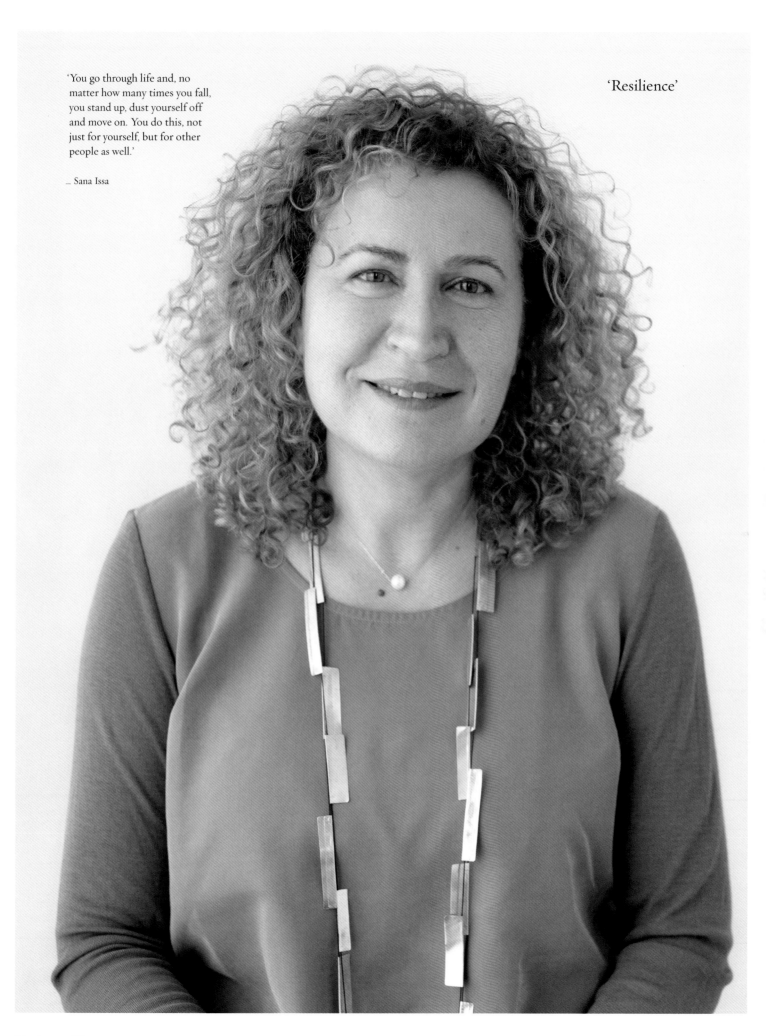

'You go through life and, no matter how many times you fall, you stand up, dust yourself off and move on. You do this, not just for yourself, but for other people as well.'

— Sana Issa

'Resilience'

Interview page 388

'Compassion'

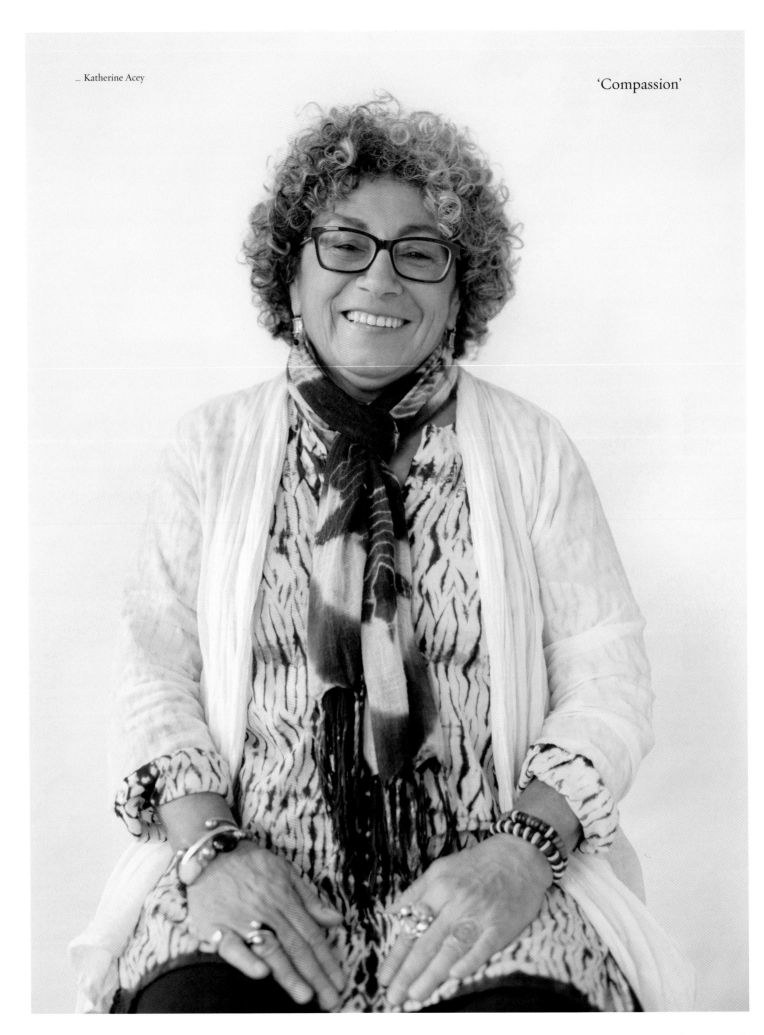

Interview page 389

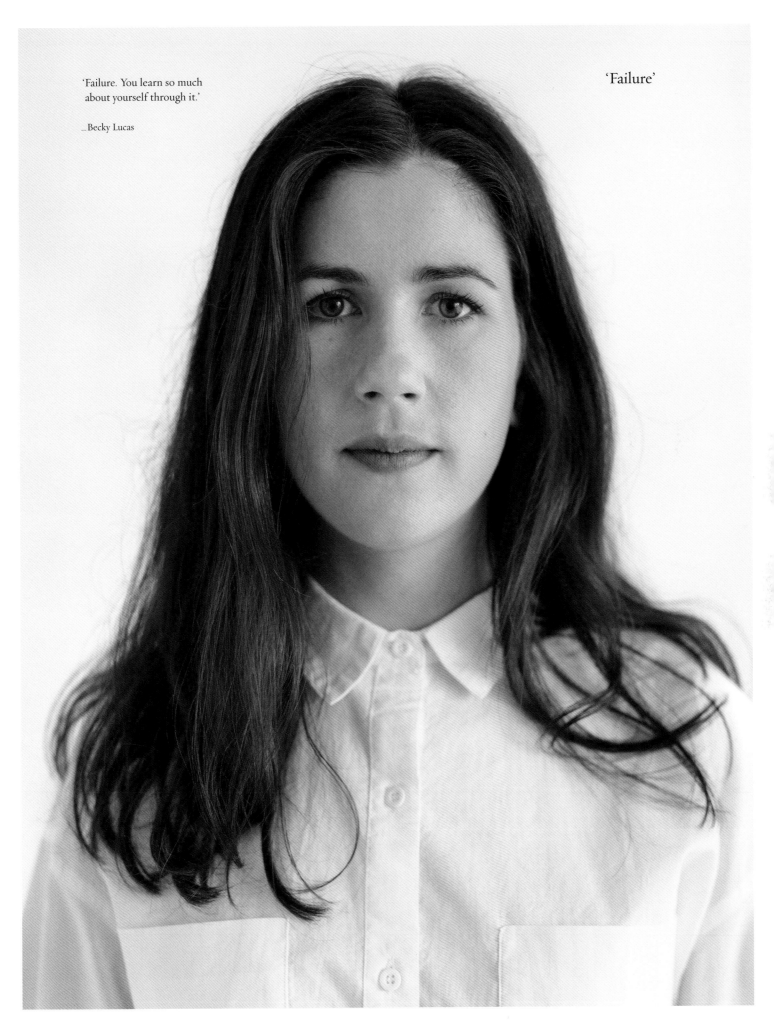

'Failure. You learn so much
about yourself through it.'

_Becky Lucas

Interview page 389

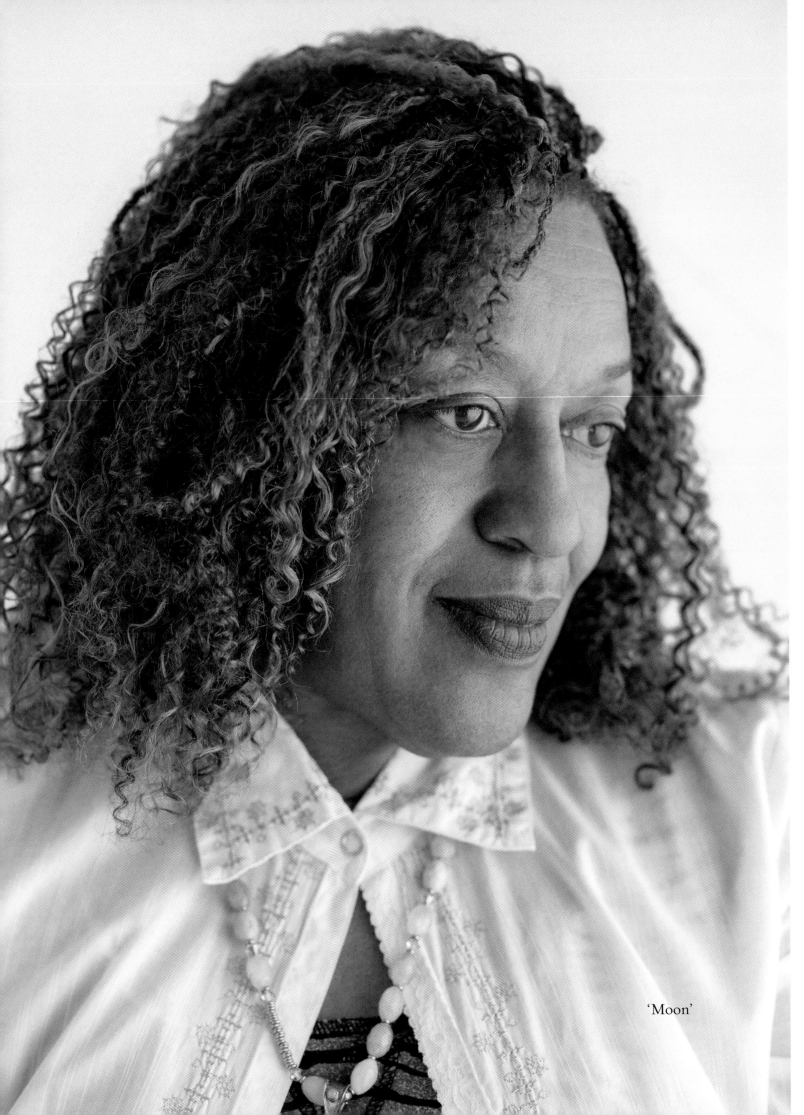

'Moon'

CCH Pounder-Koné

CCH (Carol Christine Hilaria) Pounder-Koné was born in Georgetown, Guyana. She received her bachelor of fine arts and an honourary doctorate from Ithaca College, New York. An award-winning actress and Grammy-nominated spoken-word artist, she garnered Emmy nominations for her roles in *The No. 1 Ladies' Detective Agency*, *ER*, *The X-Files* and *The Shield* and has appeared in *NCIS: New Orleans* since 2014. Her films include *Bagdad Café* and *Avatar*. A visual artist, curator, and social justice advocate, Pounder-Koné is a founding board member of the African Millennium Foundation and a co-founder of Artists for a New South Africa.

Q. What really matters to you?

Without wanting to sound sentimental or trite, it's love. Love has entered my life in a way I hadn't expected; by this, I'm not talking about being 'in love,' but rather, more about an understanding of what it means to *give* love through being of service to others.

The power of love – of service – is about the acceptance of others as they are. It is about accepting people's frailties, their meanness and their aggression without becoming engulfed by it. We can agree and engage on our commonalities, and all walk together. Although I may not understand – or even accept as truth – someone's culture or world view, I can walk with them. When it is possible for our minds to meet, I meet, and when there are things I can't tolerate, I leave alone.

I'm no missionary; I am not in the world to inspire or change anyone – I am here to work on who I want to be as a human being. Of course, it's not always easy to tolerate difference and I might keep someone at arm's length to keep myself from being burned, but I will never abandon anyone completely. That is the power of love.

My work matters to me. I was always aware of the pressure placed on an educated, black woman whose parents have worked so hard in order for their children to receive an education. But I didn't want to become a doctor, or a lawyer, or a politician – I wanted to be an actor.

As an actor in training I was acutely aware of being a foreigner, but, when I mastered my American voice, I remember so distinctly being called the n-word for the first time. It was ridiculous, because I felt simultaneously insulted and complimented; the actor in me went, 'That's an incredible compliment, because now they really think I'm from here.' The reaction was totally insane, but it was part of my introduction to American culture; it changed my perspective on belonging, because, to be a part of something, you have to take in all its cultural aspects – whether you like them or not, whether they are pretty or not.

I've been given the opportunity to take on parts originally written for white males of a certain age, so I'm very proud of the roles I'm known for playing. When I started out – as all young artists do – I played the local prostitute, the ingénue or the suffering wife. After a while, I decided I wanted to play people in authority, people with a sense of themselves. When I wanted to read for the role of a judge, I was told that there *were* no black female judges at the time and that I should stick to what I was good at – emoting suffering. I remember thinking they hadn't done their research and had just assumed it to be true. So, I found the statistics on black, female judges, lawyers and fire fighters, and took a dossier around with me until they let me read for those parts. One day, after a reading, someone said, 'Oh, you *can* do that!' And my response was, 'Yes, I *can*!'

Q. What brings you happiness?

I'm lucky, because I know that happiness is learned. I've discovered that happiness is something that I have to educate myself on and something that I have to practise. I've come to realise that it's the simple things – when I see a beautiful sunset, I'll call ten people and tell them to run outside to experience it with me: 'Go watch the sun, he's showing off today!' Happiness is the setting sun or the rising moon or the sound of the ocean. These things are small, but they figure so prominently on my happiness metre – because I can't produce them, and I do marvel at the hand that can.

Happiness is also about connecting people who need each other. I once met a person who hadn't been able to walk to school because they didn't have shoes – so, because they didn't have shoes, they weren't able to get an education and ended up working at the age of eight. I have found happiness in calling up a company and saying, 'You got any spare shoes?' Now, a hundred pairs of shoes are being sent to that person's village, and it's not just one child who is being enabled to receive an education, but a hundred children. Facilitating those kinds of engagements makes me happy; I very much believe in the principle of Each One Teach One and in doing what I can to support others.

Q. What do you regard as the lowest depth of misery?

The lowest depth of misery is when you cannot see the possibility of hope, when you don't believe in any part of yourself. It's that place where there's no one in your life to tell you that they see you, that they love you or that they appreciate you and would miss you if you were gone. I have never been to that precipice, and I find it difficult to understand, but I do believe it is misery.

Q. What would you change if you could?

I truly don't understand why life is so cruel. And I'm not just talking about human beings – there's cruelty in many facets of nature – but it does feel as though humans have created this extraordinary foundation of cruelty towards one another. I see people imposing their belief systems on others because they feel their beliefs are more powerful and worthy than those of others. That is something I'd like to change – I would sacrifice myself if it would do any good! – but, sadly, the reality is that it's not within my power to alter the minds of others.

Q. Which single word do you most identify with?

Moon. It's the most mysterious thing. Its glow is just enough for you to see, but it's not always there. It has fifty shapes. It can be bloody, it can be white. I find it to be so beautiful, but I don't want to go to it – I just want to enjoy what it does for me down here!

Sharon
Brous

Sharon Brous was born in New Jersey, USA. Ordained as a rabbi in 2001, Brous has become a leading voice in reanimating religious life in America, working to develop a spiritual roadmap for soulful, multifaith justice work around the country. In 2004, she co-founded IKAR, one of the fastest-growing Jewish congregations in the United States. IKAR is credited with sparking a rethinking of religious life in a time of declining affiliation. She works to inspire people of faith to reclaim a moral and prophetic voice in counter-testimony to the extremism prevalent in so many religious communities.

'There is a sense that suffering can hold meaning only if it's seen, shared, honoured. But to suffer alone – that may be the most profound misery.'

Q. What really matters to you?

As a rabbi and a mother, I confront the reality of life's fragility every day. I really believe that while we cannot control how long we are here, we *can* control how we use the time we are given. We can choose to live with anger, a sense of victimhood, an obsession with our vulnerabilities and limitations, or we can find hope, lead with love. Our task is to awaken to the preciousness and precariousness of it all. The truth is, we stand at the edge of the abyss all the time, and again and again we are pulled back into life with the gentle but urgent reminder that, as long as we are still alive, we need to really live.

We like to think that we are independent beings, but we're really more like the aspen trees. Above ground they appear as individual trees, but under the earth they are connected in an intricate, complex system that holds them together as one massive living organism. When one tree falls, the organism compensates for the loss by birthing another, even thousands of miles away. Isn't that like the human community? We live with a false perception of individuality and independence, but we are deeply interconnected beneath the surface. This is one of the great blessings of life – and probably the source of our resilience. That's why when Jewish people bury our dead, we say, *'U'tzrur b'tzror hachaim,'* meaning, 'May you be bound up in the bond of life.' The challenge is to honour our interdependence not only after death, but in this world: right here, right now.

Q. What brings you happiness?

I have a beautiful and wonderful family. I am so grateful.

I am also part of an extraordinary community, one that is truly a community of purpose. Together, we hold love and loss and yearning. We comfort and confront, we wrestle and challenge and support one another. There's a kind of rawness and realness in community, and a tenderness that is truly a counter-testimony to the impatience, indecency, even cruelty that is so prevalent today. At IKAR, the organising principle is Shabbat, the Sabbath. Every week we come together to sing and cry and dance and affirm the humanity that each of us holds. We remember our greatest, most audacious dreams, and affirm our capacity to move out of paralysis and act with integrity and urgency in the world.

Q. What do you regard as the lowest depth of misery?

Human beings can survive unthinkable loss, but immense, maybe even unbearable suffering emerges from the sense that none of it matters. That we – and our struggles - are not seen. Several years ago, I went to Liberia to hear the stories of the women who had helped bring peace to the country after many years of civil war. At one point, one of the women addressing our group began to weep. She said, 'I can't believe you came all this way just to hear my story.' She could not believe that she mattered enough to be heard. The fear of not mattering, I have found, is everywhere. I see it in the most rarefied, privileged communities; I see it in communities that experience daily struggle. There is a sense that suffering can hold meaning only if it's seen, shared, honoured. But to suffer alone - that may be the most profound misery. Our work is not only to alleviate suffering, but to help people recognise that their triumphs and challenges are, on some fundamental level, seen. That they matter.

Q. What would you change if you could?

I would want every child in this world to know that not only is she loved deeply, but also that she has the capacity to love deeply.

Q. Which single word do you most identify with?

Hope. So often, the reality of the world pulls our gaze down to the lowest common denominator – to the worst of human behaviour and instincts. This dulls our imagination, makes us forget what could be and live instead paralysed by what is. One of the great spiritual challenges today is reclaiming an ethos of aspiration, a sense of hope and possibility.

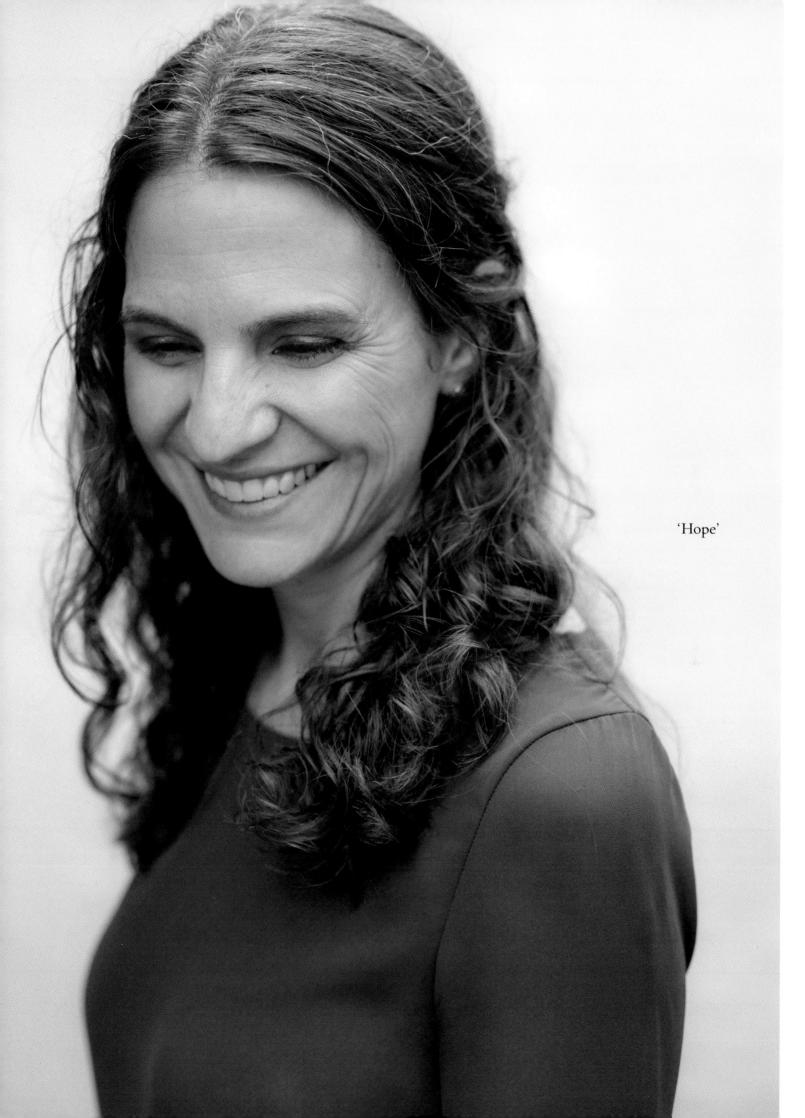

'Hope'

Anne-Sophie Mutter

————

Anne-Sophie Mutter CLH was born in Rheinfelden, Germany. She began her international violin career at age thirteen, at the 1976 Lucerne Festival, and performed as a soloist under the conductor Herbert von Karajan at the 1977 Salzburg Festival. A four-time Grammy Award winner, Mutter has performed twenty-five world premieres. She works to support next-generation musicians and is committed to numerous philanthropic projects, including the Anne-Sophie Mutter Foundation. Mutter has received numerous honours, including the Great Cross of Merit of the Federal Republic of Germany and the French Legion of Honour in the rank of Chevalier.

Q. What really matters to you?

This has changed so much over the years; since becoming a mother, my children have become what matters to me most. My husband and I had been married for six years when he died, in 1995; I was left behind with two children: a one-year-old and a three-year-old. I wouldn't have thought it possible to overcome that level of pain and grief, but the experience showed me the full extent of my capabilities and power. And something like that really changes your priorities.

A constant throughout my life, though, has been music. I discovered my passion for the violin when I was five years old. We were a very musical family and there was always music in the house – classical and jazz. The kids were always on the piano or the violin, but I was the only one who ended up turning my love into a profession. I asked for violin lessons for my fifth birthday and immediately fell in love with the feeling of being able to shape sound. It felt like I was a sculptor, engulfed in a cosmos of colours and fascinating sound dynamics, and I knew that I wanted to be a musician.

When it comes to music's potential, Europe is the perfect example of its application. There are so many different concepts and perspectives on life, religion and culture in Europe today, and, with everyone living in such close proximity to one another, these different perspectives are mingled. In this context, music is the only language we can all really share, the only language that, when 'spoken,' can be understood by us all on an emotional level. When we sing songs and play music, we are able to interact on a level that is totally natural; whether there is a celebration or we are mourning, the one thing we have in common is that our rituals are all imbued with music. And for children, music is a school of life: it teaches discipline, listening, teamwork and leadership.

A few years into my musical studies, my mother – with tears in her eyes – told me about Yehudi Menuhin's return to Germany. He was one of the great violinists and the first Jewish musician to return to Germany to play for a German audience after the Second World War. I could sense an immense gratefulness in my mother's voice – Menuhin's coming to Germany was an immense gesture of forgiveness. That's when I realised that being a musician is not only about knowing your instrument and the joy that playing it brings you, being a musician is also about creating an emotional bridge that brings people together. As a musician, you have the potential to affect thousands of people and your music can have such meaning for others – when I understood this, I began devoting some of my time to benefit projects.

I'm drawn to philanthropy. There is so much sadness and pain around me that sometimes I find it difficult to get up in the morning and face another day, but I want to spread the message that what's desperately needed today is a greater understanding of empathy. It's not a question of the average citizen donating millions, but more that we need to be aware of the extreme privilege some of us have. I live in a country where there is no war, where my children can become educated and where they have a future. However, of the almost 7.5 billion people on this planet, two thirds live in areas engulfed by armed conflicts; something has gone terribly wrong, and it matters to me that we are all aware of, and empathetic to, those affected.

Q. What brings you happiness?

Children and music. The world of classical music has become smaller over the years; it is not as popular as other art forms and it doesn't reach as many people as it once did. But, even on this small scale, I have been able to contribute to taking girls in Romania off the streets, where they are susceptible to forced prostitution or marriage. Being able to do something like that brings me happiness; having a purpose and being able to help someone else is what my life is all about.

Q. What do you regard as the lowest depth of misery?

Religious extremism has brought great misery to the world. Religion is something that is very personal and which can be a wonderful thing to practice – mind you, depending on who you are, it can also be wonderful not to practice it – but only insofar as it makes us more open, transparent and empathetic towards others. The beauty of religion is its ability to make a person more embracing of the world, not more willing to shut it out, and I have never understood why some feel their religion to be superior to those of others.

Hunger is another thing that devastates me. Money is made from holding back crops, in order to sell off later at inflated prices. And meanwhile, people are starving. This is terrible.

Q. What would you change if you could?

The basic message is: make love, not war . . . and free contraceptives to go along with it! Jokes aside, I really do feel as though humanity has become quick to revert to conflict. I have a dream of equlaity between all people.

I would also ensure that all women have the right of power over their own bodies. Something I hold against the Catholic Church is this idea that intimacy is for the purpose of producing children; it means women are bringing children into the world when they cannot ensure their safety or food security. I hope Pope Francis will address this, as he is someone who reflects empathy and is relatively open minded. I also hope he will support equality of love in the future.

Q. Which single word do you most identify with?

Passion.

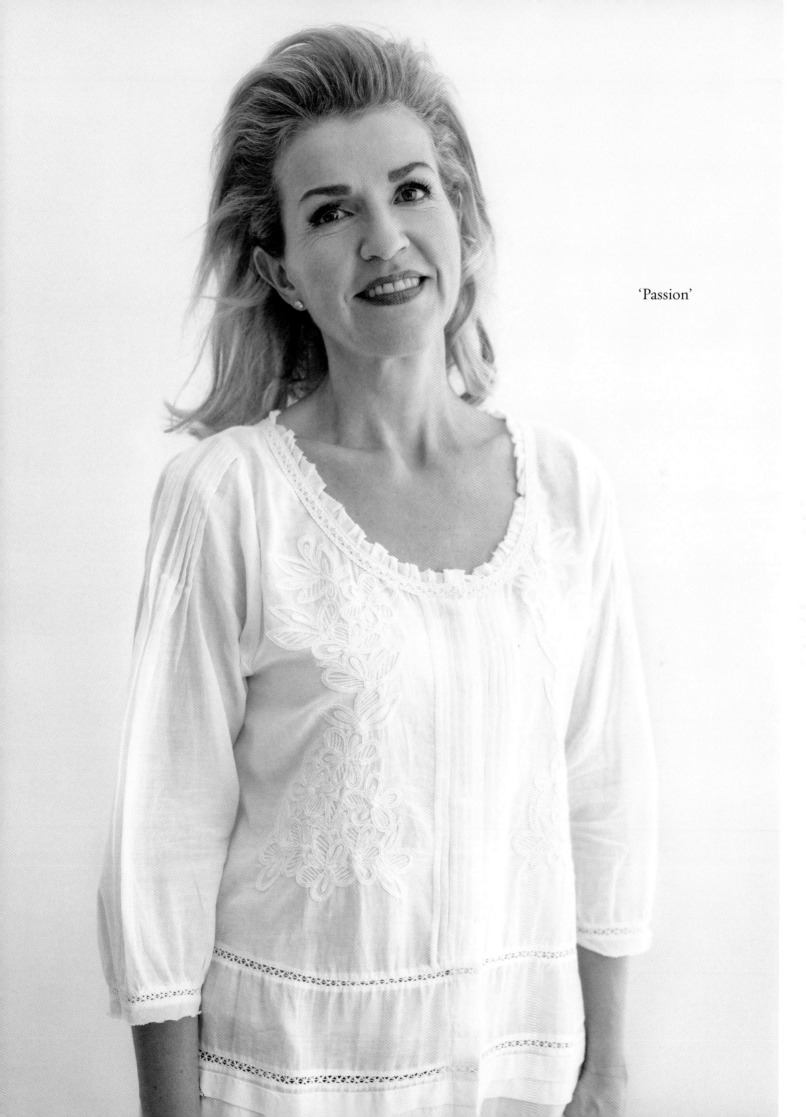

'Passion'

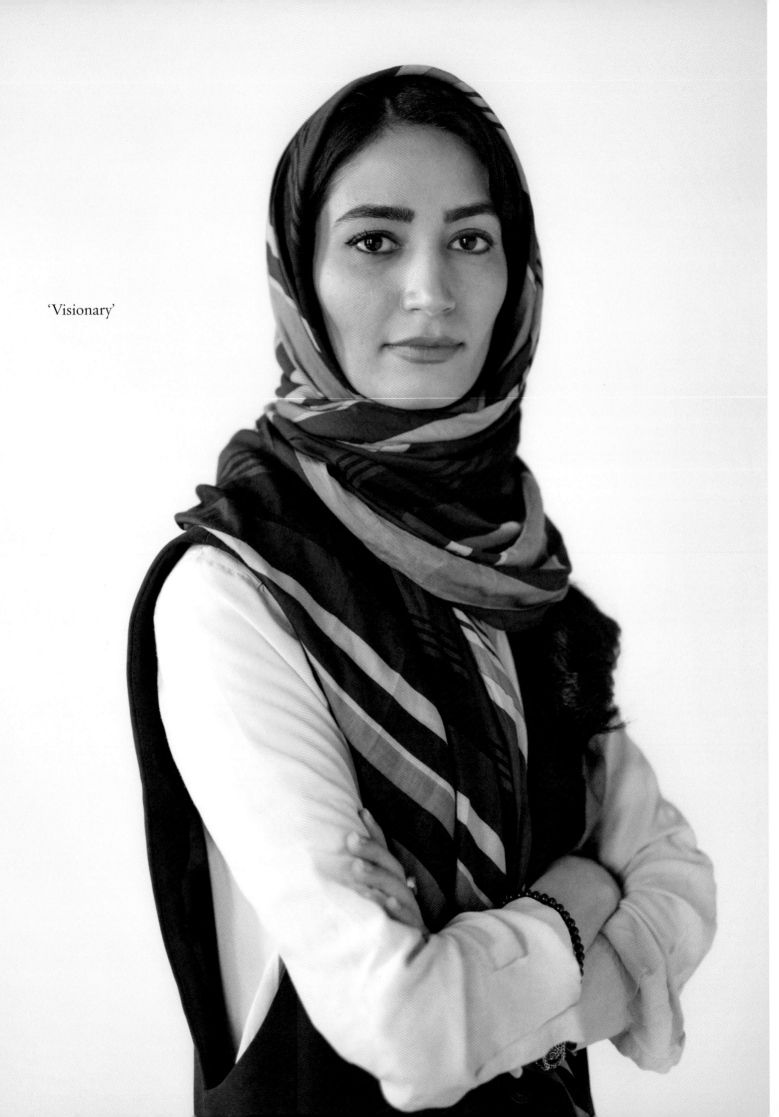

'Visionary'

Fereshteh Forough

Fereshteh Forough was born to Afghan parents in Iran. She and her family lived in Iran as refugees until, after the fall of the Taliban regime in 2001, they returned to live in Herat. Forough completed her bachelor's degree in computer science at the University of Herat before completing a master's degree in Germany. Forough is the founder of Code to Inspire, the first coding school for women in Afghanistan, and is dedicated to empowering women through education in technology.

Q. What really matters to you?

Giving back to the community. Being born a refugee taught me many lessons. Even though it was very difficult, it taught me that I don't have to wait for opportunity – that I'm still able to do my best when given the least. I was one of eight kids, and my parents had nothing. It was difficult for us to go to school, because Iran's policy was that refugees didn't have the right to education – I was deprived of that human right just because of where I came from. My mum learned to sew, so that she could afford to send us to school. I am really grateful for what I have now and what I've achieved, so I feel the responsibility to give back to the community as much as I can. This is my goal – I'm constantly asking how I can bring change and positively impact my community, especially women who have been undervalued in Afghanistan for years.

After I finished high school in Iran, the Taliban regime in Afghanistan collapsed and we moved back to Herat, my hometown. I got my bachelor's degree in computer science there, then my master's in Germany. I went back to Herat to teach and learned a lot, especially being a woman in a country where education for women – empowering women – is such a sensitive topic. I've been very vocal about women raising their voices and I think coding is such a good way for them to do it. Computer code is really a language, and learning it can connect women with people around the world; it doesn't matter who they are, or where they are, it enables them to freely express their ideas over the internet – and that's empowering. It's just the talent that matters.

Technology remains a very male-dominated field in Afghanistan. I believe equality will take time, but I have seen people come to understand that there are ways to collaborate and co-operate, and ways to overcome prejudice. I was one of the very first female student-mentors teaching their peers at the university in Herat. In my first class, teaching Java programming, only seven of the two hundred students showed up – and they were all women. Men didn't want to learn from a woman, but when they realised they might fail without my assistance, they started to come. Having just emerged from the previous regime's control, you couldn't really expect men to immediately embrace women's education and empowerment. But over time, working with men as a team, they began to appreciate women's contributions and our ideas. This brought diversity of thought to groups that were previously just made up of men.

Q. What brings you happiness?

I wake up every morning and am very conscious that I have a mission: to help people by empowering them. Every single step I take towards that goal makes me happy. It feels amazing when I see our students' tweets, their pictures, and the codes that they are writing – they are embracing the opportunity to empower and develop themselves, and that makes me joyful. Knowing that I'm contributing to empowering women in Afghanistan by educating them in the field of technology makes me happy, because they are being enabled to learn something. And not only that, it also shows people around the world a positive story about Afghanistan.

Sometimes I feel like an ambassador in America. When people find out I'm from Afghanistan, I can tell from their faces that they only have bad images in their heads. So I'm always trying to give people tonnes of good figures from back home – because it's not what they imagine. Under the Taliban, there were only nine hundred thousand university students. There were zero women at university and there was zero female participation in the workplace. Today, there are 9 million children going to school, and 4.2 million of those are female. Seventeen per cent of seats in parliament are held by women, and we have four female cabinet ministers. We've made huge progress from when I first returned to Afghanistan, so I know that change is possible. The country has a bright future, especially with this young generation – participating in that, and helping where I can, makes me happy.

Q. What do you regard as the lowest depth of misery?

The lowest depth of misery and sorrow is living in a world where human beings are being judged by their skin colour, their religious beliefs or the country that they come from. It creates a lot of barriers and makes people think differently about each other. Part of this is people's lack of information. When we don't open our hearts towards learning more about a specific thing that we are ignorant about, we begin to act against that thing. People need to learn about other cultures and about other religions – they need to have an open heart and an open mind in order to be able to embrace the hearts and minds of others. Personally, I try to educate myself on different belief systems and learn about the positive aspects of them. I've learned that none of them deliver messages of hate; they are all about peace, unity and loving each other. It's human beings who impose their agendas on belief and make it more extreme.

Q. What would you change if you could?

I want to eliminate war and make peace. It's very sad to see people leaving their beloved countries and their occupations, and having to go to other countries. They face so many difficulties on their travels, but are not accepted by the new community when they arrive.

Q. Which single word do you most identify with?

Visionary, because I dream a lot. I'm a big dreamer, but I'm a practical person, too – so I can make my dreams happen. I always try to think about the future and what I can do to improve it.

Elida
Lawton O'Connell

Elida Lawton O'Connell was born in Pristina, Kosovo. She began working as a producer for Associated Press in 1997, covering the Kosovo War for five years. Since then she has continued to work for Associated Press as a producer and editor.

'Losing my husband was the closest I've come to giving up.'

Q. What really matters to you?

My loved ones – my family, my kids and having the people that I love around me. Having children changed a lot for me; now, when I see dead children my heart breaks. I pretend that I didn't see it, and I continue to do my job – edit chopped fingers and chopped hands – but, deep down, it's all in my head.

I suppose what matters is constructing a solution to all the violence around us. I continue to fight for justice and the truth, which is tough. Being a woman war journalist was very, very difficult. Every day I knew that I could be killed, but I wanted to go out and tell the stories of what was happening out there. Those five years of war coverage changed me and taught me many things about myself: I found myself sometimes being very selfish; I found courage that I never knew I had; and the way I believed changed.

Now I'm spending a lot of time in Kosovo working with women who were raped. I myself was almost raped several times working as a journalist, so I cut my hair to look like a boy and I learned not to look anyone in the face – I learned to be as dumb as possible. My work with women in Kosovo matters to me because it's horrible that they don't know how to – or can't – say no. I've found that the first step is recognition by the women and their families that being raped is not a woman's fault. In my opinion, it's the government who needs to compensate these women for what they've encountered. They need doctors. They need psychiatrists. And there's nothing I can say to them, because I can't relate to what they went through. I can only relate in that I was threatened

with rape; it was devastating enough to look someone in the face as they say, 'I'm going to do this, this, this and this.' There are no words for men and women being subjected to systematic rape – and I've encountered a lot of men who were raped as well during the war. But although there are no words, I can help in other ways: I can report it and I can bring awareness. That is my responsibility. And I can educate other journalists so they know what to expect when they report on atrocities.

Q. What brings you happiness?

I have three children, who are fifteen, six and three years old – they are my happiness. They challenge me, and I find myself going to Google a lot with all their questions. Tennis makes me happy, too. And I love being loved and showing people love by bringing them happiness in any way: it might be by helping someone taking the rubbish out, saying how nice they look or just being there to ask how they are. If that kind of care for our neighbours stops, then humanity is gone.

In a broader sense, I still find people every day who don't give up. It's these people – who may be so different from one another, but who are defined by respect for each other no matter their colour, religion or background – who give me hope.

Q. What do you regard as the lowest depth of misery?

Personally – because I have seen death so much – I always fear losing one of my children. In the world, the saddest thing that I see is people looking at God and killing in the name of that God. The only thing that gives me hope is that there are still people out there to work against

it all. Sadly, compared to five years ago, things like sexual prejudice and racism are becoming worse in the world. But I will not take that for an answer and I still hope. I'll continue to fight. I talk to my daughter about these things a lot, to try to give her a perspective, so that hopefully she can influence others.

I met – and lost – my first husband during the war, when we were both covering stories. I was pregnant with my first child at the time. Losing my husband was the closest I've come to giving up. I thought, 'That's it. I'm going to die. I don't want to eat. I just want to die.' But, I knew I had to continue. As hard as it is, you have to keep moving until you can start breathing again. Eventually, someone you talk to will make you smile. I've learned never to give up. I've had so many bad things happen to me, but I know I've done good things in my life – when you meet a man you saved as a boy, and compare that to your sadness, it's completely eclipsed.

Q. What would you change if you could?

I would change the way some people feel about their faith. I would make it that people wouldn't kill others because they're different, so that if people change, then governments have to change. And I would bring community back – get society talking – because it is so powerful. Now we have tools and means to do this: we can show people how to respect others.

Q. Which single word do you most identify with?

Trying. I never accept 'no' for an answer. When someone tells me I can't do something, that's my word – trying.

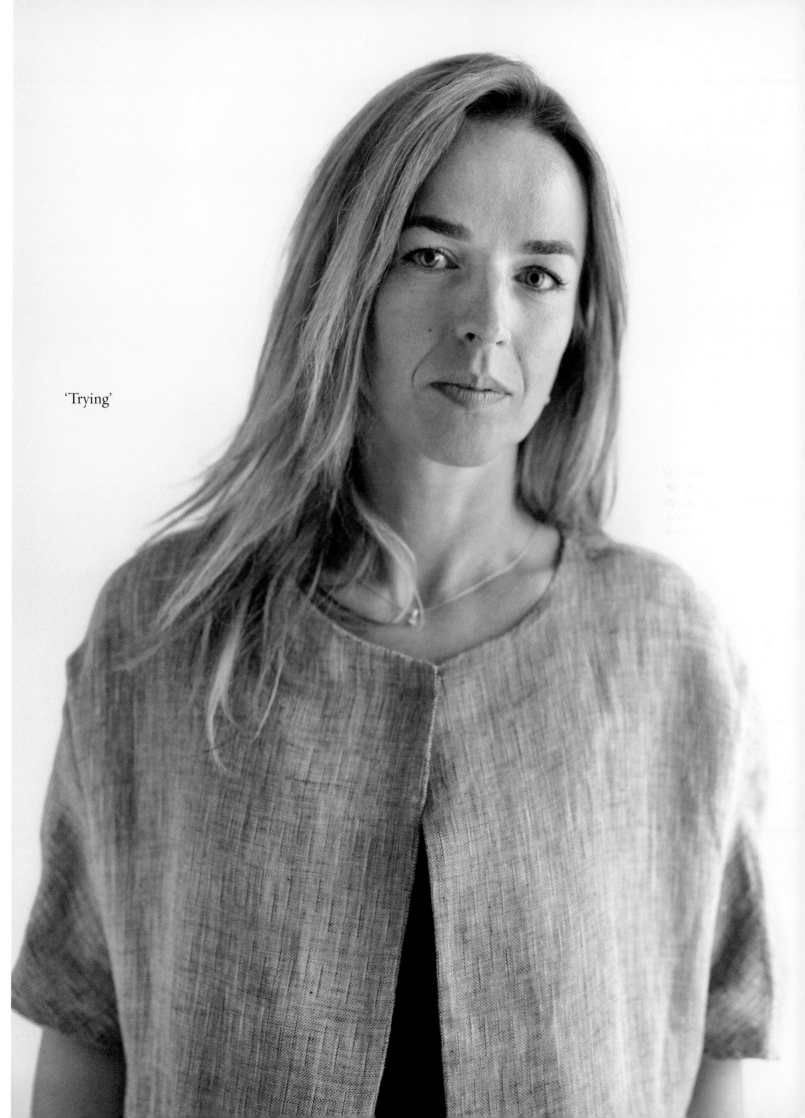

'Trying'

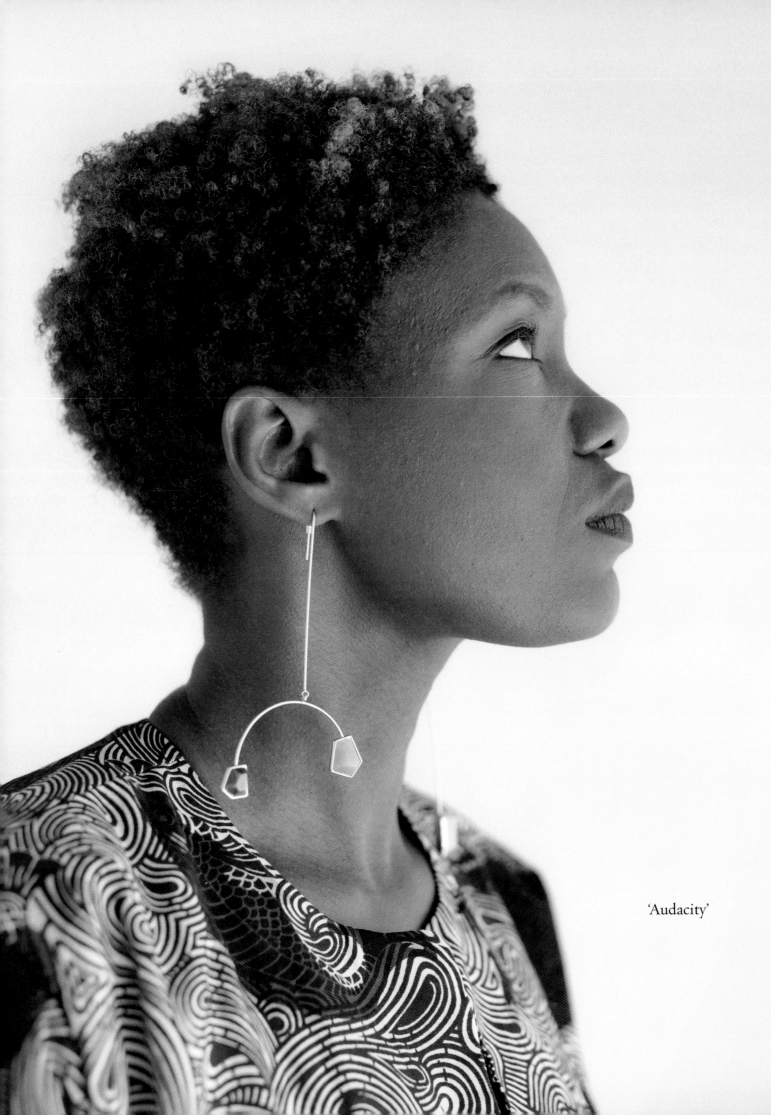

'Audacity'

Rokhaya Diallo

Rokhaya Diallo was born in Paris, France. A journalist, award-winning documentary filmmaker and activist, in 2007 Diallo co-founded Les Indivisibles, an organisation that uses parody and humour to break down racism. In 2012, she was awarded a COJEP prize for her work against racism and discrimination. Diallo is the author of seven books, including *Afro!*, which was published in 2015. She has directed four documentaries, including *Not Yo Mama's Movement*, which investigated police brutality. In 2016, Diallo was highly commended by the European Diversity Awards in the Herbert Smith Freehills Journalist of the Year category.

'It would be a great thing to live in a world without privileges, and for each and every one of us to exist fully in our own right.'

Q. What really matters to you?
The love of my family and my self-esteem.

For me, self-esteem is extremely important; it's nourished by the way people see you and by the people who surround you. I wrote *Afro!* – a book about natural hair – because I wanted young women, in particular, to be able to stand tall in the world: to say, 'No matter what kind of face or body I have – whether or not "acceptable" by prevailing standards, whether or not white, and whether short, tall, fat, young or old – I am a valuable person, and I am beautiful in the eyes of my own ego and of the people in my life.' The question of natural hair may seem completely innocuous, but it is in fact very important, because we live in a world in which beauty is extremely formulaic; this makes it extremely difficult for people who don't fit the prevailing aesthetic canons to develop a sense of self-esteem. In life, self-esteem is the ticket to happiness. In a context in which everything that is considered beautiful is contrary to what you are, feeling good about yourself – even if you don't have light skin, even if you don't have blond, straight hair – gives you an inexhaustible resource, a foundation upon which to believe in the future and face the world with a kind of inner peace.

Q. What brings you happiness?
Human relationships are a true source of joy and happiness for me. It makes me happy to be surrounded by loved ones; just knowing there are people out there who care for me is a great resource in the face of adversity. And I thrive on encounters, which is one of the reasons I love my job. My work has given me the chance to meet so many people, and to follow their lives by making films, documentaries and television reports. This brings me happiness because it nourishes me both intellectually and emotionally.

Q. What do you regard as the lowest depth of misery?
I feel saddened by suffering – by other people's distress and vulnerability. What I'm saddened by in France, today, is the issue of police brutality; every year ten to fifteen people die at the hands of the French police, and the majority of these people are young men from poor neighbourhoods who are either black or of North African origin. My work as an activist in this regard was definitely influenced by one particular event. One night in 2005, three teenage boys – who, like me, came from the working-class suburbs of Paris – were coming back from a football match; they had done nothing wrong whatsoever, but the police were pursuing them, so they decided to hide in an electrical substation. Two of the boys – Zyed Benna and Bouna Traoré – died. Following their deaths, an unprecedented wave of rioting started in Clichy-sous-Bois, Paris, and spread all over France; for me, the riots were occurring for obvious reasons – people were fed up with police brutality. I found out that the police officers had done nothing to get the boys out of the trap, and I was shocked that both the media and politicians of the day were describing them as delinquents, when in actual fact they had done absolutely nothing wrong. The two boys could have been my little brothers or my cousins, and they died because they were afraid of the police, because they were black and of North African descent. In France, if you are black or of North African origin, you are twenty times more likely to be identity-checked by the police than you are if you are white. So, even when you have done nothing at all – when you have nothing to feel guilty about – you are afraid of being arrested. It was the thought of the boys' innocence, of their fear in their final moments in the electrical substation, and the fact that they could have been saved by a simple call to the electric company, that shocked me.

Q. What would you change if you could?
I would try to carry out the promise of the French Revolution, which was the abolition of privileges. It would be a great thing to live in a world without privileges, where the promise of equality and justice are met, and where it is possible for each and every one of us to exist fully in our own right. Naturally, we are going to have to fight for this; we will have to fight to dismantle a system that gives profoundly unequal treatment to women, to people who are disabled, to people of ethnic, racial or religious minorities, to homosexuals, to transgender people and to a great many other groups of people in the world. It would be a great step forward if those with the privileges – those who do not belong to these excluded communities – were to recognise their privileges and to give them up. For me, the abolition of privileges is a critical revolutionary struggle that needs to be taken up today.

Q. Which single word do you most identify with?
Audacity.

'Freedom'

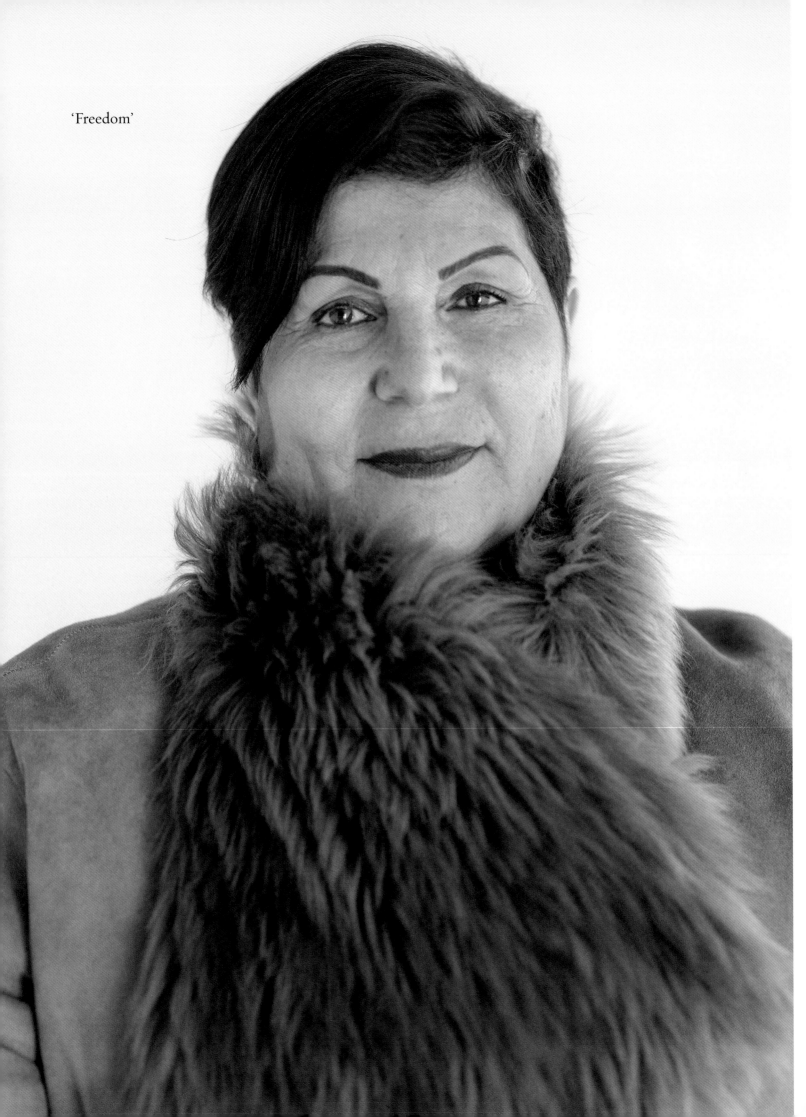

Berivan Vigoureux

Berivan Vigoureux earned a master's degree in the history of cinema, after moving to France, from the École des Hautes Études en Sciences Sociales, and a television and cinema diploma from the Conservatoire Libre du Cinéma Français. Vigoureux is a filmmaker and freelance journalist, reporting for the likes of the CAPA press agency, France 24 and *Paris Match*. She directed the 2011 documentary *Kurdistan: The Other Iraq*.

Q. What really matters to you?

Women. Women need to be empowered, because I strongly believe that it is women who are going to change the world.

Growing up in Kurdistan, I saw that women and girl children were very much confined by tradition; as a girl child, I wasn't even allowed to talk to boys, but I always had the feeling that this wasn't normal. When I was eight years old, a boy in my class asked to borrow a pencil from me and I gave it to him; my brothers told my parents I had spoken to a boy and they were horrified. As I grew older, I came to see how much our society was being crushed by tradition. I told myself I would study hard and go to university, with the ultimate goal being to put an end to this narrow-mindedness. I was always a rebel, never willing to accept the status quo. I just couldn't help asking why things were the way they were.

Once I got to university, I had greater freedom, but my family wasn't happy that I had continued with my education. My father was a good man – a kind man – but he was afraid. He was afraid because the system is an assault on families and he wanted to protect me. Families are afraid that when their daughters go to university they will begin to feel free and will start sleeping with boys.

When I became a reporter, I decided that I couldn't stay in Kurdistan; I came to France as a political refugee. Getting a resident's permit, finding work and a place to stay were a struggle, but I handled it; I had to handle it, in order to continue the fight back home. When I first came to France, I was pursuing a career as an actress, because it was hard to find work as a journalist; acting had been something I couldn't do back home, because, in Kurdistan, actresses are considered whores. But I came to realise that it made more sense to pursue journalism and my work now focusses on the struggles of women back home. I do a lot of work in Kurdistan and the border regions: Syrian Kurdistan, Iraqi Kurdistan and Turkish Kurdistan.

Women in Kurdistan are punished twice over. They are punished both by the system and by their families, who uphold that system. Women are compelled to get married, have children and stay at home; once women are confined to the home, they can't demand freedom. Men call themselves revolutionaries, but they haven't changed; when they get married, they expect their wives to stay at home. This is just another fight. We fight the system, we fight for democracy, we fight Islamic State and now we need to fight in the home. As women, we need to organise ourselves collectively – without the men. Men just fight – that's what they do. If you look at all of the statesmen in the world, you will see that the majority of them are dictators or are unable to lead. But, give power to women, and you'll see things change; wars will stop, friendships will be born and borders may even disappear.

Q. What brings you happiness?

It makes me happy to see Kurdish women showing the world that they are men's equals by fighting Islamic State together with men. It's sad that these women are not recognised as equals when they return home, but we are making progress; in Rojava, an autonomous region in northern Syria, a woman is co-president. This is phenomenal! She is modest and goes out into the streets to engage with the people. Leaders around the world could learn something from her.

In my own life, I am happy when I feel I've accomplished something positive. My happiness also comes from seeing Kurdish women being rescued from Islamic State and being able to re-enter society. Witnessing the struggles of women and telling their stories makes me happy and really motivates me.

Q. What do you regard as the lowest depth of misery?

The fact that three thousand Kurdish women are still imprisoned by Islamic State. Where are the powers that be? Why are they not helping us to rescue these women? Instead, the women Kurdish fighters on the front line are doing this themselves; they are extremely tough. Islamic State is afraid of them because, according to their logic, if they are killed by a Kurdish woman they will go straight to hell. These women have their own battle cries and Islamic State runs from them in fear. Men aren't as resilient as women – they retreat – but these women never leave the front line. Ever.

This gives me strength. I was interviewing an Islamic State fighter in prison who bragged that he'd killed thirty-nine female fighters with his sword. He said that, if he got out, he would keep doing this; I couldn't help myself, I spat in his face. I am not afraid of Islamic State; I am *not* afraid!

Q. What would you change if you could?

Women need to be empowered.

Q. Which single word do you most identify with?

It's a phrase: 'freedom for women!'

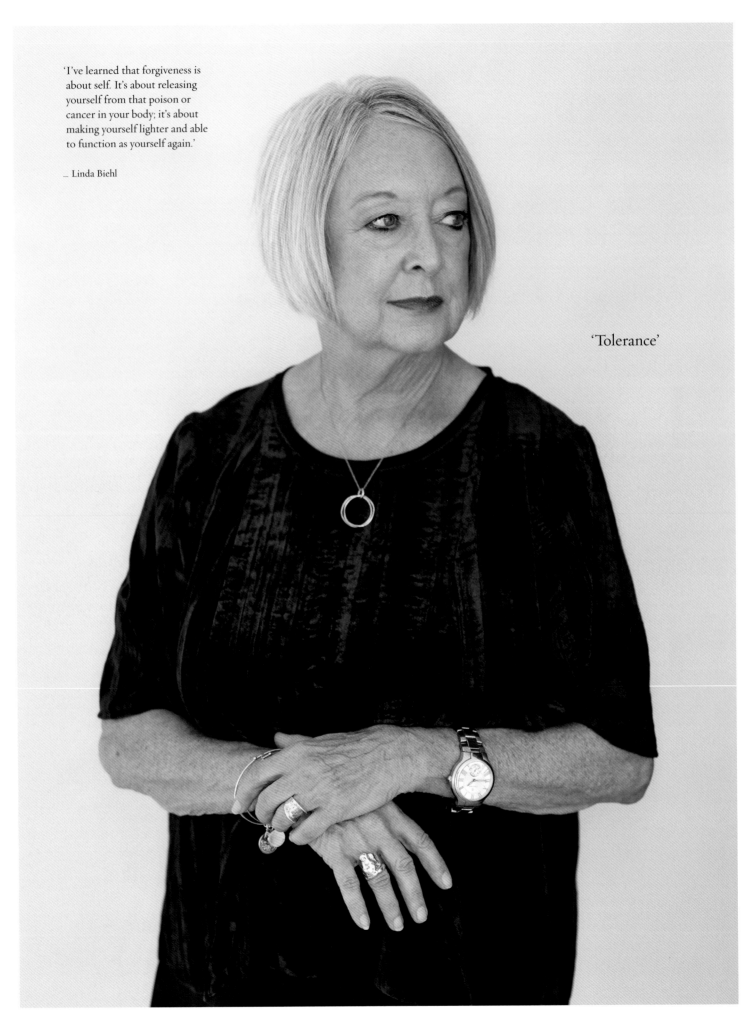

'I've learned that forgiveness is about self. It's about releasing yourself from that poison or cancer in your body; it's about making yourself lighter and able to function as yourself again.'

_ Linda Biehl

'Tolerance'

Interview page 389

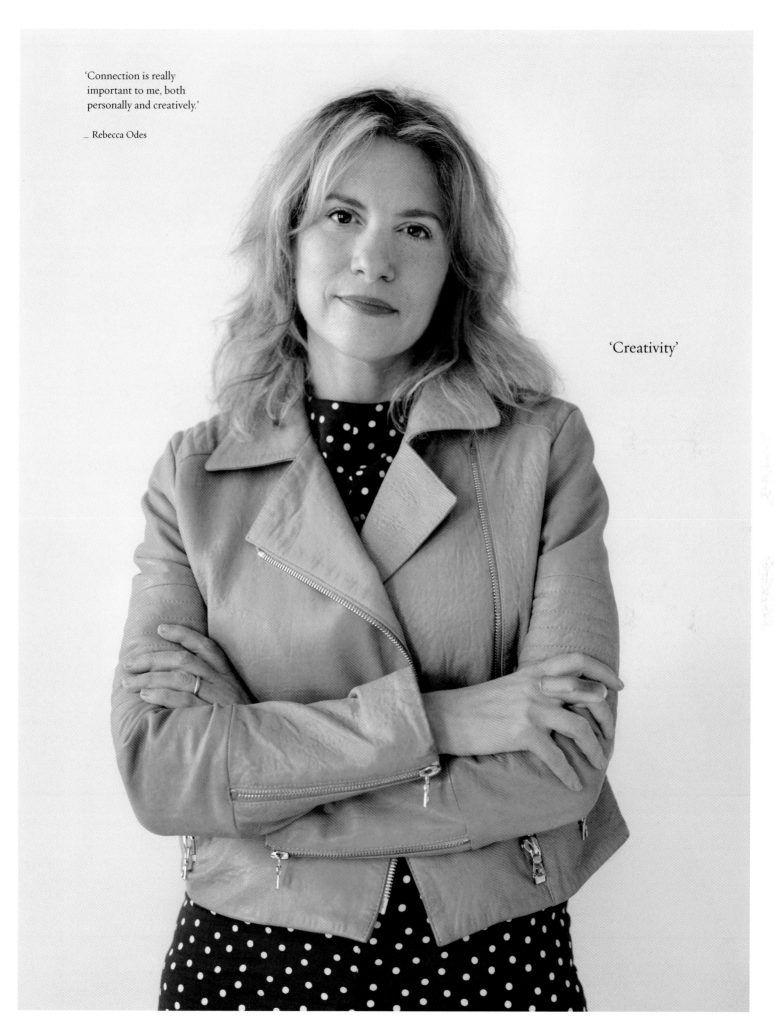

'Connection is really
important to me, both
personally and creatively.'

_ Rebecca Odes

'Creativity'

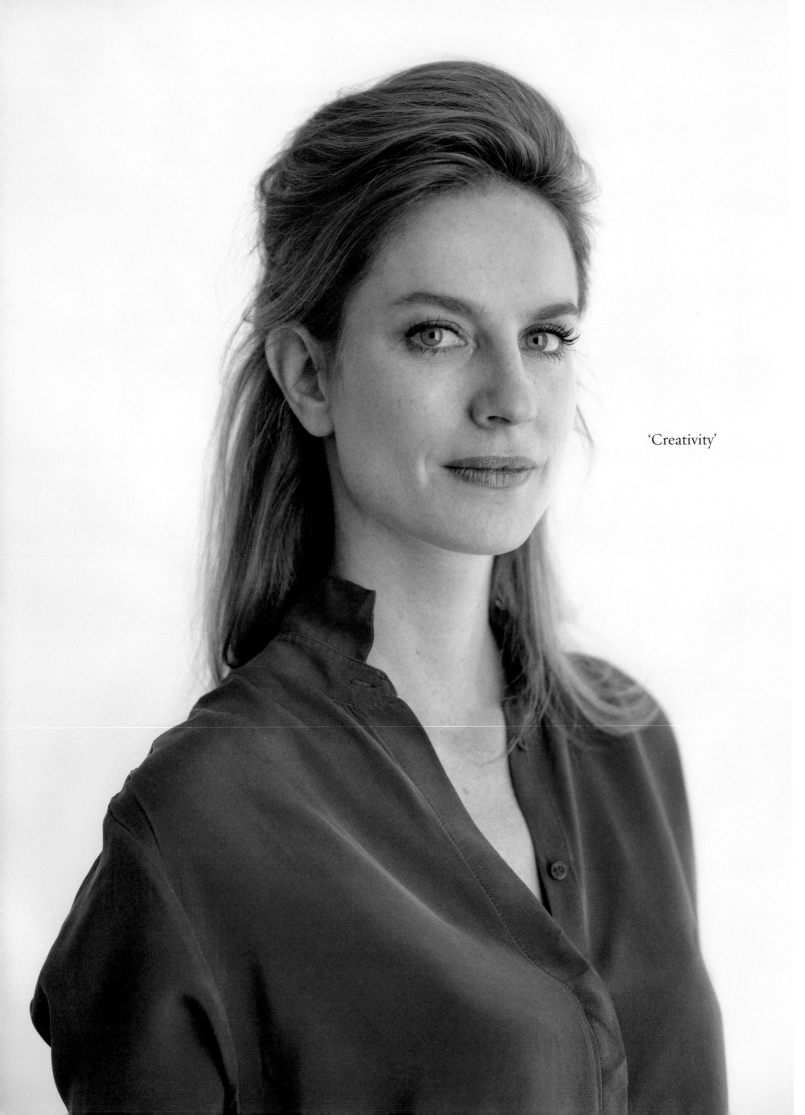

'Creativity'

Julia Leeb

_____

Julia Leeb was born in Munich, Germany. She studied international relations and diplomacy in Madrid, Arabic in Alexandria, and television and digital media in Munich. She works as a war photojournalist and filmmaker, and is the author of *North Korea: Anonymous Country*. Leeb's long-term projects have been published internationally and document political upheaval in the Democratic Republic of the Congo, Egypt, Syria, Libya, Afghanistan, South Sudan and Iran. She also produces virtual reality and 360-degree content about remote regions like Transnistria, in Moldova, and the Nuba Mountains, in Sudan.

'It's the women who keep life going; it's the women who forgive first and focus on the future.'

_____

Q. What really matters to you?

In terms of my work, what matters is being able to command attention with my photographs. It's about exposing conflict by being involved with articles, television reports and exhibitions. I love it when something positive flows from a news story. For instance, when someone decides to sponsor a school, you know it's not only those children who are being empowered, but *their* future children as well. Being part of that cycle is incredible.

What matters to me, as Goethe would say, is having elective affinities all over the world. Growing up, I was always playing with children from other countries. My mother took White Russian children into our home after the Chernobyl disaster, so, early on, I learned to live openly and arrange myself to fit in with different cultures; I learned how to communicate with people I couldn't converse with. And, throughout my childhood, I had a desire to discover the world. I was influenced by Pippi Longstocking – to break through the structures that keep you from living your life to the fullest and pursue what affects you.

Being able to find affinity with people and places around the world is a great privilege that means I never feel alone. The people I photograph give me so much – their lives existed before they meet me and carry on when I go – but, when we meet, they open up to me and we share an intimate experience. I have met the greatest people who, armed only with their will, have been able to accomplish the impossible. Through these experiences, I have learned so much: about the power of applying your mind and initiative. I have learned that a manifestation in your mind is only one step away from implementation; this has ensured that I am able to live my life on my terms.

Many people ask me whether I experience fear when I travel. The answer is, of course I do. If I didn't feel afraid, I would be behaving recklessly. But, fear is relative and can always be managed. And, my subjects are more important than the things I'm afraid of. So, I'm able to put my fears aside for those extraordinary people who stand in their power in the face of such hopelessness.

Giving a voice to women is critical in my work. One of humanity's common elements is the way it treats women, and I am trying to ensure this changes. I have noticed that women – who have the smallest voices in conflict zones – find their inner strength at the critical moment. If a school is destroyed, there is a woman who will relocate the lessons to her basement and continue on as usual. It doesn't matter where I am, it's the women I see cooking the meals and telling stories with happy endings. It's the women who keep life going; it's the women who forgive first and focus on the future. Yet, somehow, women are never sitting at the table when peace is being negotiated.

Q. What brings you happiness?

I'm happiest when I can produce something of value; creating makes me happier than consuming.

Q. What do you regard as the lowest depth of misery?

Negativity and destruction. These are not confined to war, rather, they live within each of us and have the potential to destroy us. People can be very aggressive with themselves, which leads them into self-doubt and, ultimately, selfishness. But, it's important that we don't give in to these feelings. I once read a book in which a woman talked about standing in front of a mirror and analysing her inner voice. She said that no enemy would talk to her as badly as she talked to herself. I think women are far more critical of themselves than men, and I want to live in a world in which women aren't so heavily scrutinised.

Q. What would you change if you could?

I wish people could recognise the destructive power of their impulses and counter them. I also wish people could communicate better. Some of the greatest atrocities in this world are unknown to us, because they are occurring in remote places like North Korea or the Congo. We look at these places from afar and say that we can't understand why certain things are happening. But, there's always a reason, and most often it's very conventional: someone feels misunderstood or like they have been unfairly treated, or that their pride and honour have been offended. But, the reality is that it's very easy to stop a conflict at its inception – if people could communicate better, I think they would see this.

Q. Which single word do you most identify with?

Creativity.

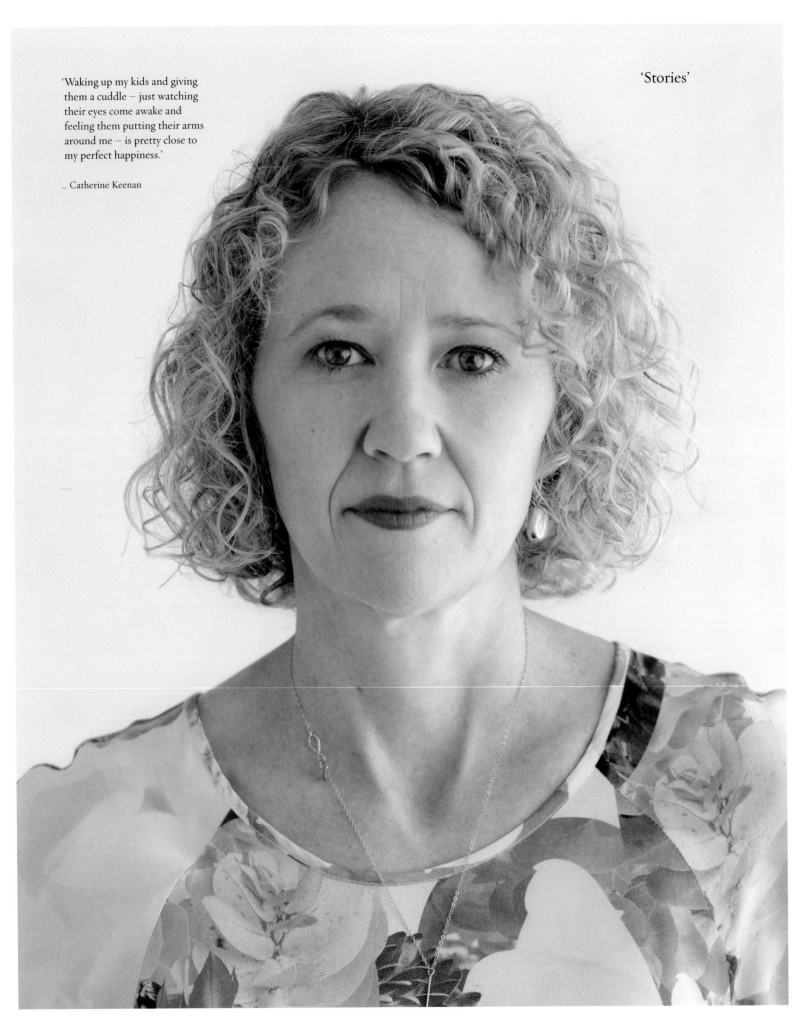

'Waking up my kids and giving them a cuddle – just watching their eyes come awake and feeling them putting their arms around me – is pretty close to my perfect happiness.'

_ Catherine Keenan

'Stories'

Interview page 390

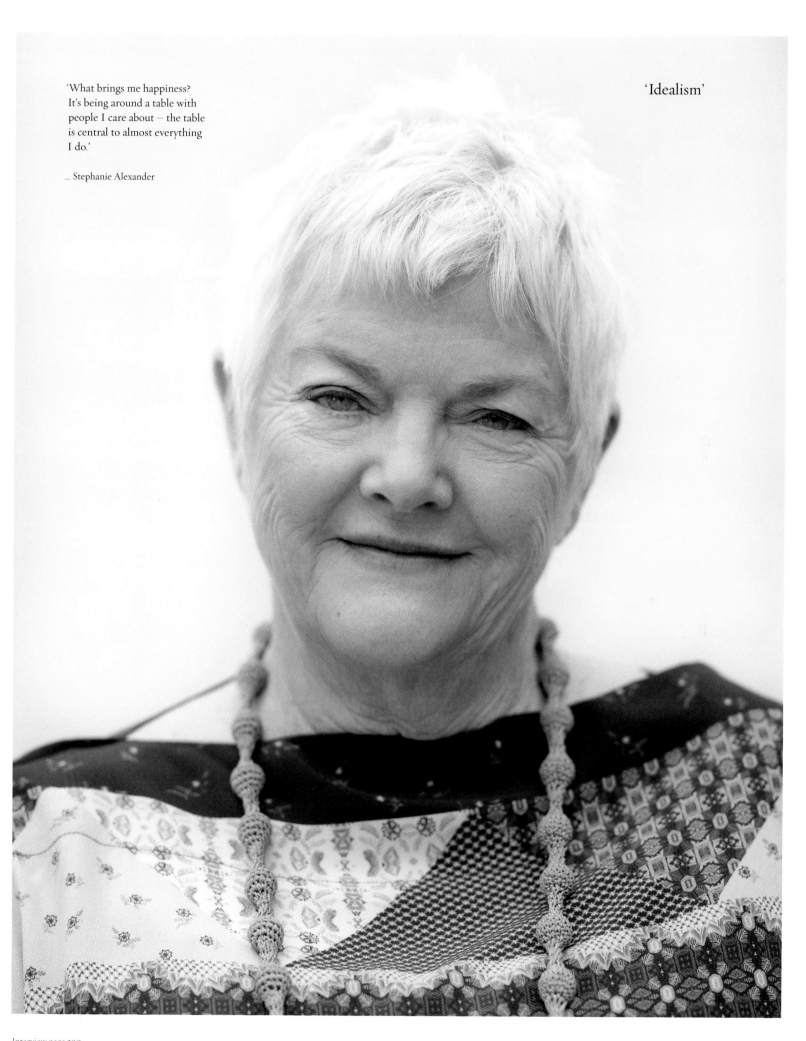

'What brings me happiness?
It's being around a table with
people I care about – the table
is central to almost everything
I do.'

_ Stephanie Alexander

'Idealism'

Interview page 390

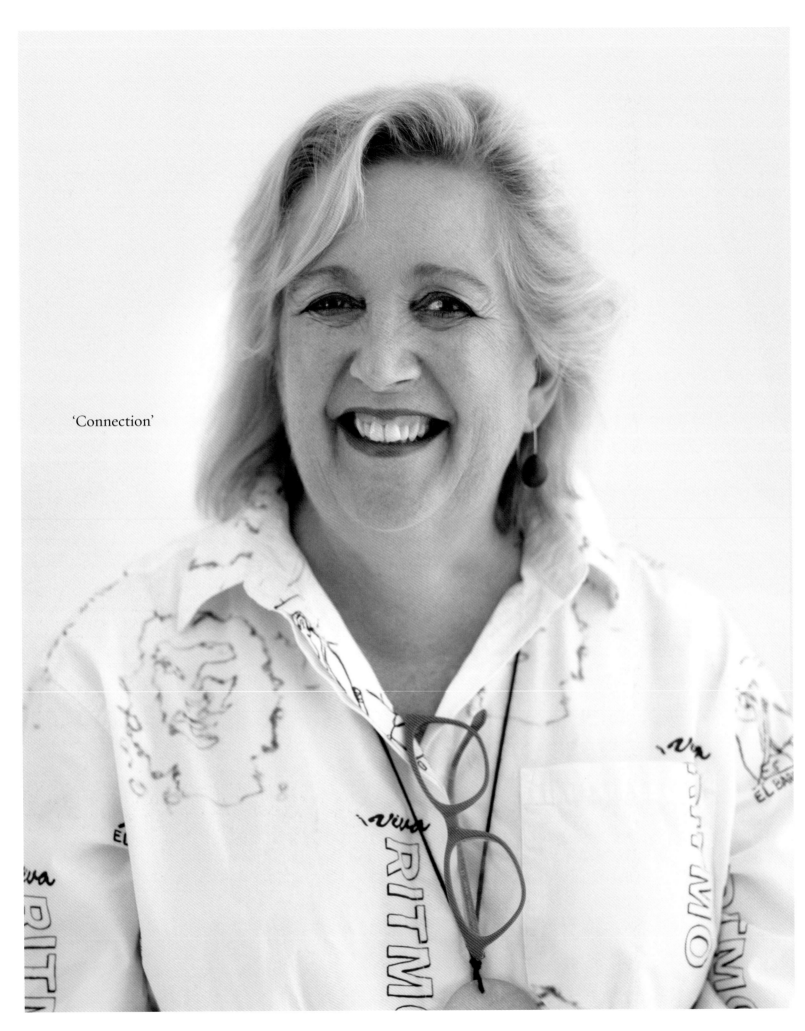

'Connection'

Jane
Caro

Jane Caro was born in London, England, and emigrated to Australia at the age of five. Caro graduated from Macquarie University with a bachelor of arts in 1977 and became an award-winning advertising copywriter. Now an author, social commentator, speaker and broadcaster, Caro appears regularly on Australian television, and has authored and co-authored eight books.

Q. What really matters to you?

I'm driven by the 'Why?' As a young woman, I struggled with an anxiety neurosis and with obsessive-compulsive disorder, so I went on a journey to understand what had led me to become so. Therapy helped me to learn about myself, which in turn helped me to learn about other people. So, I now always ask why. Why is a person reacting this way? Why do so many men regard women as objects or as something contemptible?

My work involves coming up with theories to answer all these 'whys,' then asking how the 'why' informs a person and their opinions. I can't prove my theories, but they make logical sense to me and I explore them. I am interested in finding answers that enlighten, in getting to the truthful, unvarnished core, where all pretence is lifted. Doing this allows you to accept yourself completely.

For my part, I'm as real as I can be. And I'm – I hate this word because it's become such a cliché, but I can't think of another one! – as authentic as I can be. I'm genuinely being myself, which means I have had to accept my weaknesses and my foibles – they are the pieces of me I have come to like best! In everything I need to make a decision about, I have a really, really simple philosophy; I examine whether it adds to the sum of human happiness. If so, I'll do it. If it's going to add to the sum of human misery, then it's probably better not to do it. That's as simple as it gets.

In my documentaries, I've branched out into social commentary. The theme is almost always the same: What is it to be human? What is it to be human in a long-lasting relationship? What is it to be human and have a child, or parent, of the opposite gender? What is it to be human and also be a teacher – how do colleagues, students, family and the teacher's life work together?

I'm a third-generation atheist, so, although I can see that religion is something that other people get very excited about, my curiosity lies – once again – in understanding what it is to be human. I regard religion a bit the way a non-American regards gridiron football – I can see that fans take it all very seriously, but I can't for the life of me see what the fuss is about. So, although for some people with religious faith it's about asking what it is to be a child of God, or to be spiritual, I ask: 'What is it to be the ape with the big brain?'

Feminism is a lifelong passion of mine, in part because it's about time we recognised that women are as fully human as men. Feminism is about putting a woman at the centre of her own life, rather than on the periphery of someone else's. But I don't think we're quite there yet – indeed, I wonder if we'll ever have perfect equality. But, although we may never reach nirvana, just because something has never happened before doesn't mean we should give up and allow existing inequalities to become greater – which some people do. My view is that maybe we can't solve every problem, but we do what we can to make those problems a little bit smaller; this adds to the sum of human happiness. And the more equal we can make things, the more people we can make happy.

The same goes for education, where I fight for equality of opportunity; I'm particularly passionate about public, universal, free, secular education that is open to all.

Q. What brings you happiness?

My happiness is getting to the end of a day in which I feel I've been productive and have done things that interest me, and sitting down with my husband and a glass of wine, connecting and talking about what we've both been doing.

It's playing with my grandson.

It's the ordinary, banal, human things that everybody gets an enormous amount of pleasure out of. I don't want to be anything other than ordinary, because there are such expectations around women – and expectations crucify people. Look at Hillary Clinton, people are always saying, 'Of course, she wasn't the perfect candidate.' But there has never *been* a perfect candidate, so why do we have to apologise for the woman not being perfect? Because the expectations are that, if a woman aspires, then she had better never have made a mistake or done a wrong thing. Expectations kill happiness, they kill joy and they kill courage.

Q. What do you regard as the lowest depth of misery?

Shame – it's very debilitating. Yes, some shame is necessary – we've all been in that place where we've done the wrong thing and we know it. But the sick feeling of shame is horrible. I think women have an almost constant experience of shame. We're made to feel ashamed of just being women. We're made to feel ashamed of our bodily functions. We're made to feel ashamed because we don't look the way we should, or because we look too much the way we should or because we talk too much, or too little. There is a constant measuring of how much women are allowed to do, to say, to be, to want and to aspire to. Fortunately, the older I get, the less shame I feel and the happier I become.

Q. What would you change if you could?

I would try to get rid of shame. In my view, every human being can be redeemed; it's important to condemn behaviour and opinion, but never the person who has behaved in a certain way or who has opined something foolish, or even hateful. For example, people will call certain politicians liars. But no one person is 'a liar' – we all tell lies. No one person is 'a sexist' – we are all sometimes sexist. No one person is 'a racist' – we are all sometimes prejudiced and bigoted. When you recognise this, suddenly it stops being 'us and them' and becomes just 'us.' It's that connection and 'us-ness' that I'm after.

Q. Which single word do you most identify with?

Connection.

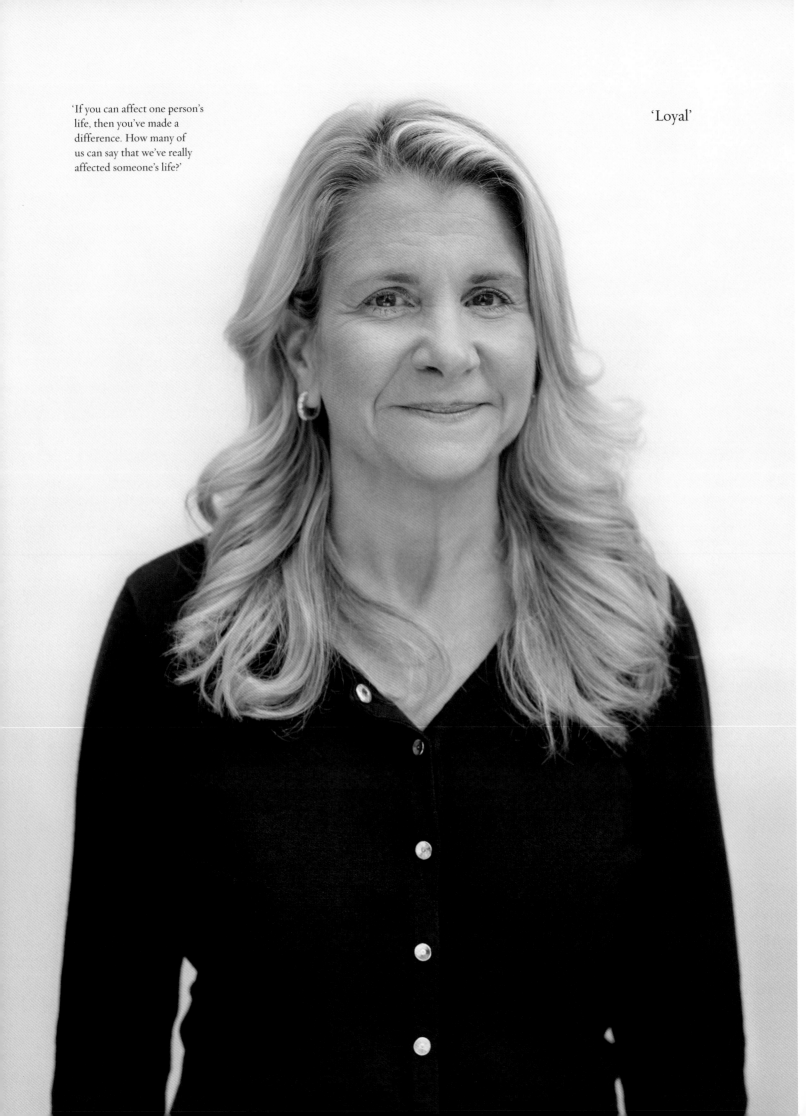

'If you can affect one person's life, then you've made a difference. How many of us can say that we've really affected someone's life?'

'Loyal'

Deana Puccio

———

Deana Puccio was born in Brooklyn in New York, USA. After becoming a lawyer, then prosecutor, she worked as assistant district attorney in the Kings County, Brooklyn, sex crimes and special victims unit. In 2001, Puccio moved to London where she taught US law. In 2012, Puccio co-founded The RAP Project to promote teenage sexual awareness, particularly in the digital landscape, and an understanding of the influence of porn and social media. Puccio is the co-author of *Sex, Likes and Social Media*, which was published in 2016.

Q. What really matters to you?

My advocacy work for young women and victims of sexual violence. New York in the seventies was not a safe place, so growing up I had this feeling of wanting to make a difference. I was lucky enough that God gave me a brain, that I had a supportive family and was able to go to decent schools. For me – as an individual and as a woman – I knew I'd been given a lot and I wanted to give something back. I became a lawyer because I wanted to become a prosecutor, specifically to work with victims of sexual assault. This has defined who I am and how I view the world vis-à-vis women and violence.

Most women I talk to have been subjected to some sort of sexual assault or harassment – or worse – some at a very early age. In my first job before law school, a senior male colleague asked me for something. When I told him I couldn't help he said, 'Well, if you don't do what I say I'm gonna undress you.' I laughed it off, but the next thing I knew his arm was around me as he unzipped my skirt. I was mortified. But when I went to my boss – a woman – she shooed me out of her office saying, 'Boys will be boys.' I knew then that, with all of my advantages, I had to do something to help women who didn't have the options I did.

When I was pregnant with my first daughter I was working on a case involving an impoverished family in Brooklyn. My victim was a sixteen-year-old girl who had been raped. She'd been manipulated and groomed by a guy who was much older. She ended up becoming pregnant from the encounter and decided to keep the child. The perpetrator took a plea because we would have his DNA. It was a relief, because trials can re-victimise the victim. And sometimes you go through a trial and the rapist gets off because of one juror with misogynistic, sexist views. One day,

after the conviction, I came back from court to find a gift at the front desk. The victim's mother had knitted me a baby blanket. For her to buy that wool, to find the money and to take the time and effort to knit that was worth more than any pay cheque, any fancy present or any expense account. Of all the baby gifts I've received – whether a Tiffany rattle or the like – the only gift I've kept and that will stay with me forever is that baby blanket, knitted for me twenty years ago by a woman in a housing project, because I helped find justice and peace for her and her daughter.

Doing things like that is what's important in life. If you can affect one person's life, then you've made a difference. How many of us can say that we've really affected someone's life? And if you can act locally, then the potential exists to make a difference globally.

I'm mother to three teenage daughters; worrying about their safety has been a hugely significant part of my life. Because of this, I started a sexual-awareness programme called The RAP Project with my friend Allison Havey. Its purpose is to educate young men and women about sex and sexuality. Professionally, it's one of the most important things I've done. It is so easy to make misogynistic comments, to participate in 'locker-room talk' or laugh at a rape joke. But we often tell young men that, if they are ever tempted to do so, they should first picture their mother, their sister or their grandmother being talked about in the same way. Their reaction is usually one of disgust. We then ask them to question why the woman they are objectifying deserves any less respect than those women in their lives do. As they acknowledge that all women are entitled to be treated with the same amount of respect and decency as their mothers, sisters and grandmothers, the process of change continues.

Q. What brings you happiness?

My three beautiful daughters. And my husband: I have a wonderful, loving partner of twenty-seven years. He is one of the most amazing people in the world and he's a proud feminist. He doesn't judge anyone. And helping young women – and now young men – makes me happy. I also love to cook; I'm Italian and Lebanese by ancestry, so to be feeding people across my kitchen table filled with family, love, friends and wine is my greatest sense of happiness.

My work has also made me very happy. When I made the decision to go to law school it was specifically to make a difference for women, so I feel extremely lucky to have been able to do that.

Q. What do you regard as the lowest depth of misery?

Having any of my children unhappy or ill. I want my daughters to be happy and confident. I want my daughters to have the confidence and self-esteem to reject society's warped standards – those societal pressures for girls to be perfect that have led to increases in eating disorders, suicide rates, self-harm and depression. I don't want my daughters to experience things I've experienced in my life – I don't want them to ride a train and be subjected to the sight of men masturbating in front of them. I want the world to be a better place for them than it was for me twenty-five years ago. But I don't think that's the case – I think the world's actually worse.

Q. What would you change if you could?

Injustice. I'd want to change economic injustice and gender injustice, to achieve an even playing field, where we treat everyone with dignity and respect, the way we actually want to be treated ourselves.

Q. Which single word do you most identify with?

Loyal.

Vidya Balan

Vidya Balan was born in Mumbai, India. She holds a bachelor's degree in sociology from St. Xavier's College, a master's degree in sociology from Bombay University (now University of Mumbai) and has passed the junior vocal examination in carnatic music at Karnataka University. Balan is an acclaimed actress in Indian cinema, whose work has been recognised with more than fifty awards, and who was on the 2013 Cannes Film Festival jury. Balan is an ambassador for the Indian government's sanitation programmes, and, in 2014, was awarded the Padma Shri Award by the Indian government.

Q. What really matters to you?

What really matters is being authentic to myself in every moment, and I would like to see every woman doing the same; we are all living by certain set standards – living to fulfil certain role obligations – and are always putting others before ourselves, but I want women to be empowered to feel, do and say whatever they wish, without pressure, fear of judgement or consequences.

In India, there is often discrimination between girls and boys, from the moment we are born. However, my sister and I were brought up in a very egalitarian atmosphere – perhaps because it was just us two girls. We were brought up to be very self-assured women. Our parents gave us the freedom to be who we wanted to be and to do what we wanted to do, and our home environment was very protective; in my parents' eyes, my sister and I were the most beautiful, the smartest and the brightest human beings.

It wasn't until I stepped out into the real world that I developed body issues. I was a very fat child, and, when I left my safe space, I came face to face with a lot of judgement that I had been kept away from – it's shocking that people are willing to use so many different parameters to judge a person by. But, when I came home, I felt secure; I didn't feel less than anyone else, than someone who was thinner or brighter – or who was a boy.

Nonetheless, I could see the difference between my family and my friends' families. I could see brothers being given more leeway than their sisters; the boys could go and get girlfriends, for instance, but the girls didn't dare. Those things bothered me a lot and informed my belief that women should not be prevented from living their lives on their own terms.

Q. What brings you happiness?

It makes me extremely happy to see anyone living their life on their own terms. In India, the social conditioning runs very deep and the family bond is very, very strong. At times we all limit ourselves because of the expectations our families have of us – we don't want to do anything that might topple the apple cart or overthrow the status quo.

There are parallel realities in India. Mumbai is the kind of city in which you can live your dreams. People come here from all over the country and fall in love with the place. In Mumbai, a girl can live her life on her own terms and with whomever she wants.

But in other parts of the country, people's struggles are very different; in a lot of small towns and villages, girls can't live their lives on their own terms. Because of a lack of resources, many families are faced with choosing which of their children to send to school. This means girls are discriminated against when their brothers are prioritised, but they cannot stand up to their fathers and speak their minds about wanting to go to school. And even when girls *are* sent to school, many drop out because there are no toilets for them to use; this remains a reality for so many girls, although our current government is doing a great job of addressing sanitation issues. I travel a lot in my work as an actor and as an ambassador for sanitation, and I'm happy to say that I see changes happening in these small towns and villages – girls are slowly gathering the courage to demand education as a right for all, rather than as privilege for the few. I also see a growing awareness that people have the right to live life on their own terms – this fills me with joy.

We are in a better place than we were ten years ago; many educated men believe themselves to be liberated and support their wives working, but I'll hear them say things like, 'She's doing so well; I've allowed her to succeed.' Excuse me? Who are you to allow anything? This is a clash between intent and conditioning, of course, but it's positive that men who are exposed to the issue of equality are part of the dialogue. It troubles me, however, that a lot of men are removed from these discussions. There are men who rape and there are men whose attitudes towards women are sometimes worse than rape. I see this a lot, and I find it very distressing.

Nonetheless, I see women in Mumbai becoming more outspoken about the issues facing them, whether that be body shaming, unfair judgement or crimes against women. It's incredible that women are saying, 'Shut up! You have no right to judge me, and, even if you think you do, I don't care, because I don't hear it!' As women, we are no one's property and our lives are ours. We can't be told what to do and are going to live our lives exactly the way we want: we will pursue our desired professions and will be single for the rest of our lives if we want to. It makes me very, very happy to see more and more women starting to feel that we are no less than those who would put us down – in fact, we are better than them.

Q. What do you regard as the lowest depth of misery?

The lack of empathy; the world has become so intolerant. When I look at the leaders being elected around the world, I see in them a reflection of the fact that we are moving backwards to a space of exclusivity. People don't want to open themselves up to others; there is a definite 'us' and 'them' in which you can see the lack of empathy. We don't have to agree on everything, but it shakes me to the core when people rule out the possibility of another's opinion.

Q. What would you change if you could?

I know it's slightly utopian, but I would love for everyone to be accepting of everyone else.

Q. Which single word do you most identify with?

Love.

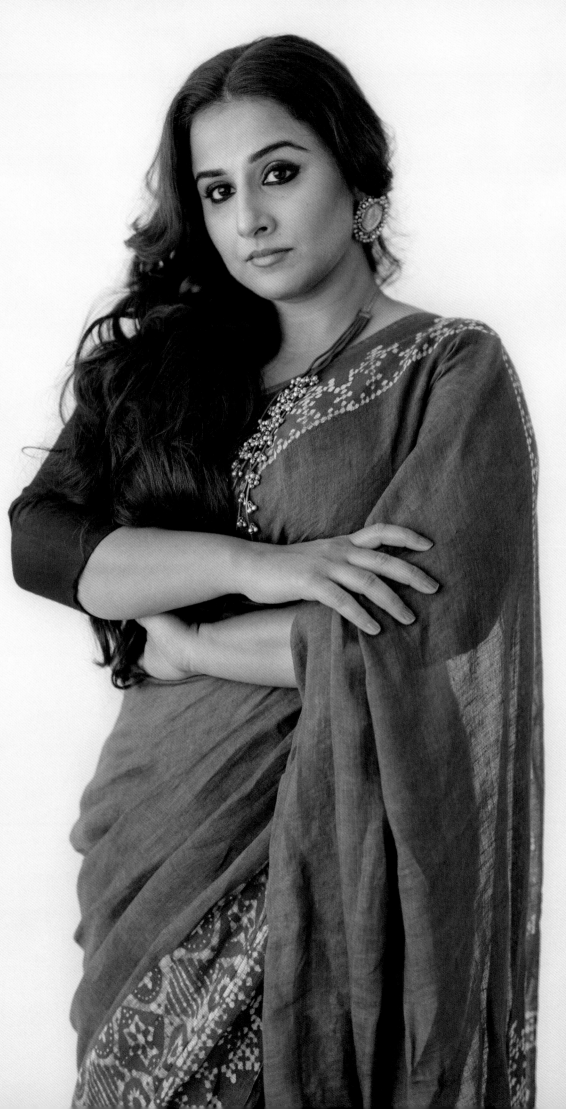

'Love'

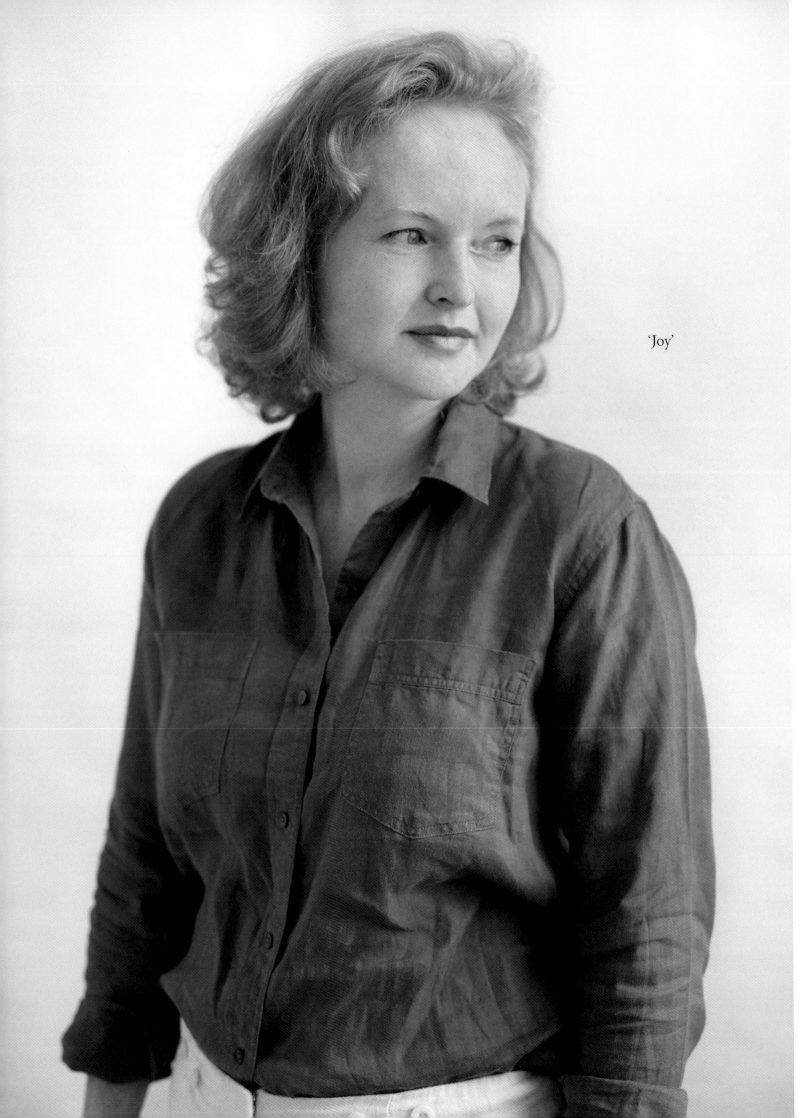

'Joy'

'When I was thirty-five, I had breast cancer, which was quite a gear-shift in my life. I'm one of the very lucky ones; I came out of it with more than I went in with. There is something very powerful about all the minutiae of life falling away.'

_ Emma Davies

Interview page 391

Nadia Remadna

Nadia Remadna was born in Créteil, France. She graduated as a special-education teaching graduate from the Institut Régional du Travail Social and is a social worker. In 2014, she founded The Mothers' Brigade, a grassroots organisation in the Paris suburb of Sevran that supports families, and that aims to save children from recruitment into lives of extremism, fundamentalism and crime. Remadna's 2016 memoir, *Comment j'ai sauvé mes enfants*, describes her experiences raising children in a suburb plagued by radicalisation.

Q. What really matters to you?

I am very passionate about, and motivated by, saving young people. Because, first and foremost, we are all human beings. And it is our duty to protect our children and young people.

I was born in Créteil, in the suburbs of Paris. When I was thirteen, my father took us to his remote Algerian village. Everybody there was a Remadna; it was like one tribe. There was no running water, and only the men were allowed to go out – all of the women stayed locked up at home. You can imagine the distress of a thirteen-year-old kid who – overnight – finds herself in the middle of nowhere, without friends or school; I had no other choice but to accept the situation and adapt.

Ten years later, though, I ran away from Algeria. It was the feast of Eid – a very important religious holiday for Muslims – and, for the first time, a praying area had been set aside in the mosque so that women could pray. I had spotted two taxis in the village, so I told my family I wanted to go to the mosque. They were delighted that I had decided to go to the mosque at last, even preparing a special meal; it was like I was getting married! In Algeria, although women didn't wear headscarves, then, they wore a small, white veil called the *haik*. I was adamant that I would go to the mosque only on one condition: that I didn't have to wear this veil. The family initially told me this was impossible, but, at last, they allowed it; they weren't happy about it, but they wanted me to go to the mosque. My aunt put a small headscarf in my bag and told me, 'You can go out without the haik, but, as soon as you get to the mosque, you have to put this on.' When we reached the mosque, there was a crowd of people so, instead of going inside, I got into one of the taxis across the road. The taxi driver had no idea what was going on; here was a young woman

he didn't know sitting in his taxi. I said, 'Take me to Algiers.' 'Algiers is far away,' he replied. So I said, 'The closest big city, then.' He agreed to take me to Sétif, in eastern Algeria. We set off, but all of a sudden we saw two cars behind us, trying to catch up. We were saved when a truck blocked the road behind us and we were able to leave.

I returned to France and studied social work; I graduated as a special-education teacher and worked as a mediator, representing women. Children being separated from their parents by force and placed in foster care was unthinkable to me, and I witnessed one scene that I'll never forget. I was helping a mother who had been the victim of domestic abuse; she had called the emergency hotline and found temporary housing, but, when she appeared before the judge, breastfeeding her child, the judge decided then and there that her children should be placed in foster care. A social worker went up to her and tore the baby from her breast – in front of the entire court. I didn't know what to do, and the scene really traumatised me: the mother was lying there on the floor, screaming; she didn't understand what was happening, because, after all, it was she who was appearing in court as a victim of domestic violence. When I tried to get to the bottom of what had happened, I found out that the hotel owner had alerted the authorities, claiming, 'Something is wrong: I hear a baby crying night after night.' It's true; the baby was sick, and all sick babies cry and scream. The hotel owner had accused the mother of negligence because, when he had knocked on the door, the mother hadn't answered. She had fallen asleep, exhausted.

There were many more stories like this, and they are why I founded The Mothers' Brigade. The association allowed me to push aside institutional violence and

barriers, so as to provide a solidarity chain of help and follow-up for families, and to give me the freedom to help people at midnight, not just during office hours. I've never met a negligent mother; I've met mothers who are exhausted and tired, but they aren't negligent. And I've never met a mother who wants her child to become a delinquent. It breaks my heart that sixteen-year-old youths are sent to prison for some petty crime; I've seen those prisons, and they are appalling. There isn't much talk about this in France, but it's a very serious issue. When all is said and done, it's always the little guys who get caught. I'm worried that, if we don't all start working together – regardless of religion, nationality, race or social status – later on these young people and kids are going to say, 'What did you ever do for us?'

Q. What brings you happiness?

When I leave the court with a mother who hugs me and says, 'Thank you, you've been so kind,' this is worth all the riches in the world.

Q. What do you regard as the lowest depth of misery?

I'm saddened by all of these young people who have no dreams or hope, young people who are filled with hatred of France and of people from different backgrounds, young people who prefer to have their brains blown out in Syria or elsewhere. I can't help wondering, 'What have we passed on? Where did we go wrong? And what could have been done about it?'

Q. What would you change if you could?

I'd make it mandatory that children – no matter how old and no matter where they live – aspire to good results. We need to aspire to creating higher standards, to raising the bar instead of lowering it.

Q. Which single word do you most identify with?

Equality.

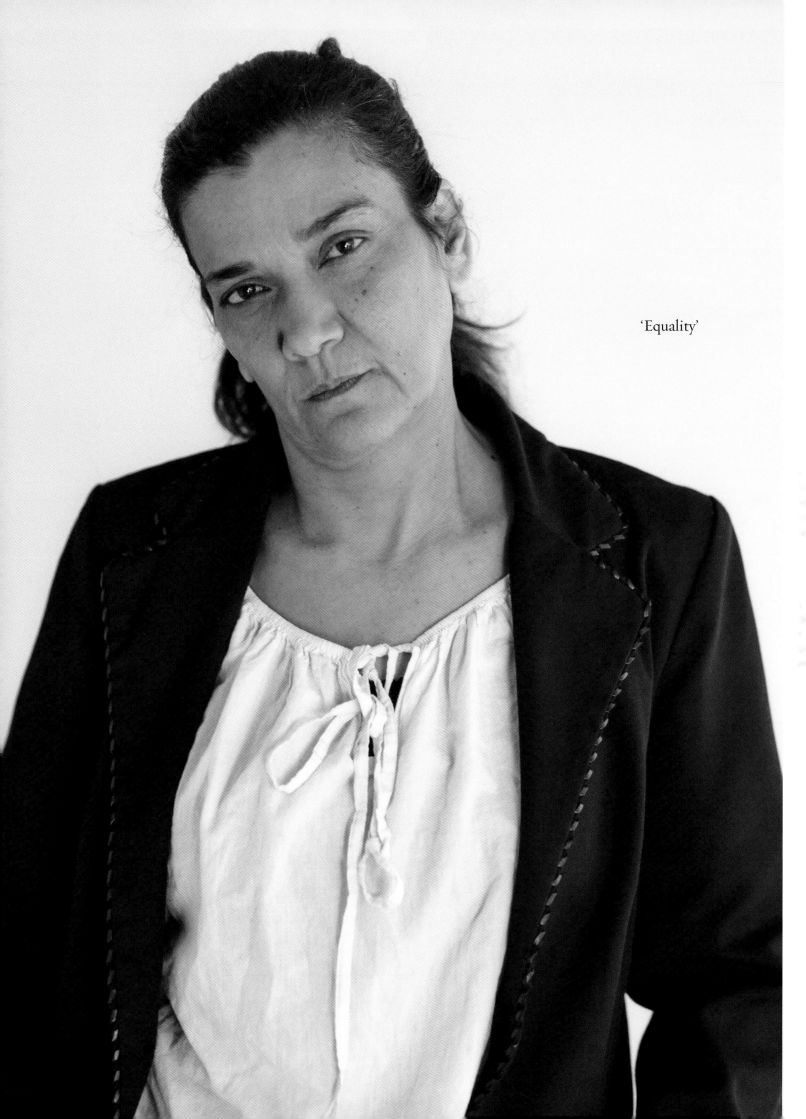

'Equality'

'Fear is the dominant ideology that divides and conquers. It is manipulated to make us hate and leave others out of our progress.'

_ Lisa VeneKlasen

Interview page 391

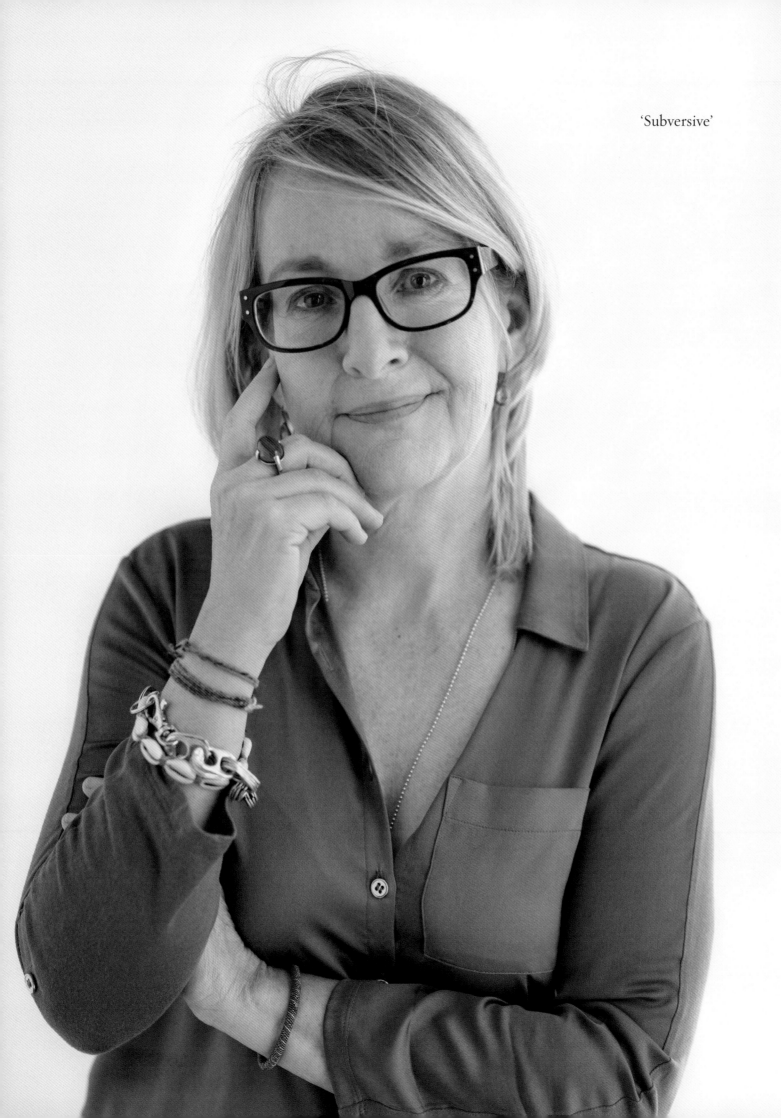

'Subversive'

'Courage!'

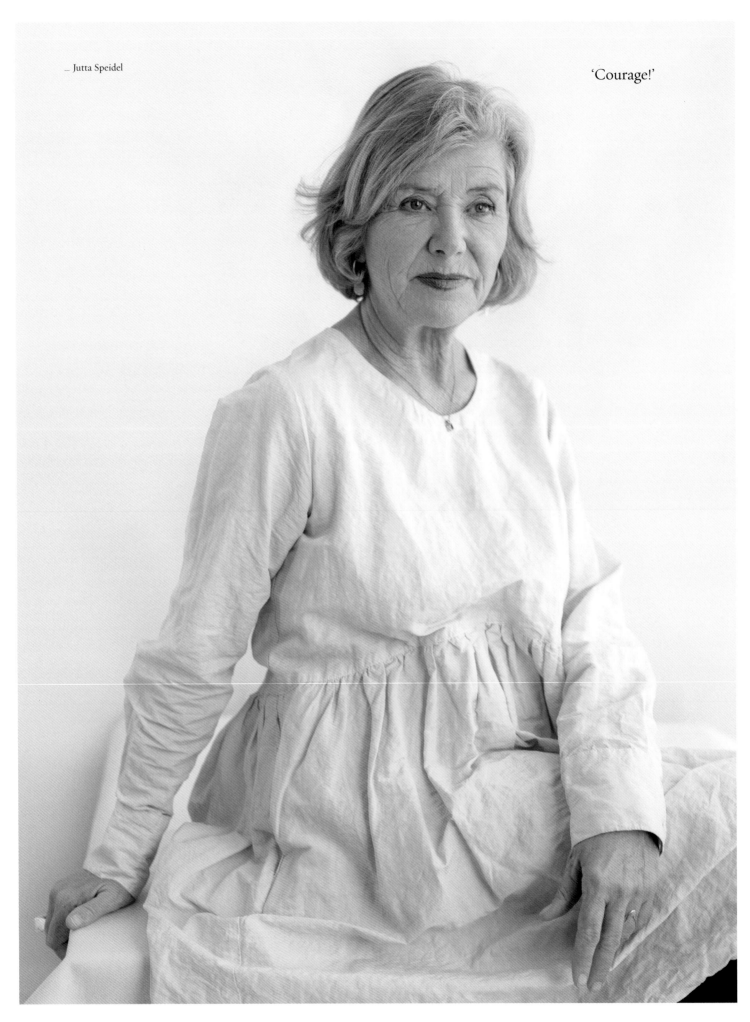

Interview page 391

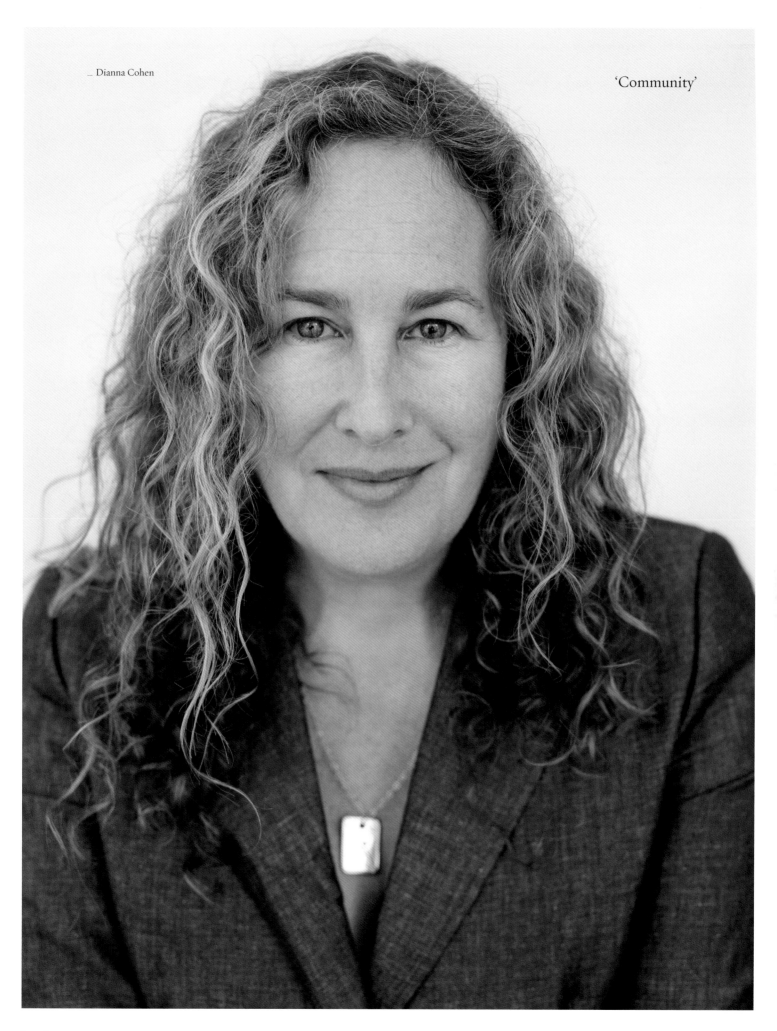

_ Dianna Cohen

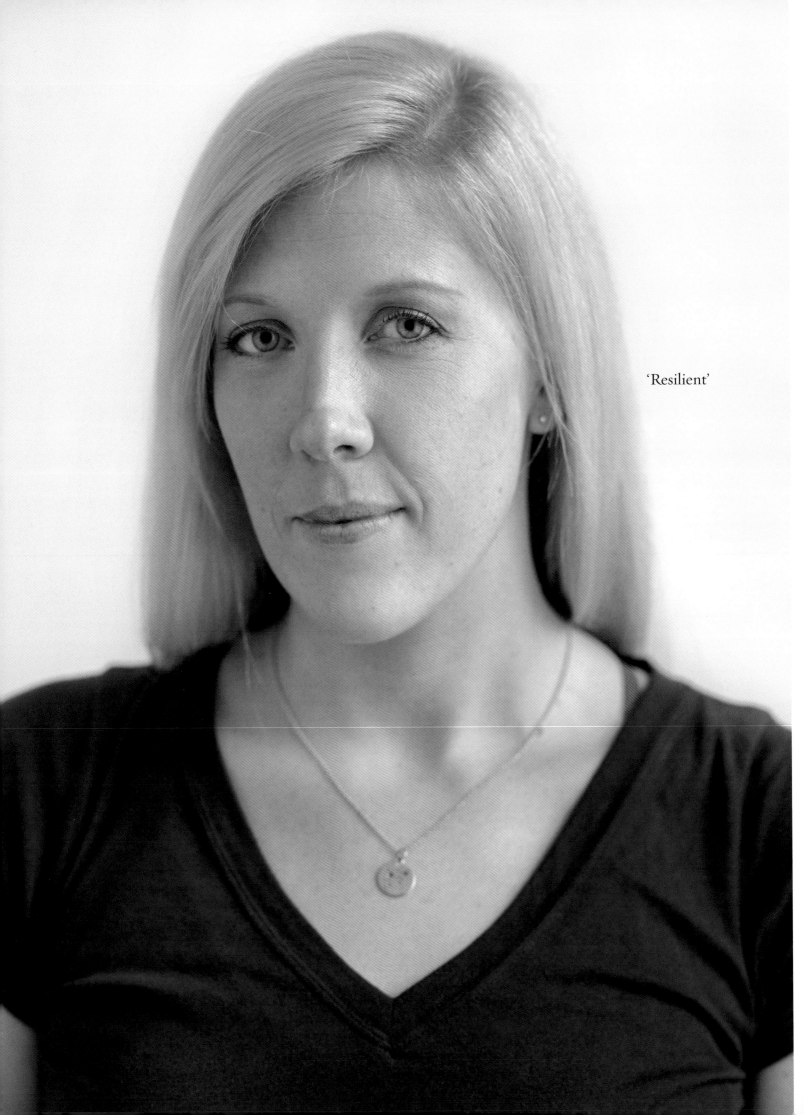

'Resilient'

Holly Bird

Holly Bird was born in Rochford in Essex, England. She attended Elam School of Fine Arts at the University of Auckland, New Zealand, before becoming a communicator in the New Zealand Police in 2009. Following her return to the United Kingdom, Bird became a member of the UK Police Service in 2013. Also a martial artist, Bird became a British kickboxing champion at the World Fight Sport and Martial Arts Council Championships in 2016. She holds a black belt in Shotokan karate, and is a qualified instructor.

Q. What really matters to you?

Making a difference matters to me. I want to affect peoples' lives by representing the police in a good light and giving them a good experience – providing reassurance to the victim of a crime can make a real difference.

My whole family – brother, cousin, uncle, mum, dad, partner – are police officers. Mum joined when she was really young and was one of the first women to drive a prisoner van. But, I never wanted to become a police officer – I wanted to go to art school. However, as I was working through my art degree, I realised that I *did* want to be a police officer as well.

As a woman in the police force, you get treated like a little sister and you know the guys will help you out if there is anything you struggle with. Similarly, you help them out; at the words 'sexual offence,' the guys run a mile. Yes, males can deal with that job, but they don't want to do it because it makes them uncomfortable and a lot of victims would prefer a female officer.

Women and men definitely deal with jobs differently, and there are differences in the responses we get as well. If there is a big brawl going on and you send in two big guys, the fight tends to kick off more – because all the lads are squaring up. But, if you send in two five-foot-two women, they are going to talk and bring the whole crowd down, as opposed to riling them up. I think the different approaches are a good thing; the guys on my team listen to my opinion and I listen to theirs.

There are no limits in the United Kingdom. As long as you can pass all the fitness tests, if you want to be a specialist officer, you can be. This is really empowering. In the country I live in, it is entirely possible to set a goal and achieve it. I don't have children, but, if I had daughters, I would want them to see that the opportunities are there for women to choose to thrive in a male-dominated environment, both professionally and physically. Yes, we might get some funny looks at times, but if we want to do it, we can do it.

Public services are a really easy target when the government needs to save money. We police officers, paramedics and firefighters do our jobs because we want to help people, so, even if our resources are stretched, we will stretch ourselves in order to meet the demands. If we're working on a job when someone else is injured or needs help, we're not going to say, 'I need to finish this job first – send someone else.' Because there is no one else. We'll say, 'I'll help that person and work overtime to finish this later.' This is what we do.

Q. What brings you happiness?

Setting myself a target and going for it, and helping other people to set targets and go for them, are definitely the happiest things for me. Making your list and ticking things off as you go is very cathartic.

Q. What do you regard as the lowest depth of misery?

I see people who are suffering from ill mental health on a daily basis, and we just don't have the resources to deal with this. This is one of the most painful things to witness. Very recently, I encountered a twenty-six-year-old girl who had taken her life. In my work, I go into houses that are disgusting, where the situations are horrible and people have been suffering from alcoholism or drug abuse for years and years. But this girl just baffled me, because she was young and she was probably one of the most beautiful people I've ever seen. She looked like a doll. In excess of twenty family members arrived at the front of the house. She appeared to have everything to live for, but she had got to that point in her life where she saw no other way out. It scares me to think how far gone she must have been, yet no one noticed.

Q. What would you change if you could?

I just don't get why people think they can justify certain types of behaviour. So, I would change the dishonesty and the unwillingness to question that lead to those behaviours. I can't get my head around people who think their cause is worth killing innocent people for. It all stems from how children just accept what is presented to them. They are told, 'Your religion is better than anyone else's and your way of doing things is better than everyone else's.' If we were teaching our kids to challenge those views, then everyone would get along better.

It sounds ridiculous, but, if we had an alien invasion, we would become Team Earth. Instead of countries and religions fighting each other, we would come together and say, 'Right: we are the human race and we are going to fight the aliens now!' It would be lovely if people could take a step back from whatever they think their cause is to remember that we are all one: one person, one planet.

Q. Which single word do you most identify with?

Resilient. There is a proverb a lot of people have shared with me over the past few years that goes, 'Fall down seven times, get up eight.'

Angela
Davis

————

Angela Davis was born in Birmingham, Alabama, USA. She holds a bachelor of arts degree from Brandeis University in Massachusetts, and a PhD in philosophy from Humboldt University of Berlin. Her work as an educator has always emphasised the importance of building communities of struggle for economic, racial, and gender justice. She is the author of ten books, including *Are Prisons Obsolete?* and *Freedom is a Constant Struggle: Ferguson, Palestine and the Foundations of a Movement.* She is a distinguished professor emerita of history of consciousness and feminist studies at the University of California, Santa Cruz.

Q. What really matters to you?

The same things that have always been important to me: justice and equality, and opposition to capitalism. I have been active in campaigns that are designed to emphasise the importance of equality among human beings, whether this be racial, gender, political or economic equality. There is no hierarchy of problems, rather, they are all interwoven, intersecting and interrelated.

My mother was a political activist and she was a very powerful influence in my early life. When I was eleven, I was involved in an interracial discussion group in our church; the building was subsequently burned down because white and black children were engaging in discourse with one another. I left Birmingham when I was fifteen years old, to finish high school in New York City. My school was very progressive; many of the teachers had been blacklisted in the public-school system, so I was exposed to Marx and Freud. I went on to study philosophy under Herbert Marcuse and came to subscribe to his view on critical theory. All of these experiences formed the person I have become.

Beyond this, I would say that the major influences in my life have been movements – movements of vast numbers of people. What started out as the freedom movement – now better known as the civil rights movement – is associated mainly with figures like Martin Luther King Jr. and Rosa Parks, but I was also very much influenced by the rank-and-file participants of that movement. I knew the four young girls who were killed in the 16th Street Baptist Church bombing, in September 1963, and that was a major turning point in my life. I became a member of Advance, which was affiliated with the communist party, of which I then also became a member. And I became active in the Black Panther Party. This has all been in aid of justice and equality.

Recently, I have focussed on issues that emanate from the vast numbers of people who have been imprisoned in the United States, by what we call the prison-industrial complex; twenty-five per cent

of the world's prison population and a third of the world's female prisoners are imprisoned in the United States. This is the work I am most passionate about today. I've been thinking about this process of imprisonment for a very long time – in 1970, I myself was arrested and spent some eighteen months in jail and on trial. I have learned to see this movement as an intersectional one, because it is very much related to struggles for equality and education, certainly to the campaigns to end racism and sexism. I have come to the conclusion – together with the many comrades, friends and others who have worked around this issue – that it really can't be fixed. There is no way to reform the prison system. How sad this is, when the very history of the prison system is a reformative one; the concept of prison was introduced as a humane alternative to existing forms of punishment, which were corporal and included the death penalty. So, we now say that the prison system must be abolished. Abolitionists argue that – as opposed to assuming that you can create a more effective penal system – you should ask a different question: What does society have to look like in order for it not to have to depend so heavily on imprisonment, policing and other forms of security that are grounded in violence? The answer is that we need to be focussing more on free education and on free healthcare – including free mental healthcare. In the United States, the three largest mental institutions are jails in New York, Chicago and Los Angeles. We say, don't fix the system, fix society, so that we are not so dependent on putting people away and using modes of violence. My views on this are very much informed by my belief that, in order to achieve any of the major goals of social justice, capitalism has to be the target of our analysis. And that, eventually, this system will have to be dismantled.

My views on feminism – the anti-racist feminism with which I identify – are integrated with my socialist outlook. Mine is a Marxist-inflected feminism that calls for social justice for everyone and requires us to think about the interconnectedness of all our social justice struggles. There

can be no end to racism unless we simultaneously envision an end to sexism, as well as an end to the pollution of the planet. The struggles of black people are interconnected with the struggles of Indigenous Peoples and the struggles of Muslims, as Islamophobia is very much linked to racism as it is evolving today. Feminism provides us with the tools to understand the interconnectedness of these issues and struggles.

I am interested in emphasising the need to make our work international, particularly here in the United States where even progressive leadership emphasises American exceptionalism and represents the United States as the centre of the world. I spend a lot of time in Australia and am affiliated with an organisation there called Sisters Inside; I have learned a great deal from that experience – especially from Aboriginal people – so, I would like to see us exercise more humility and be aware that we have so much to learn from people all over the world.

Q. What brings you happiness?

It is seeing that people are capable of coming together across the borders and lines of division that are designed to keep us apart – I am most filled with happiness when the prospect of bringing people together is fulfilled.

Q. What do you regard as the lowest depth of misery?

Donald Trump. I would never argue that history is inevitably progressive, because often we experience setbacks, but now we have someone in an elected office who assumes it is possible to return to a period before we made strides towards ending racism and many other evils. It makes me sad and very angry.

Q. What would you change if you could?

I would end capitalism. Wealth should not be concentrated in the hands of the few, rather, it should be social wealth; and education has become commoditised, to the point that the cost of so many institutions – even public ones – is prohibitive.

Q. Which single word do you most identify with?

Justice. Justice for all, that is indivisible.

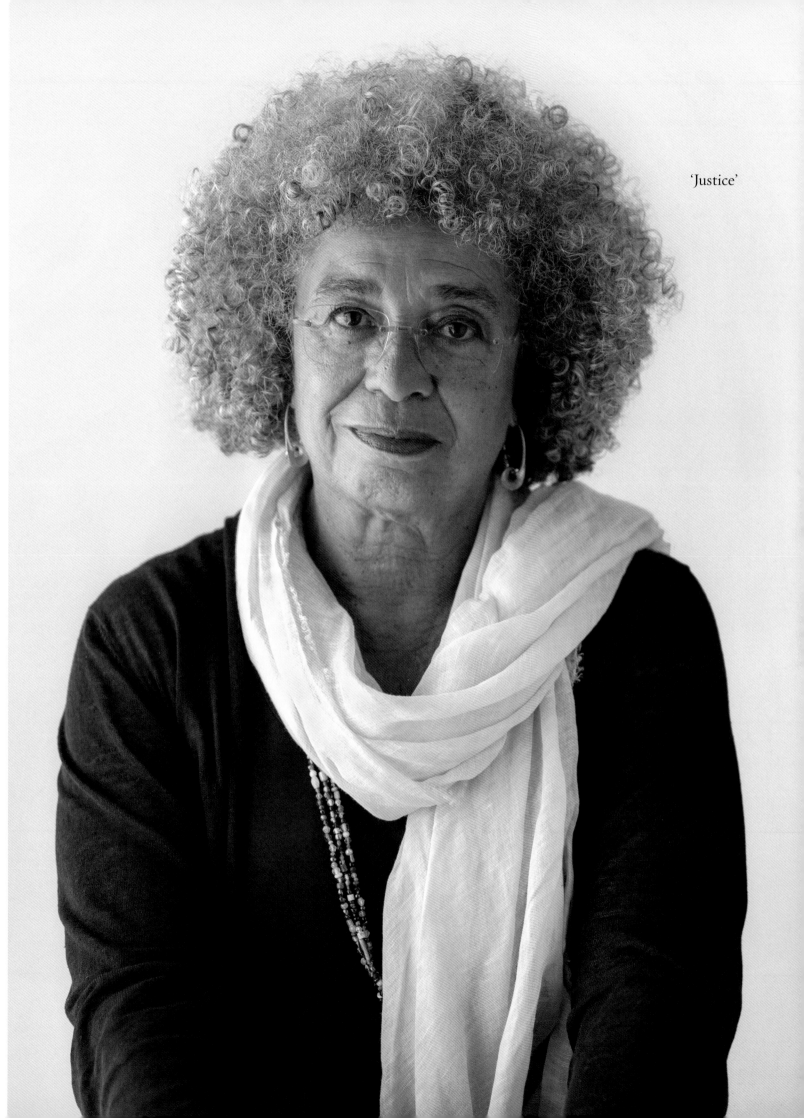

'Justice'

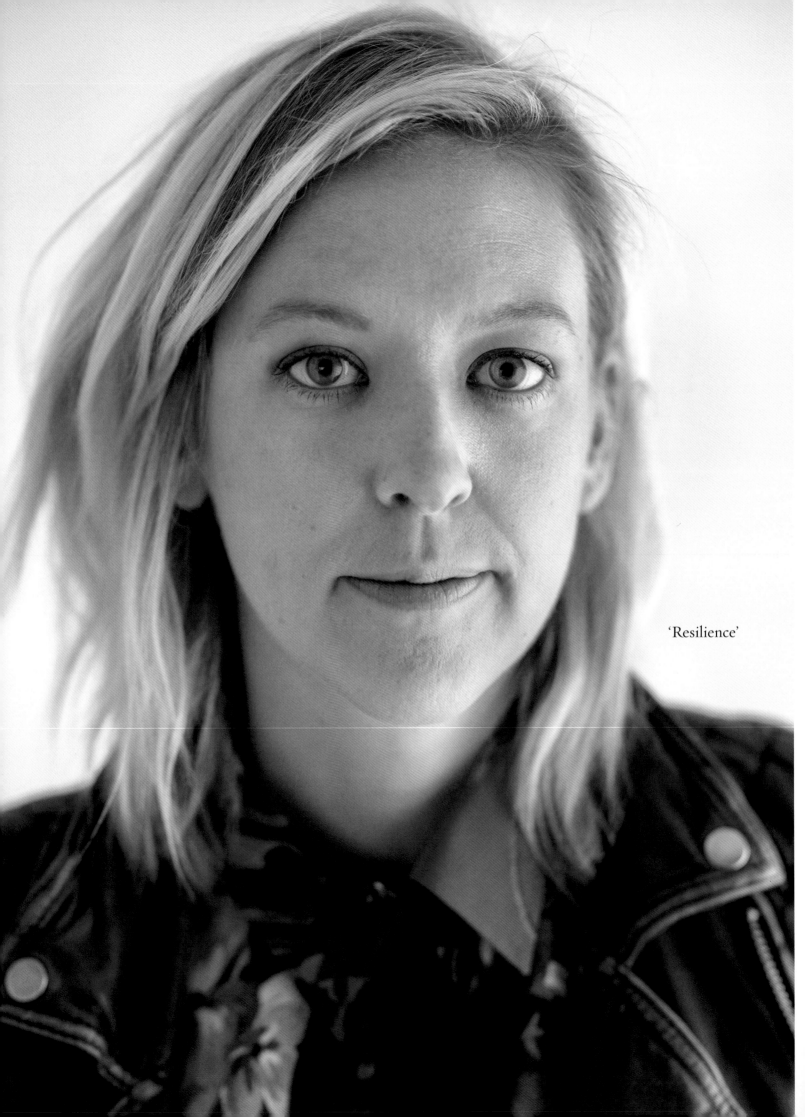

'Resilience'

Amy Stroup

Amy Stroup was born in Boston in Massachusetts, and grew up in Abilene in Texas, USA. She holds a bachelor's degree in business administration and marketing from Lipscomb University in Nashville, Tennessee. A singer-songwriter, Stroup has released three solo albums: *Chasing Greenlights*, *The Other Side of Love* and *Tunnel*, and has had more than one hundred of her songs feature in television shows and commercials, and films. In 2010, she co-founded Milkglass Creative, an independent identity and brand development studio.

Q. What really matters to you?

Wholeness. We can only appreciate the extent to which what we do affects others if we take an holistic approach to our own lives. I need to make sure that I'm centred and aligned – spiritually and physically – in order to usher the most health and love into the world that I can. I believe that many of the awful, macro problems we face in the world are created by human beings who aren't introspecting. They aren't asking themselves, 'How are the ripples of my actions affecting, or contributing to, what is happening?'

Music has a lot to do with being able to introspect, so, music matters to me. The places I grew up were all music cities: Memphis in Tennessee, Florence in Alabama and Abilene in Texas. We moved around a lot because of my father's work – he was a Christian minister. We always lived a little outside the city on acres of land – we never lived in the suburbs – so we had a lot of time to fill and we made our own fun. My mother was a librarian and there was always a lot of literature at home, but I also had a lot of time to write songs.

I wanted to be a songwriter for a long time, so, after high school, I decided to move to Nashville. Music was all around me and I knew how to write songs, but I had no idea what to do with the songs or how to reach people with them. So, I did a business degree in marketing and, in 2010, I started a company called Milkglass Creative with my friend Mary Hooper. We base our business on a value rather than on the bottom line; our value is taken from a Madeleine L'Engle quote that goes something like, 'You can either add cosmos to the chaos or chaos to the cosmos.' It means that we ask whether or not everything we do is adding loveliness, order or beauty to the world – it's a mantra that has filtered down into my outlook on life, generally. I want to add beauty and be able to highlight certain truths to the world, as opposed to just adding more noise. This is certainly something my music is imbued with. When I'm writing, I'm always looking for that 'Aha!' moment, when I realise that what I'm writing is worth being said; if I can see that it may have a negative effect, I know I have to think about it and shape it a little more before I reveal it. One of the main reasons I write music is that I hope that my songs will speak truthfully to someone's experiences and inspire them. I believe that a beautiful musical tone can create a positive effect. Yes, sometimes I'll write something that will affect someone in a way I never could have anticipated, but that's okay – I'm comfortable that, if my intentions in creating are positive, then the ripples of that will eclipse the negativity of someone's lived experience.

Q. What brings you happiness?

One of my favourite subjects in high school was humanities. One day, our teacher walked in and wrote, 'What's the difference between happiness and joy?' on the board. I was gripped by a stream of consciousness and wrote that happiness is the cheapest emotion, because it's like weather to me – there are several minutes of sunshine, then cloud eclipses the warmth and it's freezing. That's happiness – it's never constant. Joy, on the other hand, feels far more sustainable; joy is not fleeting and it's something I find in the simplest things. It brings me joy to see a man respecting a woman, to enjoy a good dinner or to see someone do something excellent. Those little things are moments of happiness, too, but I think joy is the emotion that you can actually *experience*. It's transcendent and creates the narrative you need when you receive the worst news – a narrative that tells you you'll still be all right, even when you feel you won't be.

Q. What do you regard as the lowest depth of misery?

Disconnection. Relationships are fundamentally important to the human experience, so I see misery in people disconnected from their loved ones, their communities or their spirituality. More than anything, though, I think misery comes from a disconnection with self, from feeling as though you're living a life that is not true to your self.

Q. What would you change if you could?

I would ensure that the person with everything is treated the same as the person with nothing. This means seeing the divine humanity in each human being and treating each person with dignity. If we could all do that, it would invoke much change in our culture and in our world. I remember once going along with my dad to sell our house; one of the richest men in Florence, Alabama, was buying it and was paying cash. This blew my mind as a kid; I thought, 'What guy has cash to buy a house?' We went up to this man's office, at the top of the tallest building in Florence. My dad was really kind to the man when we got the cheque; then, when we went down in the elevator and out onto the street, we came across a man who was obviously homeless – in a cardboard-box situation. My Dad said, 'Hey, Randy!' The man lit up and said, 'Hey, Jessie!' My dad shook that man's hand in the same way that he had just shaken the richest man in Florence's hand. I remember going 'Huh, that's how it's supposed to be.' I believe that, if I can treat a man of wealth the same as I treat someone with literally nothing, then that can make a huge difference in the world. One of the hardest things to do is see the dignity and the human divine in everyone, but if we could do that – if we could all look at each other with the same dignity and respect – it would change so much.

Q. Which single word do you most identify with?

Resilience.

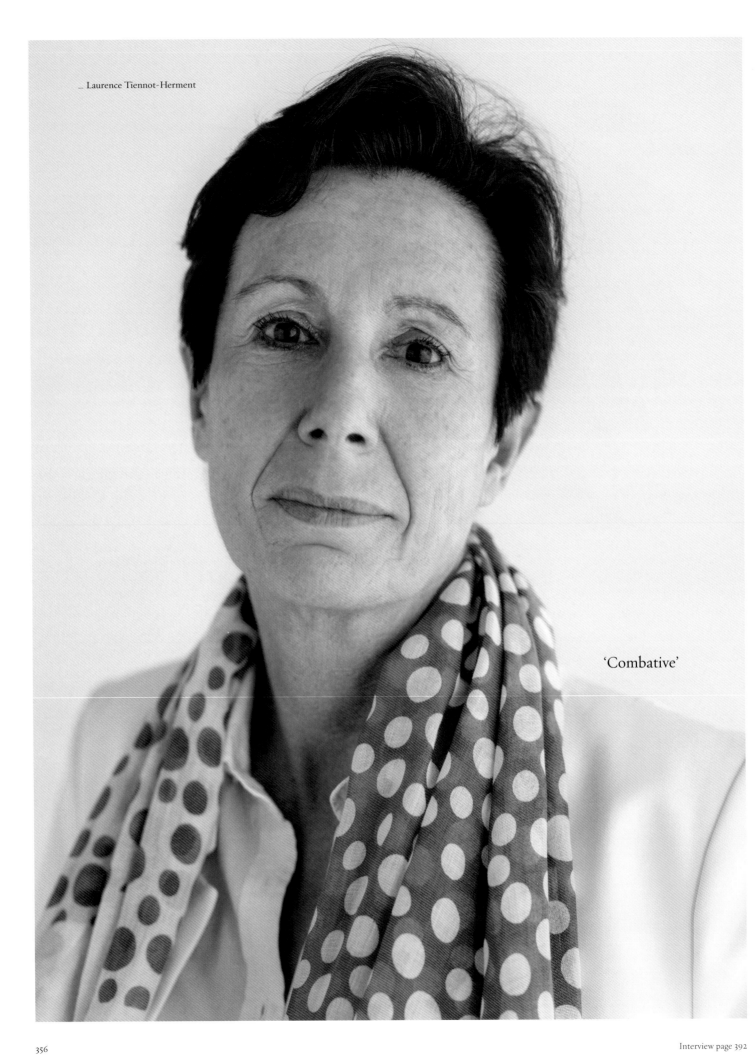

_ Laurence Tiennot-Herment

'Combative'

Interview page 392

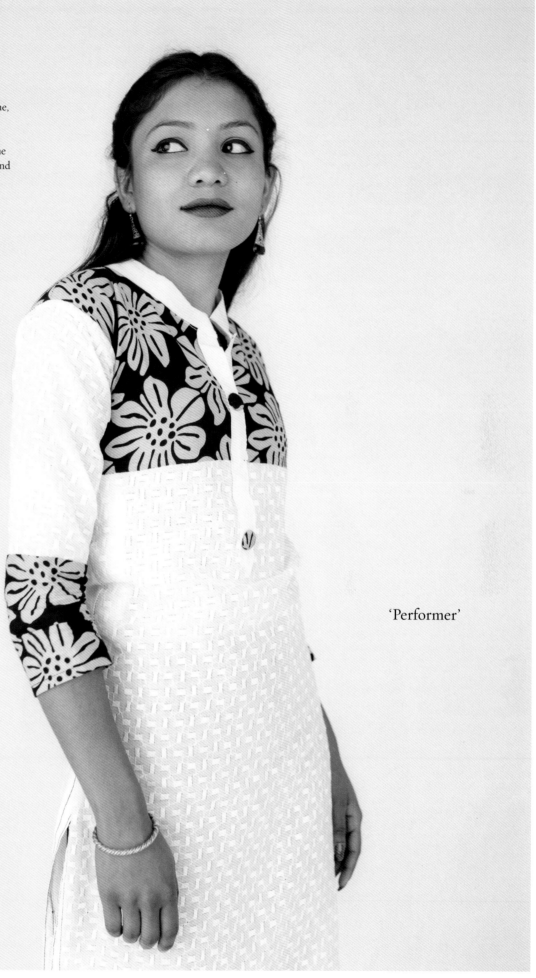

'Trust is difficult for me personally; when I was seven years old, I was sent to Kathmandu by my parents to study and to look after my grandmother. It was a sad time, but my grandmother showed me love – she is the most beautiful person and kind. She paid for me to go to school, and now I support her.'

_ Sapana Thapa

'Performer'

Interview page 392

Maria Shriver

Maria Shriver was born in Chicago in Illinois, USA. She is a mother, producer, a Peabody and Emmy Award–winning journalist and a *New York Times* bestselling author. She is the founder of Shriver Media. As California's first lady from 2003 to 2010, Shriver advocated for women, the working poor, military families and the disabled. In 2009, Shriver launched The Shriver Report, a non-partisan initiative that raises awareness around the issues women and their families face. Shriver is also a leading Alzheimer's advocate, and the founder of the Women's Alzheimer's Movement; in 2017, Shriver was awarded the Alzheimer's Association's lifetime achievement award.

Q. What really matters to you?

The most influential person in my life was my mother and the most influential person in my mother's life was *her* mother. The role of mother is the most important role I have – it completely outweighs my professional life. I am the mother of both young women and young men, and I want them to be raised the same way. I want them to experience, then pay forward, love and compassion for humanity – equally. My passion in life is humanity; within that is the understanding that women and men must be recognised as equals. But, women cannot be empowered at the expense of men, just as men cannot exist without empowered women. My goal is to empower all those who are disempowered, so that we can all be speaking the same language. Even though our brains are very different, we all have the same souls and the same hearts, and we all want the same things.

This equality is something I want all my children to feel very strongly.

Beyond my children, my family and my friends, it is my faith and my work that define me. Becoming a journalist was a natural fit for me, because I approach the world with tremendous curiosity. I'm fascinated by people and their stories – by how they got to where they are and by what they had to endure along the way. I'm constantly trying to find a story in everyone's life.

I am also passionate about working to find a cure for Alzheimer's disease. When my father was diagnosed with it, I had to watch the smartest human being I had ever met lose their mind, in real time. That experience made me incredibly curious about what goes on in the brain and about how Alzheimer's can affect such a finely tuned instrument, to the point that the sufferer no longer knows the function of a fork. So, I started teaching myself about Alzheimer's. Like everyone else I

talk to about the statistics, I was shocked and curious to discover that women are far more susceptible to the disease than men. I decided that I could be someone who sounds the alarm, who lets women know they are at risk and galvanises people, internationally, to find a cure. It has become my mission to get women to think about this and to empower their minds, with a view to saving them. I hope this will, in turn, empower their entire lives. When women put their minds to anything, the possibilities are endless, so I believe women *can* be galvanised to save others and themselves from losing their minds. My passion has always been to empower women – emotionally, physically, mentally, spiritually and financially – and so it really does feel like all my work has led me to this moment; Alzheimer's disease impacts all those areas of both a woman's life and of the life of her family, because women are at the centre of their families.

I believe that every person is inherently good and has the ability to foster change, inspire change and create change. This starts with the self; I believe that change starts within and ripples out from there. It's very easy to look around and decide that there are no good people, but, if you open your eyes and your perspective, all of a sudden you'll find them. You may have decided that someone is terrible, but, given the opportunity, that person may prove you wrong. When we open our minds, we are finally confronted by truths that force us to re-evaluate our beliefs.

It's easy to scare people and divide them, but it takes a true hero to talk about peace. We need examples of good, evolved and awakened leadership, in every country in the world. Of course, we want more women in leadership roles, but there are many progressive male leaders who are also true examples of compassion and empathy. Pope Francis talks about a revolution of tenderness – messages like

that can bring about incredible change and can inspire millions of people.

Q. What brings you happiness?

My children bring me tremendous happiness, as do my friends and being in nature. And the simple things; chips and guacamole make me happy. Beyond this, seeing other people happy and witnessing acts of kindness – the actions of those trying to make the world a better place – makes me happy; I'm always reminding myself to direct my gaze towards the good, and away from the negative, evil, divisive and cruel.

Q. What do you regard as the lowest depth of misery?

Loneliness and feeling disconnected from what's going on around you. It's miserable to not feel that you are making a meaningful contribution; I have great empathy for those who grow old and feel they are not needed by society or that they've been alienated from their families.

Q. What would you change if you could?

With my magic wand, I would create the cure for Alzheimer's, so that people could be as physically healthy and mentally strong as possible, for as long as possible.

And I would try to promote peace instead of fear, kindness instead of cruelty and compassion instead of power. There seems to be a lot of violence and anger in the world right now – I know that's been the case forever, but it feels more pronounced now. Maybe we're just more aware of it, but it definitely feels like it's encroaching on our mental and spiritual space a lot more. I'd also ask the media to report more on all the good that *is* being done, rather than on repeating the same old negativity that seems to sell.

Q. Which single word do you most identify with?

Love.

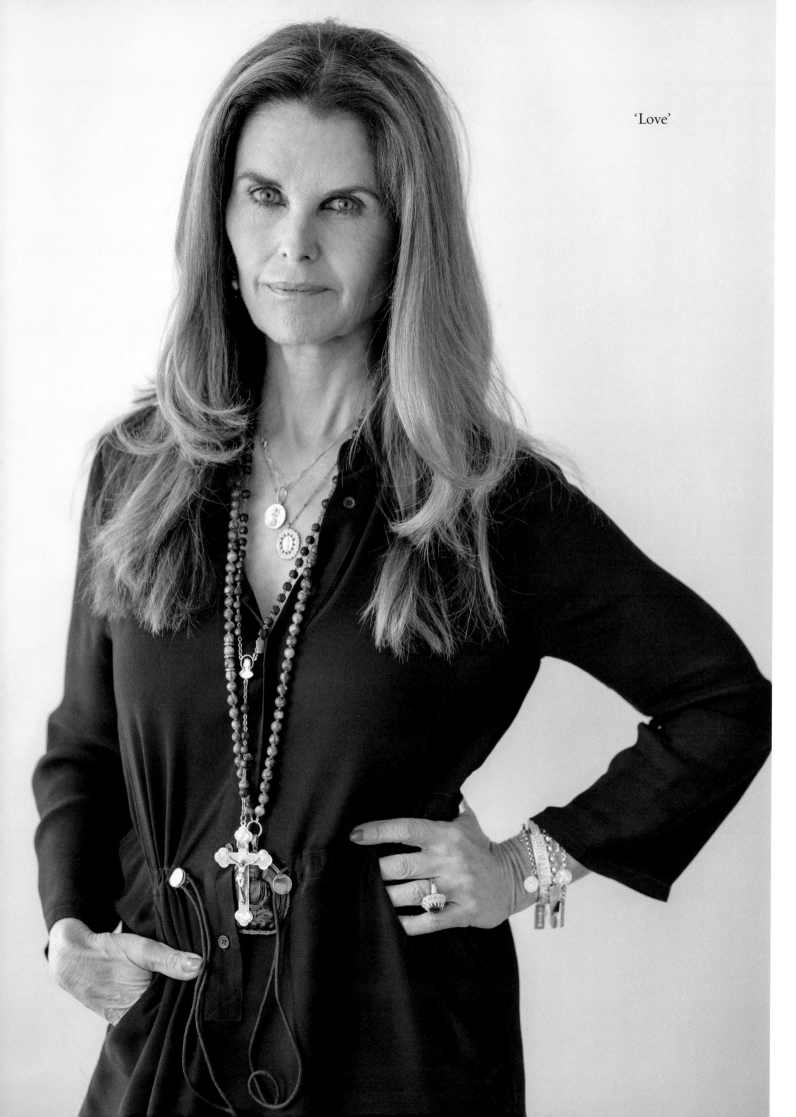

'Love'

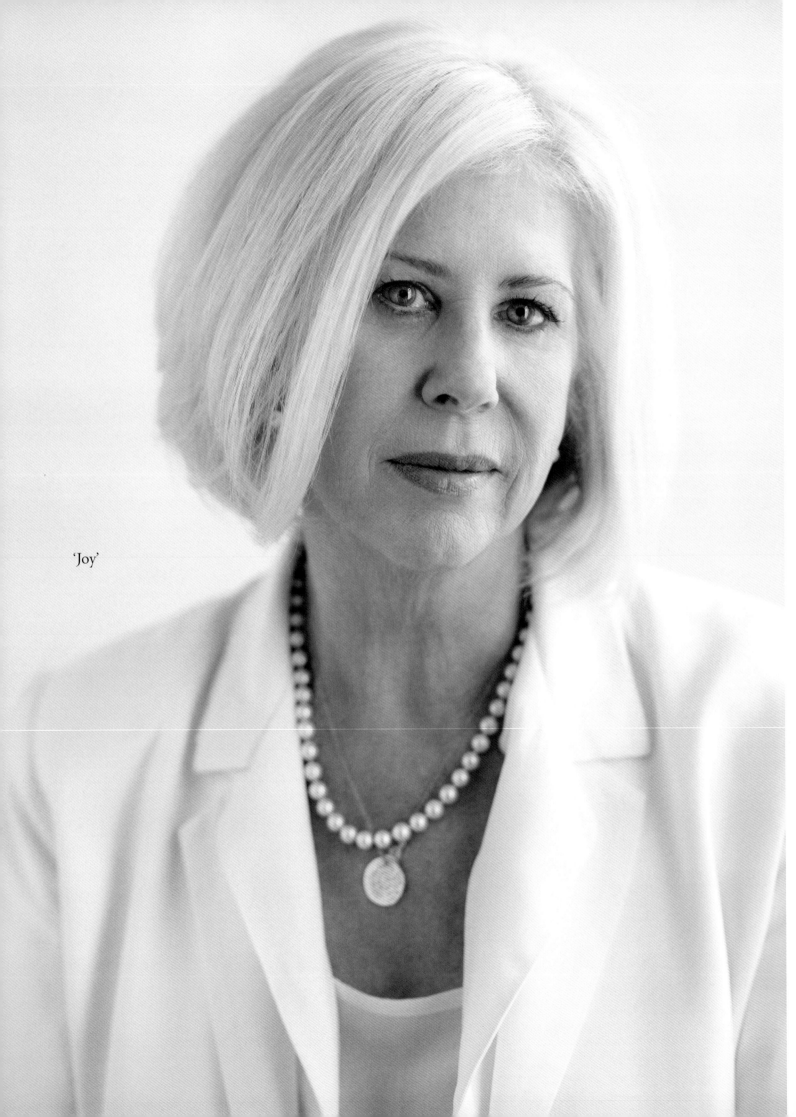

'Joy'

Callie Khouri

—

Callie Khouri was born in San Antonio in Texas, USA. Her first screenplay, 1991's *Thelma & Louise,* won critical acclaim and numerous awards, including an Academy Award, a Golden Globe and a PEN Award. A lifelong feminist, Khouri is also a lecturer and a director of films – including *Divine Secrets of the Ya-Ya Sisterhood* and *Mad Money* – and the creator of the television drama series *Nashville.* She has served two terms on the Writers Guild of America's board of directors and, in 2014, was honoured by the United States' National Women's History Museum.

Q. What really matters to you?

What matters to me most, as a human being, is that the people I experience on a daily basis feel loved. My personal relationships with my family, with the people I work with and, generally, with the people I am around are really important to me. I want the people near me to *know* how important they are to me – to know that they are appreciated.

Beyond that, I will never stop trying to make it clear that inequity is inhumane – in every single circumstance. If this world is going to survive, we have to recognise this. We cannot look out and see strangers. Because there is no room for 'them' – it *has* to be 'us.' I feel this is the overriding message of almost everything I say or do. I was thirteen when the women's movement was really getting fired up, in the seventies. That's when I started realising – looking around – that I couldn't see women in positions of power. For the first time, I felt that things for women were limited and this upset me to my core. I became aware of how women were talked about and to, and I was incensed. There was an inequity in the way women were treated and in what was expected of us – there still is.

Although the inequity wasn't something that was happening in my household, I could witness it anywhere I looked. Funnily, my father – whom I lost when I was sixteen – is the cause of and support for my feminism. I was really lucky that he was such an open-minded human being; he is the first person who ever talked to me about abortion. He was a doctor and would probably be called a conservative Republican – but he was pro-choice. He had seen the result of back-alley and botched abortions early in his career, and he found these barbaric. He thought that if someone had made the decision to terminate a pregnancy they should be able to do so safely, no matter their age. He said a twelve year old who's decided to terminate her pregnancy has had something horrible happen to her – whether she knows it or not. Such a girl shouldn't have to find a solution to her problem with the support only of her twelve-year-old best friend. We don't want youngsters deciding how to confront this issue, and we certainly don't want them – or a woman of any age – in the hands of unethical, untrained people. I had no idea about back-street abortions and the context in which they occurred, but my dad made sure I knew. He was a great man.

When I was sixteen, I picked up *Ms. Magazine.* I discovered Gloria Steinem speaking words that could have come out of my own mouth. That's when I knew I had to be working to change the way the world looks at women. I *had* to illuminate people. In this world, we have right and left, top and bottom, in and out – one doesn't exist without the other. And yet, with men and women, half are treated as second-class citizens. I'm not going to rest until that changes.

Ordinarily, I need to have a gun to my head to sit down and write; I love finishing a piece, but getting to the finish line has always been difficult. When I got the idea for *Thelma & Louise,* however, I knew I had to write it and finish it. It always had a life of its own. I would wake up in the middle of the night to write a scene – that certainly hasn't happened subsequently. I felt very strongly that it was meant for women. I could say, 'This is something I want to see. Don't you?' I wanted to watch a movie in which the women weren't objects, like they were in the forties. Those roles were ridiculous and made me not want to be a woman. I wanted to watch something that did. So, I guess *Thelma & Louise* was an answer to something I was looking for; I didn't know other women would experience it as intensely as I did, but I'm happy they did.

The movie was about two women breaking out of a box, and finally having every constraint removed by their actions and mistakes; they got bigger and bigger and bigger until the world was too small to hold them. The film was on the cover of *TIME* magazine, which was amazing, and it got glowing reviews, but it also got some really angry responses, especially from some of the male critics and social commentators. A lot of men found it incredibly threatening. I can remember the first time someone described it as 'man-hating.' I thought, 'How? How is this man-hating when it is just a reflection of how the world is for women? This is just how it is; there's nothing unusual about it. The only thing unusual is that she shot the guy! If the gun had been in the man's hand it would have been so unremarkable that it wouldn't merit comment.' I also thought, 'Wow, this film is really going to take the lid off this thing; we're *really* going to have to have this conversation now. We're going to need to talk about what hating is and then about what women-hating is.' All the men were villains? No, they weren't. And anyway, all villains are men in movies about guys. But apparently women aren't allowed to write male villains, at least on-screen. That's an insane double standard.

Q. What brings you happiness?
Dogs.

Q. What do you regard as the lowest depth of misery?
Realising that the resting state of the world is one of unfairness. There's so much darkness, violence, fear and poverty, and it's hard not to lose hope. We live an existence that was chosen for us by politicians.

Q. What would you change if you could?
If I could change one thing about human nature, I would change the propensity for violence.

Q. Which single word do you most identify with?
Joy. It's what I wish all of us could experience. We don't need to experience joy all the time, but it's important to know the real heights of emotion, and I do think joy is the overriding purpose of being a human on this earth.

Jane
Goodall

———

'It hurts that, despite being the most intellectual creature that has ever walked — the explosive development of our intellect is the main difference between us and the chimps — we are destroying the planet.'

———

Jane Goodall DBE was born in London, England. She is a primatologist, conservationist, author and environmental activist, and holds a PhD in ethology from Cambridge University. In 1960, Goodall began living with and studying chimpanzees at Gombe Stream National Park in Tanzania. She is the founder of the Jane Goodall Institute for Wildlife Research, Education and Conservation, and of Roots & Shoots, a global environmental and humanitarian education programme for young people. She became a United Nations Messenger of Peace in 2002 and was made a Dame Commander of the Order of the British Empire in 2004.

Q. What really matters to you?

The future of our planet. It matters terribly to me that people are making decisions based on questions like, 'How will this help me at the next shareholders' meeting?' Or, 'How will this help my next political campaign?' People should be asking – as Indigenous People used to – 'How will this decision benefit future generations?'

When I was ten years old, I read *Tarzan of the Apes* and fell in love with Tarzan. I decided that I would go to Africa when I grew up, to live with wild animals and write books about them. Everybody laughed at me! We didn't have any money and World War Two was raging, but my mother had always imbued me with the message that, if you really want something, you have to work hard, take advantage of opportunity and never give up.

It took a while for me to achieve my dream, because there was no money for university; there was just enough money for a secretarial course. I found it really boring, but I got a job in a London company that made documentary films. Then, the opportunity came; a school friend invited me to Kenya, where her parents had bought a farm. I worked as a waitress to raise money for the fare – it was jolly hard work! Finally, I was off to Africa by boat. There, I met Louis Leakey; somebody had said that, if you are interested in animals,

you should meet him, so I went to see him at the Natural History Museum. As chance would have it, his secretary had just left – so, that boring old secretarial training was what enabled me to follow my dream, in some ways.

I found myself among people who could talk about everything I was interested in: the animals, birds, reptiles, amphibians, insects and plants of Africa. And Leakey saw something in me. He offered me an opportunity to live with and learn from, not any old animal, but the one most like us – the chimpanzee. It was still a year before he could get money for this young, untrained girl who had never been to college; what a crazy idea! Nonetheless, a wealthy American businessman gave us money for six months' work. However, the authorities of what was then part of the crumbling British Empire wouldn't give permission for a young girl to go into the forest on her own, so, for the first four months, my amazing mother volunteered to come with me. After I observed tool use and tool making – then thought to be only human attributes - Leakey was able to get money from *National Geographic* for me to carry on with the study. They sent a photographer and filmmaker, Hugo van Lawick, whose early films and photographs took the story of 'Jane and the chimps' around the world, and who also became my first husband.

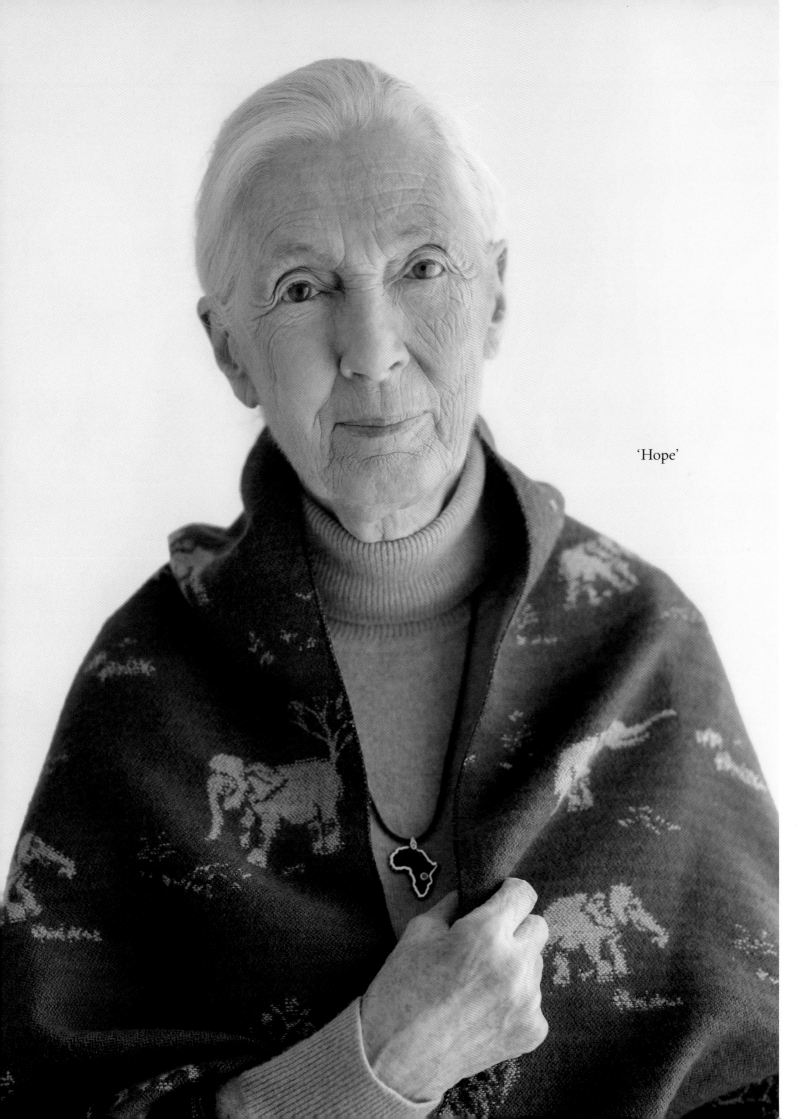

'Hope'

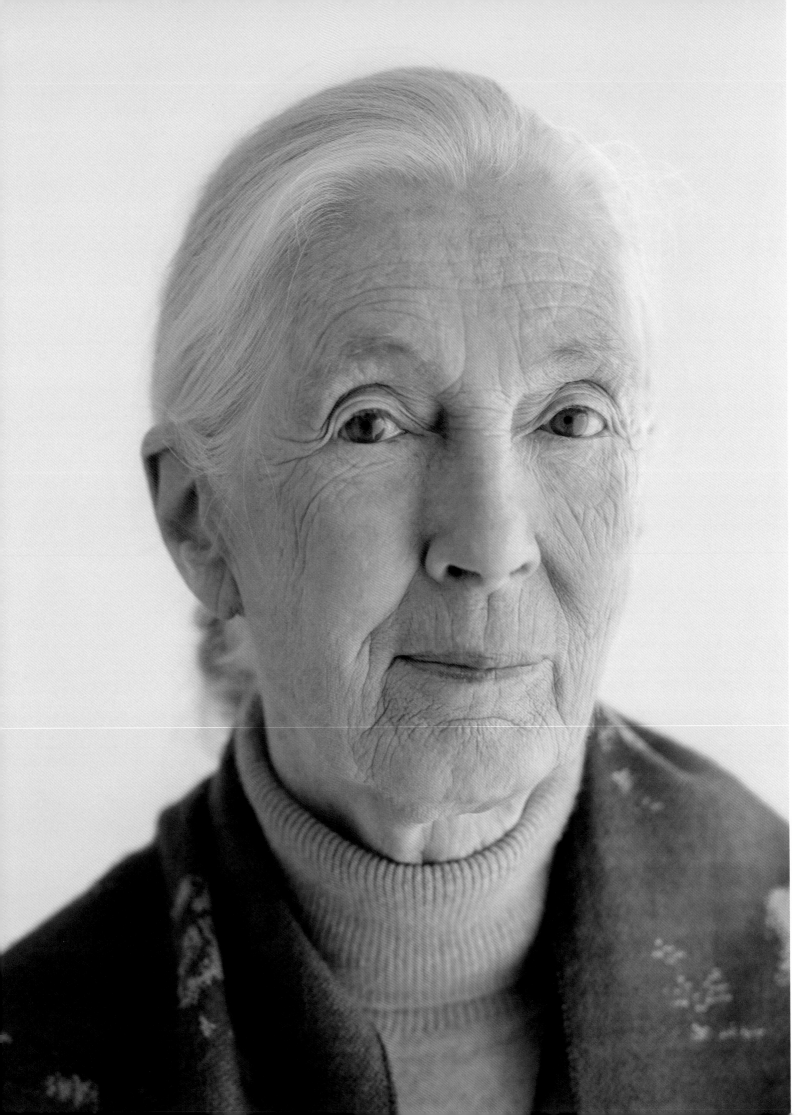

Jane Goodall

Finally, Louis Leakey wrote to tell me that I had to get a degree, but that I would have to raise my own money. And there was no time to mess about with a bachelor of arts, so he got me a place doing a PhD in ethology at Cambridge University. Never having been to college, I was extremely nervous and the professor told me I'd done my whole study wrong. He said that I should have given the chimpanzees numbers, not names, and that I couldn't talk about their personalities, minds or emotions, because only humans had those attributes. Back then, it was thought that the difference between humans and all the other animals was a difference of kind, but, in fact, it is a difference of degree, because chimps are so biologically like us. Finally, I was able to win through and today's science has largely changed its mind.

In 1986, there was a conference in Chicago that brought scientists together from around the world to discuss chimpanzees. Everywhere it was the same: chimp numbers dropping, forests disappearing, the beginnings of the bushmeat trade and the shooting of mothers to steal their babies for sale, entertainment and medical research. I went to that conference as a scientist and left as an activist. Just like that! I didn't make a decision; it just happened to me.

So, from 1986 until now, I haven't been in one place for more than three consecutive weeks. I realised that people were losing hope, which was not surprising considering how we were harming the planet. And I realised that, if young people were losing hope, we might as well all give up. So, that began JGI, the Jane Goodall Institute, which had been started by then in 1977, so we began the Roots & Shoots programme to improve the lives of the people and gradually got their trust. I got together a bit of money and went to Africa to learn more about the plight of the chimps. That is when I realised that the people were suffering, too. There were more people around Gombe than the land could support; people were too poor to buy food from elsewhere, farmland was overused and infertile, and trees were being cut down from steep slopes. It was clear to me then, that, if we didn't improve human lives, there was no way we could try and save the chimps.

There is so much left to do. People ask, 'Why aren't you slowing down? You're eighty-three!' Well, there is so much awareness to raise. I was given certain gifts and one gift was communication; I have to use that gift while I still can.

Q. What brings you happiness?
I love the planet, I love nature and I love being out in the rainforest.

Q. What do you regard as the lowest depth of misery?
What we're doing to the planet. It hurts that, despite being the most intellectual creature that has ever walked – the explosive development of our intellect is the main difference between us and the chimps – we are destroying the planet.

Q. What would you change if you could?
I would get our Roots & Shoots programme for youth into every school around the world, starting as young as possible. The main message of Roots & Shoots is that every one of us makes a difference every single day and we get to choose what sort of difference we are going to make. But, until you know something, you don't care about it and, if you don't care about it, you won't work to save it. On the one hand we have to reduce poverty, because, if you are really poor, you cut the trees down to try and grow food. On the other hand, we have to change our mindset; we have to measure success by something other than acquiring more money – acquiring more stuff.

Q. Which single word do you most identify with?
Hope. That there is time to turn things around. But this hope depends on us taking action - it will not be realised if we don't get together to do something. It is really important to remember that every single individual matters and has some kind of role to play, and that we can choose what sort of impact we will make, every single day.

'Every single individual matters and has some kind of role to play. We can choose what sort of impact we will make, every single day.'

Januka
Nepal

Januka Nepal was born in Panchkhal, Nepal. She was entered into an arranged marriage when she was eight years old and was widowed soon thereafter. In the fifty-six years that have followed her widowhood, Nepal has adhered to Nepalese traditional cultural practices, which dictated that widows remain chaste, commit to a vegetarian diet and abstain from wearing red clothes.

Q. What really matters to you?
Spending my life happily and peacefully. The earthquake in 2015 destroyed the house I shared with my brother, so we had to live in my nephew's restaurant for a time. But my nephew built a little house for us, where we now live.

I don't remember my marriage because I was so young – I was married when I was eight years old. I didn't move to my husband's home immediately, because of my age, and my husband died four months after we were married – I have been a widow ever since. There were a lot of superstitions and restrictions about widows at the time: we weren't legally allowed to remarry and had to follow mourning rituals, like wearing only white clothes and living with a husband's family a year before being allowed to return home.

I have grown old and there is very little I can do these days. I have never had a job, and I don't have the strength to do heavy work, so I just look after our goats. Other than that, I cook and I eat – and I am content.

Q. What brings you happiness?
I'm glad for the opportunities the children in my family have, because, when I was a child, there were no schools – I have never studied, and I don't know how to write; if I have to sign something, I do it with my thumb. But my 'grandson' and 'granddaughter' are going to school, so when they study hard and perform well, that makes me very happy.

Q. What do you regard as the lowest depth of misery?
The thing that I am sad about is that I can't do much work.

Q. What would you change if you could?
I can't get back my years – so I can't farm or go into business – but, if I had the opportunity, I would want to have more goats to raise.

Q. Which single word do you most identify with?
Sukha: happiness. Why do we need sadness?

Dana
Gluckstein

Dana Gluckstein was born in Los Angeles in California, USA. She is a graduate of Stanford University, where she studied psychology, painting and photography. She has photographed Indigenous Peoples worldwide as well as iconic figures that include Nelson Mandela and Muhammad Ali. Her 2010 book *DIGNITY: In Honor of the Rights of Indigenous Peoples* and its associated exhibition *DIGNITY: Tribes in Transition* have received international acclaim.

Q. What really matters to you?
My aunt, Jeanette, who died of Lupus when I was thirteen, was my deep inspiration and mentor. She taught me that it's not the material in this world which matters, but our inner light and our inner radiance. She was a very holy person who lived in a truly crippled body, but her energy transcended that body. So I, too, focus on the inner. I try – through my work and also in my life – to be a steward for voices that need to be heard. And I try to be present.

Q. What brings you happiness?
One of the great gifts is being a mother. And having an amazing husband who has believed in my work. Our world is so beautiful. Even though there is so much suffering on the planet, I see how interconnected we are; I love Desmond Tutu's description and expression of *ubuntu*. We are more alike than we are different, and that brings me great joy.

Q. What do you regard as the lowest depth of misery?
I see so much needless suffering. It pains me to see the amount of time and money that is wasted when we could be connecting people.

Q. What would you change if you could?
I really like the idea of our leaders being peacemakers. If they were committed to that, they would need to all sit in counsel together and not leave the room until they had come up with the answers. And we need more female leaders; I think that, because women carry and bear our children – feed them with our breasts – we have a deep sensitivity for life.

Q. Which single word do you most identify with?
I really love the word dignity. It encompasses everything: love, compassion and freedom, and how we honour each other.

Zamaswazi
Dlamini-Mandela

Zamaswazi Dlamini-Mandela was born in Welkom, South Africa. She is the granddaughter of Nelson Mandela and Nomzamo Nobandla Winnie Madikizela-Mandela, and of King Sobhuza II of Swaziland and Mbhono Shongwe. A business developer, public speaker and self-described serial entrepreneur, she launched her luxury fashion range, Swati by Roi Kaskara, in 2017.

Q. What really matters to you?
We need to look after each other as human beings and take it upon ourselves to make the world a better place. My grandfather's call to action when he retired many years ago was that he'd done his bit – both my grandparents have done their bit – and that it really is up to us, as a world, to make the world a better place. My grandparents have got us somewhere that is just remarkable, but, if we do not continue their work, it would be very easy for us to go back.

It's important for me to be my own person in whatever it is that I'm doing, whether it's my career or my personal relationship or being a mother. And I always like to keep things evolving, changing and moving. I open myself up so the universe can bring me something – if I feel it resonates with me, I go with it. I think my self-expression is critical, because I know that my grandmother has fought tirelessly for women to express themselves – to be whatever they want to be and do whatever they want to do. And much like my mum and grandmother taught me, I have a responsibility to teach my daughter how she can be the best version of herself.

Q. What brings you happiness?
I find my happiness in prayer, I do. It makes me cry when I think about it because it's been such a vehicle for me to release, forgive and heal.

Q. What do you regard as the lowest depth of misery?
Oppression of any kind.

Q. What would you change if you could?
I would love to teach people how to love themselves. Because it starts with the self: if you can learn to love yourself, then I don't think that you can hate your fellow human being.

Q. Which single word do you most identify with?
Love. It can eradicate hate.

Pamela Novo

Pamela Novo was born in Buenos Aires, Argentina. Her family emigrated to Australia when she was two years old. She holds a bachelor's degree in design and technology, and a master's degree in secondary education from Western Sydney University, and has completed post-graduate studies in leadership, Adobe software and information communication technologies. Since 2009, Novo has been a secondary-school computing, design and technology teacher. She is studying towards a bachelor's degree in computer science (gaming) at Charles Sturt University. In 2016, she was awarded a Westpac Bicentennial Foundation Young Technologists scholarship. In May 2017, she gave birth to her son, Valentino.

Q. What really matters to you?

My husband and our baby. And being an educator, because I do see parents who have somewhat neglected their children. That filters down into the child – it becomes apathy. In instances like that, you try to support the child and instil certain values in them – sometimes it works, sometimes it doesn't, but it makes me happy when I am able to help a child become enthusiastic about education. I use myself as an example to kids of how to continuously engage with learning; when I started school, I didn't speak a word of English. I remember standing in front of my entire class, unable to simply say, 'Teacher, can I go to the toilet.' I peed myself, which was incredibly embarrassing. So, when my kids say that they can't believe this, because my English is so good now, I tell them it's because I kept learning and kept reading.

Q. What brings you happiness?

Giving back to my parents – working for their peace and happiness. They sacrificed their lives in Argentina to give their family a better life. When I finished a university degree – something my father had started to pursue, but had never been able to finish – I was so happy; my parents were so proud of me, and we all cried with joy. My parents showered me with gifts, which is a big thing for them, and it was a really good moment to be part of.

Q. What do you regard as the lowest depth of misery?

It would be the fact that there is so much poverty, violence and general malice in the world.

Q. What would you change if you could?

I would change certain human characteristics. I would get rid of the greed, hate and malice that some humans have inside them. I think this would affect more meaningful change than any allotment of funds.

Q. Which single word do you most identify with?

Perseverance.

Cleo Wade

Cleo Wade was born in New Orleans in Louisiana, USA. As an artist, speaker and poet, Wade is an inspiring voice in today's world for gender and race equality. Her poems speak to a greater future for all women, people of colour and the LGBTQI community. Wade's work is founded on the idea that art should not only be in the name of all people, but should serve all people.

Q. What really matters to you?

I want to make the space between people more sacred, so that we can fully acknowledge and celebrate who we are. Hopefully, that makes people grow in themselves and want to do the same for their families, their communities and the world.

It matters to me that people are confident in themselves – that's something I learned from my father: when you're growing up without equal rights, what else do you have if not pride in your body and soul?

Q. What brings you happiness?

The journey of investigation – the pursuit of truth and meaning – is such a thrill for me, because, even when it makes me uncomfortable, I know that I'm gathering information that I can convert to tools for others. And I'm happy when I know I'm creating tools that can provide clarity for others.

Q. What do you regard as the lowest depth of misery?

Every day the suffering in the world makes old cracks in my heart get bigger or new ones open up. Everything is heartbreaking.

Q. What would you change if you could?

It's hard to pick one thing; as Gloria Steinem says, the issues of our world – especially those of the most marginalised people – are linked, not ranked. But, if I could change anything, it would be to plant a little flower inside everyone that incentivised them to know the world can change and to effect that change.

Q. Which single word do you most identify with?

Moon. It makes me think of so many things: 'illuminated', 'wild', 'free' and 'light.'

Santilla Chingaipe

Santilla Chingaipe was born in Livingstone, Zambia, and moved to Australia with her family when she was nine years old. A graduate of RMIT University in Melbourne, she is an award-winning journalist for Australia's SBS World News and a documentary filmmaker. Chingaipe's work has been recognised at the Victorian African Community Awards and at the Celebration of African Australians Awards, and she is also a four-time finalist for the United Nations Association of Australia Media Peace Awards.

Q. What really matters to you?

That I am doing my bit to add to my corner of the world, not take away from it. If I can add something through my work – in my own small way – then I feel like I'm living my life in the best way that I know how.

We need people to realise that when someone is suffering somewhere, it isn't that person's problem alone – it is *our* problem that we *all* need to find a solution for. I think my generation believes that others have fought for freedom and that now is the time to revel in equal rights – but it's not. In many ways, we're regressing. However, I believe that in understanding others, there is hope.

In my storytelling work, I try to challenge stereotypes. People struggle to work out my story because there's been a very singular narrative around African women that has dominated the discourse in the West. African women are seen as oppressed, but that has not necessarily been my story. For me, being African is about belonging, pride and community.

Q. What brings you happiness?

What brings me joy is the mundane, the ordinary. I take great pleasure in simple things: that first coffee in the morning.

Q. What do you regard as the lowest depth of misery?

It brings me the biggest sadness to see people being so caught up in their own view of the world that they do not want to see beyond it. How does humanity move forward if we are so stuck feeling like we're right?

Q. What would you change if you could?

The first use of my super powers would involve eliminating racism and bigotry. I would also eliminate self-hatred. A lot of weight is put on things like appearances, which prevents people from just getting on with living life.

Q. Which single word do you most identify with?

Joy. Happiness has been commodified – you have to work for it – but joy you can find in the most unexpected of places.

Karen Walker

Karen Walker CNZM was born in Auckland, New Zealand. She launched her eponymous fashion label in the late 1980s and showed at New York Fashion Week for twenty consecutive seasons from 2006 to 2016. Today her work is sold worldwide. Walker is committed to responsible, ethical sourcing, and her company partners with the African production company Artisan.Fashion to produce accessories of social significance. In 2004, she became a Member of the New Zealand Order of Merit, and, in 2014, she was made a Companion of the New Zealand Order of Merit for services to fashion design.

————

Q. What really matters to you?
It all comes down to my family and friends: to the people I love and who love me.

Q. What brings you happiness?
Feeling the love of my family and creating good work. I've always loved fashion. My grandmother and mother taught me how to sew, so I fell in love with style, making beautiful things and the effect fashion can have. It was really all I ever wanted to do. Since 2011, we've been working with the United Nations' Ethical Fashion Initiative and Artisan.Fashion for many of our accessories. We work with a team just outside Nairobi who bring us beautiful beading and metalwork. We've done about six or seven different collections of bags, jewellery or belts with them now. When I see someone with one of our Artisan.Fashion-made bags, I know they've got a bag they love, but I also know that the bag has helped make a real difference to individuals, to their families and to their communities. It's a real joy to work with these people, to be part of their lives and have them helping us tell our story. And I love seeing responses to our work and hearing what it means to people. Even seeing someone in the street wearing something of ours and looking great makes me happy!

Q. What do you regard as the lowest depth of misery?
Unfairness, fear, people being angry for no reason, a lack of calmness and people not seeing the whole picture – I find the fear all this creates for others quite distressing.

Q. What would you change if you could?
If I had a magic wand and could change anything, it would be conflict: big or small, whether between two people who should love each other or on a global scale.

Q. Which single word do you most identify with?
Honesty. I always look for honesty in a person, in an idea, in a conversation or in a relationship.

Sergut Belay

Sergut Belay was born in Addis Ababa, Ethiopia. She fled Ethiopia in 2012, after her husband became a political prisoner of the Ethiopian government; she hasn't had contact with him for five years. Belay lives in Boden, Sweden, and is a project administrator at Havremagasinet, an art gallery that exhibits Swedish, Nordic and international contemporary art. She is also a volunteer supporter of new immigrants.

————

Q. What really matters to you?
Family, health, work and happiness. Up until five years ago, I was living with my mother, my husband and our children in Ethiopia. But, when my husband was imprisoned by the government – as a political prisoner – I skipped the country. I came to Sweden, via Kenya, without my children; suddenly I was an immigrant and I was alone. The Swedish government were amazing, though; they gave me a place to live, food and money. I was placed with six other women from different countries, which was good for me, because I needed to be around people. I have learned so much from these women. In fact, I've learned a lot since coming to Sweden, especially how to live with a whole new weather system!

A year after I arrived in Sweden, I was able to bring my children over; we all needed to be together after everything we'd been through. It's difficult to talk about my husband, because I don't know how he is, where he is or even whether or not he's alive. I hope one day to meet him again. But I have a good life. There are lots of challenges in learning a new language and culture, but I'm employed and I also do volunteer work helping to settle other immigrants. And I have my children.

Q. What brings you happiness?
Getting the opportunity to help others. And freedom!

Q. What do you regard as the lowest depth of misery?
Being subjected to racism; it needs to be destroyed.

Q. What would you change if you could?
I would make sure that everybody could live in peace.

Q. Which single word do you most identify with?
Kindness. My grandmother loved to help people and that really influenced my character.

Jessica Grace Smith

Jessica Grace Smith was born in Taihape, New Zealand. She graduated from Toi Whakaari: New Zealand Drama School with a bachelor of performing arts in 2009. An actor, writer, director and producer, Smith appeared in the long-running and award-winning Australian drama series, *Home & Away*, between 2014 and 2015. Her first short film, *Everybody Else Is Taken* – the story of a young girl who refuses to let her gender define her – premiered at the New York International Children's Film Festival in 2017.

————

Q. What really matters to you?
Using my voice and my privilege to empower and encourage other women to take the podium. As a white person, that means a lot of listening and a lot of allowing space for other people to talk. In my work, it really matters to me to write strong roles for women, then cast them with a conscious effort to achieve diversity and reflect society, without this being a token gesture; it's critical to me that I really include people and am aware of my own privileges.

When you consider the inequality, the mistreatment and the prejudice experienced by New Zealand's first people, I'm very distressed by the way our country constantly pats itself on the back. And I feel the same way about the treatment of women around the world – the lack of education and male dominance is so frustrating. Women like Malala Yousafzai, who promotes the education of girls, give me hope, but I do think change is going to take a long time.

Q. What brings you happiness?
For me, it's all about connection: to the land, to my family, to my friends and to myself.

Q. What do you regard as the lowest depth of misery?
It's loss – not only the loss of a person, but of the potential of a relationship. When someone dies, you move on, but the person you lost doesn't move with you.

Q. What would you change if you could?
I would give everyone a sense of individual accountability, which would then lead to a communal accountability for our actions. People need to take responsibility for what they are consuming and for the ethics of it. Because everything we do is a vote for the world we want to live in.

Q. Which single word do you most identify with?
Restless. I'm constantly looking for the next thing to do, whether it's for myself, or as an advocate for understanding or change.

p. 62

Marita Cheng

Marita Cheng was born in Cairns, Australia. She holds a bachelor of engineering in mechatronics and a bachelor of computer science from the University of Melbourne. In 2012, Cheng was named Young Australian of the Year for her work as the founder of Robogals Global, which teaches girls robotics artifical intelligence and encourages their interest in engineering. She is the founder and chief executive officer of aubot, which builds robots that help people in their everyday lives, and a co-founder of Aipoly, an application that allows the blind to recognise objects using their mobile phones.

Q. What really matters to you?
I'm always asking whether I'm doing enough to fulfil my potential. My mother worked as a kitchen hand and put all her money into extracurricular activities for my brother and me. She wanted us to have as many experiences as possible.

Halfway through my first year at university, a friend and I started a business that won a prize for being the best undergraduate business at the University of Melbourne. After the award ceremony the head of electrical engineering told me they were looking for students to get girls interested in engineering by teaching them about robotics. So, I recruited a group of friends to start designing workshops, and that's how Robogals was founded. In the first three months we taught 124 girls from six schools in Melbourne.

When I was studying, there weren't many female students in my class, which is really what drove me to reach out to young girls. It's important to me to show people that women can create and innovate as well as men.

Q. What brings you happiness?
I think that the bigger the challenge, the greater the satisfaction afterwards. When I look back on my journey with Robogals, I see a lot of times when it was really hard. But, I also feel a lot of happiness.

Q. What do you regard as the lowest depth of misery?
Things that bring me despair are linked to time: seeing time just slip away and seeing people give up. If everyone pursued their passions then the world would be a better place.

Q. What would you change if you could?
Hearing about London exceeding the year's air-pollution limits over just five days, or seeing pictures of Beijing with smog everywhere, I've become really concerned about air pollution; I would reverse all of the damage to our air.

Q. Which single word do you most identify with?
Hope. I'm very hopeful. I build things thinking that the future will be better than the past.

p. 63

Jan Owen

Jan Owen AM was born in Brisbane, Australia. She has spent twenty-five years growing Australia's youth, social-enterprise and innovation sectors. In 2000, she was made a Member of the Order of Australia. In 2012, she was named overall winner of the inaugural *Australian Financial Review* Westpac 100 Women of Influence awards. Owen is the author of *Every Childhood Lasts a Lifetime* and *The Future Chasers*. She is also the chief executive officer of the Foundation for Young Australians and of YLab, a global youth-futures design and learning lab.

Q. What really matters to you?
My life's mission is centred around unleashing young people. My adoptive parents helped set up Lifeline in Australia, so as a child I was often in the back of a car when they drove to a domestic-violence dispute. I watched my parents walk out of houses with women and children under their arms. I learned about the power of the informal system, when the community wraps itself around someone. These experiences showed me that those episodes in people's lives don't have to dictate their destiny.

I've gone on to work with children who have spent a long time in state care. I've observed that every single young person who leaves care has the same desire to find their families. It is phenomenal how profound that need to know where you've come from is – it goes to the heart of your identity.

Q. What brings you happiness?
My happiness is tied up with my purpose of unleashing the next generation – I can't imagine doing anything else. Beyond this, I believe there are three currencies operating in life: power, which is represented in government; money, which is represented in business; then there's love, which is represented in community. I've utilised all of those, but the currency of love is my happiness.

Q. What do you regard as the lowest depth of misery?
Inequality or injustice. If we can't get to a place in which the distribution of power changes, inequality will continue to rise.

Q. What would you change if you could?
I'd flip the conversation, because we've all bought into the conversation being about the challenges rather than the opportunities.

I would ensure each citizen has access to the currencies of power, money and love. To do this, we need to unleash the next generation – they have a very strong sense of fairness and justice. They want to add value to the world; they want to see genuine democracy. I believe that, with all three currencies working together, we can unleash a new kind of global citizen.

Q. Which single word do you most identify with?
Generosity.

pp. 68–9

Valerie Van Galder

Valerie Van Galder was born in Chicago in Illinois, USA. A graduate of the University of California, Los Angeles, Van Galder has worked in the entertainment industry for over thirty years. Van Galder currently runs Depressed Cake Shop, a global pop-up concept, raising awareness and funds to help people suffering from mental health issues. She is on the board of directors of St. Joseph Center in Venice, California, an agency assisting low-income families and the homeless.

Q. What really matters to you?
Kindness matters to me. And compassion. I learned about grief and loss when my mother, and then my father, became ill, my father from severe mental health issues. When I left my job to focus on caring for him, I started taking cake-decorating classes as a way to manage my own stress and anxiety. I read about the Depressed Cake Shop, a UK event devised by a publicity guru named Emma Thomas. The idea grabbed me, because it brought together my two passions: helping people who are suffering from mental health issues . . . and cake.

After I popped up a shop in Los Angeles – donating the funds to the National Alliance on Mental Illness – I decided to continue expanding the reach of the concept. Now the Depressed Cake Shop hosts pop-ups worldwide. The events facilitate discussion on mental illness while raising money by selling customised baked goods such as misfortune cookies. We have raised more than $100,000 for mental health charities.

Mother Teresa said, "Do small things with great love." I've seen the effect tiny gestures of kindness can have. Just emailing somebody who has messaged our Facebook page and saying, 'Hey, you're not alone. We're listening, and we feel your pain,' can actually make a difference.

Q. What brings you happiness?
My greatest joy is time spent with my family – it's incredibly precious.

Q. What do you regard as the lowest depth of misery?
Seeing suffering or human cruelty and feeling powerless to do anything about it.

Q. What would you change if you could?
I would ask people who have incredible personal wealth to think about taking some of the surplus and donating it to the greater good. If those of us who have more than we actually need would look within our hearts and our pocket books, tremendous things could happen.

Q. Which single word do you most identify with?
Laughter. Because there's no better feeling than laughing until tears run down my face.

p. 76

Tabitha
St. Bernard-Jacobs

Tabitha St. Bernard-Jacobs was born in Arima, Trinidad and Tobago. After studying at St. Francis College and the Fashion Institute of Technology in New York City, she launched a zero-waste clothing label, Tabii Just. She is an outspoken advocate for ethical manufacturing and the disruption of fabric waste. In 2014, she began chronicling her experience raising an interracial child in an interfaith home. In 2016, she became the youth coordinator for the Women's March on Washington, creating the Youth Ambassador Program. She was named among *Elite Daily's* '100 Women Who Have Stood up to Trump in his First 100 Days.'

Q. What really matters to you?
Family. Love. Justice.

These are at the core of everything I do. The day after the election, I felt numb. I thought, 'This cannot be my America; this cannot be the country I dreamed of coming to when I was a child.' For me, the election signalled the need to get more active. I reached out to a friend and got involved in planning the Women's March on Washington. That was just the beginning of a truly intersectional movement of women ready to push back. I then co-led the one-day strike, A Day Without a Woman, which saw women from all over the world wear red and stand together for gender equality.

I do this work for the kids that will inherit the world we create now. The hope is that I can help give them the tools to take control through social and political engagement so that they can have a powerful say in the type of America they want to live in.

Q. What brings you happiness?
My son and my husband are responsible for my daily snippets of joy. On a larger scale, I've been particularly delighted to work with inspiring young people from all over the country on causes that matter to them. Seeing them excited about social and racial justice, and helping to create space for their voices, brings me immense happiness.

Q. What do you regard as the lowest depth of misery?
Lack of love. It lends itself to a lack of empathy, which lends itself to a lack of human connection. That is the lowest depth of misery.

Q. What would you change if you could?
I would create a system that requires every single human being, at a certain age, to live a year in somebody else's life. Most people who hurt others do so because they don't, or aren't able to, see the humanity in others.

Q. Which single word do you most identify with?
Relentless.

p. 77

Nahid
Shahalimi

Nahid Shahalimi was born in Kabul, Afghanistan. She holds degrees in international politics and Southeast Asian studies, and in fine arts from Champlain College and Concordia University in Canada. She is the founder and chairwoman of the Hope Foundation for Women and Children of Afghanistan and supports of UNICEF Germany. In 2009, she launched *We, the Women – Germany*, a book and travelling exhibition that honours strong, inspirational German women. In 2017, her book *Wo Mut die Seele trägt: Wir Frauen in Afghanistan* profiled women and girls in Afghanistan.

Q. What really matters to you?
A war that had nothing to do with us changed the course of our history and the lives of every Afghan, forever. But, it made me the person I am today, so, no matter what I do, I always try to leave a better path behind me than the one that was laid down for me.

Q. What brings you happiness?
I saw the good and bad in humanity very early in my life, and it influenced me to do what I love. So, my greatest happiness is to be allowed to love – because love is freedom.

Q. What do you regard as the lowest depth of misery?
There have been difficult moments, but aren't the lows and highs the beautiful thing about life? When the Shah – the last king of Afghanistan – was overthrown in 1973, everything changed. The war took my father away, and life became a living hell for us; being rich and female, without a male head of the family, became a curse. We had enough wealth for everyone, but some relatives were like hungry wolves waiting for my dad to die; I saw people turn into monsters for whom only money mattered. We left Afghanistan because of the war, but mainly because it was very dangerous for us as women. We left with nothing; we walked over the mountains, with nothing to eat or drink for five days. This robbed us of our childhoods, but it also made us strong. We had already hit bottom rock, so, what else was there? Death?

Q. What would you change if you could?
I believe that, if you want to do something good, you should just go and do it – you don't need permission to help somebody. And, I wish that people would find their true selves; they convince themselves that they have to fit into boxes. But for what? For whom? What are they trying to prove?

Q. Which single word do you most identify with?
Resilience.

pp. 90–1

Eva
Orner

Eva Orner was born in Melbourne, Australia. She obtained a bachelor of arts (honours) degree from Melbourne's Monash University. In 2008, Orner won an Academy Award for Best Documentary Feature as producer of *Taxi to the Dark Side*, which investigates the torture and murder of an innocent Afghan taxi driver while detained at Guantanamo Bay Detention Camp. She has directed and produced numerous other highly acclaimed, award-winning documentaries including *Chasing Asylum*, *Out of Iraq* and *The Network*.

Q. What really matters to you?
Telling stories, exposing injustices and educating people matters to me. When I produced *Taxi to the Dark Side*, I was constantly asked what motivated me. So, at the age of thirty-eight, I confronted that question for the first time. Three of my four grandparents perished in the Holocaust, and I remember 'Never Again' being a very strong message in the Australian Jewish community of the seventies and eighties. But, at the same time, I was seeing Cambodia falling apart on the news. Being a precocious child, I asked, 'Isn't it kind of happening again? It's close to us and we're not doing anything about it!' It really struck me, and I grew up wanting to do something that mattered. The work is hard, but I try not to carry it with me. I try to see beauty. Because living well matters to me, too: going to the beach, being in the sun, cultivating meaningful friendships and having love in my life.

Q. What brings you happiness?
The world is in a shitty place right now. I feel so sad about it. If I step back, I can't see joy. I see the world getting more and more conservative, xenophobic, racist, sexist and scared. I see more war and poverty. It's hard, but, when I think about happiness, I come back to the simple things like being with like-minded people and with the people you love.

Q. What do you regard as the lowest depth of misery?
It's not having freedom: whether it be freedom to choose, freedom to educate yourself, freedom to work or freedom to not have to marry at age thirteen. So many people around the world – especially women – don't have those really basic choices. It's the worst thing I can imagine.

Q. What would you change if you could?
Persecution and war, which leads to everything else.

Q. Which single word do you most identify with?
Kindness.

Lavinia
Fournier

———

Lavinia Fournier was born in Romania. She moved to France at age fourteen and holds a master's degree in international relations from the National Institute of Oriental Languages and Civilsations, at Paris-Sorbonne University, before working as a financial and administrative manager for AFGE, a French corporate-governance association, and for the not-for-profit Educateam. Fournier began helping Roma living in France in 2014 and became a social worker dedicated to reducing shantytowns on a national level in 2016.

———

Q. What really matters to you?
My goal is to no longer see Roma families living in shantytowns in France. I want to see them find work and their children become fully integrated, because this is what they want; they don't just want to make a little money to take back to Romania. I became involved with helping the Roma in 2014, when a principal who found out I was Romanian asked if I could help a family who were being expelled. The family told me, 'We've been here for a while, but we can't find work and we can't integrate into society. Our children are at school and have no trouble fitting in, but for us, it has been difficult.' I began helping them on a volunteer basis, and now I am employed as a social worker for a public limited company, working to reduce shantytowns on the national level.

Q. What brings you happiness?
The families I work with have brought me joy. These are unfortunate families who have very little to live on; they spend their days in the street scavenging materials to recycle, but they are incredibly joyful. They laugh about their problems and are full of joy. Their victories are what make me happy: when a father is overjoyed to find work, when they receive government assistance or when they find housing after months of struggle.

Q. What do you regard as the lowest depth of misery?
What makes me sad are the policies in place in France today; there is no real political will to integrate the Roma.

Q. What would you change if you could?
I would give all those families who have begun the integration process housing. Measures have been put in place to help them, but they have to wait far too long. Many families give up and leave.

Q. Which single word do you most identify with?
Humanity.

Manal
Ali

———

Manal Ali was born in Damour, Lebanon, to Palestinian parents. She was born in Damour refugee camp and now lives in Beirut's Bourj El Barajneh camp. Ali works with Soufra, a catering social enterprise, established by the Women's Program Association. Soufra employs women from Bourj El Barajneh to produce Palestinian dishes that are sold outside of the camp.

———

Q. What really matters to you?
Palestine matters to me. I was born in Lebanon, in the Damour refugee camp, and I have since lived in the Sabra and Bourj El Barajneh camps in Beirut. All I want in this life – my greatest desire – is to be able to go back to my country. When I look at the world, I know that this is impossible, but sometimes I wonder, 'How can this be?' Living outside my country for my whole life has been incredibly difficult, because here in Lebanon we Palestinians have so few rights.

As a working mother of five, my work also matters to me. I was so happy when I found out about Soufra, because I was able to start making a living with my cooking skills. It would be amazing to be able to continue to work towards expanding our business – towards making it better and better.

Q. What brings you happiness?
My family. We all live together, which I am so grateful for. To see my family happy, in spite of our surroundings, is my greatest happiness. I don't know what my children's future looks like – in fact that thought occupies my mind a lot – but I hope they will be able to have better lives than I have had.

Q. What do you regard as the lowest depth of misery?
Living like this – in this camp's unstable conditions – is the ultimate misery. You only have to look at pictures of the place to get an idea of what life is like here.

Q. What would you change if you could?
I wish I could go back to my country. But, as I know this will never be possible, I hope for a better life.

Q. Which single word do you most identify with?
Freedom!

Molly
Biehl

———

Molly Biehl was born in Santa Monica in California, USA. She holds a master's degree in sociology, as well as a bachelor's degree in political science, with an emphasis on international relations. When her sister, Amy, was killed while working in South Africa in 1993, Biehl and her family – including her mother Linda Biehl – established the Amy Biehl Foundation Trust to focus on personal development, job skills development and income-generating opportunities in South African communities. Biehl has served as an executive director for the Amy Biehl Foundation and is a contractor in the health care industry.

———

Q. What really matters to you?
Being present in every moment, being loved, feeling connected, feeling as if I can contribute no matter how small that contribution is and setting an example. I see myself as a resilient person and as a very, very grateful person; I try to focus on the gifts in my life. I love that my experiences have really shaped how I react to things. For a long time, I was just coping, though. I was a soldier trying to make sure that everything was moving forward for the people around me. It took me a really long time to get here, but I feel very calm in myself.

Q. What brings you happiness?
Some of my happiest moments have been a result of difficult moments, of realising that the magnitude of joy can, and does, far outweigh the painful things in my life. I'm grateful for difficult experiences, because they allow me to delve very deeply into myself and remember the positive things: my family, my successes. In a wider sense, the potential I see in young people brings me happiness; it makes me feel optimistic to see them seeing themselves as contributors, particularly in such a confusing time.

Q. What do you regard as the lowest depth of misery?
The thought that one person thinks they are better than another, and that their answer is more correct than another's, is the hardest for me to bear. It's not how we are going to achieve peace and understanding.

Q. What would you change if you could?
I'd like to see a shift in our education system – our world is nothing like it was and the traits that are going to be important in people, are their ability to be creative, to collaborate and to be resilient.

Q. Which single word do you most identify with?
Power. I love the idea of all of us coming into our power.

Sophie Blackall

Sophie Blackall was born in Melbourne, Australia. She earned her bachelor's degree in design with honours from the University of Technology in Sydney before relocating to Brooklyn, New York, in 2000. Blackall has illustrated more than forty children's books, including *Finding Winnie*, for which she won the 2016 Randolph Caldecott Medal. Her 2012 MTA Arts and Design subway poster was displayed in trains throughout New York City. Blackall has collaborated with UNICEF creating artwork for immunisation advocacy in the Democratic Republic of the Congo and India, and with Save the Children, promoting children's literacy in Rwanda and Bhutan.

Q. What really matters to you?
The fact that we are in this world *together* – that we are all connected. We live precariously on this fragile planet and, ultimately, that is the thing that we share more than anything else: the land we live on, the climate, and the world we will leave for our children and grandchildren. Australia and the land are very much a current that constantly runs beneath everything I do. We have this ancient landscape with its Indigenous People; we are still newcomers to the country and to the land.

The fact that we all have a story to tell also matters. We owe it to one another to listen to each other's stories. This is why I think books – and, in particular, children's books – are so important. Librarians and teachers are my heroes, because they are the people who are there right in the beginning, encouraging the reading of books and the appreciation of stories, and the empathy towards our fellow beings.

Q. What brings you happiness?
My family makes me really, really happy. I wound up with a good one, and I love spending time with them; I'm so lucky that I get to go home and see them at the end of the day. I also really love my work and the fact that I get to do it every day. I tell kids all the time that, if you can find the thing you love doing most in the world and then find a way to call it work, you are set. And I get great happiness from spending time with children; children are extraordinary and all of the clichés are true – they are full of hope, joy and honesty.

Q. What do you regard as the lowest depth of misery?
To feel unseen, unheard and unloved.

Q. What would you change if you could?
We will be nothing if we don't try and save the planet.

Q. Which single word do you most identify with?
Story.

Lisa Congdon

Lisa Congdon was born in Niskayuna in New York, USA. She spent fifteen years working in public education before embarking on a career as a writer, illustrator and fine artist. Congdon is the author of seven books, including *Whatever You Are, Be a Good One*; *Art Inc.*; *Fortune Favors the Brave*; *The Joy of Swimming*; and *A Glorious Freedom: Older Women Leading Extraordinary Lives*. Her clients include New York City's Museum of Modern Art, Harvard University and *Martha Stewart Living*. The organisation Forty Over 40 included Congdon in their 2015 list of the Forty Women Over 40 to Watch.

Q. What really matters to you?
A sense of connection to life – a sense of purpose. It matters that I get up every day and know what I am here to do. Purpose isn't something they teach you in school as a young girl, so most of us have to figure it out on our own; I figured out that I wanted to make art, to write stuff and to make a difference in the world.

When I was in my late teens I realised I was gay, which, at the time, was completely terrifying for me. I had grown up in an upper-middle-class, suburban, white world, so for the first time I was confronting being 'other.' Identifying as part of a marginalised group of people made me care about marginalised people everywhere. So, in a way, confronting my sexuality led me to become somebody who cared about social justice for all people.

Q. What brings you happiness?
I am the happiest at the beginning of any creative process. It is the 'rainbows and butterflies' phase – that imaginative phase when anything is possible.

Q. What do you regard as the lowest depth of misery?
The lowest depths of misery, for me, is a lack of connection – a feeling of separateness or of being alone. When I feel this, I know I need to figure out how I am going to reconnect.

Q. What would you change if you could?
So much pain in the world comes from fear of difference. So, if I could change one thing, it would be to make people recognise that our differences – skin colour, sexual orientation, gender identity, religion – are actually our strengths.

Q. Which single word do you most identify with?
Resilience. When hard things happen in my life, I call on my resilience to help me work through what I am stumbling up against and to help me use every hard situation as an opportunity to learn, grow and move on to whatever is next for me.

Gillian Caldwell

Gillian Caldwell was born in New York City, USA. She holds a bachelor of arts degree from Harvard University and a juris doctor degree from Georgetown University Law Center. As executive director of WITNESS, which trains and supports people using video in their fight for human rights, Caldwell helped produce over thirty documentary shorts and films. She was campaign director for the United States 1Sky climate and energy campaign. Caldwell is chief executive officer of Global Witness, a not-for-profit that exposes the hidden links between demand for natural resources, corruption, armed conflict and environmental destruction.

Q. What really matters to you?
In the wider sense, what I care about most is justice and sustainability. Here, I'm framing justice primarily in human terms – as human rights – and sustainability as the importance of living within the confines of the planetary boundaries that surround us. I'm interested in the place where justice and sustainability intersect, and in how we give people an opportunity to develop and advance: how do we get people the electricity they need in order to access the internet, be educated and participate? And how do we get people to explore new ways of sustaining themselves while paying attention to carbon loading and stewarding our limited natural resources?

Q. What brings you happiness?
My children, my family and being in nature.

Q. What do you regard as the lowest depth of misery?
I'm horrified by the greed that drives so much behaviour – at the 'profit at any price' mentality that some big corporations and individuals demonstrate in their collusion with governments, and by pay-to-play politics, whereby governments are delivering for private gain, rather than for public good. I am horrified by the collateral consequences of this greed. In January 2017, Oxfam reported that eight men now own the same wealth as the 3.6 billion people who make up the poorest half of humanity – it's preposterous. It's sad, too, because a lot of research demonstrates that wealth and power don't correlate with a sense of satisfaction and joy.

Q. What would you change if you could?
Climate change is already having catastrophic humanitarian and human-rights implications, so I would eliminate fossil-fuel subsidies, allow renewable energy to thrive, and I would ensure that multinational fossil fuel companies – some of the wealthiest in the history of *life* – pay for the full price of generating the profits they reap at the earth's expense.

Q. Which single word do you most identify with?
Integrity.

Jodi Peterson

Jodi Peterson was born in Orange County in California, USA. She earned a bachelor's degree in communications and sociology from Boston University, before working in marketing, communications and public relations. Peterson is development director of Interfaith Sanctuary Homeless Shelter in Boise, Idaho.

Q. What really matters to you?

I'm working very hard to try and close some gaps, to allow our community to successfully transition out of homelessness. A topic that's very important to me right now is helping those who are homeless get their identifications back. Many people who come out of the system – whether it's prison or foster care – end up homeless, with no way to actually say who they are. They can't do anything: they can't get a job, they can't drive a car and they can't apply to live anywhere. So they end up on the street. All this tends to lead to quite a bit of recidivism – because people have a will to survive, but if they can't do it legally, they're going to do it illegally.

Q. What brings you happiness?

I have two amazing children. They are stepping up and defending the work that we do, and they're finding their voices at a young age. They give me hope for their generation. I also have a very loving and supportive fiancé, Curtis Stigers, who works by my side to help raise much needed funds for the work that I do. He is a jazz musician who uses his amazing talent to help spread our message and connect donors to our cause.

Q. What do you regard as the lowest depth of misery?

People not understanding and people judging without spending any time talking to others. It makes me very sad when I hear people speak ill of things that they know nothing about.

Q. What would you change if you could?

My little world is Boise, and my work is with a group of chronically homeless people who are by far the most vulnerable people who live in our city. If I could raise a magic wand, Boise would have a Housing First building, a supported-living arrangement for people who are disabled and who will probably remain disabled for the remainder of their lives. Housing First would give them a place to be, a room with a lock on it, shelter, and a place to feel safe and call home. Not everyone will make it all the way back from homelessness, but, with safe shelter, a key of their own and supportive services wrapped around them, a person's chances become much greater.

Q. Which single word do you most identify with?

Family. It's where I get my strength.

Emily Uy

Emily Uy was born on the island of Cebu, in the Philippines. She immigrated to the United States in 2008. Uy is a cancer survivor and full-time caregiver, specialising in working with patients in hospice care who are suffering from the effects of a stroke or cancer. She is a member of the Pilipino Workers Centre in Los Angeles, California a non-profit that serves Filipino workers and their families.

Q. What really matters to you?

My family and my work. In 2008, we experienced major setbacks: my husband lost his job and a friend of ours caused us to lose our savings. There was no way for me to support my kids, so I moved to America to find work. I worked different jobs – making about four hundred dollars a week, which wasn't enough to send money home and still look after myself – until someone told me to become a live in caregiver; it meant I wouldn't have to commute every day and could wear scrubs all year long when I am on duty, without having to buy new clothes for work. I also joined the Pilipino Workers Centre as a way of making connections in the United States and finding a sense of belonging. They provided me with training and now I give back to them in return for what they've done for me. So, when there's a rally, I go rally. And when they are travelling to lobby for our rights, I'm there for those lobby visits – it's give and take.

When I experienced cancer and became a survivor, it changed the way I view my work. Before, it had just been a job, but I realised that my patients are like me; they are alone, their families are far away and there is no one to love them. So, my way of giving back is to care for my patients in their final days.

Q. What brings you happiness?

It's being able to help others and creating a smile.

Q. What do you regard as the lowest depth of misery?

People who are unforgiving because they can't find happiness and peace of mind.

Q. What would you change if you could?

I would end conflict: wars, certainly, but conflict of all kinds.

Q. Which single word do you most identify with?

Committed: I am committed to being a parent, a daughter, a friend and a worker.

Suha Issa

Suha Issa was born in Beirut, Lebanon, to Palestinian parents. Issa studied English language and literature at Beirut Arab University, and currently works as an English teacher to both Palestinian and Syrian refugees in Beirut. She is married and mother to four children who are all university graduates.

Q. What really matters to you?

The sense of satisfaction I get from seeing young people achieve their goals. I work as an English teacher in Beirut; in the mornings, I teach secondary-school Palestinian students at a United Nations agency, and lately I started working with primary-school Syrian refugees in the afternoons. Having my children look up to me and seek my advice – particularly now they've started their careers – matters to me as a mother.

My Palestinian teenage students are despairing because of the constraints placed on them by the Lebanese government; my role is to support them in their aspirations. This is their only chance to get out of this misery and suffering – out of *everything*.

Q. What brings you happiness?

I find happiness when people are honest, when I show a child that they *can*; when I'm doing my best to alleviate hopelessness and humiliation, especially for women and children.

Q. What do you regard as the lowest depth of misery?

The lowest depth of misery is oppression. I always keep in mind – a message all Palestinians carry forward – that even though I have never seen Palestine, it is my homeland. I tell all my students who are despairing that they *do* have a place where they belong. My own parents were born in Palestine, but fled to Lebanon: my mother was three and my father was eighteen. They have lived their lives expecting to return to Palestine. They suffered terribly, at a time when the international community knew very little of what was happening with Palestinian refugees in Lebanon. Over the years, Palestinians have become partially immersed in the Lebanese culture, but we are discriminated against in many ways. Our identity and culture are distorted, our existence marginalised. Tomorrow is never certain; we don't know what further oppression, violence or evil we may encounter. Now, even though I can never go to Palestine, I am Palestinian – I definitely don't belong here in Lebanon.

Q. What would you change if you could?

Oppression.

Q. Which single word do you most identify with?

Individuality.

p. 124

Fátima Carvalho

Fátima Carvalho was born in Mercês, an isolated village in the north-east of Brazil. She studied at the Federal University of Bahia in Salvador and started her professional career as a teacher in Brazil's public-school system. In 1989, she moved to the United Kingdom, where she began teaching Portuguese through her company, Language Connection. She is the founder of Caipirinha Club, a London-based social-networking group for speakers and students of Portuguese. Carvalho is based in London, and has lived previously in São Paulo and Johannesburg.

———

Q. What really matters to you?
Living life well and having experiences – because that's what life is all about. It's about learning new things, getting to know people and educating yourself. When I die, they'll say, 'Poor thing: she didn't leave anything.' But life is not about amassing things; it's about learning through experiences and being in charge of your own destiny.

Q. What brings you happiness?
It's being at home, where I'm cooking and surrounded by the art I love; everyone should have a home where they feel safe.

Q. What do you regard as the lowest depth of misery?
My father died when I was eleven; his loss was very sad. My mum was left alone with seven kids to raise, and she had very little money. I had to start working early on so that I would have money to do the things I enjoyed – going to the cinema, museums – because my mother didn't have enough to give these experiences to all of us. My mother is my role model. She taught me to be strong, to fight for what I want and to be an honest, positive person. My mother had no education – she didn't even finish primary school – but she became a very independent woman who always emphasised the importance of studying. She made sure we were in school and that we went to university – my life would be so different without her. Where there was misery, she created something positive for her children. She even adopted a child whose mother had lost her job. That's the thing I've learned: no matter how far down you are, your generosity doesn't need to die.

Q. What would you change if you could?
I think we should do more to reduce poverty and homelessness, and to improve the quality of education. Access to knowledge – whether through schools, the internet, other people or books – is crucial. That is what will set people free.

Q. Which single word do you most identify with?
Connection.

p. 125

Deborah Santana

Deborah Santana was born in San Francisco in California, USA. Her non-profit, Do A Little, serves women and girls in the areas of health, education and happiness. In 2005, Santana published a memoir, *Space Between the Stars*. Santana has produced five short documentary films, including four with Emmy-award winning director Barbara Rick: *Road to Ingwavuma, Girls of Daraja, School of My Dreams* and *Powerful Beyond Measure.* Santana's films highlight the work of non-profit partners in South Africa and of a free secondary boarding school for girls in Kenya. Santana is mother to three adult children: Salvador, Stella and Angelica.

———

Q. What really matters to you?
My family matters most to me: my three grown children; my husband, Carl; my sister; and our extended relatives. And my parents greatly influenced me in their lifetimes; the struggles they went through as an interracial couple in the 1940s – when it wasn't legal for them to be married in California – planted the seed of activism in me. They raised my sister and me to fight for equality and spiritual freedom, and I was taught by them and our church that everyone is in your circle. So, my family extends to Martin Luther King, Jr.'s concept of 'beloved community,' in which an all-inclusive spirit of sisterhood and brotherhood will no longer allow poverty, hunger, prejudice, discrimination and homelessness to be tolerated.

Q. What brings you happiness?
I find joy in being still, and in reading the works of people who have overcome personal strife to manifest good and live in their power. Two years ago, I finished my master's degree in women's spirituality. It was life-changing to read the multi-cultural and multi-dimensional voices of women who identify their socio-cultural, spiritual and philosophical lineages without the oppression of patriarchy. The idea stuck with me that activism can either be brash – *against* others – or it can be gentle – *for* others and standing your ground. My own activism is informed by indigenous wisdom. I call myself a 'spiritual activist' – my causes are illuminated and given foundation through prayer. The peaceful, healing energy of meditation brings me to a state of happiness.

Q. What do you regard as the lowest depth of misery?
The consciousness of divisiveness between people.

Q. What would you change if you could?
I would change the way spirituality is left out of education – not religion, but spirituality. I would have children start the day with meditation, with finding that soft, silent centre of their beings.

Q. Which single word do you most identify with?
Gratitude.

pp. 136–7

Ghada Masrieyeh

Ghada Masrieyeh was born in Beirut, Lebanon, to Palestinian parents. She was born in Sabra refugee camp and has lived in Beirut's Bourj El Barajneh refugee camp for thirty-two years. She works with Soufra, a catering social enterprise established by the Women's Program Association. Soufra employs women from Bourj El Barajneh to produce Palestinian dishes that are sold outside of the camp.

———

Q. What really matters to you?
Seeing my family happy and having work to keep me busy.

I love my work. While my husband and I were raising our children, I was a housewife. We have three sons and one daughter, and now two granddaughters. With the children grown, I had a lot of free time and grew bored. I knew Mariam Shaar (p. 172), who had a centre in the camp where people took cooking classes, and I thought that would be an interesting place to spend some time. Mariam told us she would be opening a kitchen project, and over time this developed into Soufra. We found funding and support, and began to grow. We started by giving food to schools and have gone on to buy our own food truck, selling Palestinian cuisine in the city. I am busy, with no spare time, and I love it! I feel there are always new things happening in my life; I'm always meeting new people and cooking with my friends – I am happy and so grateful.

Q. What brings you happiness?
My happiness is my family's happiness. I am also happy that I have no free time, because it means I am working. And best of all, I enjoy what I'm doing.

Q. What do you regard as the lowest depth of misery?
The context I live in is very uncertain – in fact, every day our existence feels unstable. I am always afraid of tomorrow. I am always afraid of war breaking out and of how that will affect my children: Where will they go? Will we be able to stay together? We are living in extremely difficult circumstances, with little access to clean water and constant power cuts.

Q. What would you change if you could?
I would leave the camp.

Q. Which single word do you most identify with?
Life. In spite of all the hardship I have known in life, life is beautiful.

p. 142

Véronique Vasseur

———

Véronique Vasseur was born in Paris, France. She graduated with a doctorate in medicine from Université Broussais Hotel Dieu in 1976. Vasseur worked in French medical social security before being employed at La Santé Prison, Paris, in 1992; becoming the prison's chief medical officer in 1993. Her book *Médecin-chef à la Prison de la Santé*, which recounted her experiences at La Santé, was published in 2001, and resulted in death threats and a parliamentary inquiry. Vasseur is a member of the International Observatory of Prisons, and now works in the Hôpital Saint-Antoine, a public hospital. Vasseur is also a painter.

———

Q. What really matters to you?

After my mother died, I decided to finally do something that really mattered to me. So, I entered La Santé Prison in Paris. I became part of a very particular, extremely violent world. I really loved the place and its residents, but it was a world completely apart, with its own absurd codes. So much could have been done to improve it – with very little effort and no extra resources – that I decided to write a book about it. The response was incredibly violent because, when you take on the prison administration, it's as if you are attacking the police. They have means of retaliation that are absolutely vile – extremely secret, extremely underhanded – so, after nine months of death threats, the Ministry of Health became scared that something might happen and exfiltrated me.

My driving force in writing the book was first and foremost a roar of anger; injustice incenses me, as does stupidity, and I was denouncing all the stupidity of incarceration. I was supported by the medical team and, of course, by the detainees inside the prison. I have a whole suitcase full of letters from inmates and their families, and also from more furtive sources, like the prison chaplains. My book triggered a commission of inquiry – the prison couldn't hide any more.

Q. What brings you happiness?

I find happiness in nature, beauty and art – in painting while listening to Maria Callas at full blast!

Q. What do you regard as the lowest depth of misery?

Injustice. There are way too many have-nots out there. At the hospital, practically all I see are people who can barely get by.

Q. What would you change if you could?

Wealth has to be more fairly distributed; I'm incensed that some people can barely make ends meet – are forced to go to soup kitchens – while others are having such a great time.

Q. Which single word do you most identify with?

Sincerity.

p. 143

Monika Hauser

———

Monika Hauser was born in Thal, Switzerland. She studied medicine in Innsbruck, Austria, going onto specialise in gynaecology. In 1993, in response to the mass rape of women during the Bosnian War, Hauser and a team of twenty Bosnian psychologists and doctors opened a women's therapy centre in Zenica. This evolved into Medica Mondiale, an international women's rights organisation of which Hauser remains executive member of the board. In 2008, her service was honoured with a Right Livelihood Award, and, in 2012, she was awarded the Council of Europe's North–South Prize.

———

Q. What really matters to you?

Love and respect matter, and standing together. Because, together – with the common power of like-minded people – we can move mountains; we can rid the world of institutions that permit the continuity of sexualised violence, and can support traumatised women to recover and bring their own voices to our work. This is work that concerns all of us. I first came to understand my own responsibility in this when I learned of the trauma my family suffered in World War II and of the sexualised violence several members of my family have experienced. Then the violence perpetrated against women in the Bosnian War showed me that I had to play a role – this is when I founded Medica Mondiale.

Q. What brings you happiness?

Feeling alive: walking in the sun, in a flower meadow, with my husband and our dog.

Q. What do you regard as the lowest depth of misery?

Sexualised violence and its destructive consequences: these affect all society and will have effects for generations to come. I'm furious at the ignorant politicians who create terrible situations without any sense of culpability.

Q. What would you change if you could?

I am changing something now; my colleagues and I are taking our competencies, capabilities, inner strengths and conviction that together we are strong, and using them to engage structures that perpetrate gender injustice. We are supporting survivors medically, psychosocially and legally. We support them through income-generating projects that allow the women to earn their own money and avoid relationships of dependence. I recently met one of our first clients again. When we first met, she hadn't wanted to go on with life. Now, she has started a self-help group in her village for women who aren't receiving external support and is a beautiful, strong woman. It's a wonderful story.

Q. Which single word do you most identify with?

Persistent.

pp. 148–9

Mithu Ghosh

———

Mithu Ghosh was born in Murshidabad, India. At the age of nine, she moved to Kolkata to live with her mother and aunt, who were working in the sex trade. Ghosh left school at fourteen and, after selling rotis for several years, now works as an artisan for The Loyal Workshop.

———

Q. What really matters to you?

What matters is my family and working hard for them. It matters that my son receives a great education that gives him opportunities in life, and I want to raise him well – to respect women.

When I was nine, I moved to Bowbazar, in Kolkata, to be with my mum and my aunty – they had been employed to do housework, but their place of work was actually a brothel in the red-light district and their boss was a madam. They ended up working in the sex trade and endured great suffering. My mother suffered and sacrificed so much to make sure I could receive an education. My aunty died when she covered herself in kerosene and set herself alight; witnessing the suffering that took her life and witnessing the pain that my mother experienced – I decided I would never work as a sex worker, no matter what.

Q. What brings you happiness?

My work for The Loyal Workshop. There used to be so much stress and tension in my mind, and now that's gone. And it's not just work – after all the suffering in my life, now I can buy food, wear new clothes and afford my son's tutor.

Q. What do you regard as the lowest depth of misery?

The suffering of the girls here.

Q. What would you change if you could?

I want policy changes to require that all women are respected and that men are punished appropriately if they commit crimes against women.

Q. Which single word do you most identify with?

Misti: it is the Bengali word for the sweets we have here – even if you have diabetes, you can't resist misti!

Josefine Cox

———

Josefine Cox was born in Marburg, Germany. She holds a degree in international business management from Cardiff University. She has been working in the field of corporate, product and service design solutions for more than fifteen years, and taught communication and design thinking processes at the Institute for Marketing and Communication. In 2015, Cox co-founded Musik Bewegt – meaning 'music moves' – an online donation platform through which musicians can gather support for their social endeavours and not-for-profit activities. Cox is managing director of Musik Bewegt and runs a small design consultancy.

———

Q. What really matters to you?
I was teaching communication and was working as a consultant for a not-for-profit organisation when I realised that I had to help others in need. And so I developed a concept and co-founded an online donation platform which makes it possible to donate to a variety of social projects. We wanted to build upon the emotional power of music and its ability to both trigger empathy and unite millions of people to move towards change together. People don't need a hefty bank account to contribute towards humanitarian activities or to help one another. We are all capable of effecting change, but together the change can be truly great.

Q. What brings you happiness?
When I feel that I am in any way able to help others, or to facilitate change.

Freedom and honesty are important to me. And living an autonomous life. We are lucky to have been born in freedom and peace; this is a valuable gift for which we should be grateful.

Q. What do you regard as the lowest depth of misery?
That millions of people have to suffer in fear – that they must try to survive whilst being ignored, skipped, overlooked. Also, the fact that circumstances which force people to flee their homes are primarily man-made. Too many people who are sitting in comfort and lethargy profit from social injustice – Musik Bewegt is an attempt to wake people up and to remind them of their social responsibility and their altruism. The world longs for togetherness and not for division.

Q. What would you change if you could?
I would try to diminish social inequality between people and genders, and guarantee equal access to all the world's wealth. Also, I would try to provide better access to education, clean drinking water, medical care, resources and public infrastructure. I believe the world is a big, colourful family; if one family member isn't well, it is the duty of the other family members to support them.

Q. Which single word do you most identify with?
Beherzt. Courageous.

Imany

———

Imany was born in Istres, France. She pursued a successful international modelling career before returning to France to become a singer, releasing her debut album, *The Shape of a Broken Heart,* in 2011. In 2014, Imany produced the soundtrack for the film *French Women,* and n 2016 released her second album, *The Wrong Kind of War,* which sold almost one hundred thousand copies; her song 'Don't Be So Shy' was a number-one single in France, Germany, Poland, Austria and Russia.

———

Q. What really matters to you?
Fairness, justice and kindness matter. I worry that kindness has come to be seen as a weakness, when, in fact, it is such a powerful thing; someone who is truly kind can change, not just your day, but your perspective, too.

I value honesty and truth. I don't care about imperfection – it's okay to be imperfect – but it's not okay to hide and lie. Whether it's in a piece of art or music, or in a person, what I look for is truth.

Q. What brings you happiness?
I feel very happy when I hear my sixteen-month-old baby talk and laugh. When I'm on stage I feel happy, too, because I am completely myself and that person is received by the people who come to watch me. When I was fourteen, I picked up a book by Simone de Beauvoir. Back then, my family was still very traditional: my mother was a good housewife, raising good daughters, and she told me that I had to be the perfect wife. But, when I read that book, it was like a slap in the face – it was the first time I'd heard a woman's point of view like this and it was the beginning of who I am today. It was the first time I realised I was the master of my own destiny. I realised my life was somewhere else, even though I didn't yet know where that was.

Q. What do you regard as the lowest depth of misery?
The brutality of the world right now, particularly for women.

Q. What would you change if you could?
I would change the way we raise our daughters. And, because the power is in the hands of men, I would also change how we raise our boys; I would show them that girls are just as valuable as they are.

Q. Which single word do you most identify with?
Stay.

Sasha Marianna Salzmann

———

Sasha Marianna Salzmann was born in Volgograd, Russia. In 1995, she emigrated to Germany, where she studied literature, theatre and media at the University of Hildesheim, and screenwriting at the Berlin University of the Arts. An award-winning dramatist and essayist, she was editor of *Freitext* – a German culture-and-society magazine – from 2002 to 2013. Salzmann became artistic director of Studio Я, at Berlin's Maxim Gorki Theatre, in 2013. She co-founded the New Institute for Dramatic Writing in 2014, with the goal of encouraging debate by bringing the social importance of the arts back into the public consciousness.

———

Q. What really matters to you?
Both my biological family and the people I've chosen to be my family – the people I can call when I'm struggling. Most of these people are sisters, and I feel a deep, deep connection to them. That makes me crazy happy; every time I see them, it feels like I am receiving a gift.

Q. What brings you happiness?
Writing; when I can enter this place of poetry, and it embraces me. It is a mystical place without clear paths to take you there. It's not always a bright and joyful place while writing, but when I'm finished, I always wonder why I do anything else.

Q. What do you regard as the lowest depth of misery?
Seeing people oppressed for so long that nothing is left to build trust on, and there is no dignity. This makes me want to put my hands up and say, 'I'm out of here.' But this is also the worst – just to leave the battle and say, 'I am sorry; this is hopeless.'

Q. What would you change if you could?
We have to put people who come from marginalised backgrounds into positions of power in our political, cultural and social institutions. It makes a great difference when the person at the top of a hierarchy knows her field both theoretically and practically; when she has actual experience to inform her decision-making.

Q. Which single word do you most identify with?
Silvia Calderoni once said in an interview that, to describe herself, she wished for a word that would transform or change its meaning every twenty minutes. I completely agree with her, and so without such a word, I'd choose 'transforming.'

Miss Tic

Miss Tic was born in Paris, France. She is a French street-art pioneer whose stencil work and accompanying poems have been widely exhibited internationally, in public spaces, galleries and art fairs; her works have been acquired by the likes of the Fonds Municipal d'Art Contemporain de la Ville de Paris, the Victoria and Albert Museum in London and the Museum of European and Mediterranean Civilisations in Marseilles. Miss Tic has collaborated widely, including with fashion houses Kenzo, Comme des Garçons, Longchamp and Louis Vuitton, and with the French Postal Service on a series of collector's stamps of her works for International Women's Day 2011.

Q. What really matters to you?

Being able to express myself really matters to me, as does leaving a trace; because, I think that art resists time and even death. I started painting poems and pictures in urban environments in 1985, after a trip to the United States during which I saw the emergence of hip-hop and graffiti art. When I came back to Paris, I met a lot of artists making street art there, too; it seemed like an interesting form of expression to me, and their work inspired me. I was interested in subverting, to an extent, what is normally seen on city walls. More often than not, these public spaces display advertising, so I wanted to fill them with poetry and painting. It was my way of leaving my mark – of putting in my two cents worth. And I've been doing it for thirty years now.

Q. What brings you happiness?

What gives me the most joy – I don't like the word happiness – is the desire to create. Desire, more than anything else, is what inspires me. The desire to live, the desire to create, the desire to discover and to take pleasure are my driving force.

Q. What do you regard as the lowest depth of misery?

There is another driving force for me in life; I'm angry. I've been this way since I was a child. I am very sensitive to injustice of any kind. So, inhumanity distresses me. And, instead of getting upset about it, I get angry.

Q. What would you change if you could?

Although I am a person who writes on walls, I would stop walls – whether physical, geographical or mental – being built. I draw on walls to make it possible to see beyond them.

Q. Which single word do you most identify with?

Subversion.

Dominique Attias

Dominique Attias CLH was born in Tunis, Tunisia. She holds a master's of law from Université Paris II Panthéon-Assas and a post-graduate degree in clinical psychology and psychopathology from Université Paris 8. Attias lectures at a number of French tertiary institutions and has held offices in several French legal associations as well in the Louis Chatin Association, which works to defend children's rights. In 2011, Attias was made a Knight of France's National Order of the Legion of Honour.

Q. What really matters to you?

My childhood was not particularly happy, so my children matter very much to me. And standing up for children and their rights matters. I started my career as a business lawyer, but, after a while, I became bored, because my life lacked a governing passion. I'd always been fascinated by sociology and psychology, so, when I read *L'Influence Qui Guérit*, by Tobie Nathan – a professor at Université Paris 8 – I decided to do further study. I completed a higher-education degree on practices within migrant families and became a legal expert in ethnopsychiatry. For five years, I worked with migrant families through the Georges Devereux Centre, before eventually finding my way to the children's court. It was riddled with problems, so I decided to improve what I could. I poured my efforts into child advocacy and got myself elected to the Bar Association. This experience with the legal system also confronted me with the misogyny faced by women lawyers, so I joined a group called Femmes et Droit that rails against the clan-like mentality of the patriarchy. I am inspired to open new doors in this pigeon-holed society and defend the most vulnerable.

Q. What brings you happiness?

Being free to serve – without affiliation or constraint – and being able to give without expecting anything in return.

Q. What do you regard as the lowest depth of misery?

The world's indifference. When people are dying in places that have no oil, we stand back and watch – that kind of injustice is unbearable; it makes me angry and that anger fuels me.

Q. What would you change if you could?

I would do away with fear – whether individual or collective, it does a lot of harm.

Q. Which single word do you most identify with?

It's a phrase: 'never give up.'

Clémentine Rappaport

Clémentine Rappaport CLH was born in Nantes, France. She began her career as a psychiatry assistant at Robert Ballanger Hospital in Aulnay-sous-Bois, near Paris; she founded an adolescent inpatient service at the hospital in 2000 and has led its child-psychiatry department since 2012. Rappaport was made a Knight of France's National Order of the Legion of Honour in 2017.

Q. What really matters to you?

The greatest motivating factor in my life is the fact that there are so many children suffering in this world. I work with many displaced children who have not only experienced incredible hardship in coming to France, but who are subjected to social exclusion because of this. It's inconceivable to me that children who have experienced such hardship and trauma are being confronted with unequal access to physical and mental health care. This perpetuates their suffering and is appalling. Through my work, I am dedicated to providing support for these extremely vulnerable children.

Q. What brings you happiness?

I get a lot of satisfaction from my work, which, in many ways, is political as well as medical. It brings me joy that I'm not alone in my commitment – that I have a team who share my values and goals. I also find joy in the moment when a child becomes able to access language; many children who are suffering just don't speak, so, when a child is able to articulate who they are and what they're going through, they are effectively joining the world.

Q. What do you regard as the lowest depth of misery?

Helplessness. Families with no resources who are raising children with syndromes such as autism feel absolutely helpless. This makes me sad, but it also serves as an opportunity to accompany such families and assist them in dealing with their challenges.

Q. What would you change if you could?

I know this is impossible, but I would change whatever it is about humanity that makes rivalry and hatred so many people's primary motivators; I truly believe this is the cause of inequality.

Q. Which single word do you most identify with?

Perseverance.

Märta, Karin, and Linnéa Nylund

The Nylund sisters – Märta, Karin and Linnéa – were born in Markusvinsa in Lappland, Sweden, where they still live together; their village is home to twenty people and is north of the Arctic Circle. All three women trained as teachers, with Karin specialising in the Swedish minority language, Meänkieli. Since retiring from full-time teaching, the sisters have owned and operated a restaurant and hotel in Korpilombolo, a neighbouring village. They are also the organisers of the Korpilombolo European Festival of the Night, a philosophy, literature and arts festival that is held annually between 1 and 13 December.

Q. What really matters to you?

Karin: My sisters – they are so important to me.

Märta: We were all born in our family home and have lived together most of our lives. It's been great, because we get along very well.

When we were young, although many parents wanted to speak Swedish to their children – to prepare them for school – our parents always spoke to us in our local dialect, Meänkieli. We are very grateful for this decision, because we love the language; it is a minority language, and we want it to survive.

Karin: I teach Meänkieli to children and elder pupils. It used to not be a recognised language, but that has since changed – around one hundred and sixty thousand people now speak it.

Märta: We have an amazing sense of community in this town; although it's small, it gives you a sense of being somebody – of being known. Many think that living in a small community entails a lot of accountability, but, at our age, we don't care about that! You might also think men would be in charge in a place like this, but that is not the case. With the men all working outside of the home – in the forest or wherever – the women are the ones who take care of the children, the home, the animals . . . *everything*. The women here are very skilled and strong, and that's something we identify with. We are strong.

Linnea: When I think about what matters currently, I think about the disasters of war. I was born some years after World War II, and you'd think people would have learned their lessons from that – that the United Nations would be revered as the most important apparatus of peace. But, when I look back on my sixty-six years, the conflict is worse now than it has ever been. I feel very ashamed that my country produces weapons that are used in wars all over the world – weapons that kill people. I want the Swedish government to be the first to say, 'Right, tomorrow we stop all arms production in this country.' This would set an example for other nations to follow. We need someone with the bravery to say that weapons are not being made to defend – they are being made to kill. And the money from their manufacture doesn't flow to the government or its citizens, it goes to the manufacturers.

Märta: I also see that society, generally, has too much money. When we were younger, we had no money – but we were rich. We were taught that, if you saw something you wanted to buy, you should try to make it yourself first. This was a very important lesson. We were also taught to always treat others with respect, regardless of their colour or class – regardless of all that is superfluous about a person. The only thing that matters is how you conduct yourself.

Karin: Another thing that matters to all of us, is nature. People get so stressed about so many insignificant things in today's world, and I just wish they could embrace a little more of nature's calm in their lives.

Märta: A knowledge of nature is absolutely essential if you are to appreciate its miracles. There is so much joy to be had in nature, from winter to spring.

Linnea: We were taught, from very young, that we weren't to kill animals – even ants or spiders – because they are a part of nature, and everything in creation has a right to live.

Q. What brings you happiness?

Linnea: Meeting new people and seeing young people growing up brings me a lot of joy.

And nature is a great happiness to me.

Karin: Happiness is walking through nature, being in the garden and singing along to music.

Märta: For me, happiness is our village. It's very familiar; we know everybody here, and we feel safe.

Q. What do you regard as the lowest depth of misery?

Linnea: The Syrian Civil War and the refugee crisis. It's horrible that countries across the world are rejecting these people who aren't able to stay in their homes. People from different cultures have the potential to enrich our lives, but we miss these opportunities because we are so anxious about them. Our parents were always very open-hearted – very willing to offer a room to someone – and that has stuck with us.

Karin: For me, it is war and the destruction of the environment. There is so much agricultural poison, and this worries me greatly.

Q. What would you change if you could?

Linnea: All arms factories would be shut down tomorrow, and their production lines would start creating something functional for society. And, I would end genetic research. I don't understand what scientists are trying to achieve here; they can't change anything or improve anything – it's good as it is!

Karin: I would create smaller communities. The world has become too big, and people are forgetting about each other. That's what America's problem is – it's too big.

Linnea: I would help the many women who live in very difficult situations. Most mothers have to work to feed their families, yet they are required to leave their homes to earn wages; if I were a mother, I would find it very difficult to leave my children. So, I think that women should have flexible hours, because only they can decide what works best for their families *and* for their employers.

Q. Which single word do you most identify with?

Karin: We all chose the same Meänkieli word: *luonon-kappale.* In English, it means 'piece of nature.' Everyone is a little piece of nature; if we could acknowledge that, circumstances would improve for everybody, including women and children.

Märta: It is a beautiful concept, because it encompasses everything. For me, it is about being a part of a shared heart; it's important to always be aware that everyone is equal and is therefore deserving of kindness.

Audrey Brown

Audrey Brown was born in Kliptown, South Africa. Inspired as a child by journalists such as Maud Motanyane and Don Mattera, she later obtained a bachelor's degree in journalism, African history and politics from Rhodes University and a master's degree in journalism from the University of Wales, and is now a broadcast journalist with the BBC World Service. Brown has been particularly influenced by her mother, Beatrice, a fierce Catholic divorcee; her beloved uncle, Gene; and the fact that she is the only girl in a family of five children.

Q. What really matters to you?
It matters to me that we don't have enough for everyone, and that I don't do enough about that. I am deeply thankful to people who go out of their way to do things to change the world. I thought that my job as a journalist would be something that could change the world but it doesn't always feel like it does that enough.

I want my nieces and nephews to feel special. When I was a child, it was my uncle, Gene, who made me aware of my true place in the world, and that it could be skewed by the particular ideology in South Africa at the time that was designed to tell me that I wasn't good enough. He made it clear to my brothers and me that we were exceptional human beings.

Q. What brings you happiness?
I would say the place and time when I am most happy is when I'm watching a thunderstorm in the dark, or playing swords with my nieces.

Q. What do you regard as the lowest depth of misery?
Personally, it is not knowing when next I'm going home to South Africa. I've lived in the United Kingdom for about eleven years. I'm an earthling and home is everywhere – yes – but I am a South African as well.

On the macro level, I feel unfairness and inequality very deeply. It's no accident that children say, 'That's not fair!' They recognise a lack of fairness.

Q. What would you change if you could?
We all want the world to be fairer, we all want to banish white-supremacist racist thinking. But that's not just going to happen, we're going to have to make it happen. I want human beings to be imbued with the spirit of excellence: to want to do the best that they can in any endeavour.

Q. Which single word do you most identify with?
The message I'd want to convey is, 'Be excellent.' But what sticks with me is 'kindness.' Just be kind.

Nokwanele Mbewu

Nokwanele Mbewu was born in Cala, South Africa. She manages the Mentor Mother Programme at the Philani Maternal Child Health and Nutrition Trust in Khayelitsha township in Cape Town, South Africa. The Philani Clinic provides holistic health and nutrition support to women and families in townships; its Mentor Mother Programme has been extended to South Africa's Eastern Cape, as well as to Swaziland and Ethiopia.

Q. What really matters to you?
My job and my children are who I am – I have two beautiful daughters, and their futures are so important. The care of women and children matters, it hurts me when I think about lost children and children without opportunities. When I go on home visits, I always look into the eyes of each child I visit. In those eyes something is written: it says, 'I have potential.' That potential needs to be fostered. So, fostering children's potential if and where I can matters to me.

Q. What brings you happiness?
What also makes me happy is seeing children getting better. When I first started with the Mentor Mother Programme, I met three girls on a home visit. They were living in a shack that didn't have proper walls – the walls were made of plastic. Every night, this guy was coming over, opening the home and taking a child to rape. I thought about those beautiful girls every night until they were removed by a social worker and taken somewhere that I knew they would be safe. It makes me happy to see positive change; I see so much misery in this job, but when I see things change for the better I feel such joy. The women I work with have such capacity for strength, and watching them realise that makes me so, so happy.

Q. What do you regard as the lowest depth of misery?
Knowing that there are so many people in need of help, but seeing those with the ability to help them ignore the moral obligation to do so.

Q. What would you change if you could?
We have 140 mentor mothers. Together they have a caseload of about five thousand families a year – so you can see how much vulnerability there is. We're doing what little we can, but there is just so much need. So, that's what I would change if I could – I would make sure that anyone in need received help.

Q. Which single word do you most identify with?
Care.

Patricia Grace King

Patricia Grace King was born in Charlottesville in Virginia, USA. She holds a master of fine arts from Warren Wilson College and a PhD in English from Emory University. An author, educator and cancer survivor, in the early 1990s she worked in Guatemala with the non-governmental organisation Witness for Peace, which aims to change United States policies and corporate practices that affect Latin America. She later directed a language school and cross-cultural-experience programme, CASAS, in Guatemala City. Her novella, *Day of All Saints*, reflects upon stories of refugees from Guatemala's civil war and won the 2017 Miami University Novella Prize.

Q. What really matters to you?
Being present – this is tied to having had, and recovered from, cancer; I had five months of chemotherapy, then a double mastectomy. There were elements that just sucked, but, in some ways, it was a blessed time. When we were in the middle of it, my husband said, 'Well, this is just what we're doing right now; later on we'll do something else.' This was a great way to think about it, because it helped me assess what I could take away from the experience; everything can change wildly and no moment is permanent.

Part of being present is also being conscious of what we can do from our positions of privilege. For me, that would be creating empathy and awareness of the world. My mother's family were very activist orientated. They instilled in me the idea that you don't just believe in something. You act. You try to make the world a better place. And that matters.

Q. What brings you happiness?
My marriage has been a great source of joy; sharing a vision with someone and sharing values.

And my writing is life-giving. I'm working on a novel about Guatemala; I'm still working through my time in that country. I had joined Witness for Peace while the civil war was still going on, and later I ran a language school. Going to funerals of kids killed in gang violence, whose mothers taught at my school, forced me to confront the question of what I was going to do with my life. In answer, I just started writing.

Q. What do you regard as the lowest depth of misery?
Not feeling connected to a community in any significant way; feeling unmoored or stranded in the world, especially in crisis.

Q. What would you change if you could?
I would make everybody tolerant of difference; make them be excited by it, instead of afraid of it.

Q. Which single word do you most identify with?
Gratitude.

Hlubi Mboya Arnold

Hlubi Mboya Arnold was born in Alice in Eastern Cape, South Africa. She is best known for her role in the South African Broadcasting Corporation drama *Isidingo*, in which she portrayed the long-running show's first HIV-positive character. Mboya Arnold is a social-justice activist, a social-entrepreneurship advocate, a sportswoman, an educator and a scholar, and is an executive director of two not-for-profit organisations: Future CEOs, which supports South Africans whose socioeconomic circumstances exclude them from accessing top business education and professional development opportunities; and Sunshine Cinema, a solar-powered mobile cinema that converts solar energy into social impact.

———

Q. What really matters to you?
What matters to me is protecting children; although I don't have my own kids, I lose sleep worrying about other people's children. I'm passionate about ensuring that every child receives a quality education, and, especially, that young girls reach their full potential. One of my greatest role models is Oprah Winfrey; her academy takes in girls who have nothing – girls who have experienced violence and extreme disadvantage – and is giving them the skills to converse and engage with any- and everybody. That's what I want for all girl children in Africa.

Although my name is a Xhosa name, it defies the archetypal Xhosa woman because it means 'different kind of girl.' I interpret it as representing strength, unity, passion and love of one another, and that interpretation informs my work as an activist. I'm a feminist, but I don't believe in the exclusion of men – I believe in the *in*clusion of all. In terms of gender equality, the work is all about breaking the glass ceiling. There are so many double standards in the corporate environment and there is still so much violence in the workplace – this is not limited to physical violence, it can be something as 'simple' as marginalising women.

Q. What brings you happiness?
Myself: happiness has to start within you.

Q. What do you regard as the lowest depth of misery?
Physical violence and mental health issues such as depression, anxiety, stress and suicide are big issues in the black community, so I would say pain, in all its forms.

Q. What would you change if you could?
My world is my country, so I want all my people to be educated; I want them to thrive as equals and be empowered to become their own ambassadors for change.

Q. Which single word do you most identify with?
Love: it pours out of me.

Cordelia Fine

Cordelia Fine was born in Toronto, Canada. She holds a bachelor of arts in experimental psychology from the University of Oxford, a master's in philosophy in criminology from the University of Cambridge and a PhD in psychology from University College London. She is the author of *Delusions of Gender*, *A Mind of Its Own* and *Testosterone Rex*, and is a regular contributor to popular media. A full-time academic, Fine is a professor of history and philosophy of science in the School of Historical and Philosophical Studies at the University of Melbourne.

———

Q. What really matters to you?
I care about the political implications of flawed science and the quality of scientific evidence. The science of how sex influences us has moved on hugely – in evolutionary biology, in psychology and in neuroscience – yet our beliefs about the role of biology in sex differences are sometimes based on science from the last century.

When I began looking at neuroimaging studies, I was shocked by the disconnect between what the science showed and the conclusions that were being drawn by popular writers, in particular the supposed differences in hardwiring between male and female brains were being explained in terms of very familiar gender stereotypes: men are naturally competitive, aggressive and dominant, and women are more nurturing and understanding. My aim, through my book *Delusions of Gender,* was, in part, to show how popular writers were misrepresenting, exaggerating and sometimes fabricating the science, with the goal of shoring up gender stereotypes and making us comfortable about an unequal status quo.

Q. What brings you happiness?
Freud got it right: love and work.

Q. What do you regard as the lowest depth of misery?
I feel as though I've had the most charmed life on the planet, so I can't really lay claim to have had any misery at all.

Q. What would you change if you could?
Maybe I've spent too long in the company of philosophers, but, if I could, I would impose John Rawls' veil of ignorance on society. The veil of ignorance states that, in order to prevent self-interest from dictating how resources, rights and positions in society are spread out, there is a veil of ignorance with respect to what one's personal characteristics and places in society will be. This forces policy makers to effect distributions based on moral considerations.

Q. Which single word do you most identify with?
Argument: there are a lot of strands to bringing about greater equality – gender or otherwise – and some of those have to do with rational argument.

Adele Green

Adele Green AC was born in Cairns, Australia. She studied medicine, then epidemiology at the University of Queensland and at the London School of Hygiene and Tropical Medicine. She is a senior scientist at QIMR Berghofer Medical Research Institute in Brisbane and at Cancer Research UK, Manchester Institute and Manchester University. Her focus is on researching skin cancer and melanoma causation, prevention, management and prognosis. In 2004, Green was made a Companion of the Order of Australia for service to medical research, to public health and to leadership in the wider scientific community.

———

Q. What really matters to you?
The personal welfare of my children, my family and my friends matters deeply to me; I know this is true because my world goes awry if there's any great trouble within my inner circle.

Further, it is seeing other people having good health and well-being. I find my profession so rewarding because it dovetails with my own personal deeply entrenched values and wishes; I embrace the World Health Organisation's (WHO) excellent definition of health: the state of complete physical, mental and social well-being.

Q. What brings you happiness?
Places of natural beauty. Unquestionably, being in a beautiful place far away from human touches surpasses everything else.

Great music and great literature give me deep joy, because engaging with them means touching the minds of brilliant people.

I think curiosity is the mark of a great researcher. The sense of discovery – that eureka moment of insight or epiphany when things come together in my mind and I uncover something truly great – makes me happy.

Q. What do you regard as the lowest depth of misery?
Seeing the misery of innocent victims of violence, exploitation and greed – both human and animal – who live in the most miserable circumstances.

Q. What would you change if you could?
I would banish hunger, poverty, intolerance, greed and cruelty.

In my field, I would change the overall focus from cure to prevention. Good health ultimately flows from a very sound social structure, but a lot of people are impotent because of overarching cycles of exploitation and poverty that aren't going to change until we have a more just society.

Q. Which single word do you most identify with?

Passion. If you've got good health and opportunities, you have to live life to the fullest – otherwise it's just a waste.

p. 217

Caroline Paul

Caroline Paul was born in New York City, USA. She obtained her pilot's license at twenty and eventually flew paragliders and ultralights. At twenty-three she joined an all-women whitewater team, rafting unexplored rivers in places like Borneo and Australia. A Stanford graduate, Paul joined the San Francisco Fire Department soon after, becoming the fifteenth female firefighter in a department of fifteen hundred men. She is currently a writer, and the author of four books, including *The New York Times* bestseller, *The Gutsy Girl: Escapades for Your Life of Epic Adventure.* She is the twin sister of Alexandra Paul (p. 104).

Q. What really matters to you?

When I first became a firefighter, I knew people doubted my physical strength. But what soon became clear is that they doubted my courage too! I began to realise that we don't expect bravery in women; in fact we encourage fear in our girls from an early age.

Studies show this: we warn our girls of risk – bicycles, playground equipment, tree climbs – and often step in to help the minute she gets outside her comfort zone. But we encourage our boys to go out and try things, overcome trepidations, learn how to manage fear. With that we send a message that a girl is not capable but a boy is, that being scared is cute, even feminine, that getting outside her comfort zone is unnecessary, and that she really can't rely on her own decision-making skills. Let's stop that. Bravery and resilience offer valuable life lessons, and girls should be taught these attributes just like boys are. Courageous girls grow into confident women, and that's good for the world.

Q. What brings you happiness?

Being a thousand feet in the air in my ultralight; seeing elk, coyotes and hawks are a plus.

Q. What do you regard as the lowest depth of misery?

I worry that soon this earth will be so degraded, polluted and overbuilt that we won't even be able to see the night sky. Not a single star! The human race can't forget how tiny, tiny, tiny we are. Remembering this will contain all of our terrible hubris.

Q. What would you change if you could?

I would go back to the moment where there was a choice between the mass production of gas cars and electric cars, and I'd choose the latter.

Q. Which single word do you most identify with?

Unruly. But there are way more unruly women than me, and hallelujiah for them! So, it's an aspirational word right now. Check back in a few years.

p. 222

Kanchan Singh

Kanchan Singh was born in Gurugram, India. She lives in Gurugram with her parents and brother. In 2015, Singh left her work as a delivery person and became a driver for Bikxie, an app-based bike-taxi service in Gurugram founded to provide safety and convenience to women.

Q. What really matters to you?

My family's happiness is the most important thing to me. I came to Delhi about fifteen years ago, and I live with my parents and brother; my father and I are working to support the family, while my mother keeps the home and my brother attends school. Before I joined Bikxie, I was working as a delivery person, but I applied to a job-placement agency, and they connected me with Divya Kalia (p. 220). I am now earning more money, and that helps provide for my family. They are incredibly proud and supportive of my work. I'm so grateful that their minds are at ease with the work I do.

Q. What brings you happiness?

I am very content with my life as it is. When I look at the situations of others in this world – compared to the relative comforts I have been blessed with – I am very happy.

Q. What do you regard as the lowest depth of misery?

Delhi is not a safe place for women, and that makes me so uncomfortable – and angry. The lowest depth of misery is the violence I see towards women and children. I spend my days on the road, and I see so much violence; people here get extremely agitated because of all the traffic congestion. In a traffic jam, it is absolute chaos: there is honking and people snarling at each other, and that's when incidents of road rage occur. That kind of violence just makes me so sad, because it is not necessary.

Q. What would you change if you could?

The job that I have is about driving women around to keep them safe from being accosted, so I would make this world safer for them. Wouldn't it be nice if women needn't fear being accosted or assaulted as they are going about their lives?

Q. Which single word do you most identify with?

Safety.

p. 226–7

Hélène Grimaud

Hélène Grimaud was born in Aix-en-Provence, France. She is a classical pianist. At thirteen, she was accepted into the Conservatoire de Paris, where she earned first prize in piano performance. She has performed with orchestras and conductors around the world, and has won numerous awards for her recordings. Grimaud is the founder of the Wolf Conservation Center and supports other charitable causes that include the Worldwide Fund for Nature and Amnesty International.

Q. What really matters to you?

Harmony. When you are present in the moment, in everything you do – whether it is washing the dishes or speaking to someone you will never see again – the exchange with each person, animal or action becomes the centre of your universe; you get so much more out of the day and give so much more of yourself to the people you deal with. And compassion, because it is the basis for generosity. You have to be able to put yourself in the place of another individual; if you don't, you're probably not going to be able to react in a way that will promote the world being a better place.

Q. What brings you happiness?

That sense of unfettered safety in knowing that you can freely express yourself and do the things you think are important.

Q. What do you regard as the lowest depth of misery?

Suffering from prejudice. Sometimes people feel intimidated in the face of prejudice, thinking, 'What difference am I going to make?' But we can't think that way, because we are here to make a difference; every decision we make is literally going to change the world. And if we notice something going on, it's our responsibility to intervene. Sometimes we are not even aware of the ramifications of one act of kindness, which is why we can't be ungenerous with those acts.

Q. What would you change if you could?

I would have people live in harmony with their resources, so that this amazing planet does not continue to be violated. Even if animal welfare is not your priority, you have to care about the world future generations will inherit. It is our responsibility to ensure that it is a world of biodiversity – our physical, emotional and spiritual health depends on it.

Q. Which single word do you most identify with?

Empathy. I don't think I am capable of it on a constant basis, but I like to continue to practice and improve.

p. 232

Nicole Avant

Nicole Avant was born in Los Angeles in California, USA. She graduated from California State University, Northridge. In 2009, she was named the thirteenth United States Ambassador to the Commonwealth of the Bahamas after a unanimous senate confirmation. Avant was the first African-American woman and the youngest person to hold this title. She has been honoured for her philanthropy by organisations including The Trumpet Awards and Children Mending Hearts. She is a board member for several not-for-profit organisations, including Girls Inc. and the Los Angeles County Museum of Art board of trustees.

Q. What really matters to you?
It's funny: the way people speak about their grandmothers – Jewish, Middle Eastern, Russian, African-American – you'd think they were all the same woman. When the world is unfair, grandmothers stand fiercely combating the strife caused by racism, sexism, and other forms of hate with radical love and acknowledgement.

During the Gulf War, I asked my own grandmother, who was knitting blankets to send to the troops, why she was doing this. She answered that she wanted them to know that someone was thinking of them; it didn't matter that she didn't know them personally. Her investment in others, known and unknown, is my foundation, and it informs my love for my friends and family, as well as my calling to help those in need. Showing yourself respect, love and kindness, and turning those principles into actions – extending them to the world around you – is how we march humanity forward.

Q. What brings you happiness?
Waking up with my husband and our dogs, and being healthy and able to experience the world. The ocean and the beauty of nature bring me great joy.

Q. What do you regard as the lowest depth of misery?
Self-loathing, and a refusal to take responsibility for one's own energy.

Also, people who are intentionally cruel, who enjoy seeing others fail or thrive on hurt that results from gossip and slander.

Q. What would you change if you could?
I'd see to it that all people lived safe, healthy and abundant lives. Young girls everywhere would have access to quality education and would have the freedom to live up to their full potential. When we deny women and girls an education, we hurt them for life and maim their entire communities.

Q. Which single word do you most identify with?
Yes!

p. 233

Kaylin Whittingham

Kaylin Whittingham was born in Saint Ann, Jamaica. She holds bachelor's degrees in economics and literature, and is a graduate of Northeastern University School of Law. She was staff counsel at the Attorney Grievance Committee of New York State's First Judicial Department before founding Whittingham Law, a legal ethics and alternative dispute resolution firm. She is president of the Association of Black Women Attorneys, an advisor to the American Immigration Lawyers Association's *Ethics Compendium* and sits on the New York State Bar Association's House of Delegates. In 2016, she was honoured with a Black Women of Influence Trailblazer Award.

Q. What really matters to you?
The people in my life whom I care about and whom I believe care about me – nothing else matters. I have always said that the world is cruelty outside, and then you come home. I can put up a fight day after day, and battle outside, but I never want to do that at home. It is my safe haven.

Truth and authenticity matter so much; it was best said by Jaques in Shakespeare's *As You Like It*, 'All the world's a stage, and all the men and women merely players.' There are so many people in masks, so it matters that you unmask and just be yourself. I like knowing that those around me love me and accept me for who I am, and that I don't have to pretend and can be vulnerable.

Q. What brings you happiness?
I'm still searching – I don't think I've quite found happiness as yet. But I am optimistic; there are moments, things and people that bring me joy.

I find happiness in helping others find that, yes, there *is* a way; inspiring, empowering and engaging others to believe in themselves, to believe that they, too, can accomplish.

Q. What do you regard as the lowest depth of misery?
Hopelessness: not believing that you can overcome the obstacles you're facing or when someone feels like there is no way to lift yourself up from where you are.

Q. What would you change if you could?
Poverty. As women, we need to be empowered, we need to speak and we need our voices heard, but we can get a lot done with economic empowerment. It brings us closer to where we want to go.

Q. Which single word do you most identify with?
Autonomy.

p. 236

Lynn Goldsmith

Lynn Goldsmith was born in Detroit in Michigan, USA. She graduated magna cum laude from the University of Michigan in 1968, with a bachelor of arts degree in English and psychology. Her award-winning photography has appeared in thirteen books, countless publications – including *LIFE, Newsweek, TIME, Vanity Fair, Rolling Stone, National Geographic, People, The New Yorker* and *Sports Illustrated* – and in numerous museum collections. Goldsmith is also a songwriter, an Island Records recording artist and a director, joining the Director's Guild of America in 1971; she was a director of the first-ever network-television rock show and the first 3D-animated music video.

Q. What really matters to you?
That I remember to stay in the moment. And I'd like it if everybody on the planet could do that as well. I feel that staying in the moment allows you to have compassion for people and be in touch with your humanness. Yes, it's a challenge – my mind tends to go to other places, wondering what others think of me or about a range of other things that make me feel as though there is no higher power at work. But I do think there is a higher power you experience when you're in the moment, when you give in to a lack of control and take in what's happening around you.

Q. What brings you happiness?
Other people make me happy; it makes me happy when I feel I've affected another person or have given them the courage to keep going.

Q. What do you regard as the lowest depth of misery?
Stupidity. What I mean by that is that there are so many issues in the world – famine, disease, violence, climate change – and yet we, as individuals, still don't identify as a global community. It's almost unbelievable, especially when you see that our problems are only increasing. So much of what ails this world is due to individuals not identifying with each other as human beings. It upsets me that it's taking so long for people to wake up.

Q. What would you change if you could?
Donald Trump. And I would change the human value system, so that love becomes our biggest prize. Your capacity to love is what should make you important, not your stature: as John Lennon said, 'All you need is love.' It's that simple.

Q. Which single word do you most identify with?
Limitless.

Allison Havey

Allison Havey was born in New Jersey, USA, and grew up in New York City. She has worked internationally as a journalist and producer for the likes of NBC News, Associated Press, ABC News and The Biography Channel. In 2012, she co-founded The RAP Project to promote sexual awareness for teenagers, particularly in regard to negotiating the digital landscape and understanding how porn and social media influence attitudes and expectations. Havey is a co-author of *Sex, Likes and Social Media*, which was published in 2016.

Q. What really matters to you?

My family matters the greatest deal to me: their health and happiness, their ability to love and be loved, and their ability to find something that can engage them on a passionate level.

Work has always been extremely important to me, and I feel very intensely about engaging in something that I really love. I'm now working full time as a co-founder of The RAP Project (with Deana Puccio, p. 338), which is something that I am immensely proud of. We're in over a hundred schools and we've reached twenty-five thousand teens. With the early sexualisation of nine, ten and eleven year olds, I feel very strongly that parents need to talk to their kids about sexting and hard-core porn. They might not feel comfortable doing this – I myself wasn't five years ago – but it's happening. Erotica might be natural, but hard-core pornography is not, and we don't want young men who are victims of this – nor young women – to think that it's a lovemaking manual. We're about healthy, consensual, respectful sex.

Q. What brings you happiness?

My children laughing makes me extremely happy, as does being with friends and family in a calm holiday setting. And my work makes me very happy.

Q. What do you regard as the lowest depth of misery?

On a personal level, a big sadness for me is that I lost so much time with my son as a busy single mum. I wish I knew then what I know now, because I think that my relationship with him would be better. And on a wider scale, I feel extremely sensitive and loving towards children with mental disabilities; I don't want kids to be lonely because they're different.

Q. What would you change if you could?

I would try to make our economy less disparate and more equal – we must share more.

Q. Which single word do you most identify with?

Optimistic.

Lara Bergthold

Lara Bergthold was born in Boston in Massachusetts, USA. She has a master's degree in public policy from the John F. Kennedy School of Government at Harvard University. Bergthold is a principal partner at RALLY, a communications firm that works towards influencing how people think about and respond to political and social issues.

Q. What really matters to you?

I have always cared about making change, but, when I had my own child, that shifted for me – now I see it in a much more concrete way. What matters to me is my son and his generation and the world we leave for them. The kinds of change that I look to make don't have to be big; the small changes that I make for the better in my son's life have such an impact.

Q. What brings you happiness?

Right now, the world is a complicated place that has a lot of fear. That fear is debilitating. But, I hold on to the people who are living their truth and pursuing justice; watching people face adversity is wonderful and makes me feel overwhelmed with joy.

Q. What do you regard as the lowest depth of misery?

The lowest depth of misery is fearing that you can't feed or house your child. That is a terror many people in this world are living through, and it's something we need to change. I'm a single mom, so I think a lot about the privilege that allows me not to worry about raising my child. Being the only person in my household who makes money, I'm aware of how privileged I am to have safety and security.

Q. What would you change if you could?

I've been thinking about the difference between equality and equity: equality gives everybody the same thing and says, 'Make with it what you will,' whereas equity understands that some people need a little bit more to enable them to stand on the same ground as others. If the world could better understand why equity is so important, we'd see a lot of things changed and relieved. On a different scale – and it's related to equity – young women must be raised with the power and belief that they matter as much as young men. Until that's changed, we aren't ever going to see the world the way we wish it to be.

Q. Which single word do you most identify with?

Loyal.

Christy Haubegger

Christy Haubegger was born in Houston in Texas, USA. She holds a bachelor's degree in philosophy from the University of Texas at Austin and a law degree from Stanford Law School. In 1996, Haubegger founded *Latina* magazine, serving as its publisher, president and chief executive officer until 2001. She was an associate producer of the 2003 film *Chasing Papi* and executive producer of the 2004 film *Spanglish*, and has been an executive at Creative Artists Agency since 2005. In 2000, Haubegger was inducted into the American Advertising Federation's Hall of Achievement for increasing understanding of the United States Hispanic market.

Q. What really matters to you?

I measure my life in impact; I want to be working to allocate the resource of 'me' – my time and energy – for the greatest good I can achieve. My mother was Mexican, but she couldn't look after me and put me up for adoption. I realised early on how fortunate I was to not have ended up in foster care; my gratitude for this was immense and gave me a sense of responsibility.

I want to be able to tell Hispanic stories and stories about women. I founded *Latina* magazine because, throughout my childhood, I read magazines with blonde women on the cover – it made me feel unattractive and left out. Friends of mine read *Essence*, so I wanted to start something similar for Hispanic women. I was at *Latina* for ten years before I moved into film and television, to continue to tell Hispanic women's stories. I feel that Hollywood has a responsibility to society not to perpetuate stereotypes whereby heroism seems to be implicitly reserved for men – it's dangerous.

Q. What brings you happiness?

I love experiencing people's energy – I feed off it.

Q. What do you regard as the lowest depth of misery?

Solvable problems: hunger, lack of water, inequities in the distribution of the basic things we need to live a life of dignity. Somehow, we have both an obesity and a hunger crisis in this country – but both issues are solvable. And not solving these issues is immoral.

Q. What would you change if you could?

All the talent in the United States is not limited to the 30 per cent of our population that is white and male – at least, that's unlikely. I want opportunities to be created that unlock the potential of those who have been sidelined by the 30 per cent. Who knows? Shakespeare may have had a sister of equal talent, but we'll never know!

Q. Which single word do you most identify with?

Wonder.

Kristen Visbal

Kristen Visbal was born an American citizen in Montevideo, Uruguay, daughter to a foreign service diplomat, and was raised in the United States. A bronze sculptor, she holds a bachelor of arts, summa cum laude, from Salisbury State University, Maryland, and apprenticed at the Johnson Atelier art foundry in Mercerville. Her sculptures have won numerous awards and have been exhibited at the Lincoln Center and the National Arts Club. Her well-known work, *Fearless Girl*, installed in New York City's Financial District in 2017, inspiring the empowerment of women worldwide and symbolising the call for gender diversity in leadership.

Q. What really matters to you?
I consider myself to be a very spiritual woman, and I believe I exist to make a difference with my art; it is my gift. My mother, a painter, flowed seamlessly between realism and the abstract, and so do I. The majority of my work now is realistic, easily understandable and ideal for making a statement. However, I have always felt that there is much more to who I am as a sculptor. I believe true creativity is to break the boundaries of reality and that, only by breaking these boundaries, will I be truly free.

Fearless Girl afforded me an opportunity to use art to express an idea, to make a statement and start a debate. She's shed light on women's rights issues such as equality of pay and the representation of women in leadership. *Fearless Girl* encourages people to question the status quo, and has become a catalyst for change. Making a contribution to society and effecting change is important to me. Through this project, I've enjoyed encouraging young people to dream, for this is where our biggest and best ideas spring from.

Q. What brings you happiness?
Freedom. Nature. Completing a particularly tough artistic composition. Sharing a belly laugh with someone close to me. A hug.

Q. What do you regard as the lowest depth of misery?
The total disregard for other people's lives and their right to flourish; the Holocaust, the Rwandan Genocide – we see this happening over and over again throughout history. We see a disregard born from a lack of respect for our different cultures; a disregard for the very fabric of humanity.

Q. What would you change if you could?
I would ensure everyone had food and shelter – for a start – and love, we all need love, right? So many people scowl at life because they are unfulfilled on an emotional level. Love is a part of basic sustenance, and is often overlooked.

Q. Which single word do you most identify with?
God.

Amy Eldon Turteltaub

Amy Eldon Turteltaub was born in Hampstead in London, England. When she was nineteen, her brother, Dan – who was a Reuters photographer and war correspondent – was stoned to death in Somalia. Inspired by his memory, in 1997 she and her mother, Kathy Eldon, founded the Creative Visions Foundation, dedicated to inspiring and empowering creative activism. Creative Visions' film, *Dying to Tell the Story* – in which she explored the lives of war correspondents – was nominated for a Primetime Emmy Award for Outstanding Non-Fiction Special in 1999.

Q. What really matters to you?
I grew up in Kenya, where community was a way of life, and babies were passed from one lap to another. Moving to London after that was a terrible culture shock, because people are so isolated and disconnected there by comparison. So, what matters for me is the sense of human connection: 'the God in me saluting the God in you.' My work is about empathy. It's about trying to understand the lives of others and having the ability to make a difference at some level. Connecting to others' experiences is a very important part of that.

Q. What brings you happiness?
My children bring me joy. They drive me crazy and they're amazing – they keep me present and are my spiritual teachers. I also find happiness working with extraordinary creative activists, with people who are literally in the trenches risking their lives trying to make a difference in the world.

Q. What do you regard as the lowest depth of misery?
What makes me saddest now is the refugee crisis: 69 million refugees worldwide. I think of myself pulling up on the shores of some country, with my three children and my paper bag filled with all my belongings, and no one there to greet me. I feel enormous pain for those mothers and fathers. I just can't imagine how they cope with the challenges they face. They are extraordinary.

Q. What would you change if you could?
I would change that sense of 'us' and 'them.' I wish that we could be more of a united global tribe. And, I think women are the ones to bet on! Women are the backbone of society, which is why women need to be educated. When you educate a woman, you are educating generations of people; as the primary caregivers, women feel the responsibility to pass their education on.

Q. Which single word do you most identify with?
Gratitude. Having been to the depths of sorrow – feeling the pain of losing my brother in such a horrific way – I feel grateful to now be so joyous.

Camille Crosnier

Camille Crosnier was born in La Rochelle, France. After graduating from the Lille Graduate School of Journalism, Crosnier became a journalist with Radio France and then the French commercial radio network RTL. In 2015, Crosnier joined Yann Barthès' *Petit Journal*, today known as *Quotidien*, an independent broadcast on French television and one of France's top talk shows.

Q. What really matters to you?
To keep believing and never accept defeat, regardless of how grave the circumstances are; nothing is so serious that it can justify giving up entirely. Because giving up achieves nothing and, though it might seem silly to say it, you have to stay optimistic. In France, we live in a very privileged environment; sometimes, when I hear people complaining or accepting defeat, I just want to send them to India. When I travelled there, I saw people living with absolutely nothing but still managing to keep smiling.

As a journalist, I feel a great responsibility to disseminate information. Our job is very important, because people rely on us. It matters to me that people engage with what's going on in the world around them. People mustn't be afraid of looking stupid for asking questions – they must be informed. I don't consider myself a journalist–activist, because that, for me, is militant journalism. On *Quotidien*, for political reports, we're equally forceful in our questioning of the left as we are of the right – we're just pursuing truth.

Q. What brings you happiness?
People, especially meeting new people. It makes you open up, grow and develop, and it enriches your experience of life.

Q. What do you regard as the lowest depth of misery?
I was really touched by the misery I saw when I spent three days in the Calais Jungle. I met people with histories, desires and interrupted life journeys. I met economists and athletes, people whose entire identities have been reduced to the term 'migrant.' I met a man who had travelled the entire way to Calais from Pakistan on foot.

Q. What would you change if you could?
People need to take off their blinkers. That's why I'm a journalist – I hope to broaden people's horizons.

Q. Which single word do you most identify with?
Culot. It covers a range of things – being smart, courageous, spontaneous and persistent.

p. 249

Carla Zampatti

Carla Zampatti AC, OMRI was born in Lovero, Italy, and immigrated to Australia in 1950. She founded her eponymous and award-winning fashion-design business in 1965. In 2004, Zampatti was made a Commander of the Order of Merit of the Italian Republic, and, in 2008, her achievements were recognised with the Australian Fashion Laureate Award. In 2009, Zampatti was made a Companion of the Order of Australia for service through leadership and management roles in the fashion and retail property sectors, to multicultural broadcasting, and to women as a role model and mentor.

Q. What really matters to you?

Independence. I learned to be independent at a very young age. And with independence comes control, because without control, you're not free.

As a fashion designer, I wonder if my contribution to society is frivolous. But, when women talk to me about how my clothes make them feel, I understand that it's empowering. Women say to me, 'I met my husband wearing your dress,' and, 'I went to an interview in your clothes and I got the job.' One woman told me she had gone to Russia to audition for an opera and got the part because she was wearing my evening dress.

The main thing that matters to me, though, is my three children and nine grandchildren. I'm proud that, in spite of my working very hard throughout their lives, we have wonderful relationships. I feel it's an example that women don't have to give up work and stay at home to have wonderful children. As long as you love them and give them special time when you're with them, it works.

Q. What brings you happiness?

In a wider sense, just seeing women today makes me happy, although we're still not getting the opportunities we deserve. For the most part, if you work hard and have ability, you can succeed.

Q. What do you regard as the lowest depth of misery?

That even in today's world, there is still inequality experienced by women. And that there are still hungry people and neglected children.

Q. What would you change if you could?

The mind-set of people who feel they are superior to others. I experienced a little bit of that as a newcomer to this country, but it's not right that people are treated unfairly because of their sex, colour or race.

Q. Which single word do you most identify with?

Optimism. I'm a great optimist; I really believe that the spirit of people will win through. I would like everyone to have a greater sense of optimism, because it's the only thing that you can rely upon.

p. 254—5

Dana Donofree

Dana Donofree was born in Dayton in Ohio, USA. She earned a degree in fashion design from Savannah College of Art and Design before becoming a design assistant in New York. In 2014, Donofree founded AnaOno, a lingerie and loungewear company that designs specifically for women who have had breast reconstruction, breast surgery, mastectomy, or are living with other conditions that cause pain or discomfort. Herself a breast cancer survivor, Donofree is active in the breast cancer community, serving as the co-chair on the board of Jill's Wish and as a member of the Living Beyond Breast Cancer board.

Q. What really matters to you?

I feel honoured to share some very special, intimate moments with other women. I was diagnosed with breast cancer in 2010, at which point all of my worlds collided into a kind of supernova of sorts – my experience, my passion, my life and my advocacy for young women with breast cancer – and AnaOno was born. I find it humbling when women share their stories of receiving items from AnaOno; if I've made the tiniest difference, I feel very special.

The idea behind it is not just to provide a product or a service. It is to support a woman in being a woman and in enjoying life – in feeling sexy, beautiful and like herself. What many women experience with breast cancer is that they get stripped down to the bare minimum – certainly, I felt that way. The loss of your eyelashes, eyebrows and hair is very obvious to people, but what people don't see – because these are kept shielded – is that you have also lost a sense of identity by losing your breasts to the disease. My business is about helping women to find themselves again on their journey, whatever that may mean for them.

Q. What brings you happiness?

Sunshine. I had to make a conscious effort to look at things positively after seeing the darkest moment of my life – I had to fight the blackness threatening to consume me.

Q. What do you regard as the lowest depth of misery?

The fact that we are not saving millions of women's lives, because we don't have a cure for breast cancer. The research isn't curing anybody, it's just treating them better.

Q. What would you change if you could?

I want to see a day when we are living without cancer. I hope to close my business in twenty years because there won't be a need for me anymore!

Q. Which single word do you most identify with?

Vibrant.

p. 264

Elisabeth Masé

Elisabeth Masé was born in Basel, Switzerland, and lives in Berlin. She is a graduate of the the Academy of Art and Design FHNW in Basel and is a fine artist. Her paintings and works on paper appear in public and private collections in Switzerland, Germany and the United States. She is the author of two books: *Der Hibiskus Blutet* and *Amerika: Give Me a Reason to Love You*. Masé has received numerous awards, including the SwissAward in 1987, the Manor Art Prize in 1992 and a scholarship at the Cité Internationale des Arts in Paris in 1985.

Q. What really matters to you?

Freedom, human rights and justice. When I die, I want to have the feeling that I did what I could and have no regrets about that. My mother always said, 'You can't lose something if you don't give up on it,' and that's something that informs my life.

The refugee crisis is something I care deeply about. I wanted to contribute in some way, but at the same time not in a manner that was fleetingly charitable – like giving money or food. So, I decided to bring one of my artworks of a dress to life. I brought seven German women and seven female refugees together to embroider this piece. We stitched our stories together with a red thread, which, to me, was a symbol of solidarity. Together, we made something beautiful.

Q. What brings you happiness?

Happiness is when you completely forget yourself – who you are and how that informs your actions, and how other people view you. It's the totally unselfconscious happiness experienced by a child at play. I think we experience this when we are with the people we love.

Q. What do you regard as the lowest depth of misery?

Every form of force, violence and abuse – whether I'm experiencing it myself or whether it's the lived experience of others. The way women and children are treated in this world infuriates me, as does the lack of protection offered them by those in positions of authority.

Q. What would you change if you could?

Love. If we loved each other, we would reject those things that are hurtful. There will always be a balance between good and evil, but this balance has been so disturbed that it feels as if we're tilting towards disaster.

Q. Which single word do you most identify with?

Tolerance.

p. 265

Kristin Helberg

Kristin Helberg was born in Heilbronn, Germany. She studied political science and journalism in Hamburg and Barcelona, before working as a radio journalist at Norddeutscher Rundfunk, in Hamburg, from 1995 to 2001. In that year, Helberg moved to Damascus, Syria, where she was the only accredited Western reporter for several years; she reported for radio programmes in Germany, Austria and Switzerland, as well as for television and print media, before returning to Germany in 2008. Helberg is the author of two German-language books on Syria and Syrians.

Q. What really matters to you?
Bringing light to what is happening in Syria. Today, only destroyed buildings come to mind when you think of Syria; I remember a video – a mother comforting her three-year-old child – it could have been my son, trapped between two layers of concrete, and knowing no one was coming to help him . . . When I first went to Syria, things were so different; I was welcomed by wonderful people, of all sects. The Syrians' warm-heartedness made up for the difficulties I encountered in my work. At that time, Bashar al-Assad had taken over from his father; he wasn't like Gaddafi, Mubarak or Hussein. He was soft-spoken and people hoped for reform. But Assad didn't change the authoritarian nature of the police state, he wanted to modernise Syria not reform it. He engaged in an economic liberalisation that saw some winners, and many losers. It was the losers of his policies – the people who didn't know how to feed their families anymore – who started the revolution. Once the conflict gained momentum, Assad played the sectarian card to force his population apart: to instil fear in minorities, and hate in the Sunni majority. It grieves me to see how Syrians mistrust and hate each other, because it wasn't like this before. We have to focus on the state of mind and the state of living of the Syrian people – otherwise we will never understand, and will never solve, the conflict.

Q. What brings you happiness?
Surprising people with my report; breaking up stereotypes. Being given a hug by my children.

Q. What do you regard as the lowest depth of misery?
Obvious injustice and nobody taking action against it.

Q. What would you change if you could?
I would take away the glasses – religious glasses, ideological glasses and others – through which we explain everything with a single aspect of humanity. Only by taking them off can we see each other as we are, in all of our complexity.

Q. Which single word do you most identify with?
Open-mindedness.

p. 290

Esther Duflo

Esther Duflo was born in Paris, France. She has degrees in history and economics from the École Normale Supérieure, Paris, and a PhD in economics from the Massachusetts Institute of Technology (MIT). She is a professor in the MIT department of economics, and a co-founder and co-director of the Abdul Latif Jameel Poverty Action Lab, a network of researchers whose mission is to reduce poverty by ensuring that policy is informed by scientific evidence. In 2009, she was awarded a MacArthur Foundation fellowship. Duflo is a co-author of the award-winning *Poor Economics: A Radical Rethinking of the Way to Fight Global Poverty*.

Q. What really matters to you?
My work. I'm part of a network of about 150 researchers from all over the world who are trying to understand what works, and what does not, in fighting poverty, and who are helping to design new approaches. Identifying better approaches to solve the various problems associated with poverty, and making sure that these findings inform policy, could improve the lives of every person living below the poverty line. We partner with governments, non-governmental organisations, activists, companies – whoever wants to share their ideas to address a particular issue linked to poverty. We set up rigorous evaluations of each idea, using the same methods doctors use in testing the effectiveness of a new drug – we call them randomised controlled trials.

Being part of this collective enterprise inspires me, as does being creative in designing new solutions and testing their effectiveness. We're very open about the fact that most things fail, but each failure is an important step towards understanding what *may* work – failing helps us to identify and scale up what *is* working.

Q. What brings you happiness?
I love being in the field and learning about the lives of others. And I love my kids; that feeling of having your child recover from an illness, when everything gets back to normal, gives me a great surge of happiness.

Q. What do you regard as the lowest depth of misery?
It's the contempt the rich sometimes have for the poor. Why is there so much hatred for the poor? There's no explanation other than an express intention to hurt people who are already vulnerable. I can't imagine what it must be like to have nothing and be surrounded by jeering rich people.

Q. What would you change if you could?
I would make sure that everybody had the ability to listen to, then understand, each other.

Q. Which single word do you most identify with?
Evidence.

p. 291

Katarina Pirak Sikku

Katarina Pirak Sikku was born in Jokkmokk, Sweden. She is a First Nations Sami woman. She graduated from Umeå Academy of Fine Arts in 2005. Her exhibition, *Nammaláhpán*, at the Bildmuseet comtemporary art museum in Umeå, was nominated for the Dagens Nyheters culture prize in 2015; the multimedia exhibition was the result of Pirak Sikku's ten-year study into the racial and biological nature of the Sami peoples. Her work has also been shown at Korundi House of Culture in Finland, Grafikens Hus in Sweden, Museo de Arte Moderno de Medellín in Colombia and the Árran Lule Sami Centre in Norway.

Q. What really matters to you?
What matters to me, personally, is that I'm healthy; I don't want to get sick. In terms of the world as a whole, it's climate change and freedom of speech that matter to me. Being able to express yourself without fear is so important; it worries me that censorship is becoming a part of the culture in Sweden.

I'm Sami and my culture matters to me. The Sami are the Indigenous People of the Scandinavian and Kola Peninsula arctic. I didn't learn to speak Sami until I was twenty-one, because my parents had been forbidden from speaking it when they were growing up and they spoke Swedish in our home. In school, I never read about my Indigenous history, because it wasn't something that was taught. Of course, I knew about all the Swedish kings and their wars – I knew all about a history that I didn't feel a part of. When I finally got my hands on a book about the Sami, I felt seen and understood. I wish I spoke the language better, but I've made sure that my children do. Swedes are very protective of the status quo, so, although attitudes towards the Sami are changing, you can see their exclusionary attitudes in the way they treat refugees from other parts of the world.

Q. What brings you happiness?
I love being out in nature. I love the reassurance of looking up at the stars, which are always in the same place. And there's something special about lightness and darkness that inspires me in my art.

Q. What do you regard as the lowest depth of misery?
Abuse of power: I cannot tolerate it when leaders use religion to justify inequality.

Q. What would you change if you could?
I would give everybody the opportunity to read and write.

Q. Which single word do you most identify with?
Tryekfrihet. Freedom of speech.

p. 294

Justina Machado

Justina Machado was born in Chicago, Illinois, USA. A daughter of Puerto Rican immigrants, she is a graduate of Lane Technical College Preparatory High School and studied dance at Franklin Fine Arts Center. Her acting career began at the Latino Chicago Theater Company, and she has gone on to work in film and television. She is recognised for her roles in *Six Feet Under, Queen of the South* and *Jane the Virgin,* and is the star of the 2017 remake of the sitcom *One Day at a Time.*

Q. What really matters to you?

It used to be that working and getting to a certain place in my career mattered to me – I was just going and going and going. Now, what matters to me is love, peace, happiness, family and being a person.

Q. What brings you happiness?

I can tell you what makes me happy – a good meal, travelling, wine, love, my family – but you can have all those things and still be miserable. Because I think happiness is a choice; every single day I have to choose to be happy.

Q. What do you regard as the lowest depth of misery?

Intolerance, indifference, disregard and abuse of women – the rape culture is frightening. I feel there's been a war on women going on for the last seven or eight years, trying to take away our rights and put us in our place.

Q. What would you change if you could?

Ignorance, fear, sexism, intolerance of one another. You either come from a place of love or a place of fear, and right now there's a whole lot of fear going on. But something beautiful is coming out the ugliness. Since Donald Trump was elected, I have seen this collective humanity – in the United States and in the world – getting together to fight, not just for their cause, but for everybody's causes. We all have to come together and help one another.

Q. Which single word do you most identify with?

Survivor. The best analogy is from the Olympics. You see those really brave gymnasts doing their floor work who fall, but have to get up and continue. I'm sure they think, 'I want to get the hell out of here – this is so embarrassing, this is awful.' But they get up, keep going and finish with a bang.

p. 295

Kakali Sen

Kakali Sen was born in Kolkata, India. At the age of fourteen, she began working twelve-hour days, seven days a week, in a jewellery factory. Sen now works as an artisan at The Loyal Workshop, and lives with her older sister in a red-light district of Bowbazar, Kolkata.

Q. What really matters to you?

My sister is the most important thing in my life. When I was eleven, my mother's asthma took her life; after she died, we found out she had been working as a sex worker to earn money for the family. If my sister hadn't cared for me, I would have ended up in the sex trade too.

After my mother died, our oldest sister was eager to marry me off, but my sister – who is the middle child – protected me. But, we had so many problems in the family that I had to leave school to go to work – I suffered a lot there.

At seventeen, I fell in love and was married; but my husband beat me and, when I became pregnant, tricked me into aborting the child by putting medication in my food. I got out of that terrible situation, but there is no place for a divorced woman in our culture. Single women are discarded; landlords don't want them in their buildings, and many are forced into the sex trade.

My dream had always been to study really hard and to work with my hands, to show my parents what I made and have them be proud of me. But, when I lost my mother, I thought I'd lost my dream as well. Later, though, I heard about Sarah Beisly's (p. 144) work in the red-light district and asked a friend to introduce us – Sarah gave me the opportunity to work for The Loyal Workshop. Now, I work making beautiful leather products that I can show to my father and my sister – so my dream *has* been realised.

Q. What brings you happiness?

I love wearing gold – it makes me feel beautiful!

Q. What do you regard as the lowest depth of misery?

Not having my mother's love; I miss her so much.

Q. What would you change if you could?

I would end the sex trade.

Q. Which single word do you most identify with?

Dushtu: it means cheeky or precocious. I'm very, very cheeky!

p. 302

Tracy Gray

Tracy Gray was born in Omaha in Nebraska, USA. Gray holds a bachelor's degree in mathematical science from the University of California, Santa Barbara, and dual master's degrees in business administration from the University of California, Berkeley, and Columbia University. In 2013, she founded and became managing partner of The 22 Capital Group, a Los Angeles venture-capital and advisory firm. In 2016, Gray founded We Are Enough, a not-for-profit whose mission is to educate women on investing in women-owned or women-led businesses, and how to invest with a 'gender lens.' She started her career as a systems engineer on the NASA Space Shuttle program.

Q. What really matters to you?

Justice. When I was five, I saw a mentally disabled girl being locked in the schoolyard by a group of boys. I can remember how deeply it affected me. In fact, it's an experience that birthed everything I do, think and feel today about fairness, equality and justice.

Q. What brings you happiness?

Being present. The little things: a video of a sloth or puppy-time can make me happy.

Q. What do you regard as the lowest depth of misery?

I don't have any kind of personal misery. But the misery I see in people who are homeless, children and animals in pain, and the misery being experienced in Syria and parts of Africa, really breaks my heart.

Q. What would you change if you could?

If everyone had everything they needed, the world would be a much better place. But, how hard are we going to have to work just to ensure that everybody has the basics? Why can't everyone have health care? Why can't everyone be assured that their children are healthy, safe and receiving an education? I can't understand how people are okay being five hundred times richer than what you or I would call rich. It feels criminal – and that's coming from a venture capitalist! I don't have a problem with people making money, but not at the expense of someone else. And, I don't understand how the ludicrously rich can look at what's happening with the rest of the world but continue pursuing their profits. It's unjust that there are human beings who walk miles, day after day, to fill up their buckets with water; and I want people to be able to walk out of their front door without fear of being killed. So, I would make sure there was equality, and that everyone had access to the basics.

Q. Which single word do you most identify with?

Laughter. I think we all need to laugh more.

Lennie Goodings

Lennie Goodings was born near Niagara Falls, Canada. She is the publisher at Virago, the British trailblazing feminist publishing house that was established by Carmen Callil in 1973. Goodings has worked at Virago, which is now an imprint of Little, Brown, since 1978. She is the author of the children's book *When You Grow Up* and was a contributor to the 2013 anthology *Fifty Shades of Feminism*. She is married with two children.

Q. What really matters to you?
Family. Humour. Equality. And kindness: I think it's too easy to be caustic and sarcastic.

In my work, I want to publish books that change the world. In the seventies and early eighties, the streets were alive with protests and feminism, but the publishing houses were run mainly by Oxbridge-educated men and did not reflect those politics. There were a large number of women in publishing, but they weren't in positions to decide what would be published. The person who has the power to make those decisions matters, because they reflect on manuscripts from their own perspective; they publish what speaks to them. These days, thank goodness, we have a greater variety of editors making those decisions! When Carmen Callil founded Virago, she wanted to give a voice to 53 per cent of the population – women – by taking control of what would be published. Today, I am proud that Virago continues to be known for championing women and women's talent. I think our role as inspirers is important. It's not yet ordinary for a woman to be in power in this world. I want to live in a time when women don't need to struggle to be visible.

Q. What brings you happiness?
My family and books: I feel very nourished by books.

Q. What do you regard as the lowest depth of misery?
I have been very lucky, but I will say that I am devastated by the aggression – both verbal and physical – displayed in society towards women. It's devastating the number of days on which I open a paper and read that a woman has been murdered by a man in her life.

Q. What would you change if you could?
The relationship between men and women: boys and girls *must* be educated to the same standard – at the very least we need to improve men's education to be respectful towards girls and women; I would enforce equal pay; and I would eradicate violence against women.

Q. Which single word do you most identify with?
Grace. It encapsulates everything – style, kindness, elegance, equality.

Mary Coussey

Mary Coussey was born in Plymouth, England. She has worked for the United Kingdom's Race Relations Board and its Commission for Racial Equality. For three years she was the Independent Race Monitor for the immigration service, monitoring how immigration staff treated certain nationalities prescribed by the Minister of State for Immigration on arrival in the United Kingdom. She now advocates for social justice and chairs the independent monitoring board for the Yarl's Wood Immigration Removal Centre.

Q. What really matters to you?
My number-one issue is equality, and a lot of my life has been concerned with that. When I was a child, I once saw a black woman being abused by a passenger on a bus. It upset me tremendously; she was obviously used to that kind of treatment, because she didn't react. My first job was as a personnel officer in a factory; if they thought I'd recruited too many black people, the union would approach me and tell me to stop. At another job, I was told to put a red dot next to the names of black people applying for work to 'alert' certain foremen. That kind of blatant racism infuriated me and is why I went to join the Race Relations Board.

I saw so much gender inequality when I was working in the civil service. These days it's far more subtle, but I would tell young women starting their careers now that they have to challenge discrimination and demand equal treatment.

I'm now on the independent monitoring board for an immigration removal agency, working mainly with women who have been detained for not returning to their countries. I love taking the politicians on when they visit the removal centre about the regime they're running.

Q. What brings you happiness?
Music and seeing social change.

Q. What do you regard as the lowest depth of misery?
What's going on in Syria is terrible; I was very angry about Hungary's behaviour on the question of accepting refugees. Here in the United Kingdom, too, we've not done much about refugees. And spending millions putting up walls to keep people out in Calais is outrageous.

Q. What would you change if you could?
I'd be changing our immigration policy. And I'd stay in the EU; a lot of racism has been unleashed – or revealed – by Brexit. But there's no point in nationalism, we should rather be thinking in terms of improving the world.

Q. Which single word do you most identify with?
Equality.

Sana Issa

Sana Issa was born in Beirut, Lebanon. When she was fifteen years old, her family married her to a man twenty years her senior; when she left her abusive husband, her family ostracised her. In 1982, Issa – a self-taught English speaker – began volunteering to guide aid workers and journalists visiting Beirut's refugee camps; this led to employment at *Newsweek* magazine's Beirut bureau and was the beginning of a twenty-five-year career in international journalism. In 1993, Issa moved to the United Kingdom, where she completed a master's degree at SOAS University of London. In 2016, Issa founded Agrabah Media.

Q. What really matters to you?
Home.

Buying my home was the most amazing thing for me. I was born to a traditional Palestinian family in Lebanon and grew up during the Lebanese Civil War. We were refugees several times over; our family was displaced many times. Lebanon is a difficult place for Palestinians to exist; they have no rights, they can't own property and they are barred from many jobs. Palestinians can't get out of the camps and they are treated as second-class citizens.

In my own home, I finally have a sense of belonging. Everything in my home is mine, it is filled with all the lovely things I have collected from all over the world. But, my home is more than those things that fill it: my home is me.

Q. What brings you happiness?
There is joy in a sense of belonging, in being with friends and those to whom I don't have to explain myself.

Q. What do you regard as the lowest depth of misery?
Being betrayed. Trust is an important thing for me; I treat people on the basis of trust, so it makes me very angry when I get stabbed in the back.

Q. What would you change if you could?
Violence – mental, physical, against women and children – is abhorrent and inequality plays a big part in this, so I would remove inequality.

Q. Which single word do you most identify with?
Resilience. Because you go through life and, no matter how many times you fall, you stand up, dust yourself off and move on. You do this, not just for yourself, but for other people as well.

Katherine Acey

Katherine Acey was born in Utica in New York, USA. An activist in the women's, racial justice and LGBTQI movements, Acey served as executive director of the Astraea Lesbian Foundation for Justice from 1987 to 2010. Acey is the director of strategic collaborations for GRIOT (Gay Reunion in our Time) Circle, which addresses the needs of older LGBTQI people of colour. She is a senior activist fellow emerita at the Barnard Center for Research on Women, and a board member for both the Center for Constitutional Rights and for Political Research Associates.

Q. What really matters to you?
To be engaged in a meaningful way, which means continuing to believe in the possibility that we can have a just world. Policy changes are good, but what we're really striving for is the cultural change – the change in the hearts and minds of people – and that's a tough one. I know I shouldn't be, but I'm very surprised and disappointed in people in the United States right now. We should definitely look at why so many white, working-class, decent folks are supporting somebody who is so mean, cruel and vicious. We have a responsibility as activists to understand who those people are, because we are not going to change the world if we just talk to people who are like us.

Q. What brings you happiness?
Swimming in the ocean brings me great joy – but close to shore, and I won't go in if there are waves. I only make waves in my political life!

Q. What do you regard as the lowest depth of misery?
The lowest depth of misery in the world is misery itself. There are so many people suffering unnecessarily. Society has the capacity to address these issues, but I wonder whether it has the will?

I've been an activist since I was an adolescent. When I look at where we are with issues like poverty, women's rights, reproductive justice, sexual violence, racism, the rights of Indigenous People all over the world to basics like water and land – and at my own activism for LGBTQI people, women and people of colour – I think, 'Well, we've made some progress.' But it's very hard to appreciate when you consider Black Lives Matter in the United States or lesbians subjected to corrective rape around the world – it's tough. But I carry hope with me.

Q. What would you change if you could?
If we just keep thinking in these singular, one-person, one-group, one-issue terms, we aren't going change the world – so I want to change it all!

Q. Which single word do you most identify with?
Compassion.

Becky Lucas

Becky Lucas was born in Brisbane, Australia. In 2014, she was chosen to perform as part of the Melbourne International Comedy Festival's *The Comedy Zone* showcase. She performed her debut solo comedy show, *High Tide*, in 2015, and a second full-length show, *Baby*, in 2016. Lucas has written for the International Emmy-nominated television series *Please Like Me*.

Q. What really matters to you?
People being able to have a voice. Everyone has a story and has something to say. It's important that everyone is able to speak up and be heard, and that their stories are valued. It matters to me that people learn how to listen to one another – that we move away from individualistic consciousness, towards a place of empathy.

I've always been obsessed with stories. I've always wanted to pass anything funny or interesting I heard on, to re-tell it and write it down. I love sharing something that's happened – it feels like a crime for something great to happen and for no one to hear about it. So sharing stories is part of what I do now.

Q. What brings you happiness?
I find happiness with my friends, and I find happiness in making other people happy. I think that comes from trying to keep everyone happy throughout my parents' divorce. But, I don't mind, in fact I like it, because it's a better feeling to give than to get.

Q. What do you regard as the lowest depth of misery?
Loneliness. I hate thinking of people being alone, not just physically, but in the sense of feeling like they can't connect to anyone else.

Q. What would you change if you could?
I would like to change the way we see achievements; we put way too much emphasis on them, and it makes people feel like they always need to be working to achieve a state of happiness. There's this idea that if you can only accumulate a certain number of things, or can achieve some level, then you'll have made it. But, that doesn't equate to happiness, so I would teach kids to just *be*.

Q. Which single word do you most identify with?
Failure. You learn so much about yourself through it.

Linda Biehl

Linda Biehl was born in Geneva in Illinois, USA. When Biehl's daughter Amy was killed while working in South Africa, in 1993, she and her family – including daughter Molly Corbin – established the Amy Biehl Foundation to focus on personal development, job skills development and income-generating opportunities in South African communities. Biehl now focusses on her work in the United States as chief executive officer of the Amy Biehl Foundation, USA, and works with programmes centred on human rights, forgiveness, restorative justice, and other lessons learned from South Africa.

Q. What really matters to you?
Recognising my own humanity and the humanity of others. I've never believed that I can walk in someone else's shoes, but I know I can walk beside them. When my daughter, Amy, died, our choice was to support South Africa. Amy had been researching women's roles in the transformation, and writing at the University of the Western Cape, when she was stoned and knifed to death by a group of young freedom fighters. As a family, we agreed to honour Amy by showing people that we wanted the elections to proceed. Because that's what Amy wanted. And we developed the Amy Biehl Foundation by working with people in the community and listening to their needs. In 1999, the men who killed Amy indicated that they wanted to meet us; they had started a youth group in their community and were helping people find work. They had realised they could be more beneficial if they did things positively. Eventually, they hooked up with programmes that we're involved in through our foundation. And now I walk beside them. I've learned that forgiveness is about self. It's about releasing yourself from that poison or cancer in your body; it's about making yourself lighter and able to function as yourself again.

Q. What brings you happiness?
My greatest happiness is watching my grandkids and participating in their lives – seeing them grow and evolve.

Q. What do you regard as the lowest depth of misery?
Being ignored. The Truth and Reconciliation Commission process in South Africa might not be considered very effective, but the process of healing – the process of justice – is about being heard. And that is immeasurable.

Q. What would you change if you could?
I would make people listen to others with respect and ask themselves, 'If this happened to me, how would I react?'

Q. Which single word do you most identify with?
Tolerance.

p. 331

Rebecca Odes

Rebecca Odes was born in West Orange in New Jersey, USA. She earned a bachelor of arts degree from Vassar College, studied art at the School of the Art Institute of Chicago and holds a master's degree from the Interactive Telecommunications Program at New York University. In 1996, she co-founded gURL.com, the first major website for young women. She is the co-author of four books for women and girls, including the bestselling life-guide *Deal With It!*. In 2013, Odes co-founded Wifey.tv to create and curate media by and for women.

Q. What really matters to you?
I live for my relationships, and for the sense of putting stuff out into the world that adds to goodness. This means being part of the solutions: whether it's explicitly helping to solve problems in the world – which is a big drive for a lot of my work – or whether it's just bringing beauty, telling stories that I hope other people will connect with, into the world.

I was born a feminist. My mother lived her feminism – she would go out of her way not to go out of her way to conform. This was an incredible gift to me as a girl growing into womanhood: the knowledge that you could exist outside the box. I was very confident in the idea that women should be equals – I really had no model for expecting less. But there is an overpowering structure that needs to be pushed against in order to find equilibrium. For me, this has reinforced the need for progress on sexual inequality.

Q. What brings you happiness?
Connection is really important to me, both personally and creatively.

Q. What do you regard as the lowest depth of misery?
Loss is the scariest thing – even the fear of loss can be crippling.

Q. What would you change if you could?
So many people experience so much injustice. I think about making it possible for people to live a life that is not defined by injustice and the kinds of things privileged people don't have to experience, or even know about.

Q. Which single word do you most identify with?
Creativity: it's the word I've connected with since I was a kid – it was part of needing to find a name for why I was different to people around me. It's still what I feel makes me, me.

p. 334

Catherine Keenan

Catherine Keenan was born in Perth, Australia. She holds a doctorate in English literature from Oxford University, and is a former journalist, arts writer and literary editor. In 2012, Keenan co-founded the Sydney Story Factory, a not-for-profit creative writing centre for marginalised young people. In 2016, Keenan was named Australia's Local Hero at the Australian of the Year Awards.

Q. What really matters to you?
My kids. I have a nine-year-old girl and a seven-year-old boy, and a lot of what I think about is filtered through watching them grow up.

Six years ago, my friend Tim Dick and I started the Sydney Story Factory; we fell in love with the idea of setting up a writing centre for marginalised kids, to instil in them a love of words and books. Last year, we had three thousand young people coming through, writing stories, poetry, plays and podcasts – anything that would get them engaged and interested. This work really matters to me. I get to see kids who may have a low literacy level, who really hate school and writing, suddenly get excited about telling you what happens next.

There are terrible inequalities in education in Australia, particularly for those who are Indigenous or have learning support needs, and refugees and asylum seekers. It's a tragedy that they become so frustrated when the education system is not working for them – so much possibility is cut out of their lives if they decide that they hate learning.

I believe that stories engage people and I've seen stories transform a child's sense of self. Stories give them an ability to articulate who they are and what they feel. This helps them engage with the world and with their education. Giving young people control of stories allows them to break free of others' narratives of who they are and gives them the power back. The change in them is almost physical; they stand taller and look you in the eye when they talk to you.

Q. What brings you happiness?
Waking up my kids and giving them a cuddle – just watching their eyes come awake and feeling them putting their arms around me – is pretty close to my perfect happiness.

Q. What do you regard as the lowest depth of misery?
When the people you love aren't flourishing.

Q. What would you change if you could?
I would give every child the best education they could get – in the end, that would fix every other problem.

Q. Which single word do you most identify with?
Stories.

p. 335

Stephanie Alexander

Stephanie Alexander AO was born in Melbourne, Australia. She has been owner-chef in several restaurants – including, for twenty-one years, Melbourne's acclaimed Stephanie's Restaurant – and is the author of fifteen books, among them *The Cook's Companion*, which has sold more than five hundred thousand copies. In 2004, she established the Stephanie Alexander Kitchen Garden Foundation. In 2014, Alexander was made an Officer of the Order of Australia for distinguished service to education and as an author, having previously been recognised for services to the hospitality and tourist industry, and the encouragement of apprentices, in 1994.

Q. What really matters to you?
Spending quality time with my children and my friends: having the time to talk and laugh, and always sharing beautiful food.

My food activism started with the idea that the food experience has to be pleasurable, an idea that has been missing from the public discourse around health. People are making rules – have five vegetables and two fruits a day! – designing pyramids and putting food into boxes, but all this prescriptive behaviour hasn't made any difference. It lacks any suggestion that we should cultivate wonderful, fresh food because it tastes good, is fun and because being out in the garden is a great activity. I wanted to put a programme that emphasised pleasure in place in a primary school – when children are young and curious and have masses of energy – and see if such a programme would make any difference to the way children felt about food and about the environment. So, today, through the Stephanie Alexander Kitchen Garden Foundation, I'm aiming to give children the broadest understanding about everything to do with food: about growing it, picking it, preparing it and, then, most importantly, sharing it with their friends.

Q. What brings you happiness?
It's being around a table with people I care about – the table is central to almost everything I do.

Q. What do you regard as the lowest depth of misery?
The greatest misery is the violence that's brought about by a lack of tolerance of difference, whether it be of religion, race or ethnicity.

Q. What would you change if you could?
I would like to feel that leadership within countries is the sort of leadership that encourages dialogue, promotes compromise, is pragmatic, and considers the needs and wishes of diverse groups in the community, understanding that difference is exciting, not frightening.

Q. Which single word do you most identify with?
Idealism. Being an idealist is fairly impossible, but I'm also a doer!

pp. 342–3

Emma Davies

Emma Davies was born in London, England. She is a graduate of the Corona Theatre School. A television, film and stage actor, Davies' work has included appearances in *Emmerdale, Mosley, Royal Wives at War* and *Cape Wrath.*

—————

Q. What really matters to you?
It matters that I remind myself to be present and not to miss anything, that I accept everything as it comes – whether for good or ill – and that I am ready to act. When I was thirty-five, I had breast cancer, which was quite a gear-shift in my life. I'm one of the very lucky ones; I came out of it with more than I went in with. There is something very powerful about all the minutiae of life falling away.

Q. What brings you happiness?
Collaboration. And simplicity; just a simple smile or nod can be quite powerful.

Q. What do you regard as the lowest depth of misery?
To not be able to protect your children. I cannot begin to imagine what it must be like for a mother searching for a daughter taken by Boko Haram, or who has been trafficked and enslaved.

Q. What would you change if you could?
I would ensure that every girl was educated, giving them the opportunity to plan their own futures – what they do with their bodies, who they choose to be with and how they live their lives.

I would also like to see more connectivity. If we could connect the dots and recognise the connections between global equality, fresh water, education and health care, we could do so much better. If only we could remember our connection to the animals we use, then we wouldn't put them in giant farms where they never see the light of day. If we were more connected, we wouldn't poison our oceans or fill our environment with rubbish – we would understand that all this poisons us as much as it does the planet. In a nutshell: education for all, respect for animals – plant more trees!

Q. Which single word do you most identify with?
Joy. Because it is my default position.

pp. 346–7

Lisa VeneKlasen

Lisa VeneKlasen was born in Cañon City in Colorado, USA, and grew up in New Mexico. She graduated from Smith College in Massachusetts and holds a master's degree in public policy from the John F. Kennedy School of Government at Harvard University. VeneKlasen is an activist, educator, strategist and organisation builder, who has worked with social justice and women's rights and development organisations in Asia, Africa, Latin America and Eastern Europe. She is co-founder and executive director of Just Associates, an international network dedicated to strengthening the voice, visibility and collective organising power of women.

—————

Q. What really matters to you?
A sense of belonging. It matters that I make sure people feel part of something larger. We live in an individualistic world that keeps people from connecting with each other, when what really gives us meaning is being with others, as part of something greater than our selves. My community of family and friends certainly gives me a strong foundation, and I am always wanting to bring people in to be a part of it.

Q. What brings you happiness?
Dancing! Being with my friends and family while we dance, drink and talk.

Q. What do you regard as the lowest depth of misery?
The blaming and shaming that occurs towards victims who bear the brunt of inequality brings out the uncontainable rebel-troublemaker in me. You see it in how women are controlled and dissected, and it's embedded in how our global system works. We are living in a time where insecurity is manipulated by those in power to generate all kinds of fears. Fear is the dominant ideology that divides and conquers. It is manipulated to make us hate and leave others out of our progress, and it prevents people from reaching out and trying new things.

Q. What would you change if you could?
'Smashing the Patriarchy' doesn't cover it! Personally, what I want more than anything is for things to slow down a bit. We need to pause and pay attention to how the way we are existing needs to change. We need to balance people's interests and the needs of the planet, and here's where the voices of Indigenous Peoples, especially Indigenous women, become more important than ever.

Q. Which single word do you most identify with?
Subversive. This is how I've lived and I love using this average, white-woman demeanour of mine in a way that is subversive!

p. 348

Jutta Speidel

Jutta Speidel was born in Munich, Germany. She attended film school before embarking on a successful and award-winning career as an actress in film, theatre and television. In 1997, Speidel founded HORIZONT, a non-profit organisation for homeless children and their mothers. She has received numerous awards, including the Prix Courage Woman of the Year Award in 2004, the Order of Merit of the Federal Republic of Germany Cross in 2005, the Bavarian Order of Merit in 2011 and the Bavarian Medal of Europe in 2017.

—————

Q. What really matters to you?
I want to make the world a better place. And, more than anything else, it counts for me to know that I'm doing the right thing. I have built up HORIZONT – a not-for-profit organisation for homeless mothers and children – because I felt that homelessness, especially among children, was not seriously regarded. In addition, I was very affected by the injustice with which the victims of homelessness are confronted, especially in a city like Munich. A child cannot choose the conditions into which they are born. When children and their mothers become homeless, this is usually because they have experienced *massive* domestic violence.

HORIZONT gives these people security and creates a basis for developing new perspectives. With targeted help, counselling, support and education, we work to strengthen the context of each family, and make an independent life possible for them again. This is a small drop in the ocean, but one that helps the affected families; it's a small drop that matters to me. I would be happy if more institutions could have a preventative effect, so that we can avert homelessness for mothers and children entirely.

Q. What brings you happiness?
My work with HORIZONT. When someone tells me I have helped her or that I've affected her positively in some way, I feel immensely satisfied.

Q. What do you regard as the lowest depth of misery?
Megalomania and injustice. So many politicians are malicious and corrupt. When I think about them, I have to really focus on controlling my aggressiveness.

Q. What would you change if you could?
I would send the corrupt, megalomaniacal, egocentric dictators into the desert and leave them to ruminate over their wretched lives. I would only let them return to society when they expressed remorse.

Q. Which single word do you most identify with?
Courage!

p. 349

Dianna Cohen

Dianna Cohen was born in Hollywood in California, USA. She holds a bachelor of fine arts degree from the University of California, Los Angeles (UCLA) and is a visual artist who has worked primarily with plastic bags as her material. In 2009, she co-founded the Plastic Pollution Coalition, a global alliance that aims to stop plastic pollution and that now comprises more than five hundred non-governmental organisations and businesses around the world.

Q. What really matters to you?

At this point in my life, my artwork and my work with Plastic Pollution Coalition are inextricable. I was born in the sixties, so I grew up with a lot of awareness about the environment. As a depression baby, my father was taught to save and reuse every single thing. Another thing that influences me is my mother's death from a kind of breast cancer that is oestrogen receptive; we now know that most cancers are oestrogen receptive and that chemicals that are used to make plastics – phthalates and bisphenols – are endocrine disruptors that function like synthetic oestrogen.

I've been working with plastic bags as an art form for about twenty-seven years, reworking them into two- and three-dimensional pieces. For me, combating plastic pollution is also about social justice. It is a systemic problem that I feel in my heart – it makes me emotional. Looking at the bigger picture, if we want to divest from our dependence on fossil fuels, it's absolutely essential that we reduce the production of single-use and disposable plastics which are made from petroleum. This is a very dangerous time to be alive.

Q. What brings you happiness?

I find happiness in interacting, in having a relationship to a community. I love bringing together an eclectic and diverse community of people to ruminate on a particular issue.

Q. What do you regard as the lowest depth of misery?

Social inequality and injustice: these are things that I find unfair, so I try to turn them into a positive challenge.

Q. What would you change if you could?

Social injustice is a systemic problem, and the solution has to do with education. So, I would educate people with the goal of effecting positive change. There are numerous ways of moving towards a place where children are raised to be truly colour blind, and where they don't judge others based on socio-economic differences.

Q. Which single word do you most identify with?

Community.

p. 356

Laurence Tiennot-Herment

Laurence Tiennot-Herment was born in Normandy, France. She trained as a chartered accountant. After her son, Charles-Henri, was diagnosed with muscular dystrophy in 1987, Tiennot-Herment became a volunteer for AFM-Téléthon, the French muscular dystrophy association; she became the association's president in 2003. Tiennot-Herment is a director of the Imagine Institute, a research and innovative health care institute that aims to cure genetic diseases, and a founding member of the French foundation for rare diseases.

Q. What really matters to you?

My work for muscular dystrophy matters to me – because we do not bring children into the world to teach them how to die.

I had been married for two years when I gave birth to a beautiful little boy. It was the start of a seemingly 'normal' life. But, when Charles-Henri was about eleven months old, I began to ask questions; I could sense that he wasn't very agile. A few years later, I went to see a neurologist, who said, 'I can't say for sure, but there may be a little muscular dystrophy.' I drove home, went straight to my study and opened a book – a collection on health and medicine. Under Duchenne muscular dystrophy, there were lots of pictures and a caption that read: 'Death usually occurs before the age of twenty.' I closed the book and I never opened it again. I went into battle mode. I became a volunteer for AFM-Téléthon – the French muscular dystrophy association – because two things were very clear to me: treatments had to be found and, in order to find treatments, we had to have money. I was elected the foundation's president on 4 July 2003 and Charles-Henri died a few short months later, on 30 October. The fight continues today on behalf of Charles-Henri, and on behalf of families and children everywhere, because there is nothing more unjust than losing a child to disease.

Q. What brings you happiness?

My greatest satisfaction is in our victories at AFM, when we score points against a disease.

Q. What do you regard as the lowest depth of misery?

There can be nothing more painful for a mother than seeing her son gradually drown in illness.

Q. What would you change if you could?

I would wipe out rare diseases that kill children; the helplessness in the face of these is intolerable.

Q. Which single word do you most identify with?

I have chosen two words that go together, 'combative' and 'determined.'

p. 357

Sapana Thapa

Sapana Thapa was born in Jhapa, Nepal. At the age of seven, she was sent to Kathmandu to be the primary caregiver of her grandmother. She was admitted to Bhim Sengala Secondary School, and upon graduation began working as a social worker at the Mitrataa Foundation, providing support for teachers, learners and parents.

Q. What really matters to you?

Love, trust and cooperation among people. These are the values I wholeheartedly believe in and that I want to promote in my life and in my work.

Trust is difficult for me personally; when I was seven years old, I was sent to Kathmandu by my parents to study and to look after my grandmother. It was a sad time, but my grandmother showed me love – she is the most beautiful person and kind. She paid for me to go to school, and now I support her.

I met Bec Ordish (p. 132) when I was at high school and she has been very inspiring to me; when I told her I wanted to be a social worker, she offered for me to join Mitrataa. She has helped me realise my goals and she is always teaching me about life. And these are the things I want to do for other people, which is why I am pursuing social work. It's about being supportive, about giving of my love, fostering trust and encouraging cooperation.

Q. What brings you happiness?

I am happy when I am helping others. When I can help with removing the unhappiness that others are carrying, I am happy.

Q. What do you regard as the lowest depth of misery?

My personal misery was when my parents sent me away. I felt like the unluckiest child in the world. This feeling of abandonment drives me in my work because I understand the love and support that young children need.

Q. What would you change if you could?

I would change the educational system in Nepal – I would make sure that every girl is given the opportunity to be educated, because girls are still discriminated against in terms of access to schooling.

Q. Which single word do you most identify with?

Performer: I succeed when others succeed, and, in order for others to succeed, I must perform my job well.

Index

The Charities

Ten per cent of the originating publisher's revenue received from book sales and exhibitions of *200 Women: who will change the way you see the world* will be distributed to organisations primarily devoted to protecting and advancing the rights of women. Each contributor has nominated an organisation or individual (or herself if she is in financial need) to receive her portion of the charitable pool. The beneficiaries include those listed below.

93'Or d'enfants, Service de Pédopsychiatrie, Centre Hospitalier Robert Ballanger
A Sense of Home
Aboriginal Literacy Foundation
Acid Survivors Trust International
AFM-Téléthon
Ambika Lamsal
American Civil Liberties Union
American Jewish World Service
Amy Biehl Foundation USA
Animals Australia
Apne Aap Women Worldwide
Arab American Association of New York
Association of Black Women Attorneys, New York City
Asylum Seeker Resource Centre
Barada Syrienhilfe
Berivan Vigoureux
Black Girls Code
Breast Cancer Cure
Butterfly Home
Canon Collins Educational & Legal Assistance Trust
CARE Australia
CARE International
Caster Semenya Foundation
Changing Behaviour: Creating Sanitation Change Leaders
Children's Defense Fund
Children's Hospital at Westmead
Chinese American International School, San Francisco
Code to Inspire
Collectif National des Maisons de Vie
Coppafeel
Covenant House New York
Creative Visions
Critical Resistance
Daraja Education Fund
Desmond & Leah Tutu Legacy Foundation
Deutsche Stiftung Weltbevölkerung
Divya Kalia
Doctors Without Borders
Dolores Huerta Trust
Dress for Success
Droit au Logement

Endometriosis UK
Edible Schoolyard Project
ENDOmind
Equal Access
Eva McGauley
FAIR Girls
Foundation for Young Australians
Fred Hollows Foundation
Friends of the Elizabeth Blunt School
Fund for Global Human Rights
Future Hope
Ghada Masrieyeh
Girls Not Brides
Global Witness
Good Shepherd Microfinance
Graça Machel Trust
Guttmacher Institute
Gynécologie Sans Frontières
H.E.A.L. International
Hibo Wardere
Honor the Earth
Hope Foundation for Women and Children of Afghanistan
HORIZONT
Hunger Project
Indigenous Literacy Foundation
Innovations for Poverty Action
Inspire
Interfaith Sanctuary
International Women's Development Agency
International Women's Media Foundation
Isabel Allende Foundation
James W. Foley Legacy Foundation
Jane Goodall Institute, New Zealand
Januka Nepal
Jessica Grace Smith
Just Associates
Kanchan Singh
Kids Creative
Korpilombolo European Festival of the Night
Kosovo Rehabilitation Centre for Torture Victims
L'association pour l'intégration sociale des handicapés physiques
L'association Rêves
L'Observatoire des violences policières

La Brigade des Mineurs
La Maison des Femmes
Les Restaurants du Cœur
LEYLA
Lisel Mueller Scholarship, established by Friends of Writers
Live Out Loud
Long Walk to Freedom Library Project
Louise Nicholas Trust
Loyal Workshop
MADRE
Maggie Beer Foundation
Manal Ali
Máori Women's Refuge, Gisborne
medica mondiale e.V.
METAvivor
Mitrataa Foundation
Move This World
Naidoo Pillay Fund
National Breast Cancer Foundation
National Domestic Workers Alliance
New Zealand Prostitutes Collective
Nicky Asher-Pedro
Nicole Tung
Nobel Women's Initiative
NPY Women's Council
Our Watch
OzHarvest
Padres Contra El Cáncer
People Opposing Women Abuse
Philani Family Fund
Philani Maternal, Child Health and Nutrition Project
Pilipino Workers Center
Planned Parenthood
Plastic Pollution Coalition
Political Research Associates
Population Media Center
Population Services International
Positive Exposure
Prison Insider
Public Education Foundation
Qaqamba Gubanca
RAP Project
Reaching Out – Montclair
Reeva Rebecca Steenkamp Foundation
Restaurant Opportunities Centers United, Washington, DC

Robogals
Rogbonko Village School Trust
Room To Read
Sabila Khatun
SAIL (Sudanese Australian Integrated Learning) Program
Sands (Stillbirth & neonatal death charity)
Sankofa.org
Sergut Belay
Seven Tepees Youth Program
SOS Children's Villages (Syria)
Stephanie Alexander Kitchen Garden Foundation
Sydney Community Foundation
Sydney Story Factory
Teddy Bear Clinic
Terre des Femmes
TGI (Transgender, Gender Variant, and Intersex) Justice Project
Thistle Farms
Tirzah International
Transgender Law Centre
Trey AA Simon-Pritchard
Tribes in Transition Education Fund
Tukela Organisation School
Ububele
UNICEF
UNICEF (Australia)
Vision Australia
WaterAid
We Are Enough
Winifred Nomzamo Mandela Trust
Wirringa Baiya – Aboriginal Women's Legal Centre
Wolf Conservation Centre
Women Awareness Centre Nepal, Kathmandu
Women for Women International
Women for Women International, Munich
Women's Aid, UK
Women's Alzheimer's Movement
Women's Community Shelters
Women's Programs Association
Youth Without Borders
Zizile Institute for Child Development
Zoleka Mandela Foundation
Zonta International – Fistula program

Acknowledgements

We are immensely grateful to the many generous and kind souls without whom this book would not have been possible.

First and foremost, our profound thanks and gratitude to our intrepid travelling team, including the family members we roped in. To the imperturbable Kieran E. Scott, who so selflessly put his career on hold for a year to embark on this adventure with us: your exquisite images beautifully honour these two hundred incredible women, and we simply couldn't have asked for a more passionate and assiduous partner. To Josef Scott, whose superb video captured each and every interview and faithfully recorded our travels: your musical talent and perennially genial outlook were cherished by all of us on the road. To Elizabeth Blackwell, who cajoled, choreographed and coordinated every last little thing: your diplomacy and dedication to the cause were second to none. And to Tam West: your kindness and grace added a special lustre to the touring party when you joined us.

To our editorial collaborators Sharon Gelman, Marianne Lassandro and Elisabeth Sandmann, who helped us persuade, wrangle, corral and interview: thank you for the professionalism, generosity and enthusiasm you brought to the project throughout.

We would also like to thank our many friends and colleagues who opened their address books, hearts and homes to us: Michelle Mouracade at Alfanar and Mariam Shaar at Soufra, Lebanon; Gina Belafonte; Damaris Coulter; Meryl Marshall-Daniels; Gillian Anderson; Zelda la Grange; Ruchira Gupta; Ricky Sandberg and Ingela Ögren Weinmar at Havremagasinet gallery in Boden, Sweden; Ivy Ross; Joanne Fedler; Jonny Geller; Sarah Beisly and Jake Thomas at The Loyal Workshop, Kolkata; Bec Ordish, Nimu Sherpa Ordish, Sapana Thapa and Sarita Gurung at Mitrataa, Kathmandu; Sello Hatang and Verne Harris at the Nelson Mandela Foundation; Manu and Felix Pierrot; Friedrich-Karl and Philipp Sandmann; and especially Georgie Smith and Melissa Goddard. A particular thank you to Sahm Venter and Claude Colart – your little black books never failed to deliver, and your boundless support and friendship carried us through many an uncertain moment.

Thank you also to Susan Buchanan, Miriam Dean, Claudia Edwards and Andrea Holmes for being test subjects at the outset of the project; and Genevieve Senekal from Canon New Zealand and Greg Webb from Hasselblad New Zealand for their generous assistance with advice, equipment and materials; and Daryl Simonson and Troy Caltaux from Image Centre Group.

Huge thanks to the talented publishing team at Blackwell & Ruth: Leanne McGregor, Kate Raven, Dayna Stanley, Christian Scott, Stefanie Lim, Helene Dehmer and Joyce Liu, and especially Cameron Gibb, Benjamin Harris, and Lisette du Plessis. This was a gargantuan team effort, and your commitment to excellence never fails to astonish and humble us.

Finally, to the exceptional women who grace these pages: your stories inspired us, your generosity humbled us, and your strength fortified us. Thank you from the bottom of our hearts for being part of this extraordinary project. We hope that together we will change the way people see the world.

Ruth Hobday and Geoff Blackwell

First published in the United States in 2017 by Chronicle Books LLC.

Produced and originated by Blackwell and Ruth Limited, Suite 405 IronBank,
150 Karangahape Road, Auckland 1010, New Zealand, blackwellandruth.com

Created by: Geoff Blackwell and Ruth Hobday
Publisher: Geoff Blackwell
Editor in Chief: Ruth Hobday
Photography: Kieran E. Scott
Interviewers: Geoff Blackwell, Ruth Hobday, Kieran E. Scott,
    Sharon Gelman, Marianne Lassandro and Elisabeth Sandmann
Videography: Josef Scott
Design Director: Cameron Gibb
Editorial Manager: Leanne McGregor
Project editorial: Benjamin Harris, Lisette du Plessis
Project co-ordinator: Elizabeth Blackwell

Library of Congress Cataloging-in-Publication Data available.

ISBN: 978-1-4521-6658-2

Manufactured in China.

10 9 8 7 6 5 4 3 2 1

Chronicle Books LLC
680 Second Street
San Francisco, CA 94107
www.chroniclebooks.com

This book is made with FSC®-certified paper products and is printed with soy vegetable inks.
The Forest Stewardship Council® (FSC®) is a global, not-for-profit organization dedicated to
the promotion of responsible forest management worldwide to meet the social, ecological,
and economic rights and needs of the present generation without compromising those of
future generations.

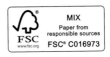

EQUALITY — Mary Crossly 2/10/16

Loyal — Lara Berghold 10/12/16

RESILIENCE — AMINATTA FORNA 20.OCT.16

COMPASSION — Katherine t. Axey 10-8-16

Freedom — Shanthini Naidoo 3/8/2016 Johannesburg

HEART — Nelson Mandela Daughter Oct 17, 2016

PERSEVERANCE! — Jeanne Weir 23/1/17

Change — Pratira Jabed Feb 26, 2017

Humanité — Fauvise L... 25/mars 17

LOVE — Swati Mandela 04/08/16

Possibility — Karin Hittican 25/1/16

TRANSFORMATION! — Jodi Flynn

LOVE

gratitude — Sahm Venter Johannesburg 3 August 2016

Mother & graditude — Zaziwe Manaway 4th August 2016 Soweto

MANAL ALI 7/3/2017

Humaniste! — Laura Huhidos 25 Mars 2017

Persévérance — Clémentin Rajjuint

STUBBORN — Ellen Bryant Voigt 10-9-16

HOPE — Zoleka Mandela South Africa 4th August 2016

Kindness — Audrey Brown

TRY — ELIDA LARTEY 01/OCT/2016

HOPE — RABBI SHARON BROUS 10.16.16

Kindness

FREEDOM

CURIOSITÉ — Claudie HAIGNERE 27.03.17

UNIT — Hodan S. Isse 4-12

invent — SAFIA SHAH 3rd October 2016

Gratitude — Patricia Grace King 1 Oct 2016

gratitude — georgie smith October 15, 2016

EMPATHY 13/05/17 ZLG

Connection — Fátima Carvalho 29.09.2016

LOVE — Nomvula Sikhakhone 3 August 2016 Johannesburg

ARGUMENT — Cordelia Fine 28/2/2017

VISION — Lynette Wallworth 13/12/16

Resilience — Soma Isa 31 March 2017

loyal — Deena 30.4.16

Justice — Gillian Slovo 30th Sept 2016

DAMARIS COULTER SERVICE 23 SEPTEMBER 2016

Optimism

Love

TOLERANCE 10/15/16

Power — Molly Corbin 10/15/16

FIGHTER — Veronique de Viguerie 28-03-2017

Si Se Puede — Dolores Huerta

Sorry — Gillian Anderson

Family — Jodi Petersen 10-14-16

Compassion — Alexandria Paul Oct 15, 2016

ENTHUSIASM! — Kathy Eldon 12th October 2016

Dignity — Dana Gluckstein 10-12-16

GRATITUDE — Yene Assegid oct 02-2016

Hope — Susan Carland

वसुधैव कुटुम्बकम् Earth Family — Vandana Shiva 2nd March 2017

KIND — Eu O'Neill

MOON — Cleo Wade

Visionary — Fereshteh Forough 10/08/2016

gratitude — Deborah Santana 10-13-16

Mercy — Liane Foley

Generosity — RUTH REICHL 10-6-16

Fuck = Noun, Verb, Adjective, Adverb. — Toby Walsh

POWER. — Christine Nixon 19/1/2017

Moon — C Giffander smith

Combattre et Déterminée — Laurence TIENMOT 27

Today — Abbey Lyons 24/01/2017

JOY! — Alfre Woodard 8 Oct '16

TRUST — JESSICA GALLAGHER 19-01-2017

Gratitude — Amy Eldon Turteltaub 10/14/16

Passionate — Renée Montagne 10-15-2016

LAUGHTER — Valerie Van Galder 10-14-16

INTEGRITY — Gillian Caldwell 28/2/2017

Perseverance — Pamela Novo

Manu-my son — Balika Das 5/3/17

PEACE — Winnie Mandela Soweto 4.8.2016!

Generosity 18/1/2017

Optimism 25.1.2017

BRAVE — Miranda Tapsell

elegant — Rosemary H. Jones 26 Jan 2017

VIVANT — Florence Aubenas 28/03/2017

Human — INNA MODJA 28 Mars 2017

Care — Irène Frachon 26 mars 2017

Liberté Pour les — Berivan Vigouroux

Excitement! — Margee Rose 20.1.2017

INTEGRITY — Marilyn J Waring

LOVE — Laura DAWN

JOY! — SANTILLA CHINGAIPE 19/01/2017

Love — Eva McGauley 6.2.17

HOPE — Marta Cheng 18-01-16

COMMUNITY — DIANNA COHEN 2016

freedom for women — Berivan Vigouroux 26 mais 2017

Persistent — Monika Hauser

FREEDOM — x PAULINE NGUYEN 23/1/17

Pugilist — Sophie Mathisen 23-1-17

Optimism — Gea Kelly 24/1/2017

Fairness — Ann Sherry 24/1/17

Failure. — Becky Lucas 12/12/16

Resilience — Carly Findlay 15/1/2017

CREATIVITY — REBECCA ODES 10.6.16

audacity — Rokhaya Diallo March 26, 2017

Culot — Camille C...